More Praise from Job Seekers for *Knock 'em Dead*

"I followed your suggestions religiously and now my job search efforts have ended most successfully—and all within a three-week period!"

— *E. V., Miami, Florida*

"I read every page of the book and after a two-month search got ten interviews with top-performing companies and six offers (five of which I declined)."

— *M. V., Millington, Tennessee*

"They were downsizing my firm . . . I just had an interview with my manager and our general manager. All the questions they asked were in your book."

— *C. M., Atlanta, Georgia*

"Thank you for writing the best and most logical approach to a job search! After reading the books and following your advice for only two weeks, I have had three interviews."

— *J. K., New Castle, Pennsylvania*

"My best investment ever! Thank you . . . I got a job one month out of college because I *knocked them dead!*"

— *A. J., Passaic, New Jersey*

"I just received the offer of my dreams with an outstanding company. Thank you for your insight. I was prepared!"

— *T. C., San Francisco, California*

"I was sending out hordes of resumes and hardly getting a nibble—and I have top-notch skills and experience in my field. I wasn't prepared for this tough job market. When I read your book, however, I immediately began applying some of your techniques. My few nibbles increased to so many job interviews I could hardly keep up with them!"

— *C. S., Chicago, Illinois*

Pg. 61-63 Compuserve; ESPAN

"I start my new job tomorrow as Purchasing Manager and am very grateful for the information contained in your books, which was a major contributor to my success."

— *J. F., Racine, Wisconsin*

"In the past two weeks I went on nine interviews and three second interviews. I got the position I wanted! Thank you, thank you, thank you! One person asked me all the questions in your book—I had all the right answers."

— *D. J., Scottsdale, Arizona*

"I read the book cover to cover and then flew to California to complete fourteen intense interviews in a two-day period. Although I was interviewing for an entry-level position with a high-tech firm, I faced few technical questions. Most of them were behavioral questions, exactly the types your book prepared me for. I had the enviable position of making a choice of which job to take!"

— *S. T., San Jose, California*

"I used the techniques you described, received multiple offers, and secured a challenging, satisfying, and well-compensated position. Thank you!"

— *G. G., San Francisco, California*

"I've just finished writing my resignation letter to the company from hell, thanks to your *Knock 'em Dead* book."

— *J. W., Pompano Beach, Florida*

"I got two job offers within a twenty-four-hour period. The information provided is as valuable as the air you breathe."

— *J. M., Greensboro, North Carolina*

1995 EDITION

KNOCK 'EM DEAD

1995 EDITION

KNOCK 'EM DEAD

THE ULTIMATE JOB-SEEKER'S HANDBOOK

MARTIN YATE

Adams Publishing
Holbrook, Massachusetts

Published by
Adams Media Corporation
260 Center Street, Holbrook, Massachusetts 02343

ISBN: 1-55850-467-2 (hardcover)
ISBN: 1-55850-433-8 (paperback)

Manufactured in the United States of America.

J   I   H   G   F   E   D   C   B   A   (hardcover)
J   I   H   G   F   E   D   C   (paperback)

Library of Congress Cataloging-in-Publication Data
Yate, Martin John.
    Knock 'em Dead :   the ultimate job seeker's handbook / Martin Yate.
        p.   cm.
    Includes index.
    ISBN 1-55850-467-2. — ISBN 1-55850-433-8 (pbk.)
    1. Employment interviewing. I. Title.
HF5549.5.I6Y37   1995
650.14—dc20   94-41716
                                                                    CIP

REAR COVER PHOTO: Nick Basillion

This book is available at quantity discounts for bulk purchases.
For more information, call 1-800-872-5627.

To your successful job hunt

Contents

III Great Answers to Tough Interview Questions   123
This section tells you not only what to answer but how to answer. It provides the real preparation for getting the job you want and deserve.

Statistics show that the last person to interview usually gets the job. Here are some steps you can take that will keep your impression strong.

Acknowledgments

My thanks to the following people, who, in different ways, have helped this book become what it is today—the only internationally published job-hunting guide of its kind.

I'd like to recognize a couple of people in the media who have given me support and encouragement over an extended period of time. These include Tony Lee and the staff of NBEW at Dow Jones, Bill Thompson of UPI, the Famous Dolans of WOR and CNBC, Fred and the gang at Morning Exchange (for putting me through my paces at the beginning of every tour, every year), and the entire editorial staff at *Working Woman*.

Of course, grateful thanks are also in order to my old friend Gary down in the Lone Star State, to Lisa Fisher, and to research director extraordinaire Karen Galletti.

From the employment services world: Dunhill Personnel System presidents—Brad Brin of Milwaukee, Warren Mahan of Maine, Leo Salzman of Columbus, Dave Bontempo of Southhampton, Paul and Pat Erickson of Shawnee Mission, Jim Fowler (and Ray Johnson) of Huntsville, Stan Hart of Troy, Mike Badgett of Cherry Hills Village, and John Webb and everyone in beautiful San Antonio.

Grateful thanks to fellow-author Bill Radin for his assistance with the chapter on the Americans with Disabilities Act.

Thanks also to Don Kipper of Ernst & Whinney, Dan O'Brien of Grumman, Amy Marglis and Kathy Seich of Merrill Lynch, Roger Villanueva of I.M.S., Victor Lindquist of Northwestern University, Ed Fitzpatrick of the University of Michigan, and Mary Giannini of Columbia University.

Gratitude is due to Eric Blume for his editorial assistance in the first three editions, and to my new editor, Brandon Toropov. Thanks go also to that man of vision, my publisher Bob Adams, and the people who got this hot little book into your hands—the tireless sales representatives of Bob Adams, Inc. And special thanks to Jill, for being the brightest star in my firmament.

Why *Knock 'em Dead?*

In 1985, when this book was first published, we began by answering a question: "Why another book about interviewing? Because the others stop at that critical point when the tough questions start flying." Sadly, that critique of the many other books out there is still valid. And with over one million *Knock 'em Dead* books in print worldwide, there seems ample evidence that readers agree with my 1985 assessment.

Still, *Knock 'em Dead* has not stood still. In the years since that first edition, this book has grown in size and scope every year; it has doubled in length and now covers the entire job search process. I am confident that it does so with a broader scope, and with more depth and originality, than any other book in the field.

The ever-expanding page count reflects my responses to the constantly changing realities of the world of work. Although we have revised the work throughout, this flexible approach is perhaps best exemplified by one of the new sections to be found in this year's edition, "When You See Clouds on the Horizon." This new chapter takes into account the sobering reality that you can no longer rely on long years of service to a single company to keep a career in high gear.

I wrote *Knock 'em Dead* because too much of the job search advice I could find on the shelves of my bookstore was infantile at best and detrimental to one's professional health at worst. The vast majority of job-hunting books lack the practical advice of what to do in the heat of battle. *Knock 'em Dead* will take you through the whole process—from putting the paperwork together to negotiating salary to your best advantage. Of course, the core of the book still helps you resolve the job-seeker's most dreaded question: "How on earth do I answer *that* one?"

Here, you'll get hundreds of the tough, sneaky, mean, and low-down questions that interviewers love to throw at you. With each question, I will show you what the interviewer wants to find out about you, and explain how you should reply. After each explanation, you'll get a sample answer and suggestions on how to customize it to your individual circumstances. The examples themselves come from real life, things people like you have done on the job that got them noticed. I'll show you how they packaged those experiences, how they used their practical experience to turn a job interview into a job offer.

Perhaps you are trying to land your first job or are returning to the workplace.

Maybe you are a seasoned executive taking another step up the ladder of success. Whoever you are, this book will help you, because it shows you how to master any interview and succeed with any interviewer. You will learn that every interviewer tries to evaluate each candidate by the same three criteria: Is the candidate *able* to do the job? Is he or she *willing* to put in the effort to make the job a success? And last but not least, is he or she *manageable*? You will learn how to demonstrate your superiority in each of these areas, under all interview conditions.

The job interview is a measured and ritualistic mating dance in which the best partners whirl away with the glittering prizes. The steps of this dance are the give-and-take, question-and-response exchanges that make meaningful business conversation. Learn the steps and you, too, can dance the dance.

Your partner in the dance, obviously, is the interviewer, who will lead with tough questions that carry subtleties hidden from the untrained ear. You will learn how to recognize those questions-within-questions. And with this knowledge, you will be cool, calm, and collected, while other candidates are falling apart with attacks of interview nerves.

How do you discover hidden meanings in questions? I recently heard a story about a young woman who was doing very well on an interview for a high-pressure job in a television studio. The interviewer wanted to know how she would react in the sudden, stressful situations common in TV, and got his answer when he said, "You know, I don't really think you're suitable for the job. Wouldn't you be better off in another company?" With wounded pride, the job-hunter stormed out in a huff. She never knew how close she was, how easy it would have been to land the job. The interviewer smiled: He had caught her with a tough question. Did the interviewer mean what he said? What was really behind the question? How could she have handled it and landed the job? The great answers to tough questions like that and many others are waiting for you in the following pages.

The job interview has many similarities to good social conversation. Job offers always go to the interviewee who can turn a one-sided examination of skills into a dynamic exchange between two professionals. In *Knock 'em Dead*, you will learn the techniques for exciting and holding your interviewer's attention, and at the same time, for promoting yourself as the best candidate for the job.

This book will carry you successfully through the worst interviews and job-hunting scenarios you will ever face. It is written in five interconnected parts. "The Well-Stocked Briefcase" gets you ready for the fray. You will quickly learn to build a resume with broad appeal and to use a unique customizing technique guaranteed to make your application stand out as something special. You will also learn how to tap into thousands of job openings at all levels that never reach the newspapers.

Once you are ready for action, "Getting to Square One" examines all the approaches to getting job interviews and teaches you simple and effective ways to set up multiple interviews. This section ends with techniques to steer you successfully through those increasingly common telephone screening interviews.

"Great Answers to Tough Interview Questions" gives you just that, and teaches you some valuable business lessons that will contribute to your future success. All successful companies look for the same things in their employees, and everything they're looking for you either have or can develop. Sound impossible? I will show you the twenty key personality traits that can convey your potential for success to any interviewer.

"Finishing Touches" assures that "out-of-sight, out-of-mind" will not apply to you after you leave the interviewer's office. You will even discover how to get a job offer after you have been turned down for the position, and how to negotiate the best salary and package for yourself when a job offer is made. Most important, the sum of those techniques will give you tremendous self-confidence when you go to an interview: No more jitters, no more sweaty palms.

The final section, "In Depth," includes new ideas for long-term career survival, proven tips for jump-starting a stalled job search, and some important advice on keeping your financial boat afloat during tough times.

If you want to know how business works and what savvy businesspeople look for in an employee, if you want to discover how to land the interview and conquer the interviewer, then this book is for you. *Knock 'em Dead* delivers everything you need to win the job of your dreams. Now get to it, step ahead in your career, and knock 'em dead.

—Martin John Yate
New York

I

The
Well-Stocked
Briefcase

Have you heard the one about the poor man who wanted to become a famous bear-slayer? Once upon a time, in a town plagued by bears, lived a man. The man had always wanted to travel but had neither the right job nor the money. If he could kill a bear, then he could travel to other places plagued with bears and make his living as a bear-slayer. Every day he sat on the porch and waited for a bear to come by. After many weeks of waiting, he thought he might go looking for bears. He didn't know much about them, except that they were out there.

Full of hope, he rose before dawn, loaded his single-shot musket, and headed for the forest. On reaching the edge of the forest, he raised the musket and fired into the dense undergrowth.

Do you think he hit a bear or, for that matter, anything else? Why was he bear-hunting with a single-shot musket, and why did he shoot before seeing a bear? What was his problem? Our hero couldn't tell dreams from reality. He went hunting unprepared and earned what he deserved. The moral of the tale is this: When you look for a job, keep a grip on reality, go loaded for bear, and don't go off half-cocked.

Out there in the forest of your profession hide many companies and countless opportunities. These are major corporations, small family affairs, and some in between. They all have something in common, and that's problems. To solve those problems, companies need people. Think about your present job function: What problems would occur if you weren't there? You were hired to take care of those problems.

Being a problem solver is good, but companies prefer to hire and promote someone who also understands what business is all about. There are three lessons you should remember on this score.

> *Lesson One:* Companies are in business to make money. People have loyalty to companies; companies have loyalty only to the bottom line. They make money by being economical and saving money. They make money by being efficient and saving time. And if they save time, they save money, and have more time to make more money.

Lesson Two: Companies and you are exactly alike. You both want to make as much money as possible in as short a time as possible. That allows you to do the things you really want with the rest of your time.

Lesson Three: There are buyer's markets (advantage: prospective employer) and there are seller's markets (advantage: prospective employee). Job offers put you in a seller's market, and give you the whip hand.

Lesson One tells you the three things every company is interested in. *Lesson Two* says to recognize that you really have the same goals as the company. *Lesson Three* says that anyone with any sense wants to be in a seller's market.

If you look for jobs one at a time, you put yourself in a buyer's market. If you implement my advice in *Knock 'em Dead*, you will have multiple job offers. And job offers, however good or bad they are, will put you in a seller's market, regardless of the economic climate.

Operating in a seller's market requires knowing who, where, and what your buyers are in the market for, then being ready with the properly packaged product.

In this section you will find out how to identify *every* company that could be in need of your services. You will learn how to discover the names of the president, those on the board, and those in management; the company sales volume; complete lines of company services or products; and the size of the outfit. You will evaluate and package your professional skills in a method guaranteed to have appeal to every employer. And you will discover highly desirable professional skills you never knew you had.

It will take a couple of days' work to get you loaded for bear. You are going to need to update your resume (or create a new one), generate some cover letters, research potential employers, and create a comprehensive marketing plan.

While I cover each of these areas in sequence, I recommend that, in the execution, you mix and match the activities. In other words, when the direct research begins to addle the gray matter, switch to resume enhancement, and so on. An hour of one activity followed by an hour of another will keep your mind fresh and your program balanced.

Your first action should be a trip to the library (taking sufficient paper and pens). On the way, purchase some push-pins, a large-scale area map, and some stick-on labels—and rustle up a three-foot piece of string. Take some sandwiches; there is no feeling in the world like eating lunch on the library steps.

1.

All Things to All People

At the library, walk in purposefully and ask for the reference section. When you find it, wander around for a few minutes before staking a claim. You will discover that libraries are a good place to watch the human race, so get the best seat in the house. Make sure you have a clear view of the librarian's desk. When you need a rest, that's where all the comic relief takes place.

Interviewers today are continually asking for detailed examples of your past performance. They safely assume you will do at least as well (or as poorly) on the new job as you did on the old one, and so the examples you give will seal your fate. Therefore you need to examine your past performance in a manner that will empower you to handle these questions in a professional and competent manner.

This chapter will show you how to identify examples of problems solved, projects completed, and contributions made that will impress any interviewer. As you complete the exercises in this chapter and concurrently proceed with your research, your added self-knowledge and confidence could well open your eyes to as-yet-unimagined professional opportunities. You will also get the correctly packaged information for a workmanlike resume. Two birds with one stone.

Resumes, of course, are important, and there are two facts you must know about them. First, you are going to need one. Second, no one will want to read it. The average interviewer has never been trained to interview effectively, probably finds the interview as uncomfortable as you do, and will do everything possible to avoid discomfort. Resumes, therefore, are used more to screen people out than screen them in. So your resume must be all things to all people.

Another hurdle to clear is avoiding too much of your professional jargon in the resume. It is a cold hard fact that the first person to see your resume is often in the personnel department. This office screens for many different jobs and cannot be expected to have an in-depth knowledge of every specialty within the company—or its special language.

For those reasons, your resume must be short, be easy to read and understand, and use words that are familiar to the reader and that have universal appeal. Most important, it should portray you as a problem solver.

While this chapter covers ways to build an effective resume, its main goal is to help you perform better at the interview. You will achieve that as you evaluate your professional skills according to the exercises. In fact, you are likely to discover skills and achievements you didn't even know you had. A few you will use in your resume (merely a preview of coming attractions); the others you will use to knock 'em dead at the interview.

A good starting point is your current or last job title. Write it down. Then, jot down all the other different titles you have heard that describe that job. When you are finished, follow it with a three- or four-sentence description of your job functions. Don't think too hard about it, just do it. The titles and descriptions are not carved in stone—this written description is just the beginning of the resume-building exercises. You'll be surprised at what you've written; it will read better than you had thought.

All attributes that you discover and develop in the following exercises are valuable to an employer. You possess many desirable traits, and these exercises help to reveal and to package them.

☐ **Exercise One**: Reread the written job description, then write down your most important duty/function. Follow that with a list of the skills or special training necessary to perform that duty. Next, list the achievements of which you are most proud in that area. It could look something like this:

> *Duty:* Train and motivate sales staff of six.
>
> *Skills:* Formal training skills. Knowledge of market and ability to make untrained sales staff productive. Ability to keep successful salespeople motivated and tied to the company.
>
> *Achievements:* Reduced turnover 7 percent; increased sales 14 percent.

The potential employer is most interested in the achievements—those things that make you stand out from the crowd. Try to appeal to a company's interests by conservatively estimating what your achievements meant to your employer. If your achievements saved time, estimate how much. If you saved money, how much? If your achievements made money for the company, how much? Beware of exaggeration—if you were part of a team, identify your achievements as such. It will make your claims more believable and will demonstrate your ability to work with others.

Achievements, of course, differ according to your profession. Most of life's jobs fall into one of these broad categories:

- sales and service;
- management and administration;
- technical and production.

While it is usual to cite the differences between those major job functions, at this point it is far more valuable to you to recognize the commonalities. In sales, dollar volume is important. In management or administration, the parallel is time saved, which is money saved; saving money is just the same as making money for your company. In the technical and production areas, increasing production (doing more in less time) accrues exactly the same benefits to the company. Job titles may differ, yet all employees have the same opportunity to benefit their employers, and in turn, themselves.

Today, companies are doing more with less; they are leaner, have higher expectations of their employees, and plan to keep it that way. The people who get hired and get ahead today are those with a basic understanding of business goals. And successful job candidates are those who have the best interests of the company and its profitability constantly in mind.

☐ **Exercise Two**: This simple exercise helps you get a clear picture of your achievements. If you were to meet with your supervisor to discuss a raise, what achievements would you want to discuss? List all you can think of, quickly. Then come back and flesh out the details.

☐ **Exercise Three**: This exercise is particularly valuable if you feel you can't see the forest for the trees.

> *Problem:* Think of a job-related problem you had to face in the last couple of years. Come on, everyone can remember one.
>
> *Solution:* Describe your solution to the problem, step by step. List everything you did.
>
> *Results:* Finally, consider the results of your solution in terms that would have value to an employer: money earned or saved; time saved.

☐ **Exercise Four:** Now, a valuable exercise that turns the absence of a negative into a positive. This one helps you look at your job in a different light and accents important but often overlooked areas that help make you special. Begin discovering for yourself some of the key personal traits that all companies look for.

First, consider actions that if not done properly would affect the goal of your job. If that is difficult, remember an incompetent co-worker. What did he or she do wrong? What did he or she do differently from competent employees?

Now, turn the absence of those negatives into positive attributes. For example, think of the employee who never managed to get to work on time. You could honestly say that someone who did come to work on time every day was punctual and reliable, believed in systems and procedures, was efficiency-minded, and cost- and profit-conscious.

If you have witnessed the reprimands and ultimate termination of that tardy employee, you will see the value of the positive traits in the eyes of an employer. The absence of negative traits makes you a desirable employee, but no one will know unless you say. On completion of the exercise, you will be able to make points about your background in a positive fashion. You will set yourself apart from others, if only because others do not understand the benefit of projecting all their positive attributes.

□ **Exercise Five:** Potential employers and interviewers are always interested in people who:

- are efficiency-minded.
- have an eye for economy.
- follow procedures.
- are profit-oriented.

Proceed through your work history and identify the aspects of your background that exemplify those traits. These newly discovered personal plusses will not only be woven into your resume but will be reflected in the posture of your answers when you get to the interview, and in your performance when you land the right job.

Now you need to take some of that knowledge and package it in a resume. There are three standard types of resumes:

> **Chronological:** The most frequently used format. Use it when your work history is stable and your professional growth is consistent. The chronological format is exactly what it sounds like: It follows your work history backward from the current job, listing companies and dates and responsibilities. Avoid it if you have experienced performance problems, have not grown professionally (but want to), or have made frequent job changes. All those problems will show up in a glaring fashion if you use a chronological resume.

> **Functional:** Use this type if you have been unemployed for long periods of time or have jumped jobs too frequently, or if your career has been stagnant and you want to jump-start it. A functional resume is created without employment dates or company names, and concentrates on skills and responsibilities. It can be useful if you have changed careers, or when current responsibilities don't relate specifically to the job you want. It is written with the most relevant experience to the job you're seeking placed first, and de-emphasizes jobs, employment dates, and job titles by placing them inconspicuously at the end. It allows you to promote specific job skills without emphasizing where or when you developed those skills.

> **Combination:** Use this format if you have a steady work history with demonstrated growth, and if you have nothing you wish to de-emphasize. A combination resume is a combination of chronological and functional resumes. It starts with a brief personal summary, then lists job-specific skills relevant to the objective, and segues into a chronological format that lists the how, where, and when these skills were acquired.

Notice that each style is designed to emphasize strengths and minimize certain undesirable traits. In today's world, all of us need a powerful resume. It is not only a door opener, it is also there long after we are gone and will almost certainly be reviewed just before the choice of the successful candidate is made by the interviewer.

Examples of each style follow; for more detailed information on assembling a winning resume, you may wish to purchase this book's companion volume, *Resumes That Knock 'em Dead*.

If you already have a resume and just want to make sure it measures up, check it against these seven basic rules of resume writing.

☐ **Rule One:** Use the most general of job titles. You are, after all, a hunter of interviews, not of specific titles. Cast your net wide. Use a title that is specific enough to put you in the field, yet vague enough to elicit further questions. One way you can make a job title specifically vague is to add the term "specialist" (e.g., Computer Specialist, Administration Specialist, Production Specialist).

☐ **Rule Two:** If you must state a specific job objective, couch it in terms of contributions you can make in that position. Do not state what you expect of the employer.

☐ **Rule Three:** Do not state your current salary. If you are earning too little or too much, you could rule yourself out before getting your foot in the door. For the same reason, do not mention your desired salary.

☐ **Rule Four:** Remember that people get great joy from getting pleasant surprises. Show a little gold now, but let the interviewer discover the motherlode at the interview.

☐ **Rule Five:** Try to keep your resume to one page; take whatever steps necessary to keep the resume no more than two pages long. No one reads long resumes— they are boring, and every company is frightened that if it lets in a windbag, it will never get him or her out again.

☐ **Rule Six:** Your resume must be typed. As a rule of thumb, three pages of double-spaced, handwritten notes make one typewritten page.

☐ **Rule Seven:** Finally, emphasize your achievements and problem-solving skills. Keep the resume general.

A Resume Only a Computer Could Love

In 1993, *78 percent* of companies surveyed had an automated resume-tracking system in place. If you're applying to a large company, or if you suspect that a potential employer is using computers instead of human beings to scan resumes, then you should prepare a computer-friendly resume as well as a more traditional version.

To prepare a resume especially for a computerized recruiter:

- Always send an original resume, never a photocopy.

- Put your name on the *first line* of your resume, and put nothing else before it.
- Use a laser jet printer or a typewriter rather than a dot matrix printer.
- Use common typefaces, such as Times, Palatino, Optima, and Courier. Avoid serif (letters with curlicues on them) or script typefaces that the computer might not recognize.
- Keep the point sizes between 10 and 14.
- If you want to use boldface, save it for headings. Never use it to type your name, address, or telephone number.
- Use few horizontal lines, and no vertical lines, if you can help it.

And *never*:

- Use double columns or other complicated layouts.
- Use any paper except white or beige, sized 8½" x 11".
- Incorporate graphics, shading, ellipses, brackets, parentheses, italics, script, underlining, or compressed type.
- Staple, fold, or fax your resume.

Keying into Buzzwords

Begin and end your computer-friendly resume with a short section of eighty words of less, called keywords, or talents. Talents encompass technical jargon and other nouns that can be used to label the job or yourself.

To compile a list of talents, check the classifieds for positions similar to the one you're looking for, and cull any recurring nouns. Make sure to put the most important words first, in case the computer is limited in the amount of buzzwords it can remember.

No Plain, No Gain

Remember, when you're preparing a resume to be scanned and understood by a computer, you are not necessarily writing one that would appeal to a human. Your goal is not to catch the recruiter's eye with fancy fonts, a jazzy layout, and exciting language, but simply to make it through the scanner intact with enough information—in the appropriate order—that when the computer is looking for somebody with your qualifications, your resume will pop up.

What follows is a selection of standard, non-computer-specific resumes for you to adapt as you see fit.

CHRONOLOGICAL RESUME

Jane Swift, 9 Central Avenue, Quincy, MA 02269. (617) 555-1212

SUMMARY: Ten years of increasing responsibilities in the employment services industry. Concentration in the high-technology markets.

EXPERIENCE: Howard Systems International, Inc.   1985-Present
Management Consulting Firm
Personnel Manager

Responsible for recruiting and managing consulting staff of five. Set up office and organized the recruitment, selection, and hiring of consultants. Recruited all levels of MIS staff from financial to manufacturing markets.

Additional responsibilities:
* coordinated with outside advertising agencies
* developed P.R. with industry periodicals—placement with over twenty magazines and newsletters
* developed effective referral programs—referrals increased 32 percent

EXPERIENCE: Technical Aid Corporation   1977-1985
National Consulting Firm. MICRO/TEMPS Division

Division Manager	1983-1985
Area Manager	1980-1983
Branch Manager	1978-1980

As Division Manager, opened additional West Coast offices, staffed and trained all offices with appropriate personnel. Created and implemented all divisional operational policies responsible for P & L. Sales increased to $20 million from $0 in 1978.

* Achieved and maintained 30 percent annual growth over seven-year period.
* Maintained sales staff turnover at 14 percent.

As Area Manager opened additional offices, hiring staff, setting up office policies and training sales and recruiting personnel.

Additional responsibilities:
* supervised offices in two states
* developed business relationships with accounts—75 percent of clients were regular customers
* client base increased 28 percent per year
* generated over $200,000 worth of free trade-journal publicity

As Branch Manager, hired to establish the new MICRO/TEMPS operation. Recruited and managed consultants. Hired internal staff. Sold service to clients.

EDUCATION: Boston University
B.S. Public Relations, 1977

FUNCTIONAL RESUME

Jane Swift
9 Central Avenue
Quincy, MA 02269
(617) 555-1212

OBJECTIVE: A position in Employment Services where my management, sales, and recruiting talents can be effectively utilized to improve operations and contribute to company profits.

SUMMARY: Over ten years of Human Resources experience. Extensive responsibility for multiple branch offices and an internal staff of forty-plus employees and 250 consultants.

SALES: Sold high-technology consulting services with consistently profitable margins throughout the United States. Grew sales from $0 to over $20 million a year.

Created training programs and trained salespeople in six metropolitan markets.

RECRUITING: Developed recruiting sourcing methods for multiple branch offices.

Recruited over 25,000 internal and external consultants in the high-technology professions.

MANAGEMENT: Managed up to forty people in sales, customer service, recruiting, and administration. Turnover maintained below 14 percent in a "turnover business."

FINANCIAL: Prepared quarterly and yearly forecasts. Presented, reviewed, and defended these forecasts to the Board of Directors. Responsible for P & L of $20 million sales operation.

PRODUCTION: Responsible for opening multiple offices and accountable for growth and profitability. One hundred percent success and maintained 30 percent growth over a seven-year period in ten offices.

WORK EXPERIENCE:

1985 to Present HOWARD SYSTEMS INTERNATIONAL, Boston, MA
National Consulting Firm
Personnel Manager

1978-1985 TECHNICAL AID CORPORATION, Needham, MA
National Consulting & Search Firm
Division Manager

EDUCATION: B.S., 1977, Boston University

REFERENCES: Available upon request

COMBINATION RESUME

EMPLOYMENT SERVICES MANAGEMENT

Jane Swift
9 Central Avenue
Quincy, MA 02269
(617) 555-1212

OBJECTIVE:

Employment Services Management

SUMMARY: Ten years of increasing responsibilities in the employment services marketplace. Concentration in the high technology markets.

SALES: Sold high-technology consulting services with consistently profitable margins throughout the United States. Grew sales from $0 to over $20 million a year.

PRODUCTION: Responsible for opening multiple offices and accountable for growth and profitability. One hundred percent success and maintained 30 percent growth over a seven-year period in ten offices.

MANAGEMENT: Managed up to forty people in sales, customer service, recruiting, and administration. Turnover maintained below 14 percent in a "turnover business." Hired branch managers, sales, and recruiting staff throughout United States.

FINANCIAL: Prepared quarterly and yearly forecasts. Presented, reviewed, and defended these forecasts to the Board of Directors. Responsible for P & L of $20 million sales operation.

MARKETING: Performed numerous market studies for multiple branch openings. Resolved feasibility of combining two different sales offices. Study resulted in savings of over $5,000 per month in operating expenses.

COMBINATION RESUME (page 2)

EXPERIENCE: Howard Systems International, Inc.   1985-Present
Management Consulting Firm
Personnel Manager

Responsible for recruiting and managing consulting staff of five. Set up office and organized the recruitment, selection, and hiring of consultants. Recruited all levels of MIS staff from financial to manufacturing markets.

Additional responsibilities:

- developed P.R. with industry periodicals—placement with over twenty magazines and newsletters
- developed effective referral programs—referrals increased 320 percent

---

Technical Aid Corporation   1977-1985
National Consulting Firm. MICRO/TEMPS Division
Division Manager   1983-1985
Area Manager   1980-1983
Branch Manager   1978-1980

As Division Manager, opened additional West Coast offices, staffed and trained all offices with appropriate personnel. Created and implemented all divisional operational policies. Responsible for P & L. Sales increase to $20 million from $0 in 1978.

- Achieved and maintained 30 percent annual growth over seven-year period.
- Maintained sales staff turnover at 14 percent.

As Area Manager opened additional offices, hiring staff, setting up office policies, training sales and recruiting personnel.

Additional responsibilities:

- supervised offices in two states
- developed business relationships with accounts—75 percent of clients were regular customers
- client base increased 28 percent per year
- generated over $200,000 worth of free trade-journal publicity

As Branch Manager, hired to establish the new MICRO/TEMPS operation. Recruited and managed consultants. Hired internal staff. Sold service to clients.

EDUCATION: B.S., 1977, Boston University

2.
The Executive Briefing

$\mathbf{A}$ general resume does have drawbacks. First, it is too general to relate your qualifications to each specific job. Second, more than one person will probably be interviewing you, and that is a major stumbling block. While you will ultimately report to one person, you may well be interviewed by other team members. When that happens, the problems begin.

A manager says to a subordinate, "Spend a few minutes with this candidate and tell me what you think." Your general resume may be impressive, but the manager rarely adequately outlines the job being filled or the specific qualifications for which he or she is looking. This means that other interviewers do not have any way to qualify you fairly and specifically. While the manager will be looking for specific skills relating to projects at hand, personnel will be trying to match your skills to the job-description-manual vagaries, and the other interviewers will fumble in the dark because no one told them what to look for. Such problems can reduce your chances of landing a job offer.

A neat trick I helped develop for the executive-search industry is the Executive Briefing. It enables you to customize your resume quickly to each specific job and acts as a focusing device for the person who interviews you.

While the Executive Briefing is only one form of cover letter, I am including it here for one very important reason—namely, that you are, in your research, going to come across "dream opportunities" before your new resume is finished. The Executive Briefing allows you to update and customize that old resume with lightning speed without delaying the rest of your research.

Like many great ideas, the Executive Briefing is beautiful in its simplicity. It is a sheet of paper with the company's requirements for the job opening listed on the left side, and your skills—matching point by point the company's needs—on the right. It looks like the following:

Executive Briefing

Dear Sir/Madam:

    While my attached resume will provide you with a general outline of my work history, my problem-solving abilities, and some achievements, I have taken the time to list your current specific requirements and my applicable skills in those areas. I hope this will enable you to use your time effectively today.

Your Requirements:	**My Skills:**
1. Management of public library service area (for circulation, reference, etc.)	1. Experience as head reference librarian at University of Smithtown
2. Supervision of fourteen full-time support employees	2. Supervised support staff of seventeen
3. Ability to work with larger supervisory team in planning, budgeting, and policy formulating	3. Responsible for budget and reformation of circulation rules during my last year
4. ALA-accredited MLS	4. ALA-accredited MLS
5. Three years' experience	5. One year with public library; two with University of Smithtown

    This briefing assures that each resume you send out addresses the job's specific needs and that every interviewer at that company will be interviewing you for the same job.

    Send an Executive Briefing with every resume; it will substantially increase your chances of obtaining an interview with the company. An Executive Briefing sent with a resume provides a comprehensive picture of a thorough professional, plus a personalized, fast, and easy-to-read synopsis that details exactly how you can help with current needs.

    The use of an Executive Briefing is naturally restricted to jobs that you have discovered through your own efforts or seen advertised. It is obviously not appropriate for sending when the requirements of a specific job are unavailable. Finally, using the Executive Briefing as a cover letter to your resume will greatly increase the chance that your query will be picked out of the pile in the personnel department and hand-carried to the appropriate manager.

3.
The Inside Track

There used to be a stigma about changing jobs or looking for a new one. Today we live in a different climate. Everyone you speak with in your job hunt has been through your experience. Career moves and unemployment are an integral part of our working lives, but how long this phase lasts is entirely up to you.

I recently met an executive who was looking for a job for the first time in twenty years. He had been looking for seven months and wasn't the least bit concerned: "I've been told that it takes a month for every ten thousand dollars of salary, so I really have another eighteen months to go." He seemed to have this mistaken idea that after two years of unemployment, someone would magically appear with another chief executive's job for him.

His method of job hunting was networking "because that is what I've been told is the best way to find jobs." It is if it works, but all too often a single-shot approach misfires.

The employment market varies from year to year. Sometimes it's a buyer's market and sometimes a seller's. But the fact remains that regardless of the state of the economy, there are good jobs out there for the job hunter who employs a systematic and comprehensive approach.

Too many job hunters rely solely on applications to the well-known companies, the IBMs of this world. They forget that the majority of growth in American industry is with small companies with less than fifty employees. Your goal is to land the best possible job for you and your needs. The problem is, you won't have the chance to pick the best opportunity unless you check them all out.

Average employee turnover in the American workplace has remained steady for some years at about 14 percent. In other words, just about every company is looking for someone during the year. What you have to do is to make sure that you are aware of the opportunity and the company, and the company in turn is aware of you when that opportunity arises.

There is a multi-pronged approach that combines active and passive job-hunting strategies that every job hunter can use to cover all the bases and tap the very best opportunities.

1. Direct research. Your future could well lie with a company you never dreamed existed.

2. Newspapers. Thousands of overlooked opportunities.

3. Employment agencies. Whoever you allow to represent you will decide who you get to meet and how seriously your initial candidacy will be considered.

4. References. The references you supply to potential employers in the later stages of the job hunt can be utilized effectively at the beginning, too.

5. College placement offices and alumni/ae organizations. Even if you have long since graduated, these organizations can be a big help.

6. Professional associations. It is sometimes said that it is not what you know, but who you know.

7. Job fairs. Home of employers in a feeding frenzy for today and tomorrow.

8. Business and trade publications. These are a much underrated resource for telling you what is happening on your profession's main street and who is making it happen.

9. Networking. It is more than an empty phrase. There are numerous networks we can all tap into effectively.

10. Job hunters' networks. If one doesn't exist, create your own.

11. Electronic databases. The newest weapon in your arsenal.

Tapping the hidden job market need not be scary if you follow a sound plan. In the following pages, you'll examine insider tricks to get you up to speed and maintain momentum in each of these areas.

4.
The Hidden Job Market

On a radio talk show earlier this year I listened to a problem from a listener. She said, "I'm in the academic field and I've been unemployed for two years, and I don't know what to do." I asked her how many organizations she had contacted, and she said 250. I asked her how many possible employers there were, and she said about 3,000. I said, "Next caller please." The world owes no one a living. You have to go out and find a job.

While I was revising this chapter, I heard from the producer of a national talk show on which I had recently appeared. She told me she used the techniques described in this part of the book to get thirty interviews in three weeks!

1. Direct Research

No job search is going to be truly comprehensive without research. As we have seen, this means visiting the local library with the best research section. It is well worth traveling a few miles to get to a major library.

There are a number of reference books you can consult; they are listed in the bibliography, so I won't waste space teaching you how to use them—the librarian will be happy to do that.

Your goal is to identify and build personalized dossiers on the companies in your chosen geographic area. Do not be judgmental about what and who they might appear to be: You are fishing for possible job openings, so cast your net wide and list them all.

Take a pad of paper, and using a separate sheet for each company, copy all the relevant company information. So that we agree on *relevant*, take a look at the example (page 40).

In the example, you see the names of the company president and chairman of the board, a description of the complete lines of company services or products, the size of the company, and the locations of its various branches. Of course, if you find other interesting information, copy it down, by all means. For instance, you might come across information on growth or shrinkage in a particular area of a company, or you might read about recent acquisitions the company has made. Write it all down.

```
Corporation, Inc.
Headquarters:
123 Main Street
Boston, MA 01234

Main phone: 617/555-1212
Personnel (Joseph Smith, Director): 617/555-1212

President: Richard Johnson (for 3 yrs.)
COO: William Jones (for 2 yrs.)

Director of Word Processing Services: Peter Lee

Company produces a complete line of office machines: calcu-
lators, adding machines, typewriters (electric, electronic,
manual), telephones, computerized switching systems, and a
wide range of peripheral equipment. Employs 1,200, all in
Massachusetts.

This location is primarily an administrative facility, but
it provides all services for the firm (research, repair, op-
erations, word processing). Manufacturing facilities located
in Worcester (calculators, telephone equipment, peripherals)
and Wakefield (typewriters, computers).

Sales (1992): $334.4 million
Profits: plus 5 percent over last five years

Recently acquired Disko, Inc. (Braintree, MA), a software
firm (looks like it's diversifying ???). Maybe has something
big in the works (possible merger with The Bigg Corpora-
tion).
```

This information will help you shine at the interview in three ways. Your knowledge creates a favorable impression at your first meeting; that you made an effort is noticed. That no one else bothers is a second benefit; you have set yourself apart from the others. And third, you are showing that you respect the company, and therefore, by inference, the interviewer; this sets a favorable tone.

All your effort has an obvious short-term value: It helps you win job offers. It also has long-term value because you are building a personalized reference work of your industry/specialty/profession that will help you throughout your career whenever you wish to make a job change.

Unfortunately, no single reference work you will find at the library is complete. The very size and scope of reference works means that they are just a little out-of-date at publication time. Also, no single reference work lists every company. Because you don't know what company has the very best job for you, you need to research as many businesses in your area as possible, and therefore you will have to look through several reference books.

Be sure to check out any specialized guides mentioned in the bibliography, including the *Standard & Poor's Register* and your state's manufacturing directory. Senior-level executives will be especially interested in volume two of this register, which gives detailed personal histories and contact information about board members and first-rank executives.

Your local *Business-to-Business Yellow Pages* is also worth a look. Information found here will range from a company name and telephone number to a full-page advertisement providing considerable "insider" data.

If you can get only names and telephone numbers, the directory can still be a valuable resource. While most directories are updated infrequently and tend only to list major players in the field, *B-to-B Yellow Pages* are updated annually. They are used extensively by growth companies as a marketing tool.

Most of our nation's economic growth (and therefore most of the promising new job opportunities) is with the small-growth companies.

Making the Battle Map

At the end of the day, pack up and head home for some well-deserved troughing and sluicing. Remember to purchase a map of your area, push-pins, and small stick-on labels for implementing the next step of your plan.

Put the map on the wall. Attach the string to a push-pin, stick the pin on the spot where you live, and draw concentric circles at intervals of one mile.

Next, take out the company biographies prepared at the library and write "#1" on the first. Find the firm's location on the map and mark it with a push-pin. Then, mark an adhesive label "#1" and attach it to the head of the pin. As you progress, a dramatic picture of your day's work appears. Each pin-filled circle is a territory that needs to be covered, and each of those pins represents a potential job. In short order you will have defaced a perfectly good map, but you'll have a physical outline of your job-hunting efforts.

It is likely you will return to the library, continuing your research work and preparing your resume. The initial research might take a few days. Your goal in this stage is to generate a couple of hundred sources, enough to get you started. Then, once your campaign is up to speed, you can visit again as prudence dictates.

Try walking to the library the next time, if practical. Not only is it cheaper (a sound reason in itself), but the exercise is important. You are engaged in a battle of wits, and the healthier you are physically, the sharper you will be mentally. You need your wits about you, because there are always well-qualified people looking for the best jobs. Yet it is not the most qualified who always get the job. It is the person who is best prepared who wins every time. Job hunters who knock 'em dead at the interview are those who do their homework. Do a little more walking. Do a little more research.

Purchasing Mailing Lists

Mailing lists can be cheap and effective. With very few exceptions there is a mailing list of exactly the types of movers and shakers you want to work for. Additionally, these lists can be broken down for you by title, geography, zip code—all sorts of ways. They are affordable, too; usually about $100 for a thousand. For a list broker, just look in your *Yellow Pages* under "Mailing List Brokers/Compilers."

As even the most up-to-date lists are out-of-date by the time they get to you, it is a good investment to call and verify that Joe Schmoe, vice president of engineering, is still there. If Joe is no longer there you can find out where he went, and you will have uncovered another opportunity for yourself.

2. Newspapers

Most people, unfortunately, use either the newspaper or reference books when job hunting, but rarely both. These people run the risk of ending up in a buyer's market. Not a good place to be.

Almost everybody looking for a new job buys the newspaper and then carefully misuses it. A recent story tells of a job hunter who started by waiting for the Sunday paper to be published. He read the paper and circled six jobs. He called about the first only to find it had already been filled, and in the process, got snubbed by someone whose voice had yet to break, requesting that in the future he write and send a resume rather than call. As anything is better than facing telephone conversations like this, the job hunter didn't call the other five companies, but took a week to write a resume that no one would read, let alone understand. He sent it, then waited a week for someone to call. Waited another week. Kicked the cat. Felt bad about that, worse about himself, and had a couple of drinks. Phone rang, someone was interested in the resume but, unfortunately, not in someone who slurred his words at lunchtime. Felt worse, stayed in bed late. Phone rang. An interview! Felt good, went to the interview. They said they'd contact him in a few days. They didn't, and when he called, everybody was mysteriously unavailable. The job hunter begins to feel like a blot on God's landscape.

This is obviously an extreme example, but the story is a little too close to home for many, and it illustrates the wrong way to use the newspaper when you're looking for a job. In today's changing economy it is not unusual for an advertisement in a local paper to draw upwards of 150 responses. I know of ads that have drawn almost two thousand responses. It is these odds of 1 in 150 or 1 in 2,000 that cause some to reject the want ads as a realistic method for finding employment. There are ways to answer want ads correctly and narrow the odds to 1 in 10 or even 1 in 5. This is exactly what I am going to show you how to do now.

While reference books give you bags of hard information about a company, they tell you little about specific job openings. Newspapers, on the other hand, tell you about specific jobs that need to be filled now, but give you few hard facts about the company. The two types of information complement each other. Often you will find ads in the newspaper for companies you have already researched. What a powerful combination of information this gives you going in the door to the interview!

Use newspaper ads to identify all companies in your field that are currently hiring, not just to identify specific openings. Write down pertinent details about each particular job opening on a separate sheet of paper, as you did earlier when using the reference books. Include the company's name, address, phone number, and contacts.

In addition to finding openings that bear your particular title, look for all the companies that regularly hire in your field. Cross-check the categories. Don't rely solely on those ads advertising for your specific job title. For example, let's say you are a graphic artist looking for a job in advertising. You should flag any advertising or public relations agency with any kind of need. The fact that your job is not being advertised does not mean a company is not looking for you; if a company is in a hiring mode, a position for you might be available. In the instances when a company is active but has not been advertising specifically for your skills, write down all relevant company contact data. Then contact the company. You could be the solution to a problem that has only just arisen or even one they have despaired of ever solving.

Virtually every newspaper has an employment edition each week (in addition to Sunday), when they have their largest selection of help-wanted ads. Make sure you always get this edition of the paper.

It is always a good idea to examine back issues of the newspapers. These can provide a rich source of job opportunities that remain unfilled from previous advertising efforts. I suggest working systematically through the want ads, going back twelve to eighteen months. React to ads as if they were fresh: answer the ones with your job title and contact companies in your field even if they appear to be seeking people with different skills.

When you contact by phone or letter, your opening gambit is not to say, "Gee whiz, Ms. Jones, I'm answering your ad from last July's *Sentinel*." No. You mention that you've "heard through the grapevine that the company might be looking" or that you "have been intrigued by their company and hope they might be looking for . . ."

Sound crazy? That's what a *Knock 'em Dead* reader said to me recently in a letter. He also said this trick landed him a $90,000-a-year job from a seven-month-old want ad. Sometimes the position will never have been filled and the employer simply despaired of getting someone through advertising. Sometimes the person hired left or didn't work out. Or perhaps they are only now starting to look for another person like the one they had advertised for earlier. They might even just be coming off a hiring freeze. Whatever the case, every old ad you follow up on won't result in an opening, but when one does, the odds can be short indeed. Smart money always goes on the short odds.

In addition to your local papers, there are regional, national, and international papers that employers favor to meet their professional needs.

National and International Newspapers:

The *Chicago Tribune*
The *New York Times*
The *Los Angeles Times*
The *Financial Times*
The *San Jose Mercury News* (if you are in the high-tech field)
The *Wall Street Journal*
The *National Business Employment Weekly (NBEW)*

The *NBEW* is of special interest to the professional. Published by the *Wall Street Journal*, *NBEW* is a weekly paper that carries hundreds of higher-level professional positions. It is packed with useful articles on job hunting and entrepreneurship, and carries a calendar of support groups' activities and employment events around the country. *Of special interest is the weekly profile of salaries by industry and function. NBEW* is available on selected newsstands, or you can subscribe for $35 for eight weeks by calling 1-800-JOB-HUNT.

Regional Newspapers:

Northeast
The *New York Times*
Newsday
The *Washington Post*
The *Philadelphia Inquirer*
The *Boston Globe*
The *Hartford Courant*

Midwest
The *Chicago Tribune*
The *Detroit Free Press*
The *Kansas City Star*
Rocky Mountain News
The *Denver Post*
The *St. Louis Post Dispatch*

West
The *San Francisco Chronicle*
The *San Francisco Examiner*
The *San Jose Mercury News*
The *Sacramento Bee*
The *Los Angeles Times*
The *San Diego Union*
The *Seattle Times*

Southwest
The *Dallas News*
The *Dallas Times*
The *New Orleans Times Picayune*

Southeast
The *Atlanta Constitution*
The *Miami Herald*

The reason you must use a combination of reference books and advertisements is that companies tend to hire in cycles. When you rely exclusively on newspapers, you miss those companies just about to start or just ending their hiring cycles. Comprehensive research is the way to tap what the business press refers to as the hidden job market. It is paramount that you have as broad a base as possible—people know people who have your special job to fill.

Adding all these companies to your map, you will have a glittering panorama of prospects, the beginnings of a dossier on each one, and an efficient way of finding any company's exact location. This is useful for finding your way to an interview and in evaluating the job offers coming your way.

Box Number Want Ads

Employed professionals are understandably leery of answering ads that give only box numbers. Unemployed professionals wonder whether it is worth the effort. There are many reasons not to answer blind ads, but the two reasons for action far outweigh the negatives.

One, if you don't respond you aren't in the game, and you have to play to win.

Two, you may not be suitable for the job advertised but may be suitable for another position.

If you are employed and skeptical about "blowing your cover," or unemployed and eager to increase your chances, try this technique. Call the main post office in the area and ask for the local office that handles zip code _____. Call the substation and speak to the local post office manager, or P.O. box manager. Introduce yourself as an employed job hunter and ask for the name of the box holder so that you won't jeopardize your current job. If you make your request pleasant and personal enough you might get the information you need. If not, try asking, "Is it my employer, _____?"

Your Own Want Ads

Better use the money to fire up your barbecue.

Consistency

Consistent research is the key to gathering speed and maintaining momentum. Without consistent research your job hunt will stall for lack of people and companies to approach.

A few years ago a neighbor of mine in the airline business found himself looking for a job. At the time, MGM Air, the airline that flies the super-rich between New York and Los Angeles, was just beginning operations. The neighbor had a friend already with the company who was going to get him a job. It took a year of not looking for work before this job hunter realized that things you want to happen often don't . . . unless you make them. Not only did he never work for MGM Air, he never worked in the airline industry again.

When you look like a penguin, act like a penguin, and hide among penguins, don't be surprised if you get lost in the flock. Today's business marketplace demands a different approach. Your career does not take care of itself; you must go out and grab the opportunities.

3. Public and Private Employment Agencies
There are essentially four categories: state employment agencies, private employment agencies and executive recruiters, temporary help organizations, and career counselors.

State Employment Agencies. These are funded by the state labor department and typically carry names like State Division of Employment Security, State Job Service, or Manpower Services. The names vary but the services remain the same. They will make efforts to line you up with appropriate jobs and will mail resumes out on your behalf to interested employers who have jobs listed with them. It is not mandatory for employers to list jobs with state agencies, but more and more are taking advantage of these free services. Once the bastion of minimum-wage jobs, positions listed with these public agencies can reach $50,000–$60,000 a year for some technical positions.

If you are moving across the state or across the country, your local employment office can plug you into what is known as a national job bank, which (theoretically) can give you access to jobs all over the nation. However, insiders agree that it can take up to a month for a particular job from a local office to hit the national system. The most effective way to use the service is to visit your local office and ask for an introduction to the office in your destination area.

Private Employment Agencies. Choose your agent, or "headhunter" as they are commonly called, with the same care and attention with which you would choose a spouse or an accountant. The caliber of the individual and company you choose could well affect the caliber of the company you ultimately join. Further, if you choose prudently, he or she can become a lifetime counselor who can guide you step by step up the ladder of success.

Understand that there are distinctly different types of employment services:

- Permanent employment agencies where you pay the fee
- Permanent agencies where the employer pays the fee
- Contingency and retained search firms

As this is the for-profit sector of the market place, the question arises: whose pocket is the profit coming from? Employment Agencies in the private sector must be registered as either an Employer Paid Fee (EPF) or an Applicant Paid Fee (APF) agency. To avoid misunderstanding, it is best to confirm which is which before entering into any relationships.

Only employment agencies and certain contingency search firms will actively market you to a large number of companies with whom they may or may not have an existing relationship. A true executive search firm will never market your services. It will only present your credentials on an existing assignment.

So what type of company is best for you? Well, the answer is simple: the one that will get you the right job offer. The problem is there are thousands of companies in each of these broad categories. So how do you choose between the good, the bad, and the ugly?

Fortunately this is not as difficult as it sounds. Let's explode one or two myths. A retained executive search firm is not necessarily any better or more professional than a contingency search firm, which in turn is not necessarily better or more professional than a regular employment agency. Each has its exemplary practitioners and its charlatans. Your goal is to avoid the charlatans and get representation by an exemplary outfit. Make the choice carefully, and having made the choice, stick with it and listen to the advice you are given.

Check on the date of the firm's establishment. If the company has been in town ever since you were in diapers, the chances are good that they are reputable.

A company's involvement in professional associations is always a good sign. It demonstrates commitment and, through extensive professional training programs, an enhanced level of competence. In the employment services industry, the National Association of Personnel Consultants (NAPC) is the premier professional organization, with state associations in all fifty states.

Involvement in independent or franchise networks of firms can also be a powerful plus. For example, an independent network like the National Personnel Associates group has over three hundred member firms around the continental United States and Europe. Membership in one of the leading franchise groups, such as Snelling & Snelling, Sanford Rose, Management Recruiters, Dunhill, or Romac is likewise positive. These networks also have extensive training programs that help assure a high-caliber consultant. Franchise offices can be especially helpful if you are looking to change jobs and move across the country (or further) at the same time, as they tend to have powerful symbiotic relationships with other network members; in fact this is often a primary reason for their being a member of that particular franchise or network. Many of the independent and franchise network members also belong to the NAPC.

To take your evaluation one step further, it is prudent to ask whether your contact has CPC designation. CPC or its international equivalent, CIPC, stands for Certified Personnel Consultant (or Certified International Personnel Consultant). The CPC and CIPC designations are recognized as a standard of excellence and commitment only achieved after rigorous training and study.

CIPC designation requires that the holder already have achieved CPC designation, and it requires adherence to an international code of ethics as designated by the International Personnel Services Association (IPSA).

Although certification can be applied for after two years of experience in the personnel consulting business, the studying involved usually means that even the newest holders of CPC have five years of experience, while your average CPC probably has seven to ten years of experience and contacts with top-notch employers under his or her belt.

Qualified CPCs can also be relied upon to have superior knowledge of the legalities and ethics of the recruitment and hiring process, along with the expertise and tricks of the trade that only come from years of hands-on experience. All of this can be put to work on your behalf.

It makes good sense to have a friend in the business with an ear to the ground on your behalf as you continue your upward climb. If you want my best advice: Find an NAPC member in good standing with CPC designation and listen to what he tells you.

Finally, don't get intimidated, and remember you are not obligated to sign anything. Neither are you obligated to guarantee an agency that you will remain in any employment for any specific length of time. Don't get put in a trick bag by the occasional cowboy in an otherwise exemplary and honored profession.

Executive Recruiters. These people rarely deal at salary levels under $70,000 per year. All the advice I have given you about employment agencies applies here (although you can take it for granted that the executive recruiter will not charge you a fee). They are going to be more interested in your resume for their files than in wanting to see you right then and there, unless you match a specific job they are trying to fill for a client. They are far more interested in the employed than in the unemployed, because an employed person is less of a risk (they often guarantee their finds to the employer for up to a year) and a more desirable commodity. Executive recruiters are there to serve the client, not to find you a job. They neither want nor expect you to rely on them for employment counseling, unless they specifically request that you do—in which case you should listen closely.

Working with a Headhunter

Few people realize it, but symbiotic relationships can be developed with headhunters in all these categories to help you professionally. Their livelihood depends on who and what they know. Perhaps you can exchange mutually beneficial information. But do be circumspect. An unethical headhunter can create further competition for you when you share information about companies you are talking to.

Select two or three firms that work in your field. Do not mass mail your resume to every agent in town. This can lead to multiple submissions of your resume to a single company and a resultant argument over which agency is due a fee. When such a situation arises, companies will sometimes choose to walk away from the candidate in question.

Ascertain network and association membership and how this might help in your job search. Determine who pays the fee and whether any contracts will need to be exchanged. Define titles and the employment levels they represent, along with geographical areas. Know what you want, or ask for assistance in defining your parameters. This will include title, style of company, salary expectations, benefits, and location.

If the professional is interested in representing you, expect a detailed analysis of your background and prepare to be honest. Do not overstate your job duties, accomplishments, or education. If there are employment gaps, explain them.

Find out first what the professional expects of you in the relationship and then explain what you expect. Reach commitments you both can live with, and stick with them. If you break those commitments, expect your representative to cease representation and to withdraw your candidacy from potential employers. They are far more interested in long-term relationships than passing nuisances.

Keep the recruiter informed about any and all changes in your status, such as salary increases, promotions, layoffs, or other offers of employment.

Don't consider yourself an employment expert. You get a job for yourself every three or four years. These people do it for a living every day of every week. Ask for their objective input and seek their advice in developing interviewing strategies with their clients.

Always tell the truth.

Temporary Help Companies. There are temporary help companies that provide corporate services to professionals at most levels, from unskilled and semi-skilled labor (referred to as light industrial in the trade) to administration, finance, technical, sales and marketing professionals, doctors, lawyers, and even interim executives up to the levels of CFOs and COOs.

Temporary help services can be a useful resource if you are unemployed. You can get temporary assignments, maintain continuity of employment and skills, and perhaps enhance your marketability in the process.

If you are changing careers or returning to work after an absence, temporary assignments can help get new or rusty skills up to speed and provide you with a current work history in your field. The temporary life can help you break out of your rut as well. It is becoming increasingly common to hear of the career-motivated professional who has been categorized and pigeon-holed in the workplace, but who finds a highly reputable temporary company and subsequently completely overhauls his skills to such an extent that a new career is possible.

In both these situations there are two other benefits:

1. You will get exposure to employers in the community who, if you really shine, could ask you to join the staff full time.

2. You will develop another group of networking contacts.

Working with a Temporary Help Company

Investigate the turnover of the temporary staff. If other temporaries have stayed with the company long term, chances are that company does a good job and has good clients.

Determine whether they are members of the National Association of Temporary Services (NATS), or of NAPC. These are the two leading industry associations.

Select a handful of firms that work in your field; this will increase the odds of suitable assignments appearing quickly.

Define the titles and the employment levels they represent, along with geographical areas they cover.

Do not overstate your job duties, accomplishments, or education.

Find out first what the temporary help professional expects of you in the relationship; then explain what you expect. Reach commitments you both can live with, and stick with them.

Judge the assignments not solely on the paycheck (although that can be important) but also on the long-term benefits that will accrue to your job search and ongoing career.

Keep the temporary help counselor informed about any and all changes in your status, such as offers of employment or acquisition of new skills.

Remember that the temporary company is your employer. They will appreciate extra effort when they really need it and will reciprocate.

Resolve key issues ahead of time. Should an employer want to take you on full time, will that employer have to pay a set amount, or will you just stay on as a temporary for a specific period and then go on the employer's payroll?

Career Counselors. Career counselors charge for their services: sometimes as little as $200 for a resume and a half an hour's advice, sometimes up to $10,000. For this you get assistance in your career realignment or job search skill development. What you don't get is a guarantee of employment.

If you consider this route, speak to a number of counselors and check multiple references on all of them. As you are unlikely to be given poor references, you will want to check secondary and tertiary references. This is simple to do. Check the half dozen references you request and then ask each of the referees to refer someone else they know who used the service. Then check that reference as well.

It could also be prudent to check out potential counselors with your local Better Business Bureau to see whether any complaints have been registered against them.

Find out how long the company has been in business; ascertain a complete work history of the individual counselor who is likely to be assisting you. A number of people have been known to slip into this area of the employment services business for a quick buck with little expertise and commitment.

The person who can offer you the best advice in this area is the professional who has both corporate personnel experience *and* employment agency or retained search experience. This exposure should be mandatory for anyone willing to charge you for career and employment assistance.

All the Players

To provide you with the widest possible choice of employment services, here are some contact data for the most comprehensive lists and directories available.

National Association of Personnel Services
3133 Mount Vernon Avenue
Alexandria, VA 22305
703-684-0180
National Directory of Personnel Consultants, $22.95. Identifies companies by

occupational specialization and geographical coverage. Includes employment agencies, contingency and retained search companies, and temporary help organizations in membership. The industry's premier organization. Thousands of reputable contacts. Also available as printed labels and on disk. Price on request.

Directory of Executive Recruiters
Kennedy Publications
Templeton Road
Fitzwilliam, NH 03447
603-585-6544 or 800-531-0007
Directory of Executive Recruiters, $39.95. Details 2,000 retained and contingency firms throughout the USA, Canada, and Mexico. Labels, not available on disk.

National Association of Temporary Services
119 South Saint Asaph Street
Alexandria, VA 22314
703-549-6287
Directory with 7,300 entries by city and state. $135. A SASE with a polite request will get you a free listing of temporary help companies by city for the state of your choice. Disk. Prices on request.

The Recruiting & Search Report
Ken Cole, President
Box 9433
Panama City Beach, FL 32417
904-235-3733
This organization sells data. It should be known as legwork central. The company provides many of the research services offered by the top outplacement firms only for the individual consumer. Among its unique and exciting products for the job hunter:

- Over one hundred industry-specific directories of top contingency and retained research firms throughout the United States. Updated quarterly. Provides pinpoint accuracy for $11 per category, with a minimum of three categories. Just specify your industry and get the heavy hitters by return mail. This is a great deal.

- *Executive Research Directory.* $88 (the seventh edition was published in November of 1994). This is a tremendous resource for the senior-level executive. Perhaps you need contact information for the board members of, say, artificial intelligence's fifty largest firms. Well, here are the researchers who can find this information for you. At the highest levels, it is paramount that your references be sound. This directory provides resources who will check your references for you.

- Senior executive research package. Includes the *Executive Search Research Directory* and a printout of the four hundred research directors at many of the nation's leading search firms. $125.

- Dun & Bradstreet Database. NJCRC has acquired this database of 230,000 firms. This combined with their state-of-the-art word processing capabilities means that they can offer direct-mail services for specifically targeted markets. Price upon request.
- Labels. Mailing lists customized by geography, occupation, and industry. Price upon request. Disks not available.

Don't restrict yourself to any single category in this area. Executives, especially, should not turn their noses up at local employment agencies. Often that local agency has better rapport and contacts with the local business community than the big-name search firm. I have also known more than one employment agency that regularly placed job candidates earning in excess of $250,000 per year. Don't get hung up on agency versus search firm labels without researching the outfits in question; you could miss some great career opportunities.

4. Your References as a Resource

As a rule, we have faith in ourselves and are confident that our references will speak well of us. The fact is that some will speak well of us, some will speak excellently, and some, we might be surprised to hear, bear us no good will.

The wrong references at a critical juncture could spell disaster. At the very start of your job hunt you need to identify as many potential references as possible. The more options you have, the better your likelihood of coming up with excellent references. When you are currently employed, however, unless you want your employer to know you are actively engaged in making a career move, you will want to avoid using current managers and co-workers as references.

Yet at this point of the job search, excellent references, though important, are simply an added bonus. Your hidden agenda is to use these contacts as job search leads.

The process is simplicity itself, starting with an introduction: "Bob, this is _____. We worked together at Acme between 1985 and 1992. How's it going?" It is appropriate here to catch up on gossip and the like. Then broach the subject of your call.

"John, I wanted to ask your advice." (Everyone loves to be asked for an expert opinion.) "We had some cutbacks at Fly-By-Night Finance, as you probably heard," or "The last five years at Bank of Crooks and Criminals International have been great, and the _____ project we are just winding down has been a fascinating job. Nevertheless, I have decided that this would be a perfect time for a career move to capitalize on my experience."

Then, "John, I realize how important references can be and I was wondering if you would have any reservations about my using you as a reference?" It's better to find out now rather than down the line when it could blow a job offer.

The response will usually be positive, so then you move to the next step. "Thanks, John, I hoped you would feel able to. Let me update you about what I have been doing recently and tell you about the type of opportunity I'm looking for." Then proceed in less than two minutes to give a capsule of what has passed since you worked together and what you are looking for. With co-workers or past managers, be sure to restate why you left your last job, since the reference is likely to be asked.

You can then, if appropriate and time allows, tell the reference some of the questions he might be asked. These might include the time he has known you, your relationship to each other, the title you worked under (be sure to remind your reference of promotions and title changes), your five or six most important duties, the key projects you worked on, your greatest strengths, your greatest weaknesses, your attitude toward your job, your attitude toward your peers, your attitude toward management, the timeliness, quality, and quantity of your work, your willingness to achieve above and beyond the call of duty (remind him of all those weekends you worked), whether he would rehire you (if company policy forbids rehiring, make sure your reference will mention this), your earnings, and any additional comments the reference would like to make.

Once all this has been covered, ask the reference for one further piece of assistance and then recycle the conversation through your networking presentation. (See item #8 below.)

When references are about to be checked for a specific job, get back to your chosen references, reacquaint them with any relevant areas the employer might wish to discuss, and tell them to expect a call. I have even known professionals who, with the approval of the potential employer, have their references call in with recommendations.

Some smart job hunters also take the precaution of having a friend do a dummy check on all references just to confirm what they will say when the occasion arises. This way you can distinguish the excellent references from the merely good. (For guaranteed peace of mind you could call Taylor Review at (810) 651-0286, and have them check your references for you. For a modest fee you'll know in advance just who will be your best spokespeople.)

5. College Placement Offices and Alumni/ae Associations

College Placement Offices. If you are leaving school or college, take advantage of this resource. Remember that the college placement office is not a substitute for your mother; it is not there to provide for you or hand you job offers. Rather, you will find there a wealth of experience that will accelerate the process and aid you in finding your own job.

Placement offices and their staffs are horrendously overworked, and merely keeping pace with the Herculean task of providing assistance to the student body as a whole is more than a full-time job. Take the time to make yourself known here and stress your sincerity and willingness to listen to good advice. Act on it; then, when you come back for more, you will have earned the placement director's respect and as such will begin to earn yourself that extra bit of attention and guidance that winners always manage for themselves.

Don't wait until the last minute, especially if you are hoping to gain your foothold on the ladder of success from on-campus recruiters who represent the big corporations. These recruiters go to society and association meetings on campus all year long. Take an active part in campus affairs and you may well find them coming after you. I know of one campus recruiter for a major accounting firm who swears she has selected all her prime choices before the campus recruiting season even opens. How do such campus recruiters pick the winners from the also-rans? Simple. They all maintain very close working relationships with the placement office, so an endorsement at the right time can mean an important introduction rather than a closed door.

Alumni/ae Associations. Even when your school days are in the misty distant past, this isn't the time to forget the people of the old school tie. People hire people like themselves, people with whom they share something in common. Your school or college alumni/ae association is a complete and valuable network just waiting for you.

As a member of the alumni/ae association you are likely to have access to a membership listing. Additionally, many of the larger schools have alumni/ae placement networks, so you may want to check with the alma mater and tap into the old-boy and -girl network.

6. Professional Associations

Professional associations provide excellent networks for your benefit. Almost all committed professionals are members of at least one or two professional networks. Their membership is based on:

a) Commitment to the profession.

b) The knowledge that people who know people know where the opportunities are hidden.

If you never got around to joining, or your membership has lapsed, it is time to visit the library and check out the *Encyclopedia of Associations* (published by Bowker). It tells you about all known associations for your profession and provides contact information and other relevant data.

You might also check out another important resource: *The Directory of Directories.* This reference work lists all the available directories in the country and details their content. For example, if you are an oil and gas geologist, you'll learn that there is a directory of geologists with 11,000 plus entries that includes full biographical and contact data. *The Directory of Directories* can be a major lead generator and significant professional networking resource for almost anybody.

Some professions have multiple associations, all of which could be of value to the serious job hunter. For example, if you happen to be in retail, you will find thirty national associations and fifty state associations. Together these associations represent one and a half million retailers who provide employment for over fourteen million people. And these are just retail associations that are members of the American Retail Federation. You may well discover even more.

There are two ways to make memberships in professional organizations work. The first is the membership directory, which provides you with a direct networking resource for direct verbal contact and mail campaigns. All associations supply their members with a directory of contact information for all other members. Additionally, all associations schedule regular meetings, which provide further opportunities to mingle with your professional peers on an informal basis, as well as opportunities to get involved on a volunteer basis with organizing such meetings or speaking at a meeting. Networking at the meetings and using an association's directory for contacts are wise and accepted uses of membership.

Professional associations all have newsletters. In addition to using the help-wanted section, you will be able to utilize them in other ways by following the advice on trade and business publications later in this chapter.

It is often one's active membership in professional associations that leads other disgruntled job hunters to mutter, "It's not what you know, it's who you know." (Membership in professional associations is also an excellent way to maintain long-term career stability; see chapter 29.)

7. Job Fairs

Job fairs and career days are occasions where local or regional companies that are actively hiring get together, usually under the auspices of a job fair promoter or local employment agency to attract large numbers of potential employees.

There aren't many of these occasions, so they won't be taking much of your time, but you shouldn't miss them when they do occur. They are always advertised in the local newspapers and frequently on the radio. Many also appear in the *National Business Employment Weekly's* events calendar.

When the job fair is organized by a promoter, entrance is either free or nominal. When it is organized by a local employment service, it helps to be on their mailing list.

In addition to the exhibit hall, there are likely to be formal group presentations by employers. As all speakers love to get feedback, move in when the crush of presentor groupies has died down; you'll get more time and closer attention. You will also have additional knowledge of the company and the chance to spend a few minutes customizing the emphasis of your skills to meet the stated needs and interests of the employer in question.

When you attend job fairs, go prepared. Take:

- Business cards. (If employed, remember to request the courtesy of confidentiality in calls to the workplace.)
- Resumes—as many as there are exhibitors times two. You'll need one to leave at the exhibit booth and an additional copy for anyone you have a meaningful conversation with.
- Note pad and pen, preferably in a folder.

Go with specific objectives in mind.

- Visit every booth, not just the ones with the flashing lights and professional models stopping traffic.
- Talk to someone at every booth. Since they are the ones who are selling,

you have a slight advantage. You can walk up and ask questions about the company, who they are, and what they are doing, before you talk about yourself. This allows you to present yourself in the most relevant light.

- Collect business cards from everyone you speak to so that you can follow up with a letter and a call when they are not so harried. Very few people actually get hired at job fairs. For most companies the exercise is usually one of collecting resumes so that meaningful meetings can take place in the ensuing weeks. But be "on" in case someone wants to sit down and give you a serious interview on the spot. This is most likely to happen when you least expect it, so be prepared.
- Collect company brochures and collateral materials.
- Arrange times and dates to follow up with each employer. "Ms. Jones, I realize you are very busy today, and I would like to speak to you further. Your company sounds very exciting. I should like to set up a time when we could meet to talk further or perhaps set a time to call you in the next few days."
- Dress for business. You may be meeting your new boss, and you don't want the first impression to be less than professional.

Job fairs provide opportunity for administrative, professional, and technical people up to the middle management ranks. However, this doesn't mean that the senior executive should feel such an event beneath her. The opportunity still exists to have meaningful conversations with tens or hundreds of employers in a single day, from which may come further fruitful conversations.

On leaving each booth, and at the end of the day, go through your notes while everything is still fresh in your mind. Review each company and what possibilities it holds for you. Then review all the companies as a whole to see what you might glean about industry needs or marketplace shifts and long-term staffing needs. Make notes.

8. Trade and Business Magazines

This resource includes professional association periodicals, trade magazines, and the general business press. They can all be utilized in a similar fashion: by contacting the individuals and companies mentioned and using the article to begin discussion.

In these publications you may find the following:

- Focus articles about interesting companies, which can alert you to specific growth opportunities.
- Industry overviews and market development pieces, which can tip you off to subtle shifts in your professional marketplace and thereby alert you to opportunities—and provide you with the chance to customize your letters, calls, and resume for specific targets.
- Quotations. "The art of press writing demands frequent quotes, and by necessity, attributions," says Peregrine McCoy, senior partner of Connem,

Covertrax and Splitt. Contacting the person quoted is flattering and shows that you have your finger on the pulse of your profession.

- Articles by industry professionals. When contacting the author of an article, you might include how much you agree with what was said, a little additional information on the subject, or words to the effect that "It's about time someone told it like it is." Never say anything in the vein of, "Hey, the article is great but you missed . . ."

- Opportunities to write the editors of the publication. The editors themselves are always on the lookout for quotable letters, so a flattering note about an article with a line or two about your background in the field may get you some valuable free publicity down the line.

- Columns on promotions, executive moves, and obituaries. If someone has just received a promotion, there are reasonable odds that somewhere in the chain is an opening. If executive A has moved to company B, it could mean the first company is looking for someone. The same applies to obituaries.

- Help-wanted sections. Many employers will give the general newspapers only token attention when it comes to filling hard-to-find professional and trade positions. They will concentrate their advertising budgets instead on the trade press.

- Advertisements for new products can tell you about companies that are making things happen, and that need people who can make things happen.

In all of the above instances it is advisable to clip and keep, in retrievable fashion, all the items that generate leads. There are two reasons for this: You can send a copy to the person you intend to approach, and you will have a copy on file to refresh your memory before any direct communication.

In short, just about every page of your average trade journal holds a valuable job lead. You just need to know how and where to look. Then having found something, you need to take action.

9. Networking

People frequently think networking means annoying the hell out of your friends until they stop taking your calls. What it should mean is using others to assist in your job search. You will find it surprising how willing friends, colleagues, and even strangers are to help you.

The bad news is that networks need nurturing and development. Networking is more than calling your relatives and waiting for them to call back with job offers. People know people, not just in your home town but all over the country and sometimes the world.

I used the word *networks*, not *network*. We all have a number of networks, any of which may produce that all-important job offer. Here are the typical networks we can all tap into.

- Family and relatives. This includes your spouse's family and relatives.

- Friends. This includes neighbors and casual acquaintances.
- Co-workers. This includes professional colleagues past and present. You will especially want to ask about headhunters they know or might hear from, and professional affiliations they have found valuable.
- Managers, past and present. A manager's success depends on tapping good talent. Even if a particular manager can't use you, a judicious referral to a colleague can gain goodwill for the future.
- Service industry acquaintances. This includes your banker, lawyer, insurance agent, realtor, doctors, and dentist.
- Other job hunters.
- Other professionals in your field.

Over a period of a few days you need to develop the most extensive lists you can in each of these categories. Start lists and add to them every day. The experienced professional should be able to come up with a minimum of twenty names for, say, the service industry network list, and upward of a couple of hundred professional colleagues.

Here are some tips for writing networking letters or making calls asking for assistance.

- Establish connectivity. Recall the last memorable contact you had or mention someone you both knew whom you have spoken to recently.
- Tell why you are writing or calling: "It's time for me to make a move. I just got laid off with one thousand others, and I'm taking a couple of days to catch up with old friends."
- Ask for advice and guidance about your tactics, what the happening companies are, and whether the person can take a look at your resume—because you really need an objective opinion and have always respected his viewpoint. Don't ask specifically, "Can you or your company hire me?" If there is some action available, he will let you know.
- Don't rely on a contact with a particular company to get you into that company. Mount and execute your own plan of attack. No one is as interested as you are to put bread on your table.
- Let contacts know what you are open for. They will usually want to help, but you have to give them a framework within which to target their efforts.
- Discuss the profession, the industry, the areas of opportunity, and the people worthwhile to contact. If you comport yourself in a professional manner most fellow professionals will come up with a lead. If they can't think of a person, back off and ask them about companies. Everyone can think of a company. If they come up with a company, respond, "Hey, that's a great idea. I never thought of those people," even if you have just spoken to that outfit. Then after a suitable pause, ask for another company. When people see that their advice is appreciated, they will often come up with more.

When you have gathered two or three company names, backtrack with, "Do you know of anyone I could speak to at _____ [company A, B, C]?" Every time you get a referral be sure to ask whether you can use your contact's name as an introduction. The answer will invariably be yes, but asking demonstrates professionalism and will encourage your contact to come up with more leads.

Remember to ask for information about and specific leads from your targeted companies.

- At the end of the call make sure the contact knows how to get in touch with you. I find the nicest and most effective way of doing this is to say something like, "Mack, I really appreciate your help. I'd like to leave you my name and number in the hope that one day in the future I can return the favor." Not only is this a supremely professional gesture, it ensures that your contact information is available to that individual should openings arise within his sphere of influence. Say you hope you'll get to see each other again soon, that you look forward to doing something together. Invite the contact over for drinks, dinner, or a barbecue.

- When you do get help, say thank you. And if you get it verbally, follow it up in writing. The impression is indelible and just might get you another lead. Include a copy of your resume with the thank-you letter.

- Keep an open mind. You never know who your friends are. You will be surprised at how someone you always regarded as a real pal won't give you the time of day and how someone you never thought of as a friend will go above and beyond the call of duty for you.

- Whether your contacts help you or not, let them know when you get a job and maintain contact at least once a year. A career is a long time. It might be next week or a decade from now when a group of managers (including one from your personal network) are talking about filling a new position and the first thing they'll do is ask "Who do we know?" That could be you. (This topic is discussed in detail in chapter 29.)

Networking is more than one call or letter to each person on your list. Once the first conversation is in the bag, another call in a couple of months won't be taken amiss. For examples of networking cover letters, see the book *Cover Letters That Knock 'em Dead*.

When you get referrals as a result of your networking, use your source as an introduction: "Jane, my name is Martin Yate. Our mutual friend George Smith suggested I call, so before I go any further I must pass on George's regards."

10. The Job Hunter's Network
In your job hunt you will invariably find that companies are looking for everyone but you. The recent graduate is told to come back when she has experience, the experienced professional is told that only entry-level people are being hired. That's the luck of the draw, but one person's problem is another's opportunity.

The solution is to join or create a support group and job-hunting network of your own with people in the same situation as you are.

Existing Support Groups. In many communities these are sponsored by church or other social organizations. They meet, usually on a weekly basis, to discuss ideas, exchange tips and job leads, and provide encouragement and the opportunity to support and be supported by others in the same situation.

One national organization is known as the 40 Plus Club. The only requirements for membership are that you be a mature professional in your field. The 40 Plus Club has chapters around the country. You can find a comprehensive listing of these, other support groups, and networking opportunities in the weekly edition of the *National Business Employment Weekly.*

Creating Your Own Support Group. All this takes is finding someone in the same situation as yourself. Among your neighbors and friends someone probably knows someone who has the same needs as you do; all it takes is two. Your goals are quite simple: You meet on a regular basis to exchange ideas and tips; review each other's resumes, letters, and verbal presentations; and check on each other's progress. This means that if I tell you that in the last five days I've sent out only three resumes and made only two follow-up calls, you are obliged to get on my case. The purpose of such a group is to provide the pressure to perform that you experience at work.

You can advertise for members in your local penny saver. The paper might even be talked into running the ad for free as a community service.

Once you are involved in a group, you will meet others with different skill levels and areas of expertise. Then when an employer tells you she is hiring only accountants this month, you can offer a referral to the employer or give the lead to your accountant friend. In turn the accountant will be turning up leads in your field. If these openings don't make themselves known during your conversations, you can tag on a question of your own when the conversation is winding down: "John, I'm a member of an informal job-hunting network. If you don't have a need for someone with my background right now, perhaps one of my colleagues could be just what you are looking for. What needs do you have at present and in the forseeable future?"

Becoming an active member in an existing group or creating one of your own can get you leads and provide a forum for you to discuss your fears and hopes with others who understand your concerns.

With all of this chapter's networks working for you, you will have maximum coverage and will have minimized the chances of your exhausting any one member or network through overworking their good will and patience. Do it. You have nothing to lose and everything to gain.

11. The Electronic Job Hunt
There's a new weapon in your arsenal.

You can use your modem and personal computer to access important job information. Savvy job hunters can now tap into huge reservoirs of on-line data before launching a search in earnest or going on an interview. This approach is a new one that may well help you gain an edge over your competition.

There have been many changes recently in the world of on-line information. Gale's *Directory of Databases* indicates that there continues to be strong growth in the database industry; the totals for databases, records, on-line searches, database entries, database producers, and vendors are all up. The industry is showing no signs of leveling off; nor do consumers appear to be at a loss when it comes to finding new ways to use the information available. Using an on-line service is a little like walking into the biggest library in the world and being able to get anything you want without having to walk anywhere (and without having to wait in line). Some services even offer affordable practice forums for developing on-line skills.

The flexibility of on-line services makes them extremely valuable. Through one of the new online database services, you can request a list of all the companies in a certain geographic region; you can specify that you want to see only companies in a certain area that do business in your field of choice; you can further narrow the list by asking to see a list that highlights only firms with a sales level of x dollars or more. It's all up to you. If you need to get a list of all the hospitals in Kansas with five hundred beds or more that boast a state-of-the-art magnetic resonance imaging system, all you have to do is punch in your requirements or explain them to a database representative. The data is all there waiting for you, in over a dozen established business information databases; you'll probably be able to secure names and contact information for key company executives as well.

Many libraries provide walk-in use of on-line fee-based services. Additionally, most will conduct searches for you based on your specific needs. So, if you're a computerphobe, you can get all the benefits without ever touching a keyboard. If your local library doesn't have these services, explain your needs and ask for information on how to contact a library or other database access point that does.

Of course, there is no guarantee that your nearest database access point has the information you want to find. Enter the *Directory of Fee-Based Information Services*, an invaluable resource listing around 440 U.S. and Canadian library systems. This book will provide the details of which library will allow you to access what; you can ask for it at the library or order it direct from the American Library Association at 800-545-2433. Many of the libraries listed in this directory will either conduct a company search for you or provide a full-service business library where you can run your own search for the price of a few photocopies. The retail cost of the most recent edition is $65.00. (*Note:* A much shorter list detailing some of the major databases and the types of data each can generate appears as an appendix at the end of this book.)

Conducting Your Own Search
On-line searching is a tricky task, but one that can open the doors to the employment world in seconds. Even with all the excitement you may feel at the prospect of entering the computer age with your job search, however, a few caveats are in order before you plunge in.

First and foremost, I would issue the warning that time is money when you're on-line; many job seekers, of course, are in short supply of both. If you're one of them, and if you aren't familiar with the sometimes perplexing world of on-line computer searching, *don't take on the job of cruising this ocean of information yourself.* Either have the search conducted for you by a computer-friendly navigator, or use your local library.

If you *are* familiar with both computer procedures and the on-line world, get ready for some exciting news about CompuServe. (And if you aren't, get ready to pass this part of the book on to your navigator.) The Knowledge Index available through CompuServe, offered from 6:00 P.M. to 6:00 A.M., contains over a hundred databases—featuring full text, abstracts, or summaries—for only forty cents a minute. Like most databases, this one is word-oriented, but managing the database with CompuServe's menu-assisted windows is pretty easy. This database does *not* charge a "per page" surcharge for the pages of text downloaded. It offers a variety of useful information, including a full-text Standard and Poor's directory of company information, a full-text newspaper database, a full-text *Who's Who* directory, and addresses, phone numbers, and information about key employees of the companies you're searching for. Add to this plenty of data on subsidiaries, financial performance, and any number of other important topics, and you have an avalanche of information that will help you distinguish yourself from the competition.

If you've worked up a little experience with this sort of thing, the average company search will run approximately five minutes on line. That's just $2.00 in database charges per lead. For an additional eighteen minutes of on-line time (read: $7.20), we were able to find and download over a hundred recent news articles about our target company using our 2400-baud modem. In short, we got a small library of invaluable interview-preparation information for under ten bucks. Not a bad value, eh?

Through its BIZ FILE option, CompuServe also offers access to consumer and business phone directories for just twenty-five cents a minute. We searched for the word "resume" and the database prompted us with "resume services." We then asked for a listing of all such companies in twenty major cities across the United States. In about an hour, we had downloaded a fifty-page booklet of names, addresses, and phone numbers; some of the cities had over two hundred resume companies each. Similarly, if you're searching for all the divisions of, say, Ford Motor Company operating in Southern California, you can conduct the same search by going into BIZ FILE and asking the computer to search for all Ford divisions in the applicable regions.

CompuServe, of course, is not the only operation offering such services. Many services do, and there is a bewildering array of access requirements and charges. A good number of the databases are cheaper in the evening; be sure to doublecheck the rates you are quoted for this feature. Some on-line databases are designed to keep professional people informed of developments in their field. These are usually cheaper than other services; typically, they are offered at non-peak hours and are not always available in full-text format. If you find an entry abstract (rather than the material itself) on-line through one of these sources, you can usually do one of two things: build up a bibliography of articles and pop into the full-text index for the article you want, or head to the library, find the right copy of the publication in question, and make a copy of the article for five or ten cents a sheet on the library photocopier. The second option takes more time, but then again, the premium rate for printing an article in some on-line magazine or newspaper databases can run as high as $1.50 per page, plus on-line time and surcharges. Experts may (or may not) be able to make the longer searches for articles cost-effective; newcomers are once again advised to avoid paying for a costly—and, often, frustrating—learning-curve experience.

Classifieds on Your Screen

Among the most exciting developments in electronic databases has been E-Span, through which employers are effectively screening out the dinosaurs of the corporate world and zeroing in on the successful professionals of today. E-Span is essentially a national classified help-wanted database; it is also a service tailored to those growth industries of the future where computer literacy is an unspoken requirement for any job.

The ads run from entry-level through senior executive positions, and cover sixteen major professional groupings ranging from accounting to sales. Each of these major groupings has subheadings: the sales grouping, for instance, includes separate sections for advertisings, communications/public relations, customer service, and of course straight sales positions.

A great plus for the job hunter in comparison with a "real" help-wanted section is E-Span's lack of a newspaper's space restrictions. I noticed advertisements running one to two pages in length that gave job requirements in incredible detail. This can give you a substantial edge; it allows you to customize paperwork and focus your expertise in the appropriate direction.

The ads are national in nature, and will not necessarily feature opportunities in your own backyard. By the same token, some of the larger firms may have unadvertised opportunities in your area that you can track through E-Span.

E-Span is available through a number of media, including CompuServe; call 800-682-2901 for more information. This service can be an invaluable aid to your job search. I was able to pick out an ad that profiled a certain company; I then did an article search (through a separate on-line service) to get the latest breaking news on that firm, and I discovered three recent deals it had signed. Finally, I was able to pull up a quarterly interim balance sheet and get a breakdown on the company's worldwide core businesses. I started with nothing, discovered a specific job opening not likely to be advertised in the mainstream press, and gathered eight pages of first-rate analysis of the company.

If you can't get access to a computer, you can still find out what's cooking on E-Span. When we last checked with the service, you could order a disk of the current ads, then take the disk to your local library or copy shop for printout. The last we heard, disks were updated every two weeks. Call the E-Span number above for more information. (Words to the wise: Be sure to specify the working environment in which the disks will be printed out—usually IBM or Macintosh—and the disk size required.)

Close Encounters

As you can see, using on-line research services can do much more than provide extensive contact lists for your mail or phone campaigns. In a tightly run job race, being able to ace the "What do you know about us?" question could make all the differences. On-line services can often yield more detailed information about a specific company than you'd ever imagined possible.

Imagine for a moment that you're a corporate galley slave with an interview slated with 3M in Minneapolis for the day after tomorrow. You decide to call Nexis Express, a service of the Nexis/Lexis databases, both of which are divisions of Mead Data Central. You pick up the phone, dial 800-227-9597, and give them the specifics, asking them to fax the data to a local copy shop for you to pick up.

The total cost is quite reasonable, considering the purpose for which you'll be using the information. The most recent pricing schedules are as follows: $6.00 per minute of on-line search time, four cents per line printing charge, and twenty-five cents per page if the information is faxed to you. If you want the material sent to you by Federal Express, add another fifteen bucks. There is no charge for information sent to you via the U.S. Mail, but you may decide that receiving your data in this way defeats the purpose of *express service*, which is presumably what led you to call in the first place.

What you get for your money is truly remarkable: Over fifteen pages of data providing a complete overview of 3M from its inception to the present day, including contact information, officers and directors, the number of employees, subsidiaries of the company, corporate product lines and services, stock performance records, earnings and finances, and more. And you got it in no time flat. How's that for an advantage to carry into the heat of battle?

But you don't stop there. You call again to take advantage of the service's extensive article search capabilities. You ask for all the business articles run in the past year that featured 3M as the main topic and receive fourteen and a half more pages of material. (If you'd asked for everything about 3M, period, with no restrictions, you could have accessed literally thousands of articles, but you're pressed for time.) The entire process took ninety seconds on the phone and a few minutes of transmission time to your corner copy shop. The total cost for the article search and delivery is the same as for your company search; you can expect to pay $40.00 or a little more for each. Add it all up and you're cruising toward the hundred-dollar line, which is probably a little steep for that practice interview at Last Chance Electronics (where you don't want to work anyway), but may be perfectly appropriate for the Big Interview You've Been Waiting For at 3M.

Within ten minutes the company representative was inviting me in for an interview—and two hours earlier, I could have fit all I knew about microchips on the back of a Doritos package! Imagine what this kind of additional data could do for you if you had some idea what you were talking about in the first place; it would be blindingly obvious at the interview that you were twice as sharp as any other applicant. While this kind of edge is desirable at any level, the seeming omniscience that comes with doing better research than anyone else is all the more important when applying for executive positions. For job seekers at all levels, Nexis gets you what you need—and quick.

Similarly mindboggling is the service available through Standard and Poor's *Research Reports*, which provides in-depth analyses of specific publicly traded companies. I ran across a job opening at Reebok, the major sports shoe manufacturer, called Standard and Poor's to request a report, and received ten pages of great information guaranteed to knock the socks off any interviewer in the place. You can order through Standard and Poor's *Research Reports* by calling 800-642-2858. They offer a quick company report for $9.95, plus a $3.00 faxing charge. Within ninety minutes you'll have pages of information on your target company.

The New Resume Databases

Another revolutionary job-hunting technology is emerging: the public resume database. Under this system, you pay a nominal amount (usually between $10 and $30) to have your resume loaded onto a database. Access to this resume bank is then sold to corporations; they pay a few hundred to a few thousand dollars for unlimited access.

The employer logs on, detailing exactly what qualifications are being sought. If the company has asked for someone with four years of experience with Corel desktop publishing software, the computer searches the scanned-in resume text for words such as "Corel" and "four years." (This means that you should check with the database service on guidelines for composing your resume in such a way that it is properly retrieved!) The employer receives hard-copy resumes that exactly meet its criteria. No one in human resources has to scan five hundred resumes; your resume reaches the right person. Everyone benefits.

To the employer, the new system provides a brand-new, cost-effective recruiting and initial screening tool; to the job-hunter, it provides yet another great way to get that resume under the noses of forward-thinking employers. Of course, there is the added benefit that all resumes generated from the search are already perceived to be good matches. Consequently, your candidacy is likely to receive more serious initial evaluation and consideration.

There are currently about a dozen resume database companies in operation. Most claim to be national; none of them really are, at least not by my standards. I don't feel comfortable endorsing any specific companies at this point, but considering the low dollar amounts involved you probably can't go wrong with this method unless you rely on it as your sole means of generating interviews. As one of your many resources, resume banks are certainly worth a shot.

That's the picture now. I predict that by the turn of the century, however, registering one's resume on at least one public database will be a standard component of any professional job search. The savviest job hunters will keep their resumes permanently registered, on the theory that you can only turn down an opportunity if you have heard about it.

Getting the Word Out

So much for the eleven paths most likely to lead you to the hidden job market. Remember, there is no single approach to landing your dream job. Friends may tell you that the only effective way is the way that worked for them. Of course, we are all different people, and some things will be harder for you than others.

Although each of these techniques has proven effective, no single one is guaranteed for any one individual. Your plan of attack must be balanced and comprehensive. It should include elements of every technique discussed in this section. A man who goes fishing and puts one hook in the water has but one chance of catching any one of the millions of fish in the sea; a man with two hooks in the water has double the chances of getting a bite. At this stage of the game you are looking for bites. The more hooks you have in the water, the better your chances.

In the end, of course, you will want to know how to contact the companies you learn about through your various types of research. You have two basic approaches to choose from: the verbal approach, usually by telephone, and the written approach, usually including a letter and resume.

One of these is likely to appeal to you more than the other. However, in execution you will see that they both simply become different steps in the same process. When you send out letters and resumes, you will invariably find yourself following up with phone calls. When you make phone contact, you will inevitably be following up with letters and resumes. Your program needs to maintain a delicate balance between the two, so that your calls force you to follow up in writing and your resumes and letters force you to follow up with phone calls.

The trick is not to overemphasize the approach that is easiest for you (say, networking with friends and colleagues) at the expense of other approaches (say, direct research calls). Now while ultimately it is the conversations, not the letters, that get you interviews, I recommend that you begin your campaign by researching contacts in every single category I have discussed; then begin with a combination of mailings and direct calls, because every letter and every resume and every call is another hook in the water. We will examine the written part of the campaign now; initial phone calls will be the topic of the next few chapters.

Letters

Must you send out hundreds or even thousands of letters in the coming weeks? Yes and no. The goal is to mail as much as you need in your field and no more. Two employer contacts a week will not get you accelerating along that career path again. Only if you approach and establish communication with every possible employer will you create the maximum opportunity for yourself. *Two contacts a week is the behavior of the long-term unemployed.*

On the other hand, I am not recommending that you immediately make up a list of seven hundred companies and mail letters to them today. That isn't the answer either. Your campaign needs strategy. While every job-hunting campaign is unique, you will want to maintain a balance between the *number* of letters you send out on a daily and weekly basis and the *types* of letters you send out. Start off with balanced mailings and your phone contacts will maintain equilibrium, too.

The key is to send out a balanced mailing representing all the different types of leads, and to send them out regularly and in a volume that will allow you to make follow-up calls. Many headhunters manage their time so well that they average over fifty calls per day, year in and year out. While you may aim at building your call volume up to this number, I recommend that you start out with more modest goals. Send five to ten letters per day in each of the following areas:

- In response to newspaper advertisements
- To friends
- To professional colleagues
- To research contacts from reference works, newspapers, etc.
- To headhunters

With adequate research and the resources I have mentioned, there are literally thousands of contacts waiting to be made. So this breakdown of contacts is a daily quota. If it seems a bit steep to begin with, scale down the numbers until they are achievable and gradually build up the volume. But remember, the lower the volume, the longer the job search.

Do you need to write more than one letter? Almost certainly. There is a case to be made for having letters and resumes in more than one format. There is no need to waste precious time crafting your written communication entirely from scratch when templates exist. The key is to do each variation once and to do it right. This means doing your work on a computer if possible and keeping it comprehensively backed up on disk. This way you'll be loaded for bear regardless of when opportunity comes knocking on your door. More information on creating and managing an effective direct-mail campaign can be found in *Cover Letters That Knock 'em Dead*.

Multiple Submissions

You may sometimes find it valuable to send half a dozen contact letters to a given company, to assure that all the important players know of your existence. Let's say you are a young engineer who wants to work for Last Chance Electronics. It is well within the bounds of reason to mail cover or broadcast letters to any or all of the following people (each addressed by name so the letter doesn't end up in the trash): the company president, the vice president of engineering, the chief engineer, the engineering manager, the vice president of human resources, the technical engineering recruitment manager, and the technical recruiter.

A professionally organized and conducted campaign will proceed on two fronts.

Front One. A carefully targeted rifle approach to a select group of companies. You will have first identified these super-desirable places to work when you researched your long list of potential employers. You will continue to add to this primary target list as you unearth fresh opportunities in your day-to-day research efforts.

In this instance you have two choices:

1. Mail to everyone at once, remembering that the letters have to be personalized and followed up.

2. Start your mailings off with one to a line manager and one to a contact in human resources. Follow up in a few days and repeat the process to other names on your list.

Front Two. A carpet bombing approach to every possible employer in the area. After all, you won't know what opportunities exist unless you go find out.

Here you will begin with a mailing to one or two contacts within the company and then repeat the mailings to other contacts when your initial follow-up calls result in referrals or dead ends. Remember, just because Harry in engineering says there are no openings in the company doesn't necessarily make it so. Besides, any one of the additional contacts you make could well be the person *who knows the person* who is just dying to meet you.

Once your campaign is in motion and you have received some responses to your mailings and scheduled some interviews from your calls (how to make the calls is covered in the next chapter), your emphasis will change. Those contacts and interviews will require follow-up letters and conversation. You will be spending time preparing for the interviews.

This is exactly the point at which most job hunts stall. We get so excited about the interview activity that we convince ourselves that "This will be the offer." Experienced headhunters know that the offer that can't fail always will. The offer doesn't materialize, and we are left sitting with absolutely no interview activity. We let the interview funnel empty itself.

The more letters you send out, the more follow-up calls you can make to schedule interviews. The more direct calls you make, the more interviews you will schedule and the more leads you will generate. The more interviews you get, the better you feel and the better you get at interviewing. The better you get at interviewing, the better the offers you get—and the *more* offers you get.

So no matter how good things look, you must continue the campaign. While you have to maintain activity with those companies you are negotiating with, you must also make yourself maintain your daily marketing schedule. Write letters in *each* of the following areas:

- In response to newspaper ads
- To associations, alumni/ae, colleagues
- To direct research contacts
- To headhunters
- Follow-up letters

Small but consistent mailings have many benefits. The balance you maintain is important because most job hunters are tempted to send the easy letters and make the easy calls (networking with old friends). But this will knock your job hunt out of balance and kick you into a tailspin.

Don't stop searching even when an offer is pending, and your potential boss says, "Robin, you've got the job and we're glad you can start on Monday. The offer letter is in the mail." Never accept any "yes" until you have it in writing, you have started work, and the first paycheck has cleared at the bank! Until then keep your momentum building: it is the professional and circumspect thing to do.

It is no use mailing tens or even hundreds of resumes without following up on your efforts. If you are not getting a response with one resume format, you might want to redo it; try changing from a chronological to a functional or combination format, just as you would change the bait if the fish weren't taking what you had on the hook.

Keep things in perspective. Although your 224th contact may not have an opening for you, with a few polite and judicious questions she may well have a good lead. You will learn how to do this in the chapter entitled "Getting Live Leads from Dead Ends."

In the job hunt there are only two "yeses": Their "yes-I-want-you-to-work-for-us" and your "yes-I-can-start-on-Monday." Every "no" brings you closer to the big "yes." Never take rejections of your resume or your phone call as rejections of yourself; just as every job is not for you, you aren't right for every job.

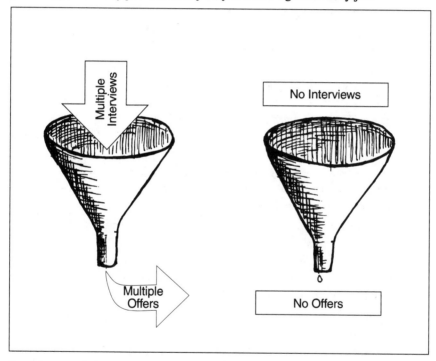

Stacking the Odds in Your Favor

We all have 168 hours a week to become bagmen or billionaires and to make our lives as fulfilling as they can be. For some of us this means a better job, for others it means getting back to work to keep a roof over our heads.

How we manage these hours will determine our success. These Job Hunting Commandments will see you successfully through the job change process or career transition.

- Those in the professional employment field reckon an average of seven hundred fresh contacts is required per job placement. You should anticipate at least this number. In a forty-hour week these professionals average approximately thirty-five to fifty contacts per day. Build to this momentum.

- Work at getting a new job. Work at least forty hours per week at it. Divide your time between contacting potential employers and generating new leads. Never stop the research and job-hunting process until you have a written job offer in hand and you have accepted that job in writing with an agreed-upon start date.

- Research the companies you contact. In a tightly run job race the candidate who is most knowledgeable about the employer has a distinct advantage.

- Contact and recontact your job leads. Follow up on the resumes you send out. Resubmit your resume after six weeks. Change the format of your resume and resubmit yet again. (See my book *Resumes That Knock 'em Dead* for specific ideas on how to do this.)

- Stay in regular telephone contact with your job leads on a monthly basis to maintain top-of-the-mind awareness.

- Take off the blinkers. We all have two specific skills: our professional/technical skills—say, computer programming—and our industry skills—say, banking. Professional/technical skills can be transferable to other industries—say, manufacturing; and industry skills can open up other opportunities in your industry—say, as a technical trainer for programmers and/or technophobes.

- Develop examples of the personality traits that make you special—say, determination. Rehearse building these examples into your interview responses. (See chapter 14.)

- Send follow-up notes with relevant news clippings, cartoons, and so on to those in your networks.

- Work on your self-image. Use this time to get physically fit. Studies show that unfit, overweight people take longer to find suitable work. The more you do today the better you will feel about yourself.

- Maintain a professional demeanor during the work week (clothing, posture, personal hygiene).

- Use regular business hours for making contacts. Use the early morning, lunch time, after 5 P.M., and Saturday for doing the on-going research to maintain momentum.

- Don't feel guilty about taking time off from your job-hunting job. Just do it conscientiously. If you regularly spend Saturday morning in the library doing research, you can take Wednesday afternoon off.

- Maintain records of your contacts. They will benefit not only this job search but maybe those in the future, too.

- Remember: It's all up to you. There are many excuses not to make calls or send resumes on any given day. There are many excuses to get up later or knock off earlier. There are many excuses to back off because this one's in the bag. There are no real reasons. There are no jobs out there for those who won't look. There are countless opportunities for those who assiduously turn over the stones.

Contact Trackers

Job hunting requires multiple contacts with employers and others. You will call an employer and schedule a follow-up conversation for a specific time and date next week, you will send a resume today, and you need to schedule a follow-up call four to eight days later. When you get up to speed, important opportunities will fall through the cracks unless you maintain a contact tracker like the one on page 73.

How to Use the Contact Tracker

I recommend you make 365 copies of this, date each one, and put them in a ring binder. Once you have been going a couple of weeks, your days will plan themselves. Of course you probably won't use anywhere near all 365, but as we say in New York, "such a problem I should have."

Before making a day's mailing, fill out the contact tracker with the company name, telephone number, and contact name. This will help you structure your job-hunting days. A mailing today will allow you to have a follow-up plan set and ready to go at the appropriate time. As a rule of thumb, a mailing today is ripe for follow-up four to eight days later. Much sooner and you can't guarantee the mail has arrived; much later and it will already be lost in an in-box or passed on.

You will know that your job hunt is on track when you are filling one of these out every day as a result of a mailing, and filling a second one out as a result of your follow-up calls.

Every month I hear from people who use these techniques effectively. Just last week I had a gentleman speak to me on a radio show in Texas who explained that he had been out of work for six months. He said he had bought the *Knock 'em Dead* books just five weeks earlier, had followed my advice to the letter, and had since generated four job offers. Follow my advice in letter and spirit and the same good fortune can be yours.

Network Index Sheets

As you develop your multiple networks, they too will become unwieldy and you will need some form of record keeping. Network index sheets will help you stay on top of the problem. The sheets should be developed on every good contact you make.

Good contacts from the Contact Tracker will be forwarded to a future date for follow up; then, as you develop a history on that person, on a network index sheet you can add a memory jogger to the Contact Tracker.

Follow-up: The Key Ingredient

In theory the perfect letters you send cold or as a result of phone calls will receive a response rate of one hundred percent. Unfortunately there is no perfect letter or call in this less-than-perfect world. If you sit there like some fat Buddha waiting for the world to beat a path to your door, you may wait a long time.

While I was writing this chapter, a pal of mine advertised for a programmer analyst, a two-line ad in the local paper. By Wednesday of the following week he had over one hundred responses. Ten days later he was still plowing through them when he received a follow-up call (the only one he received) from one of the respondents. The job hunter was in the office within two hours, returned the following morning, and was hired before lunchtime.

The story? The candidate's paperwork was simply languishing there in the pile, waiting to be discovered. The follow-up phone call got it discovered. The call made the interviewer sort through the enormous pile of paper, pull out the letter and resume, and act on it. Follow-up calls, and follow-up calls on the follow-up calls, do work.

The best managers maintain a private file of great professionals whom they can't use today but want to keep available. I know of someone who got a top job as a result of being in these files. She got an interview and job offer from a broadcast letter she had sent *three years earlier.*

Grant yourself the right to pick and choose among many job offers with this approach. Because you are in control, it is possible to set your multiple interviews close together. This way your interviewing skills improve from one meeting to the next. And soon, instead of scheduling multiple interviews, you can be weighing multiple job offers.

Date: _____

CONTACT TRACKER

	Company	Tel #	Contact Name	Result	F/U Date	Sent Resume
1.						
2.						
3.						
4.						
5.						
6.						
7.						
8.						
9.						
10.						
11.						
12.						
13.						
14.						
15.						
16.						
17.						
18.						
19.						
20.						

NETWORK INDEX SHEET

Name: _____

Relationship: _____

How known: _____

Time known: _____

People in common: _____

_____

Telephone: (H) _____,   (O) _____

Home address: _____

_____

Office address: _____

_____

Secretary: _____

Leads given: _____

_____

_____

BIOGRAPHICAL INFORMATION

Spouse: _____

Children: _____

Interests: _____

_____

Affiliations: _____

_____

Professional experience: _____

_____

_____

Date last contacted: _____

Result: _____

_____

_____

II

Getting to Square One

With the grunt work completed, you are loaded for bear and ready to knock 'em dead. So how do you begin?

It bears repeating that you must take the initiative when it comes to finding a job. You must do so in a distinctive way. What is your first instinct when you must "go look for a job?" Read the want ads? Everybody else does. Apply for jobs listed with the unemployment office? Everybody else does. Send resumes to companies on the off-chance they have a job that fits your resume? Everybody else does. Or, of course, you can wait for someone to call you. Employ those tactics as your main thrust for hunting down the best jobs in town, and you will fail, as do millions of others who fall into the trap of using such outdated job-hunting techniques.

Today's business marketplace demands a different approach. Your career does not take care of itself—you must go out and grab the opportunities.

"Hello, Mr. Smith? My name is Martin Yate. I am an experienced training specialist. . . ."

It's as easy as that.

Guide your destiny by speaking directly to the professionals who make their living in the same way you do. A few minutes spent calling different companies from your research dossier, and you will have an interview. When you get one interview from making a few calls, how many do you think could be arranged with a day's concerted effort?

5.
Painting the Perfect Picture
on the Phone

Before making that first nerve-wracking telephone call, you must be prepared to achieve one of these three goals. They are listed in order of priority.

- I will arrange a meeting.
- I will arrange a time to talk further on the phone.
- I will ask for a lead on a promising job opening elsewhere.

Always keep these goals in mind. By the time you finish the next four chapters, you'll be able to achieve any one of these goals quickly and easily.

To make the initial phone call a success, all you need to do is paint a convincing word picture of yourself. To start, remember the old saying: "No one really listens; we are all just waiting for our turn to speak." With this in mind, you shouldn't expect to hold anyone's attention for an extended period, so the picture you create needs to be brief yet thorough. Most of all, it should be specifically vague: specific enough to arouse interest, to make the company representative prick up his ears and yet vague enough to encourage questions, to make him pursue you. The aim is to paint a representation of your skills in broad brush strokes with examples of the money-making, money-saving, or time-saving accomplishments all companies like to hear about.

A presentation made over the telephone must possess four characteristics to be successful. These can best be remembered by an old acronym from the advertising world: *AIDA*.

A—You must get the company representative's **Attention**.
I—You must get the company representative's **Interest**.
D—You must create a **Desire** to know more about you.
A—You must encourage the company representative to take **Action**.

With AIDA you get noticed. The interest you generate will be displayed by the questions that are being asked: "How much are you making?" "Do you have a degree?" "How much experience do you have?" By giving the appropriate answers to these and other questions (which I will discuss in detail), you will change interest into a desire to know more and then parlay that desire into an interview.

The types of questions you are asked also enable you to identify the company's specific needs, and once they are identified, you can gear the ongoing conversation toward those needs.

Here are the steps in building your AIDA presentation:

Step One: This covers who you are and what you do. It is planned to get the company representative's attention, to give the person a reason to stay on the phone. This introduction will include your job title and a brief generalized description of your duties and responsibilities. Use a nonspecific job title, as you did for your resume. Remember, getting a foot in the door with a generalized title can provide the occasion to sell your superior skills.

Tell just enough about yourself to whet the company's appetite and cause the representative to start asking questions. Again, keep your description a little vague. For example, if you describe yourself as simply experienced, the company representative must try to qualify your statement with a question: "How much experience do you have?" You have established a level of interest. But if you describe yourself as having four years of experience, while the company is looking for seven, you are likely to be ruled out before you are even aware a job exists. Never specify exact experience or list all your accomplishments during the initial presentation. Your aim is just to open a dialogue.

Example:
"Good morning, Mr. Smith. My name is Joan Jones. I am an experienced office equipment salesperson with an in-depth knowledge of the office products industry. Have I caught you at a good time?"

Never ever ask if you have caught someone at a bad time. You are offering your contact an excuse to say "yes." By the same token, asking whether you have caught someone at a good time will usually get you a "yes." Then you can go directly into the rest of your presentation.

Step Two: Now you are ready to generate interest, and from that, desire; it's time to sell one or two of your accomplishments. You already should have identified these during earlier resume-building exercises. Pull out no more than two items and follow your introductory sentence with them. Keep them brief and to the point, without embellishments.

Example:
"As the #3 salesperson in my company, I increased sales in my territory 15 percent to over $1 million. In the last six months, I won three major accounts from my competitors."

Step Three: You have made the company representative want to know more about you, so now you can make him take action. Include the reason for your call and a request to meet. It should be carefully constructed to finish with a question that will bring a positive response, which will launch the two of you into a nuts-and-bolts discussion.

Example:
"The reason I'm calling, Mr. Smith, is that I'm looking for a new challenge, and having researched your company, I felt we might have some areas for discussion. Are these the types of skills and accomplishments you look for in your staff?"

Your presentation ends with a question that guarantees a positive response, and the conversation gets moving.

□   □   □

Your task before calling is to write out a presentation using these guidelines and your work experience. Knowing exactly what you are going to say and what you wish to achieve is the only way to generate multiple interviews and multiple job offers. When your presentation is prepared and written, read it aloud to yourself, and imagine the faceless company representative on the other end of the line. Practice with a friend or spouse, or use a tape recorder to critique yourself.

After you make the actual presentation on the phone, you'll really begin to work on arranging a meeting, another phone conversation, or establishing a referral. There will likely be a silence on the other end after your initial pitch. Be patient. The company representative needs time to digest your words. If you feel tempted to break the silence, resist; you do not want to break the person's train of thought, nor do you want the ball back in your court.

This contemplative silence may last as long as twenty seconds, but when the company representative responds, only three things can happen.

1. The company representative can agree with you and arrange a meeting.

2. The company representative can ask questions that show interest: "Do you have a degree?" "How much are you earning?"
   (Any question, because it denotes interest, is considered a buy signal. Handled properly, it will enable you to arrange a meeting.)

3. The company representative can raise an objection: "I don't need anyone like that now." "Send me a resume."

These objections, when handled properly, will also result in an interview with the company, or at least a referral to someone else who has job openings. In fact, you will frequently find that objections prove to be terrific opportunities.

□   □   □

I hope you can handle the first option, "I'd like to meet with you," with little assistance; for obvious reasons, it doesn't get its own chapter.

It will sometimes happen that an overly officious receptionist or secretary will try to thwart you in your efforts to present your credentials directly to a potential employer. At least it appears that way to you.

In fact, it is very rare that these corporate gatekeepers, as they are known, are specifically directed to screen calls from professionals seeking employment, as to do so can only increase employment costs to the company. What they are there to do is to screen the nuisance calls from salespeople and the like.

However, to arm you for the occasional objectionable gatekeeper standing between you and making a living, you might try the following techniques used by investigative reporters, private eyes, and headhunters.

Go up the Ladder

If you can't get through to the person you want to speak to, say the accounting manager, go up the ladder to the controller or the vice president of finance. Interestingly enough, the higher you go, the more accessible people are. In this instance the senior manager may well not schedule an interview with you but instead refer you back down to the appropriate level. Which means that to the pesky gatekeeper you can now say, "Mr. Bigshot, your divisional vice president of finance, asked me to call your Mr. Jones. Is he there?" Or if you didn't get through, and Bigshot's secretary referred you down the ladder, you say, "Mr. Bigshot's office recommended . . ." Then the conversation with your target can begin with your standard introduction, but be sure to mention first that so-and-so suggested you call.

Preempt

Most gatekeepers are trained at most to find out your name and the nature of your business. But when they are asking the questions, they control the conversation. You can remain in control by preempting their standard script. "Hi, I'm Mr. Yate [always use your surname for the intimidation value]. I need to speak to Ms. Jones about an accounting matter. Is she there?" Should a truly obnoxious gatekeeper ask snidely, "Perhaps I can help you?" you can effectively utilize any of the following options: "Thank you, but I'd rather discuss it with Ms. Jones." "It's personal." (Well, it's your livelihood isn't it?) Or you can blind them with science. "Yes, if you can talk to me about the finer points of release 6.2 of Lotus 1-2-3," which invariably they can't, so you're in like Flynn.

When you are clear about who you want to speak to and can predict possible screening devices, you are usually assured of getting through. When you don't have the name, try these techniques.

Explain to gatekeepers that you need to send a letter to (title) and ask for the correct spelling of the name. There is usually more than one person worth speaking to at any company, so ask for more than one name and title. In the finance area, and depending on your title, any or all of the following could provide useful contacts: the accounting supervisor, the accounting manager, the assistant controller, the controller, the vice president of finance, the executive vice president, the COO, the CEO, and the chairman.

Anyone who will give you one name will invariably give you more. Some years ago in Colorado I sat with a job hunter using this technique who gathered 142 names in one hour!

In companies where security is at a premium, the gatekeepers are expressly forbidden to give out names and titles. In this case use some of my blind-siding techniques: There are certain people in every company who by the very nature of their jobs have contacts with people at all levels of the company, and who are not given the responsibility to screen calls. These include people in the mail room, the gate house, guards, shipping and receiving employees, second-, third-, and fourth-shift employees, new or temporary employees, advertising and public relations people, sales and marketing people, travel center, Q/A, or customer service employees.

Automatic Phone Systems

Automatic phone systems are on the increase. If the techniques I've mentioned don't turn the trick for you, these will. When the recorded voice tells you to enter the extension key, keep keying until you hit one that is on the money. It doesn't matter who answers as long as someone does. The conversation goes like this:

"Jack speaking."

"Jack, this is Martin Yate. I'm calling from outside and I'm lost on this damn telephone system." This usually gets a smile. "I'm trying to get hold of (title). Could you check who that would be for me?"

or,

"Jack, this is Martin Yate. I'm lost on this damn telephone system. I need some help. Can you spare me a minute?"

Whichever technique you use, be sensitive to the person in a rush and don't leave numerous messages. Try to get the extension of the person you want, rather than letting yourself be transferred.

6.
Responding to Buy Signals

With just a touch of nervous excitement you finish your presentation: "Are these the types of skills and accomplishments you look for in your staff?" There is silence on the other end. It is broken by a question. You breathe a sigh of relief because you remember that any question denotes interest and is a buy signal.

Now, conversation is a two-way street, and you are most likely to win an interview when you take responsibility for your half. Just as the employer's questions show interest in you, your questions should show your interest in the work done at the company. By asking questions of your own in the normal course of conversation—questions usually tagged on to the end of one of your answers—you will forward the conversation. Also, such questions help you find out what particular skills and qualities are important to the employer. Inquisitiveness will increase your knowledge of the opportunity at hand, and that knowledge will give you the power to arrange a meeting.

The alternative is to leave all the interrogation to the employer. That will place you on the defensive and at the end of the talk, you will be as ignorant of the real parameters of the job as you were at the start. And the employer will know less about you than you might want.

Applying the technique of giving a short answer and finishing that reply with a question will carry your call to its logical conclusion: The interviewer will tell you the job specifics, and as that happens, you will present the relevant skills or attributes. In any conversation, the person who asks the questions controls its outcome. You called the employer to get an interview as the first step in generating a job offer, so take control of your destiny by taking control of the conversation.

Example:
Joan Jones: "Good morning, Mr. Smith. My name is Joan Jones. I am an experienced office equipment salesperson with an in-depth knowledge of the office products industry. Have I caught you at a good time? . . . . As the #3 salesperson in my company, I increased sales in my territory 15 percent to over $1 million. In the last six months, I won three major accounts from my competitors. The reason I'm calling, Mr. Smith, is that I'm looking for a new challenge, and having researched your company, I felt we might have areas for discussion. Are these the types of skills and accomplishments you look for in your staff?"

[Pause.]

Mr. Smith: "Yes, they are. What type of equipment have you been selling?" *[Buy signal!]*

J: "My company carries a comprehensive range, and I sell both the top and bottom of the line, according to my customers' needs. I have been noticing a considerable interest in the latest fax and scanning equipment." *[You've made it a conversation; you further it with the following.]* "Has that been your experience recently?"

S: "Yes, especially in the color and acetate capability machines." *[Useful information for you.]* "Do you have a degree?" *[Buy signal!]*

J: "Yes, I do." *[Just enough information to keep the company representative chasing you.]* "I understand your company prefers degreed salespeople to deal with its more sophisticated clients." *[Your research is paying off.]*

S: "Our customer base is very sophisticated, and they expect a certain professionalism and competence from us." *[An inkling of the kind of person they want to hire.]* "How much experience do you have?" *[Buy signal!]*

J: "Well, I've worked in both operations and sales, so I have a wide experience base." *[General but thorough.]* "How many years of experience are you looking for?" *[Turning it around, but furthering the conversation.]*

S: "Ideally, four or five for the position I have in mind." *[More good information.]* "How many do you have?" *[Buy signal!]*

J: "I have two with this company, and one and a half before that. I fit right in with your needs, don't you agree?" *[How can Mr. Smith say "no"?]*

S: "Uhmmm . . . What's your territory?" *[Buy signal!]*

J: "I cover the metropolitan area. Mr. Smith, it really does sound as if we might have something to talk about." *[Remember, your first goal is the face-to-face interview.]* "I am planning to take Thursday and Friday off at the end of the week. Can we meet then?" *[Make Mr. Smith decide what day he can see you, rather than whether he will see you at all.]* "Which would be best for you?"

S: "How about Friday morning? Can you bring a resume?"

Your conversation should proceed with that kind of give-and-take. Your questions show interest, carry the conversation forward, and teach you more about the company's needs. By the end of the conversation you have an interview arranged and several key areas to promote when you arrive:

- The company sees growth in the latest fax and scanning equipment, especially those with color and acetate capabilities.
- They want business and personal sophistication.
- They ideally want four or five years' experience.
- They are interested in your metropolitan contacts.

The above is a fairly simple scenario, but even though it is constructive, it doesn't show you the tricky buy signals that can spell disaster in your job hunt. These are questions that appear to be simple buy signals, yet in reality are a part of every interviewer's arsenal called "knock-out" questions—questions that can save the interviewer time by quickly ruling out certain types of candidates. Although these questions most frequently arise during the initial telephone conversation, they can crop up at the face-to-face interview; the answering techniques are applicable throughout the interview cycle.

Note: We all come from different backgrounds and geographical areas. So understand that while my answers cover correct approaches and responses, they do not attempt to capture the regional and personal flavor of conversation. You and I will never talk alike, so don't learn the example answers parrot-fashion. Instead, you should take the essence of the responses and personalize them until the words fall easily from your lips.

Buy Signal:
"How much are you making/do you want?"
This is a direct question looking for a direct answer, yet it is a knock-out question. Earning either too little or too much could ruin your chances before you're given the opportunity to shine in person. There are a number of options that could serve you better than a direct answer. First, you must understand that questions about money at this point in the conversation are being used to screen you in or screen you out of the "ballpark"—the answers you give now should be geared specifically toward getting you in the door and into a face-to-face meeting. (Handling the serious salary negotiations that are attached to a job offer are covered extensively in chapter 23, "Negotiating the Offer.") For now, your main options are as follows.

☐ **Put yourself above the money**: "I'm looking for a job and a company to call home. If I am the right person for you, I'm sure you'll make me a fair offer. What is the salary range for the position?"

☐ **Give a vague answer**: "The most important things to me are the job itself and the company. What is the salary range for the position?"

☐ **Or you could answer a question with a question:** "How much does the job pay?"

When you are pressed a second time for an exact dollar figure, be as honest and forthright as circumstances permit. Some people (often, unfortunately, women) are underpaid for their jobs when their work is compared to that of others in similar positions. It is not a question of perception; these women in fact make less money than they should. If you have the skills for the job and you are concerned that your current low salary will eliminate you before you have the chance to show your worth, you might want to add into your base salary the dollar value of your benefits. If it turns out to be too much, you can then simply explain that you were including the value of your benefits. Or, you could say, "Mr. Smith, my previous employers felt I am well worth the money I earn due to my skills, dedication, and honesty. Were we to meet, I'm sure I could demonstrate my value and my ability to contribute to your department. You'd like an opportunity to make that evaluation, wouldn't you?"

Notice the "wouldn't you?" at the end of the reply. A reflexive question such as this is a great conversation-forwarding technique because it encourages a positive response. Conservative use of reflexive questions can really help you move things along. Watch the sound of your voice, though. A reflexive question can sound pleasantly conversational or pointed and accusatory; it's not really what you say, but how you say it.

Such questions are easy to create. Just conclude with "wouldn't you?" "didn't you?" "won't you?" "couldn't you?" "shouldn't you?" or "don't you?" as appropriate at the end of virtually any statement, and the interviewer will almost always answer "yes." You have kept the conversation alive, and moved it closer to your goal. Repeat the reflexive questions to yourself. They have a certain rhythm that will help you remember them.

Buy Signal:
"Do you have a degree?"

Always answer the exact question; beware of giving unrequested (and possibly excessive) information. For example, if you have a bachelor's degree in fine arts from New York University, your answer is "Yes," not "Yes, I have a bachelor's degree in fine arts from NYU." Perhaps the company wants an architecture degree. Perhaps the company representative has bad feelings about NYU graduates. You don't want to be knocked out before you've been given the chance to prove yourself.

"Yes, I have a degree. What background are you looking for?" Or, you can always answer a question with a question: "I have a diverse educational background. Ideally, what are you looking for?"

When a degree is perceived as mandatory and you barely scraped through grade school, don't be intimidated. As Calvin Coolidge used to say, "The world is full of educated layabouts." You may want to use the "Life University" answer. For instance: "My education was cut short by the necessity of earning a living at an early age. My past managers have found that my life experience and responsible attitude is a valuable asset to the department. Also, I intend to return to school to continue my education."

A small proportion of the more sensitive employers are verifying educational credentials, and if yours are checked it means the employer takes such matters seriously, so an untruth or an exaggeration could cost you a job. Think hard and long before inflating your educational background.

Buy Signal:
"How much experience do you have?"

Too much or too little could easily rule you out. Be careful how you answer and try to gain time. It is a vague question, and you have a right to ask for qualifications.

"Could you help me with that question?" or, "Are you looking for overall experience or in some specific areas?" or, "Which areas are most important to you?" Again, you answer a question with a question. The employer's response, while gaining you time, tells you what it takes to do the job and therefore what you have to say to get it, so take mental notes—you can even write them down, if you have time. Then give an appropriate response.

You might want to retain control of the conversation by asking another question, for example: "The areas of expertise you require sound very interesting, and it sounds as if you have some exciting projects at hand. Exactly what projects would I be involved with in the first few months?"

After one or two buy signal questions are asked, ask for a meeting. Apart from those just outlined, questions asked over the phone tend not to contain traps. If you simply ask, "Would you like to meet me?" there are only two possible responses: "yes" or "no." Your chances of success are greatly decreased. When you intimate, however, that you will be in the area on a particular date or dates—"I'm going to be in town on Thursday and Friday, Mr. Smith. Which would be better for you?"— you have asked a question that moves the conversation along dramatically. Your question gives the company representative the choice of meeting you on Thursday or Friday, rather than meeting you or not meeting you. By presuming the "yes," you reduce the chances of hearing a negative, and increase the possibility of a face-to-face meeting.

7.
Responding to Objections

Even with the most convincing word picture, the silence may be broken not by a buy signal, but by an objection. An objection is usually a statement, not a question: "Send me a resume," or, "I don't have time to see you," or, "You are earning too much," or, "You'll have to talk to personnel," or, "I don't need anyone like you right now."

Although these seem like brush-off lines, often they are really disguised opportunities to get yourself a job offer—handled properly, almost all objections can be parlayed into interviews. This section will teach you to seize hidden opportunities successfully; notice that all your responses have a commonality with buy-signal responses. They all end with a question, one that will enable you to learn more about the reason for the objection, overcome it, and once again lead the conversation toward a face-to-face interview.

In dealing with objections, as with differences of opinion, nothing is gained by confrontation, though much is to be gained by appreciation of the other's viewpoint. Most objections you hear are best handled by first demonstrating your understanding of the other's viewpoint. Always start your response with "I understand," or, "I can appreciate your position," or, "I see your point," or, "Of course," followed by, "However," or, "Also consider," or a similar line that puts you back into consideration.

Remember, these responses should not be learned merely to be repeated. You need only to understand and implement their meaning, to understand their concept and put the answers in your own words. Personalize all the suggestions to your character and style of speech.

□   □   □

Objection:
"Why don't you send me a resume?"

Danger here. The company representative may be genuinely interested in seeing your resume as a first step in the interview cycle; or it may be a polite way of getting you off the phone. You should identify what the real reason is without causing antagonism. At the same time, you want to open up the conversation. A good reply would be: "Of course, Mr. Smith. Would you give me your exact title and the full address? . . . . Thank you. So that I can be sure that my qualifications fit your needs, what skills are you looking for in this position?"

Notice the steps:

- Apparent agreement to start
- A show of consideration
- A question to further the conversation

Answering in that fashion will open up the conversation. Mr. Smith will relay the aspects of the job that are important to him, and with this knowledge, you can sell Smith on your skills over the phone. Also, you will be able to use the information to draw attention to your skills in the future, in:

- Following conversations
- The cover letter to your resume
- Your executive briefing
- Your face-to-face meeting
- Your follow-up after the meeting

The information you glean will give you power and will increase your chances of receiving a job offer.

□   □   □

Objection:

"I don't have time to see you."

If the employer is too busy to see you, he or she has a problem, and by recognizing that, perhaps you can show yourself as the one to solve it. You should avoid confrontation, however—it is important that you demonstrate empathy for the speaker. Agree, empathize, and ask a question that moves the conversation forward.

"I understand how busy you must be; it sounds like a competent, dedicated, and efficient professional [whatever your title is] could be of some assistance. Perhaps I could call you back at a better time, to discuss how I might make you some time. When are you least busy, in the morning or afternoon?"

The company representative will either make time to talk now, or will arrange a better time for the two of you to talk further.

Here are some other ideas you could use to phrase the same objection:

"Since you are so busy, what is the best time of day for you? First thing in the morning, or is the afternoon a quieter time?" or, "I will be in your area tomorrow, so why don't I come by and see you?"

Of course, you can combine the two: "I'm going to be in your part of town tomorrow, and I could drop by and see you. What is your quietest time, morning or afternoon?" By presuming the invitation for a meeting, you make it harder for the company representative to object. And if he or she is truly busy, your consideration will be appreciated and will still make it hard to object.

□ □ □

Objection:

"You are earning too much."

You should not have brought up salary in the first place. Go straight to jail. If the company representative brought up the matter, that's a buy signal, which was discussed in the last chapter. If the job really doesn't pay enough, you got (as the carnival barker says) close, but no cigar! How to make a success of this seeming dead-end is handled in the next chapter. You may also refer to helpful information covered in chapter 23, "Negotiating the Offer."

□ □ □

Objection:

"We only promote from within."

Your response could be: "I realize that, Mr. Smith. Your development of employees is a major reason I want to get in! I am bright, conscientious, and motivated. When you do hire from the outside, what assets are you looking for?"

The response finishes with a question designed to carry the conversation forward, and to give you a new opportunity to sell yourself. Notice that the response assumes that the company is hiring from the outside, even though the company representative has said otherwise. You have called his bluff, but in a professional, inoffensive manner.

□ □ □

Objection:

"You'll have to talk to personnel."

Your reply is: "Of course, Mr. Smith. Whom should I speak to in personnel, and what specific position should I mention?"

You cover a good deal of ground with that response. You establish whether there is a job there or whether you are being fobbed off to personnel to waste their time and your own. Also, you move the conversation forward again while changing the thrust of it to your advantage. Develop a specific job-related question to ask while the company representative is answering the first question. It can open a fruitful line for you to pursue. If you receive a nonspecific reply, probe a little deeper. A simple phrase like, "That's interesting, please tell me more," or, "Why's that?" will usually do the trick.

Or you can ask: "When I speak to personnel, will it be about a specific job you have, or is it to see whether I might fill a position elsewhere in the company?"

Armed with the resulting information, you can talk to personnel about your conversation with Mr. Smith. Remember to get the name of a specific person with whom to speak, and to quote the company representative.

Example:

"Good morning, Mr. Johnson. Mr. Smith, the regional sales manager, suggested we should speak to arrange an interview."

That way, you will show personnel that you are not a waste of time; because you know someone in the company, you won't be regarded as one of the frequent "blind" calls they get every day. As the most overworked, understaffed department in a company, they will appreciate that. Most important, you will stand out, be noticed.

Don't look at the personnel department as a roadblock; it may contain a host of opportunities for you. Because a large company may have many different departments that can use your talents, personnel is likely to be the only department that knows all the openings. You might be able to arrange three or four interviews with the same company for three or four different positions!

☐   ☐   ☐

Objection:

"I really wanted someone with a degree."

You could respond to this by saying: "Mr. Smith, I appreciate your position. It was necessary that I start earning a living early in life. If we meet, I am certain you would recognize the value of my additional practical experience."

You might then wish to ask what the company policy is for support and encouragement of employees taking night classes or continuing-education courses, and will naturally explain how you are hoping to find an employer who encourages employees to further their education. Your response will end with: "If we were to meet, I am certain you would recognize the value of my practical experience. I am going to be in your area next week. When would be the best time of day to get together?"

☐   ☐   ☐

Objection:

"I don't need anyone like you now."

Short of suggesting that the employer fire someone to make room for you (which, incidentally, has been done successfully on a few occasions), chances of getting an interview with this particular company are slim. With the right question, however, that person will give you a personal introduction to someone else who could use your talents. Asking that right question or series of questions is what networking and the next chapter are all about. So on the occasions when the techniques for answering buy signals or rebutting objections do not get you a meeting, "Getting Live Leads from Dead Ends" will!

8.
Getting Live Leads from Dead Ends

There will be times when you have said all the right things on the phone, but hear, "I can't use anyone like you right now." Not every company has a job opening for you, nor are you right for every job. Sometimes you must accept a temporary setback and understand that the rejection is not one of you as a human being. By using these special interview development questions, though, you will be able to turn those setbacks into job interviews.

The company representative is a professional and knows other professionals in his or her field, in other departments, subsidiaries, even other companies. If you approach the phone presentation in a professional manner, he or she, as a fellow professional, will be glad to advise you on who is looking for someone with your skills. Nearly everyone you call will be pleased to point you in the right direction, but only if you *ask*! And you'll be able to ask as many questions as you wish, because you will be recognized as a colleague intelligently using the professional network. The company representative also knows that his good turn in referring you to a colleague at another company will be returned in the future. And, as a general rule, companies prefer candidates to be referred this way over any other method.

But do not expect people to be clairvoyant. There are two sayings: "You get what you ask for," and "If you don't ask, you don't get." Each is pertinent here.

When you are sure that no job openings exist within a particular department, ask one of these questions:

- "Who else in the company might need someone with my qualifications?"
- "Does your company have any other divisions or subsidiaries that might need someone with my attributes?"
- "Whom do you know in the business community who might have a lead for me?"
- "Which are the most rapidly growing companies in the area?"
- "Whom should I speak to there?"
- "Do you know anyone at the ABC Electronics Company?"
- "When do you anticipate an opening in your company?"

- "Are you planning any expansion or new projects that might create an opening?"
- "When do you anticipate change in your manpower needs?"

Each one of those interview-development questions can gain you an introduction or lead to a fresh opportunity. The questions have not been put in any order of importance—that is for you to do. Take a sheet of paper and, looking at the list, figure out what question you would ask if you had time to ask only one. Write it down. Do that with the remaining questions on the list. As you advance, you will develop a comfortable set of prioritized questions. Add questions of your own. For instance, the type of computer or word-processing equipment a company has might be important to some professions, but not to others, and a company representative might be able to lead you to companies that have your machines. Be sure that any question you add to your list is specific and leads to a job opening. Avoid questions like, "How's business these days?" Time is valuable, and time is money to both of you. When you're satisfied with your list of interview development questions, put them on a fresh sheet of paper and store it safely with your telephone presentation and resume.

Those interview development questions will lead you to a substantial number of jobs in the hidden job market. You are getting referrals from the "in" crowd, who know who is hiring whom long before that news is generally circulated.

By being in with the "in" crowd, you establish a very effective referral network.

When you get leads on companies and specific individuals to talk to, be sure to thank your benefactor and ask to use his or her name as an introduction. The answer, you will find, will always be "yes," but asking shows you to be someone with manners—in this day and age, that alone will set you apart.

You might also suggest to your contact that you leave your telephone number in case he or she runs into someone who can use you. You'll be surprised at how many people call back with a lead.

With personal permission to use someone's name on your next networking call, you have been given the greatest of job-search gifts: a personal introduction. Your call will begin with something like:

"Hello, Ms. Smith. My name is Jack Jones. Joseph McDonald recommended I give you a call. By the way, he sends his regards." [Pause for any response to this.] "He felt we might have something valuable to discuss."

Follow up on every lead you get. Too many people become elated at securing an interview for themselves and then cease all effort to generate additional interviews, believing a job offer is definitely on its way. Your goal is to have a choice of the best jobs in town, and without multiple interviews, there is no way you'll have that choice. Asking interview-development questions ensures that you are tapping all the secret recesses of the hidden job market.

Networking is a continuous cycle:

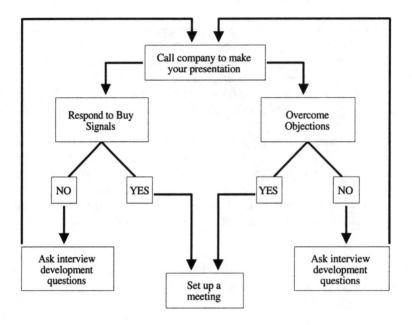

Make a commitment to sell yourself, to make telephone calls, to make a referral network, and to recognize buy signals and objections for what they really are—opportunities to shine. Make a commitment to ask interview development questions at every seeming dead end: They will lead you to all the jobs in town.

9.
The Telephone Interview

In this glorious technological age, the first substantive contact with a potential employer is virtually always by telephone. It's the way business is done today.

It happens in one of three ways:

- You are networking, and the company representative goes into a screening process immediately because you have aroused his or her interest.

- A company calls unexpectedly as a result of a resume you have mailed and catches you off-guard.

- You or a headhunter who has agreed to take you on has set up a specific time for a telephone interview.

Whatever circumstance creates the telephone interview, you must be prepared to handle the questioning and use every means at your disposal to win the real thing—the face-to-face meeting. The telephone interview is the trial run for the face-to-face and is an opportunity you must not bumble; your happiness and prosperity may hinge on it.

This, the first contact with your future employer, will test your mental preparation. Remember: You can plant in your mind any thought, plan, desire, strategy, or purpose, and translate it into reality. Put your goal down on paper and read it aloud to yourself every day, because the constant reiteration will crystallize your aims, and clear goals provide the most solid base of preparation.

Being prepared for a telephone interview takes organization. You never know when a company is going to call once you have started networking and sending your resume out (the word gets around more quickly than you think if it's a resume that knocks 'em dead). Usually the call comes at the worst of times, such as 8 o'clock Monday morning when you are sleeping late, or 4:56 in the afternoon, just as you return from walking the dog. You can avoid being caught completely off-guard by keeping your resume and alphabetized company dossiers by the telephone.

The most obvious (and often most neglected) point to remember is this: During the interview, the company representative has only ears with which to judge you, and that is something you must overcome. Here are some tips.

- **Take a surprise call in stride.** If you receive a call as a result of a mailed resume or a telephone message you left, and you are unprepared, be calm. Sound positive, friendly, and collected: "Thank you for calling, Mr. Smith. Would you wait just a moment while I close the door?"

    Put the phone down, take three deep breaths to slow your heart down, pull out the appropriate company dossier and your resume, put a smile on your face (it improves the timbre of your voice), and pick up the phone again. Now you are in control of yourself and the situation.

- **Beware of over-familiarity.** You should always refer to the interviewer by his or her surname until invited to do otherwise.

- **Allow the company representative to do most of the talking**—to ask most (but not all) of the questions. Keep up your end of the conversation—this is, after all, a sales presentation, so be sure to ask a few questions of your own that will reveal you as an intelligent person and provide you the opportunity to promote your candidacy. For example, ask what immediate projects the interviewer's department is involved in, or the biggest challenges that are being tackled. When the interviewer answers your question, you will either have a clear picture of how to sell yourself, or you will ask a follow-up question for clarification.

    For example: "What specific skills and personality traits do you think are necessary for a person to succeed with those challenges?" Everyone hires a problem solver—find the problem and you are already halfway toward the offer.

- **Beware of giving yes/no answers.** They give no real information about your abilities.

- **Be factual in your answers.** Brief yet thorough.

- **Speak directly into the telephone.** Keep the mouthpiece about one inch from your mouth. Do not smoke or eat while on the phone. Numbered among the mystical properties of our telephone system is its excellence at picking up and amplifying background music and voices, especially young ones. That is excelled only by its power to transmit the sounds of food or gum being chewed or smoke being inhaled or exhaled. Smokers, take note: there are no laws about discriminating against smokers, and therefore, all nonsmokers naturally discriminate. They will assume that even if you don't actually light up at the interview, you'll have been chain-smoking beforehand and will carry the smell with you as long as you are around. Taking no chances, they probably won't even give you a chance to get through the door once they hear you puffing away over the phone.

- **Take notes.** They will be invaluable to you in preparing for the face-to-face meeting. Were it not for the recent furor over the clandestine use of tape recorders, I would have recommended that you buy a cheap tape recorder and a phone attachment from your local electronics store and tape the whole conversation.

If, for any reason, the company representative is interrupted, jot down the topic under discussion. When he or she gets back on the line, you can helpfully recap: "We were just discussing . . ." That will be appreciated and will set you apart from the others.

The company representative may talk about the corporation, and from the dossier in front of you, you will also know facts about the outfit. A little flattery goes a long way: Admire the company's achievements and you are, in fact, admiring the interviewer. Likewise, if any areas of common interest arise, comment on them, and agree with the interviewer when possible—people hire people like themselves.

If the interviewer does not give you the openings you need to sell yourself, be ready to salvage the situation and turn it to your advantage. Have a few work-related questions prepared—for example, "What exactly will be the three major responsibilities in this job?" or, "What will be the first job I get my teeth into?" While you are getting the explanation, wait for a pause so that you can tell the interviewer your appropriate skills: "Would it be of value if I described my experience in the area of office management?" or, "Then my experience in word processing should be a great help to you," or, "I recently completed an accounting project just like that."

Under no circumstances, though, should you ask about the money you want, or benefits and vacation time; that comes later.

Remember that your single objective at this point is to sell yourself and your skills; if you don't do that, you may never get the face-to-face interview.

The telephone interview has come to an end when you are asked whether you have any questions. Ask any more questions that will improve your understanding of the job requirements. If you haven't asked before, now is the time to establish what projects you would be working on in the first six months. By discovering them now, you will have time before the face-to-face meeting to package your skills to the needs at hand, and to create the appropriate Executive Briefing.

And if you have not already asked or been invited to meet the interviewer, now is the time. Take the initiative.

"It sounds like a very interesting opportunity, Ms. Smith, and a situation where I could definitely make a contribution. The most pressing question I have now is, when can we get together?" (*Note:* Even though the emphasis throughout has been on putting things in your own words, do use "make a contribution." It shows pride in your work—a key personal trait.)

Once the details are confirmed, finish with this request: "If I need any additional information before the interview, I would like to feel free to get back to you." The company representative will naturally agree. No matter how many questions you get answered in the initial conversation, there will always be something you forgot. This allows you to call again to satisfy any curiosity—it will also enable you to increase rapport. Don't take too much advantage of it, though: One well-placed phone call that contains two or three considered questions will be appreciated; four or five phone calls will not.

Taking care to ascertain the correct spelling and pronunciation of the interviewer's name shows your concern for the small but important things in life—it will be noticed. This is also a good time to establish who else will be interviewing you, their titles, and how long the meeting is expected to last.

Follow with a casual inquiry as to what direction the meeting will take. You might ask, "Would you tell me some of the critical areas we will discuss on Thursday?" The knowledge gained will help you to package and present yourself, and will allow you time to bone up on any weak or rusty areas.

It is difficult to evaluate an opportunity properly over the telephone. Even if the job doesn't sound right, go to the interview. It will give you practice, and the job may look better when you have more facts. You might even discover a more suitable opening elsewhere within the company when you go to the face-to-face interview.

10.
Dressing for Interview Success

The moment we set eyes on someone, our minds make evaluations and judgments with lightning speed. The same is true for the potential employers who must assess us.

"What you see is what you get!"
"If a candidate can't put himself together in a professional manner, why should you assume he can put it all together on the job? Unless you look the part, don't expect an offer!" It may sound harsh, but that's an accurate summary of most employers' feelings on this issue. It's a fair estimate that nine out of ten of today's employers will reject an unsuitably dressed applicant without a second thought. Similarly dispiriting odds confront those who expect promotions but wear less than appropriate attire on the job. Like it or not, your outward image, your attitude, your confidence level, and your overall delivery are all affected by the clothes you wear.

The respect you receive at the interview is in direct proportion to the respect your visual image earns for you before you have the chance to say a word. If you wear clothes that are generally associated with leisure activities, you may be telling those who see you that you do not take your career seriously, and therefore are not committed to your work. Similarly, if you report for work the first day on a new job wearing clothes that undercut your perceived effectiveness, personal skills, and professionalism, it will be hard for you to be seen as a major contributor—no matter what you do between nine and five.

Employers rarely make overt statements about acceptable dress codes to their employees, much less to interviewees; more often there is an unspoken dictum that those who wish to climb the professional career ladder will dress appropriately . . . and that those who don't, won't.

There are some areas of employment where on-the-job dress (as opposed to interview dress) is somewhat less conservative than in the mainstream: Fashion, entertainment, and advertising are three examples. In these and a few other fields, there is a good deal of leeway with regard to personal expression in workplace attire. But for most of us, our jobs and our employers require a certain minimal level of professionalism in our dress. Interviewees must exceed these standards. This is not to say that you must dress like the chairman of the board (although that probably won't hurt), but you should be aware that dressing for the Friday night Lambada party on the day of your interview is not in your best professional interests.

Dressing Sharp: Your Interviewing Advantage

Our appearance tells people how we feel about ourselves as applicants, as well as how we feel about the interviewer(s), the company, and the process of interviewing itself. By dressing professionally, we tell people that we understand the niceties of corporate life, and we send a subtle "reinforcing" message that we can, for example, be relied upon to deal one-on-one with members of a company's prized client base.

More to the point, the correct image at an interview will give you a real edge over your competition. In fact, your overall appearance and presentation may well leave a more tangible impression than the words you say, since memory is rooted most strongly in pictures and impressions. At the very least, you can expect what you say to be strongly influenced in the mind of your interviewer by the way you present yourself.

Of course, the act of taking time to present an attractive professional image before you interview will add to your own sense of self-esteem and confidence. That is perhaps the greatest advantage of all.

The Look

The safest look for both men and women at interviews is traditional and conservative. This makes life fairly easy for the men: their professional fashions tend not to change much from year to year. A man can usually interview with confidence and poise in his three-year-old Brooks Brothers suit, provided that it isn't worn to a shine.

For women, the matter is a little more complicated. Appropriate female attire for the interview should ideally reflect the current fashion if the applicant is to be taken seriously. Rarely, if ever, can a woman feel comfortable interviewing in something she bought several years ago. Moreover, in selecting her current professional "uniform" the female applicant must walk a thin line, combining elements of both conformity (to show she belongs) and panache (to show a measure of individuality and style).

The key for both sexes is to dress for the position you want, not the one you have. This means that the upwardly mobile professional might need to invest in the clothes that project the desired image. The woman who dresses like a long-term member of the steno pool is unlikely ever to leave the secretarial ranks; the man who dresses like one of the corporate walking wounded will never be invited to move to Mahogany Row. Positions of responsibility are awarded to those who demonstrate that they are able to shoulder the burden. Looking capable will inspire others with the confidence to give you the most visible challenges.

The correct appearance alone probably won't get you a job offer, but it will go a long way toward winning attention and respect. When you know you look right, you can stop worrying about the impression your clothes are making and concentrate on communicating your message.

To be sure, every interview and every interviewer is different; because of this, it isn't possible to set down rigid guidelines for exactly what to wear in each situation. There is, however, relevant broadly based counsel that will help you make the right decision for your interview.

As we have seen, much of what we believe about others is based on our perception of their appearance; this chapter will help you insure that you are perceived as practical, well educated, competent, ethical, and professional.

General Guidelines

Appropriate attire, as we have noted, varies from industry to industry. The college professor can sport tweed jackets with elbow patches on the job, but is nevertheless likely to wear a suit to an interview. The advertising executive may wear wild ties as a badge of creativity (that is what he is being paid for), but he too is likely to dress conservatively for an interview. In all instances, our clothes are sending a message about our image, and the image we want to convey is one of reliability, trustworthiness, and attention to detail.

Most of us are far more adept at recognizing the dress mistakes of others than at spotting our own sartorial failings. When we do look for a second opinion, we often make the mistake of only asking a loved one. It's not that spouses, lovers, and parents lack taste; these people are, however, more in tune with our positive qualities than the rest of the world, and frequently they do not recognize how essential it is to reflect those qualities in our dress. Better candidates for evaluation of your interview attire are trusted friends who have proved their objectivity in such matters, or even a colleague at work.

Whenever possible, find out the dress code of the company you are visiting. For example, if you are an engineer applying for a job at a high-tech company, a blue three-piece suit might be overpowering. It is perfectly acceptable to ask someone in personnel about the dress code (written or informal) of the company. In the example we just used, you might be perfectly comfortable showing up *for work* in a sports coat or blazer; nevertheless, you are advised to wear a suit, at least for the first interview.

You may simply decide to change your look somewhat after learning of a more informal atmosphere with regard to dress at the firm you visit. If you are told that everyone works in shirt-sleeves and that there is never a tie in sight, a prudent and completely acceptable approach is to opt for your less formal brown or beige suit, rather than blues, grays, or pinstripes.

One final piece of advice: Avoid 100 percent synthetic garments at all costs. Their sheen makes them unattractive and they often retain body odor despite many washings.

Men

Following are the best current dress guidelines for men preparing for a professional interview.

Men's Suits

The most acceptable colors for men's suits are navy through teal blue and charcoal through light gray, followed at some distance by brown and beige. The fabric should be 100 percent wool; wool looks and wears better than any other material. Stay away from European designer suits, as they tend to be cut tighter and are often too flashy for the conservative world we live in. Two-piece suits are completely acceptable today, whereas only a few years ago one had to wear a three-piece suit to an interview.

The darker the suit, the more authority it carries (but beware: a man should *not* wear a black suit to an interview unless applying for an undertaker's job). Solid colors and pinstripes are both acceptable, so long as the stripes themselves are muted and very narrow. Of the solids, dark gray, navy, or teal blue are equally acceptable. Some feel that a dark solid suit is the best option, because it gives authority to the wearer and is less intimidating than a pinstripe suit.

Men's Shirts

The principles here are simple.

> *Rule One:* Always wear a long-sleeved shirt.
> *Rule Two:* Always wear a white or pale-blue shirt.
> *Rule Three:* Never violate Rules One or Two.

By "white," I do not mean to exclude, for instance, shirts with very thin red or blue pinstripes: these "white" shirts are acceptable, although not really first-rate. There is something about a solid white shirt that conveys honesty, intelligence, and stability; it should be your first choice. It is true that artists, writers, engineers, and other creative types are sometimes known to object to white shirts; for them pale blue may be the best option. Remember that the paler and more subtle the shade, the better the impression you will make.

While monograms are common enough in this country, those who don't accept them usually feel strongly about the implied ostentation of stylized initials on clothing. If you can avoid it, don't take the chance of giving your interviewer the chance to find fault in this area. (On the other hand, if your choice is between wearing your monogrammed shirt or pulling out the old Motley Crue tee-shirt, then your choice should be clear, and so should your conscience.)

Cotton shirts look better and hold up under perspiration more impressively than their synthetic counterparts; if at all possible, opt for a cotton shirt that's been professionally cleaned and starched. A cotton and polyester blend can be an acceptable alternative, but keep in mind that the higher the cotton content, the better the shirt will look. While these blend shirts wrinkle less easily, you are advised to ignore the "wash-and-wear-no-need-to-iron" claims you'll read on the front of the package when you purchase them. Experience has shown that *any* shirt you wear to an interview must be ironed and starched by a professional.

Men's Neckwear: Ties

While an expensive suit can be ruined by a cheap-looking tie, the right tie can do a lot to pull the less-than-perfect suit together for a professional look. When you can't afford a new suit for the interview, you can upgrade your whole look with the right tie.

A pure silk tie makes the most powerful professional impact, has the best finish and feel, and is easiest to tie well. Linen ties are too informal, wrinkle too easily, and may only be worn during warmer weather. (What's more, they can only be tied once between cleanings because they wrinkle so easily.) A wool tie is casual in appearance and has knot problems. Man-made fibers are shiny, make colors look harsh when you want them to look subtle, and may undercut your professional image. A pure silk tie, or a fifty-fifty wool and silk blend (which is almost wrinkle-proof), should be your choice for the interview.

The tie should complement your suit. This means that there should be a physical balance: the rule of thumb is that the width of your tie should approximate the width of your lapels. The prevailing standard, which has held good for over a decade now, is that ties can range in width between 2¾" and 3½". Wearing anything wider may mark you as someone still trapped in the disco era.

While the tie should complement the suit, it should not *match* it. You would never, for instance, wear a navy blue tie with a navy blue suit. Choose an appropriate tie that neither vanishes into nor does battle with your suit pattern; the most popular and safest styles are found within the categories of solids, foulards, stripes, and paisleys.

Do not wear ties with large polka dots, pictures of animals such as leaping trout or soaring mallards, or sporting symbols such as golf clubs or (God forbid) little men on polo ponies. Never wear any piece of apparel that has a manufacturer's symbol emblazoned on the front as part of the decoration. It is difficult to project an image of competent, balanced professionalism when you are acting as a walking billboard for some fashion designer.

Other considerations include the length of the tie (it should, when tied, extend to your trouser belt), the size of the knot (smaller is better), and whether you should wear a bow tie to an interview (you shouldn't).

Men's Shoes

Shoes should be either black leather or brown leather. Stay away from all other materials and colors: They are too risky.

Lace-up wing tips are the most conservative choice and are almost universally acceptable. Slightly less conservative, but equally appropriate, are slip-on dress shoes—not to be confused with boating shoes. The slip-on, with its low, plain vamp or tassel, is versatile enough to be used for both day and evening business wear. (The lace-up wing tip can look a bit cloddish at dinner.)

In certain areas of the South, Southwest, and West, heeled cowboy boots are not at all unusual for business wear, and neither are those Grand Ole Opry versions of the business suit. But beware: Outside of such specifically defined areas, you will attract only puzzled stares—and few if any professional career opportunities—with these wardrobe selections.

Men's Socks

Socks should complement the suit; accordingly, they are likely to be blue, black, gray, or brown. They should also be long enough for you to cross your legs without showing off lots of bare shin, and should not fall in a bunch toward the ankle as you move. Elastic-reinforced, over-the-calf socks are your best bet.

Men's Accessories

The right accessories can enhance the professional image of any applicant, male or female; the wrong accessories can destroy it.

The guiding principle here is to include nothing that could conceivably be misconstrued or leave a bad impression. Never, for instance, should you wear religious or political insignias in the form of rings, ties, or pins. If you would not initiate a conversation about such topics at a job interview (and you shouldn't), why send smoke signals asking your interviewer to do so?

The watch you wear should be simple and plain. This means Mickey Mouse is out, as are sports-oriented and Swatch-style watches. No one is impressed by digital watches these days; don't be afraid to wear a simple analog model with a leather strap. (Besides, you don't want people wondering whether you can really tell time, do you?) Avoid cheap-looking pseudo-gold watchbands at all costs.

Your briefcase, if you carry one, can make a strong professional statement about you. Leather makes the best impression, while all other materials follow far behind. Brown and burgundy are the colors of choice. The case itself should be plain, although some very expensive models offer a host of embellishments that only detract from the effect you want.

A cotton or linen handkerchief should be part of every job hunter's wardrobe. Plain white is best. Your handkerchief can also be used to relieve the clammy-hands syndrome so common before the interview. Anything to avoid the infamous "wet fish" handshake!

(By the way, avoid the matching-tie-and-pocket-square look at all costs. It's hideous and inappropriate for a professional interview.)

Belts should match or complement the shoes you select. Accordingly, a blue, black, or gray suit will require a black belt and black shoes, while brown, tan, or beige suits will call for brown. With regard to materials, stick with plain leather. The most common mistake made with belts is the buckle: an interview is not the place for your favorite Harley Davidson, Grateful Dead, or Bart Simpson buckle. Select a small, simple buckle that doesn't overwhelm the rest of your look.

Jewelry

Men may wear a wedding band, if applicable, and a small pair of subdued cuff-links (if wearing French cuffs, of course). Anything more is dangerous. Even fraternity rings—much less bracelets, neck chains, or medallions—can send the wrong message.

Overcoats

The safest and most utilitarian colors for overcoats are beige and blue; stick to these two exclusively. If you can avoid wearing an overcoat, do so (it's an encumbrance and adds to clutter).

Makeup

It is inadvisable for a man to wear makeup to an interview or at any other time during his professional life.

Women

Following are the best current dress guidelines for women preparing for a professional interview.

Women's Suits

You have more room for creativity in this area than men do, but also more room for mistakes. Of course, your creativity must stay within certain accepted guidelines created not by me, nor even by the fashion industry, but by the consensus of the business world. And that is a world, alas, that tends to trail behind the rest of us, and so the options for imaginative masterstrokes are limited.

Limit your creativity to materials, patterns, and cuts. A woman's business wardrobe need no longer be simply a pseudo-male selection of drab grey skirts and blouses. (Recent advice that women should avoid pinstripes or ties is probably insecure and dated. With the right cuts, pinstripes and ties can look both stylish and professional.)

Wool and linen are both accepted as the right look for professional women's suits, but there is a problem. Wool wrinkles so quickly that you may feel as though you leave the house dressed for success and arrive at your destination destined for bag-ladyhood. Cotton-polyester blends are great for warm climates: They look like linen but lack the "wrinklability" factor.

Combinations of synthetics and natural fabrics do have their advantages: suits made of such material will certainly retain their shape better. The eye trained to pay attention to detail, however, (read: your interviewers') may well detect the type of fabric, say a cheap polyester blend, and draw unwarranted conclusions about your personality and taste. The choice is up to you; if you do opt for natural fabrics, you will probably want to stay with wool. It provides the smartest look of all, and is most versatile and rugged.

While men are usually limited to either solid or pinstripe suits, a woman can add to this list the varied category of plaids. The Prince of Wales plaid, for instance, is attractive and is utterly acceptable for businesswomen (no doubt because of its regal namesake).

How long a skirt should you wear? Any hard-and-fast rule I could offer here would be in danger of being outdated almost immediately, as the fashion industry demands dramatically different looks every season in order to fuel sales. (After all, keeping the same hemlines would mean that last season's clothes could last another season or two.)

It should go without saying that you don't want to sport something that soars to the upper thigh if you want to be taken seriously as an applicant. Your best bet is to dress somewhat more conservatively than you would if you were simply showing up for work at the organization in question. Hemlines come and go, and while there is some leeway as to what is appropriate for everyday wear on the job, the safest bet is usually to select something that falls just a little below the knee.

Colors most suitable for interview suits include charcoal, medium gray, steel gray, black, and navy blue. All of these look smart with a white blouse. A navy suit can also look good with a gray or beige blouse (but see the notes on blouse color selection below). You may be tempted to select a burgundy blouse with that navy blue outfit, but save it for a dinner date; it is inappropriate at an interview. In the second tier come beige, tan, and camel suits; these look best with blue blouses.

Of all these looks, the cleanest and most professional is the simple solid gray suit (either medium or charcoal) with a white blouse.

Blouses

With regard to blouses, long sleeves will project the authoritative, professional look you desire. Three-quarter-length sleeves are less desirable, and they are followed in turn by short sleeves. *Never* wear a sleeveless blouse to an interview. (You may be confident that there is absolutely no chance that you will be required to remove your jacket, but why take the risk?)

Solid colors and natural fabrics (particularly cotton and silk) are the best selections for blouses. Combinations of natural and synthetic fabrics, while wrinkle-resistant, do not absorb moisture well.

The acceptable color spectrum is wider for blouses than for men's shirts, but it is not limitless. The most prudent choices are still white or pale blue; these offer a universal professional appeal. Pink and gray may also be suitable in certain situations (say, at a "creative" company such as an advertising firm for pink, or at an investment bank in a metropolitan area for gray).

The blouse with a front-tie bow is most acceptable; it always works well with a suit. Asymmetrically-closing blouses, as well as those with the bow at the side, are also good choices for a job interview. The button-down collar always looks great; the more conservative the company or industry, the more positive its impression will be.

Women's Neckwear: Scarves

While a woman might choose to wear a string of pearls instead of a scarf to an interview, the scarf can still serve as a powerful status symbol.

Just as you would expect, a good outfit can be ruined by a cheap-looking scarf. Opting to wear a scarf means that the scarf will be saying something dramatic about you: make sure it's something dramatically positive.

A pure silk scarf will offer a conservative look, a good finish, and ease in tying. Some of the better synthetic blends achieve an overall effect that is almost as good.

While some books on women's clothing will recommend buying blouses that have matching scarves attached to the collar, there is an increasingly vocal lobby of stylish businesswomen who feel this is the equivalent of mandating that a man wear a clip-on bow tie. As with men's ties, the objective is to complement the outfit, not match it. Avoid overly flamboyant styles, and stick with the basics: solids, foulards, small polka dots, or paisleys.

Women's Shoes

Female applicants have a greater color selection in footwear than do their male counterparts. The shoes should still be of leather, but in addition to brown and black a woman is safe in wearing navy, burgundy, black, or even, if circumstances warrant, red.

It is safest to stay away from faddish or multicolored shoes (even such classics as two-toned oxfords). There are two reasons for this: First, all fashion is transitory, and even if you are up-to-date, you cannot assume that your interviewer is; second, many interviewers are male and thus likely to exhibit an inability to appreciate vivid color combinations. As with the rest of your wardrobe, stay away from radical choices and opt for the easily comprehensible professional look.

Heel height is important, as well. Flats are fine; a shoe with a heel of up to about $1\frac{1}{2}$" is perfectly acceptable. Stay away from high heels: At best you will wobble slightly, and at worst you will walk at an angle. Unless you're an Olympic ski jumper, it's hard to maintain an "in-control" image when you are tipped forward at a forty-five degree angle!

The pump or court shoe, with its closed toe and heel, is perhaps the safest and most conservative look. A closed heel with a slightly open toe is acceptable, too, as is the sling-back shoe with a closed toe.

Stockings or Pantyhose

These should not make a statement of their own. Select neutral skintones in most cases. You may be an exception if you are interviewing for a job in the fashion industry, in which case you might coordinate colors with your outfit, but be very sure of the company standard already in place. Even in such an instance, avoid loud or glitzy looks. A bold black, of course, is out entirely.

Pantyhose and stockings are prone to developing runs at the worst possible moment. Keep an extra pair in your purse or briefcase.

Accessories

Because a briefcase is a symbol of authority, it is an excellent choice for the female applicant. Do not, however, bring both your purse and a briefcase to the interview. (You'll look awkward juggling them around.) Instead, transfer essential items to a small clutch bag you can store in the case. In addition to brown and burgundy (recommended colors for the men), you may include blue and black as possible colors for your case, which should be free of expensive and distracting embellishments.

With regard to belts, the advice given for men holds for women as well. Belts should match or complement the shoes you select; a blue, black, or grey suit will require a black belt and black shoes, while brown, tan, or beige suits will call for brown. In addition, women may wear snakeskin, lizard, and the like. Remember that the belt is a functional item; if it is instantly noticeable, it is wrong.

Jewelry

As far as jewelry goes, less is more. A woman should restrict rings to engagement or wedding bands if these are applicable, but she can wear a necklace and earrings, as long as these are subdued and professional-looking. (I should note that some men are put off by earrings of any description in the workplace, so if you wear them keep them small, discreet, and in good taste. Avoid fake or strangely colored pearls, anything with your name or initials on it, and earrings that dangle or jangle.) In addition, a single bracelet on the woman's wrist is acceptable; anything around the ankle is not. Remember, too much of the wrong kind of jewelry can keep a woman from receiving an offer she might otherwise receive, or inhibit her promotional opportunities once on the team.

Makeup

Take care never to appear overly made-up. Natural is the key word; eye makeup should be subtle, so as not to overwhelm the rest of the face. As a general rule, I advise against lipstick at an interview because it can cause negative reactions in some interviewers, and because it can smudge and wear off, as the hours wear on. (Who can say, going in, how long the meeting will last?) However, as women advance into their thirties and beyond, the natural pinkness of the lips can fade; you might feel you look pale and washed out without lipstick. So if you feel "undressed" without your lipstick, use some; but apply it sparingly and carefully, using a subdued color.

For Men and Women: A Note on Personal Hygiene

It should go without saying that bad breath, dandruff, body odor, and dirty nails have the potential to undo all your efforts at putting across a good first impression. These and related problems denote an underlying professional slovenliness, which an interviewer will feel is likely to reflect itself in your work. You want to show yourself to be appealing, self-respecting, and enjoyable to be around. You can't do that if the people you meet with have to call on exceptional powers of self-control in order to stay in the same room with you. (For a more detailed discussion of personal hygiene, see chapter 27.)

Don't ask yourself whether any friend or colleague has actually come out and suggested that you pay more attention to these matters; ask yourself how you felt the last time *you* had to conduct business of any sort with a person who had a hygiene problem. Then resolve never to leave that kind of impression.

11.
Body Language

Given the choice of going blind or going deaf, which would you choose?

If you are like nine out of ten other people, you would choose to go deaf. The vast majority of us rely to a remarkable degree on our ability to gather information visually. This really is not all that surprising: While speech is a comparatively recent development, humans have been sending and receiving nonverbal signals from the dawn of the species.

In fact, body language is one of the earliest methods of communication we learn after birth. We master the spoken word later in life, and in so doing we forget the importance of nonverbal cues. But the signals are still sent and received (usually at a subconscious level), even if most of us discount their importance.

It is common to hear people say of the body language they use, "Take me or leave me as I am." This is all very well if you have no concern for what others think of you. For those seeking professional employment, however, it is of paramount importance that the correct body language be utilized. If your mouth says "Hire me," but your body says something quite different, you are likely to leave the interviewer confused. "Well," he or she will think, "the right answers all came out, but there was something about that candidate that just rubbed me the wrong way." Such misgivings are generally sufficient to keep any candidate from making the short list.

When we are in stressful situations (and a job interview is certainly right there in Stress Hell), our bodies react accordingly. The way they react can send unintentional negative messages. The interviewer may or may not be aware of what causes the concern, but the messages will be sent, and our cause will suffer.

Of course, interviewers can be expected to listen carefully to what we say, too. When our body language doesn't contradict our statements, we will generally be given credence. When our body language complements our verbal statements, our message will gain a great deal of impact. But when our body language *contradicts* what we say, it is human nature for the interviewer to be skeptical. In short, learning to control negative body movements during an interview—and learning to use positive body signals—will greatly increase the chances for job interview success.

Under the Microscope

What is the interviewer watching us for during the interview? The answer is: clues. The mystery for the interviewer is, what kind of an employee would we make? It is incumbent on us to provide not just any old clues but the ones most likely to prompt a decision to hire.

Let's begin at the beginning. When we are invited in to an interview, we are probably safe in assuming that our interviewer believes we meet certain minimum standards, and could conceivably be hired. (Otherwise, why take the time to interview?) Once in the door, we can assume that we will be scrutinized in three main areas:

- Ability (Can we do the job?)
- Willingness (Will we do the job?)
- Manageability (Will we be a pleasure or a pain to have around?)

Appropriate control and use of our gestures can help us emphasize positive features of our personality in these key areas—and also project integrity, honesty, attention to detail, and the like.

The adage that actions speak louder than words appears to be something we should take quite literally. Studies done at the University of Chicago found that over 50 percent of all effective communication relies on body language. Since we can expect interviewers to respond to the body language we employ at the interview, it is up to us to decide what messages we want them to receive.

There are also studies that suggest that the impression we create in the first few minutes of the interview are the most lasting. Since the first few minutes after we meet the interviewer is a time when he or she is doing the vast majority of the talking, we have very little control over the impression we create with our words: We can't say much of anything! It is up to our bodies, then, to do the job for us.

The Greeting

Giving a "dead fish" handshake will not advance one's candidacy; neither will the opposite extreme, the iron-man bonecrusher grip.

The ideal handshake starts before the meeting actually occurs. Creating the right impression with the handshake is a three-step process. Be sure that:

1. Your hands are clean and adequately manicured.

2. Your hands are warm and reasonably free of perspiration. (There are a number of ways to ensure this, including washing hands in warm water at the interview site, holding one's hand close to the cheek for a few seconds, and even applying a little talcum powder.)

3. The handshake itself is executed professionally and politely, with a firm grip and a warm smile.

Remember that if you initiate the handshake, you may send the message that you have a desire to dominate the interview; this is not a good impression to leave with one's potential boss. Better to wait a moment and allow the interviewer to initiate the shake. (If for any reason you do find yourself initiating the handshake, do not pull back; if you do, you will appear indecisive. Instead, make the best of it, smile confidently, and make good eye contact.)

The handshake should signal cooperation and friendliness. Match the pressure extended by the interviewer—never exceed it. Ideally, the handshake should last for between three and five seconds, and should "pump" for no more than six times. (The parting handshake may last a little longer. Smile and lean forward very slightly as you shake hands before departing.)

Certain cultural and professional differences should be considered with regard to handshakes, as well. Many doctors, artists, and others who do delicate work with their hands can and do give less enthusiastic handshakes than other people. Similarly, the English handshake is considerably less firm than the American, while the German variety is more firm.

Use only one hand; always shake vertically. Do not extend your hand parallel to the floor, with the palm up, as this conveys submissiveness. By the same token, you may be seen as being too aggressive if you extend your flat hand outward with the palm facing down.

Taking Your Seat

> *Some thirty inches from my nose*
> *The frontier of my person goes.*
> *Beware of rudely crossing it;*
> *I have no gun, but I can spit.*
> (With apologies to W. H. Auden)

Encroaching on another's "personal zone" is a bad idea in any business situation, but it is particularly dangerous in an interview. The thirty-inch standard is a good one to follow: It is the distance that allows you to extend your hand comfortably for a handshake. Maintain this distance throughout the interview, and be particularly watchful of intrusions during the early stages when you meet, greet, and take a seat.

Applying this principle may seem simple enough, but how often have you found yourself dodging awkwardly in front of someone to take a seat before it has been offered? A person's office is an extension of sorts of his personal zone; this is why it is not only polite but also sound business sense to wait until the interviewer offers you a seat.

It is not uncommon to meet with an interviewer in a conference room or other supposedly "neutral" site. Again, wait for the interviewer to motion you to a spot, or, if you feel uncomfortable doing this, tactfully ask the interviewer to take the initiative: "Where would you like me to sit?"

Facial/Head Signals

Once you take your seat, you can expect the interviewer to do most of the talking. You can also probably expect your nervousness to be at its height. Accordingly, you must be particularly careful about the nonverbal messages you send at this stage.

Now, while all parts of the body are capable of sending positive and negative signals, the head (including the eyes and mouth) is under closest scrutiny. Most good interviewers will make an effort to establish and maintain eye contact, and thus you should expect that whatever messages you are sending from the facial region will be picked up, at least on a subliminal level.

Our language is full of expressions testifying to the powerful influence of facial signals. When we say that someone is shifty-eyed, is tight-lipped, has a furrowed brow, flashes bedroom eyes, stares into space, or grins like a Cheshire cat, we are speaking in a kind of shorthand, and using a set of stereotypes that enables us to make judgments—consciously or unconsciously—about the person's abilities and qualities. Those judgments may not be accurate, but they are usually difficult to reverse.

Tight smiles and tension in the facial muscles often bespeak an inability to handle stress; little eye contact can communicate a desire to hide something; pursed lips are often associated with a secretive nature; and frowning, looking sideways, or peering over one's glasses can send signals of haughtiness and arrogance. Hardly the stuff of which winning interviews are made!

The Eyes

Looking at someone means showing interest in that person, and showing interest is a giant step forward in making the right impression. (Remember, each of us is our own favorite subject!)

Your aim should be to stay with a calm, steady, and nonthreatening gaze. It is easy to mismanage this, and so you may have to practice a bit to overcome the common hurdles in this area. Looking away from the interviewer for long periods while he is talking, closing your eyes while being addressed, repeatedly shifting focus from the subject to some other point: These are likely to leave the wrong impression.

Of course, there is a big difference between looking and staring at someone! Rather than looking the speaker straight-on at all times, create a mental triangle incorporating both eyes and the mouth; your eyes will follow a natural, continuous path along the three points. Maintain this approach for roughly three-quarters of the time; you can break your gaze to look at the interviewer's hands as points are emphasized, or to refer to your note pad. These techniques will allow you to leave the impression that you are attentive, sincere, and committed. Staring will only send the message that you are aggressive or belligerent.

Be wary of breaking eye contact too abruptly, and of shifting your focus in ways that will disrupt the atmosphere of professionalism. Examining the interviewer below the head and shoulders, for instance, is a sign of overfamiliarity. (This is an especially important point to keep in mind when being interviewed by someone of the opposite sex.)

The eyebrows send messages as well. Under stress, one's brows may wrinkle; as we have seen, this sends a negative signal about our ability to handle challenges in the business world. The best advice on this score is simply to take a deep breath and collect yourself. Most of the tension that people feel at interviews has to do with anxiety about how to respond to what the interviewer will ask. As a reader of *Knock 'em Dead*, you will be prepared with credible responses for even the toughest queries. Relax.

The Head

Rapidly nodding your head can leave the impression that you are impatient and eager to add something to the conversation—if only the interviewer would let you. Slower nodding, on the other hand, emphasizes interest, shows that you are validating the comments of your interviewer, and subtly encourages him to continue. Tilting the head slightly, when combined with eye contact and a natural smile, demonstrates friendliness and approachability. The tilt should be momentary and not exaggerated, almost like a bob of the head to one side. (Do not overuse this technique!)

The Mouth

One guiding principle of good body language is to turn upward rather than downward. Look at two boxers after a fight: the loser is slumped forward, brows knit and eyes downcast, while the winner's smiling face is thrust upward and outward. The victor's arms are raised high, his back is straight, his shoulders are square. In the first instance the signals we receive are those of anger, frustration, belligerence, and defeat; in the second, happiness, openness, warmth, and confidence.

Your smile is one of the most powerful positive body signals in your arsenal; it best exemplifies the up-is-best principle, as well. Offer an unforced, confident smile as frequently as opportunity and circumstances dictate. *Avoid at all costs* the technique some applicants use: grinning idiotically for the length of the interview, no matter what. This will only communicate that you are either insincere or not quite on the right track.

It's worth remembering that the mouth provides a seemingly limitless supply of opportunities to convey weakness. This may be done by touching the mouth frequently (and, typically, unconsciously); "faking" a cough when confronted with a difficult question; and/or gnawing on one's lips absentmindedly. Employing any of these "insincerity signs" when you are asked about, say, why you lost your last job, will confirm or instill suspicions about your honesty and effectiveness.

Glasses

Those who wear glasses sometimes leave them off when going on an interview in an attempt to project a more favorable image. There are two main difficulties with this. The first is that farsighted people who don't wear their glasses will (unwittingly) seem to stare long and hard at the people they converse with, and this, as we have seen, is a negative signal. The second problem is that leaving the glasses at home—even if you replace them with contacts—will actually undercut your cause in most cases. Many studies have shown that those who wear glasses are perceived as being more intelligent than those who don't. Why not take advantage of this effect? The issue is really not *whether* you should wear your glasses—you should—but how best to make them work for you.

Peering over the top of your glasses—even if you wear reading glasses and have been handed something to read and subsequently asked a question—carries professorial connotations that are frequently interpreted as critical. (If you wear glasses for reading, you should remove them when conversing, replacing them only when appropriate.)

Wearing dark glasses to an interview will paint you as secretive, cold, and devious. Even if your prescription glasses are tinted, the effect will be the same. Try to obtain nontinted glasses for your interview; if you are unable to do so, you are likely to be faced with the only case where contacts are preferable to eyeglasses.

Body Signal Barricades

Folding or crossing the arms, or holding things in front of the body, is a wonderful way to send negative messages to the interviewer. The signal is, essentially, "I know you're there, but you can't come in. I'm nervous and closed for business."

It is bad enough to feel this way, but worse to express it with blatant signals. Don't fold your arms or "protect" your chest with hands, clipboard, briefcase, or anything else during the interview. (These positions, in fact, should be avoided in any and every business situation.)

Hands

As we have seen, a confident and positive handshake breaks the ice and gets the interview moving in the right direction. Proper use of the hands throughout the rest of the interview will help to convey an above-board, "nothing-to-hide" message.

Watch out for hands and fingers that take on a life of their own, fidgeting with themselves or other objects such as pens, paper, or your hair. Pen tapping is interpreted as the action of an impatient person; this is an example of an otherwise trivial habit that can take on immense significance in an interview situation. (Rarely will an interviewer ask you to stop doing something annoying; instead, he'll simply make a mental note that you are an annoying person, and congratulate himself for picking this up before making the mistake of hiring you.)

Negative hand messages are legion. Some of the most dangerous are listed below.

- You can demonstrate smugness and superiority by clasping your hands behind your head. (You'll also expose any perspiration marks that are under your arms.)
- A man can show insecurity by simply adjusting his tie, and that's not the worst of it: when interviewing with a woman, his gesture will show something other than a businesslike interest in the interviewer.
- Slouching in your chair, with hands in pockets or thumbs in belt, can brand you as insolent and aggressive—and when this error is made in the pres-

ence of an interviewer of the opposite sex, it carries sexually aggressive overtones as well. (Beware, too, of sending these signals while you are walking on a tour of the facility.)

- Pulling your collar away from your neck for a moment may seem like an innocent enough reaction to the heat of the day, but the interviewer might assume that you are tense and/or masking an untruth. (The same goes for scratching the neck during, before, or after your response to a question.)

- Moving the hands toward a feature one perceives as deficient is a common unconscious reaction to stress. A man with thinning hair, for example, may thoughtlessly put his hand to his forehead when pondering how to respond to the query, "Why aren't you earning more at your age?" This habit may be extremely difficult for you to detect in the first place, much less reverse, but make the effort. Such protective movements are likely to be perceived—if only on a subliminal level—as acknowledgments of low status.

- Picking at invisible bits of fluff on one's suit looks like what it is: a nervous tic. Keep your focus on the interviewer. (If you do have some bit of lint somewhere on your clothing, the best advice is usually to ignore it rather than call attention to it by brushing it away.)

By contrast, employing the hands in a positive way can further your candidacy. Here are some of the best techniques.

- Subtly exposing your palms now and then as you speak can help to demonstrate that you are open, friendly, and have nothing to hide. (The technique is used to great effect by many politicians and television talk show hosts; watch for it.)

- When considering a question, it can sometimes be beneficial to "steeple" your fingers for a few seconds as you think and when you first start to talk. Unless you hold the gesture for long periods of time, it will be perceived as a neutral demonstration of your thoughtfulness. (Of course, if you overuse this or hold the position for too long, you may be taken as condescending.) Steepling will also give you something constructive to do with your hands; it offers a change from holding your pad and pen.

Seating

The signals you send with your body during an interview can be affected by the type of chair you sit in. If you have a choice, go with an upright chair with arms. Deep armchairs can restrict your ability to send certain positive signals, and encourage the likelihood of negative ones. (They're best suited for watching television, not for projecting the image of a competent professional.)

There is only one way to sit during an interview; bottom well back in the chair and back straight. Slouching, of course, is out, but a slight forward leaning posture will show interest and friendliness toward the interviewer. Keep your hands on the sides of the chair; if there are no arms on the chair, keep your hands in your lap or on your pad of paper.

Crossed legs, in all their many forms, send a mixture of signals; most of them are negative.

- Crossing one ankle over the other knee can show a certain stubborn and recalcitrant outlook (as well as the bottom of your shoe, which is not always a pretty sight). The negative signal is intensified when you grasp the horizontally crossed leg or—worst of all—cross your arms across your chest.

- Crossed ankles have often been assumed to indicate that the person doing the crossing is withholding information. However, some dress fashions encourage decorous ankle crossing. Of course, since the majority of interviews take place across a desk, crossed ankles will often be virtually unnoticeable. The best advice on this body signal is that it is probably the most permissible barrier you can erect; if you must allow yourself one body language vice, this is the one to choose.

- When sitting in armchairs or on sofas, crossing the legs may be necessary to create some stability amid all the plush upholstery. In this instance, the signals you send by crossing your legs will be neutral, as long your crossed legs point toward, rather than away from, the interviewer.

Feet

Some foot signals can have negative connotations. Women and men wearing slip-on shoes should beware of dangling the loose shoe from the toes; this can be quite distracting and, as it is a gesture often used to signal physical attraction, it has no place in a job interview. Likewise, avoid compulsive jabbing of floor, desk, or chair with your foot; this can be perceived as a hostile and angry motion, and is likely to annoy the interviewer.

Walking

Many interviews will require that you walk from point A to point B with the interviewer, either on a guided tour of facilities or to move from one office to another. (Of course, if you are interviewing in a restaurant, you will have to walk with your interviewer to and from the dining facility.) How long these walks last is not as important as how you use them to reinforce positive traits and impressions.

Posture is the first concern. Keep your shoulders back, maintain an erect posture, smile, and make eye contact when appropriate. Avoid fidgeting with your feet as you move, rubbing one shoe against the other, or kicking absentmindedly at the ground as you stand: these signals will lead others to believe that you are anxious and/or insecure. Crossing your arms or legs while standing carries the same negative connotations as it does when you are sitting. Putting your hands in your pockets is less offensive—assuming you don't jangle keys or coins—but men must be careful not to employ the hands-on-hips or thumbs-in-belt postures discussed earlier. These send messages that you are aggressive and dominating.

Seven Signals for Success

So far we have focused primarily on the pitfalls to avoid; but what messages *should* be sent, and how? Here are seven general suggestions on good body language for the interview.

1. Walk slowly, deliberately, and tall upon entering the room.

2. On greeting your interviewer, give (and, hopefully, receive) a friendly "eyebrow flash": that brief, slight raising of the brows that calls attention to the face, encourages eye contact, and (when accompanied by a natural smile) sends a strong positive signal that that interview has gotten off to a good start.

3. Use mirroring techniques. In other words, make an effort—subtly!—to reproduce the positive signals your interviewer sends. (Of course, you should never mirror negative body signals.) Say the interviewer leans forward to make a point; a few moments later, you lean forward slightly in order to hear better. Say the interviewer leans back and laughs; you "laugh beneath" the interviewer's laughter, taking care not to overwhelm your partner by using an inappropriate volume level. This technique may seem contrived at first, but you will learn that it is far from that, if only you experiment a little.

4. Maintain a naturally alert head position; keep your head up and your eyes front at all times.

5. Remember to avert your gaze from time to time so as to avoid the impression that you are staring; when you do so, look confidently and calmly to the right or to the left; never look down.

6. Do not hurry any movement.

7. Relax with every breath.

Putting It All Together

We have discussed the individual gestures that can either improve or diminish your chances of success at the interview. Working in our favor is the fact that positive signals reinforce one another; employing them in combination yields an overwhelming positive message that is truly greater than the sum of its parts. Now it is time to look at how to combine the various positive elements to send a message of competence and professionalism.

Here is the best posture to aim for during the interview.

- Sit well back in the chair; allow the back of it to support you and help you sit upright. Increase the impression of openness ("I have nothing to hide!") by unbuttoning your jacket as you sit down. Keep your head up. Maintain eye contact a good portion of the time, especially when the interviewer begins to speak and when you reply. Smile naturally whenever the opportunity arises. Avoid folding your arms; it is better to keep them on the arms of your chair. Remember to show one or both of your palms occasionally as you make points, but do not overuse this gesture.

Open for Business

The more open your body movements during the interview, the more you will be perceived as open yourself. Understanding and directing your body language will give you added power to turn interviews into cooperative exchanges between two professionals.

Just as you interpret the body language of others, both positive and negative, so your body language makes an indelible impression on those you meet. It tells them whether you like and have confidence in yourself, whether or not you are pleasant to be around, and whether you are more likely to be honest or deceitful. Like it or not, our bodies carry these messages for the world to see.

Job interviews are reliable in one constant: They bring out insecurities in those who must undergo them. All the more reason to consciously manage the impressions the body sends!

12.
The Curtain Goes Up

Backstage in the theater, the announcement "Places, please" is made five minutes before the curtain goes up. It's the performers' signal to psych themselves up, complete final costume adjustments, and make time to reach the stage. They are getting ready to go on stage and knock 'em dead. You should go through a similar process.

Winning that job offer depends not only on the things you do well but also on the absence of things you do poorly. As the interview date approaches, settle down with your resume and the exercises you performed in building it. Immerse yourself in your past successes and strengths. This is a time for building confidence. A little nervousness is perfectly natural and healthy, but channel the extra energy in a positive direction by beginning your physical and mental preparations.

First, you should assemble your interview kit.

- **The company dossier.**
- **Two or three copies of your resume and executive briefing, one for you and one or two for the interviewer.** It is perfectly all right to have your resume in front of you at the interview; it shows that you are organized. It also makes a great cheat sheet (after all, the interviewer is using it for that reason)—you can keep it on your lap during the interview with pad and pencil. It is not unusual to hear, "Mr. Jones wasn't hired because he didn't pay attention to detail and could not even remember his employment dates." And those are just the kinds of things you are likely to forget in the heat of the moment.
- **A pad of paper and writing instruments.** These articles have a twofold purpose. They demonstrate your organization and interest in the job and they give you something constructive to do with your hands during the interview. Bring along a blue or black ballpoint for filling out applications.
- **Contact telephone numbers.** If you get detained on the way to the interview, you can call and let the company representative know.
- **Reference letters**. Take the sensible precaution of gathering these from your employers, on the off-chance they are requested.

- **A list of job-related questions.** During the interview is the time when you gather information to evaluate a job (the actual evaluation comes when you have an offer in hand). At the end of the interview, you will be given the opportunity to ask additional questions. Develop some that help you understand the job's parameters and potential.

  You might ask: "Why is the job open?" "Where does the job lead?" "What is the job's relationship to other departments?" "How do the job and the department relate to the corporate mission?"

For a longer list of questions that might be valuable to ask along those lines, see chapter 23, "Negotiating the Offer." Understand, though, that some of those will obviously only be appropriate in the context of a serious negotiation talk. You can also find good questions to ask in the answer to "Do you have any questions?" at the end of chapter 14, "How to Knock 'em Dead."

- **Any additional information you have about the company or the job.** If time permits, ask the interviewer's secretary to send you some company literature. Absorb whatever you can.

- **Directions to the interview.** Decide on your form of transportation and finalize your time of departure. Check the route, distance, and travel time. Write it all down legibly and put it with the rest of your interview kit. If you forget to verify date, time, and place (including floor and suite number), you might not even arrive at the right place, or on the right day, for your interview.

□   □   □

First impressions are the strongest you make, and they are based on your appearance. There is only one way to dress for the first meeting: clean-cut and conservative. You may or may not see yourself that way, but how you see yourself is not important now—your only concern is how others see you. As you could be asked to appear for an interview at a scant couple of hours notice, you must be in a constant state of readiness. Keep your best two suits of clothing freshly cleaned, your shirts or blouses wrinkle-free, and your shoes polished. Never wear these outfits unless you are interviewing.

Here are some more tips:

- Regardless of sex or hairstyle, take it to the lawn doctor once a month.

- While a shower or bath prior to an interview is most desirable, and the use of an unscented deodorant advisable, the wearing of after-shave or perfume should be avoided. You are trying to get hired, not dated.

- You should never drink alcohol the day before an interview. It affects eyes, skin pallor, and your wits.

- Nails should be trimmed and manicured at all times, even if you work with your hands.

III
Great Answers
to
Tough
Interview Questions

"Like being on trial for your life" is how many people look at a job interview. They are probably right. With the interviewer as judge and jury, you are at least on trial for your livelihood. Therefore, you must lay the foundation for a winning defense. F. Lee Bailey, America's most celebrated defense attorney, attributes his success in the courtroom to preparation. He likens himself to a magician going into court with fifty rabbits in his hat, not knowing which one he'll really need, but ready to pull out any single one. Bailey is successful because he is ready for any eventuality. He takes the time to analyze every situation and every possible option. He never underestimates his opposition. He is always prepared. F. Lee Bailey usually wins.

Another famous attorney, Louis Nizer, successfully defended all of his fifty-plus capital offense clients. When lauded as the greatest courtroom performer of his day, Nizer denied the accolade. He claimed for himself the distinction of being the *best prepared.*

You won't win your day in court just based on your skills. As competition for the best jobs increases, employers are comparing more and more applicants for every opening and asking more and more questions. To win against stiff competition, you need more than just your merits. When the race is close, the final winner is often as not picked for a comparative lack of negatives when ranged against the other contenders. Like Bailey and Nizer, you can prove to yourself that the prize always goes to the best prepared.

During an interview, employers ask you dozens of searching questions. Questions that test your confidence, poise, and desirable personality traits. Questions that trick you into contradicting yourself. Questions that probe your quick thinking and job skills. They are all designed so that the interviewer can make decisions in some critical areas:

- Can you do the job?
- Will you complement or disrupt the department?
- Are you willing to take the extra step?
- Are you manageable?
- Is the money right?

Notice that only one of the critical areas has anything to do with your actual job skills. Being able to do the job is only a small part of getting an offer. Whether you will fit in and make a contribution, and whether you are manageable, are just as important to the interviewer. Those traits the company probes for during the interview are the same that will mark a person for professional growth when on board. In this era of high unemployment and high specialization, companies become more critical in the selection process and look more actively for certain traits, some of which cannot be ascertained by a direct question or answer. Consequently, the interviewer will seek a pattern in your replies that shows your possession of such traits—I discuss them in detail in the next chapter.

The time spent in "court" on trial for your livelihood contains four deadly traps:

- your failure to listen to the question;
- annoying the interviewer by answering a question that was not asked;
- providing superfluous information (you should keep answers brief, thorough, and to the point);
- attempting to interview without preparation.

The effect of those blunders is cumulative, and each reduces your chances of receiving a job offer.

The number of offers you win in your search for the ideal job depends on your ability to answer a staggering array of questions in terms that have value and relevance to the employer: "Why do you want to work here?" "What are your biggest accomplishments?" "How long will it take you to make a contribution?" "Why should I hire you?" "What can you do for us that someone else cannot do?" "What is your greatest weakness?" "Why aren't you earning more?" and, "What interests you least about this job?" are just some of the questions you will be asked.

The example answers in the following chapters come from across the job spectrum. Though the example answer might come from the mouth of an administrator, while you are a scientist or in one of the service industries, the commonality of all job functions in contributing to the bottom line will help you draw the parallel to your job.

You will also notice that each of the example answers teaches a small yet valuable lesson in good business behavior—something you can use both to get the job and to make a good impression when you are on board.

And remember, the answers provided in the following chapters should not be repeated word for word, exactly as they come off the page. You have your own style of speech (not to mention your own kind of business experience), so try to put the answers in your own words.

13.

The Five Secrets of the Hire

Before we examine the "dos and don'ts" advice on interviewing contained in the next chapter, it's a good idea to review the interview process from the employer's perspective. As we have observed, there is a fallacy that all that is necessary for success at the interview is for you to show that you have what it takes to do the job. There's a lot more to it than that.

The First Secret: Ability and Suitability
Saying, "Hey, I can do this job—give me a shot and I'll prove it to you" is not enough anymore. Today you have to *prove* ability and suitability.

Every working professional has a combination of skills that broadly define his or her ability and suitability. How well you program that computer, service that client, or sew up that appendix is part of the picture; knowing the steps involved well enough *to be able to explain them clearly and simply to others* is another part.

Itemize your technical/professional skills as they parallel the requirements of the job. Then recall an incident to illustrate each of those skills. When you have done this, and not before, you will be in a position to begin justifying your ability and suitability to an employer.

If you are applying for a job in an industry with which you are familiar, you should also consider highlighting your industry sensibilities. Industry sensibilities means knowing "how we do it here." A good computer programmer working in a bank has technical and professional skills; that is, the ability to program a computer is required by the employer. That same programmer has knowledge of how to get things done *in the industry in which he or she operates*; that is, the ability to work well with bankers, which is quite different than being able to work well with, say, public television fundraisers.

Demonstrating both professional/technical and industry skills will set you apart from the vast majority of candidates. Show that you understand these combinations and you will stand out from the pack.

The Second Secret: Willingness
Ten years ago, if a woman were asked during an interview whether she would be willing to make coffee, she might have experienced some awkwardness in answer-

ing. Nowadays that awkwardness is less common, as she is likely to know that she is within her rights in asking whether the duties were part of her job description. But in doing so, she might be losing an opportunity to demonstrate her readiness to pitch in at any task. This question is being used more and more by potential employers who want to gauge *willingness*—and have no intention of sending applicants off to brew the perfect cup of Good Morning America. Male applicants, too, are well advised to consider an answer along the lines of "Yes, and how would you like your eggs?"

Today, the issue isn't whether you are prepared to do demeaning tasks. It is whether you are the kind of person who is prepared to do whatever it takes to help the team survive and prosper. Can you take the rough with the smooth? Are you prepared to go that extra mile? You are? Great. Think of a time when you did. Figure out how your doing so helped the company. Now rehearse the story until you can tell it in about ninety seconds.

The Third Secret: Manageability and Teamwork

There isn't a manager in the world who enjoys a sleepless night caused by an unmanageable employee. Avoiding such nights is a major concern for managers, who develop, over time, a remarkable sixth sense when it comes to spotting and cutting out mavericks.

Manageability is defined in different ways: the ability to work alone; the ability to work with others; the ability to take direction and criticism when it is carefully and considerately given; and, perhaps dearest to the manager's heart, the ability to take direction when it *isn't* carefully and considerately given, often because of a crisis. Also crucial is a willingness to work with others regardless of their sex, age, religion, physical appearance, abilities or disabilities, skin color, or national origin.

Such "manageability" considerations make a job interview tricky. Yes, you should certainly state your strongly held convictions—after all, you don't want to appear wishy-washy—but you should do *so only as long as they are professional in nature and relate to the job at hand.*

Let me give you an example of what I mean. A number of people have asked me about what they perceive as discrimination as a result of their being born-again Christians. However, each discussion invariably ends in the conclusion that a job interview is simply no place to bring up personal beliefs. Today's managers will usually go well out of their way to avoid even the perception of intolerance toward sincerely held spiritual beliefs. Yet, by the same token, they are deeply suspicious of any strident religious rhetoric that surfaces in a professional setting. (This also holds true of political, ethnic, or other inappropriate issues raised by a candidate during an interview.) The potential employer's caution in these circumstances, far from representing discrimination, is a sign of concern that the candidate might not be tolerant of the views of others—and might thereby become an obstacle to a harmonious work group.

The rules here are simple. Don't bring up religious, political, or racial matters during the job interview. Even a casual reference to such topics can put a potential employer on the spot, since he or she could subject the company to a lawsuit if a racial or religious topic is perceived as having influenced a hiring decision. The interview is a potential paycheck; don't mess with it.

You're a team player, someone who gets along well with others and has no problem tolerating other opinions or beliefs. Demonstrate that with your every word and action.

The Fourth Secret: Professional Behavior

I emphasize *professional* behavior throughout this book because, to a large extent, the traits that are most desirable to employers are learned and developed as a result of our experiences in the workplace.

As you will see in the next chapter, there are twenty universally admired behavioral traits common to successful people in all fields. Once you review them, you will no doubt find that they are important to you, too, since just understanding what they are will give you up to twenty unique points to make about your candidacy. But understanding the traits is only part of the secret.

Harry works in Shipping and Receiving. He reads the list of traits, comes across the category labeled "Determination," and thinks, "Yeah, that's me. I'm a determined guy." On its own, though, he knows this is not enough. Then Harry recalls the time he came in over the weekend to clear the warehouse in time to make room for the twenty-ton press due in Monday morning at seven. When he tells this story to the interviewer, he gets a lot further than he would if he simply said, "Hire me; I'm determined." The interviewer, instead of a bland, unsubstantiated claim that would be forgotten almost the instant it left Harry's mouth, gets a mental movie of the event that's hard to forget: Harry coming in on the weekend to make room for that press. Actually, the interviewer *really* sees something much more important, namely Harry applying the same level of determination and extra effort on the behalf of the interviewer's company.

Simple statements don't leave any lasting impression on employers. Anecdotes that prove a point do.

The Fifth Secret: Everyone Hires for the Same Job

Surprised? Here's another, related news flash: No one in the history of industry and commerce has ever been added to a payroll for the love of mankind.

Regardless of job or profession, we are all, at some level, *problem solvers.* That's the first and most important part of the job description for anyone who has ever been hired for any job, at any level, in any organization, anywhere in the world. This fifth secret is absolutely key to job hunting and career success in any field.

Think of your profession in terms of its problem-solving responsibilities. Once you have identified the particular problem-solving business you are in, you will have gone a long way toward isolating what the interviewer will want to talk about. Identify and list for yourself the typical problems you tackle for employers on a daily basis. Come up with plenty of specific examples. Then move on to the *biggest and dirtiest* problems you've been faced with. Again, recall specifically how you solved them.

Here's a technique used by corporate outplacement professionals to help people develop examples of their problem-solving skills and the resultant achievements.

1. *State the problem.* What was the situation? Was it typical of your job, or had something gone wrong? If the latter, be leery of apportioning blame.

2. *Isolate relevant background information.* What special knowledge or education were you armed with to tackle this dilemma?

3. *List your key qualities.* What professional skills and personal behavior traits did you bring into play to solve the problem?

4. *Recall the solution.* How did things turn out in the end? (If the problem did not have a successful resolution, do not use it as an example.)

5. *Determine what the solution was worth.* Quantify the solution in terms of money earned, money saved, or time saved. Specify your role as a team member or as a lone gun, as the facts demand.

With an improved understanding of what employers seek in employees, you will have a better understanding of yourself and what you have to offer in the way of specific problem-solving abilities. If you follow the steps outlined above, you will develop a series of illustrative stories for each key area. Remember, stories help interviewers visualize you solving *their* problems—as a paid member of the team.

Here's a story for you. It's based on a real-life interview pattern, although the names are fictional.

Mr. Wanton Grabbit, eighty-year-old senior partner at the revered Washington law firm of Sue, Grabbit, and Runne, ran a help-wanted advertisement in The *Washington Post* for a word processing specialist. He was looking for someone with five years of experience in W.P. and the same amount working in a legal environment. He also wanted someone with experience in using the office computer system, a Bambleweeney 5000.

Grabbit interviewed ten candidates with exactly the experience the advertisement demanded. Each of them came away from the interview convinced that a job offer was imminent. None of them got the job. The person who did get the job had *three* years of experience and had *never before set foot* inside a law office.

Sue Sharp, the successful candidate, understood the fifth secret and asked a few intelligent questions of her own during the interview. Specifically, she asked, "What are the first projects I will be involved with?" This led Mr. Grabbit to launch into a long discourse on his desire to see the law firm rush headlong into the 20th century by the year 2001. The first project, he explained, would be to load the firm's approximately 4,000 manual files onto the Bambleweeney.

Now, although Sue had never worked in a law firm before, she had, on her last job, automated a cumbersome manual filing system. Having faced the *problem* before, even though she had done so in the "wrong" setting, she was able to demonstrate an understanding of the challenges the position presented. Furthermore, she was able to tell the illustrative stories from her last job that enabled Mr. Grabbit to see her, in his mind's eye, tackling and solving his immediate, specific, short-term problems successfully.

We get two very special benefits when we understand and apply the fifth secret. First, we show that we possess the problem-solving abilities of a first-rate professional in the field. Second, when we ask about the problems, challenges, projects, deadlines, and pressure points that will be tackled in the early months, we show that we will be able to hit the ground running on those first critical projects.

□   □   □

Integrate the five secrets of the hire as you read the rest of this section. You will reap the rewards—while your competition must resign themselves to harvesting sour grapes.

14.

How to Knock 'em Dead

- "Describe a situation where your work or an idea was criticized."
- "Have you done the best work you are capable of doing?"
- "What problems do you have getting along with others?"
- "How long will you stay with the company?"
- "I'm not sure you're suitable for the job."
- "Tell me about something you are not very proud of."
- "What are some of the things your supervisor did that you disliked?"
- "What aspects of your job do you consider most crucial?"

Can you answer all these questions off the top of your head? Can you do it in a way that will set your worth above the other job candidates? I doubt it—they were *designed* to catch you off guard. But they won't after you have read the rest of *Knock 'em Dead*.

Even if you could answer some of them, it would not be enough to assure you of victory: The employer is looking for certain intangible assets as well. Think back to your last job for a moment. Can you recall someone with fewer skills, less professionalism, and less dedication who somehow leveraged his or her career into a position of superiority to you? He or she was able to do that only by cleverly projecting a series of personality traits that are universally sought by all successful companies. Building those key traits into your answers to the interviewer's questions will win you any job and set the stage for your career growth at the new company.

There are twenty universally admired key personality traits; they are your passport to success at any interview. Use them for reference as you customize your answers to the tough questions in the following chapters.

☐ ☐ ☐

Personal Profile:
The interviewer searches for personal profile keys to determine what type of person you really are. The presence of these keys in your answers tells the company

representative how you feel about yourself, your chosen career, and what you would be like to work with. Few of them will arise from direct questions—your future employer will search for them in your answers to specific job-performance probes. The following words and phrases are those you will project as part of your successful, healthy personal profile.

- **Drive:** A desire to get things done. Goal-oriented.
- **Motivation:** Enthusiasm and a willingness to ask questions. A company realizes that a motivated person accepts added challenges and does that little bit extra on every job.
- **Communication Skills:** More than ever, the ability to talk and write effectively to people at all levels in a company is a key to success.
- **Chemistry:** The company representative is looking for someone who does not get rattled, wears a smile, is confident without self-importance, gets along with others—who is, in short, a team player.
- **Energy:** Someone who always gives that extra effort in the little things as well as important matters.
- **Determination:** Someone who does not back off when a problem or situation gets tough.
- **Confidence:** Not braggadocio. Poise. Friendly, honest, and open to employees high or low. Not intimidated by the big enchiladas, nor overly familiar.

Professional Profile:
All companies seek employees who respect their profession and employer. Projecting these professional traits will identify you as loyal, reliable, and trustworthy.

- **Reliability:** Following up on yourself, not relying on anyone else to ensure the job is well done, and keeping management informed every step of the way.
- **Honesty/Integrity:** Taking responsibility for your actions, both good and bad. Always making decisions in the best interests of the company, never on whim or personal preference.
- **Pride:** Pride in a job well done. Always taking the extra step to make sure the job is done to the best of your ability. Paying attention to the details.
- **Dedication:** Whatever it takes in time and effort to see a project through to completion, on deadline.
- **Analytical Skills:** Weighing the pros and cons. Not jumping at the first solution to a problem that presents itself. The short- and long-term benefits of a solution against all its possible negatives.
- **Listening Skills:** Listening and understanding, as opposed to waiting your turn to speak.

Achievement Profile:

Earlier, I discussed that companies have very limited interests: making money, saving money (the same as making money), and saving time (which does both). Projecting your achievement profile, in however humble a fashion, is the key to winning any job.

- **Money Saved:** Every penny saved by your thought and efficiency is a penny earned for the company.
- **Time Saved:** Every moment saved by your thought and efficiency enables your company to save money and make more in the additional time available. Double bonus.
- **Money Earned:** Generating revenue is the goal of every company.

Business Profile:

Projecting your business profile is important on those occasions when you cannot demonstrate ways you have made money, saved money, or saved time for previous employers. These keys demonstrate you are always on the lookout for opportunities to contribute, and that you keep your boss informed when an opportunity arises.

- **Efficiency:** Always keeping an eye open for wastage of time, effort, resources, and money.
- **Economy:** Most problems have two solutions: an expensive one, and one the company would prefer to implement.
- **Procedures:** Procedures exist to keep the company profitable. Don't work around them. That also means keeping your boss informed. You tell your boss about problems or good ideas, not his or her boss. Follow the chain of command. Do not implement your own "improved" procedures or organize others to do so.
- **Profit:** All the above traits are universally admired in the business world because they relate to profit.

□   □   □

As the requirements of the job are unfolded for you at the interview, meet them point by point with your qualifications. If your experience is limited, stress the appropriate key profile traits (such as energy, determination, motivation), your relevant interests, and your desire to learn. If you are weak in just one particular area, keep your mouth shut—perhaps that dimension will not arise. If the area is probed, be prepared to handle and overcome the negative by stressing skills that compensate and/or demonstrate that you will experience a fast learning curve.

Do not show discouragement if the interview appears to be going poorly. You have nothing to gain by showing defeat, and it could merely be a stress interview tactic to test your self-confidence.

If for any reason you get flustered or lost, keep a straight face and posture;

gain time to marshal your thoughts by asking, "Could you help me with that?" or, "Would you run that by me again?" or, "That's a good question; I want to be sure I understand. Could you please explain it again?"

□　　□　　□

Now it is time for you to study the tough questions. Use the examples and explanations to build answers that reflect your background and promote your skills and attributes.

"What are the reasons for your success in this profession?"
With this question, the interviewer is not so much interested in examples of your success—he or she wants to know what makes you tick. Keep your answers short, general, and to the point. Using your work experience, personalize and use value keys from your personal, professional and business profiles. For example: "I attribute my success to three reasons: the support I've always received from co-workers, which always encourages me to be cooperative and look at my specific job in terms of what we as a department are trying to achieve. That gives me great pride in my work and its contribution to the department's efforts, which is the second factor. Finally, I find that every job has its problems that need solutions, and while there's always a costly solution, there's usually an economical one as well, whether it's in terms of time or money." Then give an example from your experience that illustrates those points.

"What is your energy level like? Describe a typical day."
You must demonstrate good use of your time, that you believe in planning your day beforehand, and that when it is over, you review your own performance to make sure you are reaching the desired goals. No one wants a part-time employee, so you should sell your energy level. For example, your answer might end with: "At the end of the day when I'm ready to go home, I make a rule always to type one more letter [make one more call, etc.] and clear my desk for the next day."

"Why do you want to work here?"
To answer this question, you must have researched the company and built a dossier. Your research work from Chapter 1 is now rewarded. Reply with the company's attributes as you see them. Cap your answer with reference to your belief that the company can provide you with a stable and happy work environment—the company has that reputation—and that such an atmosphere would encourage your best work.
"I'm not looking for just another paycheck. I enjoy my work and am proud of my profession. Your company produces a superior product/provides a superior service. I share the values that make this possible, which should enable me to fit in and complement the team."

"What kind of experience do you have for this job?"

This is a golden opportunity to sell yourself, but before you do, be sure you know what is most critical to the interviewer. The interviewer is not just looking for a competent engineer, typist, or what-have-you—he or she is looking for someone who can contribute quickly to the current projects. When interviewing, companies invariably give everyone a broad picture of the job, but the person they hire will be a problem-solver, someone who can contribute to the specific projects in the first six months. Only by asking will you identify the areas of your interviewer's greatest urgency and therefore interest.

If you do not know the projects you will be involved with in the first six months, you must ask. Level-headedness and analytical ability are respected, and the information you get will naturally let you answer the question more appropriately. For example, a company experiencing shipping problems might appreciate this answer: "My high-speed machining background and familiarity with your equipment will allow me to contribute quickly. I understand deadlines, delivery schedules, and the importance of getting the product shipped. Finally, my awareness of economy and profit has always kept reject parts to a bare minimum."

"What are the broad responsibilities of a [e.g.] systems analyst?"

This is suddenly becoming a very popular question with interviewers, and rightly so. There are three layers to it. First, it acknowledges that all employees nowadays are required to be more efficiency- and profit-conscious, and need to know how individual responsibilities fit into the big picture. Second, the answer provides some idea of how much you will have to be taught or re-oriented if and when you join the company. Third, it is a very effective knock-out question—if you lack a comprehensive understanding of your job, that's it! You'll be knocked out then and there.

While your answer must reflect an understanding of the responsibilities, be wary of falling afoul of differing corporate jargon. A systems analyst in one company, for instance, may be only a programmer trainee in another. With that in mind, you may wish to preface your answer with, "While the responsibilities of my job title vary somewhat from company to company, at my current/last job, my responsibilities included . . ." Then, in case your background isn't an exact match, ask, "Which areas of relevant expertise haven't I covered?" That will give you the opportunity to recoup.

"Describe how your job relates to the overall goals of your department and company."

This not only probes your understanding of department and corporate missions, but also obliquely checks into your ability to function as a team member to get the work done. Consequently, whatever the specifics of your answer, include words to this effect: "The quality of my work directly affects the ability of others to do their work properly. As a team member, one has to be aware of the other players."

"What aspects of your job do you consider most crucial?"

A wrong answer can knock you out of the running in short order. The executive who describes expense reports as the job's most crucial aspect is a case in point. The question is designed to determine time management, prioritization skills, and any inclination for task avoidance.

"Are you willing to go where the company sends you?"

Unfortunately with this one, you are, as the saying goes, damned if you do and damned if you don't. What is the real question? Do they want you to relocate or just travel on business? If you simply answer "no," you will not get the job offer, but if you answer "yes," you could end up in Monkey's Eyebrow, Kentucky. So play for time and ask, "Are you talking about business travel, or is the company relocating?" In the final analysis, your answer should be "yes." You don't have to accept the job, but without the offer you have no decision to make. Your single goal at an interview is to sell yourself and win a job offer. Never forget, only when you have the offer is there a decision to make about that particular job.

"What did you like/dislike about your last job?"

The interviewer is looking for incompatibilities. If a trial lawyer says he or she dislikes arguing a point with colleagues, such a statement will only weaken—if not immediately destroy—his or her candidacy.

Most interviews start with a preamble by the interviewer about the company. Pay attention: That information will help you answer the question. In fact, any statement the interviewer makes about the job or corporation can be used to your advantage.

So, in answer, you liked everything about your last job. You might even say your company taught you the importance of certain keys from the business, achievement, or professional profile. Criticizing a prior employer is a warning flag that you could be a problem employee. No one intentionally hires trouble, and that's what's behind the question. Keep your answer short and positive. You are allowed only one negative about past employers, and only then if your interviewer has a "hot button" about his or her department or company; if so, you will have written it down on your notepad. For example, the only thing your past employer could not offer might be something like "the ability to contribute more in different areas in the smaller environment you have here." You might continue with, "I really liked everything about the job. The reason I want to leave it is to find a position where I can make a greater contribution. You see, I work for a large company that encourages specialization of skills. The smaller environment you have here will, as I said, allow me to contribute far more in different areas." Tell them what they want to hear—replay the hot button.

Of course, if you interview with a large company, turn it around. "I work for a small company and don't get the time to specialize in one or two major areas." Then replay the hot button.

"What is the least relevant job you have held?"

If your least relevant job is not on your resume, it shouldn't be mentioned. Some people skip over those six months between jobs when they worked as soda jerks just to pay the bills, and would rather not talk about it, until they hear a question like this one. But a mention of a job that, according to all chronological records, you never had, will throw your integrity into question and your candidacy out the door.

Apart from that, no job in your profession has been a waste of time if it increases your knowledge about how the business works and makes money. Your answer will include: "Every job I've held has given me new insights into my profession, and the higher one climbs, the more important the understanding of the lower-level, more menial jobs. They all play a role in making the company profitable. And anyway, it's certainly easier to schedule and plan work when you have first-hand knowledge of what others will have to do to complete their tasks."

"What have you learned from jobs you have held?"

Tie your answer to your business and professional profile. The interviewer needs to understand that you seek and can accept constructive advice, and that your business decisions are based on the ultimate good of the company, not your personal whim or preference. "More than anything, I have learned that what is good for the company is good for me. So I listen very carefully to directions and always keep my boss informed of my actions."

"How do you feel about your progress to date?"

This question is not geared solely to rate your progress; it also rates your self-esteem (personal profile keys). Be positive, yet do not give the impression you have already done your best work. Make the interviewer believe you see each day as an opportunity to learn and contribute, and that you see the environment at this company as conducive to your best efforts.

"Given the parameters of my job, my progress has been excellent. I know the work, and I am just reaching that point in my career when I can make significant contributions."

"Have you done the best work you are capable of doing?"

Say "yes," and the interviewer will think you're a has-been. As with all these questions, personalize your work history. For this particular question, include the essence of this reply: "I'm proud of my professional achievements to date, especially [give an example]. But I believe the best is yet to come. I am always motivated to give my best efforts, and in this job there are always opportunities to contribute when you stay alert."

"How long would you stay with the company?"

The interviewer might be thinking of offering you a job. So you must encourage him or her to sell you on the job. With a tricky question like this, end your answer with a question of your own that really puts the ball back in the interviewer's court. Your reply might be: "I would really like to settle down with this company. I take direction well and love to learn. As long as I am growing professionally, there is no reason for me to make a move. How long do you think I would be challenged here?"

"How long would it take you to make a contribution to our company?"

Again, be sure to qualify the question: In what area does the interviewer need rapid contributions? You are best advised to answer this with a question: "That is an excellent question. To help me answer, what do you anticipate my responsibilities will be for the first six or seven months?" or, "What are your greatest areas of need right now?" You give yourself time to think while the interviewer concentrates on images of you working for the company. When your time comes to answer, start with: "Let's say I started on Monday the seventeenth. It will take me a few weeks to settle down and learn the ropes. I'll be earning my keep very quickly, but making a real contribution . . . [give a hesitant pause] Do you have a special project in mind you will want me to get involved with?" That response could lead directly to a job offer, but if not, you already have the interviewer thinking of you as an employee.

"What would you like to be doing five years from now?"

The safest answer contains a desire to be regarded as a true professional and team player. As far as promotion, that depends on finding a manager with whom you can grow. Of course, you will ask what opportunities exist within the company before being any more specific: "From my research and what you have told me about the growth here, it seems operations is where the heavy emphasis is going to be. It seems that's where you need the effort and where I could contribute toward the company's goals." Or, "I have always felt that first-hand knowledge and experience open up opportunities that one might never have considered, so while at this point in time I plan to be a part of [e.g.] operations, it is reasonable to expect that other exciting opportunities will crop up in the meantime."

"What are your qualifications?"

Be sure you don't answer the wrong question. Does the interviewer want job-related or academic job qualifications? Ask. If the question concerns job-related information, you need to know what problems must be tackled first before you can answer adequately. If you can determine this, you will also know what is causing the manager most concern. Then, if you can show yourself as someone who can contribute to the solution of those projects or problems, you have taken a dramatic step ahead in the race for the job offer. Ask for clarification, then use appropriate value keys from all four categories tied in with relevant skills and achievements. You might say: "I can give you a general answer, but I feel my answer might be more valuable if you could tell me about specific work assignments in the early months."

Or: "If the major task right now is to automate the filing system, I should tell you that in my last job I was responsible for creating a computerized database for a previously uncomputerized firm."

"What are your biggest accomplishments?"

Keep your answers job related; from earlier exercises, a number of achievements should spring to mind. If you exaggerate contributions to major projects, you will be accused of suffering from "coffee-machine syndrome," the affliction of a junior clerk who claimed success for an Apollo space mission based on his relationships with certain scientists, established at the coffee machine. You might begin your reply with: "Although I feel my biggest achievements are still ahead of me, I am proud of my involvement with . . . I made my contribution as part of that team and learned a lot in the process. We did it with hard work, concentration, and an eye for the bottom line."

"How do you organize and plan for major projects?"

Effective planning requires both forward thinking ("Who and what am I going to need to get this job done?") and backward thinking ("If this job must be completed by the twentieth, what steps must be made, and at what time, to achieve it?"). Effective planning also includes contingencies and budgets for time and cost overruns. Show that you cover all the bases.

"How many hours a week do you find it necessary to work to get your job done?"

No absolutely correct answer here, so again, you have to cover all the bases. Some managers pride themselves on working nights and weekends, or on never taking their full vacation quota. Others pride themselves on their excellent planning and time management that allows them never to work more than regular office hours. You must pick the best of both worlds: "I try to plan my time effectively and usually can. Our business always has its rushes, though, so I put in whatever effort it takes to get the job finished." It is rare that the interviewer will then come back and ask for a specific number of hours. If that does happen, turn the question around: "It depends on the projects. What is typical in your department?" The answer will give you the right cue, of course.

"Tell me how you moved up through the organization."

A fast-track question, the answer to which tells a lot about your personality, your goals, your past, your future, and whether you still have any steam left in you. The answer might be long, but try to avoid rambling. Include a fair sprinkling of your key personality traits in your stories (because this is the perfect time to do it). As well as listing the promotions, you will want to demonstrate that they came as a result of dedicated, long-term effort, substantial contributions, and flashes of genius.

"Can you work under pressure?"

You might be tempted to give a simple "yes" or "no" answer, but don't. It reveals nothing, and you lose the opportunity to sell your skills and value profiles. Actually, this common question often comes from an unskilled interviewer, because it is closed-ended. (How to handle different types of interviewers is covered in Chapter 16, "The Other Side of the Desk.") As such, the question does not give you the chance to elaborate. Whenever you are asked a closed-ended question, mentally add: "Please give me a brief yet comprehensive answer." Do that, and you will give the information requested and seize an opportunity to sell yourself. For example, you could say: "Yes, I usually find it stimulating. However, I believe in planning and proper management of my time to reduce panic deadlines within my area of responsibility."

"What is your greatest strength?"

Isolate high points from your background and build in a couple of the key value profiles from different categories. You will want to demonstrate pride, reliability, and the ability to stick with a difficult task yet change course rapidly when required. You can rearrange the previous answer here. Your answer in part might be: "I believe in planning and proper management of my time. And yet I can still work under pressure."

"What are your outstanding qualities?"

This is essentially the same as an interviewer asking you what your greatest strengths are. While in the former question you might choose to pay attention to job-specific skills, this question asks you to talk about your personality profile. Now while you are fortunate enough to have a list of the business world's most desirable personality traits at the beginning of this chapter, try to do more than just list them. In fact, rather than offering a long "laundry list," you might consider picking out just two or three and giving an illustration of each.

"What interests you most about this job?"

Be straightforward, unless you haven't been given adequate information to determine an answer, in which case you should ask a question of your own to clarify. Perhaps you could say, "Before answering, could I ask you to tell me a little more about the role this job plays in the departmental goals?" or, "Where is the biggest vacuum in your department at the moment?" or, "Could you describe a typical day for me?" The additional information you gather with those questions provides the appropriate slant to your answer—that is, what is of greatest benefit to the department and to the company. Career-wise, that obviously has the greatest benefit to you, too. Your answer then displays the personality traits that support the existing need. Your answer in part might include, "I'm looking for a challenge and an opportunity to make a contribution, so if you feel the biggest challenge in the department is _____, I'm the one for the job." Then include the personality traits and experience that support your statements. Perhaps: "I like a challenge, my background demonstrates excellent problem-solving abilities [give some examples], and I always see a project through to the finish."

"What are you looking for in your next job?"

You want a company where your personal profile keys and professional profile keys will allow you to contribute to business value keys. Avoid saying what you want the company to give you; you must say what you want in terms of what you can give to your employer. The key word in the following example is "contribution": "My experience at the XYZ Corporation has shown me I have a talent for motivating people. That is demonstrated by my team's absenteeism dropping 20 percent, turnover steadying at 10 percent, and production increasing 12 percent. I am looking for an opportunity to continue that kind of contribution, and a company and supervisor who will help me develop in a professional manner."

"Why should I hire you?"

Your answer will be short and to the point. It will highlight areas from your background that relate to current needs and problems. Recap the interviewer's description of the job, meeting it point by point with your skills. Finish your answer with: "I have the qualifications you need [itemize them], I'm a team player, I take direction, and I have the desire to make a thorough success."

"What can you do for us that someone else cannot do?"

This question will come only after a full explanation of the job has been given. If not, qualify the question with: "What voids are you trying to eradicate when you fill this position?" Then recap the interviewer's job description, followed with: "I can bring to this job a determination to see projects through to a proper conclusion. I listen and take direction well. I am analytical and don't jump to conclusions. And finally, I understand we are in business to make a profit, so I keep an eye on cost and return." End with: "How do these qualifications fit your needs?" or, "What else are you looking for?"

You finish with a question that asks for feedback or a powerful answer. If you haven't covered the interviewer's hot buttons, he or she will cover them now, and you can respond accordingly.

"Describe a difficult problem you've had to deal with."

This is a favorite tough question. It is not so much the difficult problem that's important—it's the approach you take to solving problems in general. It is designed to probe your professional profile; specifically, your analytical skills.

"Well, I always follow a five-step format with a difficult problem. One, I stand back and examine the problem. Two, I recognize the problem as the symptom of other, perhaps hidden, factors. Three, I make a list of possible solutions to the problem. Four, I weigh both the consequences and cost of each solution, and determine the best solution. And five, I go to my boss, outline the problem, make my recommendation, and ask for my superior's advice and approval."

Then give an example of a problem and your solution. Here is a thorough example: "When I joined my present company, I filled the shoes of a manager who had been fired. Turnover was very high. My job was to reduce turnover and increase performance. Sales of our new copier had slumped for the fourth quarter in a row, partly due to ineffective customer service. The new employer was very concerned, and he even gave me permission to clean house. The cause of the problem? The customer-service team never had any training. All my people needed was some intensive training. My boss gave me permission to join the American Society for Training and Development, which cost $120. With what I learned there, I turned the department around. Sales continued to slump in my first quarter. Then they skyrocketed. Management was pleased with the sales and felt my job in customer service had played a real part in the turnaround; my boss was pleased because the solution was effective and cheap. I only had to replace two customer-service people."

"What would your references say?"

You have nothing to lose by being positive. If you demonstrate how well you and your boss got along, the interviewer does not have to ask, "What do you dislike about your current manager?"

It is a good idea to ask past employers to give you a letter of recommendation. That way, you know what is being said. It reduces the chances of the company representative checking up on you, and if you are asked this question you can pull out a sheaf of rousing accolades and hand them over. If your references are checked by the company, it must by law have your written permission. That permission is usually included in the application form you sign. All that said, never offer references or written recommendations unless they are requested.

"Can we check your references?"

This question is frequently asked as a stress question to catch the too-smooth candidate off guard. It is also one that occasionally is asked in the general course of events. Comparatively few managers or companies ever check references—that astounds me, yet it's a fact of life. On the other hand, the higher up the corporate ladder you go, the more likely it is that your references will be checked. There is only one answer to this question if you ever expect to get an offer: "Yes."

Your answer may include: "Yes, of course you can check my references. However, at present, I would like to keep matters confidential, until we have established a serious mutual interest [i.e., an offer]. At such time I will be pleased to furnish you with whatever references you need from prior employers. I would expect you to wait to check my current employer's references until you have extended an offer in writing, I have accepted, we have agreed upon a start date, and I have had the opportunity to resign in a professional manner." You are under no obligation to give references of a current employer until you have a written offer in hand. You are also well within your rights to request that reference checks of current employers wait until you have started your new job.

"What type of decisions did you make on your last job?"

Your answer should include reference to the fact that your decisions were all based on appropriate business profile keys. The interviewer may be searching to define your responsibilities, or he or she may want to know that you don't overstep yourself. It is also an opportunity, however humble your position, to show your achievement profile.

For example: "Being in charge of the mailroom, my job is to make sure people get information in a timely manner. The job is well defined, and my decisions aren't that difficult. I noticed a year or two ago that when I took the mail around at

10 A.M., everything stopped for twenty minutes. I had an idea and gave it to my boss. She got it cleared by the president, and ever since, we take the mail around just before lunch. Mr. Gray, the president, told me my idea improved productivity, saved time, and that he wished everyone was as conscientious."

"What was the last book you read (or movie you saw)? How did it affect you?"

It doesn't really matter what you say about the latest book or movie, just as long as you have read or seen it. Don't be like the interviewee who said the name of the first book that came to mind—*In Search of Excellence*—only to be caught by the follow-up, "To what extent do you agree with Peters' simultaneous loose/tight pronouncements?" Also, by naming such a well-known book, you have managed only to say that you are like millions of others, which doesn't make you stand out in the crowd. Better that you should name something less faddish—that helps to avoid nasty follow-up questions. And you needn't mention the most *recent* book or movie you've seen. Your answer must simply make a statement about you as a potential employee. Come up with a response that will set you apart and demonstrate your obvious superiority. Ideally you want to mention a work that in some way has helped you improve yourself; anything that has honed any of the twenty key personality traits will do.

"How do you handle tension?"

This question is different from "Can you handle pressure?"—it asks *how* you handle it. You could reply, "Tension is caused when you let things pile up. It is usually caused by letting other areas of responsibility slip by for an extended period. For instance, if you have a difficult presentation coming up, you may procrastinate in your preparations for it. I've seen lots of people do things like that—a task seems so overwhelming they don't know where to begin. I find that if you break those overwhelming tasks into little pieces, they aren't so overwhelming any more. So I suppose I don't so much handle tension as handle the causes of it, by not letting things slip in other areas that can give rise to it."

"How long have you been looking for another position?"

If you are employed, your answer isn't that important—a short or long time is irrelevant to you in any follow-up probes, because you are just looking for the right job, with the right people and outfit that offers you the right opportunities. If, on the other hand, you are unemployed at the time of the question, how you answer becomes more important. If you say, "Well, I've been looking for two years now," it isn't going to score you any points. The interviewer thinks, "Two years, huh? And no one else wanted him in that time. I'm certainly not." So if you must talk of months or more be careful to add something like, "Well, I've been looking for about a year now. I've had a number of offers in that time, but I have determined that as I spend most of my waking hours at work, the job I take and the people I work with have got to be people with values I can identify with. I made the decision that I just wasn't going to suffer clock-watchers and work-to-rule specialists anymore."

"Have you ever been fired?"

Say "no" if you can; if not, act on the advice given to the next question.

"Why were you fired?"

If you were laid off as part of general workforce reduction, be straightforward and move on to the next topic as quickly as possible. If you have been terminated with cause, however, this is a very difficult question to answer. Like it or not, termination with cause is usually justified, because the most loathed responsibility of any manager is to take away someone's livelihood. Virtually no one fires an employee for the heck of it.

Looking at that painful event objectively, you will probably find the cause of your dismissal rooted in the absence of one or more of the twenty profiles. Having been fired also creates instant doubt in the mind of the interviewer, and greatly increases the chances of your references being checked. So if you have been fired, the first thing to do is bite the bullet and call the person who fired you, find out why it happened, and learn what he or she would say about you today.

Your aim is to clear the air, so whatever you do, don't be antagonistic. Reintroduce yourself, explain that you are looking (or, if you have been unemployed for a while, say you are "still looking") for a new job. Say that you appreciate that the manager had to do what was done, and that you learned from the experience. Then ask, "If you were asked as part of a pre- or post-employment reference check, how would you describe my leaving the company? Would you say that I was fired or that I simply resigned? You see, every time I tell someone about my termination, whoosh, there goes another chance of getting another paycheck!" Most managers will plump for the latter option (describing your departure as a resignation). After all, even testy managers tend to be humane after the fact, and such a response saves them potential headaches and even lawsuits.

Whatever you do, don't advertise the fact you were fired. If you are asked, be honest, but make sure you have packaged the reason in the best light possible. Perhaps: "I'm sorry to say, but I deserved it. I was having some personal problems at the time, and I let them affect my work. I was late to work and lost my motivation. My supervisor (whom, by the way, I still speak to) had directions to trim the workforce anyway, and as I was hired only a couple of years ago, I was one of the first to go."

If you can find out the employee turnover figures, voluntary or otherwise, you might add: "Fifteen other people have left so far this year." A combination answer of this nature minimizes the stigma. You have even managed to demonstrate that you take responsibility for your actions, which shows your analytical and listening skills. If one of your past managers will speak well of you, there is nothing to lose and everything to gain by finishing with: "Jill Johnson, at the company, would be a good person to check for a reference on what I have told you."

I would never advise you to be anything but honest in your answers to any interview question. If, however, you have been terminated by a manager who is still vindictive, take heart: Only about 10 percent of all successful job candidates ever get their references checked.

"Have you ever been asked to resign?"

When someone is asked to resign, it is a gesture on the part of the employer: "You can quit, or we will can you, so which do you want it to be?" Because you were given the option, though, that employer cannot later say, "I had to ask him to resign"—that is tantamount to firing and could lead to legal problems. In the final analysis, it is safe to answer "no."

"Were you ever dismissed from your job for a reason that seemed unjustified?"

Another sneaky way of asking, "Were you ever fired?" The sympathetic phrasing is geared to getting you to reveal all the sordid details. The cold hard facts are that hardly anyone is ever fired without cause, and you're kidding yourself if you think otherwise. With that in mind, you can quite honestly say, "No," and move on to the next topic.

"In your last job, what were some of the things you spent most of your time on, and why?"

Employees come in two categories: goal-oriented (those who want to get the job done), and task-oriented (those who believe in "busy" work). You must demonstrate good time management, and that you are, therefore, goal-oriented, for that is what this question probes.

You might reply: "I work on the telephone like a lot of businesspeople; meetings also take up a great deal of time. What is more important to me is effective time management. I find more gets achieved in a shorter time if a meeting is scheduled, say, immediately before lunch or at the close of business. I try to block my time in the morning. At four o'clock, I review what I've achieved, what went right or wrong, and plan adjustments and my main thrust of business for tomorrow."

"In what ways has your job prepared you to take on greater responsibility?"

This is one of the most important questions you will have to answer. The interviewer is looking for examples of your professional development, perhaps to judge your future growth potential, so you must tell a story that demonstrates it. The following example shows growth, listening skills, honesty, and adherence to procedures. Parts of it can be adapted to your personal experience. Notice the then-and-now aspect of the answer.

"When I first started my last job, my boss would brief me morning and evening. I made some mistakes, learned a lot, and got the jobs in on time. As time went by I took on greater responsibilities, [list some of them]. Nowadays, I meet with her every Monday for breakfast to discuss any major directional changes, so that she can keep management informed. I think that demonstrates not only my growth, but also the confidence my management has in my judgment and ability to perform consistently above standard."

"In what ways has your job changed since you originally joined the company?"

You can use the same answer here as for the previous question.

"How does this job compare with others you have applied for?"

This is a variation of more direct questions, such as, "How many other jobs have you applied for?" and "Who else have you applied to?" but it is a slightly more intelligent question and therefore more dangerous. It asks you to compare. Answer the question and sidestep at the same time.

"No two jobs are the same, and this one is certainly unlike any other I have applied for." If you are pressed further, say, "Well, to give you a more detailed answer, I would need to ask you a number of questions about the job and the company. Would now be a good time to do that or would it be better later in the interview process?"

"What makes this job different from your current/last one?"

If you don't have enough information to answer the question, say so, and ask some of your own. Behind the question is the interviewer's desire to uncover experience you are lacking—your answer could be used as evidence against you. Focus on the positive: "From what I know of the job, I seem to have all the experience required to make a thorough success. I would say that the major differences seem to be. . ." and here you play back the positive attributes of the department and company as the interviewer gave them to you, either in the course of the interview or in answer to your specific questions.

"Do you have any questions?"

A good question. Almost always, this is a sign that the interview is drawing to a close, and that you have one more chance to make an impression. Remember the adage: People respect what you inspect, not what you expect. Create questions from any of the following.

- Find out why the job is open, who had it last, and what happened to him or her. Did he or she get promoted or fired? How many people have held this position in the last couple of years? What happened to them subsequently?
- Why did the interviewer join the company? How long has he or she been there? What is it about the company that keeps him or her there?
- To whom would you report? Will you get the opportunity to meet that person?
- Where is the job located? What are the travel requirements, if any?
- What type of training is required, and how long is it? What type of training is available?
- What would your first assignment be?
- What are the realistic chances for growth in the job? Where are the opportunities for greatest growth within the company?
- What are the skills and attributes most needed to get ahead in the company?
- Who will be the company's major competitor over the next few years? How does the interviewer feel the company stacks up against them?
- What has been the growth pattern of the company over the last five years?

Is it profitable? How profitable? Is the company privately or publicly held?

- If there is a written job description, may you see it?
- How regularly do performance evaluations occur? What model do they follow?

15.
"What Kind of Person Are You Really, Mr. Jones?"

Will you reduce your new employer's life expectancy? The interviewer wants to know! If you are offered the job and accept, you will be working together fifty weeks of the year. Every employer wants to know whether you will fit in with the rest of the staff, whether you are a team player, and most of all: Are you manageable?

There are a number of questions the interviewer might use to probe this area. They will mainly be geared to your behavior and attitudes in the past. Remember: It is universally believed that your past actions predict your future behavior.

"How do you take direction?"

This is really two questions. "How do you take direction?" and, "How do you take criticism?" Your answer will cover both points. "I take direction well and believe there are two types: carefully explained direction, when my boss has time to treat me with honor and respect; then there is the other, a brusque order or correction. While most people get upset with that, personally I always believe the manager is troubled with bigger problems and a tight schedule. As such, I take the direction and get on with the job without taking offense so my boss can get on with her job. It's the only way."

"Would you like to have your boss' job?"

It is a rare boss who wants his or her livelihood taken. On my very first interview, my future boss said, "Mr. Yate, it has been a pleasure to meet you. However, until you walked in, I wasn't looking for a new job."

By the same token, ambition is admired, but mainly by the ambitious. Be cautiously optimistic. Perhaps: "Well, if my boss were promoted over the coming years, I would hope to have made a strong enough contribution to warrant his recommendation. I'm looking for a manager who will help me develop my capabilities and grow with him."

"What do you think of your current/last boss?"

Short, sweet, and shut up. People who complain about their employers are recognized to be the same people who cause the most disruption in a department. This question means the interviewer has no desire to hire trouble. "I liked her as a person, respected her professionally, and appreciated her guidance." The question is often followed by one that tries to validate your answer.

"Describe a situation where your work or an idea was criticized."

A doubly dangerous question. You are being asked to say how you handle criticism and to detail your faults. If you are asked this question, describe a poor idea that was criticized, not poor work. Poor work can cost money and is a warning sign, obviously, to the interviewer.

One of the wonderful things about a new job is that you can leave the past entirely behind, so it does not matter how you handled criticism in the past. What does matter is how the interviewer would like you to handle criticism, if and when it becomes his or her unpleasant duty to dish it out; that's what the question is really about. So relate one of those it-seemed-like-a-good-idea-at-the-time ideas, and finish with how you handled the criticism. You could say: "I listened carefully and resisted the temptation to interrupt or defend myself. Then I fed back what I heard to make sure the facts were straight. I asked for advice, we bounced some ideas around, then I came back later and represented the idea in a more viable format. My supervisor's input was invaluable."

"Tell me about yourself."

This is not an invitation to ramble on. You need to know more about the question before giving an answer. "What area of my background would be most relevant to you?" That enables the interviewer to help you with the appropriate focus, so you can avoid discussing irrelevancies. Never answer this question without qualifying whether the interviewer wishes to hear about your business or personal life.

However the interviewer responds to your qualifying question, the tale you tell should demonstrate one or more of the twenty key personality profiles—perhaps honesty, integrity, being a team player, or determination. If you choose "team player," part of your answer might include this: "I put my heart into everything I do, whether it be sports or work. I find that getting along with your peers and being part of the team makes life more enjoyable and productive."

"Rate yourself on a scale of one to ten."

A stupid question. That aside, bear in mind that this is meant to plumb the depths of your self-esteem. If you answer ten, you run the risk of portraying yourself as insufferable; on the other hand, if you say less than seven, you might as well get up and leave. You are probably best claiming to be an eight or nine, saying that you always give of your best, but that in doing so you always increase your skills and therefore always see room for improvement.

"What kinds of things do you worry about?"

Some questions, such as this one, can seem so off-the-wall that you might start treating the interviewer as a father confessor in no time flat. Your private phobias have nothing to do with your job, and revealing them can get you labeled as unbalanced. It is best to confine your answer to the sensible worries of a conscientious professional. "I worry about deadlines, staff turnover, tardiness, back-up plans for when the computer crashes, or that one of my auditors burns out or defects to the competition—just the normal stuff. It goes with the territory, so I don't let it get me down."

"What is the most difficult situation you have faced?"

The question looks for information on two fronts: How do you define difficult? and, what was your handling of the situation? You must have a story ready for this one in which the situation both was tough and allowed you to show yourself in a good light. Avoid talking about problems that have to do with co-workers. You can talk about the difficult decision to fire someone, but emphasize that once you had examined the problem and reached a conclusion you acted quickly and professionally, with the best interests of the company at heart.

"What are some of the things that bother you?" "What are your pet hates?" "Tell me about the last time you felt anger on the job."

These questions are so similar that they can be treated as one. It is tremendously important that you show you can remain calm. Most of us have seen a colleague lose his or her cool on occasion—not a pretty sight and one that every sensible employer wants to avoid. This question comes up more and more often the higher up the corporate ladder you climb, and the more frequent your contact with clients and the general public. To answer it, find something that angers conscientious workers. "I enjoy my work and believe in giving value to my employer. Dealing with clock-watchers and the ones who regularly get sick on Mondays and Fridays really bothers me, but it's not something that gets me angry or anything like that." An answer of this nature will help you much more than the kind given by a California engineer, who went on for some minutes about how he hated the small-mindedness of people who don't like pet rabbits in the office.

"What have you done that shows initiative?"

The question probes whether you are a doer, someone who will look for ways to increase sales, save time, or save money—the kind of person who gives a manager a pleasant surprise once in a while, who makes life easier for co-workers. Be sure, however, that your example of initiative does not show a disregard for company policies and procedures.

"My boss has to organize a lot of meetings. That means developing agendas, letting employees around the country know the dates well in advance, getting materials printed, etc. Most people in my position would wait for the work to be given them. I don't. Every quarter, I sit down with my boss and find out the dates of all his meetings for the next six months. I immediately make the hotel and flight arrangements and then work backwards. I ask myself questions like, 'If the agenda for the July meeting is to reach the field at least six weeks before the meeting, when must it be finished by?' Then I come up with a deadline. I do that for all the major activities for all the meetings. I put the deadlines in his diary; and mine, only two weeks earlier. That way I remind the boss that the deadline is getting close. My boss is the best organized, most relaxed manager in the company. None of his colleagues can understand how he does it."

"What are some of the things about which you and your supervisor disagreed?"
It is safest to state that you did not disagree.

"In what areas do you feel your supervisor could have done a better job?"
The same goes for this one. No one admires a Monday-morning quarterback.
You could reply, though: "I have always had the highest respect for my supervisor. I have always been so busy learning from Mr. Jones that I don't think he could have done a better job. He has really brought me to the point where I am ready for greater challenges. That's why I'm here."

"What are some of the things your supervisor did that you disliked?"
If you and the interviewer are both non-smokers, for example, and your boss isn't, use it. Apart from that: "You know, I've never thought of our relationship in terms of like or dislike. I've always thought our role was to get along together and get the job done."

"How well do you feel your boss rated your job performance?"
This is one very sound reason to ask for written evaluations of your work before leaving a company. Some performance-review procedures include a written evaluation of your performance—perhaps your company employs it. If you work for a company that asks you to sign your formal review, you are quite entitled to request a copy of it. You should also ask for a letter of recommendation whenever you leave a job: You have nothing to lose. While I don't recommend thrusting recommendations under unwilling interviewers' noses (they smell a rat when written endorsements of any kind are offered unrequested), the time will come when you are asked and can produce them with a flourish. If you don't have written references, perhaps: "My supervisor always rated my job performance well. In fact, I was always rated as being capable of accepting further responsibilities. The problem was there was nothing available in the company—that's why I'm here."
If your research has been done properly you can also quote verbal appraisals of your performance from prior jobs. "In fact, my boss said only a month ago that I was the most valuable [e.g.] engineer in the workgroup, because. . ."

"How did your boss get the best out of you?"
This is a manageability question, geared to probing whether you are going to be a pain in the neck or not. Whatever you say, it is important for your ongoing happiness that you make it clear you don't appreciate being treated like a dishrag.

You can give a short, general answer: "My last boss got superior effort and performance by treating me like a human being and giving me the same personal respect with which she liked to be treated herself." This book is full of answers that get you out of tight corners and make you shine, but this is one instance in which you really should tell it like it is. You don't want to work for someone who is going to make life miserable for you.

"How interested are you in sports?"

A recently completed survey of middle- and upper-management personnel found that the executives who listed group sports/activities among their extracurricular activities made an average of $3,000 per year more than their sedentary colleagues. Don't you just love baseball suddenly? The interviewer is looking for your involvement in groups, as a signal that you know how to get along with others and pull together as a team.

"I really enjoy most team sports. Don't get a lot of time to indulge myself, but I am a regular member of my company's softball team." Apart from team sports, endurance sports are seen as a sign of determination: swimming, running, and cycling are all okay. Games of skill (bridge, chess, and the like) demonstrate analytical skills. Being a Grand Master of Dungeons and Dragons doesn't demonstrate a damned thing.

"What personal characteristics are necessary for success in your field?"

You know the answer to this one: It's a brief recital of key personality profiles.

You might say: "To be successful in my field? Drive, motivation, energy, confidence, determination, good communication, and analytical skills. Combined, of course, with the ability to work with others."

"Do you prefer working with others or alone?"

This question is usually used to determine whether you are a team player. Before answering, however, be sure you know whether the job requires you to work alone. Then answer appropriately. Perhaps: "I'm quite happy working alone when necessary. I don't need much constant reassurance. But I prefer to work in a group—so much more gets achieved when people pull together."

"Explain your role as a group/team member."

You are being asked to describe yourself as either a team player or a loner. Most departments depend on harmonious teamwork for their success, so describe yourself as a team player, by all means: "I perform my job in a way that helps others to do theirs in an efficient fashion. Beyond the mechanics, we all have a responsibility to make the workplace a friendly and pleasant place to be. That means everyone working for the common good and making the necessary personal sacrifices toward that good."

"How would you define a conducive work atmosphere?"

This is a tricky question, especially because you probably have no idea what kind of work atmosphere exists in that particular office. So, the longer your answer, the greater your chances of saying the wrong thing. Keep it short and sweet. "One where the team has a genuine interest in its work and desire to turn out a good product/deliver a good service."

"Do you make your opinions known when you disagree with the views of your supervisor?"

If you can, state that you come from an environment where input is encouraged when it helps the team's ability to get the job done efficiently. "If opinions are sought in a meeting, I will give mine, although I am careful to be aware of others' feelings. I will never criticize a co-worker or a superior in open forum; besides, it is quite possible to disagree without being disagreeable. However, my past manager made it clear that she valued my opinion by asking for it. So, after a while, if there was something I felt strongly about, I would make an appointment to sit down and discuss it one on one." You might choose to end by turning the tables with a question of your own: "Is this a position where we work as a team to solve problems and get the job done, or one where we are meant to be seen and not heard and speak when spoken to?"

"What would you say about a supervisor who was unfair or difficult to work with?"

For this job, you'll definitely want to meet your potential supervisor—just in case you have been earmarked for the company Genghis Khan without warning. The response, "Do you have anyone in particular in mind?" will probably get you off the hook. If you need to elaborate, try: "I would make an appointment to see the supervisor and diplomatically explain that I felt uncomfortable in our relationship, that I felt he or she was not treating me as a professional colleague, and therefore that I might not be performing up to standard in some way—that I wanted to right matters and ask for his or her input as to what I must do to create a professional relationship. I would enter into the discussion in the frame of mind that we were equally responsible for whatever communication problems existed, and that this wasn't just the manager's problem."

"Do you consider yourself a natural leader or a born follower?"

Ow! How you answer depends a lot on the job offer you are chasing. If you are a recent graduate, you are expected to have high aspirations, so go for it. If you are already on the corporate ladder with some practical experience in the school of hard knocks, you might want to be a little more cagey. Assuming you are up for (and want) a leadership position, you might try something like this: "I would be reluctant to regard anyone as a natural leader. Hiring, motivating, and disciplining other adults and at the same time molding them into a cohesive team involves a number of delicately tuned skills that no honest people can say they were born with. Leadership requires first of all the desire; then it is a lifetime learning process. Anyone who reckons they have it all under control and has nothing more to learn isn't doing the employer any favors."

Of course, a little humility is also in order, because just about every leader in every company reports to someone, and there is a good chance that you are talking to such a someone right now. So you might consider including something like, "No matter how well developed any individual's leadership qualities, an integral part of the skills of a leader is to take direction both from his or her immediate boss, and also to seek the input of the people being supervised. The wise leader will always follow good advice and sound business judgment wherever it comes from. I would say that given the desire to be a leader, the true leader in the modern business world must embrace both." How can anyone disagree with that kind of wisdom?

"Why do you feel you are a better [e.g.] secretary than some of your co-workers?"

If you speak disparagingly of your co-workers, you will not put yourself in the best light. That is what the question asks you to do, so it poses some difficulties. The trick is to answer the question but not to accept the invitation to show yourself from anything other than a flattering perspective. "I think that question is best answered by a manager. It is so difficult to be objective, and I really don't like to slight my co-workers. I don't spend my time thinking about how superior I am, because that would be detrimental to our working together as a team. I believe, however, some of the qualities that make me an outstanding secretary are . . ." and you go on to illustrate job-related personal qualities that make you a beacon of productivity and a joy to work with.

"You have a doctor's appointment arranged for noon. You've waited two weeks to get in. An urgent meeting is scheduled at the last moment, though. What do you do?"

What a crazy question, you mutter. It's not. It is even more than a question—it is what I call a question shell. The question within the shell—in this instance, "Will you sacrifice the appointment or sacrifice your job?—can be changed at will. This is a situational-interviewing technique, which poses an on-the-job problem to see how the prospective employee will respond. A Chicago company asks this question as part of its initial screening, and if you give the wrong answer, you never even get a face-to-face interview. So what is the right answer to this or any similar shell question?

Fortunately, once you understand the interviewing technique, it is quite easy to handle—all you have to do is turn the question around. "If I were the manager who had to schedule a really important meeting at the last moment, and someone on my staff chose to go to the doctor's instead, how would I feel?"

It is unlikely that you would be an understanding manager unless the visit were for a triple bypass. To answer, you start with an evaluation of the importance of the problem and the responsibility of everyone to make some sacrifices for the organization, and finish with: "The first thing I would do is reschedule the appointment and save the doctor's office inconvenience. Then I would immediately make sure I was properly prepared for the emergency meeting."

"How do you manage to interview while still employed?"

As long as you don't explain that you faked a dentist appointment to make the interview you should be all right. Beware of revealing anything that might make you appear at all underhanded. Best to make the answer short and sweet and let the interviewer move on to richer areas of inquiry. Just explain that you had some vacation time due, or took a day off in lieu of overtime payments. "I had some vacation time, so I went to my boss and explained I needed a couple of days off for some personal business, and asked her what days would be most suitable. Although I plan to change jobs, I don't in any way want to hurt my current employer in the process by being absent during a crunch."

"When do you expect a promotion?"

Tread warily, show you believe in yourself, and have both feet firmly planted on the ground. "That depends on a few criteria. Of course, I cannot expect promotions without the performance that marks me as deserving of promotion. I also need to join a company that has the growth necessary to provide the opportunity. I hope that my manager believes in promoting from within and will help me grow so that I will have the skills necessary to be considered for promotion when the opportunity comes along."

If you are the only one doing a particular job in the company, or you are in management, you need to build another factor into your answer. For example: "As a manager, I realize that part of my job is to have done my succession planning, and that I must have someone trained and ready to step into my shoes before I can expect to step up. That way I play my part in preserving the chain of command." To avoid being caught off guard with queries about your having achieved that in your present job, you can finish with: "Just as I have done in my present job, where I have a couple of people capable of taking over the reins when I leave."

"Tell me a story."

Wow. What on earth does the interviewer mean by that question? You don't know until you get him or her to elaborate. Ask, "What would you like me to tell you a story about?" To make any other response is to risk making a fool of yourself. Very often the question is asked to see how analytical you are: People who answer the question without qualifying show that they do not think things through carefully. The subsequent question will be about either your personal or professional life. If it is about your personal life, tell a story that shows you like people and are determined. Do not discuss your love life. If the subsequent question is about your professional life, tell a story that demonstrates your willingness and manageability.

"What have your other jobs taught you?"

Talk about the professional skills you have learned and the personality traits you have polished. Many interviewees have had success finishing their answer with: "There are two general things I have learned from past jobs. First, if you are confused, ask—it's better to ask a dumb question than make a stupid mistake. Second, it's better to promise less and produce more than to make unrealistic forecasts."

"Define cooperation."

The question asks you to explain how to function as a team player in the workplace. Your answer could be: "Cooperation is a person's ability to sacrifice personal wishes and beliefs whenever necessary to assure the department reaches its goals. It is also a person's desire to be part of a team, and by hard work and goodwill make the department greater than the sum of its parts."

"What difficulties do you have tolerating people with different backgrounds and interests from yours?"

Another "team player" question with the awkward inference that you do have problems. Give the following answer: "I don't have any."

"In hindsight, what have you done that was a little harebrained?"

You are never harebrained in your business dealings, and you haven't been harebrained in your personal life since graduation, right? The only safe examples to use are ones from your deep past that ultimately turned out well. One of the best to use, if it applies to you, is this one: "Well, I guess the time I bought my house. I had no idea what I was letting myself in for, and at the time, I really couldn't afford it. Still, I managed to make the payments, though I had to work like someone possessed. Yes, my first house—that was a real learning experience." Not only can most people relate to this example, but it also gives you the opportunity to sell one or two of your very positive and endearing traits.

□   □   □

If you think the interview is only tough for the interviewee, it's time to take a look at the other side of the desk. Knowing what's going on behind those Foster Grants can really help you shine.

16.
The Other Side of the Desk

There are two terrible places to be during an interview—sitting in front of the desk wondering what on earth is going to happen next, and sitting behind the desk asking the questions. The average interviewer dreads the meeting almost as much as the interviewee, yet for opposite reasons.

American business frequently yields to the mistaken belief that any person, on being promoted to the ranks of management, becomes mystically endowed with all necessary managerial skills. That is a fallacy. Comparatively few management people have been taught to interview; most just bumble along and pick up a certain proficiency over a period of time.

There are two distinct types of interviewers who can spell disaster for you if you are unprepared. One is the highly skilled interviewer, who has been trained in systematic techniques for probing your past for all the facts and evaluating your potential. The other is the totally incompetent interviewer, who may even lack the ability to phrase a question adequately. Both are equally dangerous when it comes to winning the job offer.

The Skillful Interviewer
Skillful interviewers know exactly what they want to discover. They have taken exhaustive steps to learn the strategies that will help them hire only the best for their company. They follow a set format for the interview process to ensure objectivity in selection and a set sequence of questions to ensure the facts are gathered. They will definitely test your mettle.

There are many ways for a manager to build and conduct a structured interview, but all have the same goals:

- To ensure a systematic coverage of your work history and applicable job-related skills.
- To provide a technique for gathering all the relevant facts.
- To provide a uniform strategy that objectively evaluates all job candidates.
- To determine ability, willingness, and manageability.

Someone using structured interview techniques will usually follow a standard format. The interview will begin with small talk and a brief introduction to relax you. Following close on the heels of that chit-chat comes a statement geared to assure you that baring your faults is the best way to get the job. Your interviewer will then outline the steps in the interview. That will include you giving a chronological description of your work history, and then the interviewer asking specific questions about your experience. Then, prior to the close of the interview, you will be given an opportunity to ask your own questions.

Sounds pretty simple, huh? Well, watch out! The skilled interviewer knows exactly what questions to ask, why they will be asked, in what order they will be asked, and what the desired responses are. He or she will interview and evaluate every applicant for the job in exactly the same fashion. You are up against a pro.

Like the hunter who learns to think like his or her prey, you will find that the best way to win over the interviewer is to think like the interviewer. In fact, take that idea a little further: You must win, but you don't want the other guys to realize you beat them at their own game. To do that, you must learn how the interviewer has prepared for you; and by going through the same process you will beat out your competitors for the job offer.

The dangerous part of this type of structured interview is called "skills evaluation." The interviewer has analyzed all the different skills it takes to do the job, and all the personality traits that complement those skills. Armed with that data, he or she has developed a series of carefully-sequenced questions to draw out your relative merits and weaknesses.

Graphically, it looks like this:

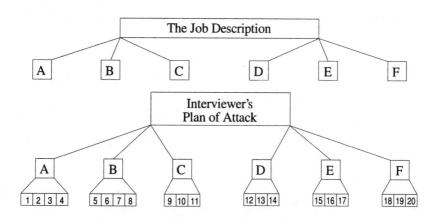

Letters A–F are the separate skills necessary to do the job; numbers 1–20 are questions asked to identify and verify that particular skill. This is where many of the tough questions will arise, and the only way to prepare effectively is to take the interviewer's viewpoint and complete this exercise in its entirety. That effort requires a degree of objectivity, but will generate multiple job offers.

☐ Look at the position you seek. What role does it play in helping the company achieve its corporate mission and make a profit?

☐ What are the five most important duties of that job?

☐ From a management viewpoint, what are the skills and attributes necessary to perform each of these tasks?

Write it all down. Now, put yourself in the interviewer's shoes. What topics would you examine to find out whether a person can really do the job? If for some reason you get stuck in the process, just use your past experience. You have worked with good and bad people, and their work habits and skills will lead you to develop both the potential questions and the correct answers.

Each job skill you identify is fertile ground for the interviewer's questions. Don't forget the intangible skills that are so important to many jobs, like self-confidence and creativity, because the interviewer won't. Develop a number of questions for each job skill you identify.

Again, looking back at co-workers (and still wearing the manager's mask), what are the personal characteristics that would make life more comfortable for you as a manager? Those are also dimensions that are likely to be probed by the interviewer. Once you have identified the questions you would ask in the interviewer's position, the answers should come easily.

That's the way managers are trained to develop structured interview questions—I just gave you the inside track. Complete the exercise by developing the answers you would like to hear as a manager. Take time to complete the exercise conscientiously, writing out both the questions and the appropriate answers.

☐   ☐   ☐

These sharks have some juicy questions to probe your skills, attitude, and personality. Would you like to hear some of them? Notice that these questions tend to lay out a problem for you to solve, but in no way lead you towards the answer. They are often two- and three-part questions as well. The additional question that can be tagged onto them all is, "What did you learn from this experience?" Assume it is included whenever you get one of these questions—you'll be able to sell different aspects of your success profile.

"You have been given a project that requires you to interact with different levels within the company. How do you do this? What levels are you most comfortable with?"

This is a two-part question that probes communication and self-confidence skills. The first part asks how you interact with superiors and motivate those working with and for you on the project. The second part of the question is saying, "Tell me whom you regard as your peer group—help me categorize you." To cover those bases, you will want to include the essence of this: "There are basically two types of people I would interact with on a project of this nature. First, there are those I report to, who bear the ultimate responsibility for its success. With them, I determine deadlines and how they will evaluate the success of the project. I outline my approach, breaking the project down into component parts, getting approval on both the approach and the costs. I would keep my supervisors up-to-date on a regular basis, and seek input whenever needed. My supervisors would expect three things from me: the facts, an analysis of potential problems, and that I not be intimidated, as that would jeopardize the project's success. I would comfortably satisfy those expectations.

"The other people to interact with on a project like this are those who work with and for me. With those people, I would outline the project and explain how a successful outcome will benefit the company. I would assign the component parts to those best suited to each, and arrange follow-up times to assure completion by deadline. My role here would be to facilitate, motivate, and bring the different personalities together to form a team.

"As for comfort level, I find this type of approach enables me to interact comfortably with all levels and types of people."

"Tell me about an event that really challenged you. How did you meet the challenge? In what way was your approach different from others'?"

This is a straightforward two-part question. The first probes your problem-solving abilities. The second asks you to set yourself apart from the herd. First of all, outline the problem. The blacker you make the situation, the better. Having done that, go ahead and explain your solution, its value to your employer, and how it was different from other approaches.

"My company has offices all around the country; I am responsible for seventy of them. My job is to visit each office on a regular basis and build market-penetration strategies with management, and to train and motivate the sales and customer-service force. When the recession hit, the need to service those offices was more important than ever, yet the traveling costs were getting prohibitive.

"Morale was an especially important factor; you can't let outlying offices feel defeated. I re-apportioned my budget and did the following: I dramatically increased telephone contact with the offices. I instituted a monthly sales-technique letter—how to prospect for new clients, how to negotiate difficult sales, and so forth. I bought and rented sales training and motivational tapes and sent them to my managers with instructions on how to use them in a sales meeting. I stopped visiting all the offices. Instead, I scheduled weekend training meetings in central locations throughout my area: one day of sales training and one day of management training, concentrating on how to run sales meetings, early termination of low producers, and so forth.

"While my colleagues complained about the drop in sales, mine increased, albeit a modest six percent. After two quarters, my approach was officially adopted by the company."

"Give me an example of a method of working you have used. How did you feel about it?"

You have a choice of giving an example of either good or bad work habits. Give a good example, one that demonstrates your understanding of corporate goals, your organizational skills, analytical ability, or time management skills.

You could say: "I believe in giving an honest day's work for a day's pay. That requires organization and time management. I do my paperwork at the end of each day, when I review the day's achievements; with this done, I plan for tomorrow. When I come to work in the morning, I'm ready to get going without wasting time. I try to schedule meetings right before lunch; people get to the point more quickly if it's on their time. I feel that is an efficient and organized method of working."

"When you joined your last company and met the group for the first time, how did you feel? How did you get on with them?"

Your answer should include: "I naturally felt a little nervous, but I was excited about the new job. I shared that excitement with my new friends, and told them that I was enthusiastic about learning new skills from them. I was open and friendly, and when given the opportunity to help someone myself, I jumped at it."

"In your last job, how did you plan to interview?"

That's an easy one. Just give a description of how the skilled interviewer prepares.

"How have you benefited from your disappointments?"

Disappointments are different from failures. It is an intelligent—probably trained—interviewer who asks this one; it is also an opportunity for the astute interviewee to shine. The question itself is very positive—it asks you to show how you benefited. Note also that it doesn't ask you to give specific details of specific disappointments, so you don't have to open your mouth and insert your foot. Instead, be general. Edison once explained his success as an inventor by claiming that he knew more ways not to do something than anyone else living; you can do worse than quote him. In any event, sum up your answer with, "I treat disappointments as a learning experience; I look at what happened, why it happened, and how I would do things differently in each stage should the same set of circumstances appear again. That way, I put disappointment behind me and am ready with renewed vigor and understanding to face the new day's problems."

A side note. A person with strong religious beliefs may be tempted to answer a question like this in terms of religious values. If you benefit from disappointments in a spiritual way, remember that not everyone feels the same as you do. More important, the interviewer is, by law, prohibited from talking about religion with you, so you can unwittingly put the interviewer in an awkward position of not knowing how to respond. And making an interviewer feel awkward in any way is not the way to win the job offer.

"What would you do when you have a decision to make and no procedure exists?"

This question probes your analytical skills, integrity, and dedication. Most of all, the interviewer is testing your manageability and adherence to procedures—the "company way of doing things." You need to cover that with: "I would act without my manager's direction only if the situation were urgent and my manager were not available. Then, I would take command of the situation, make a decision based on the facts, and implement it. I would update my boss at the earliest opportunity." If possible, tell a story to illustrate.

"That is an excellent answer. Now to give me a balanced view, can you give me an example that didn't work out so well?"

There are two techniques that every skilled interviewer will use, especially if you are giving good answers. In this question, the interviewer looks for negative balance; in the follow-up, the person will look for negative confirmation. Here, you are required to give an example of an inadequacy. The trick is to pull something from the past, not the present, and to finish with what you learned from the experience. For example: "That's easy. When I first joined the workforce, I didn't really understand the importance of systems and procedures. There was one time when I was too anxious to contribute and didn't have the full picture. There was a sales visit report everyone had to fill out after visiting a customer. I always put a lot of effort into it until I realized it was never read; it just went in the files. So I stopped doing it for a few days to see if it made any difference. I thought I was gaining time to make more sales for the company. I was so proud of my extra sales calls I told the boss at the end of the week. My boss explained that the records were for the long term, so that should my job change, the next salesperson would have the benefit of a full client history. It was a long time ago, but I have never forgotten the lesson: There's always a reason for systems and procedures. I've had the best-kept records in the company ever since."

To look for negative confirmation, the interviewer then may say something like, "Thank you. Now can you give me another example?" He or she is trying to confirm a weakness. If you help, you could well do yourself out of a job. Here's your reaction: You sit deep in thought for a good ten seconds, then look up and say firmly, "No, that's the only occasion when anything like that happened." Shut up and refuse to be enticed further.

The Unconscious Incompetent

Now you should be ready for almost anything a professional interviewer could throw at you. Your foresight and strategic planning will generate multiple offers of employment for you in all circumstances except one, and that's when you face the unconsciously incompetent interviewer. He or she is probably more dangerous to your job-offer status than everything else combined.

The problem is embodied in the experienced manager who is a poor interviewer, but who does not know it. He or she, consciously or otherwise, bases hiring decisions on "experience" and "knowledge of mankind" and "gut feeling." In any event, he or she is an unconscious incompetent. You have probably been interviewed by one in your time. Remember leaving an interview and, upon reflection, feeling the interviewer knew absolutely nothing about you or your skills? If so, you know how frustrating that can be. Here, you'll see how to turn that difficult situation to your advantage. In the future, good managers who are poor interviewers will be offering jobs with far greater frequency than ever before. Understand that a poor interviewer can be a wonderful manager; interviewing skills are learned, not inherited or created as a result of a mystical corporate blessing.

The unconscious incompetents abound. Their heinous crime can only be exceeded by your inability to recognize and take advantage of the proffered opportunity.

As in handling the skilled interviewer, it is necessary to imagine how the unconscious incompetent thinks and feels. There are many manifestations of the poor interviewer. After each of the next examples, follow instructions for appropriate handling of the unique problems each type poses for you.

☐ **Example One:** The interviewer's desk is cluttered, and the resume or application that was handed to him or her a few minutes before cannot be found.

Response: Sit quietly through the bumbling and searching. Check out the surroundings. Breathe deeply and slowly to calm any natural interview nerves. As you bring your adrenaline under control, you bring a certain calming effect to the interviewer and the interview. (This example, by the way, is usually the most common sign of the unconscious incompetent.)

☐ **Example Two:** The interviewer experiences constant interruptions from the telephone or people walking into the office.

Response: This provides good opportunities for selling yourself. Make note on your pad of where you were in the conversation and refresh the interviewer on the point when you start talking again. He or she will be impressed with your level head and good memory. The interruptions also give time, perhaps, to find something of common interest in the office, something you can compliment. You will also have time to compose the suitable value key follow-up to the point made in the conversation prior to the interruption.

☐ **Example Three:** The interviewer starts with an explanation of why you are both sitting there, and then allows the conversation to degenerate into a lengthy diatribe about the company.

Response: Show interest in the company and the conversation. Sit straight, look attentive (the other applicants probably fall asleep), make appreciative murmurs, and nod at the appropriate times until there is a pause. When that occurs, comment that you appreciate the background on the company, because you can now see more clearly how the job fits into the general scheme of things; that you see, for example, how valuable communication skills would be for the job. Could the interviewer please tell you some of the other job requirements? Then, as the job's functions are described, you can interject appropriate information about your background with: "Would it be of value, Mr. Smith, if I described my experience with . . . ?"

☐ **Example Four:** The interviewer begins with, or quickly breaks into, the drawbacks of the job. The job may even be described in totally negative terms.

That is often done without giving a balanced view of the duties and expectations of the position.

Response: An initial negative description often means that the interviewer has had bad experiences hiring for the position. Your course is to empathize (not sympathize) with his or her bad experiences, and make it known that you recognize the importance of (for example) reliability, especially in this particular type of job. (You will invariably find in these instances that what your interviewer has lacked in the past is someone with a serious understanding of value keys.) Illustrate your proficiency in that particular aspect of your profession with a short example from your work history. Finish your statements by asking the interviewer what some of the biggest problems to be handled in the job are. The questions demonstrate your understanding, and the interviewer's answers outline the areas from your background and skills to which you should draw attention.

☐ **Example Five:** The interviewer spends considerable time early in the interview describing "the type of people we are here at XYZ Corporation."

Response: Very simple. You have always wanted to work for a company with that atmosphere. It creates the type of work environment that is conducive to a person really giving his or her best efforts.

☐ **Example Six:** The interviewer asks closed-ended questions, ones that demand no more than a yes/no answer (e.g., "Do you pay attention to detail?"). Such questions are hardly adequate to establish your skills, yet you must handle them effectively to secure the job offer.

Response: A yes/no answer to a closed-ended question will not get you that offer. The trick is to treat each closed-ended question as if the interviewer has added, "Please give me a brief yet thorough answer." Closed-ended questions also are often mingled with statements followed by pauses. In those instances, agree with the statement in a way that demonstrates both a grasp of your job and the interviewer's statement. For example: "That's an excellent point, Mr. Smith. I couldn't agree more that the attention to detail you describe naturally affects cost containment. My track record in this area is . . . ."

☐ **Example Seven:** The interviewer asks a continuing stream of negative questions (as described in chapter 17, "The Stress Interview").

Response: Use the techniques and answers described earlier. Give your answers with a smile and do not take the questions as personal insults; they are not intended that way. The more stressful the situations the job is likely to place you in, the greater the likelihood of your having to field negative questions. The interviewer wants to know if you can take the heat.

☐ **Example Eight:** The interviewer has difficulty looking at you while speaking.

Response: The interviewer is someone who finds it uncomfortable being in the spotlight. Try to help him or her to be a good audience. Ask specific questions about the job responsibilities and offer your skills in turn.

□   □   □

Often a hiring manager will arrange for you to meet with two or three other people. Frequently, the other interviewers have been neither trained in appropriate interviewing skills nor told the details of the job for which you are interviewing. So you will take additional copies of your executive briefing with you to the interview to aid them in focusing on the appropriate job functions.

When you understand how to recognize and respond to these different types of interviewer, you will leave your interview having made a favorable first impression. No one forgets first impressions.

17.
The Stress Interview

$\mathbf{F}$or all intents and purposes, every interview is a stress interview: The interviewer's negative and trick questions can act as the catalyst for your own fear. And the only way to combat that fear is to be prepared, to know what the interviewer is trying to do, to anticipate the various tacks he or she will take. Only preparedness will keep you cool and collected. Whenever you are ill-prepared for an interview, no one will be able to put more pressure on you than yourself. Remember: A stress interview is just a regular interview with the volume turned all the way up—the music's the same, just louder.

You've heard the horror stories. An interviewer demands of a hapless applicant, "Sell me this pen," or asks, "How would you improve the design of a teddy bear?" Or the candidate is faced with a battery of interviewers, all demanding rapid-fire answers to questions like, "You're giving a dinner party. Which ten famous people would you invite and why?" When the interviewee offers evidence of foot-in-mouth disease by asking, "Living or dead?" he receives his just desserts in reply: "Ten of each."

Such awful-sounding questions are thrown in to test your poise, to see how you react under pressure, and to plumb the depths of your confidence. Many people ruin their chances by reacting to them as personal insults rather than the challenge and opportunity to shine that they really represent.

Previously restricted to the executive suite for the selection of high-powered executives, stress interviews are now established throughout the professional world. And they can come complete with all the intimidating and treacherous tricks your worst nightmare can devise. Yet your good performance at a stress interview can mean the difference between a job in the fast lane and a stalled career. The interviewers in a stress interview are invariably experienced and well-organized, with tightly structured procedures and advanced interviewing techniques. The questions and tension they generate have the cumulative effect of throwing you off balance and revealing the "real" you—rather than someone who can respond with last night's rehearsed answers to six or seven stock questions.

Stress questions can be turned to your advantage or merely avoided by your nifty footwork. Whichever, you will be among a select few who understand this line of questioning. As always, remember with the questions in this chapter to build a personalized answer that reflects your experience and profession. Practice them aloud—by doing that, your responses to these interview gambits will become part of you, and that enhancement of your mental attitude will positively affect your confidence during an interview. You might even consider making a tape of tough questions, spacing them at intervals of thirty seconds to two minutes. You can then play the tape back and answer the questions in real time.

As we will see in this chapter, reflexive questions can prove especially useful when the heat is on. Stress questions are designed to sort out the clutch players from those who slow down under pressure. Used with discretion, the reflexives (". . . don't you think?") will demonstrate to the interviewer that you are able to function well under pressure. At the same time, of course, you put the ball back in the interviewer's court.

One common stress interview technique is to set you up for a fall: A pleasant conversation, one or a series of seemingly innocuous questions to relax your guard, then a dazzling series of jabs and body blows that leave you gibbering. For instance, an interviewer might lull you into a false sense of security by asking some relatively stressless questions: "What was your initial starting salary at your last job?" then, "What is your salary now?" then, "Do you receive bonuses?" etc. To put you on the ropes, he or she then completely surprises you with, "Tell me what sort of troubles you have living within your means," or "Why aren't you earning more at your age?" Such interviewers are using stress in an intelligent fashion, to simulate the unexpected and sometimes tense events of everyday business life. Seeing how you handle simulated pressure gives a fair indication of how you will react to the real thing.

The sophisticated interviewer talks very little, perhaps only twenty percent of the time, and that time is spent asking questions. Few comments, and no editorializing on your answers, means that you get no hint, verbal or otherwise, about your performance.

The questions are planned, targeted, sequenced, and layered. The interviewer covers one subject thoroughly before moving on. Let's take the simple example of "Can you work under pressure?" As a reader of *Knock 'em Dead*, you will know to answer that question with an example, and thereby deflect the main thrust of the stress technique. The interviewer will be prepared for a simple yes/no answer; what follows will keep the unprepared applicant reeling.

☐ *"Can you work under pressure?"* A simple, closed-ended question that requires just a yes/no answer, but you don't get off so easy.

☐ *"Good, I'd be interested to hear about a time when you experienced pressure on your job."* An open-ended request to tell a story about a pressure situation. After this, you will be subjected to the layering technique—six layers in the following instance. Imagine how tangled you could get without preparation.

☐ *"Why do you think this situation arose?"*

☐ *"When exactly did it happen?"* Watch out! Your story of saving thousands from the burning skyscraper may well be checked with your references.

☐ *"What in hindsight were you most dissatisfied with about your performance?"* Here we go. You're trying to show how well you perform under pressure, then suddenly you're telling tales against yourself.

☐ *"How do you feel others involved could have acted more responsibly?"* An open invitation to criticize peers and superiors, which you should diplomatically decline.

☐ *"Who holds the responsibility for the situation?"* Another invitation to point the finger of blame.

☐ *"Where in the chain of command could steps be taken to avoid that sort of thing happening again?"*

You have just been through an old reporters' technique of asking why, when, who, what, how, and where. That technique can be applied to any question you are asked and is frequently used to probe those success stories that sound just too good to be true. You'll find them suddenly tagged on to the simple closed-ended questions, as well as to the open-ended ones, starting, "Share with me," "Tell me about a time when," or, "I'm interested in finding out about," and requesting specific examples from your work history.

After you've survived that barrage, a friendly tone will conceal another zinger: "What did you learn from the experience?" It's a question that is geared to probing your judgment and emotional maturity. Your answer will be to emphasize whichever of the key personality traits your story was illustrating.

When the interviewer feels you were on the edge of revealing something unusual in an answer, you may well encounter "mirror statements." Here, the last key phrase of your answer will be repeated or paraphrased, and followed by a steady gaze and silence: "So, you learned that organization is the key to management." The idea is that the quiet and expectant look will work together to keep you talking. It can give you a most disconcerting feeling to find yourself rambling on without quite knowing why. The trick to that is knowing when to stop. When the interviewer gives you the expectant look, expand your answer (you have to), but by no more than a couple of sentences. Otherwise, you will get that creepy feeling that you're digging yourself into a hole.

There will be times when you face more than one interviewer at a time. When it happens, remember the story of one woman attorney who had five law partners all asking questions at the same time—as the poor interviewee got halfway through one answer, another question would be shot at her. Pausing for breath, she smiled and said, "Hold your horses, ladies and gentlemen. These are all excellent questions, and given time, I'll answer them all. Now who's next?" In so doing, she showed the interviewers exactly what they wanted to see and what, incidentally, is behind every stress interview and every negatively phrased question—finding the presence of poise and calm under fire, combined with a refusal to be intimidated.

You never know when a stress interview will raise its ugly head. Often it can be that rubber-stamp meeting with the senior V.P. at the end of a series of grueling meetings. That is not surprising: While other interviewers are concerned with determining whether you are able, willing, and manageable for the job in question, the senior executive who eventually throws you for a loop is the one who is probing you for potential promotability.

The most intimidating stress interviews are recognizable before the interviewer speaks: no eye contact, no greeting, either silence or a noncommittal grunt, no small talk. You may also recognize such an interviewer by his general air of boredom, lack of interest, or thinly veiled aggression. The first words you hear could well be, "O.K., so go ahead. I don't have all day." In these situations, forewarned is forearmed, so here are some of the questions you can expect to follow such openings.

"What is your greatest weakness?"

This is a direct invitation to put your head in a noose. Decline the invitation.

If there is a minor part of the job at hand where you lack knowledge—but knowledge you will obviously pick up quickly—use that. For instance: "I haven't worked with this type of spreadsheet program before, but given my experience with six other types, I don't think it should take me more than a couple of days to pick it up." Here you remove the emphasis from weakness and put it onto a developmental problem that is easily overcome. Be careful, however: This very effective ploy must be used with discretion.

Another good option is to give a generalized answer that takes advantage of value keys. Design the answer so that your weakness is ultimately a positive characteristic. For example: "I enjoy my work and always give each project my best shot. So when sometimes I don't feel others are pulling their weight, I find it a little frustrating. I am aware of that weakness, and in those situations I try to overcome it with a positive attitude that I hope will catch on."

Also consider the technique of putting a problem in the past. Here you take a weakness from way back when, and show how you overcame it. It answers the question but ends on a positive note. An illustration: "When I first got into this field, I always had problems with my paperwork—you know, leaving an adequate paper trail. And to be honest, I let it slip once or twice. My manager sat me down and explained the potential troubles such behavior could cause. I really took it to heart, and I think you will find my paper trails some of the best around today. You only have to tell me something once." With that kind of answer, you also get the added bonus of showing that you accept and act on criticism.

Congratulations! You have just turned a bear of a question into an opportunity to sell yourself with your professional profile. In deciding on the particular answer you will give, remember that the interviewer isn't really concerned about your general weaknesses—no one is a saint outside of the interview room. He or she is simply concerned about any red flags that might signal your inability to perform the job or be manageable in the performance of your duties.

"With hindsight, how could you have improved your progress?"

Here's a question that demands, "Tell me your mistakes and weaknesses." If you can mention ways of improving your performance without damaging your candidacy, do so. The end of your answer should contain something like: "Other than that, I don't know what to add. I have always given it my best shot." Then shut up.

"What kinds of decisions are most difficult for you?"

You are human, admit it, but be careful what you admit. If you have ever had to fire someone, you are in luck, because no one likes to do that. Emphasize that having reached a logical conclusion, you act. If you are not in management, tie your answer to key profiles: "It's not that I have difficulty making decisions—some just require more consideration than others. A small example might be vacation time. Now, everyone is entitled to it, but I don't believe you should leave your boss in a bind at short notice. I think very carefully at the beginning of the year when I'd like to take my vacation, and then think of alternate dates. I go to my supervisor, tell him what I hope to do, and see whether there is any conflict. I wouldn't want to be out of the office for the two weeks prior to a project deadline, for instance. So by carefully considering things far enough in advance, I don't procrastinate, and I make sure my plans jibe with my boss and the department for the year."

Here you take a trick question and use it to demonstrate your consideration, analytical abilities, and concern for the department—and for the company bottom line.

"Tell me about the problems you have living within your means."

This is a twister to catch you off guard. Your best defense is first of all to know that it exists, and secondly to give it short shrift. "I know few people who are satisfied with their current earnings. As a professional, I am continually striving to improve my skills and to improve my living standard. But my problems are no different from that of this company or any other—making sure all the bills get paid on time and recognizing that every month and year there are some things that are prudent to do and other expenses that are best deferred."

"What area of your skills/professional development do you want to improve at this time?"

Another tell-me-all-your-weaknesses question. You should try to avoid damaging your candidacy by tossing around careless admissions. One effective answer to this is to say, "Well, from what you told me about the job, I seem to have all the necessary skills and background. What I would really find exciting is the opportunity to work on a job where . . ." At this point, you replay the interviewer's hot buttons about the job. You emphasize that you really have all the job-related skills and also tell the interviewer what you find exciting about the job. It works admirably.

Another safe response is to reiterate one or two areas that combine personal strengths and the job's most crucial responsibilities, and finish with saying, "These areas are so important that I don't think anyone can be too good or should ever stop trying to polish skills."

"Your application shows you have been with one company a long time without any appreciable increase in rank or salary. Tell me about this."

Ugh. A toughie. To start with, you should analyze why this state of affairs does exist (assuming the interviewer's assessment is accurate). Then, when you have determined the cause, practice saying it out loud to yourself as you would say it during an actual interview. It may take a few tries. Chances are that no matter how valid your explanation really is, it will come off sounding a little tinny or vindictive without some polishing. Avoid the sour grapes syndrome at all costs.

Here are some tactics you can use. First of all, try to avoid putting your salary history on application forms. No one is going to deny you an interview for lack of a salary history if your skills match those the job requires. Of course, you should never put such trivia on your resume.

If the interviewer is intent, and asks you outright for this information, you'll find a great response in the section on payment histories in chapter 23.

Now then. We address next the delicate matter of "hey-wait-a-minute-why-no-promotions?" This is one case where saying the wrong thing can get you in just as much trouble as failing to say the right thing. The interviewer has posed a truly negative inquiry; the more time either of you spend on it, the more time the interviewer gets to devote to concentrating on negative aspects of your candidacy. Make your answer short and sweet, then shut up. For instance, "My current employer is a stable company with a good working environment, but there's minimal growth there in my area—in fact, there hasn't been any promotion in my area since _____. Your question is the reason I am meeting here with you; I have the skills and ability to take on more responsibility and I'm looking for a place to do that."

"Are you willing to take calculated risks when necessary?"

First, qualify the question: "How do you define calculated risks? What sort of risks? Give me an example of a risk you have in mind; what are the stakes involved?" That will show you exactly the right analytical approach to evaluating a calculated risk, and while the interviewer is rattling on, you have bought time to come up with an answer. Whatever your answer, you will include, "Naturally, I would never take any risk that would in any way jeopardize the safety or reputation of my company or colleagues. In fact, I don't think any employer would appreciate an employee at any level taking risks of any nature without first having a thorough briefing and chance to give input."

"See this pen I'm holding? Sell it to me."

Not a request, as you might think, that would be asked only of a salesperson. In today's business world, everyone is required to sell—sometimes products, but more often ideas, approaches, and concepts. As such, you are being tested to see whether you understand the basic concepts of features-and-benefits selling, how quickly you think on your feet, and how effective your verbal communication is. For example, the interviewer holds up a broad-tip yellow highlighter. You say calmly, "Let me tell you about the special features of this product. First of all, it's a highlighter that will emphasize important points in reports or articles, and that will save you time in recalling the important features. The casing is wide enough to enable you to use it comfortably at your desk or on a flip chart. It has a flat base you can stand it up on. At one dollar, it is disposable—and affordable enough for you to have a handful for your desk, briefcase, car, and at home. And the bright yellow color means you'll never lose it."

Then close with a smile and a question of your own that will bring a smile to your interviewer's face: "How many gross shall we deliver?"

"How will you be able to cope with a change in environment after [e.g.] five years with your current company?"

Another chance to take an implied negative and turn it into a positive. "That's one of the reasons I want to make a change. After five years with my current employer, I felt I was about to get stale. Everyone needs a change of scene once in a while. It's just time for me to make some new friends, face some new challenges, and experience some new approaches; hopefully, I'll have the chance to contribute from my experience."

"Why aren't you earning more at your age?"

Accept this as a compliment to your skills and accomplishments. "I have always felt that solid experience would stand me in good stead in the long run and that earnings would come in due course. Also, I am not the type of person to change jobs just for the money. At this point, I have a solid background that is worth something to a company." Now, to avoid the interviewer putting you on the spot again, finish with a question: "How much should I be earning now?" The figure could be your offer.

"What is the worst thing you have heard about our company?"

This question can come as something of a shock. As with all stress questions, your poise under stress is vital: If you can carry off a halfway decent answer as well, you are a winner. The best response to this question is simple. Just say with a smile: "You're a tough company to get into because your interviews and interviewers are so rigorous." It's true, it's flattering, and it shows that you are not intimidated.

"How would you define your profession?"

With questions that solicit your understanding of a topic, no matter how good your answer, you can expect to be interrupted in mid-reply with "That has nothing to do with it," or, "Whoever put that idea into your head?" While your response is a judgment call, 999 times out of a thousand these comments are not meant to be taken as serious criticisms. Rather, they are tests to see how well you would be able to defend your position in a no-holds-barred conversation with the chairman of the board who says exactly what he or she thinks at all times. So go ahead and defend yourself, without taking or showing offense.

Your first response will be to gain time and get the interviewer talking. "Why do you say that?" you ask, answering a question with a question. And turning the tables on your aggressor displays your poise, calm, and analytical skills better than any other response.

"Why should I hire an outsider when I could fill the job with someone inside the company?"

The question isn't as stupid as it sounds. Obviously, the interviewer has examined existing employees with an eye toward their promotion or reassignment. Just as obviously, the job cannot be filled from within the company. If it could be, it would be, and for two very good reasons: It is cheaper for the company to promote from within, and it is good for employee morale.

Hiding behind this intimidating question is actually a pleasant invitation: "Tell me why I should hire you." Your answer follows two steps. The first is a simple recitation of your skills and personality profile strengths, tailored to the specific requirements of the job.

For the second step, realize first that whenever a manager is filling a position, he or she is looking not only for someone who can do the job, but also for someone who can benefit the department in a larger sense. No department is as good as it could be—each has weaknesses that need strengthening. So in the second part of your answer, include a question of your own: "Those are my general attributes. However, if no one is promotable from inside the company, that means you are looking to add strength to your team in a special way. In what ways do you hope the final candidate will be able to benefit your department?" The answer to this is your cue to sell your applicable qualities.

"Have you ever had any financial difficulties?"

The potential employer wants to know whether you can control not only your own finances, but finances in general. If you are in the insurance field, for example—claims, accounting, supervision, management—you can expect to hear this one. The question, though, is not restricted to insurance: Anyone, especially the person who handles money in day-to-day business, is fair game.

Remember that for someone to check your credit history, he or she must have your written consent. That is required under the 1972 Fair Credit and Reporting Act. When you fill out an application form, sign it, and date it, invariably somewhere on the form is a release permitting the employer to check your credit history. If you have already filled out the form, you might not hear the question, but your creditors might. I should note here that the reader who asked me about this question also described how she'd handled it during the interview: by describing her past problems with bankruptcy in every detail. However, in trying to be open and honest, she had actually done herself a disservice.

The interviewer does not want to hear sob-stories. Concentrate on the information that will damage your candidacy least and enhance it most. You might find it appropriate to bring the matter up yourself if you work in an area where your credit history is likely to be checked. If you choose to wait until the interviewer brings it up, you might say (if you had to file for bankruptcy, for instance), "I should tell you that some years ago, for reasons beyond my control, I was forced into personal bankruptcy. That has been behind me for some time. Today, I have a sound credit rating and no debts. Bankruptcy is not something I'm proud of, but I did learn from the experience, and I feel it has made me a more proficient account supervisor." The answer concentrates on today, not past history.

"How do you handle rejection?"

This question is common if you are applying for a job in sales, including face-to-face sales, telemarketing, public relations, and customer service. If you are after a job in one of these areas and you really don't like the heavy doses of rejection that are any salesperson's lot, consider a new field. The anguish you will experience will not lead to a successful career or a happy life.

With that in mind, let's look behind the question. The interviewer simply wants to know whether you take rejection as rejection of yourself or whether you simply accept it as a temporary rejection of a service or product. Here is a sample answer that you can tailor to your particular needs and background: "I accept rejection as an integral part of the sales process. If everyone said 'yes' to a product, there would be no need for the sales function. As it is, I see every rejection as bringing me closer to the customer who will say 'yes.'" Then, if you are encouraged to go on: "I regard rejection as simply a fact of life, that the customer has no need for the product today. I can go on to my next call with the conviction that I am a little closer to my next sale."

"Why were you out of work for so long?"

You must have a sound explanation for any and all gaps in your employment history. If not, you are unlikely to receive a job offer. Emphasize that you were not just looking for another paycheck—you were looking for a company with which to settle and to which to make a long-term contribution.

"I made a decision that I enjoy my work too much just to accept another paycheck. So I determined that the next job I took would be one where I could settle down and do my best to make a solid contribution. From everything I have heard about this company, you are a group that expects people to pull their weight, because you've got a real job to do. I like that, and I would like to be part of the team. What have I got to do to get the job?"

You answer the question, compliment the interviewer, and shift the emphasis from you being unemployed to how you can get the job offer.

"Why have you changed jobs so frequently?"

If you have jumped around, blame it on youth (even the interviewer was young once). Now you realize what a mistake your job-hopping was, and with your added domestic responsibilities you are now much more settled. Or you may wish to impress on the interviewer that your job-hopping was never as a result of poor performance, and that you grew professionally as a result of each job change.

You could reply: "My first job was a very long commute. I soon realized that, but I knew it would give me good experience in a very competitive field. Subsequently, I found a job much closer to home where the commute was only an hour each way. I was very happy at my second job. However, I got an opportunity to really broaden my experience base with a new company that was starting up. With the wisdom of hindsight, I realize that was a mistake; it took me six months to realize I couldn't make a contribution there. I've been with my current company a reasonable length of time. So I have broad experience in different environments. I didn't just job-hop, I have been following a path to gain broad experience. So you see, I have more experience than the average person of my years, and a desire to settle down and make it pay off for me and my employer."

Or you can say: "Now I want to settle down and make all my diverse background pay off in my contributions to my new employer. I have a strong desire to contribute and am looking for an employer that will keep me challenged; I think this might be the company to do that. Am I right?"

"Tell me about a time when you put your foot in your mouth."
Answer this question with caution. The interviewer is examining your ability and willingness to interact pleasantly with others. The question is tricky because it asks you to show yourself in a poor light. Your answer will downplay the negative impact of your action and will end with positive information about your candidacy. The best thing to do is to start with an example outside of the workplace, and show how the experience improved your performance at work.

"About five years ago, I let the cat out of the bag about a surprise birthday party for a friend, a terrific *faux pas*. It was a mortifying experience, and I promised myself not to let anything like that happen again." Then, after this fairly innocuous statement, you can talk about communications in the workplace. "As far as work is concerned, I always regard employer/employee communications on any matter as confidential unless expressly stated otherwise. So, putting my foot in my mouth doesn't happen to me at work."

"Why do you want to leave your current job?" or, *"Why did you leave your last job?"*
This is a common trick question. You should have an acceptable reason for leaving every job you have held, but if you don't, pick one of the six acceptable reasons from the employment industry formula, the acronym for which is CLAMPS:

- Challenge: You weren't able to grow professionally in that position.
- Location: The commute was unreasonably long.
- Advancement: There was nowhere for you to go. You had the talent, but there were too many people ahead of you.
- Money: You were underpaid for your skills and contribution.
- Pride or prestige: You wanted to be with a better company.
- Security: The company was not stable.

For example: "My last company was a family-owned affair. I had gone as far as I was able. It just seemed time for me to join a more prestigious company and accept greater challenges."

"What interests you least about this job?"
This question is potentially explosive, but easily defused. Regardless of your occupation, there is at least one repetitive, mindless duty that everyone groans about and that goes with the territory. Use that as your example in a statement of

this nature: "Filing is probably the least demanding part of the job. However, it is important to the overall success of my department, so I try to do it with a smile." This shows that you understand that it is necessary to take the rough with the smooth in any job.

"What was there about your last company that you didn't particularly like or agree with?"

You are being checked out as a potential fly in the ointment. If you have to answer, it might be the way the company policies and/or directives were sometimes consciously misunderstood by some employees who disregard the bottom line— the profitability of the corporation.

Or: "You know how it is sometimes with a big company. People lose awareness of the cost of things. There never seemed to be much concern about economy or efficiency. Everyone wanted his or her year-end bonus, but only worried about it in December. The rest of the year, nobody gave a hoot. I think that's the kind of thing we could be aware of most every day, don't you agree?"

Or: "I didn't like the way some people gave lip-service to 'the customer comes first,' but really didn't go out of their way to keep the customer satisfied. I don't think it was a fault of management, just a general malaise that seemed to affect a lot of people."

"What do you feel is a satisfactory attendance record?"

There are two answers to this question—one if you are in management, one if you are not. As a manager: "I believe attendance is a matter of management, motivation, and psychology. Letting the employees know you expect their best efforts and won't accept half-baked excuses is one thing. The other is to keep your employees motivated by a congenial work environment and the challenge to stretch themselves. Giving people pride in their work and letting them know you respect them as individuals have a lot to do with it, too."

If you are not in management, the answer is even easier: "I've never really considered it. I work for a living, I enjoy my job, and I'm rarely sick."

"What is your general impression of your last company?"

Always answer positively. Keep your real feelings to yourself, whatever they might be. There is a strong belief among the management fraternity that people who complain about past employers will cause problems for their new ones. Your answer is, "Very good" or, "Excellent." Then smile and wait for the next question.

"What are some of the problems you encounter in doing your job, and what do you do about them?"

Note well the old saying, "A poor workman blames his tools." Your awareness that careless mistakes cost the company good money means you are always on the lookout for potential problems. Give an example of a problem you recognized and solved.

For example: "My job is fairly repetitive, so it's easy to overlook problems.

Lots of people do. However, I always look for them; it helps keep me alert and motivated, so I do a better job. To give you an example, we make computer-memory disks. Each one has to be machined by hand, and once completed, the slightest abrasion will turn one into a reject. I have a steady staff and little turnover, and everyone wears cotton gloves to handle the disks. Yet about six months ago, the reject rate suddenly went through the roof. Is that the kind of problem you mean? Well, the cause was one that could have gone unnoticed for ages. Jill, the section head who inspects all the disks, had lost a lot of weight, her diamond engagement ring was slipping around her finger, and it was scratching the disks as she passed them and stacked them to be shipped. Our main client was giving us a big problem over it, so my looking for problems and paying attention to detail really paid off."

The interviewer was trying to get you to reveal weak points; you avoided the trap.

"What are some of the things you find difficult to do? Why do you feel that way?"

This is a variation on a couple of earlier questions. Remember, anything that goes against the best interests of your employer is difficult to do. If you are pressed for a job function you find difficult, answer in the past tense; that way, you show that you recognize the difficulty, but that you obviously handle it well.

"That's a tough question. There are so many things that are difficult to learn in our business if you want to do the job right. I used to have forty clients to sell to every month, and I was so busy touching bases with all of them, I never got a chance to sell to any of them. So I graded them into three groups. I call on the top 20 percent with whom I did business every three weeks. The next group were those I sold to occasionally. I called on them once a month, but with a difference—each month, I marked ten of them to spend time with and really get to know. I still have difficulty reaching all forty of my clients in a month, but my sales have tripled and are still climbing."

"Jobs have plusses and minuses. What were some of the minuses on your last job?"

A variation on the question, "What interests you least about this job?" which was handled earlier. Use the same type of answer. For example, "Like any salesperson, I enjoy selling, not doing the paperwork. But as I cannot expect the customer to get the goods, and me my commission, without following through on this task, I grin and bear it. Besides, if I don't do the paperwork, that holds up other people in the company."

If you are not in sales, use the salesforce as a scapegoat. "In accounts receivable, it's my job to get the money in to make payroll and good things like that. Half the time, the goods get shipped before I get the paperwork because sales says, 'It's a rush order.' That's a real minus to me. It was so bad at my last company, we tried a new approach. We met with sales and explained our problem. The result was that incremental commissions were based on cash in, not on bill date. They saw the connection, and things are much better now."

"What kinds of people do you like to work with?"

This is the easy part of a tricky three-part question. Obviously, you like to work with people who have pride, honesty, integrity, and dedication to their work. Now—

"What kinds of people do you find it difficult to work with?"

The second part of the same question. You could say: "People who don't follow procedures, or slackers—the occasional rotten apples who don't really care about the quality of their work. They're long on complaints, but short on solutions." Which brings us to the third part of the question:

"How have you successfully worked with this difficult type of person?"

This is the most difficult part to answer. You might reply: "I stick to my guns, keep enthusiastic, and hope some of it will rub off. I had a big problem with one guy—all he did was complain and always in my area. Eventually, I told him how I felt. I said if I were a millionaire, I'd have all the answers and wouldn't have to work, but as it was, I wasn't, and had to work for a living. I told him that I really enjoyed his company, but I didn't want to hear it any more. Every time I saw him after that, I presented him with a work problem and asked his advice. In other words I challenged him to come up with positives, not negatives."

You can go on that sometimes you've noticed that such people simply lack enthusiasm and confidence, and that energetic and cheerful co-workers can often change that. If the interviewer follows up with an inquiry about what you would do if no amount of good effort on your part solved the problem, respond, "I would maintain cordial relations, but not go out of my way to seek more than a businesslike acquaintance. Life is too short to be demotivated by people who always think their cup is half empty."

"How did you get your last job?"

The interviewer is looking for initiative. If you can, show it. At the least, show determination.

"I was actually turned down for my last job as having too little experience. I asked the manager to give me a trial before she offered it to anyone else. I went in and asked for a list of companies they'd never sold to, picked up the phone, and in that hour I arranged two appointments. How did I get the job? In a word, determination!"

"How would you evaluate me as an interviewer?"

The question is dangerous, maybe more so than the one asking you to criticize your boss. Whatever you do, of course, don't tell the truth if you think the interviewer is an unconscious incompetent. It may be true, but it won't get you a job offer. This is an instance where honesty is not the best policy. It is best to say, "This is one of the toughest interviews I have ever been through, and I don't relish the prospect of going through another. Yet I do realize what you are trying to achieve." Then go on to explain that you understand the interviewer wants to know whether you can think on your feet, that there is pressure on the job, and that he or she is trying to simulate some of that real-life pressure in the interview. You may choose to finish the answer with a question of your own: "How do you think I fit the profile of the person you need?"

"I'm not sure you're suitable for the job."

Don't worry about the tone of the question—the interviewer's "I'm not sure" really means, "I'd like to hire you, so here's a wide-open opportunity to sell me." He or she is probing three areas from your personal profile: your confidence, determination, and listening profiles. Remain calm and put the ball straight back into the interviewer's court: "Why do you say that?" You need both the information and time to think up an appropriate reply, but it is important to show that you are not intimidated. Work out a program of action for this question; even if the interviewer's point regarding your skills is valid, come back with value keys and alternate compatible skills. You counter with other skills that show your competence and learning ability, and use them to show you can pick up the new skills quickly. Tie the two together and demonstrate that with your other attributes you can bring many plusses to the job. Finish your answer with a reflexive question that encourages a "yes" answer.

"I admit my programming skills in that language are a little light. However, all languages have similarities, and my experience demonstrates that with a competence in four other languages, getting up to speed with this one will take only a short while. Plus, I can bring a depth of other experience to the job." Then, after you itemize your experience: "Wouldn't you agree?"

If the reason for the question is not a lack of technical skills, it must be a question about one of your key profile areas. Perhaps the interviewer will say, "You haven't convinced me of your determination." This is an invitation to sell yourself, so tell a story that demonstrates determination.

For example: "It's interesting you should say that. My present boss is convinced of my determination. About a year ago we were having some problems with a union organization in the plant. Management's problem was our 50 percent Spanish monolingual production workforce. Despite the fact that our people had the best working conditions and benefits in the area, they were strongly pro-union. If they were successful, we would be the first unionized division in the company. No one in management spoke Spanish, so I took a crash Berlitz course—two hours at home every night for five weeks. I got one of the maintenance crew to help me with my grammar and diction. Then a number of other production workers started saying simple things to me in Spanish and helping me with the answers. I opened the first meeting with the workforce to discuss the problems. My 'Buenos dias. Me llamo Brandon,' got a few cheers. We had demonstrated that we cared enough to try to communicate. Our division never did unionize, and my determination to take the extra step paid off and allowed my superiors to negotiate from a position of caring and strength. That led to English lessons for the Spanish-speaking, and Spanish classes for the English-speaking. We are now a bilingual company, and I think that shows we care. Wouldn't you agree my work in that instance shows determination?"

"Wouldn't you feel better off in another firm?"

Relax, things aren't as bad as you might assume. This question is usually asked if you are really doing quite well, or if the job involves a certain amount of stress. A lawyer, for example, might well be expected to face this one. The trick is not to be intimidated. Your first step is to qualify the question: Relax, take a breath, sit back, smile, and say, "You surprise me. Why do you say that?" The interviewer must then talk, giving you precious time to collect your wits and come back with a rebuttal.

Then answer "no" and explain why. All the interviewer wants to see is how much you know about the company and how determined you are to join its ranks. Your earlier research and knowledge of personal profile keys (determination) will pay off again. Overcome the objection with an example, and show how that will help you contribute to the company; end with a question of your own. In this instance, the question has a twofold purpose: one, to identify a critical area to sell yourself; and two, to encourage the interviewer to consider an image of you working at the company.

You could reply: "Not at all. My whole experience has been with small companies. I am good at my job and in time could become a big fish in a little pond. But that is not what I want. This corporation is a leader in its business. You have a strong reputation for encouraging skills-development in your employees. This is the type of environment I want to work in. Now, coming from a small company, I have done a little bit of everything. That means that no matter what you throw at me, I will learn it quickly. For example, what would be the first project I would be involved with?"

And you end with a question of your own that gets the interviewer focusing on those immediate problems. You can then explain how your background and experience can help.

"What would you say if I told you your presentation this afternoon was lousy?"

"If" is the key here, with the accusation only there for the terminally neurotic. The question is designed to see how you react to criticism, and so tests manageability. No company can afford the thin-skinned today. You will come back and answer the question with a question of your own.

An appropriate response would be: "First of all, I would ask which aspects of my presentation were lousy. My next step would be to find out where you felt the problem was. If there'd been miscommunication, I'd clear it up. If the problem was elsewhere, I would seek your advice and be sure that the problem was not recurrent." This would show that when it is a manager's duty to criticize performance, you are an employee who will respond in a businesslike and emotionally mature manner.

The Illegal Question

Of course, one of the most stressful—and negative—questions is the illegal one, a question that delves into your private life or personal background. Such a question will make you uncomfortable if it is blatant, and could also make you angry.

Your aim, however, is to overcome the discomfort and to avoid anger: You want to get the job offer, and any self-righteousness or defensive reaction on your part will ensure that you *don't* get it. You may feel angry enough to get up and walk out, or say things like, "These are unfair practices; you'll hear from my lawyer in the morning." But the result will be that you won't get the offer, and therefore won't have the leverage you need. Remember, no one is saying you can't refuse the job once it's offered to you.

But what is an illegal question? Title VII is a federal law that forbids employers from discriminating against any person on the basis of sex, age, race, national origin, or religion. In addition, many states have laws that protect people who fall into other categories, such as the physically challenged. Here are some general guidelines interviewers must follow.

☐ An interviewer may not ask about your religion, church, synagogue, parish, the religious holidays you observe, or your political beliefs or affiliations. He or she may not ask, for instance, "Does your religion allow you to work on Saturdays?" *But*, the interviewer may ask something like, "This job requires work on Saturdays. Is that a problem?"

☐ An interviewer may not ask about your ancestry, national origin, or parentage; in addition, you cannot be asked about the naturalization status of your parents, spouse, or children. The interviewer cannot ask about your birthplace. *But*, the interviewer may ask (and probably will, considering the current immigration laws) whether you are a U.S. citizen or a resident alien with the right to work in the U.S.

☐ An interviewer may not ask about your native language, the language you speak at home, or how you acquired the ability to read, write, or speak a foreign language. *But*, he or she may ask about the languages in which you are fluent, if knowledge of those languages is pertinent to the job.

☐ An interviewer may not ask about your age, your date of birth, or the ages of your children. *But*, he or she may ask you whether you are over eighteen years old.

☐ An interviewer may not ask about maiden names or whether you have changed your name; your marital status, number of children or dependents, or your spouse's occupation; or whether (if you are a woman) you wish to be addressed as Miss, Mrs., or Ms. *But*, the interviewer may ask about how you like to be addressed (a common courtesy) and whether you have ever worked for the company before under a different name. (If you have worked for this company or other companies under a different name, you may want to mention that, in light of the fact that this prospective manager may check your references and additional background information.)

As you consider a question that seems to verge on illegality, you should take into account that the interviewer may be asking it innocently, and may be unaware of the laws on the matter. Your best bet is to be polite and straightforward, as you would in any other social situation. You also want to move the conversation to an examination of your skills and abilities, not your status. Here are some illegal questions—and some possible responses. Remember, your objective is to get job offers; if you later decide that this company is not for you, you are under no obligation to accept the position.

"What religion do you practice?"

If you do practice, you can say, "I attend my church/synagogue/mosque regularly, but I make it my practice not to involve my personal beliefs in my work. The work for the company and my career are too important for that."

If you do not practice a religion, you may want to say something like, "I have a set of personal beliefs that are important to me, but I do not attend any organized services. And I do not mix those beliefs with my work, if that's what you mean."

"How old are you?"

Old-age discrimination is still prevalent, but with older people joining the workforce every day and the increasing need for experienced workers, you will hear this question less and less. Answer the question in terms of your experience. For example: "I'm in my fifties and have more than twenty-five years of experience in this field." Then list your skills as they apply to the job.

"Are you married?"

If you are, the company is concerned with the impact your family duties and future plans will have on your tenure there. Your answer could be, "Yes, I am. Of course, I make a separation between my work life and my family life that allows me to give my all to a job. I have no problem with travel or late hours—those things are part of this line of work. I'm sure my references will confirm this for you."

"Do you plan to have children?"

This isn't any of the interviewer's business, but he or she wants to know whether you will leave the company early to raise a family. You can answer "no," of course. If you answer "yes," you might add, "But those plans are for the future, and they depend on the success of my career. Certainly, I want to do the best, most complete job for this company I can. I consider that my skills are right for the job and that I can make a long-range contribution. I certainly have no plans to leave the company just as I begin to make meaningful contributions."

If the questions become too pointed, you may want to ask—innocently— "Could you explain the relevance of that issue to the position? I'm trying to get a handle on it." That response, however, can seem confrontational; you should only use it if you are *extremely* uncomfortable, or are quite certain you can get away with it. Sometimes, the interviewer will drop the line of questioning.

Illegal questions tend to arise, not out of brazen insensitivity, but rather out of an interest in you. The employer is familiar with your skills and background, feels you can do the job, and wants to get to know you as a person. Outright discrimination these days is really quite rare. With illegal questions, your response must be positive—that's the only way you're going to get the job offer, and getting a job offer allows you to leverage other jobs. You don't have to work for a discriminatory company, but you can certainly use the firm to get to something better.

□   □   □

Interviewers may pull all kinds of tricks on you, but you will come through with flying colors once you realize that they're trying to discover something extremely simple—whether or not you can take the heat. After all, those interviewers are only trying to sort out the good corporate warriors from the walking wounded. If you are asked and successfully handle these trick and negatively phrased questions, the interviewer will end up looking at you favorably. Stay calm, give as good as you get, and take it all in good part. Remember that no one can intimidate you without your permission.

18.
Strange Venues

Why are some interviews conducted in strange places? Are meetings in noisy, distracting hotel lobbies designed as a form of torture? What are the real reasons that an interviewer invites you to eat at a fancy restaurant?

For the most part, these tough-on-the-nerves situations happen because the interviewer is a busy person, fitting you into a busy schedule. Take the case of a woman I know. She had heard stories about tough interview situations but never expected to face one herself. It happened at a retail convention in Arizona, and she had been asked to meet for a final interview by the pool. The interviewer was there, taking a short break between meetings, in his bathing suit. And the first thing the interviewer did was suggest that my friend slip into something comfortable.

That scenario may not lurk in your future, but the chances are that you will face many tough interview situations in your career. They call for a clear head and a little gamesmanship to put you ahead of the competition. The interviewee at the pool used both. She removed her jacket, folded it over the arm of the chair and seated herself, saying pleasantly, "That's much better. Where shall we begin?"

It isn't easy to remain calm at such times. On top of interview nerves, you're worried about being overheard in a public place, or (worse) surprised by the appearance of your current boss. That last item isn't too far-fetched. It actually happened to a reader from San Francisco. He was being interviewed in the departure lounge at the airport when his boss walked through the arrivals door. Oops—he had asked for the day off "to go to the doctor."

Could he have avoided the situation? Certainly, if he had asked about privacy when the meeting was arranged. That would have reminded the interviewer of the need for discretion. The point is to do all you can in advance to make such a meeting as private as possible. Once that's done, you can ignore the rest of the world and concentrate on the interviewer's questions.

Hotel Lobbies and Other Strange Places

Strange interview situations provide other wonderful opportunities to embarrass yourself. You come to a hotel lobby in full corporate battle dress: coat, briefcase, perhaps an umbrella. You sit down to wait for the interviewer. "Aha," you think to yourself, opening your briefcase, "I'll show him my excellent work habits by delving into this computer printout."

That's not such a great idea. Have you ever tried rising with your lap covered with business papers, then juggling the briefcase from right hand to left to accommodate the ritual handshake? It's quite difficult. Besides, while you are sitting in nervous anticipation, pre-interview tension has no way of dissipating. Your mouth will become dry, and your "Good morning, I'm pleased to meet you" will come out sounding like the cat being strangled.

To avoid such catastrophes in places like hotel lobbies, first remove your coat on arrival. Then, instead of sitting, walk around a little while you wait. Even in a small lobby, a few steps back and forth will help you reduce tension to a manageable level. Keep your briefcase in your left hand at all times—it makes you look purposeful, and you won't trip over it when you meet the interviewer.

If, for any reason, you must sit down, make a conscious effort to breathe deeply and slowly. This will help control the adrenaline that makes you feel jumpy.

A strange setting can actually put you on equal footing with the interviewer. Neither of you is on home turf, so in many cases, the interviewer will feel just as awkward as you do. A little gamesmanship can turn the occasion to your advantage.

To gain the upper hand, get to the meeting site early to scout the territory. By knowing your surroundings, you will feel more relaxed. Early arrival also allows you to control the outcome of the meeting in other subtle ways. You will have time to stake out the most private spot in an otherwise public place. Corners are best. They tend to be quieter, and you can choose the seat that puts your back to the wall (in a practical sense, that is). In this position, you have a clear view of your surroundings and will feel more secure. The fear of being overheard will evaporate.

The situation is now somewhat in your favor. You know the locale, and the meeting place is as much yours as the interviewer's. You will have a clear view of your surroundings, and odds are that you will be more relaxed than the interviewer. When he or she arrives, say, "I arrived a little early to make sure we had some privacy. I think over here is the best spot." With that positive demonstration of your organizational abilities, you give yourself a head start over the competition.

The Meal Meeting
Breakfast, lunch, or dinner are the prime choices for interviewers who want to catch the seasoned professional off guard. In fact, the meal is arguably the toughest of all tough interview situations. The setting offers the interviewer the chance to see you in a nonoffice (and therefore more natural) setting, to observe your social graces, and to consider you as a whole person. Here, topics that would be impossible to address in the traditional office setting will naturally surface, often with virtually no effort on the part of the interviewer. The slightest slip in front of that wily old sea pirate opposite—thinly disguised in a Brooks Brothers suit—could get your candidacy deep-sixed *tout de suite*.

Usually you will not be invited to an "eating meeting" until you have already demonstrated that you are capable of doing the job. It's a good sign, actually: An invitation to a meal means that you are under strong consideration, and, by extension, intense scrutiny.

The meeting is often the final hurdle and could lead directly to the job offer—assuming, of course, that you properly handle the occasional surprises that arise. The interviewer's concern is not whether you can do the job, but whether you have the growth potential that will allow you to fill more senior slots as they become available.

But be careful. Many have fallen at the final hurdle in a close-run race. Being interviewed in front of others is bad enough; eating and drinking in front of them at the same time only makes it worse. If you knock over a glass or dribble spaghetti sauce down your chin, the interviewer will be so busy smirking that he or she won't hear what you have to say.

To be sure that the interviewer remains as attentive to the positive points of your candidacy as possible, let's discuss table manners.

Your social graces and general demeanor at the table can tell as much about you as your answer to a question. For instance, over-ordering food or drink can signal poor self-discipline. At the very least, it will call into question your judgment and maturity. High-handed behavior toward waiters and buspeople could reflect negatively on your ability to get along with subordinates and on your leadership skills. Those concerns are amplified when you return food or complain about the service, actions which, at the very least, find fault with the interviewer's choice of restaurant.

By the same token, you will want to observe how your potential employer behaves. After all, you are likely to become an employee, and the interviewer's behavior to servers in a restaurant can tell you a lot about what it will be like on the job.

☐ **Alcohol:** Soon after being seated, you will be offered a drink—if not by your host, then by the waiter. There are many reasons to avoid alcohol at interview meals. The most important reason is that alcohol fuzzes your mind, and research proves that stress increases the intoxicating effect of alcohol. So, if you order something to drink, try to stick with something nonalcoholic, such as a club soda or simply a glass of water. If pressed, order a white-wine spritzer, a sherry, or a light beer—it depends on the environment and what your host is drinking.

If you do have a drink, never have more than one. If there is a bottle of wine on the table, and the waiter offers you another glass, simply place your hand over the top of your glass. It is a polite way of signifying no.

You may be offered alcohol at the end of the meal. The rule still holds true—turn it down. You need your wits about you even if the interview seems to be drawing to a close. Some interviewers will try to use those moments, when your defenses are at their lowest, to throw in a couple of zingers.

☐ **Smoking:** Smoking is another big problem that is best handled by taking a simple approach. Don't do it unless encouraged. If both of you are smokers, and you are encouraged to smoke, follow a simple rule: Never smoke between courses, only at the end of a meal. Even most confirmed nicotine addicts, like the rest of the population, hate smoke while they are eating.

☐ **Utensils:** Keep all your cups and glasses at the top of your place setting and well away from you. Most glasses are knocked over at a cluttered table when one stretches for the condiments or gesticulates to make a point. Of course, your manners will prevent you from reaching rudely for the pepper-shaker.

When you are faced with an array of knives, forks, and spoons, it is always safe to start at the outside and work your way in as the courses come. Keep your elbows at your sides and don't slouch in the chair. When pausing between mouthfuls (which, if you are promoting yourself properly, should be frequently), rest your knife and fork on the plate this way.

The time to start eating, of course, is when the interviewer does; the time to stop is when he or she does. At the end of a course or the meal, rest your knife and fork together on the plate, at five o'clock.

Here are some other helpful hints:

- Never speak with your mouth full.
- To be on the safe side, eat the same thing, or close to it, as the interviewer. Of course, while this rule makes sense in theory, the fact is that you probably will be asked to order first, so ordering the same thing can become problematic. Solve the problem before you order by complimenting the restaurant during your small talk and then, when the menus arrive, asking, "What do think you will have today?"
- Do not change your order once it is made, and never send the food back.
- Be polite to your waiters, even when they spill soup in your lap.
- Don't order expensive food. Naturally, in our heart of hearts, we all like to eat well, especially on someone else's tab. But don't be tempted. When you come right down to it, you are there to talk and be seen at your best, not to eat.
- Eat what you know. Stay away from awkward, messy, or exotic foods (e.g., artichokes, long pasta, and escargot, respectively). Ignore finger foods,

such as lobster or spare ribs. In fact, you should avoid eating with your fingers altogether, unless you are in a sandwich joint, in which case you should make a point of avoiding the leaky, over-stuffed menu items.

- Don't order salad. The dressing can often get messy. If a salad comes with the meal, request that the dressing be on the side. Then, before pouring it on, cut up the lettuce.

- Don't order anything with bones. Stick with filets; there are few simple, gracious ways to deal with any type of bone.

☐ **Checks and Goodbyes:** I know an interviewer whose favorite test of composure is to have the waiter, by arrangement, put the bill on the interviewee's side of the table. She then chats on, waiting for something interesting to happen. If you ever find yourself in a similar situation, never pick up the check, however long it is left by your plate. When ready, your host will pick it up, because that's the simple protocol of the occasion. By the same token, you should never offer to share payment.

When parting company, always thank the host for his or her hospitality and the wonderful meal. Of course, you should be sure to leave on a positive note by asking good naturedly what you have to do to get the job.

☐   ☐   ☐

Strange interview situations can arise at any time during the interview cycle, and in any public place. Wherever you are asked to go, keep your guard up. Your table manners, listening skills, and overall social graces are being judged. The question on the interviewer's mind is: Can you be trusted to represent the company graciously?

19.
Welcome to the Real World

Of all the steps a recent graduate will take up the ladder of success over the years, none is more important or more difficult than getting a foot on the first rung. And the interviewing process designed for recent graduates is particularly rigorous, because management regards the hiring of entry-level professionals as one of its toughest jobs.

When a company hires experienced people, there is a track record to evaluate. With recent graduates, there is little or nothing. Often, the only solid things an interviewer has to go on are high-school, SAT, and/or college grades. That's not much on which to base a hiring decision—grades don't tell the interviewer whether you will fit in or make a reliable employee. Many recruiters liken the gamble of hiring recent graduates to laying down wines for the future: They know that some will develop into full-bodied, reliable vintages, but that others will be disappointments. So, recruiters have to find different ways to predict your potential accurately.

After relying, as best they can, on school performance to evaluate your ability, interviewers concentrate on questions that reveal how willing you are to learn and get the job done, and how manageable you are likely to be, both on average days and when the going gets rough.

Your goal is to stand out from all the other entry-level candidates as someone altogether different and better. For example, don't be like thousands of others who, in answer to questions about their greatest strength, reply lamely, "I'm good with people," or, "I like working with others." As you know by now, such answers do not separate you from the herd. In fact, they brand you as average. To stand out, a recent graduate must recount a past situation that illustrates how good he or she is with people, or one that demonstrates an ability to be a team player.

Fortunately, the key personality traits discussed throughout the book are just as helpful for getting your foot on the ladder as they are for aiding your climb to the top. They will guide you in choosing what aspects of your personality and background you should promote at the interview.

It isn't necessary to have snap answers ready for every question, because you never will. In fact, it is more important for you to pause after a question and collect your thoughts before answering: You must show that you think before you speak. That way, you will demonstrate your analytical abilities, which age feels youth has in short supply.

By the same token, occasionally asking for a question to be repeated is useful to gain time and is quite acceptable, as long as you don't do it with every question. And if a question stumps you, as sometimes happens, do not stutter incoherently. It is sometimes best to say simply, "I don't know." Or, you might say, "I'd like to come back to that later"—the odds are even that the interviewer will forget to ask again; if he or she doesn't, at least you've had some time to come up with an answer.

Knowing everything about a certain entry-level position is not necessary, because business feels it can teach you most things. But, as a vice president of Merrill Lynch once said, "You must bring to the table the ability to speak clearly." So, knowing what is behind those questions designed especially for recent graduates will give you the time to build informative and understandable answers.

"How did you get your summer jobs?"

All employers look favorably on recent graduates who have any work experience, no matter what it is. "It is far easier to get a fix on someone who has worked while at school," says Dan O'Brien, head of employment at Grumman. "They manage their time better, are more realistic, and more mature. Any work experience gives us much more in common." So, as you make your answer, add that you learned that business is about making a profit, doing things more efficiently, adhering to procedures, and putting out whatever effort it takes to get the job done. In short, treat your summer jobs, no matter how humble, as any other business experience.

In this particular question, the interviewer is looking ideally for something that shows initiative, creativity, and flexibility. Here's an example: "In my town, summer jobs were hard to come by, but I applied to each local restaurant for a position waiting tables, called the manager at each one to arrange an interview, and finally landed a job at one of the most prestigious. I was assigned to the afternoon shift, but with my quick work, accurate billing, and ability to keep customers happy, they soon moved me to the evening shift. I worked there for three summers, and by the time I left, I was responsible for the training and management of the night-shift waiters, the allotment of tips, and the evening's final closing and accounting. All in all, my experience showed me the mechanics of a small business and of business in general."

"Which of the jobs you have held have you liked least?"

The interviewer is trying to trip you up. It is likely that your work experience contained a certain amount of repetition and drudgery, as all early jobs in the business world do. So beware of saying that you hated a particular job "because it was boring." Avoid the negative and say something along these lines: "All of my jobs had their good and bad points, but I've always found that if you want to learn, there's plenty to be picked up every day. Each experience was valuable." Then describe a seemingly boring job, but show how it taught you valuable lessons or helped you hone different aspects of your personality profile.

"What are your future vocational plans?"

This is a fancy way of asking, "Where do you want to be five years from now?" The trap all entry-level professionals make is to say, "In management," because they think that shows drive and ambition. It has become such a trite answer, though, that it immediately generates a string of questions that most recent graduates can't answer: What is the definition of management? What is a manager's prime responsibility? A manager in what area? Your safest answer identifies you with the profession you are trying to break into, and shows you have your feet on the ground. "My vocational plans are that I want to get ahead. To do that I must be able to channel my energies and expertise into those areas my industry and employer need. So given a couple of years I hope to have become a thorough professional with a clear understanding of the company, the industry, and where the biggest challenges, and therefore opportunities, lie. By that time, my goals for the future should be sharply defined." An answer like that will set you far apart from your contemporaries.

"What college did you attend, and why did you choose it?"

The college you attended isn't as important as your reasons for choosing it— the question is trying to examine your reasoning processes. Emphasize that it was your choice, and that you didn't go there as a result of your parents' desires or because generations of your family have always attended the Acme School of Welding. Focus on the practical. "I went to Greenbriar State—it was a choice based on practicality. I wanted a school that would give me a good education and prepare me for the real world. State has a good record for turning out students fully prepared to take on responsibilities in the real world. It is [or isn't] a big school, but/and it has certainly taught me some big lessons about the value of [whatever personality values apply] in the real world of business."

If the interviewer has a follow-up question about the role your parents played in selection of your school, be wary—he or she is plumbing your maturity. It is best to reply that the choice of the school was yours, though you did seek the advice of your parents once you had made your selection, and that they supported your decision.

"Are you looking for a permanent or temporary job?"

The interviewer wants reassurance that you are genuinely interested in the position and won't disappear in a few months to pursue post-doctoral studies in St. Tropez. Try to go beyond saying simply "yes." Explain why you want the job. You might say, "Of course, I am looking for a permanent job. I intend to make my career in this field, and I want the opportunity to learn the business, face new challenges, and learn from experienced professionals." You will also want to qualify the question with one of your own at the end of your answer: "Is this a permanent or a temporary position you are trying to fill?" And don't be scared to ask. The occasional unscrupulous employer will hire someone fresh out of school for a short period of time—say, for one particular project—and then lay them off.

"How did you pay for college?"

Avoid saying "Oh, Daddy handled all of that," as it probably won't create quite the impression you'd like. Your parents may well have helped you out, but you should explain, if it's appropriate, that you worked part-time and took out loans (as most of us must during college).

"We have tried to hire people from your school/your major before, and they never seem to work out. What makes you different?"

Here's a stress question to test your poise and analytical skills. You can shout that, yes, of course you are different and can prove it. So far, though, all you know is that there was a problem, not what caused the problem. Respond this way: "First, may I ask you exactly what problems you've had with people from this background?" Once you know what the problem is (if one really exists at all—it may just be a curve ball to test your poise) then you can illustrate how you are different. But only then. Otherwise, you run the risk of your answer being interrupted with, "Well, that's what everyone else said before I hired them. You haven't shown me that you are different."

"I'd be interested to hear about some things you learned in school that could be used on the job."

While specific job-related courses could form part of your answer, they cannot be all of it. The interviewer wants to hear about "real-world" skills, so oblige by explaining what the experience of college taught you rather than a specific course. In other words, explain how the experience honed your relevant personality profiles. "Within my major and minor I tried to pursue those courses that had most practical relevance, such as . . . However, the greatest lessons I learned were the importance of . . ." and then list your personality profile strengths.

"Do you like routine tasks/regular hours?"

A trick question. The interviewer knows from bitter experience that most recent graduates hate routine and are hopeless as employees until they come to an acceptance of such facts of life. Explain that, yes, you appreciate the need for routine, that you expect a fair amount of routine assignments before you are entrusted with the more responsible ones, and that that is why you are prepared to accept it as necessary. As far as regular hours go you could say, "No, there's no problem there. A company expects to make a profit, so the doors have to be open for business on a regular basis."

"What have you done that shows initiative and willingness to work?"

Again, tell a story about how you landed or created a job for yourself, or even got involved in some volunteer work. Your answer should show initiative in that you both handled unexpected problems calmly and anticipated others. Your willingness is demonstrated by the ways you overcame obstacles. For example: "I worked for a summer in a small warehouse. I found out that a large shipment was due in a couple of weeks, and I knew that room had to be made. The inventory system was outdated, and the rear of the warehouse was disorganized, so I came in on a Saturday, figured out how much room I needed, cleaned up the mess in the rear, and catalogued it all on the new inventory forms. When the shipment arrived, the truck just backed in. There was even room to spare."

Often after an effort above and beyond the call of duty, a manager might congratulate you, and if it had happened to you in this instance, you might conclude your answer with the verbal endorsement. "The divisional manager happened along just when I was finishing the job, and said he wished he had more people who took such pride in their work."

"Can you take instructions without feeling upset or hurt?"

This is a manageability question. If you take offense easily or bristle when your mistakes are pointed out, you won't last long with any company. Competition is fierce at the entry level, so take this as another chance to set yourself apart. "Yes, I can take instructions—and more important, I can take constructive criticism without feeling hurt. Even with the best intent, I will still make mistakes, and at times someone will have to put me back on the right track. I know that if I ever expect to rise in the company, I must first prove myself to be manageable."

"Have you ever had difficulties getting along with others?"

This is a combination question, probing willingness and manageability. Are you a team player or are you going to disrupt the department and make the interviewer's life miserable? This is a closed-ended question that requires only a yes/no answer, so give one and shut up.

"What type of position are you interested in?"

This again is one of those questions that tempts you to mention management. Don't. Say you are interested in what you will be offered anyway, which is an entry-level job. "I am interested in an entry-level position that will enable me to learn this business inside and out, and will give me the opportunity to grow when I prove myself, either on a professional or a managerial ladder."

"What qualifications do you have that will make you successful in this field?"

There is more to answering this question than reeling off your academic qualifications. In addition you will want to stress relevant work experience and illustrate your strong points as they match the key personality traits as they apply to the position you seek. It's a simple, wide-open question that says, "Hey, we're looking for an excuse to hire you. Give us some help."

"Why do you think you would like this type of work?"

This is a deceptively simple question because there is no pat answer. It is usually asked to see whether you really understand what the specific job and profession entails on a day-to-day basis. So, to answer it requires you to have researched the company and job functions as carefully as possible. Preparation for this should include a call to another company in the field and a request to speak to someone doing the job you hope to get. Ask what the job is like and what that person does day to day. How does the job fit into the department? What contribution does it make to the overall efforts of the company? Why does he or she like that type of work? Armed with that information, you will show that you understand what you are getting into; most recent graduates do not.

"What's your idea of how industry works?"

The interviewer does not want a long dissertation, just the reassurance that you don't think it works along the same lines as a registered charity. Your understanding should be something like this: "The role of any company is to make as much money as possible, as quickly and efficiently as possible, and in a manner that will encourage repeat business from the existing client base and new business from word of mouth and reputation." Finish with the observation that it is every employee's role to play as a team member in order to achieve those goals.

"What do you know about our company?"

You can't answer this question unless you have enough interest to research the company thoroughly. If you don't have that interest, you should expect someone who has made the effort to get the job.

"What do you think determines progress in a good company?"

Your answer will include all the positive personality traits you have been illustrating throughout the interview. Include allusions to the listening profile, determination, ability to take the rough with the smooth, adherence to systems and procedures, and the good fortune to have a manager who wants you to grow.

"Do you think grades should be considered by first employers?"

If your grades were good, the answer is obviously "yes." If they weren't, your answer needs a little more thought. "Of course, an employer should take everything into consideration, and along with grades will be an evaluation of willingness and manageability, an understanding of how business works, and actual work experience. Combined, such experience and professional skills can be more valuable than grades alone."

□　□　□

Many virtuous candidates are called for entry-level interviews, but only those who prepare themselves to answer the tough questions will be chosen. Interviews for recent graduates are partly sales presentations. And the more you interview, the better you get, so don't leave preparing for them until the last minute. Start now and hone your skills to get a headstart on your peers. Finally, here's what a professor from a top-notch business school once told me: "You are taking a new product to market. Accordingly, you've got to analyze what it can do, who is likely to be interested, and how you are going to sell it to them." Take some time to get to know yourself and your particular values as they will be perceived in the world of business.

20.
The Graceful Exit

To paraphrase Shakespeare, all the employment world's a stage, and all the people on it merely players making their entrances and exits. Curtains rise and fall, and your powerful performance must be capped with a professional and memorable exit. To ensure you leave the right impression, this chapter will review the do's and don'ts of leaving an interview.

A signal that the interview is drawing to a close comes when you are asked whether you have any questions. Ask questions, and by doing so, highlight your strengths and show your enthusiasm. Your goal at the interview is to generate a job offer, so you should find it easy to avoid the crimes that damage your case.

Don'ts:

1. **Don't discuss salary, vacation, or benefits**. It is not that the questions are invalid, just that the timing is wrong. Bringing such topics up before you have an offer is asking what the company can do for you—instead, you should be saying what you can do for the company. Those topics are part of the negotiation (handled in chapter 23, "Negotiating the Offer"); remember, without an offer you have nothing to negotiate.

2. **Don't press for an early decision.** Of course you should ask, "When will I know your decision?" But don't press it. And don't try to use the "other-opportunities-I-have-to-consider" gambit as leverage when no such offers exist—that annoys the interviewer, makes you look foolish, and may even force you to negotiate from a position of weakness. Timing is everything; the issue of how to handle other opportunities as leverage is explored in detail later.

3. **Don't show discouragement.** Sometimes a job offer can occur on the spot. Usually it does not. So don't show discouragement if you are not offered the job at the interview, because discouragement shows a lack of self-esteem and determination. Avoiding a bad impression is merely the foundation of leaving a good one, and the right image to leave is one of enthusiasm, guts, and openness—just the traits you have been projecting throughout the interview.

4. **Don't ask for an evaluation of your interview performance.** That forces the issue and puts the interviewer in an awkward position. You *can* say that you want the job, and ask what you have to do to get it.

Dos:

1. **Ask appropriate job-related questions.** When the opportunity comes to ask any final questions, review your notes. Bring up any relevant strengths that haven't been addressed.

2. **Show decisiveness.** If you are offered the job, react with enthusiasm. Then sleep on it. If it's possible to do so without making a formal acceptance, lock the job up now and put yourself in control; you can always change your mind later. But before you make any commitment with regard to compensation, see chapter 23, "Negotiating the Offer."

3. **When you are interviewed by more than one person, be sure you have the correct spelling of their names.** "I enjoyed meeting your colleagues, Ms. Smith. Could you give me the correct spelling of their names, please?" This question will give you the names you forgot in the heat of battle and will demonstrate your consideration.

4. **Review the job's requirements with the interviewer.** Match them point by point with your skills and attributes.

5. **Find out whether this is the only interview.** If so, you must ask for the job in a positive and enthusiastic manner. Find out the time frame for a decision and finish with: "I am very enthusiastic about the job and the contributions I can make. If your decision will be made by the fifteenth, what must I do in the meantime to assure I get the job?"

6. **Ask for the next interview.** When there are subsequent interviews in the hiring procedure, ask for the next interview in the same honest and forthright manner. "Is now a good time to schedule our next meeting?" If you do not ask, you do not get.

7. **Keep yourself in contention.** A good leading question to ask is, "Until I hear from you again, what particular aspects of the job and this interview should I be considering?"

8. **Always depart in the same polite and assured manner you entered.** Look the interviewer in the eye, put on a smile (there's no need to grin), give a firm handshake, and say, "This has been an exciting meeting for me. This is a job I can do, and I feel I can contribute to your goals, because the atmosphere here seems conducive to doing my very best work. When will we speak again?"

IV

Finishing Touches

The successful completion of every interview is a big stride toward getting job offers, yet it is not the end of your job hunt.

A company rarely hires the first competent person it sees. A hiring manager will sometimes interview as many as fifteen people for a particular job, but the strain and pace of conducting interviews naturally dim the memory of each applicant. Unless you are the last person to be interviewed, the impression you make will fade with each subsequent interview the interviewer undertakes. And if you are not remembered, you will not be offered the job. You must develop a strategy to keep your name and skills constantly in the forefront of the interviewer's mind. These finishing touches often make all the difference.

Some of the suggestions here may not seem earth-shattering, just simple, sensible demonstrations of your manners, enthusiasm, and determination. But remember that today all employers are looking for people with that extra little something. You can avoid the negative or merely indifferent impression and be certain of creating a positive one by following these guidelines.

21.
Out of Sight, Out of Mind

The first thing you do on leaving the interview is breathe a sigh of relief. The second is to make sure that "out of sight, out of mind" will not apply to you. You do this by starting a follow-up procedure immediately after the interview.

Sitting in your car, on the bus, train, or plane, do a written recap of the interview while it's still fresh in your mind. Answer these questions.

- Whom did you meet? (Names and titles.)
- What does the job entail?
- What are the first projects, the biggest challenges?
- Why can you do the job?
- What aspects of the interview went poorly? Why?
- What is the agreed-upon next step?
- What was said during the last few minutes of the interview?

Probably the most difficult—and most important—thing to do is to analyze what aspects of the interview went poorly. A person does not get offered a job based solely on strength. On the contrary, many people get new jobs based on their relative lack of negatives as compared to the other applicants. So it is mandatory that you look for and recognize any negatives from your performance. That is the only way you will have an opportunity to package and overcome those negatives in your follow-up procedure and during subsequent interviews.

The next step is to write the follow-up letter to the interviewer to acknowledge the meeting and to keep you fresh in his or her mind. Writing a follow-up letter also shows that you are both appreciative and organized, and it refreshes the urgency of your candidacy at the expense of other candidates. But remember that a canned follow-up form letter could hurt your candidacy.

☐ **1. Type the letter.** It exhibits greater professionalism. If you don't own a typewriter, the local library will frequently allow the use of theirs. If not, a typing service will do it for a nominal fee. If, for any reason, the letter cannot be typed, make sure it is legibly and neatly written. The letter should make four points clear to the company representative:

- You paid attention to what was being said.
- You understood the importance of the interviewer's comments.
- You are excited about the job, can do it, and want it.
- You can contribute to those first major projects.

☐ **2. Use the right words and phrases in your letter.** Here are some you might want to use.

- "Upon reflection," or, "Having thought about our meeting . . ."
- Recognize—"I recognize the importance of . . ."
- Listen—"Listening to the points you made . . ."
- Enthusiasm—Let the interviewer catch your enthusiasm. It is very effective, especially as your letter will arrive while other applicants are nervously sweating their way through the interview.
- Impressed—Let the interviewer know you were impressed with the people/product/service/facility/market/position, but do not overdo it.
- Challenge—Show that you feel you would be challenged to do your best work in this environment.
- Confidence—There is a job to be done and a challenge to be met. Let the interviewer know you are confident of doing both well.
- Interest—If you want the job (or next interview), say so. At this stage, the company is buying and you are selling. Ask for the job in a positive and enthusiastic manner.
- Appreciation—As a courtesy and mark of professional manners, you must express appreciation for the time the interviewer took out of his or her busy schedule.

☐ **3. Whenever possible and appropriate, mention the names of the people you met at the interview.** Draw attention to one of the topics that was of general interest to the interviewers.

☐ **4. Address the follow-up letter to the main interviewer.** Send a copy to personnel with a note of thanks as a courtesy.

☐ **5. Don't gild the lily.** Keep it short—less than one page—and don't make any wild claims that might not withstand close scrutiny.

☐ **6. Mail the letter within twenty-four hours of the interview.** If the decision is going to be made in the next couple of days, hand-deliver the letter or make a strong point by sending a mailgram. The follow-up letter will help to set you apart from other applicants and will refresh your image in the mind of the interviewer just when it would normally be starting to dim.

☐ **7. If you do not hear anything after five days (which is quite normal), put in a telephone call to the company representative.** Reiterate the points made in the letter, saying that you want the job (or next interview), and finish your statements with a question: "Mr. Smith, I feel confident about my ability to contribute to your department's efforts, and I really want the job. Could you tell me what I have to do to get it?" Then be quiet and wait for the answer.

☐ ☐ ☐

Of course, you may be told you are no longer in the running. The next chapter will show you that that is a great opportunity to snatch victory from the jaws of defeat.

22.
Snatching Victory from the Jaws of Defeat

During the interviewing process, there are bound to be interviewers who erroneously come to the conclusion that you are not the right person for the job they need to fill. When that happens, you will be turned down. Such an absurd travesty of justice can occur in different ways:

- At the interview.
- In a letter of rejection.
- During your follow-up telephone call.

Whenever the turn-down comes, you must be emotionally and intellectually prepared to take advantage of the opportunity being offered to you.

When you get turned down for the only opportunity you have going, the rejection can be devastating to your ego. That is why I have stressed the wisdom of having at least a few interviews in process at the same time.

You will get turned down. No one can be right for every job. The right person for a job doesn't always get it, however—the best prepared and most determined often does. While you may be responsible in part for the initial rejection, you still have the power to correct the situation and win the job offer. What you do with the claimed victory is a different matter—you will then be in a seller's market with choice and control of your situation.

To turn around a turn-down often requires only willpower and determination. Almost every job you desire is obtainable once you understand the hiring process from the interviewer's side of the desk. Your initial—and temporary—rejection is attributable to one of these reasons:

- The interviewer does not feel you can do the job.
- The interviewer feels you lack a successful profile.
- The interviewer did not feel your personality would contribute to the smooth functioning of the department—perhaps you didn't portray yourself as either a team player, or as someone willing to take the extra step.

With belief in yourself, you can still succeed. Repeat to yourself constantly through the interview cycle: "I will get this job, because no one else can give as much to this company as I can!" Do that and implement the following plan immediately when you hear of rejection, whether in person, via mail, or over the telephone.

☐ **Step One:** Thank the interviewer for the time and consideration. Then ask politely: "To help my future job search, why wasn't I chosen for the position?" Assure the interviewer that you would truly appreciate an honest, objective analysis. Listen to the reply and do not interrupt regardless of the comments. Use your time constructively and take notes furiously. When the company representative finishes speaking, show you understood the comments. (Remember, understanding and agreeing are different animals.)

"Thank you, Mr. Smith, now I can understand the way you feel. Because I am not a professional interviewer, I'm afraid my interview nerves got in the way. I'm very interested in working for your company [use an enthusiastic tone] and am determined to get the job. Let me meet with you once again. This time, when I'm not so nervous, I am confident you will see I really do have the skills you require" [then provide an example of a skill you have in the questionable area]. "You name the time and the place, and I will be there. What's best for you, Mr. Smith?"

End with a question, of course. An enthusiastic request like that is very difficult to refuse and will usually get you another interview. An interview, of course, at which you must shine.

☐ **Step Two:** Check your notes and accept the company representative's concerns. Their validity is irrelevant; the important point is that the negative points represent the problem areas in the interviewer's perception of you. List the negative perceptions, and using the techniques, exercises, and value keys discussed throughout the book, develop different ways to overcome or compensate for every negative perception.

☐ **Step Three:** Reread part 3 of this book.

☐ **Step Four:** Practice aloud the statements and responses you will use at the interview. If you can practice with someone who plays the part of the interviewer, so much the better. That will create a real interview atmosphere and be helpful to your success. Lacking a role-play partner, you can create that live answer by putting the anticipated objections and questions on a tape and responding to them.

☐ **Step Five:** Study all available information on the company.

☐ **Step Six:** Congratulate yourself continually for getting another interview after initial rejection. This is proof of your self-worth, ability, and tenacity. You have nothing to lose and everything to gain, having already risen phoenix-like from the ashes of temporary defeat.

☐ **Step Seven:** During the interview, ask for the job in a positive and enthusiastic manner. Your drive and staying power will impress the interviewer. All you must do to win the job is overcome the perceived negatives, and you have been given the time to prepare. Go for it.

☐ **Step Eight:** Even when all has failed at the subsequent interview, do not leave without a final request for the job. Play your trump card: "Mr. Smith, I respect the fact that you allowed me the opportunity to prove myself here today. I am convinced I am the best person for the job. I want you to give me a trial, and I will prove on the job that I am the best hiring decision you have made this year. Will you give us both the opportunity?"

A reader once wrote to me as I was revising *Knock 'em Dead*. The letter read in part, "I read the chapter entitled 'Snatching Victory from the Jaws of Defeat' and did everything you said to salvage what appeared to be a losing interview. My efforts did make a very good impression on the interviewer, but as it was finally explained to me, I really did not have equal qualifications for the job, and finally came in a close second. I really want to work for this growing company, and they say they have another position coming up in six months. What should I do?"

I know of someone in the airline business who wanted a job working on that most prestigious of aircraft, the Concorde. He had been recently laid off and had high hopes for a successful interview. As it happened, he came in second for the Concorde position. He was told that the firm would speak to him again in the near future. So he waited—for eight months. Finally, he realized that waiting for the job could only leave him unemployed. The moral of the story is that you must be brutally objective when you come out second-best, and whatever the interviewer says, you must sometimes assume that you are getting the polite brush-off.

With that in mind, let's see what can be done on the positive side. First of all, send a thank-you note to the interviewer, acknowledging your understanding of the state of affairs and reaffirming your desire to work for the company. Conclude with a polite request to bear you in mind for the future.

Then, keep an eye out for any news item about the company in the press. Whenever you see something, cut it out and mail it to the interviewer with a very brief note that says something like: "I came across this in *Forbes* and thought you might find it interesting. I am still determined to be your next account manager, so please keep me in mind when the next opening occurs."

You can also call the interviewer once every couple of months, just to check in. Remember, of course, to keep the phone call brief and polite—you simply want to keep your name at the top of the interviewer's mind.

And maybe something will come of it. Ultimately, however, your only choice is to move on. There is no gain waiting on an interviewer's word. Go out and keep looking, because chances are that you will come up with an even better job. Then, if you still want to work for that company that gave you the brush-off, you will have some leverage.

Most people fail in their endeavors by quitting just before the dawn of success.

Follow these directions and you can win the job. You have proved yourself to be a fighter, and that is universally admired. The company representative will want you to succeed because you are made of stuff that is rarely seen today. You are a person of guts, drive, and endurance—the hallmarks of a winner. Job turn-downs are an opportunity to exercise and build your strengths, and by persisting, you may well add to your growing number of job offers, now and in the future.

23.
Negotiating the Offer

The crucial period after you have received a formal offer and before you accept is probably the one point in your relationship with an employer at which you can say with any accuracy that you have the whip hand. The advantage, for now, is yours. They want you but don't have you; and their wanting something they don't have gives you a negotiating edge. An employer is also more inclined to respect and honor a person who has a clear understanding of his or her worth in the marketplace—they want a savvy and businesslike person.

You don't have to accept or reject the first offer, whatever it is. In most instances you can improve the initial offer in a number of ways, but you have to know something about the existing market conditions for those employed in your area of endeavor. If you are female, bear in mind that simply settling for a few points above your current rate of pay is bad advice for anyone and downright crazy for you. A word or two on the sober topic of pay discrimination is in order here.

The Women's Bureau of the U.S. Department of Labor tells us that men outearn women in nearly every field. (For what it's worth, my research could not turn up a single industry in which this was not the case.) Even if a woman's responsibilities, background, and accomplishments are exactly the same as those of her male colleague, she is statistically unlikely to take home a paycheck equal to his.

According to the Women's Bureau, male engineers make 14.3 percent more than their female counterparts. Male mathematicians make 16.3 percent more. Male advertising and public relations professionals make 28 percent more. Male lawyers and judges make 28 percent more. And male editors and reporters make a whopping 43 percent more than women performing the same or comparable work.

Those are big discrepancies, and they're just the tip of the iceberg. On average, a woman earns seventy cents for every dollar a man performing the same work earns. That's up from fifty-nine cents, which was the figure back in 1981, but it's still a depressing figure for women in the workplace today. At this rate, American industry will not be able to reach gender-based pay equity until the year 2020.

Is this a conscious male conspiracy against women? I think not. My personal belief is that much of the gap can be attributed to a simple lack of knowledge of professional negotiating skills, and that women in the workplace are picking these skills up fast. A recent *Industry Week* survey showed that 75 percent of men believe their firms pay men and women equally, even though only a little over half of all American corporations have standardized pay scales. This indicates that qualified female hires are now in a position, at least at the majority of firms, to receive fair consideration of their requests for equitable pay rates. But they have to ask.

Man or woman, there is no guarantee that you are being paid what you are worth. The simple facts are these: If you don't get it while they want you and don't have you, you sure as shootin' can't count on getting it once they do have you. When a thirty-year-old undernegotiates his or her salary by just $2,000 on a new job, it will cost that person a minimum of $70,000 over the course of a career. And remember, every subsequent raise will come from a proportionately lower base; real dollars lost over an entire career span could actually be double this figure.

To get what you have coming at the negotiating table, you must take the time to understand what you have achieved, what you have to offer, and what you are worth to the employer. You should be able to get a better handle on that final item by doing good research, but remember that regional influences can affect pay levels, as can current business conditions.

Everything in this book has been written toward maximizing your professional worth, and salary negotiation is certainly no exception. Please bear in mind that there are no shortcuts. The ideas presented in this chapter will be helpful to you if they represent the culmination of your successful campaign to set yourself apart from the competition, but you cannot negotiate a terrific salary package if an employer is not convinced that you are in the top tier of applicants.

Follow this three-step procedure in planning your salary discussions with employers.

☐ **Step One:** Before getting into negotiation with any employer, work out your minimum cash requirements for any job; you must know what it is going to take to keep a roof over your head and bread on the table. It's necessary to know this figure, but you need never discuss it with anyone—knowing it is the foundation of getting both what you need and what you are worth.

☐ **Step Two:** Get a grip on what your skills are worth in the current market. There are a number of ways to do that. Consider the resources and methods outlined below.

- You may be able to find out the salary range for the level above you and the level beneath you at the company in question.

- You can get information from the Bureau of Labor Statistics in Washington, DC, which keeps stats on hundreds of job titles. Be warned, however, that those titles are often a little out of date.

- Your state labor office may have salary ranges available for you to review.

- Ask headhunters—they know better than anyone what the market will bear. You should, as a matter of career prudence, establish an ongoing relationship with a reputable headhunter, because you never know when his or her services will come in handy.

- Many professional journals publish annual salary surveys you can consult.
- The *National Business Employment Weekly*, a magazine published by The *Wall Street Journal*, runs ongoing salary surveys by profession; back issues are available.

☐ **Step Three:** This is the fun part. Come up with the figure that would make you smile, drop dead, and go to heaven on the spot. (But try to keep it somewhere within the bounds of reality—multimillion-dollar offers with stock options being in relatively short supply for most of us.)

☐   ☐   ☐

You now have three figures: a minimum, a realistic midpoint desired salary, and a dream salary.

Your minimum is, as I have said, for personal consumption—never discuss it with anyone. Put it aside, and what do you have left? A salary range, just like the one every employer has for every interview you attend. Yours extends from your midpoint to your dream salary. Yes, that range represents the "top half" of what you want or, more accurately, could conceivably accept—but there's a reason for that. In the event, you will find that it is far easier to negotiate down than it is to negotiate up, and you must find a starting point that gives you every possible advantage.

Negotiate When You Can

I have said throughout *Knock 'em Dead* that your sole aim at the interview is to get the job offer, because without it you have nothing to negotiate. Once the offer is extended, the time to negotiate has arrived, and there will never be a more opportune time. Your relationship with the potential employer has gone through a number of distinct changes—from, "Perhaps we should speak to this one," to, "Yes, he might be able to do the job," through, "This is the top candidate, we really like him and want to have him on board." But now is the only point in the relationship when you will have the upper hand. Enjoy it while you can.

Although questions of salary are usually brought up after you are under serious consideration, you must be careful to avoid painting yourself into a corner when you fill out the initial company application form that contains a request for required salary. Usually you can get away with "open" as a response; sometimes the form will instruct you not to write "open," in which case you can write "negotiable," or "competitive."

☐   ☐   ☐

So much for basic considerations. Let's move on to the money questions that are likely to be flying around the room.

The salary/job negotiation begins in earnest in two ways. The interviewer can bring up the topic with statements like:

- "How do you think you would like working here?"

- "People with your background always fit in well with us."
- "You could make a real contribution here."
- "Well, you certainly seem to have what it takes."

Or, if it is clearly appropriate to do so, you can bring on the negotiating stage. In that case, you can make mirror images of the above, which make the interviewer face the fact that you certainly are able to do the job, and that the time has therefore come to talk turkey:

- "How do you think I would fit in with the group?"
- "I feel my background and experience would definitely complement the workgroup, don't you?"
- "I think I could make a real contribution here. What do you think?"
- "I know I have what it takes to do this job. What questions are lingering in your mind?"

Now then. What do you do when the question of money is brought up before you have enough details about the job to negotiate from a position of knowledge and strength? Postpone money talk until you have the facts in hand. Do that by asking something like: "I still have one or two questions about my responsibilities, and it will be easier for me to talk about money when I have cleared them up. Could I first ask you a few questions about . . . ?"

Then proceed to clarify duties and responsibilities, being careful to weigh the relative importance of the position and the individual duties to the success of the department you may join.

The employer is duty-bound to get your services as reasonably as possible, while you have an equal responsibility to do the best you can for yourself. Your goal is not to settle for less than will enable you to be happy on the job—unhappiness at work can taint the rest of your life. It is far easier to negotiate down than it is to negotiate up. The value of the offer you accept depends on your performance throughout the interview and hiring cycle, and especially the finesse you display in the final negotiations. The rest of the chapter is going to address the many questions that might be asked, or that you might ask, to bring matters to a successful conclusion.

"What is an adequate reward for your efforts?"

A glaring manageability question and money probe all in one. The interviewer probably already has a typist on staff who expects a Nobel Prize each time he or she gets out a faultless letter. Your answer should be honest and cover all bases. "My primary satisfaction and reward comes from a job well done and completed on time. The occasional good word from my boss is always welcome. Last but not least, I think everyone looks forward to a salary review."

"What is your salary history?" or, *"What was your salary progress on your last job?"*

The interviewer is looking for a couple of things here. First, he or she is looking for the frequency, percentage, and dollar-value of your raises, which in turn tell him or her about your performance and the relative value of the offer that is about to be made. What you want to avoid is tying the potential offer to your salary history—the offer you negotiate should be based solely on the value of the job in hand. Again, this is even more important if you are a woman.

Your answer needs to be specifically vague. Perhaps: "My salary history has followed a steady upward path, and I have never failed to receive merit increases. I would be glad to give you the specific numbers if needed, but I shall have to sit down and give it some thought with a pencil and paper." The odds are that the interviewer will not ask you to do that; if he or she does, nod in agreement and say that you'll get right to it when you get home. Don't begin the task until you are requested a second time, which is unlikely.

If for any reason you do get your back against the wall with this one, be sure to include in the specifics of your answer that "one of the reasons I am leaving my current job is that raises were standard for all levels of employees, so that despite my superior contributions, I got the same percentage raise as the tardy employee. I want to work in an environment where I will be recognized and rewarded for my contributions." Then end with a question: "Is this the sort of company where I can expect that?"

"What were you making on your last job?"
A similar but different question. It could also be phrased, "What are you making now?" or, "What is your current salary?"

While I have said that your current earnings should bear no relation to your starting salary on the new job, it can be difficult to make that statement clear to the interviewer without appearing objectionable. Although the question asks you to be specific, you needn't get too specific. Instead, you should try to draw attention to the fact that the two jobs are different. A short answer might include: "I am earning $X, although I'm not sure how that will help you in your evaluation of my worth for this job, because the two jobs are somewhat different."

It is important to understand the "areas of allowable fudge." For instance, if you are considerably underpaid, you may want to weigh the dollar-value of such perks as medical and dental plans, pay in lieu of vacation, profit-sharing and pension plans, bonuses, stock options, and other incentives. For many people, those can add between 20 to 35 percent to their base salary—you might honestly be able to mention a higher figure than you at first thought possible. Also, if you are due for a raise imminently, you are justified in adding it in.

It isn't common for current or previous salaries to be verified by employers, although certain industries, because of legal requirements, check more than others do (for instance, the stock market or the liquor business). Before your "current salary" disappears through the roof, however, you should know that the interviewer can ask to see a payroll stub or W2 form at the time you start work, or could make the offer dependent on verification of salary. After you are hired, the new employer may request verbal or written confirmation from previous employers, or might use an outside verification agency. In any instance where the employer contacts someone verbally or in writing, the employer must by law have your written permission to do so. That small print on the bottom of the job application form followed by a request for your signature usually authorizes the employer to do just that.

"Have you ever been refused a salary increase?"

This implies that you asked. An example of your justifiable request might parallel the following true story. An accountant in a tire distributorship made changes to an accounting system that saved $65,000 a year, plus thirty staff hours a week. Six months after the methods were obviously working smoothly, he requested a salary review, was refused, but was told he would receive a year-end bonus. He did: $75. If you can tell a story like that, by all means tell how you were turned down for a raise. If not, it is best to play it safe and explain that your work and salary history showed a steady and marked continual improvement over the years.

"How much do you need to support your family?"

As we have seen, your best advice is to find some way to sidestep this by discussing your midpoint desired salary.

This question is sometimes asked of people who will be working in a sales job, where remuneration is based upon a draw against forthcoming commissions. If this scenario describes your income patterns, be sure you have a firm handle on your basic needs before you accept the position.

For salaried positions, this question is of questionable relevance. It implies the employer will try to get you at a subsistence salary, which is not why you are there. In this instance, give a range from your desired high-end salary down to your desired mid-point salary.

"How much will it take to get you?" "How much are you looking for?" "What are your salary expectations?" "What are your salary requirements?"

You are being asked to name a figure here. Give the wrong answer and you can get eliminated. It is always a temptation to ask for the moon, knowing you can come down later, but there are better approaches. It is wise to confirm your understanding of the job and its importance before you start throwing numbers around, because you will have to live with the consequences. You need the best possible offer without pricing yourself out of the market, so it's time to dance with one of the following responses.

"Well, let's see if I understand the responsibilities fully . . ." You then proceed to itemize exactly what you will be doing on a daily basis and the parameters of your responsibilities and authority. Once that is done you will seek agreement: "Is this the job as you see it or have I missed anything?" Remember to describe the job in its most flattering and challenging light, paying special attention to the way you see it fitting into the overall picture and contributing to the success of department, workgroup, and company. You can then finish your response with a question of your own: "What figure did you have in mind for someone with my track record?" or, "What range has been authorized for this position?" Your answer will include, in part, something along the lines of, "I believe my skills and experience will warrant a starting salary between _____ and _____."

You also could ask, "What would be the salary range for someone with my experience and skills?" or, "I naturally want to make as much as my background and skills will allow. If I am right for the job, and I think my credentials demonstrate that I am, I am sure you will make me a fair offer. What figure do you have in mind?"

Another good response is: "I would expect a salary appropriate to my experience and ability to do the job successfully. What range do you have in mind?"

Such questions will get the interviewer to reveal the salary range, and concentrate his or her attention on the challenges of the job and your ability to accept and work with those challenges.

When you are given a range, you can adjust your money requirements appropriately, latching on to the upper part of the range. For example, if the range is $30,000–$35,000 a year, you can come back with a range of $34,000–$37,000.

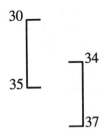

Consequently, your response will include: "That certainly means we have something to talk about. While your range is $30,000-$35,000, I am looking for a minimum of $34,000 with an ideal of $37,000. Tell me, what flexibility is there at the top of your salary range?" You need to know this to put yourself in the strongest negotiating position, and this is the perfect time and opportunity to gain the information and the advantage.

All this fencing is aimed at getting the interviewer to show his or her hand first. Ask for too much, and it's "Oh dear, I'm afraid you're overqualified"—to which you can reply, "So overpay me." (Actually, that works when you can carry it off with an ingratiating smile.) If your request is too low, you are likely to be ruled out as lacking the appropriate experience.

When you have tried to get the interviewer to name a range and failed, you must come up with specific dollars and cents. At this point, the key is to understand that all jobs have salary ranges attached to them. Consequently, the last thing you will ever do is come back with a specific dollar figure—that traps you. Instead, you will mention your own range, which will not be from your minimum to your maximum but rather from your midpoint to your maximum. Remember, you can always negotiate down, but can rarely negotiate up.

"What kind of salary are you worth?"

This is a how-much-do-you-want question with a slight twist. It is asking you to name a desired figure, but the twist is that it also asks you to justify that figure.

It requires that you demonstrate careful analysis of your worth, industry norms, and job requirements. You are recommended to try for a higher figure rather than a lower one. "Having compared my background and experience with industry norms and salary surveys, I feel my general worth is in the region of $X to $Y. My general background and credentials fit your needs, and my first-hand knowledge of the specific challenges and projects I would face in this job are an exact match, so I feel worthy of justifying an offer toward the top of this range. Don't you agree?"

After your response to a salary question, you can expect to hear, "That's too much," or, "Oh, that is more than we were hoping to pay," or, "That would be stretching the budget to the breaking point." When that happens, accept it as no more than a negotiating gambit and come back with your own calm rebuttal: "What did you have in mind?"

"What do you hope to be earning two to five years from now?"

A difficult question. The interviewer is probing your desired career and earning path and is trying to see whether you have your sights set high enough—or too high. Perhaps a jocular tone doesn't hurt here: "I'd like to be earning just about as much as my boss and I can work out!" Then, throw the ball back with your own question: "How much is it possible to make here?"

If you give a specific figure, the interviewer is going to want justification. If you come up with a salary range, you are advised also to have a justified career path to go along with it.

You could also say, "In two years, I will have finished my C.P.A. requirements, so with that plus my additional experience, industry norms say I should be earning between $X and $Y. I would hope to be earning at least within that range, but hopefully with a proven track record of contributions, I would be making above the norm." The trick is to use industry statistics as the backbone of your argument, express confidence in doing better than the norm, and whenever possible stay away from specific job titles unless pressed.

"Do you think people in your occupation should be paid more?"

This one can be used prior to serious salary negotiation to probe your awareness of how your job really contributes to the bottom line. Or it can occur in the middle of salary negotiations to throw you off balance. The safe and correct answer is to straddle the fence. "Most jobs have salary ranges that reflect the job's relative importance and contribution to a company. And those salary ranges reflect the norm for the great majority of people within that profession. That does not mean, however, that the extraordinary people in such a group are not recognized for the extra performance and skills. There are always exceptions to the rule."

Good Offers, Poor Offers

After a period of bantering back and forth like this, the interviewer names a figure, hopefully meant as a legitimate offer. If you aren't sure, qualify it: "Let me see if I understand you correctly: Are you formally offering me the position at $X a year?"

The formal offer can fall into one of two categories.

☐ **It sounds fair and equitable:** In that case, you still want to negotiate for a little more—employers almost expect it of you, so don't disappoint them. Mention a salary range again, the low end of which comes at about the level of their offer and the high end somewhat above it. You can say, "Well it certainly seems that we are close. I was hoping for something more in the range of $X to $Y. How much room do we have for negotiation here?"

No one will withdraw an offer because you say you feel you are worth more. After all, the interviewer thinks you are the best person for the job, and has extended a formal offer, and the last thing he or she needs now is to start from square one again. The employer has a vested interest in bringing the negotiation to a satisfactory conclusion. In a worst-case scenario, the interviewer can stick to the original offer.

☐ **It isn't quite what you expected:** Even if the offer isn't what you thought it would be, you still have options other than accepting or rejecting the offer as it stands. But your strategy for now is to run the money topic as far as you can in a calm and businesslike way; then once you have gone that far, you can back off and examine the other potential benefits of the job. That way you will leave yourself with an opening, if you need it, to hit the money topic once more at the close of negotiations.

If you feel the salary could do with a boost, say so. "I like the job, and I know I have what it takes to be successful in it. I would also be prepared to give you a start date of [e.g.] March 1 to show my sincerity. But quite honestly, I couldn't justify it with your initial salary offer. I just hope that we have some room for negotiation here."

Or you can say, "I could start on March 1, and I do feel I could make a contribution here and become an integral part of the team. The only thing standing in the way is my inability to make ends meet based on your initial offer. I am sincerely interested in the opportunity and flattered by your interest in me. If we could just solve this money problem, I'm sure we could come to terms. What do you think can be done about it?"

The interviewer will probably come back with a question asking how much you want. "What is the minimum you would be prepared to work for?" he or she might ask. Respond with your range again—with your minimum really your midpoint—and the interviewer may well then come back with a higher offer and ask for your concurrence. This is the time to be noncommittal but encouraged, and to move on to the benefits included with the position: "Well, yes, that is a little better. Perhaps we should talk about the benefits."

Alternatively, the interviewer may come back with another question: "That's beyond our salary range for this job title. How far can you reduce your salary needs to fit our range?"

That question shows good faith and a desire to close the deal, but don't give in too easily—the interviewer is never going to want you as much as he or she does now. Your first response might be: "I appreciate that, but if it is the job title and its accompanying range that is causing the problem, couldn't we upgrade the title, thereby putting me near the bottom of the next range?" Try it—it often works. If is doesn't, it is probably time to move to other negotiable aspects of the job offer.

But not before one last try. You can take that final stab by asking, "Is that the best you can do?" With this question, you must look the interviewer directly in the eye, ask the question, and maintain eye contact. It works surprisingly well. You should also remember to try it as a closing gambit *at the very end of negotiations* when you have received everything you can hope for. You may get a surprise.

Negotiating Your Future Salary

At this point, you have probably ridden present salary as hard as you reasonably can (for a while, anyway)—so the time has come to shift the conversation to future remuneration.

"Even though the offer isn't quite what I'd hoped for to start the job, I am still interested. Can we talk about the future for a while?" Then you move the conversation to an on-the-job focus. Here are a few arrangements corporate headhunters frequently negotiate for their recruits.

☐ **A single, lump-sum signing bonus.** Nice to have, though it is money here today and gone tomorrow. Don't make the mistake of adding it onto the base. If you get a $2,500 signing bonus, that money won't be figured in for your year-end review—your raise will be based on your actual salary, so the bonus is a little less meaningful than it appears.

☐ **A 60-, 90-, or 120-day performance review with raise attached.** You can frequently negotiate a minimum percentage increase here, if you have confidence in your abilities.

☐ **A title promotion and raise** after two, three, or four months.

☐ **Bonus.** When you hear talk about a year-end bonus, don't rely on "what it's going to be this year" or "what it was last year," because the actual bonus will never bear any resemblance to either figure. Base the realism of any bonus expectations on a five-year performance history.

☐ **Things other than cash.** Also in the realm of real disposable income are things like a company car, gas, maintenance, and insurance. They represent hard dollars you would not have to spend. It's not unusual to hear of employers paying car or insurance allowances, picking up servicing bills for your personal automobile, or paying gas up to a certain amount each month. But if you don't ask, you can never expect an employer to offer. What have you got to lose? Remember, though, to get any of those unusual goodies in writing—even respectable managers in respected companies can suffer amnesia.

Questions to Leverage and Evaluate the Offer

No two negotiations are going to be alike, so there is no absolute model you can follow.

Nevertheless, when you have addressed present and future remuneration, this might be the time to get some more information on the company and the job itself.

Even if you haven't agreed on money, you are probably beginning to get a feeling as to whether or not you can put the deal together; you know the employer wants to. Many of the following questions will be appropriate here; some might even be appropriate at other times during the interview cycle.

Full knowledge of all the relevant facts is critical to your successful final negotiation of money and benefits. Your prudent selection of questions from this list will help you negotiate the best offers and choose the right job for you. (At this point, asking some pertinent questions from the following list also serves as a decompression device of sorts for both parties.)

□ □ □

The questions come in these categories:

- Nuts-and-bolts job clarification.
- Job and department growth.
- Corporate culture.
- Company growth and direction.

The following section is also worth reading between first and second interviews.

Nuts and Bolts
First, if you have career aspirations, you want to land in an outfit that believes in promoting from within. To find out, ask a few of these questions.

How long has the job been open? Why is it open? Who held the job last? What is he doing now? Promoted, fired, quit? How long was he in that job? How many people have held this job in the last three years? Where are they now? How often and how many people have been promoted from this position—and to where?

Other questions that might follow would include:

"What is the timetable for filling the position?"
The longer the job has been open and the tighter the timeframe for filling it, the better your leverage. That can also be determined by asking, "When do you need me to start? Why on that date particularly?"

"What are the first projects to be addressed?" or, "What are the major problems to be tackled and conquered?"

"What do you consider the five most important day-to-day responsibilities of this job? Why?"

"What personality traits do you consider critical to success in this job?"

"How do you see me complementing the existing group?"

"Will I be working with a team, or on my own? What will be my responsibilities as a team member? What will be my leadership responsibilities?"

"How much overtime is involved?"

"How much travel is involved?" and, *"How much overnight travel?"*

With overnight travel you need to find out the number of days per week and month; and more important, whether you will be paid for weekend days or given comp time. I have known companies who regularly expect you to get home from a long weekend trip at one o'clock in the morning and be at work at 8:30 A.M. on Monday—all without extra pay or comp time.

"How frequent are performance and salary reviews? And what are they based on—standard raises for all, or are they weighted toward merit and performance?

How does the performance appraisal and reward system work? Exactly how are outstanding employees recognized, judged, and rewarded?"

"What is the complete financial package for someone at my level?"

Job and Department Growth

Not everyone wants a career path—in fact, careers and career paths are fairly new to business and are a phenomenon of the latter part of the twentieth century. The fast track may or may not be for you. Gauging the potential for professional growth in a job is very important for some; for others, it comes slightly lower down the list. Even if you aren't striving to head the corporation in the next few years, you will still want to know what the promotional and growth expectations are so that you don't end up with a company expecting you to scale the heights.

"To what extent are the functions of the department recognized as important and worthy of review by upper management?"

If upper management takes an interest in the doings of your workgroup, rest assured you are in a visible position for recognition and reward.

"Where and how does my department fit into the company pecking order?"

"What does the department hope to achieve in the next two to three years? How will that help the company? How will it be recognized by the company?"

"What do you see as the strengths of the department? What do you see as weaknesses that you are looking to turn into strengths?"

"What role would you hope I would play in these goals?"

"What informal/formal benchmarks will you use to measure my effectiveness and contributions?"

"Based on my effectiveness, how long would you anticipate me holding this position? When my position and responsibilities change, what are the possible titles and responsibilities I might grow into?"

"What is the official corporate policy on internal promotion? How many people in this department have been promoted from their original positions since joining the company?"

"How do you determine when a person is ready for promotion?"

"What training and professional development programs are available to help me grow professionally?"

"Does the company encourage outside professional development training? Does the company sponsor all or part of any costs?"

"What are my potential career paths within the company?"

"To what jobs have people with my title risen in the company?"

"Who in the company was in this position the shortest length of time? Why? Who has remained in this position the longest? Why?"

Corporate Culture
All companies have their own way of doing things—that's corporate culture. Not every corporate culture is for you.

"What is the company's mission? What are the company's goals?"

"What approach does this company take to its marketplace?"

"What is unique about the way this company operates?"

"What is the best thing you know about this company? What is the worst thing you know about this company?"

"How does the reporting structure work? What are the accepted channels of communication and how do they work?"

"What kinds of checks and balances, reports, or other work-measurement tools are used in the department and company?"

"What do you and the company consider important in my fitting into the corporate culture—the way of doing things around here?"

"Will I be encouraged or discouraged from learning about the company beyond my own department?"

Company Growth and Direction

For those concerned about career growth, a healthy company is mandatory; for those concerned about stability of employment, the same applies.

"What expansion is planned for this department, division, or facility?"

"What markets does the company anticipate developing?"

"Does the company have plans for mergers or acquisitions?"

"Currently, what new endeavors is the company actively pursuing?"

"How do market trends affect company growth and progress? What is being done about them?"

"What production and employee layoffs and cutbacks have you experienced in the last three years?"

"What production and employee layoffs and cutbacks do you anticipate? How are they likely to affect this department, division, or facility?"

"When was the last corporate reorganization? How did it affect this department? When will the next corporate reorganization occur? How will it affect this department?"

"Is this department a profit center? How does that affect remuneration?"

The Package

Take-home pay is the most important part of your package. (You'll probably feel that the only thing wrong with your pay is that it gets taxed before you get to take it home!) That means you must carefully negotiate any possible benefits accruing to the job that have a monetary value but are nontaxable, and/or add to your physical and mental happiness. The list is almost endless, but here is a comprehensive listing of commonly available benefits. Although many of these benefits are available to all employees at some companies, you should know that, as a rule of thumb, the higher up the ladder you climb, the more benefits you can expect. Because the corporate world and its concepts of creating a motivated and committed workforce are constantly in flux, you should never assume that a particular benefit will not be available to you.

The basic rule is to ask—if you don't ask, there is no way you will get. A few years ago, it would have been unthinkable that anyone but an executive could expect something as glamorous as an athletic-club membership in a benefits package. In the 1990s, however, more companies have a membership as a standard benefit; an increasing number are even building their own health-club facilities. In New York you can easily pay between $250 and $700 for membership in a good club. What's this benefit worth in your area? Call a club and find out.

Benefits Your Package May Include

- 401K and other investment matching programs
- "Cafeteria" insurance plans—you pick the insurance benefits you want
- Car allowance
- Car insurance or an allowance
- Car maintenance and gas or an allowance
- Car
- Compensation days—for unpaid overtime/business travel time
- Country club or health club membership
- Accidental death insurance
- Deferred compensation
- Dental insurance—note deductibles and the percentage that is employer-paid
- Employment contract and/or termination contract
- Expense account
- Financial planning help and tax assistance
- Life insurance
- Medical insurance—note deductibles and percentage that is employer-paid
- Optical insurance—note deductibles and percentage that is employer-paid
- Paid sick leave
- Pension plans
- Personal days off
- Profit sharing
- Short- or long-term disability compensation plans
- Stock options
- Vacation

Evaluating the Offer

Once the offer has been negotiated to the best of your ability, you need to evaluate it—and that doesn't have to be done on the spot. Some of your requests and questions will take time to get answered, and very often the final parts of negotiation—

"Yes, Mr. Jones, we can give you the extra $20,000 and six months of vacation you requested"—will take place over the telephone. Regardless of where the final negotiations are completed, never accept or reject the offer on the spot.

Be positive, say how excited you are about the prospect and that you would like a little time (overnight, a day, two days) to think it over, discuss it with your spouse, consult your tarot cards, whatever. Not only is this delay standard practice, but it will also give you the opportunity to leverage other offers, as discussed in the next chapter.

Use the time you gain to speak to your mentors or advisors. But a word of caution: In asking advice from those close to you, be sure you know exactly where that advice is coming from—you need clear-headed objectivity at this time.

Once the advice is in, and not before, weigh it along with your own observations—no one knows your needs and aspirations better than you do. While there are many ways of doing that, a simple line down the middle of a sheet of paper, with the reasons to take the job written on one side and the reasons to turn it down on the other, is about as straightforward and objective as you can get.

You will weigh salary, future earnings and career prospects, benefits, commute, lifestyle, and stability of the company, along with all those intangibles that are summed up in the term "gut feelings." Make sure you answer these questions for yourself:

- Do you like the work?
- Can you be trained in a reasonable period of time, thus having a realistic chance of success on the job?
- Are the title and responsibilities likely to provide you with challenge?
- Is the opportunity for growth in the job compatible with your needs and desires?
- Are the company's location, stability, and reputation in line with your needs?
- Is the atmosphere/culture of the company conducive to your enjoying working at the company?
- Can you get along with your new manager and immediate workgroup?
- Is the money offer and total compensation package the best you can get?

Notice that money is but one aspect of the evaluation process. There are many other factors to take into account as well. Even a high-paying job can be less advantageous than you think. For instance, you should be careful not to be foxed by the gross figure. It really is important that you get a firm handle on those actual, spendable, after-tax dollars—the ones with which you pay the rent. Always look at an offer in the light of how many more spendable dollars a week it will put in your pocket.

Evaluating the New Boss
When all that is done, you must make a final but immensely important determination—whether or not you will be happy with your future manager. Remember, you

are going to spend the majority of your waking hours at work, and the new job can only be as good as your relationship with your new boss. If you felt uncomfortable with the person after an interview or two, you need to evaluate carefully the kind of discomfort and unhappiness it could generate over the coming months and years.

You'll want to know about the manager's personal style: Is he or she confrontational, authoritarian, democratic, hands-off? How would reprimands or differing viewpoints be handled? Does he or she share information on a need-to-know basis, the old military-management style of keep-'em-in-the-dark? When a group member makes a significant contribution, who gets the credit as far as senior management is concerned—the person, the manager, or the group? You can find out some of that information from the manager; other aspects you'll need to review when you meet team members, or the people from personnel.

Accepting New Jobs, Resigning from Others

Once your decision is made, you should accept the job verbally. Spell out exactly what you are accepting: "Mr. Smith, I'd like to accept the position of engineer at a starting salary of $42,000. I will be able to start work on March 1. And I understand my package will include life, health, and dental insurance, a 401K plan, and a company car." Then you finish with: "I will be glad to start on the above date pending a written offer received in time to give my present employer adequate notice of my departure. I'm sure that's acceptable to you."

Until you have the offer in writing, you have nothing. A verbal offer can be withdrawn—it happens all the time. That's not because the employer suddenly doesn't like you, but because of reasons that affect, but bear no real relationship to, your candidacy. I have known of countless careers that have stalled through reneged verbal offers—they lead to unemployment, bitterness, and even lawsuits. So avoid the headaches and play it by the numbers.

Once you have the offer in writing, notify your current employer in the same fashion. Quitting is difficult for almost everyone, so you can write a pleasant resignation letter, walk into your boss's office, hand it to him or her, then discuss things calmly and pleasantly once he or she has read it.

You will also want to notify any other companies who have been in negotiation with you that you are no longer on the market, but that you were most impressed with meeting them and would like to keep communications open for the future. (Again, see the next chapter for details on how to handle—and encourage—multiple job offers.)

24.
Multiple Interviews, Multiple Offers

False optimism and laziness lead many job hunters to be content with only one interview in process at any given time. That severely reduces the odds of landing the best job in town within your chosen time frame. Complacency guarantees that you will continue to operate in a buyer's market.

The recommended approach is to generate as many interviews as possible in a two- to three-week period. Interviewing skills are learned and consequently improve with practice. With the improved skills comes a greater confidence, and those natural interview nerves disperse. Your confidence shows through to potential employers, and you are perceived in a positive light. And because other companies are interested in you, everyone will move more quickly to secure your services. That is especially important if you are unfortunate enough to be unemployed. Being out of work is when you need money the most and is the time when the salary you can command on the open market is substantially reduced. The interview activity you generate will help offset this.

By generating multiple interviews, you bring the time of the first job offer closer and closer. That one job offer can be quickly parlayed into a number of others. And with a single job offer, your unemployed status has, to all intents and purposes, passed.

Immediately, you can call every company with whom you've met, and explain the situation. "Mr. Johnson, I'm calling because while still under consideration with your company I have received a job offer from one of your competitors. I would hate to make a decision without the chance of speaking with you again. I was very impressed by my meeting with you. Can we get together in the next couple of days?" End, of course, with a question that carries the conversation forward.

If you were in the running at all, your call will usually generate another interview; Mr. Johnson does not want to miss out on a suddenly prized commodity. Remember: It is human nature to want the very things one is about to lose. So you see, your simple offer can be multiplied almost by the number of interviews you have in process at the time.

A single job offer can also be used to generate interviews with new firms. It is as simple as making your usual telephone networking presentation, but you end it differently. You would be very interested in meeting with them because of your knowledge of the company/product/service, but also because you have just received a job offer—would it be possible to get together in the next couple of days?

Relying on one interview at a time can only lead to prolonged anxiety, disappointment, and, possibly, unemployment. That reliance is due to the combination of false optimism, laziness, and fear of rejection. Those are traits that cannot be tolerated except by confirmed defeatists, for defeat is the inevitable result of those traits. As Heraclitus said, "Character is destiny." Headhunters say, "The job offer that cannot fail will."

Self-esteem, on the other hand, is vital to your success, and happiness is found with it. And with it you will begin to awake each day with a vitality previously unknown. Vigor will increase, your enthusiasm will rise, and desire to achieve will burn within. The more you do today, the better you will feel tomorrow.

Even when you follow this plan to the letter, not every interview will result in an offer. But with many irons in the fire, an occasional firm "no" should not affect your morale. It won't be the first or last time you face rejection. Be persistent, and above all, close your mind to all negative and discouraging influences. The success you experience from implementing this plan will increase your store of willpower and determination, affect the successful outcome of your job hunt, and enrich your whole life. Start today.

The key to your success is preparation. Remember, it is necessary to plan and organize in order to succeed. Failing is easy—it requires no effort. It is the achievement of success that requires effort; and that means effort today, not tomorrow, for tomorrow never comes. So start building that well-stocked briefcase today.

25.
What If I Am Asked
to Take a Drug Test?

"*Would you be willing to take a drug test as a condition of employment?*"

Rightly or wrongly, drug testing as a condition of employment is much more common than in years past; it is likely to remain part of the job-search landscape for the foreseeable future. We can reasonably expect that by the mid-nineties, up to one out of every three jobs will require some form of drug testing as part of the selection process.

The Supreme Court has upheld drug testing programs for federal employees holding law enforcement positions and for customs personnel involved in drug interdiction activities. While there is no direct link between these governmental policies and private industry hiring, the rulings have been interpreted as reflecting our society's general acceptance of drug testing.

Recently, the U.S. Chamber of Commerce estimated that half of all *Fortune* 500 companies engage in some form of drug testing, either in the selection process or as part of random testing programs subsequent to hiring. As it turns out, the vast majority of testing is done to screen potential employees; the Employment Management Association has concluded that once hired, you are less likely to be subjected to drug testing than you were as an applicant (unless, of course, you exhibit signs of drug abuse on the job).

Perhaps you are reading this section out of curiosity, because drugs and drug testing are in the news these days. You may even think to yourself, "Well, this is all very interesting, but *I* don't take drugs; none of this applies to me." Unfortunately, you couldn't be more wrong.

Drug testing is everyone's business, because even those who have no problem with abusing controlled substances can be maligned by a false reading on a drug test. Such readings are, alas, all too common. Drug testing as it is practiced in today's workplace is rife with false positives, or, stated somewhat less clinically, mistakes. These mistakes provide seemingly authoritative "evidence" that you use illicit drugs when you do not.

What causes false positives? There are a number of factors, but of greatest interest here is the way many everyday foods, liquids, and over-the-counter drugs can set off alarms meant to identify serious drug abuse. By taking a pain reliever that contains ibuprofen, for instance—as millions do for relief of any number of aches and pains—you are increasing the risk that you will test positive for marijuana use. If you suffer from a cold and want to be sure to get the sleep necessary to put in a good day at work tomorrow, you may decide to take a nighttime cold medication; but if there is a surprise drug test the next day, you may learn to your surprise that you are an abuser of amphetamines!

False positives can occur as the result of asthma medications you receive on prescription, or because of cross-reacting chemicals in that doctor-prescribed and controlled diet plan. Has your physician instructed you to take the sedative Valium? If you do, a drug test could earn you a reputation as an angel dust fan. You are likely to show up as a morphine addict if you've suffered a bad cold or cough and have been prescribed codeine or certain other medications. This may also happen if you indulge in that most wicked of all addictions: lust for poppy seed bagels. That's what two bagel-hefting Navy doctors discovered recently: their careers nearly ran aground when two consecutive tests branded them as users of morphine. A few weeks later, however, the Navy discovered the error and traced it to the ship's commissary. The consumption levels of the bagels in question, the Navy eventually admitted, were well within the range of "normal dietary use."

The pharmaceutical companies that sell the tests list the *known* substances that are *proven* to cross-react, but that doesn't mean that those administering the tests can always be depended upon to possess this information or use it wisely. It should be noted, too, that the test manufacturers admit the tests are sometimes just plain wrong, poppy seeds or no poppy seeds; currently, the line is that urinalysis carries no more than a 5 percent inaccuracy rate. (This is misleading, however, as we shall see.)

Five percent doesn't seem like much, does it? Many businesses and organizations seem to have deemed that error rate to be an acceptable level of risk. Stop for a moment, though, and ask yourself this: What happens if you are the unlucky one out of twenty wrongly identified as a drug abuser? Remember, the mere presence of a positive on your test is usually enough to brand you as a person with a drug problem. By contrast, a breathalyzer test for alcohol is designed to determine whether you have consumed *too much* liquor. Drug testing recognizes no such niceties: If the buzzer goes off, you're one of the bad guys.

A little background is probably in order here. Drug testing recognizes (or, at any rate, is meant to recognize) whether miniscule traces of a certain substance are present in the urine. While marijuana, which accounts for over 90 percent of all positive findings, stays in an average-sized body for about three weeks, the length of time any substance stays in your system is affected by your actual body weight.

Now then. Since the question is not whether you *decided* to put a substance in your body, but whether it is *present*, an interesting set of issues arises. We are all well aware of the ongoing conflict over second-hand cigarette smoke; current evidence indicates that even those who don't smoke tobacco can, if they breathe air polluted by cigarette smoke, suffer adverse health effects as a result. The smoke still enters the body, even if you don't have a cigarette between your lips. Well, marijuana makes smoke, too. And you don't have to smoke it for it to show up in your system; just go to a party where someone else is smoking it, or sit next to a puffing Wall Streeter at a Grateful Dead concert, and you could have your professional reputation destroyed by an "accurate" drug test the next day!

What's more, the 5 percent accuracy rate claimed by the manufacturers of urinalysis tests is, while true in the strict sense, not meaningful in practical terms. In clinical testing conditions, these tests have indeed been shown to perform at or under 5 percent where errors are concerned. But your drug test will not be conducted in clinical testing conditions. It will be conducted "in the field"—out in the real world, where things aren't monitored quite so closely. When the lab's emphasis is on weeding out drug users (rather than on research), the error rate can be expected to balloon to 14 percent, according to estimates made in the *Journal of Analytic Toxicology*.

But why should we rely on estimates? The Center for Disease Control (CDC) and the National Institute on Drug Abuse (NIDA) ran a nine-year study on the accuracy of private-sector laboratories. Private-sector labs, where your specimen is most likely to be handled, hardly inspire confidence: they don't have to be licensed, they usually operate under no legislated employee training requirements, and they are often staffed by workers receiving only minimum wage. The results of the study? Brace yourself.

When the labs knew the specimens in question came from the CDC and the NIDA, the results were extremely impressive and could serve as a model for any testing program. But when the labs did not know who the specimens were coming from—when the specimen, in other words, could have been yours—a very different picture emerged. Up to sixty-six out of a hundred samples showed false positives. That translates to two-thirds of a given group of people having their reputations and careers destroyed for no particular reason. At the same time, the inaccuracy rate for screening known abusers under these "blind" conditions was shown to rise to as high as 100 percent! Translation: the labs gave a clean bill of health to up to 100 percent of the sample specimens *known* to contain traces of illegal drugs.

It's quite clear, then, that the claims of the pharmaceutical industry notwithstanding, there is cause for considerable concern when it comes to accuracy in urinalysis testing. In theory, the numbers may border on acceptable (though they are not iron-clad by any means); in practice, however, the record is horrendous.

What causes the inaccuracy? First of all, juggling urine specimens all day long is not exactly everyone's idea of ultimate career fulfillment; it is not surprising that the quality of work is less than exemplary. Second, urine testing is easy to do incorrectly. The specimens go stale quickly and react poorly to extremes of heat and cold. In addition, urine that is too acidic or too alkaline can skew the test results; these problems can be caused simply by the subject's eating spicy foods.

Bearing all of this depressing news in mind, then, how are you supposed to answer when asked whether you would submit to a drug test?

If you want the job offer—and at the early stage of the game the offer is all that's important—your short answer is "Yes." There is nothing at all wrong with answering in this way and using whatever offer may arise to negotiate with other employers, as outlined earlier in this book. Remember that being asked *whether* you would take a test is not the same thing as being asked *when* you would take a test. Initially, the question is invariably placed on a hypothetical footing: "Would you have any problem with taking a drug test?" And once you assent to the testing, you have about a fifty-fifty chance of making it through without actually being asked to provide a specimen.

When it appears that the drug test is about to move from the hypothetical into the realm of stark reality, though, you will need to protect yourself. Your good reputation could be in jeopardy.

Prior to the testing, an ethical company will give you a form to read, fill in, and sign. This formalizes your permission to conduct the test, and affirms your willingness to comply with company policies on the matter. The form should also list all the over-the-counter and prescription drugs—and other ingestible substances—known to cross-react with the test that will be used. Be sure to indicate on the form any of these substances and all drugs and medications you have taken recently. (The form often asks you to note what has been taken "within the week," but you should also list any medications you have taken in the past few weeks. Depending on your body weight, one week may not be enough to flush the residues from your system.)

Do not fail to note *every* applicable item! Five minutes ago you had no idea that a bagel or a cold medication could earn you a reputation as a lowlife; nothing is "innocent" when it comes to cross-reaction with drug tests. And all tests cross-react with something!

If the above-mentioned ethical courtesies are not extended to you prior to the test, cover yourself by saying something along the following lines.

> "Yes, I would of course be willing to take a drug test as part of the condition of employment. However, I have seen some reliable reporting that says many of these tests could show me to be a drug abuser if I have taken something as innocuous as a headache pill. I have been assured that you will not take offense if I ask what medications the test is known to cross-react with."

Again, if you are provided with the list, you should add whatever medications you have been taking, whether or not they appear on the list. If the company is unable or unwilling to give you the list you will be faced with a judgment call. Only you can say how important your good name is. In this case, you might ask whether, under the circumstances, the company would be willing to have your personal physician administer the test.

If the test should show a positive result, ethical organizations will agree to guarantee you a backup test *of another type* because of the chance of a false reading. Reputable pharmaceutical companies and laboratories recommend an additional test upon the first occurrence of a positive; you are well within your rights to ask whether you will be given this basic consideration. If the company in question refuses to offer you a backup test, there is a good chance it is because they are costly and the company is short-sighted enough to want to scrimp in this area. It is your decision whether or not to interview or work at such a firm.

There is, unfortunately, more bad news you should be aware of when it comes to corporate drug-testing policies. A number of companies have shown themselves to be less than ethical in their handling of samples received as a result of drug testing; people have unwittingly been tested for asthma, diabetes, epilepsy, and even pregnancy. Check the form carefully before signing it, and if there appear to be loopholes you'd rather see closed, point them out.

Suppose that, somewhere during the process, someone at the firm comments suspiciously that you seem remarkably well briefed on this topic. You might reply along these lines.

> "Yes, I am; this is because I realize that there is only one thing more important to a professional than his or her competence, and that is reputation. Being a person who is attentive to detail and proud of it, I took the time to research this issue thoroughly."

Your demeanor is all-important; if you act like you have something to hide, people will assume that you do. Stay calm, and express your concerns from a position of self-assured professionalism.

So much for the preliminaries. We move now to the question of what to do if you have decided it is in your best interests to take a drug test. If you are, rightly or wrongly, identified as a drug user, there will be three pertinent questions to answer.

- Will word reach your colleagues in the professional community, and if so, when?
- Will word reach your neighborhood, and if so, when?
- If you are branded as a drug abuser, just how long will it take you to get another job?

They aren't pleasant questions to have to answer; my feeling is that you should give yourself every advantage before the test, so that you will reduce your chances of ever having to face these quandaries. I am not saying you should "cheat"; as we have seen, the problem is not so much people cheating on drug tests as drug tests cheating innocent people out of rightful opportunity. You should, in my view, do everything in your power to avoid being placed in a compromising position. Following are suggestions of some things you can do to put the odds in your favor before you take the test.

The moment you learn that you may have to take a test, your objective should be to flush your body out. Drink lots and lots of water; seize every opportunity to void yourself the day of the test. If you can, schedule the test for after work; claim that it is impossible for you to get away in the morning. The most concentrated urine specimens are those generated first thing in the morning; those given later in the afternoon are less potent.

You will want to make use of as many diuretics (items that promote urination) as you can work into your diet. Coffee, tea, and juices are excellent diuretics; so is beer, but you should not drink alcohol prior to an interview, for reasons I have outlined elsewhere in this book.

Jogging or working out makes you sweat, which helps clean out the system. Exercise also improves alertness and physical agility. (Anyone in pursuit of a new job should exercise on a regular basis, anyway.)

Saunas and steam baths will help remove impurities from your system, as well as increase your need to consume liquids. What's more, they are relaxing, rejuvenating, and good for the skin.

Finally, you may want to pick up a bottle of B-complex vitamins and take some for the few days preceding your test date. They are good for you, of course, and will leave all sorts of wholesome stuff in your specimen, but they will also give the little glass jar you pass in a healthy yellow glow that fairly shouts: "This one is no crack addict!" (Well, appearances do count for something.)

□ □ □

Remember, in the early stages, your goal is to generate offers; you want people bidding for your services. Even an offer you don't want can be leveraged into another and better offer elsewhere. Once you know you want to work at a given company, you will have to decide for yourself whether it is worth undergoing the rigors and uncertainties of drug testing to obtain a job there. Many people decide that it is, and for reasons that are perfectly valid for them. I would suggest, though, that you bear in mind that potential employers are on their best behavior when wooing new recruits; if you have to go through all of this prior to the wedding, what sort of marriage is it likely to be?

By the way, if you do decide *against* working for a company that insists on drug testing, you might consider writing the higher-ups in the firm to tell them—politely—the reasons underlying your decision. Many of these executives have no idea how difficult or degrading undergoing a drug test can be. An argument can certainly be made that they should be exposed to the concerns of the people whose lives their decisions affect; too often, company policies are established in an insulated environment that does not take basic human sensibilities into account.

Corporate America is currently wringing its collective hands over the perceived fickleness and lack of loyalty in today's work force; but those in authority really should not be surprised if this is the case. Loyalty is a two-way street; today, employees and potential employees are sometimes so casually assumed to be guilty before proven innocent that they cannot be faulted for seeking to make a contribution elsewhere.

26.
How to Beat the Psychological Tests

In late 1989, Congress banned most private-sector applications of the polygraph test, voice stress analysis, and other electronic screening methods. While many government personnel (for instance, those involved in drug interdiction activities) are still subject to these tests, many private employers have had to change their ways, and are increasingly turning to psychological testing to weed out what they consider to be undesirable job applicants. These tests may be known as aptitude tests, personality profiles, or some other name, but in the end they are all the same thing: the next-best thing to the old, now-illegal methods for finding out whether you show signs of being a "risky" hire.

Actually, although the 1989 legislation has led to new popularity for the psychological tests, they have been around for decades. Psychological exams come in two flavors: One is a face-to-face meeting with a psychologist, and the other (far more common) is a written test, often multiple choice.

In any discussion of this issue, we should bear in mind that psychology is, by the admission of its own practitioners, an inexact science. It cannot yield any definitive litmus test on your potential employability. Yet many companies are pretending that it can, and are grafting the imprecise discipline of psychological testing onto the equally imprecise one of employment selection. The result is an essentially insight-free mess that is, nevertheless, easy to administer, relatively cheap, and increasingly popular. Those seeking employment are often asked to answer "a few routine questions" that end up being anything but routine. The tests, which are (in theory) not to be used as the sole basis for a hiring decision, can nevertheless have a huge effect on people's livelihoods.

The whole concept of psychological testing is fraught with controversy. Some view the tests as an intrusion into private life, and with good reason: They often ask blatantly illegal questions about, say, your religious beliefs. Others request information about your sexuality, and many of these queries are illegal in states that have adopted legislation protecting freedom of sexual preference. Laws or no laws, however, there the questions are, in black and white. If you refuse to take a test that is a "required" part of the selection process, you will almost certainly be denied employment. (Not surprisingly, several court cases have been initiated by disgruntled applicants.)

It isn't surprising that many of the companies using the tests are concerned about the potential honesty of prospective employees. Each year American industry loses an estimated $40 billion from employee theft. But while honesty is often one of the behavioral profiles examined, the tests tend to emphasize the examination of aptitude and suitability. Often, the exams are geared to evaluating the amount of energy a person might bring to the job, how he or she would handle stress, and what attitude toward job, peers, and management would be likely to be prevalent.

Unfortunately, answering a psychological test with complete personal honesty may very well threaten your chance of being offered employment. That's the bad news. Here's the good news: you can beat the tests without having to compromise your personal integrity.

Not long ago I did an in-house employee selection and motivation seminar for a large corporation; I was asked for my opinion on the subject of psychological testing. I replied that the tests were often used inappropriately as a pass/fail criterion for hiring, and that anyone with half a mind could come up with the desired or correct answers. "The question is," I concluded, "how many people who could have served you well will you miss out on because of a test?"

The managers assured me that they had a test in use that was "virtually infallible" in helping to identify strong hires, and certainly not subject to the machinations of the average applicant. They asked if I would be prepared to take it. I not only agreed, but also promised to prove my point. "Let me take the test twice," I said. "The first profile you get will tell you to hire me; the second will say I'm a bad risk."

I took the test twice that day. "Applicant #1" came back with a strong recommendation for hire. "Applicant #2" came back with a warning to exercise caution before considering taking him on.

How was this possible? Well, there is something the tests ignore: None of us is the same person in the workplace as in our personal life. Over a period of time at work, we come to understand the need for different behavioral patterns and different ways of interacting with people.

Sometimes our more considered, analytical, logical approaches pass over from our "professional self" into the personal realm. However, in the world of work, we are not expected to try to override the "corporate way" of doing things with our personal preferences. When this happens, and personal preferences take precedence over existing corporate theories of behavior, we get warnings and terminations. In other words, as professionals we are inculcated with a set of behavioral patterns that are supplied to us over the years to enable us to be successful and productive for our employers.

Did I really "fool" the test? No. I was completely honest both times. The "winning" test was the one in which I viewed myself—and, thus, described myself—as the thoroughly professional white-collar worker in the job for which I was applying. The "losing" test was the one I used to describe myself as the kind of person I see myself in my personal life.

This was not a hoax perpetrated by a smart aleck. I am that person they would have hired, and I possess a strong track record to back up my claim. I learned the behaviors necessary to succeed, adopted them, and made them my own—just as you have undoubtedly done.

Many of the tests simply lack an awareness of the complexity of the human mind. They seem to miss the point when they ask us to speak honestly about our feelings and beliefs. They do not take into account that our learned behaviors in our professional lives are, invariably, quite distinct from the behaviors we accept in our personal lives.

The secret of my success—and of yours, if you must take a psychological test—is really quite simple.

How to Prepare for, Read, and Answer the Tests
Born independently wealthy, very few of us would be doing the jobs we do. But we *are* doing them, and we have learned certain sets of skills and behavioral traits that are critical to our ability to survive and succeed professionally. The first thing you must do, then, is identify and separate the professional you from the personal you.

☐ **Step One: Never consider answering a test from the viewpoint of your innermost beliefs.** Instead, use your learned and developed professional behavior traits and modus operandi. Ask yourself, "How has my experience as a professional _____ taught me to think and respond to this?"

To do this effectively (and to understand ourselves a little better in the process), we need some further insights into the three critical skill sets that every professional relies on to succeed.

- Professional/technical skills (whether you're a secretary or a senior vice president)
- Industry skills (such as—if you happen to be in banking—your overall knowledge of the world of banking: how things work, how things get done, what is accepted within the industry, and so on)
- Professional behavior traits (the traits, discussed in chapter 14 of this book, that all employers look for, and that will get you ahead once you are on the job)

☐ **Step Two: Look at yourself from the employer's point of view.** (Review "The Five Secrets of the Hire," and "The Other Side of the Desk" for some helpful ideas.) Evaluate what traits come into play that enable you to discharge your duties effectively. Examine the typical crises/emergencies that are likely to arise: What supportive behavioral traits are necessary to overcome them? As you do this, you will almost certainly relive some episodes that seemed to put you at a disadvantage for a time. When it was tough to do things the right way, you had to buckle down and see the problem through, even though doing so did not necessarily "come naturally." The fact is, though, you overcame the obstacle. Remember *how* you did so, and keep that in mind as you answer the questions.

Conversely, you will want to look at those instances where a crisis had a less-than-successful outcome. What traits did you swear you would develop and use for next time?

Highlighting such traits simply constitutes your acknowledgment of the supremacy of learned behavior in the workplace. It does *not* constitute lying. (Why do you think so many professionals strive to keep their business lives separate from their personal lives? What is the point of such a separation if the two lives are identical?)

☐ **Step Three: Think of people you've known who have failed on the job.** Why did they fail? What have you learned from their mistakes and made a part of the "professional you"?

☐ **Step Four: Think of people you've known who have succeeded on the job.** Why did they succeed? What have you learned from their success and made a part of the "professional you"?

Once you have completed this exercise in detail, you will have effectively determined how a professional _____ would react in a wide range of circumstances, and identified the ways in which you have, over time, developed a "professional self" to match that profile.

Getting Ready for the Test

Any test can be nerve-wracking, but when it comes to psych tests your livelihood is in the balance. Desperate times, of course, call for desperate measures. Accordingly, you should be sure, as you enter the testing area, that you are armed with the ultimate failsafe. If at all possible, carry with you the one object that will guarantee you the chance to make the best possible impression as you take the test: a cup of coffee. (Yes, I am serious; the reasoning here will become clear very soon.)

The tests instruct you to answer quickly, offering the first response that comes to mind. Don't. Following this path may well cost you a job. Instead, look at the test in terms of the exercises outlined above; provide reasoned responses from the viewpoint of the "professional you."

Time limits are usually not imposed; on the contrary, those administering the test will often begin the proceedings with a soothing "Take your time, there's no pressure." (Except, of course, the minor pressure of knowing a job offer is on the line!)

In a face-to-face meeting with a psychologist, use the same techniques we have discussed throughout *Knock 'em Dead* to qualify the questions before answering them; when you suspect a trap, employ the tricks that will help you clarify things and buy time.

Beware: the written tests may contain "double blinds," where you are asked a question on page one, and then asked a virtually identical one thirty or forty questions later. The technique is based on the belief that most of us can tell a lie, but few of us can remember that lie under stress, and are therefore likely to answer differently later. This is held to show the potential for untruthfulness. The problem isn't that one answer is likely to deny you employment; the questions are asked in patterns to evaluate your behavior and attitudes on different topics.

So: Read the test through before you start answering questions! (There's "plenty of time" and "no pressure," remember?) Review the material at least three times, mentally flagging the questions that seem similar. This way you will be assured of consistency.

Of course, you are likely to encounter ethics questions. "Have you ever stolen anything?" "Have you ever felt guilty?" "Have you ever told a lie?" Avoid the temptation to respond impulsively with something like "Lies? No, I prefer to chop down the damned cherry tree." The truth is we have all done these things in our lives. When you are asked, for instance, whether there is anything you would ever change about yourself, or whether you think everyone is dishonest to some degree, the overwhelming likelihood is that your own honesty is being tested: The best answer is probably "yes."

If you must address ethics matters in a face-to-face encounter, you can explain your answer, placing it far in the past where appropriate, and explain what you learned from the experience. If such questions must be answered on paper, the best approach is to follow the dictates of your own conscience and try to bring the issue up after the test. You might say something like this:

> "Gee, that question about lying was a tough one. I guess every-
> one has told a lie at some time in the past, and I wanted to be
> truthful, so I said 'yes.' But I'd be lying if I didn't tell you it
> made me nervous. You know, I saw a show on television re-
> cently about these tests. It told the story of someone who lost a
> job because of answering a question just like that; the profile
> came back with an untrustworthy rating."

This should reduce the odds of your being denied the job in the same way. If the test does come back with a question about your honesty, you will at least have sown seeds of doubt about the validity of such a rating in the interviewer's mind. That doubt, and your disarming honesty, might just turn the tables in your favor.

Resist any temptation to project an image of yourself as an interesting person by the answers you select. These tests are not designed to reward eccentricity; think sliced white bread. You are happy at work and home. You enjoy being around people. You don't spend all your evenings watching movies (unless your name is Siskel or Ebert). You don't spend your weekends with a computer or pursuing other solitary pastimes (unless you are a programmer or an aspiring Trappist monk). You have beliefs, but not too strong. You respect the beliefs of all others, regardless of their age, sex, race, or religion.

When you finish the test, read through your answers a few times; if you don't like one or two, change them. Don't change too many; if you do, you will risk appearing indecisive. However, if you have a lot of changes, just spill your coffee over the test (I told you there was a reason to bring that cup in with you). Throw the test in the trash—near the top, of course, where its condition can be verified— and ask for another copy. Since you will likely have some measure of privacy for taking the test, you can take on the new test with the added benefit of having the old one in front of you. (You don't mind retrieving that slightly sodden document for the sake of your career, do you?)

□   □   □

All of what I have said here takes for granted that the overriding goal of the employer is to determine whether or not you are suitable for the job. If you can give an accurate affirmative answer to that question, then the approach you take in doing so is—to my way of thinking, anyway—of little consequence. If you have learned and applied what it takes to prosper in your profession, then it is emphatically your right to provide an honest profile of your professional self, in whatever forum you are to be evaluated.

V

In Depth

What if things aren't clicking?

It has happened to more than one job search. A strong start encounters an occasional obstacle, then a somewhat-more-than-occasional obstacle, then a series of increasingly predictable obstacles, and finally a steady rain of obstacles. On some days, it looks like there is considerably more obstacle to your campaign than anything else. Lethargy and discouragement set in. What's more, bills maintain a nagging habit of requiring payment, which can be tiresome even if you are still employed—and downright crushing if you're not. Rejection, pressure, withering self-esteem: You know them better than you'd ever imagined you would. Nobody else on earth seems to have a sense of humor about all this. Why should you?

Similar obstacles, of course, can arise on the job. Careers get stalled, promotions fail to materialize, jobs demand change. While there's nothing particularly amusing about career problems, you should bear in mind that your biggest potential asset and/or liability in the search is the person staring back at you from the bathroom mirror each morning. That person is a walking, talking advertisement—pro or con—of your professionalism. If the face you see is drawn, pale, aggravated, or simply tired, you need to stop and take stock. You may be short-circuiting your own efforts.

In this section of the book, we'll look at a number of different ways to rescue a stalled job hunt, as well as some techniques for making the financial pinch you may be feeling a little more bearable. Finally, we'll examine the best ways to maintain strong career growth and stability once you actually get the position you want.

27.
How to Jump-Start a Stalled Job Search

Okay. You've been out of work for a while. You're low on ideas, and your get-up-and-go gas tank reads "empty." You don't know which way to turn. The things you've done so far just haven't panned out. It's time to take it from the top.

Believe it or not, you can start over again, and you have certain advantages in doing so. At least some of the people who screened you out so many months ago have, in all likelihood, moved on to another place (hopefully a hot and fetid one in the hereafter). Sure, most of the jobs you applied for have been filled, but a whole new batch has now opened up. And if there were ill economic winds blowing through an industry you took a fancy to, perhaps things aren't looking quite so bad anymore for some of the companies that were on your list.

With little adjustments here and there, and a bit more attention to a few key points, this can be a whole new ballgame. Following are some suggestions on how to rescue a faltering job search campaign.

Get a New Resume
White collar or blue collar, executive V.P. or electrician, you should throw out what you've got and start over from scratch. The current version isn't working. Your resume must get your foot in the door, set the tone for the interview, and, after all the shouting, act as your last and most powerful advocate when the final hiring decision is being made. Build one from ground up that does this.

Write at least two new drafts. One should be in chronological format; the other should be in either functional or combination format. Although there is helpful advice on resume writing in this book, at this stage I recommend that you complete the detailed questionnaire in the first part of *Resumes That Knock 'em Dead*, which will help you evaluate exactly what you have to offer potential employers.

Don't pooh-pooh the idea of rewriting your resume by claiming that "getting your foot in the door hasn't been the problem." It is entirely possible that your resume is strong enough to get you in the race, but doesn't pack enough punch to get over the finish line ahead of the competition.

Rewrite Your Cover Letter

Adhering to a single, bland, "one-size-fits-all" cover letter is a common mistake. Remember, different circumstances require different letters. There are over a dozen different categories of cover and follow-up letters; they are detailed in my book *Cover Letters That Knock 'em Dead.* By following the advice there you will be able to craft a unique, memorable set of professional letters.

I would advise you to make a commitment to send follow-up letters with religious zeal if you are not already doing so. This may seem like a minor detail, but it is one of the most important—and easiest—ways for you to stand out from the competition.

When it comes to cover and follow-up letters, the whole really is greater than the sum of its parts. Employers maintain dossiers on every candidate during the selection process; your coordinated written campaign makes you stand out from the other contenders as someone who pays a little bit more attention to detail, who goes a little further to get the job done. Armed with your improved resume and cover letter, reread chapter 4 ("The Hidden Job Market") and follow its advice to the letter. Don't worry about sending your new resume to companies you've already contacted. A new resume means a new you.

Work as a Temporary

Get hold of a temporary employment directory for your area. (See chapter 4 for details on this resource.) Contact every appropriate temporary-help company listed and offer your services.

There are two benefits to working with a temporary help company. First, while you retain adequate time to pursue a structured job hunt, you get some work and a paycheck—thereby keeping your skills current and, just as important, the wolf from the door. Second, you may be able to upgrade that temp job into a full-time position. (At the very least, you can expand your contact network.)

Today, there are temporary companies that represent professionals at virtually all levels. Some even specialize solely in management people, and high-level ones at that, because companies are increasingly inclined to "test-drive" executives before making a permanent commitment to them. Interim Management Corporation (IMCOR) is typical of this new breed of temporary company; almost 40 percent of their assignments result in full-time employment.

Check Your References and Credit Rating

Do it now. Don't let a mystery problem sabotage an offer at the last moment. You'd be surprised how many otherwise qualified candidates eventually learn that they were taken out of the running by flunking the "tiebreaker" test. Two or more people are under final consideration; management decides to run a credit check and/or call references to help them decide who will get the job. If you have not attended to these areas, you should. Credit problems can undo months of preparatory work on your part; mediocre (or worse) references can be just as problematic.

Chapter 4 covers the topic of references in detail. (And remember, *all* of the references you give must be sterling!) For some ideas on repairing a negative credit report, see chapter 28.

Widen the Scope of Your Job Search

Under what other job titles could you work? Can you commute an extra twenty minutes for the right job? Consider relocation to another city, but bear in mind that for most of us this is an extremely costly proposition, and that you should not depend on a firm's picking up your moving expenses. On the other hand, if you are single and can fit all your earthly possessions in the back seat of your Festiva, some far-flung operation may be worth serious consideration.

Twenty Keys to Success

If you are having trouble at the interview, odds are you have not thoroughly assimilated chapter 14 of this book, which highlights the twenty key personality traits employers love and shows you how to project them. Reread this chapter.

Smokestack

This used to mean keeping an eye out for smokestacks over the course of the day. Today it more commonly means remembering to incorporate job hunting as part of your daily routine. Stop in and see what firms are in that office building you pass every morning. Perhaps there are opportunities there for you.

Of course, you are not going to get far by simply appearing at the reception desk and demanding an interview. Be a little more circumspect. Ask—politely—about the firm in question. What does it do? Who is in charge of hiring? Are there any circulars, advertisements, or company reports you can take home with you? After your initial visit, you can incorporate this information into a new research file for the company and add the firm to your database of leads.

Body Check

This topic was covered briefly in the earlier section on dressing for interview success, but if you find yourself running into brick walls on the job search front it's a good idea to look at the most important points more thoroughly. Remember, one's personal friends often have trouble bringing up this subject; people in a position to hire simply move on to the next applicant.

If you do not brush and floss regularly, you have bad breath, and this will not aid your candidacy. If you eat a lot of spicy foods (onions, garlic, cilantro), you may be aware of the importance of keeping your breath fresh after a pungent meal, but this is not, alas, your only worry. These foods typically sour your sweat and taint your clothing. Change your diet and have your interview clothes cleaned before every wearing. (But note that polyester and other synthetic fabrics are notorious for retaining body odors even after cleaning—one of many reasons to avoid them.)

Have you put on a few pounds while looking for work? Many people use eating as a response to stress. Turn off the TV once a day and get some exercise; Nick at Nite will still be there after you work out. Couch potatoes don't make good candidates—period. Regular physical activity will improve your appearance *and* your mindset, so don't skip it.

These suggestions may be difficult for you to implement if they run counter to long-established patterns, but being in a permanent job-search mode is, you must admit, a much more daunting prospect. If you need motivation, recall the statistical truth that overweight and malodorous people are always the last to get hired or promoted.

Prepare, Prepare, Prepare
It may seem obvious, but all too often this is the step that people take for granted. When you walk into the interview, you should be ready to answer all the questions you could ever be asked, as well as all the ones you couldn't. Relevant portions of this book, especially Part 4, "Finishing Touches," will be invaluable on this score.

Don't make the mistake of preparing only for the questions you want to hear!

Follow Up
I worked for some years as a headhunter and corporate personnel director. I can't count the number of times managers told me that there was really nothing to distinguish Candidate A (who got the job) from Candidate B (who didn't)—*except that Candidate A showed an unusual level of determination and attention to detail.* The way Candidate A conveyed this, of course, was usually through a dogged follow-up campaign.

After every job interview, review the recommended follow-up procedure in chapter 21, "Out of Sight, Out of Mind," and implement it.

Remember: There Are Dream Jobs and There Is the Dream of a Job
Even though this has been touched on earlier in this book, it bears repeating in this context. If you have been unemployed for a significant period of time, you might find it fiscally prudent to accept that less-than-perfect job. That's okay. By the same token, there is a big difference between settling for less than your dreams and making the wrong job your life's work. If circumstances force you to take a temporary detour from your ultimate career goal, give an honest day's work for an honest day's pay and continue to pursue other opportunities.

Remember: You're the Most Important Part of This
Maintain ongoing motivational input. Reading this book and its two companion books, *Resumes That Knock 'em Dead* and *Cover Letters That Knock 'em Dead* is a good start; you should also keep an eye on the *National Business Employment Weekly* (NBEW), available at newsstands. It is full of help wanted ads and features motivational, how-to, career, and job-hunting articles. NBEW also provides a weekly list of self-help group events. Additionally, you should consider visiting the library to check out motivational tapes and related materials. You're worth it.

You are not a loser; you got blindsided. The trick is to get back in the saddle. If you climb up and grip the reins, tomorrow you'll see all kinds of opportunities you didn't see before.

28.
Keeping the Financial Boat Afloat

For too many of us, it actually takes losing a job in tough times to illustrate how close to the economic edge we usually live. To be sure, we take on financial obligations of our own free will—but the media, the society we live in, and, yes, our erstwhile employers all encourage standards of consumption we quickly learn to take for granted.

If you are reading this in a state of shock because you have recently been terminated, have a seat and take a deep breath. Things are probably not as bad as they seem right about now, but even if they were, you would need to keep your wits about you. Rash decisions, decisions made in desperation, are the ones we end up regretting. Take some time to decompress.

When Still inside the Building . . .
If, on the other hand, you are lucky enough to be reading this before your termination has been finalized, you should be very careful how you approach matters. It goes without saying that you should check your instinct to settle old scores or to lash out at the firm that is letting you go, but there are other important pieces of advice you should follow as well. Most of what follows is meant for those who have fallen victim to staffing cuts, but some of the ideas can be adapted to those who are terminated under less than favorable conditions—especially Rule Number One.

Rule Number One is simple: *Don't sign anything* until you are convinced you have everything the law, ethical considerations, and good old-fashioned guilt can elicit from the employer.

Ask about outplacement services. Outplacement firms are companies that provide you with job-hunting assistance ranging from a one-day seminar to "as-long-as-it-takes" counseling. This type of program is increasingly common; don't feel guilty about asking for it.

Negotiate the best-possible severance package. A week's severance pay for every year of service is the standard, inadequate though it is. Whatever you are offered, try to wheedle a little more. Point out that times are tough; if the unemployment rate is high, say so, and use actual numbers if you can. Remember, guilt works. Those that don't ask, don't get.

Find out what your benefits will be over the next months. Murphy's law, which states that whatever can go wrong will, applies with double force to the unemployed. Under the current insurance laws, you can continue the health plan your employer provided for you at a subsidized rate for up to eighteen months, after which time you can continue on the same plan at a (much higher) personal rate.

Determine the company policy on providing references. Sometimes companies will give no more than salary and dates of employment to those who call asking about your tenure there, regardless of your level of performance; this can adversely affect your job hunt. If you learn that this is the policy in your case, get a written letter to that effect to show to potential employers. If at all possible, you should obtain a written testimonial from your manager before you sign anything or leave the company.

You and I know, of course, that a reference is essentially the same thing as a letter testifying to your character. It is gratifying, however, how many superiors bidding a reluctant adieu to a team member are willing to forget this point. If you run into "company policy" trouble here, you can point out that you are not asking for an official reference, but the supervisor's personal evaluation of you as one professional discussing another. The fact that the personal reference need not appear on company stationery is usually a plus in obtaining the letter.

Request that the employer tell callers that you are unavailable, rather than unemployed, and that you will return all calls. Obviously, you won't be able to make this last forever, but you may be able to maintain at least the appearance of gainful employment. Every little bit helps.

If it isn't part of your outplacement package, try asking for desk space and telephone cost reimbursement for your job hunt. Of course, this is only feasible if you work in an appropriate office environment. Asking for desk space and telephone time in, say, a retail setting will do nothing but brand you as a head case. Assuming the circumstances are favorable for such a request, you may be able to get two or three months worth of help, or perhaps a flat cash payment. You certainly shouldn't rely on this, but it could be worth asking about.

Ask for professional financial counseling. In case the employer hasn't thought of this (a good bet), call an accountant for an estimate of the amount of money involved; the *Yellow Pages* are a good resource to use if you don't already know of a reputable accountant. Say, "I've just been laid off; I'm married, with two kids and a mortgage. I want to know how much you'd charge to help me create a liveable, pared-down budget." Then go to the employer with the figure. If a number of people are being let go, you may be able to get the employer to spring for a seminar for everyone.

Once You've Left the Building . . .

The time for all of the above has passed. You and the employer have parted company, and you must make some sense of the financial picture before you. If you don't face up to the financial problems of unemployment in a timely fashion, you may end up losing everything except the shopping cart. So face the facts early— and if you didn't do it early, do it now. Immediate action will only help you reach the point where problems are rectified all the sooner. Procrastination can only worsen your situation.

If you have stocks or stock options, you may want to consider cashing them in. However, you should be prepared to pay a capital gains tax on your profits. If you have a vested company-sponsored pension plan, this will merit your close attention, as well. I have heard of employees who had to sue to get monies owed them through these plans, but this problem generally arises only with smaller employers. Check with an accountant or financial advisor for all the details.

You may have the option of having your severance moneys paid out to you on a regular basis, approximating the payment pattern of your wages, or in a lump sum. Arguments run in two directions on this. Some feel that it is to your advantage to have the payments spread out because this realistically defines you as being on the payroll and, therefore, at least technically employed. Others argue, though, that such a ruse is often of marginal aid, and point out that in a time of severe financial stress, you should at least earn some interest on your money.

Your best course is probably to ask to have the money paid out over a period, if you see a realistic prospect of an offer on the horizon, and if that offer will be aided by your being able to claim, legitimately, that you are still on someone's payroll. Otherwise, bank it all. If you do choose to deposit all the money, look at your calendar before the check is cut; for tax reasons, you will almost certainly want to avoid receiving huge sums late in the year.

That lump sum can be dangerous if you're not used to dealing with large amounts of cash; beware of the Payday Millionaire Syndrome. Now is not the time to use "all that money" to refinish your basement or get a new car. Be prudent with your cash. Strike that: Be *miserly* with your cash. Bear in mind that some authorities estimate it will take you, on average, one month of job hunting for every ten thousand dollars of yearly salary in your desired job. Whether or not that is accurate, you should prepare yourself for quite a wait between paychecks!

No matter how bad things get or how tempted you may be, avoid cashing in any IRAs you have—you will pay huge tax penalties. Instead, look into a loan against your IRA or any other tax-deferred annuity.

If you consider refinancing your home mortgage, take into account not only the new interest rates you will pay and your likelihood of moving within five years, but also any closing fees you will encounter. Closing costs on refinanced mortgages typically run between three and six thousand dollars as of this writing. There may also be tax issues to consider, and these could add to the cost of refinancing as well. You may end up pursuing savings that are illusory; check with a qualified financial adviser before refinancing.

Get a handle on your credit card use. *This is a vitally important point.*

It is natural to avoid the unpleasant, and no one enjoys the business of downgrading one's lifestyle expectations. But as bad as the picture may be, it can't be half as depressing as turning a blind eye to your problems. Avoid, at all costs, maintaining a false standard of living by pushing your credit card limits to the upper ionosphere. As will be detailed later in this chapter, your best course for now is simply to cut all existing cards (but one) in half.

Getting into credit difficulties will undermine your confidence, strain your personal relationships, put a big dent in your morale, and, most important of all, *stop you from getting hired!* You will remember from past experience, no doubt, that virtually all professional interviews these days are preceded by an application form with a space for your signature beneath a block of minute type. In that unreadable thicket of words, required by the Fair Credit Reporting Act of 1972, is an authorization for the employer to check your references and your credit history. Employers are usually quite content to process your application if they have your resume, your name, your address, and your signature on the application form. This signature, they will tell you, is simply something they "need for their records."

Uh-huh.

Credit agencies make a business of marketing their files to corporate employers, who use them as tools for evaluation of potential employees. The service is popular because credit information is seen as an indicator of future performance. This, of course, is based on the premise that knowing how a potential employee handles fiscal obligations provides a preview of that person's likelihood of stealing from the company, acting irresponsibly, or otherwise compromising the employer. Whether or not you agree with this idea, you should know that a bad credit rating has the potential to blow your candidacy right out of the water—and that it can do so even if *all* the other variables point to a successful outcome for your job search.

You can find out more about your credit rating by contacting the major national credit rating bureaus.

CSC Credit Services, Inc. (Houston, Texas): 713/878-4840
TransUnion Credit Information (Chicago, Illinois): 312/408-1050
CBI/Equifax (Atlanta, Georgia): 1-800/685-1111
TRW Consumer Assistance (Cleveland, Ohio): 1-800/682-7654

The last entry on that list may be the most useful to you. If you write TRW Consumer Assistance (the address is P.O. Box 2350, Chatsworth, California, 91313), you can get a printout of your credit report; this is free for the asking. The only limitation is that you can receive only one free report per year.

Credit bureaus are legally obligated to update reports containing factual errors, so be sure to notify the appropriate companies immediately if you find any mistakes. Even if you do not find outright misstatements on your report, you have some options. Many experts recommend that you send the credit bureau a letter explaining that your late or incomplete payments resulted from the loss of a job—a temporary state of affairs that is a world away from simple fiscal irresponsibility.

Starting Over
If you are in or are getting into debt as a result of losing your job, you should by all means face the problem squarely.

Sit down (with your family, if this is applicable) and review the situation. Air any unresolved issues and thoroughly examine your situation. Then work out your current monthly financial picture with a form something like the one reproduced below.

MONTHLY INCOME

Earnings	_____
Severance	_____
Spouse's salary	_____
Unemployment benefits*	_____
Withdrawal from savings	_____
Dividends	_____
Interest	_____
Gifts	_____
TOTAL INCOME:	_____

MONTHLY OBLIGATIONS/PAYMENTS

Rent/mortgage	_____
Taxes	_____
Groceries	_____
Clothing	_____
Household	_____
Loan repayments	_____
Car expenses	_____
Insurance	_____
Recreation	_____
Charitable contributions/dues/gifts	_____
Medical expenses	_____
Auto-related expenses	_____
Credit card repayments	_____
Job-search-related expenses	_____
Mortgage	_____
Home-equity loan	_____
Miscellaneous	_____
TOTAL OUTGOING:	_____

---

* If you have worked and received unemployment benefits in the same tax year, those unemployment benefits will be regarded as taxable income.

Once you know where you stand, there comes the dreaded task of taking action.

I said a little earlier on that you should, if you find yourself in financial difficulties while conducting your job search, simply cut your credit cards in half—all but one of them, at any rate. The one exception is to allow the member of the family who is conducting the job search to have some flexibility in obtaining stationery supplies, strategically selected interview wear, printing services, and the like. But even this carries with it a warning: Make your plastic job-search purchases prudent ones! This is not the time to update your entire wardrobe on the vague idea that you'll be going on *lots* of interviews and will therefore need *lots* of great clothes.

Treat your remaining credit card with the wary respect you would accord an adversary who has become a temporary ally—that is, someone who still very much bears watching. Bear in mind that it is misuse of credit cards, more than anything else, that is responsible for plunging the professional into hopeless levels of debt.

If your financial situation is giving you cause for concern, you might consider contacting the non-profit National Foundation for Consumer Credit at 301/589-5600. They have been providing free and low-cost counseling to people in financial hot water for over thirty years. With branches throughout the country, they can assist you in creating a workable budget and realistic plans for debt repayment, and they can even contact creditors on your behalf. Another good organization to contact is the National Center for Financial Education, which can be reached by calling 619/232-8811. They can advise you on a wide range of financial issues, including repairing your credit.

If Things Don't Look Good . . .
You might want to consider a debt consolidation loan. This is an arrangement whereby a loan is taken out to pay off all debts, giving you just one simple bill to deal with per month.

Such a loan looks like a great hassle eradicator, but it can cause more problems than it solves if you're not careful. Some people have taken out consolidation loans and gotten everything ship-shape—only to use the new "breathing room" they've won to charge their credit cards back up to the limit and push their home equity lines to dangerous levels. The result is not a reprieve from financial woes, but a doubling of their severity.

Whatever you do, watch out for the "credit repair" companies that offer to "fix" all your credit problems for a substantial but (considering the stakes) seemingly reasonable fee. The Federal Trade Commission has been all over these fly-by-night outfits, and with good reason. The overwhelming majority do nothing but take your money, dazzle you with words, and baffle you with B.S.—and I'm not talking undergraduate degrees here.

If the situation deteriorates to the point where bankruptcy seems to be a realistic prospect, I recommend that you contact creditors to negotiate even smaller payments than the ones you've been making. You may be surprised at their eagerness to work with you. Tell them what you can pay; if it's interest plus something, there is probably a deal to be worked out. Using the legitimate threat of bankruptcy to get creditors to offer you more favorable settlement arrangements is a powerful tool; credit card companies have been known to accept a fraction of what is owed them under these circumstances. The reason is simple: Once you go into bankruptcy, the creditors are likely to get nothing whatsoever from you. (By the way, this maneuver is one you can use but once in a lifetime. Sadly, it cannot be employed as an annual cost-cutting measure.)

For more information on personal bankruptcy, consult your attorney or contact the local bar association, which is listed in your phone directory and can refer you to a bankruptcy specialist in your price range.

On a more positive note, remember that there are many steps you can take to generate some interim cash that will see you through the tough times. You can:

- Rent out a room in your house.
- Get a part-time or temp job.
- Take out an ad in the local penny saver promoting your services as a repairperson (if you've always been good with your hands).
- Sell your professional services as a consultant.
- Turn a hobby into a profitable occupation. (A friend of mine lost her income and, being an artist, started an after-school art program for kids. Now she has three employees, is looking for more space, and is making over $60,000 per year. Very wisely, she contacted SCORE, the Service Corps of Retired Executives, for free counseling on how to start and operate her business. SCORE is sponsored by the Small Business Administration and has offices just about everywhere. For women and minorities, there are numerous low-interest loan programs available through the Small Business Administration. Contact your local office.)

Debt Collectors
If you're seriously considering talking to an attorney about filing for bankruptcy, chances are you are also being dunned by debt collectors, a fearsome species to say the least. People in this profession generally do not attend charm school as part of their training, so don't be surprised if you are addressed in a way that oversteps the *social* niceties. On the other hand, you should know when these people overstep their *legal* bounds.

The Fair Debt Collection Practices Act of 1977 protects you and your loved ones from illegal, rude, unfair, and unreasonable collection practices. Some of the specific limitations under which the debt collection industry must act are listed below.

- Debt collectors are forbidden to ask you for your telephone number, salary, payment dates, or place of employment. (But they may still use their own best efforts to locate you, and they can be depended upon to come after you when you find a new job.)

- Debt collectors can only speak to others about you in the context of determining your whereabouts. They cannot discuss with anyone the nature of their business with you unless you give them permission to do so.
- Debt collectors can contact you in person, by phone, or by letter—but only at times and places convenient to you.
- Debt collectors cannot harass or abuse you or anyone connected with you (such as a spouse or other family member) about the collection of your debt. This means telephone harassment, abusive language, and threats of violence are all out.

In all fairness to debt collectors, they have a job to do and bosses to pacify just like everyone else. Treat them with respect and they will probably return the favor. If you keep the channels of communication open, you probably won't have to worry about any of the above-mentioned horrors. But if you do have problems in any of these areas, don't hesitate to talk to a lawyer.

The Second Time Around
Time passes. (It always does.) Life continues, crises recede. This is a tough stretch, but it won't last forever. Once you make it through to the other side—and you will—take a look around and prepare yourself for a surprise. You will probably be a better person for all of this. The next time you're on a career roll, you will likely find it easier to forget the myriad admonishments we all receive to "live up to our income." The next time, you might be perfectly positioned to live up to your dreams instead.

29.
The Seven Secrets of Long-Term Career Survival

We talk about "job security," but in fact the only long-term career security you have sits between your ears. Even if you land the greatest job in the world, you must live your life in a world in which nothing, ultimately, is guaranteed. In this chapter we will cover some of the important truths that underlie any attempt to endure and prosper in a time of rapid technological and economic change.

Before we get into the specifics, a few words on mindset are in order. You will be happier if you do not view your career as an even tradeoff—your unquestioning loyalty for the employer's promise to require your services always. This unwavering relationship may have been the standard twenty or thirty years ago, but it is not so now. People should certainly have a measure of loyalty to the firms for which they work, but these days lifetime commitment is for altars, not cubicles.

After all, companies only have loyalty to the bottom right-hand corner of the quarterly profit and loss statement. (If they didn't have that loyalty, your paycheck would bounce.) It may seem harsh, but the fact is that you are a plentiful and renewable resource. You are, in a word, expendable.

But if a company has a responsibility to survive, you do too. This fact has not been lost on many of today's career writers and counselors, who have advised the development of a single area of high performance, one that transfers easily from one company (or industry) to another. Slogans such as "Become a specialist" and "Develop an expertise" have been offered as answers to the rapidly changing career picture so many emergent careerists face. Yet these are only partially correct responses to the problem.

Recognition in your "specialty" can actually get you pigeonholed and damage your future employability. The problem is that "specialists" all too often repeat a single year's experience, year in and year out. With the rapid technological changes in our world, the "specialist" may, ten years on, have the marketable equivalent of one year of experience repeated ten times—in an obsolete area of expertise, no less! This is not positioning yourself in a seller's market, not by a long shot.

No matter how stellar your performance, no matter how shrewdly you focus your efforts, you remain open to the risk that economic and technological changes will undermine your career. Of course, the "specialize" crew is right in pointing out that you can no longer expect the modern corporation to guarantee your employment. But there are seven important ways you can protect your *employability* over the long haul, ways you don't usually hear or read about. Here they are.

Secret #1: Join the Inner Circle

I have written in other books about the inner circles that develop in every department and in every company. These are the people whose input is requested on key decisions, and who are likely to have the best sense of *why* a given initiative is being pursued, rather than just *what* steps are being delegated to carry them out.

How do you get the invitation to that inner circle—which carries with it visibility, raises, plum assignments, and, most important for our purposes, the greatest possible relevant experience, stability, and future employability? There is a step-by-step approach you can follow.

During your first few days on the job, sit down with your boss and explain how much you want to make a success of your new position. Add that you are prepared to do whatever it takes to make your goal of becoming a valuable member of the team a reality (and mean it). There isn't a manager in the world who wouldn't like to hear this.

Continue by stressing that you want to maximize your strengths and minimize any weaknesses related to your inexperience by turning them into strengths. With this in mind, ask whether it would be possible for you and your boss to sit down on a regular basis over the first few months to make sure you are on the right track.

It should go without saying that, having begun in such a remarkable fashion, you must follow your plan to the letter and assiduously follow up any suggestions or guidance you receive. (Be forewarned: This plan is not recommended for members of the "4:59-and-I'm-outta-here" club!) Once the first three months have passed, tell your boss that you are so appreciative of the help you've received that you would like to continue the process on an informal basis by sitting down for a few minutes every two or three months to get feedback on your performance.

Several very interesting things happen when you take this approach. If you've been working for any length of time, you've probably noticed that, once a year, you have a formal performance review meeting with your manager—who typically knows little or nothing about the actual quality of your work. If you follow the advice I've just given, that same manager will be meeting with you six times more frequently than with anyone else in your department. You will also be the beneficiary of a great deal of one-on-one attention and positive feedback, not to mention the possibility of exposure to important information that might not otherwise come your way. As you travel down the road, you'll be picking up points and protecting your future at the same time.

Secret #2: Achieve Twenty-first Century Literacy

If you expect to be employable a decade from now, you had better set about achieving basic computer literacy. The bare minimum for anyone aspiring to a professional position will be an ability to execute daily communications at the terminal.

There is simply no excuse now for inability to function with a computer. Note that, by taking the minimal time to learn how to operate, say, a popular word processing program such as Microsoft Word, you will experience the added benefit of having a far more efficient and professional job search the next time you are out of work.

Secret #3: Mend Your Patchwork Quilt

The typical working professional is still clinging to an "updated" version of the same resume created to meet the needs of that first professional job hunt. After five, ten, or fifteen years of carefully adding subsequent jobs, the resulting document is less a resume than a patchwork quilt. Quilts don't win jobs nowadays.

Take the time to update your resume by rewriting it from scratch to reflect the dictates of the current employment environment. You never know when you will need it; don't procrastinate! Prudence dictates that we expect the best in our lives and prepare for the worst. Do it now.

Secret #4: The In Crowd

Have you noticed that all the really top-notch people in a given field seem to know one another—or at least are no more than a handful of phone calls from anyone in the business they have to contact?

How did these people get in the enviable position of being "in with the in crowd"? It's a little far-fetched to delude ourselves that they are all sons and daughters of *Fortune* 500 executives!

The truth is more prosaic. The top people in every field got that way by concerted long-term effort, and by making a point of communicating with and learning from their peers. These people have done many inspired things, and maintaining membership in at least one professional association is virtually always one of them. The theory is simple: If you can't have the opportunity to get to know everyone within the context of your job, you *can* get to know just about everyone of consequence by working with them at the same association meetings and functions.

When an employment need arises at a company, the first thing management does is scratch its collectively balding head and mutter, "Who do we know?" Then, apart from everyone management has worked with in the past, a mental spotlight shines on those extra special professionals, those folks who go that extra mile, the people who demonstrate their commitment and dedication to the profession with big infusions of time and effort. The people who come to mind are those met at association meetings.

Fortunately for you, finding and joining appropriate associations requires little more than thirty minutes in the local library. There you will examine a big fat book called the Encyclopedia of Associations, which details thousands of national and regional associations with appropriate contact information.

Don't get discouraged by that old saying, "It's not what you know, it's who you know." That only goes halfway. It should really end like this: " . . . it's who you get to know."

Secret #5: Reach Out and Touch Someone

Having amended the saying we discussed in Secret #4, let's do it again: "It's not just what you know, it's who you get to know *and who you stay in touch with.*"

Have you ever had someone call you for career help, someone you've stayed in touch with over the years? Isn't your instinct to try to move heaven and earth to help that person? Now think of someone who calls *just* to ask you for help—that's the only context in which the two of you communicate. If you're like most of us, the assistance you offer in this situation is cursory at best.

The idea here is to make as many professional contacts *for their own sake* as you can over the years. Make it a daily priority. Collect business cards from everyone you meet during the general run of business: at conventions, during sales presentations, at seminars, and so on. Note on those cards, for future reference, the circumstances under which you met the person.

Talk to each of your contacts at least once a year just to stay in touch and see how things are going. The dividend comes down the line when you need help, or when you receive a call from someone who says, "Carol, we're starting a search for a [position], and we wondered whether you could refer us to anyone." Make no mistake; the caller is discreetly asking if you are interested.

Reach out and touch lots of people so they can reach out and help you. It's called safety networking.

Secret #6: Work on the Day of Rest

Every Sunday, remove and file the Help Wanted section of your major metropolitan newspaper. You may not need it today or even this year, but at some point you will be in need of job leads, and this collection of want ads will provide you with an essential roadmap of where the jobs are in your area. A company that needed an accountant a year ago could just be starting a search for another one today.

As discussed in chapter 4, even aged want-ads give you specifics about exactly what kind of experience a particular company looks for. The "hidden job market" should perhaps be renamed the "forgotten job market," since a review of advertising in a national or metropolitan daily will give you the skinny on virtually all types of jobs in your field. For you, however, it won't be a forgotten market at all. It will be nestling safely in your bottom drawer.

Secret #7: Say Hello to Harry the Headhunter

My career began with a long stint as a headhunter, and a couple of things about daily life in that particular salt mine have always amused me. I noticed that entry-level professionals tended to be offended that a headhunter would try to lure them away from a current position for another one with better opportunities and rewards, while more senior people appreciated the opportunity to keep their options open. I also noticed that line managers and human resources professionals would have conniption fits on finding a fox in the chicken coop—but that those same managers would change their feelings entirely when it came to their personal career options.

My advice, then, is that you never blow off a headhunter. Provide assistance to them when it cannot hurt you and when you are confident of the headhunter's professional integrity. After all, you never know when they will have the perfect job for you. Most successful professionals have "a friend in the business." You should, too.

☐   ☐   ☐

Some call me cynical, but I prefer to think of myself as a practical urban survivalist. Give your employer the very best you can, every day and in every way—and do the same for yourself.

Yes. All of this is depressing. But for the companies involved, these changes are often unavoidable. In many cases, keeping the guillotine sharpened is the only alternative to shutting the doors and laying *everyone* off.

Your ability to keep your head—and keep yourself employed—will depend on your ability to accept some facts about today's work and world. First, you must accept that the idea that you will work for one employer for the bulk of your career is no longer viable. Check the demographics yourself; employers have shown no hesitation in laying off mid- to senior-level managers short of retirement by a few years, months, or even days. Continued employment no longer depends on company loyalty, but rather on your ability to change with the time.

A Watchful Eye

By continuously assessing the health of your employer, you will be able to make informed decisions about what kind of changes you must make. In some cases, you will find the company so troubled that looking for another job before the ax falls is the best course of action. In other situations, adapting to a new way of doing business may be a sure-fire way to be among those valued employees in the irreducible core. Only you will be able to tell.

While restructuring does not necessarily mean that a company is planning a major layoff, it's a pretty darned good indication. Call it better-than-even odds that the one follows the other. Once you see evidence of unspecified Bug Changes on the Horizon, your diagnosis of the situation—and your ability to adapt to it—should come into play. As corporations flatten their structure to become more efficient, employees are asked to work and think in new ways. Those who are unable to adapt to the new structure, or whose roles are found to be untenable in the new organization, will be the first to go.

Unfortunately, many people (and particularly those with a long history at the company) ignore what is going on right under their noses. Witness the case of the flight engineer who worked for a major airplane manufacturer. He saw his own name on a list of people the organization had determined it could do without—and refused to believe it. When he was handed his pink slip, he was speechless with shock.

As an employee, you probably have as much access to information as you need to make an informed judgment about what's on the horizon. When it comes to your own corner of the organization's universe, you know as much as the C.E.O. and probably a good deal more. An accountant can see that revenues are not meeting expenditures. A salesperson knows when quotas aren't being met. Think carefully about the events that affect your department or position, and (discreetly, of course) investigate them further whenever you can.

On the brink of a disaster? Or poised for explosive growth to which you can contribute? You must find out into which category your company falls. But some changes in the company may be difficult to interpret. For instance, your company might use attrition—simply not filling vacated positions—as a way to cut costs. The next step might be to reduce administrative or support staff. You have to determine whether the company is sincerely attempting to improve efficiency and productivity, or whether these actions are leading to deeper staff cuts.

The signs will differ depending on the size of your employer, and you may have to put on your Sherlock Holmes hat to get the type of information you need. Then again, learning more about your company, your industry, and your market will also make you a better and more valuable employee. More important, it will enhance your career buoyancy.

Let's say you work for a publicly held corporation. By watching the price of your employer's stock over a specific period, you should be able to get an idea of the firm's performance and standing in the marketplace. It's simple enough to check the price of your company's stock (and, for comparison, that of its competitors) in a daily newspaper. Your firm's annual report may have similarly useful information, such as long-term plans and recent successes and failures. Has the company consolidated any of its operations? This may be a clue to future downsizing plans.

Many public libraries have CD-ROM services that allow you to access a massive volume of published material in a very short period of time; you can use this resource to scan articles about your company. Are the pieces positive or negative in tone? Do they relate, directly or indirectly, to your work? Read about your employer's competitors as well; you'll be in a better position to understand your company's moves. Trade and business publications are excellent sources of information about your company and its competitors; they will also give you an indication of the overall condition of the market.

During the middle eighties, one professional woman in the petroleum industry saw the bid rates for consulting work drop dramatically due to an overabundance of workers. Virtually every company in the industry, it seemed, was either laying off employees or going out of business. By understanding the market, she was able to begin her job hunt long before the bottom fell out of the industry in the late eighties. She's now happily employed in another field.

Knowing the strategic advantages your company holds in the market can also be helpful. If you see these advantages disappearing (either because of new technology or other unexpected developments, such as sudden demographic changes or a natural disaster), collapse may be inevitable. If this is the case, you are well advised to start looking for another job *now*. Don't talk yourself into believing that things will eventually get better; they almost certainly won't.

Unfortunately, the downward spiral of a large corporation may be slow and subtle. In many cases, you may have to do more than simply read the trade papers. By successfully building a network of contacts throughout the organization, you may be able to find out exactly what is going on in departments far removed from your own. Developing a strong ally or two in the Human Resources department is often a good first step; people in this area will know in advance about any workforce changes. By knowing and understanding what the company's plans are for the next one to five years, you will be better able to judge your employer's stability.

If you work for a large corporation, and you find that the firm is planning for next year, next quarter, or next month—but has no idea where it is going in five years, a red flag should go up immediately. There's a problem somewhere. Either management is simply inept, flying by the seat of its collective pants, or it is in a firefighting mode, living from one day's crisis to the next. You will have to make your own judgment as to whether or not the people at the top will be able to get their act together.

What about a smaller or mid-sized organization? Some clues are bound to be more obvious in a close-knit environment, where people often wear several hats. Look for bills that don't get paid, new work that doesn't come in, and old contracts that end without renewals or new work to take their place. You should also keep an eye on your workload and that of your fellow employees. If the company is shuffling people around more than usual, or if job responsibilities are changing significantly or frequently in a short period of time, there may be trouble ahead.

With work wrapping up on the two key projects in which he was involved, a highway engineer found himself shuffled between southern California, Milwaukee, and his home office in Phoenix several times in one year. He knew that, when things were going well, he rarely traveled, because he had enough work to keep him in the office. From these clues, he deduced that his number was up. Not long after the new travel pattern emerged, his employer asked him to take early retirement.

Dramatically increased or decreased travel can be one sign that new initiatives affecting you may be on the way; there are others. A sudden change in your performance evaluations may indicate some behind-the-scenes politicking—or a more straightforward attempt to discredit you and justify your dismissal.

Similarly, any indication that your boss's position is shaky may mean that your job is at risk as well. Changes in top leadership often mean a shakeup of philosophies, standard operating procedures, and staffing levels. Your value to members of the "old guard" may prove to be of little consequence to the incoming "new guard." However, proving yourself valuable to the organization in general may help stall your demise—and buy you the time you need to look for another job. (It may also provide you with better referrals, or a chance to be redeployed elsewhere in the company.)

The Hammer Falls
Some layoffs are completely unavoidable. Perhaps the company is no longer involved in the part of the business in which you have worked, or it cannot support more than the most elementary operations.

If you are asked to leave, it's in your best interest to keep your cool. Resist the temptation to blow up at your employer. Sure, it's unlikely you'll ever be asked back to your job, but there is that saying about burning bridges, remember? Concentrate on getting the best severance package (and future references) you can.

Ready for a surprise? You might be in a good negotiating position when it comes to that severance package. There are a number of reasons for this. First, it's likely that the employer is feeling guilty about the layoff. Second, other employees will watch how you're treated when you leave. It's bad for company morale if you're treated unfairly at this stage, and the employer knows it. Finally, there are pragmatic reasons to be fair. Who knows where you'll find yourself after you leave the company? Someday, when you make it to the top, your former boss may even approach *you* for a job!

When a severance package is presented to you, listen calmly. Once the details have been laid out, you will probably want to ask for more. Unless the company's employee handbook clearly details the benefits you are entitled to, it is almost certainly to your advantage to attempt to negotiate a higher severance figure. But how and when you ask are the key.

You may want to take more time to think about a severance package before signing anything. By then, you will have had time to think clearly, assess your situation, and figure out your financial needs. (See chapter 28, "Keeping the Financial Boat Afloat," for more details on this.) Taking a little extra time also allows you a "chill-out" period, which will reduce the likelihood that you will come across as angry and irrational when you present your arguments.

Whether or not you decide to ask for time to think about the severance offer, you should approach any attempt to increase the severance package in a non-threatening manner. Be sure to begin by saying, "I'm certain that you're making every effort to be fair." Then summarize your contribution to the company so the employer knows exactly why you deserve the increased consideration.

Try for benefits that are already in the company's budget, such as magazine and newspaper subscriptions or professional association membership renewals. You might even be able to talk your former employee into continued use of a company car for a time.

As helpful as it may have been in helping you forecast the rough weather you are now negotiating, the Human Resources department, with its rulebooks and set policies, is unlikely to be your greatest ally in this cause. You should try to avoid negotiating you severance package solely through this office. Instead, co-opt your former supervisor, who is likely to feel much more guilt. Granted, the meeting may not be one you look forward to with great enthusiasm, but then again, this is not about getting mad or becoming vindictive; this is about survival. The best recipe calls for generous amounts of calm objectivity and carefully measured doses of despair.

The Emotional Costs

Take time to mourn the loss of your job, as you would any other loss. Don't tough it out. Admit that this hurts. The degree to which you effectively work through the shock will determine how quickly you can get back on your feet and mount a successful job search.

The aftereffects of job loss are similar to the stages of grieving that follow divorce or the death of a loved one: denial, bargaining, anger, depression, and acceptance. Dealing with these can be difficult, and may require more time than you would think.

Finding support is crucial to your success in landing another job. Consider joining community job-search clubs or meeting with an ad hoc group of other people in your situation. (Perhaps there are others who were laid off at the same time you were at your old firm.) By following these steps, you will expand your opportunities and maintain some perspective on the situation.

When you're ready, turn this horrible experience into a growth opportunity. Assess the experience and be honest with yourself. Did you inadvertently contribute to the situation? Was there anything you might have done differently? Did you learn anything that you can apply in your next job?

Appendix B
Conducting a Job Search while
You're Still Employed

Make No Mistake

Looking for a great way to get fired? Leave the original copy of your resume in the office photocopier. It was bad news five years ago, before the downsizing boon. Today it's like signing your own death warrant. Well, who would you lay off, the guy who really wants to work at the company or the one who has demonstrated his intent to leave?

Most prudent people conduct a job search while they're still gainfully employed. In fact, if you suspect a layoff is imminent (see "When You See Clouds on the Horizon," page 264, for some of the early warning signs), you must start looking or get caught in a glut when five hundred others get the pink slip. Maybe you have a dead-end job, are employed in an industry that's doomed in the technological age, or suspect that you have more professional potential than your current employer can tap. Maybe you took a lesser job to put food on the table and keep a roof over your head. No matter what the reason, if your job doesn't seem long for this world, now is the time to start looking around.

Just don't get caught.

Before you start looking for a job while you're still employed, look at your motives.

If you intend to use a job offer from the outside to get a counter-offer from your current employer, forget it. Even if you get a raise, you will likely only benefit in the short-term. Sooner or later, the fact that you strong-armed your employer is likely to catch up with you, when the next round of downsizing comes along, as we both know it will.

Home Is Where the Office Is

Use your home rather than the office. You won't you be tempted to leave your resume in the photocopier, and you can work with maximum privacy.

For efficiency, set up your home-based office as though you were running a business. Designate a room as yours, and allow no phone calls, TV sets, visitors, or other distractions during work hours.

269

When job hunting while you're still employed, the last thing you want at your current job is inquiries from potential employers. So you must have a means to take calls from potential employers that will present you in a fashionable light.

You might be able to talk your spouse into taking on the role of receptionist. Or you can have a special hotline installed and give that number exclusively to prospective employers. Keep an appropriate message on your answering machine for the duration of the job search, and make sure that family members and roommates answer the phone professionally at all times.

Stick to It

You might be working for yourself in an informal environment, but there are still some rules. And you're in charge of setting them and implementing them.

Once you've established a plan for your job search, stick to it. Decide what your work-at-home hours will be, whether it's thirty minutes before dinner or two hours before bedtime each night, and then set the schedule in stone.

Since your job search probably won't be a matter of public record, work to keep yourself motivated. Reward yourself for your successes. Decide on a movie you'll see, a restaurant you'll go to, or whatever works for you, to celebrate sending out the twentieth, fiftieth, or hundredth batch of letters, going on your first interview, and so on.

And be persistent. I remember, years ago, my friend, Dennis, had a hook for his jacket on the back of his office door. When he put it on every evening, the last thing he saw was a message that read, "Keep Writing." It was a reminder for him to continue his job-hunting campaign when he got home. When the going gets tough, remember your goal—a more interesting job, better pay, increased job security, etc.—and don't let anything deter you!

Get Organized

Since you have a job already, you don't have the luxury of spending forty hours a week on a job search. So you have to make the most of every moment.

Take some time to research everything you've been wanting to know about the industry you're working in but haven't had time to find out recently. See who the important players are, which companies are prospering, and who's been promoted. Catch up on old contacts. Contact or join trade organizations and associations, and make friends throughout your industry; attend trade shows and conventions. Or, if you prefer, learn all you can about an up-and-coming industry that might make for an interesting career move, and find out how your skills might be applied toward it.

Stretching Your Job-Search Hours

To maximize your time, you might want to engage the services of employment agencies. (Use employer-paid services only—see page 46.) That way you can have headhunters do some of the legwork for you—and it always helps to have job-search allies.

The key to stretching your job-search hours is to make the most of every moment you do have available instead of lamenting about the time you don't have. Use lunch hours, weekends, holidays, personal days, and any other off-the-clock time you have available to conduct research. (If, by the way, you're conducting an after-hours electronic job search—see *Electronic Job Hunt*, pages 284–287—your rates will be even cheaper than they would be during business hours.)

Check out job fairs and college or alumni offices for job listings. You might also try your hand at writing (and publishing) magazine articles related to your profession, or securing public-speaking engagements to boost your exposure to large groups of people in your field. The easiest way to get started with either of these tactics is to become an active member of your professional association. That gives you access to trade newsletters, magazines, meetings, and so on.

Market Yourself

Direct mail shots with cover letters and resumes are an effective use of your time when you're looking for a job while you're still employed. Your short-term goal is to turn your home-based office into a direct mail house with one product: you. The selling points? Your skills and experience. And the customers? Any and all prospective employers.

Spend time creating a targeted mailing list composed of the companies most likely to hire you. Then identify the needs of each, so you can market your services appropriately. Use a computer to research companies (for more information on *The Electronic Job Hunt*, see pages 284–287) on line. Today, vast amounts of data and contact information are available to you by computer.

Because job hunting while employed is less frantic than the alternative, you will have time to learn about companies and contacts through your research, and you can learn where each company is headed and what each really needs. Then you can use this information to send a perceptive and powerful cover letter with your resume. (For more information about cover letters, see my book, *Cover Letters That Knock 'em Dead*.)

How to Keep Your Job while You're Looking Elsewhere

Do whatever is necessary so that you don't get your walking papers before you decide to walk.

- Don't let anyone in the office know that you're looking for another job, if you can help it. Even if you tell no one besides your best friend, you've told one co-worker too many. Word has a way of getting around, and if management finds out, you've had it.

- Make sure everything seems the same. When you're at the office, dress the way you've always dressed, contribute to meetings what you've always contributed, keep the same hours, and so on. Don't let anybody suspect that you're meeting recruiters during lunch hours, losing interest in your job, or taking time off for interviews. Everything should go on as before.

- If anything, do your job better than you have before, and become an even more valuable worker.

- Keep office items at the office. Don't pack up your belongings, even if they're personal things such as photographs, until you're ready to leave.

- The great advantage of job hunting while employed is the relative lack of urgency. You have time to research companies and people, time to rebuild your resume, time to craft *Knock 'em Dead* cover letters, time to become part of your professional resume. You will be more focused and informed. The result will not always be a better job but will certainly be a more career-buoyant you.

How to Resign

Once you've accepted a job offer and you're ready to resign, do it graciously. Now is not the time to pay back your employer for years of grief; save the bridge burning for your fantasies and go about the business of severing relations professionally. You never know when you'll run into your former employer or when you'll need the old so-and-so again.

Although employees who are terminated are expected to clean out their desks and leave immediately, resigning workers are generally required to give proper notice. Helping make a smooth transition for your remaining colleagues builds bridges for the future. You can even offer to hire and train a replacement—and you can promise to be available to answer questions even after you leave. Be sure and follow through if you do so.

An important tip: It's okay to be happy, but keep your mirth under control while you're in the office. Save the rip-roaring celebration for family and friends. Even your closest colleagues can resent your good fortune, so don't do anything to encourage them to believe you might be gloating. Remember, those you offend on the way up could very well show you the way down sometime in the future.

Appendix C
What Disabled Job Seekers Should Know

Discrimination—in the workplace and in practically every other aspect of everyday life—has been no stranger to the estimated forty-three million disabled Americans. Unemployment among people with disabilities, in fact, is higher than that in any other demographic group.

Many talented people with disabilities, denied employment and a chance at independence, find themselves forced to live as second-class citizens, ignored by society and forced to depend on the financial support of friends and relatives. Until recently, there was no national civil rights law that addressed the problems of the disabled in (or out) of the workplace.

Exactly why this lapse went unremedied for so long remains something of a mystery. Any able-bodied person, of course, could join the ranks of those with substantial physical or mental impairment at any time and with no warning. A traffic accident on the way home from work can rob a sighted person of eyesight or mobility. The sudden onset of a long-undiagnosed illness such as multiple sclerosis can leave the accountant who moaned about the expense of the company's wheelchair-access program with a different state of mind entirely.

Of course, no one chooses to be disabled. Similarly, no one wants to be unemployed. Today, however, if you are both disabled and out of work, that doesn't mean you are out of luck.

The New Rules
In 1990, the Americans with Disabilities Act (ADA), which bans most employment discrimination against disabled people, became the law of the land. (Previously only companies that did more than $2,500 worth of business per year with the federal government were prohibited from discrimination against disabled job applicants and employees.)

Title I of ADA (the part of the statute that deals with disabled job hunters) takes an across-the-board approach to weeding out discriminatory practices. It states that private employers, state and local governments, employment agencies, and labor organizations may not discriminate against job seekers because of their disabilities. It requires nondiscrimination in job application procedures, hiring, advancement, pay, job training, assignments, benefits, and other privileges of employment. And ADA makes it illegal to retaliate against any applicant or employee who asserts his or her rights under the ACT.

Employers with twenty-five or more workers were required to comply with the provisions of ADA as of July, 1992, and employers of fifteen or more must comply beginning as of July, 1994. Private membership clubs (except labor unions) are exempted.

ADA guarantees you equal rights in the workplace if you are disabled that is, if you have a substantial physical or mental impairment that limits a major life activity (hearing, seeing, speaking, walking, and so on) in the long term. It also protects you if you have a history of a disability, if an employer believes you are disabled (regardless of whether or not you are), and if you're married to, or have a relationship with, someone who is disabled.

A few words are in order on that last issue. Specifically, the ADA forbids discrimination based on "relationship or association." That means an employer cannot refuse to hire you because he or she feels that your relationship with a person who has a disability would affect your job performance. So, if your spouse is disabled, you cannot be denied a job because the interviewer believes that you would require excessive amounts of sick time to care for him or her. By the same token, you can't be discriminated against because you do volunteer work for people who have disabilities, such as AIDS.

In addition, ADA protects people with AIDS and those who are HIV-positive. It also applies to alcoholics. While it does not protect current illegal drug users, ADA does extend protection to recovering drug users and those who are participating in supervised drug-rehabilitation programs and no longer using controlled substances.

ADA also deals with non-workplace issues. It prohibits discrimination against the disabled in public accommodations, including hotels, restaurants, stores, theaters, museums, and public transportation. The ACT also bans discrimination in any activity or service either operated or funded by federal, state, or local government and requires some businesses to adjust their operations to meet the needs of the disabled. Telephone companies, for instance, must provide relay services for people who use keyboard devices, enabling people with speech or hearing impairments to communicate with people and businesses that use conventional voice phones.

It should be noted here that ADA does not *mandate the hiring* of any individuals who fall into one of the protected categories; rather, it forbids discrimination by employers in cases where the disability would not affect the employee's job performance, or where the disability could be accommodated to enable the employee to perform the essential functions of the job. We'll look at this theme throughout this section.

ADA also does not extend protection to individuals with short-term disabilities, such as a broken arm. In a case such as this, although there is a physical impairment, it is not one that will interfere with a major life activity in the long term. The ACT does, however, protect diabetics. Even though the condition of diabetes can be controlled through medication and, in most cases, does not adversely affect one's performance in any noticeable way, it still viewed as a disability that substantially limits a major life activity.

Persons with infectious diseases *can* be refused positions that involve handling food. Who, you might well ask, falls into this category? Well, anyone with a disease that appears on the list maintained by the Department of Health and Human Services. A person with tuberculosis would qualify as having a communicable disease; a person with AIDS, or one who is HIV-positive, would not.

If this all sounds a bit confusing, that's because it is. Many provisions of ADA are ambiguous, and parts of the law are currently being wrangled over in the courts. It may be many years (and lawsuits) before the final ramifications of the ACT are clear. In the meantime, if you need clarification on a particular point, see the "Resources" section that follows this one. There you'll find many agencies and organizations that will be able to help answer your questions.

Other Laws That May Affect You

Other federal laws, such as those associated with the Occupational Safety and Health Administration, may have requirements that affect the disabled. Employers must still conform to these laws; ADA does not override them.

If there are state or local safety laws that conflict with ADA requirements, the ADA *may* override them. For example, if a state or local law excludes a disabled person from a job because of a perceived safety risk, the employer must still abide by the ADA and determine whether an actual and serious risk exists, and whether the risk can be reduced to an acceptable level or eliminated with a reasonable accommodation.

As a general rule, it is against the law for an employer to ask you specifically whether you are disabled or inquire into the nature of your disability. However, federal contractors and subcontractors who are affected by the affirmative action requirements of SECTION 503 of the Rehabilitation Act of 1973 may ask applicants to identify themselves on job application forms or during an interview. (Other federal laws or regulations, such as those that apply to disabled veterans, might necessitate preemployment inquiries about disabilities.)

Are You Protected by ADA? If So, How?

To be protected under Title I of ADA, you must be qualified to do the job in question. This means that you must possess whatever education, experiences, skills, or licenses would be required of any other applicant. You must also be able to perform the responsibilities of the job you're seeking. ADA does not protect the person with no legs who would like to be a firefighter—as a result of the disability, that person would be incapable of executing essential firefighting tasks. Nor does it help the blind person who wants to be a bus driver, even though that person may have driven a bus before his or her disability.

Gather as much information as you can about the requirements of the job before the interview; you can do this with intelligent questions during the telephone interview, if there is one. Employers are not required by law to develop and maintain written job descriptions, but many do. An applicant may use a written job description—if one exists—as evidence in a later discrimination claim.

You should understand that, while ADA is a comprehensive civil rights act, it is not in any way an "affirmative action" program. ADA will entitle you to get to the interview, and will protect you from discrimination due to your disability once you get there, but it will not hand you the job on a platter. You'll still have to earn it. If more than one qualified person applies for the job, an employer isn't under any obligation to hire the candidate who is disabled. The employer is entitled to hire whichever applicant he or she prefers.

If you are hired, you can be held to the same standards of productivity and performance as similarly employed individuals without disabilities. However, this only applies to areas that are considered essential to the job. For instance, a deaf delivery person who works for a bottling company would not be required to perform marginal functions associated with the position (such as telephone work). Job restructuring may be an appropriate accommodation in some cases to ensure that disabled workers are not penalized if they are unable to perform extraneous duties.

If your disability requires reasonable accommodation—such as equipment, interpreters, or readers—the employer is required to provide them. *That goes for the period of time that you are applying for the job, as well as after you are hired.* Reasonable accommodations might also include making facilities accessible to persons with disabilities, incorporating part-time or adaptable work schedules, making reassignments to vacant positions, and modifying training materials and policies.

An employer may also be required to adapt an existing applicant or employee examination so that it measures a person's ability to perform the job—and *not* the limitations caused by a disability. The format of the tests should not require the use of skills that may be impaired (sensory, speaking, or manual ability, for instance) to demonstrate competence in an essential area of the position that does not require those skills. Put more simply, if the job does not require, say, the applicant's sight as far as essential functions are concerned, the employer should be prepared to adapt a written test designed for sighted people (by, perhaps, changing it to an oral test).

An employer may also need to make reasonable accommodations in nonwork areas, including cafeterias, lounges, or transportation that the employer provides. It is against the law for the employer to penalize you as a result of these changes. The ADA forbids the employer from lowering your salary or paying you less than other employees who do the same job because you need an accommodation.

There are limits to an employer's responsibility to provide accommodations; reasons such as prohibitive expense or undue hardship may waive some obligations. These claims are weighed against such issues as the actual cost of the accommodation, the size of the business, its financial resources, the number of facilities, and the workforce structure. Generally speaking, though, an employer must have a very good reason to deny a job applicant's or employee's request for an accommodation.

If the employer makes a legitimate claim that it is impossible to provide the accommodation you need, you have the option of providing the accommodation yourself or paying for part of it. But there is less reason to plead poverty when it comes to making accommodations than many employers might think. Financial assistance and a special tax credit may be available to help employers make accommodations to comply with ADA. (If anyone asks you about this, you can refer him or her to the local IRS office, or the Job Accommodation Network, the phone number of which is 1-800-526-7234.) The smart disabled job hunter will have verified his own eligibility with these resources prior to the job hunt. When this is done, questions of cost, financial assistance, or tax credit can be raised in a follow-up letter or interview as circumstances dictate.

Obviously, the specifics of accommodations will vary. Each person's situations and needs are unique. If you need an accommodation for your disability, it is your responsibility to bring that need to the attention of your employer or potential employer. You may be in the best position to suggest an appropriate accommodation, but the process of identifying and implementing an accommodation is ideally an interactive one, with both you and your employer participating in a dialogue. If you have more questions on this score, contact your local Equal Opportunity Employment Commission or local vocational rehabilitation agencies; you'll find contact information in your phone directory. Another good bet is the aforementioned Job Accommodation Network.

Should You Bring up the Subject of Your Disability?

You may or may not want to bring up the subject or your disability before you are hired. That's a matter of personal preference. However, since employers are required only to accommodate "known" disabilities, many employers do recommend that you "self-identify" during the interview. Richard Torockio, General Manger of the Host Travel Plaza Division of the Marriott Corporation, says, "If the applicant tells us what special accommodations he or she will need, it's a big plus. We like to know what changes will need to be made in advance."

Of course, you must find an appropriate time to bring up the topic of accommodations. Paul L. Scher, CRC, a partner at Jordon & Scher Associates, suggests you take the following approach: "When the interviewer asks whether you did this kind of work at your last job, take the opportunity to explain how well you performed and which special accommodations have helped you in the past." In other words, apply the *Knock 'em Dead* philosophy!

We saw earlier that, as a result of the specific requirements of certain preexisting federal laws and regulations, very few employers may legally ask you questions during the application process concerning your disability. Under most circumstances, an interviewer may not ask whether you are disabled or question you about the severity of your disability during a job interview. However, the employer can (and probably will) ask you whether or not you can perform the essential responsibilities of the job. And he or she can also ask you to describe or demonstrate how you can perform those duties.

Your Interview

It is important that you give positive answers with illustrations and examples. Simple "yes" or "no" answers are guaranteed to keep you from leading the field. The idea is not to hide behind the law and your rights, but rather to use it as foundation for open communication. Don't allow a disability to give you a blind spot when it comes to an employer's real needs. See chapter 13, "The Five Secrets of the Hire."

You must win this job on your own merits, not as a result of your status as a disabled person! But you do face certain special challenges. Along with knowing how to answer all the questions put to you and how to hold up under pressure, you will have to take care to put the interviewer at ease.

Your potential employer may feel awkward because of your disability, or even feel unnerved by the implications of ADA. What can you do about it? Do the unexpected! Take your interviewer by surprise and make light of your disability. Show that you have a sense of humor. A blind friend of mine was interviewed for a job over lunch at an Indian restaurant—but soon sensed that his companion was having second thoughts about his choice, given the complex plate arrangements and exotic presentations of some of the menu items the waiter recited. To put the interviewer at ease, my friend quipped, "Would it be okay with you if I just ordered a rice dish?" Later, when his potential employer asked what his greatest weakness was, he confessed, "Well, I suppose it may not be a good idea for me to pour everyone's morning coffee!"

Use whatever positive personality traits you have developed the most highly. Drive, motivation, communication skills, energy, confidence. . . find the most flattering aspect of your work identity and showcase it to the fullest. It is likely that you have more than your share determination. Now is the time to use it to your advantage.

Stress your similarities with the interviewer rather than your differences. One deaf woman who has been through the process suggests, "Instead of saying, 'I'm the same as you,' show it. Simply express your professional opinions and attitudes, and let the interviewer see how 'normal' you are."

Do feel free to be diplomatically pushy when necessary. It's okay to refuse to take no for an answer. Help the interviewer see ADA as an opportunity to find a way to let you, a potentially valuable employee, perform for his or her company.

One more important note on interview preparation. Don't be afraid to ask for help with your personal appearance before you head out to meet the prospective employer. When you dress for an interview, always look (and smell) your best. Charles Rich, a paraplegic writer and broadcaster, suggests that you consider each interview you go on as a date. "You didn't get used to your disability in the first fifteen minutes. You can't expect your interviewer—your 'date'—to either." Take the time you need to get ready. Look your best, and give the employer the time and opportunity to see the real you; ADA has at last provided him or her with the motivation to do so.

Success Stories
Here are a few true stories of disabled job applicants who were able to showcase their talents to prospective employers and land the jobs they wanted.

- One newspaper columnist went out and made an opportunity for himself. He told a managing editor that it was about time the paper had a column about people with disabilities. As a deaf person, he naturally felt that he was uniquely qualified to do the job. And he got it!

- A young man with Crohn's disease who has arthritis of the hips and back was homebound for two and a half years. Here's how he reentered the workforce: "I prepared a great resume and got a letter of reference from my physician. Then I simply convinced my employer that I was very creative and a hard worker."

- Another disabled applicant wrote a short story about his determination to succeed, detailing the steps he took to triumph over adversity. The piece got him hired.

- In 1989, a manufacturing firm hired a woman who was deaf and blind. She had previously been evaluated by a rehabilitation service organization professional as being incapable of any competitive employment. Since joining the company, she has been cross-trained to perform more jobs than anyone else in the organization. "We've *had* to cross-train her in so many jobs just to keep work in front of her," her manager confesses. "It's because she's so quick. In fact, she can outwork me!"

- Before he became a quadriplegic, Tony was a shoe buyer. Now he's a full-time market-research analyst; he uses special software that allows him to operate a computer without using a keyboard. He's been so successful that his former boss recently asked whether he'd consider moving back to his old position.

Bear in mind that most employers view all job seekers, disabled or otherwise, in the same way. The big question is: What can you do for our company? Your past performance, skills, and ability to do the job are what will make the most bottom-line difference to the interviewer, not you limitations.

We have the same success rate in hiring disabled people that we have with the general population," says Mariott's Richard Torockio. "Some people work out, some don't. We don't want to hear 'I'm good because I'm disabled.' We like to hear, 'I'm good because I'm me.'"

Carole Rogers, Director of Employment Activities at McDonald's, agrees. "We look for the ability and skills needed to do the job," she notes, "and the experience that relates to what we're trying to accomplish. We look for the same things in people with disabilities that we look for in people without disabilities."

Remain upbeat and friendly throughout the interview. As Susan Brake, Director of Human Resources at Pizza Hut, puts it, "We look for a good attitude and flexibility—someone who's excited about working for us."

The Insurance Question

Health insurance is a topic that is on the minds of many Americans these days, and it's a safe bet that it is also on the minds of many disabled job applicants as they head into the interview room.

ADA, unfortunately, is not a cure for health insurance problems. The ACT does require that employers allow all employees access to health insurance. But employers *are* entitled to offer only health insurance policies that feature clauses excluding pre-existing conditions. Obviously, such clauses affect the disabled more than any other employees.

By the time you read this, the picture may well have changed significantly— but not as a result of ADA. As this book goes to press, published reports indicate that the Clinton Administration will include as part of its proposed health care reform plan new regulations forbidding insurers from withholding coverage for persons with preexisting medical conditions.

Physical Exams and Questions about Your History

Can the employer ask you to take a physical exam? Only if he or she is willing to give you the job first! An employer may not require a medical exam until *after* a job offer has been made, and then only if the company requires physicals of all employees who are starting similar jobs. (Note, however, that ADA does permit tests for illegal drug use administered in accordance with existing laws. Drug tests are not considered medical examinations under the ACT, and an employer may legally conduct drug tests and make hiring decisions based on the results.)

An employer may not rescind your job offer because of information revealed by a physical exam unless the reasons for the rejection are strictly job-related. Thus, the employer would have to show, for example, the physical exam revealed that you would be unable to perform the essential functions of the job even with a reasonable accommodation, or that no accommodation exists that would enable you to perform the job. Another example is medical evidence showing that, by virtue of your disability, you would pose a direct threat to the health and safety of yourself or others in the workplace. The direct threat must be actual, current, and serious, rather than based on stereotype, fear, or prejudice. Moreover, the employer must demonstrate that the threat could not be reduced to an acceptable level or eliminated by a reasonable accommodation.

Any information resulting from your physical exam must be kept confidential, in a file separate from personnel records. These files should be available only under extremely limited conditions. An employer may, however, submit medical information to state workers' compensation offices without violating ADA confidentiality requirements.

What does all this boil down to? Your medical records are your business, that's what. You cannot be refused a job (or fired) simply because an employer suspects that your disability may cause increased workers' compensation costs. But beware! An employer *can* terminate consideration of your employment or fire you if you lie in an answer to a legal question about your condition or workers' compensation history.

How, you may ask, can an employer legally pose such questions? Well, the key fact to bear in mind here is that a person who is receiving workers' compensation, or is receiving benefits under another disability law, is *not necessarily also considered disabled under ADA*. Work-related injuries do not always "significantly limit" a major life activity. Many on-the-job injuries are temporary, and do not cause severe long-term mental or physical impairment. If yours is one of them, you should be prepared to answer questions about your past medical history if they come up.

And remember, it's not at all in your interests to sign on or continue with a job for which you are not suited. Even if it means considering a lifestyle or career change, you should make an honest assessment of your abilities. Janet is a firefighter who was recently diagnosed with multiple sclerosis, an illness that could potentially cause risk to herself and others if she were to attempt to continue as before in her career. She decided that it was absolutely necessary to tell her superiors about the condition on her own initiative. "The most important thing I did," she says, "was provide education about the disease, and let my reputation as an honest, open person stand for itself. My peers know that I will not do anything that will jeopardize anyone." She was eventually transferred to a position with which both she and her supervisors felt comfortable.

The Long View

You don't have to give up your life's ambitions simply because of a disability. With modern technology—which includes such devices as robotic arms, braille printers, word-prediction software programs, voice-recognition systems, optical readers, and telecommunications devices—more disabled people than ever before are benefiting from their success.*

You can make success *your* reality, as well. Stay active in churches, professional organizations, community organizations, and groups for the disabled. Not only is every person you meet a potential job contact, but some employers are more receptive to hiring disabled people who are backed by an organization. This is especially true if the group is one that offers job coaching for the first few weeks of work, when intensive training may be needed. And, of course, there are some important morale considerations related to keeping active in this way.

You are a valuable, empowered person. Never sell yourself short. (If all else fails, remind yourself that job discrimination is illegal, and that the suits are currently being settled at a three-to-one rate in favor of the disabled applicant.)

If you do need an extra shot of self-confidence, consider the observation of Brent Stull, Plant Manager at Kreonite Corporation. "In integrated workforces," Stull observes, "I find that turnover rates decrease, attendance rates go up, and re-work rates decrease." Managers pay attention to things like that. Although you may have been denied the chance to work in the past, you have a chance now to make a real difference—not only in your own life, but in the workplace as well.

Don't spend time poking holes in your own self-esteem if you get turned down for jobs a few times. It happens to everyone! Remember, the more interviews and

---

* Let the record show I speak not in the abstract, but from experience. As a result of recent hires related to the research required for this section, *half* of my own team here at Peregrine McCoy is now disabled. I'm ecstatic with the results and I'm sure the experience is being replicated throughout the business world. When it comes to productivity, loyalty and extra effort, I've been simply blown away. Give me a team of so-called "challenged" people with a sense of humor and I'll conquer the world. You can quote me on this!

prospects you initiate, the more opportunities you'll have. Follow a plan as its outlined here and remain optimistic.

When you do land the right job, remember that you don't have to work twice as hard as the person next to you just because you're disabled. As writer/broadcaster Charles Rich says, "You are as entitled as any other employee to look tired every now and then. You can even be out sick once in a while. You don't have to prove yourself every hour of every day."

If You Have to Use ADA to Obtain a Legal Remedy . . .

ADA has made job discrimination against disabled persons illegal—but it has not abolished that discrimination. If you feel you have been discriminated against as the result of a disability, you can fight back. If you decide to do so, you will have the power of the federal government behind you.

Contact the Equal Employment Opportunity Commission (see the "Resources" section that follows for contact information) within 180 days of the incident you feel was discriminatory. Under some state and local laws, you may have a bit more time to file a charge: up to three hundred days. Call for details. The number is 1-800-669-EEOC (voice) or 1-800-800-3302 (TDD).

The EEOC will investigate and attempt to resolve the charge through conciliation. The same procedures used to handle charges of discrimination filed under Title VII of the Civil Rights Act of 1964—the law that covers race, color, sex, national origin, and religious discrimination—apply. (Note: the EEOC is responsible for handling discrimination charges for actions that took place on or after July 26, 1992. If the incident took place before that date, you should still contact the Commission for information on what agencies to get in touch with next.)

If it is found that you have in fact been discriminated against on account of your disability and in violation of the ADA, you will be entitled to a remedy that may include: hiring, promotion, reinstatement, back pay, or a reasonable accommodation (such as reassignment). You may also be entitled to attorney's fees.

The EEOC can provide you with more detailed summaries of the ADA and other federal requirements for nondiscrimination. Call them at the numbers provided above for additional information if you need it.

Resources

ADA Regional Disability and Business Technical Assistance Centers

Connecticut, Maine, Massachusetts, New Hampshire, Rhode Island, and Vermont: New England Disability and Business Technical Assistance Center, 145 Newbury Street, Portland ME 04101. 207/874-6535 (voice/TDD).

New Jersey, New York, Puerto Rico, and Virgin Islands: Northeast Disability and Business Technical Assistance Center, 354 South Broad Street, Trenton NJ 08608. 609/392-4004 (voice), 609/392-7044 (TDD).

Delaware, District of Columbia, Maryland, Pennsylvania, Virginia, and West Virginia: Mid-Atlantic Disability and Business Technical Assistance Center, 2111 Wilson Boulevard, Suite 400, Arlington VA 22201. 703/525-3268 (voice/TDD).

Alabama, Florida, Georgia, Kentucky, Mississippi, North Carolina, South Carolina, and Tennessee: Southeast Disability and Business Technical Assistance Center, 1776 Peachtree Street, Suite 310 North, Atlanta, GA 30309. 404/888-0022 (voice/TDD).

Illinois, Indiana, Michigan, Minnesota, Ohio, and Wisconsin: Great Lakes Disability and Business Technical Assistance Center, 1640 West Roosevelt Road (M/C 627), Chicago, IL 60608. 312/413-1407 (voice/TDD).

Arkansas, Louisiana, New Mexico, Oklahoma, and Texas: Southwest Disability and Business Technical Assistance Center, 2323 South Shepherd Boulevard, Suite 1000, Houston, TX 77019. 713/520-0232 (voice), 713/520-5136 (TDD).

Iowa, Kansas, Nebraska, and Missouri: Great Plains Disability and Business Technical Assistance Center, 4816 Santana Drive, Columbia MO 65203. 314/882-3600 (voice/TDD).

Colorado, Montana, North Dakota, South Dakota, Utah, and Wyoming: Rocky Mountain Disability and Business Technical Assistance Center, 3630 Sinton Road, Suite 103, Colorado Springs CO 80907-5072. 719/444-0252 (voice/TDD).

Arizona, California, Hawaii, and Nevada: Pacific Coast Disability and Business Technical Assistance Center, 440 Grand Avenue, Suite 500, Oakland, CA 94610. 510/465-7884 (voice), 510/465-3167 (TDD).

Other Resources
Job Accommodation Network, P.O. Box 6123, 809 Allen Hall, Morgantown WV 26505-6123. 800/526-7234 (voice/TDD).

The President's Committee on Employment of People with Disabilities, 1331 F Street NW, Washington, DC 20004. 202/376-6200 (voice), 202/376-6205 (TDD).

U.S. Department of Justice, Civil Rights Division, Office on the Americans with Disabilities Act, P.O. Box 66118, Washington, DC 20035-6118. 800/514-0301 (voice), 800/514-0383 (TDD).

Appendix D
Electronic Job-Hunting Resources

To use an on-line service for your job search, you can subscribe directly to one or visit your local library. There are many public and university libraries that provide walk-in uses of on-line services; some will conduct the search for you at a nominal cost. Some fee-based services offer same-day turnaround for customized research, or even one-hour rush service. An invaluable resource guide called *The Directory of Fee-Based Information Services* lists more than four hundred U.S. and Canadian library systems that provide fee-based search services. The price of the directory is $29.00. For more information, call FYI Service at 800/582-1093.

In the first part of this section of *Knock 'em Dead*, the "Electronic Database Public Access Directory," you will find information on universities or public libraries that offer complete research and document delivery services, from in-library research to on-line services with hard-copy delivery. We have provided regional listings, and only a handful in most major metropolitan areas. You can also find out the facility closest to you by calling your public library (or one of the full service libraries listed here) and asking for information on the nearest library that offers "on-line information services and a public-access computer center." (Use that wording exactly; it will save you some time.)

The next series of listings is the "Electronic Record Database Directory," which lists on-line databases in most major U.S. cities. Some are quite specialized; others offer services of interest to most job hunters. Typically, these services will charge subscription dues, password fees, access charges, or a combination of these. Phone costs are extra.

□ □ □

Whether you own your own personal computer, would use a library's computer, or plan on having a search done for you, the resources are waiting for you. Even if you are intimidated by computers, you should consider calling some of the organizations listed in this part of the book. Many of these facilities will allow you to take advantage of all the benefits of cutting-edge technology without ever touching a keyboard.

Important Note: Before you dive headlong into the world of electronic information, a word of caution is in order. Electronic job hunting (EJH) can be very effective, but it can also be very expensive. In EJH, time is money. The more information you gather, the longer it will take to print out or fax to you; the more time you spend on the line, the more you will pay in telephone and access charges. EJH can be more comprehensive and faster than regular hard-copy methods of finding leads, but as of this writing it is best viewed as a judiciously used supplement to standard research methods.

Electronic Database Public Access Directory

An asterisk (*) by a listing indicates that the library in question specializes in business research.

If a university or public library in your area isn't listed, call your local library and ask about "on-line computer services available to the general public" in your area. The services you come up with may not be equipped to run the search for you, but they will probably have computers and several on-line resources available for your use.

Arizona State University*
602/965-3415

Boston University Metropolitan College Corporate Education Center
(CD-ROM or customized research only)
508/649-9731

Brandeis University
617/736-4721

Broward County Library (Ft. Lauderdale, FL)
305/357-7444

Buffalo and Erie County Public Library
716/858-8900

Carnegie-Mellon University Engineering and Science Library
412/268-2426

Cleveland Public Library
216/623-2999

County of Los Angeles Public Library*
310/868-4003

Data Center Search Service (Oakland, CA)
510/835-4692

Denver Public Library
303/640-8846

Fairfax County (VA) Public Library
703/222-3155

Fairleigh Dickinson University*
201/692-2100

George Washington University*
202/994-6973

Georgia Institute of Technology*
404-894-4511

Highsmith Co., Inc. (Fort Atkinson, WI)*
414/563-9571

James J. Hill Reference Library* (St. Paul, MN)
612/227-9531

ICFAR-ARAC (Indianapolis, IN)
(NASA's Industrial Engineering Center)
317/262-5003

Industrial Technology Institute (Ann Arbor, MI)*
313/769-4000

Lewis & Clark Law School
503/768-6600

Los Angeles Public Library*
213/612-3200

Louisville Free Public Library
502/547-1600

Moraine Valley Community College
708/974-5234

National Ground Water Well Association
(Customized environmental research on all groundwater-related topics.)
614/761-1711

New Jersey State Library
609/292-6220

New York Academy of Medicine Library
212/876-8200

New York Public Library
212/930-0800

North Dakota State University
701/237-8900

North York Public Library (Ontario, Canada)
416/395-5579

Ohio State University
(Medical and health information)
614/292-9810

Ohio University
614/593-2931

Purdue University
317/494-2831

Rice University*
713/528-3553

Seltzer Daley Companies, Inc. (Princeton, NJ)
(Customized research for hospitals, healthcare systems, and health-related businesses.)
609/924-2420

South Dakota State Library*
605/773-3131

Temple University/Paley Library
215/787-3836

Texas Tech University
806/742-2265

Tulsa City (OK) County Library
918/596-7991

University of Alberta (Canada)
403/492-2728

University of California at Irvine
714/856-6654

University of California at Riverside
909/787-1012

University of Central Florida
407/823-2562

University of Colorado at Colorado Springs
719/593-3295

University of Florida*
(Southern Technology Applications Center, Alachua, FL)
800/225-0308

University of Georgia
706/542-0604

University of Illinois at Urbana-Champaign*
217/333-6202

University of Michigan at Ann Arbor
313/763-5060

University of Minnesota Biomedical Information Service
612/626-3730

University of Minnesota: ESTIS Service
612/624-2356

University of New Mexico
(Science and Engineering)
505/277-5054

University of Oklahoma R.M. Bird Health Sciences Library
405/271-2343

University of Oregon at Eugene
503/346-1818

University of Pittsburgh
412/648-7000

University of Richmond Business School Library
804/289-8666

University of South Florida—Tampa*
813/974-4880

University of Southern California*
(NASA's Regional Technology Transfer Center with access to over 500 databases)
213/743-6132

University of Texas at Dallas
214/690-2999

University of Wisconsin at Madison
608/262-5913

Wayne State University Science and Engineering Library
313/577-4373

Electronic Record Database Directory

Accessing any one of the following databases for the first time will probably make you feel as though you're walking into the biggest library in the world. The specialties and fee structures of the various services vary widely, however, and we cannot do full justice to any of them in our allotted space. For additional information, call the numbers listed. (Many are toll-free.)

ADP
ADP Network Services, 175 Jackson Plaza,
Ann Arbor, MI 48106
313/769-6800.

CD Plus Technologies
333 Seventh Ave., 4th Floor, New York, NY
10001
212/263-3006
800/950-2035
Fax: 212/563-3784

CompuServe
CompuServe Information Service, 5000
Arlington Centre Boulevard, P.O. Box 20212,
Columbus, OH 43220
614/457-8600
800/848-8199

Corporate Jobs Outlook!
Jack Plunket, Publisher, P.O. Drawer 670466,
Dallas, TX 75367
210/755-8810
Fax: 214/692-0105

Datatimes
Datatimes, Inc., 14000 Quail Springs Parkway,
Suite 450, Oklahoma City, OK 73134
405/751-6400

Dialog Information Services
Dialog Information Services, Inc., 3460
Hillview Avenue, Palo Alto, CA 94304-1396
415/858-3785
800/334-2564
Fax: 415/858-7069
In Canada: 800/668-9215
Fax in Canada: 416/445-3508

Dun's Electronic Business Directory
Dun & Bradstreet, Three Sylvan Way,
Parsippany, NJ 07054
201/605-6000
800/526-0651
Fax: 201/605-6921

G.E. Information Services (GENIE)
Client Services, 401 North Washington Street,
Rockville, MD 20850
800/638-9636

Human Resources Information Network
ETSI/Timeplace, 1200 Quince Orchard
Boulevard, Gaithersburg, MD 20878
301/590-2300

Medlars
U.S. National Library of Medicine, 8600
Rockville Pike, Bethesda, MD 20894
800/638-8480

NewsNet
NewsNet, Inc., 945 Haverford Road, Bryn
Mawr, PA 19010
610/527-8030
800/345-1301
Fax: 610/527-0338

Lexis Nexis
Mead Data Central, P.O. Box 933, Dayton, OH
45401-9964
513/865-6800
800/227-9597
Fax: 513/865-7894

Orbit/Questel
Info-pro Technologies, 8000 Westpark Drive,
McLean, VA 22102
703/442-0900
800/456-7248
Fax: 703/893-4632

Prodigy
Prodigy Services Company, 445 Hamilton
Avenue, White Plains, NY 10601
914/448-8000
800/776-3449

Reuters Accountline
Reuters Information Services, 1333 H Street
NW, Suite 410, Washington, DC 20005
202/898-8300

Standard & Poor's On-Line Services
Standard & Poor's Corporation, 25 Broadway
New York, NY 10004
212/208-8300
Fax: 212/412-0498

Technical Employment News **Job Listings**
Publications and Communications, Inc., 12416
Hymeadow Drive, Austin, TX 78750
512/250-9023
800/678-9724
Fax: 512/331-3900

Vu/Text
Knight-Ridder Corporation, 75 Wall Street,
22nd Floor, New York, NY 10005
212/269-1110
800/533-8139

Wilsonline
H.W. Wilson Company, 950 University Avenue
Bronx, NY 10452
718/588-8400
800/367-6770
Fax: 718/590-1617

Appendix E
Printed Job-Hunting Resources

The Adams Jobs Almanac
Adams Media Corporation, Holbrook, MA.
Detailed information on over ten thousand major employers, including, for most companies, jobs commonly filled, experience required, and even benefits packages offered. Also includes regional economic forecasts, industrial outlooks, and projections of employment growth by occupation.

The Almanac of American Employers
Corporate Jobs Outlook, Boerne, TX.
Lists five hundred of the country's most successful large companies; profiles salary ranges, benefits, financial stability, and advancement opportunities.

American College of Healthcare Executives Directory
American Association of Healthcare, Chicago, IL.
Lists over sixteen thousand healthcare executives in public and private organizations. Published every other year.

America's Fastest Growing Employers
Adams Media Corporation, Holbrook, MA.
A national career guide for those seeking employment with the most rapidly-growing firms in the country. Includes names, addresses, and vital statistics for more than two hundred seventy-five companies that are thriving in today's economy. Each profile gives key facts about the company's growth and development.

The Capitol Source
National Journal, Inc., Washington, DC.
Includes names, addresses, and phone numbers for key figures in the District of Columbia; also features information about corporations, interest groups, think tanks, labor unions, real estate organizations, financial institutions, trade and professional groups, law firms, political consultants, advertising and public relations firms, private clubs, and the media. Published twice a year.

Congressional Yellow Book
Monitor Publishing Co., New York, NY.
Gives detailed information on congressional staff positions, committees and subcommittees, and top staff in congressional support agencies. Published annually.

Corporate Jobs Outlook
Corporate Jobs Outlook, Inc., Dallas, TX.
Each issue reviews fifteen to twenty major (five thousand employees or more) firms. The report rates the firms and provides information on: salaries and benefits, current and projected development, where to apply for jobs, potential layoffs, benefit plans, the company's record for promoting women or minorities to executive positions, and college reimbursement packages. Also includes personnel contact information for each firm. Published bimonthly; a yearly subscription is $159.99. Call 210/755-8810.

Note: This resource is also available on-line through NewsNet (800-345-1301) or the Human Resources Information Network (800-638-8094). Call for more details.

Corporate Technology Directory
CorpTech, Woburn, MA.
Lists over thirty-five thousand businesses and one hundred ten thousand executives. Describes products and services in such fields as automation, biotechnology, chemicals, computers and software, defense, energy, environment, manufacturing equipment, advanced materials, medical, pharmaceuticals, photonics, subassemblies and components, testing and measurements, telecommunications, transportation and holding companies. Published annually.

CorpTech Fast 5,000 Company Locator
CorpTech, Woburn, MA.
Lists over five thousand of the fastest-growing companies listed in the *Corporate Technology Directory*, but includes addresses and phone numbers, number of employees, sales, and industries by state. Published annually.

COSLA Directory
The Council of State Governments, Lexington, KY.
Provides information on state library agencies, consultant and administrative staff, plus ALANET numbers, electronic mail letters and fax numbers. Published annually.

Directory of Corporate Affiliations
Reed Reference Publishing Company, New Providence, NJ
Lists key personnel in 4,700 parent companies and forty thousand divisions, subsidiaries, and affiliates. Includes addresses and phone numbers of key executives and decision makers. Published once a year, with quarterly updates. For more information, call 800-323-6772.

Directory of Environmental Information
Government Institutes, Rockville, MD.
Lists federal and state government resources, trade organizations, and professional and scientific newsletters, magazines, and databases. Published every other year.

Directory of Federal Libraries
Includes library's administrator and selected staff for three thousand special and general, presidential and national libraries, as well as library facilities in technical centers, hospitals, and penal institutions.

Directory of Legal Aid and Defender Offices in the U.S. and Territories
National Legal Aid and Defender Association, Washington, DC.
Lists legal aid and public defender offices across the U.S. Published annually.

Directory of Leading Private Companies
National Register Publishing Company, Wilmette, IL.
Profiles over seven thousand U.S. private companies in the service, manufacturing, distribution, retail, and construction fields. Includes companies in such areas as healthcare, high technology, entertainment, fast-food franchises, leasing, publishing, and communications. Published annually.

Encyclopedia of Associations
Gale Research, Inc., Detroit, MI.
Published in three volumes. Volume 1 lists national organizations in the U.S. and includes over twenty-two thousand associations, including hundreds for government professions. Volume 2 provides geographic and executive indexes. Volume 3 features full entries on associations that are not listed in Volume 1.
   Note: This resource is also available on-line through Dialog Information Services (800-334-2564). Call for more information.

Environmental Telephone Directory
Governmental Institutes, Rockville, MD.
Lists detailed information on governmental agencies that deal with the environment. The directory also identifies the environmental aides of U.S. Senators and Representatives. Published every other year.

Federal Careers for Attorneys
Federal Reports, Inc., Washington, DC.
A guide to legal careers with over three hundred U.S. government general counsel and other legal offices in the U.S. Explains where to apply, the types of legal work common to each field, and information on special recruitment programs.

Federal Executive Directory
Carroll Publishing Co., Washington, DC.
Profiles a broad range of agencies, both executive and legislative, including cabinet departments, federal administrative agencies, and congressional committee members and staff. The directory also outlines areas of responsibility for legal and administrative assistants. Published six times a year; an annual subscription is $178. Call 202/333-8620 for more information.

Federal Organization Service: Military
Carroll Publishing Co., Washington, DC.
Lists direct-dial phone numbers for 11,500 key individuals in fifteen hundred military departments and offices. Updated every six weeks; an annual subscription is $625. Call 202-333-8620 for more information.

Hospital Phone Book
U.S. Directory Service, Miami, FL.
Provides information on over 7,940 government and private hospitals in the U.S.

International Directory of Corporate Affiliations
National Register Publishing Company, Wilmette, IL.
Lists over fourteen hundred major foreign companies and their thirty thousand U.S. and foreign holdings. Published annually.

The JobBank Series
Adams Media Corporation, Holbrook, MA.
A top-notch series of paperback local employment guides. The 1995 editions profile virtually every local company with over fifty employees in a given metro area. Company listings
are arranged by industry for easy use; also included is a section on the region's economic
outlook and contact information for local professional associations, executive search firms,
and job placement agencies. The series covers twenty major metropolitan areas: Atlanta,
Boston, the Carolinas, Chicago, Dallas/Ft. Worth, Denver, Detroit, Florida, Houston, Los
Angeles, Minneapolis/St.Paul, New York, Ohio, Philadelphia, Phoenix, St. Louis, San Francisco, Seattle, Tennessee, and Washington, D.C. Many listings feature contact names, common positions hired for, educational backgrounds sought, benefits, fax numbers, internship
information, staff size, and more. Available at most bookstores. Updated yearly.

Judicial Staff Directory
Staff Directories, Ltd., Mt. Vernon, VA.
Lists over eleven thousand individuals employed in the 207 federal courts, as well as thirteen
thousand cities and their courts. The book also has information on court administration, U.S. mar-
shalls, U.S. attorneys, and the U.S. Department of Justice. Includes eighteen hundred biographies.

National Association of County Health Officials Sustaining Membership Directory
National Association of County Health Officials, Washington, DC.
Lists national health officials for almost every county in the U.S. Published annually. $10.
Call 202-783-5550 for more information.

The National JobBank
Adams Media Corporation, Holbrook, MA.
The 1995 edition includes over sixteen thousand company profiles. Many listings feature
contact names, common positions hired for, educational backgrounds sought, benefits, fax
numbers, internship information, staff size, and more. Updated annually.

National Trade and Professional Associations of the United States
Columbia Books, Washington, DC.
Lists information on over 6,500 trade and professional associations. Published annually.

Nationwide Jobs in Dietetics
Jobs in Dietetics, Santa Monica, CA.
Lists jobs nationwide in the field of dietetics. Published monthly; an annual subscription is
$84. Call 310/453-5375 for more information.

NDAA Membership Directory
National District Attorneys Association, Alexandria, VA.
Lists all district attorneys' offices across the U.S. $15 for nonmembers, $10 for members.
Call 703/549-9222 for more information.

Paralegal's Guide to Government Jobs
Federal Reports, Inc., Washington, DC.
Explains federal hiring procedures for both entry-level and experienced paralegals. The volume describes seventy law-related careers for which paralegals qualify and lists over one
thousand federal agency personnel offices that hire the most paralegal talent. Also profiles
special hiring programs.

Sales Guide to High-Tech Companies
CorpTech, Woburn, MA.
Covers over three thousand company profiles and twelve thousand executive contacts. Includes specific details on each company's products and services. Published quarterly; a yearly subscription is $185. Call 617-932-3939 for more information.

Transportation Officials and Engineers Directory
American Road and Transportation Builders Association, Washington, DC.
Lists over four thousand state transportation officials and engineers at local, state, and federal levels. Published annually.

U.S. Medical Directory
U.S. Directory Service, Miami, FL.
Over one thousand pages of information on doctors, hospitals, nursing facilities, medical laboratories, and medical libraries.

Washington Information Directory
Congressional Quarterly Inc., Washington, DC.
Provides important information on the federal government as a whole, and on each federal department and agency. The volume also provides details on regional federal information sources, non-governmental organizations in the Washington area, and congressional committees and subcommittees. Published annually.

Washington '92
Columbia Books, New York, NY.
Contains addresses, phone numbers, and profiles of key institutions in the city. Includes chapters on the federal government, the media, business, national associations, labor unions, law firms, medicine and health, foundations and philanthropic organizations, science and policy research groups, and educational, religious, and cultural institutions. Published annually.

Who's Who in Special Libraries and Information Centers
Gale Research Inc., Detroit, MI.
Lists special libraries alphabetically and geographically. Published annually.

Appendix F
Index to the Questions

How do you handle rejection? See page 175.
How do you handle tension? See page 144.
How do you interact with people at different levels? See page 160.
How do you manage to interview while still employed? See page 155.
How do you organize and plan for major projects? See page 140.
How do you take direction? See page 149.
How does this job compare with others you have applied for? See page 147.
How have you benefited from your disappointments? See page 162.
How interested are you in sports? See page 153.
How long have you been looking for another position? See page 144.
How long would it take you to make a contribution to our company? See page 139.
How long would you stay with the company? See page 139.
How many hours a week do you find it necessary to work to get your job done? See page 140.
How many other jobs have you applied for? See page 147.
How much are you looking for? See pages 85, 214.
How much are you making? See pages 85, 214.
How much do you need to support your family? See page 214.
How much do you want? See pages 85, 214.
How much experience do you have? See pages 87, 136.
How much will it take to get you? See page 214.
How old are you? See page 183.
How well do you feel your boss rated your job performance? See page 152.
How will you be able to cope with a change in environment? See page 173.
How would you define a conducive work atmosphere? See page 153.
How would you define your profession? See page 173.
How would you evaluate me as an interviewer? See page 179.
I'd be interested to hear about some things you learned in school that could be used on the job. See page 193.
[Illegal interview questions] See pages 181–183.
I'm not sure you're suitable for the job. See page 180.
In hindsight, what have you done that was a little harebrained? See page 157.
In what areas do you feel your supervisor could have done a better job? See page 152.
In what ways has your job changed since you originally joined the company? See page 146.
In what ways has your job prepared you to take on greater responsibility? See page 146.
In your last job, how did you plan to interview? See page 162.
In your last job, what were some of the things you spent most of your time on, and why? See page 146.
People from your school or major never work out here. What makes you different? See page 193.
Rate yourself on a scale of one to ten. See page 150.
See this pen I'm holding? Sell it to me. See page 150.
Tell me about a time when you experienced pressure on the job. See page 168.
Tell me about a time when you put your foot in your mouth. See page 176.
Tell me about an event that really challenged you. See page 161.
Tell me about the last time you felt anger on the job. See page 151.
Tell me about the problems you have living within your means. See page 171.
Tell me about yourself. See page 150.
Tell me a story. See page 156.
Tell me how you moved up through the organization. See page 140.

Index

Ability, demonstrating, 127
Accessories
  men's , 104
  women's, 107
Accomplishments, discussing, 140
Achievements and resume, 26-27
Adams Job Almanac, 288
ADA Regional Disability and Business Technical Centers,
  list of, 282-283
ADP, 287
AIDA formula, 78-80
AIDS, 274
Alberta, University of, 286
Alcohol, at interview, 187
Alcoholics, protection of, 274
Almanac of American Employers, 288
Alumni Associations, 38, 53-54
American College of Healthcare Executives Directory, 288
American Library Association, 61
American Management Association survey, 264
Americans with Disabilities Act (ADA), 273-282
America's Fastest Growing Employers, 288
Analytical skills, importance of, 133
Anecdotes, value of, 129
Arizona State University, 285
Attendance record, discussing, 177
Automatic telephone systems, 82

Bailey, F. Lee, 125
Bankruptcy, 253-254
Benefits, 222-223
  See also Salary, Negotiation
BIZ FILE, 62
Blouses, 106
Body language, 109-118
  positive, 116-118
Boston University, 285
Brake, Susan, 279
Brandeis University, 285
Briefcase
  men's, 104
  women's, 107
Broward County Library, 285
Buffalo and Erie County Public Library, 285
Bureau of Labor Statistics, 210
Business magazines, 38, 56-57
Business to Business Yellow Pages, 41
Buy signals, 83-87
Buzzwords, in resume, 30

California, University of, 286
Capitol Source, The, 288
Career counselors, 50
Carnegie-Mellon University, 285
CD Plus Technologies, 287
Center for Disease Control (CDC) study, 230
Central Florida, University of, 286
Certified Personnel Consultant, 47-48
Challenges, discussing, 161

Checks, at restaurant interviews, 189
Chemistry (personal), importance of, 133
Chicago, University of, communication study, 110
Chronological resume, 28, 31
Civil Rights Act of 1964, Title VII, 182, 282
Cleveland Public Library, 285
Closed-end questions, 165
Clothing. *See* Dress
College, discussing, 192-193
College placement offices, 38, 53-54
Colorado at Colorado Springs, University of, 286
Combination resume, 28, 33-34
Commandments, of job hunting, 69-71
Communication skills, importance of, 133
Companies, lessons about, 23-24
CompuServe, 62-63, 287
Computerized recruiter, 29-30
Computer literacy, importance of, 257-258
Computers and resumes, 29-30
Confidence, importance of, 133
Congressional Yellow Book, 288
Consistency, importance of, 45-46
Contact trackers, 71, 73
Conversation, controlling, 83-87
Coolidge, Calvin, 86
Cooperation, discussing, 157
Corporate Jobs Outlook, 287, 289
Corporate Technology Directory, 289
CorpTech Fast 500 Company Locator, 289
COSLA Directory, 289
Cover letter
  for stalled search, 245
  See also Executive briefing
Cover Letters That Knock 'em Dead, 59, 67, 245, 247
Credit cards, use of, 250, 253
Credit history, 174
Credit rating, 245, 250-251
  bureaus, list of, 251

Databases, and resumes, 65
Data Center Search Service, 285
Datatimes, 287
Debt. *See* Finances
Debt collectors, 254-255
Decision making, discussing, 171
Dedication, importance of, 133
Denver Public Library, 285
Determination, importance of, 133
Diabetics, protection of, 274-275
Dialog Information Services, 287
Directory of Corporate Affiliations, 289
Directory of Databases, 61
Directory of Directories, 54
Directory of Environmental Information, 289
Directory of Executive Recruiters, 51
Directory of Federal Libraries, 289
Directory of Fee-Based Information Services, 61, 284
Directory of Leading Private Companies, 290
Directory of Legal Aid and Defender Offices, 289

Direct research, 37, 39-42
Disabled job seekers, 273-283
    accommodations for, 276-281
    and health insurance, 279-280
    resources for, 282-283
Disappointments, discussing, 162
Discrimination
    and disabled, 273-283
    pay, 209-210
Dress, 99-108
    codes, 101
    for men, 101-105
    for women, 100, 105-108
Drive, importance of, 133
Drug tests, 228-233
    and ADA, 280
    false positives in, 228-232
    flushing system prior to, 232-233
Dun & Bradstreet Database, 52
Dun's Electronic Business Directory, 287

Earnings, discussing, 173
    See also Salary, Negotiations
Economy, importance of, 134
Edison, Thomas, A., 162
Education, questions about, 86-87, 91, 192-193
Efficiency, importance of, 134
Electronic database directory, 285-287
Electronic job hunt, 38, 60-65, 284-285
    resources for, 284-287
Employer
    evaluating, 219-222, 224-225
    "secret" needs of, 127-131
Employment agencies, 38
    private, 46-52
    public, 46
Employment dates and resumes, 28
Employment Management Association drug study, 228
Encyclopedia of Associations, 54, 258, 290
Energy (personal), importance of, 133
Environmental research, 285
Environmental Telephone Directory, 290
Equal Employment Opportunity Commission (EEOC), 277, 282
E-Span, 63
Evaluation criteria, 18
Executive briefing, 35-36, 97
Executive recruiters, 48
Executive Research Directory, 51
Experience, discussing, 87
Eye contact, 112-113

Facial signals, 112, 113
Fair Credit Reporting Act of 1972, 174, 251
Fair Debt Collection Practices Act of 1977, 254
Fairfax County (VA) Public Library, 285
Fairleigh Dickinson University, 285
False positives in drug test, 228-233
Federal Careers for Attorneys, 290
Federal Executive Directory, 290
Federal Organization Service: Military, 290
Feet, 116
Finances, personal
    discussing, 174
    during unemployment, 248-255
Financial counseling, 249
Florida, University of, 286
Follow-up, 247
    importance of, 71-72
    to interview, 202-204
Follow-up letters, 245
40 Plus Club, 60
Functional resume, 28, 32
Future, discussing, 139, 191-192

Gatekeepers, handling of, 81-82
G.E. Information Services (GENIE), 287
George Washington University, 285
Georgia, University of, 286
Georgia Institute of Technology, 285
Glasses, 113-114
Goals, use of, 95
Graduates, recent, 190-195
Greeting, 110-111, 121
Grumman Aerospace, 191

Hands, 114-115
Handshake, 110-111
Headhunters, 48-49, 259-260
Head signals, 112, 113
Healthcare research, 286
Heraclitus, 227
Hidden job market, 37-74
Highsmith Co., Inc., 285
Hill Reference Library, 285
Home office, 269-270
Honesty, importance of, 133
Hospital Phone Book, 290
Hot button, 137
Human Resources Information Network, 287
Hygiene, personal, 108, 246-247

ICFAR-ARAC (NASA), 285
Illegal questions, 181-183
    examples of, 181
    handling, 183
Illinois at Urbana-Champaign, University of, 286
Industrial Technology Institute, 285
Industry Week survey, 209-210
Inner circle, joining, 257
Interim Management Corporation (IMCOR), 245
International Directory of Corporate Affiliations, 290
International Personnel Services Association (IPSA), 47
Interview
    do's and don'ts for ending, 196-197
    from employer's perspective, 127-131
    follow-up to, 202-204
    inappropriate topics for, 128-129
    kit, 119-120
    preparation for, 99-121
    questions, common, 135-157, 160-184, 191-195
    in restaurant, 186-189
    stress, 167-184
    telephone, 95-98
Interviewer
    evaluation of, 179
    incompetent, 163-165
    skillful, 158-163

Jewelry
    men's, 104
    women's, 107-108
Job Accommodation Network, 277
JobBank Series, 291
Job changes, discussing, 28, 175-176
Job experience, discussing, 136
Job fairs, 38, 55-56
Job market
    buyer's vs. seller's, 24
    hidden, 37-74
Job objectives, 29
Job offer
    evaluating, 216-218, 223-224
    single, 226-227
Job search
    commandments of, 69-71
    and disabled, 273-283
    discussing length of, 144
    electronic resources for, 284-287

Your Two Cents' Worth

Comments, questions, or suggestions? Please complete this questionnaire and mail it to me:

Martin Yate
c/o Adams Media Corporation
260 Center St.
Holbrook, MA 02343

Hey Martin,

Here's how I used *Knock 'em Dead*:

By the way, I'm thinking of changing my will and naming you as my major beneficiary if you . . .

1. Give me some additional information about the following issue.

   _____

2. Tell me how to find the resource described below, since I drew a blank. (Circle one: This is something I came up with. / You mentioned it on page _____.)

   _____

3. Add a chapter on the following topic, since it would really be helpful to people like me.

   _____

I guess that's it. No, wait—please SEND ME/DO NOT SEND ME some information on your *Career Survivalist* newsletter.

And, oh yeah, stick my name in the hat when you're done reading this. I deserve a shot at a free dinner for two at the restaurant of my choice as much as anyone else who fills this out.

Name: _____

Address: _____

_____

Daytime phone: _____

Evening phone: _____

Occupation: _____

Also by Martin Yate

Cover Letters That Knock 'em Dead
Completely revised and updated. The final word on not just how to write a "correct" cover letter, but how to write a cover letter that offers a powerful competitive advantage in today's tough job market. *Cover Letters That Knock 'em Dead* gives the essential information on composing a cover letter that wins attention, interest, and job offers. 8 ¹/₂" by 11"; 224 pages, paperback, $9.95.

Resumes That Knock 'em Dead
Completely revised and updated. Every single one of the 110 resumes in this book is based on a resume that was successfully used to obtain a job. Many of the resumes included were used to change careers; others resulted in dramatically higher salaries. Some produced both. Yate reviews the marks of a great resume, what type of resume is right for each applicant, what always goes in, what always stays out, and why. 8 ¹/₂" by 11"; 224 pages, paperback, $9.95.

Hiring the Best: A Manager's Guide to Effective Interviewing (4th ed.)
Contrary to popular belief, not all managers are mystically endowed with the ability to hire the right people. Interviewing is a skill that must be developed, and Martin Yate shows just how to identify the person who provides the best "fit" for any given position. Includes sections on interviewing within the law and hiring clerical help, as well as prewritten interview outlines. 6" x 9"; 240 pages, paperback, $9.95.

Also of interest from Adams Publishing

The Adams Jobs Almanac, 1995. Editors of Adams Publishing.
Updated annually, *The Adams Jobs Almanac, 1995* provides an unprecedented amount of information on nationwide career opportunities and strategies. This best-selling book includes names and addresses for over ten thousand leading employers; information on which job each company commonly hires for; industry forecasts and geographical cross-references; a close look at over forty popular professions; a detailed forecast of 21st-century careers; and advice on preparing resumes and shining at interviews. It's the most comprehensive national career reference guide available! 5 ¹/₂" x 8 ¹/₂", 928 pages, paperback, $15.00.

America's Fastest Growing Employers: The Complete Guide to Finding Jobs with Over 300 of America's Hottest Companies, Second Edition. Carter Smith.

"If you want to know who's doing the hiring now, pick up a copy of *America's Fastest Growing Employers*." —The *Wall Street Journal*

The all-new, revised edition examines which companies are thriving in today's ultra-competitive market conditions. It contains expanded profiles of today's leading companies, as well as a survey of the hottest industries in terms of hiring. 6" x 9", 330 pages, paperback, $16.00.

If you cannot find a book at your local bookstore, you may order it directly from the publisher. Please send payment including $4.50 for shipping and handling (for the entire order) to: Adams Publishing, 260 Center Street, Holbrook, MA 02343. Credit card holders may call 1-800-USA-JOBS (in Massachusetts, 617-767-8100). Please check your local bookstore first.

Get the latest current job listings from Adams JobBank Online—free!

If you have a computer with a modem, you can take advantage of **Adams JobBank Online**, the most powerful electronic job search tool available today. You'll enjoy the benefits of unlimited online access, without high installation fees or monthly online service charges.

Explore *current* job opportunities with top employers nationwide—free!

Listings cover a range of openings in many different industries from leading employers throughout the U.S. Listings typically include: company background, benefits, contact person, and training programs.

Get online tips from top career experts—free!

Get answers to your career and job-search questions from nationally recognized experts, such as Martin Yate, author of the *Knock 'em Dead* books, by visiting the Job Hunting Conferences.

Visit the Online Career Service Center—free!

In addition, you can read cutting-edge career articles, book excerpts, and software; get valuable tips on networking, interview preparation, and career management; and read offer-winning resumes and cover letters.

Adams JobBank Online is also available on our home page at http://www.adamsonline.com

OXFORD WORLD'S CLASSICS

IRISH WRITING

THIS is an anthology of Irish writing in English from the revolutionary era of the 1790s to the early years of the Irish Free State in the 1930s. It spans 150 years of modern Irish culture, from the dawning of a powerful nationalist consciousness inspired by Wolfe Tone and the United Irish movement to the waning of the Irish Literary Revival and the last poems of W. B. Yeats. In that traumatic century and a half, the struggle for political independence found expression in songs and stories, poems and plays, as well as in essays, speeches, and memoirs. It was in these years that Ireland produced a new and distinctive national literature in which questions of origin, identity, and destiny were of paramount importance. This emerging tradition of Irish literature was all the more remarkable for being written in English at a time when the Irish language was being steadily eroded. The determination of Irish writers to forge a tradition of their own and to use the English language in new and often subversive ways produced a literature of startling imaginative vitality and stylistic experimentation. Selected authors include Edmund Burke, Maria Edgeworth, Thomas Moore, Oscar Wilde, Augusta Gregory, J. M. Synge, W. B. Yeats, James Joyce, Seán O'Casey, Elizabeth Bowen, Samuel Beckett, and Louis MacNeice.

STEPHEN REGAN is Professor of English at Durham University.

OXFORD WORLD'S CLASSICS

*For over 100 years Oxford World's Classics have brought
readers closer to the world's great literature. Now with over 700
titles—from the 4,000-year-old myths of Mesopotamia to the
twentieth century's greatest novels—the series makes available
lesser-known as well as celebrated writing.*

*The pocket-sized hardbacks of the early years contained
introductions by Virginia Woolf, T. S. Eliot, Graham Greene,
and other literary figures which enriched the experience of reading.
Today the series is recognized for its fine scholarship and
reliability in texts that span world literature, drama and poetry,
religion, philosophy and politics. Each edition includes perceptive
commentary and essential background information to meet the
changing needs of readers.*

OXFORD WORLD'S CLASSICS

Irish Writing
An Anthology of Irish Literature in English 1789–1939

Edited with an Introduction and Notes by
STEPHEN REGAN

OXFORD
UNIVERSITY PRESS

OXFORD
UNIVERSITY PRESS

Great Clarendon Street, Oxford OX2 6DP

Oxford University Press is a department of the University of Oxford.
It furthers the University's objective of excellence in research, scholarship,
and education by publishing worldwide in

Oxford New York

Auckland Bangkok Buenos Aires Cape Town Chennai
Dar es Salaam Delhi Hong Kong Istanbul Karachi Kolkata
Kuala Lumpur Madrid Melbourne Mexico City Mumbai Nairobi
São Paulo Shanghai Singapore Taipei Tokyo Toronto

Oxford is a registered trade mark of Oxford University Press
in the UK and in certain other countries

Published in the United States
by Oxford University Press Inc., New York

Selection and editorial matter © Stephen Regan 2004
Other copyright information appears on pages 544–6.

The moral rights of the author have been asserted

Database right Oxford University Press (maker)

First published as an Oxford World's Classics paperback 2004
Reissued 2008

British Library Cataloguing in Publication Data

Data available

Library of Congress Cataloging in Publication Data

Data available

ISBN 978–0–19–954982–5

13

Typeset in Ehrhardt
by RefineCatch Limited, Bungay, Suffolk
Printed and bound in Great Britain
by Clays Ltd, Elcograf S.p.A.

CONTENTS

IRISH WRITING

PART ONE: WRITINGS 1789–1890

1. POLITICAL WRITINGS AND SPEECHES

2. REFLECTIONS ON IRISH CULTURE

INTRODUCTION

'The seas of literature are full of the wrecks of Irish anthologies.'
With this cheering thought, W. B. Yeats set afloat his own anthology,
A Book of Irish Verse, in 1895.[1] Yeats fervently believed that his book
was a genuine contribution to a tradition of Irish writing in English,
as well as a personal record of what he considered to be the best in
Irish verse, but he also realized that the very word 'Irish' would
summon critics with more ardent nationalist sentiments than his
own. His concern was that the image of Ireland that his anthology
conveyed would be regarded as insufficiently patriotic and that the
times might demand a more heroic and more explicitly political
representation of national identity. Any new anthology of Irish writing still runs the risk of censure for what its selection of material
might suggest about Ireland and Irishness. Today, however, critics
are wary of impassioned talk about tradition and identity. Anthologies are suspect because they are, by their very nature, part of a
tradition-making process and tradition is often invoked as a way of
defining and declaring identity. Anthologies can, of course, also
acknowledge diversity and plurality.

Many of the writings in this anthology *are* overtly nationalist.
This is hardly surprising, given the historical circumstances in which
they were composed. Political speeches, songs, and memoirs are
included here, along with stories, plays, and poems. Questions about
national destiny and national identity are paramount in all of these
works, but they do not as a body of writing constitute some mono-
lithic notion of Ireland or promote some essentialist idea of what it is
to be Irish. What these writings frequently reveal are the startling
instabilities and uncertainties that accompany debates about identity
and nationality, especially in times of violent political conflict and
difficult social transition. Images of Ireland in the writings of
Edmund Burke, Maria Edgeworth, J. M. Synge, W. B. Yeats, James
Joyce, Elizabeth Bowen, and others are not necessarily flattering
or positive images. One of the strongest dissenting voices towards
the end of the period represented here is that of Louis MacNeice

[1] W. B. Yeats, *A Book of Irish Verse* (London: Methuen & Co., 1895), p. x.

provocatively asking, 'Why should I want to go back | To you, Ireland, my Ireland?'.

This is an anthology of Irish writing in English from the revolutionary era of the late eighteenth century to the formative years of the Irish Free State in the early decades of the twentieth century. It spans 150 years of modern European history, from the French Revolution, which impacted so powerfully on Irish nationalist aspirations, to the outbreak of the Second World War, in which the newly independent Irish Free State maintained its neutrality. In that traumatic century and a half, the struggle for political independence inspired patriotic speeches, songs, and stories, and these in turn gave fresh inspiration to new generations of nationalist writers and activists. The voices of Wolfe Tone and Robert Emmet are heard in the uproar of Easter 1916 and later. Other voices, of course, are inflected in different ways and not always in support of revolutionary change. There are voices of loyalist fervour as well as nationalist aspiration, voices of bewilderment as well as assurance, and voices of lament as well as celebration. Throughout the writings of this troubled century and a half, there is an intense preoccupation with Ireland itself: with issues of national identity, political liberty, sectarian conflict, territorial possession, and linguistic inheritance. This preoccupation is inflected in different ways in a variety of literary forms: in travel writing and Gothic fiction as much as in autobiographical essays and translations of early Irish poems.

Modern Irish literature: beginnings

In the years between 1789 and 1939, Irish writing gathers a powerful sense of momentum and direction, and it does so when complex cultural issues find appropriate form in equally complex rhetorical structures. This is not to suggest that there is a definitive canon of Irish writing with clearly marked characteristics, but simply to observe an emerging body of writing with a familiar set of conventions and concerns. There are discernible influences and lines of descent, from Maria Edgeworth to Elizabeth Bowen, for instance, or from William Carleton to James Joyce. In terms of its earliest and latest dates of publication, the anthology stretches from the early translations in Charlotte Brooke's _Reliques of Irish Poetry_ to the _Last Poems_ of W. B. Yeats, tracing what Yeats himself regarded as a national tradition of Irish writing in English. That Irish writers should have produced such an extensive and imposing body of writing in the English language is itself a remarkable phenomenon, and a high degree of self-consciousness about the political implications of adopting an imposed colonial language is a significant feature of some of the writings included here.

There were, of course, many notable Irish writers working in the English language prior to 1789, including Oliver Goldsmith and Jonathan Swift, but the French Revolution and the United Ireland movement focused the concerns of Irish writers in new and unprecedented ways. No writer records the impact of the French Revolution on Irish politics more acutely or more powerfully than Edmund Burke. While Burke is comprehensively committed to preserving political equanimity in Europe and throughout the Empire, he also retains a special affection, as well as a profound anxiety, for his native Ireland. Born in Dublin and raised in Cork, Burke considered Ireland to be 'the Country to which I am bound by my earliest instincts'.[2] He was brought up as a Protestant, but was also an ardent supporter of Catholic rights. He had close contact with the Catholic community through his mother's family in Cork, and his wife was also a Catholic. Burke's deep conviction was that Irish Catholics, under continuing duress and exclusion from political power, would become increasingly vulnerable to the spread of French revolutionary principles. It was a conviction that found dramatic confirmation in the Irish Rebellion of 1798.

As Seamus Deane has argued, Burke's *Reflections on the Revolution in France* (1790) is a foundational modern Irish text.[3] In the first place, it provides the crucial contrasting terms—'tradition' and 'modernity'—by which the progress of Ireland, as well as France, might be measured and understood. More generally, though, it prompts a debate about cultural identity and political destiny, about national character and civil liberty, and in doing so it establishes the terms on which future narratives of the nation might be constructed. Written so soon after the events it describes, the book has a striking immediacy of address. In Burke's opinion, the French Revolution

---

[2] R. B. McDowell (ed.), *The Writings and Speeches of Edmund Burke*, ix (Oxford: Clarendon Press, 1991), 389.

[3] Seamus Deane, *Strange Country: Modernity and Nationhood in Irish Writing since 1790* (Oxford: Clarendon Press, 1997), 1.

has had a terminal and irreversible effect on European civilization: 'the glory of Europe is extinguished for ever' and 'the old manners and opinions' of traditional society have been swept away by 'a savage and brutal humanity'. At the same time, Burke's text is an exercise in damage limitation—an impassioned attempt to counter any further swell of revolutionary ardour. The revolution gives *all* Europe 'too close and connected a concern in what is done in France'. In the case of Ireland, Burke came to see that the rigidity of Protestant conservatives in the face of growing demands for Catholic enfranchisement would ignite a similarly violent rebellion.

Burke's fearful account of 'the atrocious spectacle of the sixth of October 1789' and his perception of tragic drama in the ordeal of Marie Antoinette ought to remind us that he was also the author of *A Philosophical Enquiry into the Origin of our Ideas of the Sublime and the Beautiful* (1757). In Burke's political theory, revolution is equated with the sublime emotions of fear and dread, while order is consonant with what is beautiful, lovely, and serene. Accordingly, national cohesion and solidarity depend on bonds of affection and on the appreciation of loveliness: 'To make us love our country, our country ought to be lovely.' Ireland's distress undermines any secure sense of well-being that Burke envisages for the rest of Europe beyond revolutionary France. The alarming contradiction in Burke's theory is that the British civil society that he seeks to defend for its decency and nobility is the same that condones the abuse of civil rights among Catholics in Ireland.

The problem, as Burke saw it, lay in the continuing opposition to Catholic relief among the so-called Protestant 'Ascendancy' (a term that was still very new when Burke gave it his attention in the 1790s). This is the substance of the troubled, unfinished letter that he addressed to his son Richard in 1792. His son was an agent of the Catholic Committee in Dublin and later a leader of the Catholic Association of Ireland, and his father pays tribute to him as one 'engaged in the relief of an oppressed people'. In recognizing the Ascendancy as a persecuting faction, Burke emphatically makes a political as well as a religious distinction between Catholics and Protestants. Burke's writings, then, acknowledge and inform the sectarian politics that increasingly dominate discussions of national identity from the 1790s onwards.

At the same time, Burke is clearly alert to comparisons between the Ascendancy in Ireland and the East India Company in India. If he enables political discussion of Ireland's future within the immediate context of revolutionary Europe, he also acutely registers the predicament of Ireland within a long and continuing history of Empire. Even so, Ireland remains a special case, and one of the problems facing Burke and later Irish writers is how to articulate Ireland's difference from England and other constituent parts of the Empire. If, in some obvious respects, Ireland seems an extension of the British system, sharing similar values and ideals, it is also in other respects profoundly different, resistant to foreign ways, and implacably opposed to the imposition of colonial institutions and regulations.

Burke and later writers saw that 'Ireland was being treated as an irredeemably strange country', both familiar and alien, both known and unknown.[4] While Burke continued to hope that Ireland might have a peaceful and secure role in the British imperial system, he also ruefully acknowledged the injustices and inequities that made such a prospect unlikely. Burke's impact on modern Irish culture is profound. In seeking to establish the appropriate conditions for a harmonious civil society in Ireland, he gives serious consideration to questions of national identity and national character. His work provides the impulse for the Protestant Ascendancy to authenticate its political power by rooting itself in tradition, and in this respect it can be seen to anticipate the Literary Revival spearheaded by W. B. Yeats and his contemporaries a century later.[5] In equally lasting ways, however, Burke provides a model of Irish eloquence in the English language and sets a standard of linguistic opulence in those rhetorical skills for which he is justly remembered: 'his vivid vocabulary, his profusion of epithets, his ready resort to metaphor, his exuberance in praise, denunciation, and ridicule, his infusion of poetry into the exposition of political practicalities.'[6]

Burke's fears about the vulnerability of Ireland in the wake of the French Revolution were not exaggerated. He accurately predicted that Catholic demands for religious toleration and civil liberties would be joined and supported by expressions of discontent among

---

[4] Deane, *Strange Country*, 16.

[5] The point is well made by Declan Kiberd in *Irish Classics* (Cambridge, Mass.: Harvard University Press, 2000), 219.

[6] McDowell (ed.), *The Writings and Speeches of Edmund Burke*, ix. 391.

radical Protestant dissenters, including Belfast Presbyterians. This alliance on revolutionary principles between two disaffected groups provided the impulse behind the United Irish movement of 1797–8. That alliance is memorably celebrated by Wolfe Tone in 'An Argument on Behalf of the Catholics of Ireland' (1791) and proudly recalled in his autobiography: 'To unite the whole people of Ireland, to abolish the memory of all past dissentions, and to substitute the common name of Irishman in place of the denominations of Protestant, Catholic and Dissenter—these were my means.'

There are good reasons for seeing the 1790s as 'the pivotal decade in the evolution of modern Ireland'. The United Irish movement sought to transcend sectarian differences and establish a political system founded on universal ideas of equality and justice. The suppression of those aspirations by the British state was to have profound consequences, both in terms of subsequent constitutional arrangements and in terms of the direction that popular republican and loyalist sentiment would take. As Kevin Whelan and other historians of the period have argued, what has since proved elusive is 'an agreed political structure, capable of representing Irish people in all their inherited complexities'.[7] If the events of the 1790s were crucial to the evolution of modern Ireland, they also impacted in significant ways on the imaginative and artistic life of the country.

Reading Tone's autobiography in the knowledge of his certain failure in the Irish rebellion of 1798 is a poignant experience. The revolutionary excitement and promise of the 1790s, however, are given popular expression in songs and ballads of the time, including 'The Croppy Boy' and 'The Wearin' o' the Green', as well as in much later literary works, including Ethna Carbery's 'Rody McCorley' and that controversial play of the Irish Literary Revival, *Cathleen ni Houlihan* (1902). In the aftermath of rebellion, the extirpation of French revolutionary ideals was accompanied by a more pragmatic governmental attempt at pacification: the Act of Union in 1800. Direct control from Westminster did not, however, prevent a further uprising by another United Irishman of Protestant background, though Robert Emmet insisted in his 'Speech in the Dock' that he was 'no emissary' of France but the advocate of a proudly independent Ireland. Emmet and Tone together provide a

---

[7] Kevin Whelan, *Fellowship of Freedom: The United Irishmen and 1798* (Cork: Cork University Press, 1998), p. ix.

model of exemplary patriotism for the abject Yeats in his poem of mourning for a lost Romantic Ireland, 'September 1913'.

Yeats was clearly less impressed by Daniel O'Connell, whose redoubtable energies helped to mobilize Catholic opinion on a massive scale and achieve emancipation in 1829. His 'Speech at Tara' is a powerful demonstration of his skills in rhetoric, as well as a compelling example of his insistent call for the repeal of the Union. O'Connell's constitutional endeavours contrast markedly, however, with the militant republicanism of James Fintan Lalor and the emerging Fenian Brotherhood. The difference in outlook is, in part, a consequence of the Famine years, during which almost a million people died from starvation and disease and a million and a half sought emigration as an escape from desperate circumstances. Lalor articulates the uncompromising nationalism of an Ireland suffering the dire social and economic consequences of the Famine and intent on dealing with issues of land ownership and reform. If Lalor revives the republican spirit of Wolfe Tone, he also anticipates the militant politics of Patrick Pearse and the patriots of Easter 1916.

Political essays, speeches, letters, and memoirs were instrumental in the making of an Irish national literature, and so, too, were works of travel writing and cultural anthropology. There is a special sense in which Burke's *Reflections on the Revolution in France* might be regarded as a work of travel writing, and this ought to remind us that travel writing often functions as social and political critique.[8] In late eighteenth-century and early nineteenth-century Europe, there are numerous works of journeying and observation inspired by an Enlightenment curiosity in social and cultural differences. What prompts these works of travel writing is a desire to know a country and to find appropriate ways of rendering it knowable. Ireland stirs the imagination of the traveller/anthropologist in peculiar ways. Even when the traveller is an insider like John Gamble or William Carleton, Ireland is rendered phantasmagorically strange. When the traveller is an outsider, the representation is sometimes startling in its novelty.

One of the most remarkable travel books from the revolutionary 1790s is *A Frenchman's Walk Through Ireland* (1797), the work of Chevalier de la Tocnaye, a Breton officer and Royalist supporter

---

[8] Again, I am indebted to Seamus Deane's *Strange Country* (see pp. 4–6).

who fled his country in 1792 and arrived in London, not knowing English. His 'promenade dans l'Irlande' is sharply responsive to the contrasting grandeur and misery of Dublin, but it also reports from remoter places like 'the neighbourhood of Armagh' on 'the subject of the troubles, which for so long have desolated this beautiful country'. The book offers a French Royalist perspective on both sectarian grievances and United Irish solidarity in the north at a time of immense political uncertainty. In contrast, John Gamble and William Carleton, both writing in the early decades of a new century, are intent on recording the spiritual as well as the political life of the people. Both writers, in the essays included here, depict a Gaelic peasant Ireland holding stubbornly to its own rituals, customs, and superstitions. A century later, a similar kind of writing would help to lay the foundations of the Irish Literary Revival, and John Millington Synge would follow these earlier writers in converting the stuff of his observations in the Aran Islands and the Wicklow Hills into powerful creative works like *Riders to the Sea* (1904). Indeed, for Yeats and Synge and other Revivalists caught up in debates about identity and nationhood, the very act of wandering becomes not only a means of observation but a mode of self-definition and self-realization.

Irish fiction and political crisis

Gamble's *Sketches of History, Politics, and Manners, in Dublin, and the North of Ireland, in 1810* belongs to a polite genre of writing popular with English readers. The aesthetic delicacy of 'sketches' and the ostensible concern with 'manners' position the writer as a mediator between very different styles of life. The preface to the book confirms this in its declaration that the author 'endeavours to make known a very peculiar people, and a state of society, unhappily unparalleled on the civilised earth'.[9] Gamble's moving account of an Irish wake, preceded by the cry of the Banshee, is astutely observant and impeccably detailed, but it also shows his flair for telling a good tale. Like Carleton, he prepares the ground on which the Irish tale is transformed into printed literary forms, including novels.

Carleton, too, has a fondness for telling a good tale, but the title of

---

[9] John Gamble, *Sketches of History, Politics, and Manners, in Dublin, and the North of Ireland, in 1810*, new edn. (London: Baldwin, Cradock and Joy, 1826), p. v.

his *Traits and Stories of the Irish Peasantry* points to a particular interest in the exploration of national character. In the preface to that book (a new edition of which was published in 1843–4), Carleton presents his writings as 'works which may be said to treat exclusively of a people who form such an important and interesting portion of the empire as the Irish peasantry do'. He claims, as author, to be concerned with 'removing many absurd prejudices which have existed for time immemorial against his countrymen', though it might be argued that his account of Catholic ritual in 'A Pilgrim at Lough Derg' is itself a work of comic absurdity and one that reinforces as many prejudices as it seeks to dispel.[10]

In other respects, however, 'A Pilgrim at Lough Derg' was of crucial importance both to Carleton and his successors. It constituted his 'début in literature', but it also prompted him to forsake his vocation as a Catholic priest. It was, he says, 'the cause of changing the whole destiny of my subsequent life'. The wealth of characterization, the shrewdness of observation, and the vigorous delivery of Irish speech all point towards significant developments in the history of Irish fiction. Ironically, Carleton renders the Irish peasant knowable in print only by transforming himself: by adopting the Protestant faith and appealing to his readers through an educated English syntax and diction. Even in the passage describing his abandoned vocation, the transformation appears inevitable and complete: 'I had nothing for it now but to forget my sacerdotal prospects.'[11] Paul Muldoon has made the excellent point that as well as representing 'an extraordinary straddling of the two main religio-political traditions in Ireland', Carleton shows a powerful combination of intimacy with, and enmity towards, his subject-matter that anticipates the work of James Joyce.[12]

Over a century and a half later, Carleton comes back to inspire and instruct the pilgrim poet Seamus Heaney in *Station Island* (1984). The dialogue between them is an act of mutual confession, with Heaney telling Carleton's shade, 'Your *Lough Derg Pilgrim* | haunts me every time I cross this mountain | . . . A lot of what you wrote | I heard and did', and Carleton acknowledging his 'old fork-tongued

---

[10] William Carleton, *Traits and Stories of the Irish Peasantry*, new edn. (Dublin: William Curry & Co., 1843–4), p. i.

[11] Ibid., p. xvi.

[12] Paul Muldoon, *To Ireland, I* (Oxford: Oxford University Press, 2000), 25.

turncoat' tendencies. Carleton is 'an aggravated man | raving on about nights spent listening for | gun butts to come cracking on the door'. He is deeply dismayed to find that nothing has changed. He offers a lesson to Heaney in being true to oneself: 'It is a road you travel on your own.'[13] Heaney's marvellous encounter with Carleton is just one instance of how the earlier writer's predicament continues to haunt a generation of later writers.

Irish fiction, with the help of prolific practitioners like Carleton, gained immense popularity among English readers in the nineteenth century. As well as representing Ireland to readers unfamiliar with its topography and culture, the fiction of the time provided an appropriate space for imaginative explorations of national identity and political unity. The Act of Union in 1800 prompted fresh consideration of power relations between Protestant and Catholic, and between Anglo-Irish Ascendancy and Irish peasant society, and these were frequently cast in fictional form. Some of the best-known novels of the time seem to function as moral fables in which questions of leadership and government are intricately caught up with issues of land ownership, legal rights, and family lineage. The pressing concerns of *Castle Rackrent* (1800) are still apparent in later novels such as *The Real Charlotte* (1894) and *The Last September* (1929), all novels by women writers who were both privileged enough to be part of the Ascendancy ethos and yet ironically disposed towards the uses and abuses of power around them. One of the peculiar and distinctive features of Irish fiction in the nineteenth century is the disparity between its insistence on telling the truth or showing things as they are and its actual instability and profound uncertainty about its capacity for realist verisimilitude. This element of indeterminacy is palpably evident in some of the popular Irish novels of the time, including *Castle Rackrent*, *The Wild Irish Girl* (1806), and *Hurrish* (1886).

Castle Rackrent was published shortly before the Act of Union was passed in 1800, though it was probably written in the closing years of the 1790s during a time of revolutionary disturbance. It purports, however, to be a tale of Irish life at the beginning of the 1780s, recounting the decline and fall of the Rackrent family in that earlier decade. The narrator of the story, Thady Quirk, is a dutiful servant

---

[13] Seamus Heaney, *Station Island* (London: Faber and Faber, 1984), 64–6.

whose personal loyalty to the family contrasts markedly with the opportunistic attitude of his son, Jason. The novel's extended chronology helps to conceal its more immediate concern with the fate of the Protestant Ascendancy in the context of recent political rebellion and allows a retrospective view on a class that has lost its claims to leadership over Ireland's benighted peasantry. What gives complexity to the narrative is its subtle combination of ironic critique and intimate lament.

The moral and political anxieties embodied in *Castle Rackrent* can be readily identified and understood in relation to the events of the 1790s, especially in the light of Burke's similar concerns about the responsibilities of the Ascendancy. What is perhaps harder to comprehend is the curiously unstable and indeterminate nature of its narrative structure. To characterize the work as an early regional novel on the basis of its realist interest in local place and local speech is to overlook the extent to which it flagrantly displays its various fictional devices. The illiterate Thady's story, supposedly dictated to an editor, is complemented and extended by a preface, a glossary, and a series of scholarly footnotes, but in straining for an impression of editorial control and objectivity, the novel risks collapsing into incoherence.

The Wild Irish Girl likewise creates an impression of realist veracity and simultaneously undermines it. In this case, the use of epistolary conventions and polite English diction are compounded with scenes of romantic extravagance that strain credulity. Mortimer, the son of an absentee landlord, encounters the old Gaelic civilization and seeks in marriage a way of reconciling Irish tradition and English modernity. The ancestral ruins of Inismore and the wild landscape around it contribute to the novel's exploration of Irishness. The extravagant description of the Irish landscape is matched only by the elaborate description of the people who live there. An Irish Chieftain, a man 'gigantic in stature', with 'limbs of Herculean mould', wears 'a triangular mantle of bright *scarlet* cloth, embroidered and frayed round the edges' and 'fastened at the breast with a large circular golden brooch of a workmanship most curiously beautiful'. James Joyce was to seize on these exuberant descriptions of Irish nobility in his comic undermining of an idealized ancient Ireland in *Ulysses*.

Joyce also gave extended comic life to the 'broad-shouldered, loose-limbed, genial-faced giant' known as Hurrish in the 1886 novel of that title by Emily Lawless.[14] *Hurrish* opens with a powerful evocation of the wild Atlantic coast of the west of Ireland and suggests a correlation between this landscape and the wild Irish who dwell there. Hurrish's mother, the ardent patriot, Bridget O'Brien, is 'black-browed' and 'witch-like ... an elderly bird of prey ... with claws ever upon the watch to tear'. Remarkably, the book was praised for its accurate depiction of Ireland and the Irish. The London *St James Gazette* insisted on the novel's objectivity: 'At a time when the eyes of all men are turned upon Ireland, a vivid and striking picture of the Irish peasant as he really is – a description coloured by no political or partisan motive – is doubly valuable.' The *Dublin Irish Times* agreed that *Hurrish* offered 'A realistic and truthful depiction of existing conditions in Ireland', while the British Prime Minister, William Ewart Gladstone, considered the novel essential reading for anyone who wished to understand contemporary Irish politics and the raging Land Wars in the 1880s.[15]

Castle Rackrent, *The Wild Irish Girl*, and *Hurrish* all contain incidental details of setting and characterization that might loosely be identified as Gothic.[16] Wildness and strangeness at the level of description are often accompanied by heightened emotions of fear and terror, sporadic violence, and supernatural visitings. These are also the characteristic features of other European Gothic novels, but it might be argued that in Irish fiction they are bound up in a complex psychological way with political insecurity and the waning of colonial power. The title of 'first Irish Gothic novelist' is usually reserved for Charles Robert Maturin, whose Faustian hero Melmoth embodies a profound sense of dislocation and alienation. Sebastian Melmoth was the pseudonym adopted by Oscar Wilde as he embarked on his troubled wanderings after release from Reading

---

[14] See, for instance, Joyce's description of the 'longheaded deepvoiced bareknneed brawnyhanded hairylegged ruddyfaced, sinewyarmed hero' in the Cyclops episode of *Ulysses*. James Joyce, *Ulysses*, ed. Jeri Johnson (Oxford: Oxford University Press, 1993), 284.

[15] Quotations from reviews included in the preliminary pages of *Hurrish: A Study*, 3rd edn. (London and Edinburgh: William Blackwood & Sons, 1887).

[16] For an excellent account of Irish Gothic, see W. J. McCormack, *Dissolute Characters: Irish Literary History through Balzac, Sheridan Le Fanu, Yeats and Bowen* (Manchester: Manchester University Press, 1993), and also his introduction to 'Irish Gothic and After 1820–1945', in *The Field Day Anthology of Irish Writing*, ed. Seamus Deane (Derry: Field Day Publications, 1991), ii. 831–45.

Gaol in 1897. In the earlier period of the 1820s, however, Melmoth signifies the growing crisis of a Protestant Ascendancy collapsing in ruins and increasingly alienated by the shifting balance of power.

The House by the Church-yard (1863), Sheridan Le Fanu's macabre tale, also deserves its place in the haunted halls of Irish Gothic, even if the more obvious sensationalist aspects of the fiction sometimes detract from other areas of critical interest. As one of his editors remarked, 'his gusto for lively eccentric character might have made him an Irish Dickens if the ghosts had not dominated him'.[17] The proliferation of Irish Gothic writing should not come as a surprise. Edmund Burke's early writings on beauty gave aesthetic sanctioning to the sublime emotions of terror and fear, and Wolfe Tone (as good a name as any for a Gothic novelist) is thought to have tried his hand at the genre. A preoccupation with psychic disturbance and the supernatural persists in Irish writing, finding notorious expression in Bram Stoker's *Dracula* (1897), but also featuring significantly in the writings of Oscar Wilde, W. B. Yeats, and James Joyce. The celebrated closing story of Joyce's *Dubliners*, 'The Dead', takes on the lineaments of a ghost story when read within this context of Irish supernaturalism.

Songs and poems: enshrining the nation

Irish fiction in the nineteenth century provides an imaginative space for narratives riven with political insecurity and uncertainty. Irish poetry and Irish song, however, seem to strive for a more buoyant and assertive view of national identity and national destiny. The lyric potential of poetry is put to the service of an inspiring and enduring national spirit. Ironically, a new sense of national pride is furbished from the fragmented remains of a disappearing Gaelic culture. What is often regarded as antiquarianism provides a vital impulse for cultural nationalism throughout the nineteenth century. As Yeats and Augusta Gregory were to discover at the end of the century, the Literary Revival depended heavily on literary retrieval. One of the principal works informing this process of cultural recovery was Charlotte Brooke's *Reliques of Irish Poetry* (1789), which brought together a selection of Irish poems with translations for the benefit

---

[17] Introduction to *The House by the Church-yard* (Dublin: The Parkside Press, 1945), 3.

of an English-speaking audience. Brooke, like later revivalists, sees poetry as 'the vital soul of the nation' and wishes to convey an impression of Irish bardic refinement and nobility. Her cultural project, however, is to encourage a closer union between countries: 'The British muse is not yet informed that she has an elder sister in this isle; let us then introduce them to each other! Together let them walk abroad from their bowers, sweet ambassadresses of cordial union between two countries that seem formed by nature to be joined by every bond of interest, and of amity.' Later revivalists and translators like Samuel Ferguson would seek to perpetuate the spirit of *entente cordiale*, while Patrick Pearse and others would place their knowledge of Ireland's distinctive cultural heritage in the service of an uncompromising political separatism.

The idea that the 'spirit' of Gaelic culture might be preserved and conveyed through the English language was given widespread popular expression in Thomas Moore's *Irish Melodies*, published in ten parts between 1807 and 1834. Moore knew little Irish, but his success involved a certain kind of translation in fusing simple, affecting English lyrics with melancholic Irish airs. From the outset, Moore faced accusations that he had transformed the old Gaelic culture into drawing-room songs for easy consumption by the privileged few. William Hazlitt famously remarked that Moore 'converts the wild harp of Erin into a musical snuff-box'.[18] Intriguingly, however, the political resonance and potential of the songs seem all the greater for their willingness to risk sentimentality and nostalgia. The nationalist appeal of the songs derives, in part, from their quiet insistence on secrecy and solidarity, a technique that is aptly demonstrated in the title of Moore's impassioned tribute to Robert Emmet: 'Oh! breathe not his name.' The emotional force of Moore's lamentation for Ireland's betrayed and bewildered idealists left a powerful impact on the young James Joyce and the *Melodies* are recalled in his fiction as a shaping influence on the hearts and minds of several generations of Dubliners.

A similar conviction that songs might revive and sustain the spirit of the nation was central to the Young Ireland movement of the 1840s under the guidance of Thomas Davis. With two Catholic friends, Charles Gavan Duffy and John Blake Dillon, the Protestant

---

[18] P. P. Howe (ed.), *The Complete Works of William Hazlitt*, 21 vols. (London: J. M. Dent & Sons, 1930–4), vii. 234.

Davis founded *The Nation*, a journal that received wide ecumenical support. His own songs, among which the best known are probably 'The West's Asleep' and 'A Nation Once Again', undoubtedly owe something to Moore's example, though their nationalist sentiment is more brusque and overt than the mournful patriotic spirit of the *Melodies*. Like Moore, Davis appreciated the popular educative role of song in restoring national pride, but his role as an educator extended to many other spheres of Irish culture, including history, painting, and architecture. Davis provides a powerful stimulus for the Irish Literary Revival later in the century, even though Yeats and others resisted what they saw as an overtly dogmatic style. As well as seeking an alliance between peasant Ireland and the Protestant Ascendancy in the interests of political independence, his work provides an ideal of cultural nationalism that draws a sharp distinction between Irish imagination and creativity and English commercialism and philistinism.

Among the poets encouraged by Davis and his editorship of *The Nation* was James Clarence Mangan, whose legendary strangeness has tended to inhibit a full and serious consideration of his prodigious linguistic achievements. With his green spectacles, conical hat, and battered umbrella, and with a self-destructive propensity for alcohol and opium, Mangan provided a perfect image of the *poète maudit*. It is perhaps too easy to establish a correspondence between Mangan's tormented imagination and the political turmoil of his day. Even so, there is no doubt that his struggle for artistic integrity and recognition was caught up with the peculiar circumstances of being an Irish writer working with the English language in the charged political and cultural climate of the 1830s and 1840s. Mangan's earliest critics and biographers were inclined to present him as either an unworldly aesthete or a committed nationalist, but it was precisely the uncertain relationship between these roles and possibilities that informed a good deal of Mangan's work and fascinated W. B. Yeats and James Joyce, both of whom saw Mangan as a motivating force in the history of Irish writing.

In his 1902 and 1907 lectures on Mangan, Joyce acknowledges the poet as 'the type of his race', whose work embodies 'nobly suffered misfortunes' and 'irreparable devastations of the soul', but he also regards him as the type of the outcast artist and internal exile, 'a stranger in his country, a rare and bizarre figure in the streets'.[19] This dual response to Mangan epitomizes Joyce's own divided instincts concerning the role of the writer in modern Ireland. On the one hand, Mangan appears to be the unfortunate vessel for the great traditions of his race: 'love of sorrow, desperation, high-sounding threats'; on the other hand, he is 'one of those strange aberrant spirits who believe that the artistic life should be nothing other than the continuous and true revelation of the spiritual life'. It is Mangan's struggle between national and aesthetic priorities that prompts Joyce to see him as 'a would-be herald, a prototype for a would-be nation'.[20] Like Joyce's own Stephen Dedalus in *A Portrait of the Artist as a Young Man* (1914), Mangan's role is to forge anew 'the uncreated conscience' of his race.[21] Ultimately, Joyce's essay gives unstinting and unqualified praise to Mangan as 'the most distinguished poet of the modern Celtic world and one of the most inspired poets of any country ever to make use of the lyric form'.[22]

Mangan's lyric amplitude and felicity tend to conceal the fact that many of his best-known poems, including 'Dark Rosaleen' and 'Kathaleen Ny-Houlihan', are neither original compositions nor direct translations from the Irish. They are essentially reworkings or reinventions of Irish poems presented to Mangan in literal English versions already prepared by other scholars. This realization in no way diminishes the immediate political force of a poem like 'Dark Rosaleen', published in *The Nation* in 1846, during the most desperate months of the Great Famine. Mangan embodies that strange inverse proportion in modern Irish culture between the wealth of linguistic and imaginative resources and the deprivation of social and material existence. Brian Friel gives that predicament a memorable dramatic realization in his 1980 play *Translations*, when he has a hedge-school master, Hugh O'Donnell, tell a British soldier that 'certain cultures expend on their vocabularies and syntax acquisitive energies and ostentations entirely lacking in their material lives'.[23]

Set in the 1830s at a time when the Irish language is being rapidly

[19] James Joyce, *Occasional, Critical, and Political Writing*, ed. Kevin Barry (Oxford: Oxford University Press, 2000), 59, 135, 131.

[20] Ibid. 136, 134.

[21] James Joyce, *A Portrait of the Artist as a Young Man* (1916), ed. Jeri Johnson (Oxford: Oxford University Press, 2000), 213.

[22] Joyce, *Occasional, Critical, and Political Writing*, 130.

[23] Brian Friel, *Translations* (London: Faber and Faber, 1981), 42.

displaced by the introduction of a national school system promoting the English language, Friel's play explores the psychic and cultural consequences of linguistic dispossession. One of his characters, a young woman called Maire, who dreams of emigrating to America, cites Daniel O'Connell's verdict that 'the old language is a barrier to modern progress'.[24] At the same time, however, the play is sensitive to what has been lost and to what the country is about to suffer in the Famine years. The Famine hastened the decline of the Irish language so rapidly that by 1851 only 23 per cent of the population spoke Irish, and of these only 5 per cent were monoglot. Many writers would then have little choice but to declare with Yeats that 'Gaelic is my national language, but it is not my mother tongue'.[25] Translation gives only a fleeting impression of those qualities that Friel acknowledges when his hedge-school master pays ironic tribute to a language 'full of the mythologies of fantasy and hope and self-deception—a syntax opulent with tomorrows'.

The Irish Literary Revival: Yeats and Joyce

The impulse that generated the Irish Literary Revival at the end of the nineteenth century came largely from Protestant idealists such as W. B. Yeats, Augusta Gregory, J. M. Synge, Douglas Hyde, and George Russell. As Catholic nationalism intensified and Home Rule for Ireland became a strong possibility, it was imperative for these writers to have their say on matters of identity and nationality; and as Protestant power began to wane, it seemed that supremacy might be retained in the realm of culture if not practical politics. The Abbey Theatre, which opened in December 1904 and included *Cathleen ni Houlihan* and *Riders to the Sea* among its first productions, was a lasting realization of the desire that Yeats and others expressed for an Irish literary theatre. Yeats had a powerful role as poet, dramatist, folklorist, essayist, and critic in articulating the idea of a distinctive national literature. He was fond of quoting his friend and mentor, John O'Leary, on this issue: 'There is no great literature without nationality, no great nationality without literature.'[26] The

---

[24] Ibid.
[25] W. B. Yeats, 'A General Introduction for my Work' (1937), *Essays and Introductions* (London: Macmillan, 1961), 520.
[26] W. B. Yeats, *Letters to the New Island* (London: Macmillan, 1989), 30.

emphatic nature of this declaration disguises both the profound uncertainty about what constituted nationality in late nineteenth-century Ireland and the problematic attempt by writers like Yeats to embody national characteristics in literature.

One of the obvious problems confronting Yeats and his contemporaries was how to create an Irish national literature in the English language. There was no easy consensus on this issue. Opposition came from the likes of D. P. Moran, intent on promoting 'the philosophy of Irish Ireland', and from Irish language revivalists in the Gaelic League, founded on 31 July 1893. In a lecture to the National Literary Society in November 1892, the future president of the Gaelic League, Douglas Hyde, had spoken of 'the necessity for de-Anglicising Ireland'.[27] Yeats's response was to ask, 'Can we not build up a national tradition, a national literature, which shall be none the less Irish in spirit from being English in language?'[28] The most thoroughgoing exploration of this ideal was to appear later in Thomas MacDonagh's *Literature in Ireland: Studies Irish and Anglo-Irish*, published in the year he was executed by the British as one of the leaders of the 1916 rebellion. MacDonagh, to whom Yeats pays tribute in 'Easter 1916' ('So sensitive his nature seemed, | So daring and sweet his thought'), proposes an ideal of Irish writing in English that possesses sound patterns and rhythmic qualities reminiscent of the older Gaelic culture. There was no simple return to the past in any of this, but vigorous debate and a revolutionizing of tradition.

Yeats's early poem, 'The Lake Isle of Innisfree', shows how the syllabic measures and stresses of Gaelic poetry might be reproduced in English. This hybrid quality is evident in the title (an Anglicized version of the Gaelic place name 'Inis Fraoigh'), which both roots the poem topographically in Ireland and conveniently evokes the spirit of freedom. At the same time, however, the poem is written from an implied perspective of distance and remoteness from its subject. Yeats claimed that the poem came to him while he was walking homesick through Fleet Street in London. It is, essentially, a poem of willed return. Edward Said's post-colonial reading of early

[27] See D. P. Moran, *The Philosophy of Irish Ireland* (Dublin: James Duffy & Co., 1905), and Douglas Hyde, 'The Necessity for De-Anglicising Ireland', in *The Revival of Irish Literature*, ed. C. G. Duffy, G. Sigerson, and D. Hyde (London: T. Fisher Unwin, 1894).

[28] John Kelly and Eric Domville (eds.), *The Collected Letters of W. B. Yeats*, i: *1865–1895* (Oxford: Clarendon Press, 1986), 338.

poems by Yeats identifies a strong liberationist and utopian impulse in their geographical imagination—a seeming desire to recover lost territory—but just as powerful is the Protestant insistence on duty and responsibility in the resounding echo of Luke's Gospel (15: 18) in the King James Bible: 'I will arise and go to my father.'[29] The prodigal son is just one of a number of wandering figures with whom Yeats identifies in the early writings. His nationalism is both propelled and restrained by the peculiar estrangement and displacement of the Irish Protestant class to which he belonged.

'To Ireland in the Coming Times' (1892) is a revealing instance of Yeats's complicated nationalist sentiments. The forthright address and imperative mood of the opening lines create an impression of undivided commitment and unwavering loyalty:

> *Know, that I would accounted be,*
> *True brother of a company*
> *That sang, to sweeten Ireland's wrong,*
> *Ballad and story, rann and song . . .*

The poem's relationship with Irish national culture, however, is more complex than at first appears. Each stanza of the poem involves both a declaration of allegiance to national tradition and a declaration of difference:

> *Nor may I less be counted one*
> *With Davis, Mangan, Ferguson,*
> *Because, to him who ponders well,*
> *My rhymes more than their rhyming tell*
> *Of things discovered in the deep,*
> *Where only body's laid asleep.*

The pursuit of the red rose of spiritual beauty and an occultist fascination for 'things discovered in the deep' have to be reconciled with 'thoughts of Ireland'. The ancient past provides the most obvious meeting ground. Yeats's desire to 'Sing of old Eire and the ancient ways' was to be sorely tested, even within the early years of the 1890s.[30] In September 1894 he wrote to Alice Milligan that 'My experience of Ireland, during the last three years, has changed my

---

[29] Edward Said, *Yeats and Decolonization* (Derry: Field Day, 1988). This Field Day Pamphlet is reprinted in a slightly revised form in *Culture and Imperialism* (London: Chatto and Windus, 1993).

[30] This line is from Yeats's 1892 poem 'To the Rose upon the Rood of Time'.

views very greatly'. His belief now is that the role of the Irish man of letters is 'not so much to awaken or quicken or preserve the national ideal among the mass of the people but to convert the educated classes to it' and 'to fight for moderation, dignity, & the rights of the intellect among his fellow nationalists'.[31]

Loss of faith in a popular national literature and growing disillusionment with divisive nationalist politics are defiantly registered in Yeats's later poems. Heartfelt words and goodwill gestures for 'the dim coming times' are displaced by the more strident and acerbic idiom of poems like 'To a Shade' and 'September 1913' in the aptly titled volume, *Responsibilities* (1914). Both are profoundly elegiac poems, mourning the loss of a dignified civic idealism typified by Charles Stewart Parnell and John O'Leary respectively. Modern democracy and the lure of 'the greasy till' have spoiled an earlier pristine image of nationhood: 'Romantic Ireland's dead and gone, | It's with O'Leary in the grave'. The poem's refrain suggests an irrecoverable loss, yet in other ways the poem is strangely buoyant. What rescues it from defeatist gloom is its sheer rhetorical brilliance. In a beautifully cadenced shift of mood and register, the poem recalls both a seemingly lost heroism and an attitude of reverence that it once inspired. Among 'The names that stilled your childish play' are those of Robert Emmet and Wolfe Tone.

'To a Shade' dismisses the ghost of Parnell from the streets of modern Dublin, but the assertion that the time 'has not come' keeps alive a flicker of hope. In his 1923 Nobel Prize acceptance speech, Yeats looked back on Parnell's troubled career and saw in his demise a turning from parliamentary politics to other means of persuasion and coercion:

The modern literature of Ireland, and indeed all that stir of thought which prepared for the Anglo-Irish war, began when Parnell fell from power in 1891. A disillusioned and embittered Ireland turned from parliamentary politics; an event was conceived; and the race began, as I think, to be troubled by that event's long gestation.[32]

In the curious formulation of 'all that stir of thought' Yeats would appear to be including not just the modern literature of the Revival but the extra-parliamentary, revolutionary ideas of Patrick Pearse,

---

[31] Kelly and Domville (eds.), *The Collected Letters of W. B. Yeats*, i: *1865–1895*, 399.
[32] W. B. Yeats, *Autobiographies* (London: Macmillan, 1955), 559.

James Connolly, Maud Gonne, Constance Markiewicz, and others. The event 'conceived' is the Easter 1916 rebellion and the terms in which Yeats acknowledges that event are consonant with those in his poem 'Easter 1916', in which the uprising 'troubles' the living stream of history and 'A terrible beauty is *born*'.

To read Yeats's famous poem alongside other accounts of Easter 1916, including James Stephens's meticulous day-by-day rendering of events in *The Insurrection in Dublin*, is to be reminded of how strategically and stylishly Yeats mythologizes the rebellion and gives himself a place on the stage of an unfolding tragic drama. Easter 1916 did, of course, prove Yeats wrong in the assumptions that inform 'September 1913'. Another elegy with a different roll-call had then to be devised from the names of those who had only recently occupied the same Dublin haunts and thoroughfares as the urbane speaker of the poem: 'MacDonagh and MacBride | And Connolly and Pearse'. Pearse had written of 'the terrible, beautiful voice that comes out of the heart of battles', though Sheridan Le Fanu had earlier used the phrase 'a terrible beauty'.[33] In other respects, the poem is Burkean in its response to political violence. As well as grasping the 'terrible beauty' that Burke acknowledges in his treatise on the sublime and the picturesque, it resonates with an unmistakable echo of Burke's *Reflections on the Revolution in France*: 'All changed, changed utterly.' Burke's insistence that 'now all is to be changed' provides a touchstone for Yeats in his own changing world, and it surfaces again in the autumnal reflections of that great post-revolutionary poem, 'The Wild Swans at Coole'. Yeats continued to invoke the names of Robert Emmet and Wolfe Tone in poems like 'Parnell's Funeral' (1934), but it is Edmund Burke who hovers over the ancestral houses of his later civil war poetry and provides his most 'Befitting emblems of adversity'.

Burke is also a presiding spirit in the Irish literary tradition that Joyce constructs in his 1907 Italian lectures. Surveying developments in Irish literature written in the English language during the eighteenth century, Joyce applauds 'the so-called English Demosthenes, Edmund Burke, considered even by English critics as the most profound orator ever to speak in the Chamber of Deputies, and one of the most learned men of state even among the crafty ranks of

---

[33] See John Wilson Foster, 'Yeats and the Easter Rising', *Colonial Consequences: Essays in Irish Literature and Culture* (Dublin: Lilliput Press, 1991), 140.

the politicians of blonde Albion'.[34] Joyce also shares with Yeats a deep and abiding respect for Parnell, as well as a troubled dismay at some manifestations of nationalist sentiment in the period following the demise of Irish parliamentary fortunes.

There is a tantalizing glimpse of Joyce's thoughts on literature and nationalism in the remaining fragment of his 1907 lecture on the Irish Literary Renaissance. He notes how 'the youth of Ireland, disillusioned by the moral assassination of Parnell, aligns itself increasingly with a nationalism that is broader and, at the same time, more severe'. Despite sharing some political and cultural allegiances with Yeats, Joyce harboured very different notions of Irish nationality and was sharply critical of what he described as 'a revival in another guise of the ancient civilisation of the Celt'. Joyce felt no compunction to 'Sing of old Eire and the ancient ways'. In the third of his 1907 lectures, 'Ireland: Island of Saints and Sages', he makes the point emphatically: 'Just as ancient Egypt is dead, so is ancient Ireland. Its dirge has been sung and the seal set upon its gravestone.' The alternative conception of nationality that Joyce proposes is pluralistic, flexible, and accommodating: 'Our civilization is an immense woven fabric in which very different elements are mixed ... In such a fabric, it is pointless searching for a thread that has remained pure, virgin and uninfluenced by other threads nearby.'[35]

Throughout his fiction, Joyce ironically exposes essentialist notions of Irishness and comically undermines the heroic ideal of the Celt. His method in *Dubliners* (1914) is to counter prevailing images of a romantic Ireland with a sobering naturalistic truthfulness. Urging his publisher Grant Richards to proceed with the printing of his stories, Joyce insisted that his work would function as a moral corrective to the false consciousness of the time: 'I seriously believe you will retard the course of civilisation in Ireland by preventing the Irish people from having one good look at themselves in my nicely-polished looking-glass.'[36] Joyce's collection of short stories is not only an unflattering depiction of a stagnating colonial city, it is also an intensely psychological study of defeated aims and desires in the people who live there. 'A Painful Case', for instance, is a squalid narrative of drunkenness and suicide, but it also points to hidden

[34] Joyce, *Occasional, Critical, and Political Writing*, 123.
[35] Ibid. 137, 125, 118.
[36] *The Letters of James Joyce*, ed. Stuart Gilbert (London: Faber, 1957; 1966), 64.

depths of repression beyond the representational capacity of language.

In *Ulysses* (1922), the 'nicely polished looking-glass' is exchanged for 'the cracked lookingglass of a servant', a more appropriate symbol of Irish art and one that is borrowed from Oscar Wilde. In the opening episode of the novel, the looking-glass is literally a servant's mirror, but it is also a fitting emblem of colonial servitude and an indication that Irish fiction must now break decisively with the stable realist modes of the English novel. What Joyce then devises is 'a narrative frame . . . flexible enough to endure vertiginous variations of style'.[37] In doing so he liberates Irish fiction from any lingering sense of colonial inferiority to the English novel and gives to Irish writers a new freedom of experimentation with the English language. Seamus Heaney spoke for many of his contemporaries when he remarked that Joyce had shown how 'the English language was no longer an imperial humiliation but a native weapon'.[38]

The opening episode of *Ulysses* also plays satirically with familiar images of ancient Ireland and Revivalist hopes for the preservation of the Irish language. The old woman who arrives at the Martello tower and respectfully takes payment for her milk is both the Athenian messenger of Greek legend and the Shan Van Vocht of Irish legend. Ironically, though, she is unable to speak any Irish and cannot distinguish between French and Irish when the Englishman Haines demonstrates his linguistic skills: 'I don't speak the language myself. I'm told it's a grand language by them that knows.' Between *Dubliners* and *Ulysses* Joyce perfects a comic, satirical mode of writing in close alliance with a sceptical apprehension of the idealized, romantic aspects of cultural nationalism in his own day. At the same time, as Andrew Gibson reminds us, Joyce was deeply influenced by 'the pervasive hostility to England within Irish political and cultural nationalism', and his laughter is often the antagonistic laughter of the ironist or trickster. From the outset, *Ulysses* 'pits Stephen against the English presence in Ireland' and shows him resisting both the patronage of Haines and the complicity of Mulligan.[39]

[37] Seamus Deane, *A Short History of Irish Literature* (London: Hutchinson, 1986; 1989), 183.

[38] Seamus Heaney, 'The Interesting Case of John Alphonsus Mulrennan', *Planet*, 41 (Jan. 1978), 40.

[39] Andrew Gibson, *Joyce's Revenge: History, Politics, and Aesthetics in Ulysses* (Oxford: Oxford University Press, 2003), 4, 23.

Disillusion and reconstruction

The glamour of ancient civilization and the bright hopes of the
Revival continue to fade in Irish literature written after the mid-
1920s. Joyce's influence on a new generation of writers, including
Samuel Beckett and Flann O'Brien, was considerable in this respect,
but the country Joyce left behind was, in any case, a profoundly
different place. The momentous changes Yeats observed in the
aftermath of Easter 1916 ignited the War of Independence and led to
the founding of the Free State, partition of the country on sectarian
grounds, and ferocious civil war. The new generation was one that
felt acutely the thwarted nationalist aspirations and disappointed
ideals of the time. Yeats in *The Tower* (1928) is compelled to
reconsider his earlier artistic ideals as military conflict intrudes upon
his dwelling place, but the violence of armed struggle in the 1920s
is a subject that other writers turn to from a variety of perspectives.
It is present in the short stories of Seán O'Faoláin and Liam
O'Flaherty, in the plays of Seán O'Casey, in the memoirs of
Earnán O'Malley, and in the fiction of Elizabeth Bowen.

A strong mood of disillusionment seeps into many of the literary
works of the 1920s and 1930s as a newly independent state, severely
shaken by civil war, enters a period of sober reconstruction and
pragmatic reassessment. It might seem surprising, then, that this
should also be a time of comic exuberance, though the comedy of
Beckett, O'Brien, and O'Casey often seems to be wrung from a
depressed and restrictive social milieu or else satirically aimed at the
oppressive provincialism of post-revolutionary Ireland. Joyce's
comic spirit continues to provide an impulse here, as does that of
Oscar Wilde. If Wilde's best-known play, *The Importance of Being
Earnest* (1895) partakes of a fine tradition of Irish satire directed at
the English, his less well-known memoir, *De Profundis* (1905), joins
an equally honourable tradition of prison journals by Irish writers.
Wilde's assessment of himself and his fellow inmates evokes the
spirit of Irish tragicomedy: 'We are the zanies of sorrow. We are
clowns whose hearts are broken.' O'Casey catches that spirit with
impressive dramatic power and colloquial vigour in *Juno and the
Paycock* (1924) and the other plays in his *Dublin Trilogy*. So too, in
a more reflective mode, does Elizabeth Bowen, whose 1929 novel,
The Last September, is both a sombre elegy for the Anglo-Irish

Ascendancy in its moment of collapse and a zestful comic satire directed at the folly and complacency of that same class.

In short fiction, too, there is a comic style that tends towards ironic critique and often closes in melancholic reflection. It can be seen at work in Frank O'Connor's artfully crafted story, 'The Majesty of the Law', which gently weighs the claims of an isolated private morality against an officially sanctioned law and order, at the same time sedulously avoiding any dogmatic conclusion. O'Connor and his contemporaries look for the signs of social and moral integrity in a country that seems caught between small-town provincialism and metropolitan modernity. The title of Seán O'Faoláin's 'Lilliput' carries suggestions of Swiftian satire and points to the seemingly absurd conditions that prevail in a small town caught up in the War of Independence. The diminished revolutionary hopes of the time are evident in this early story, and the same can be said of Liam O'Flaherty's story, 'The Mountain Tavern', in which a frozen landscape seems emblematic of disappointed nationalist ideals. O'Flaherty's story both insists on a sense of continuity with the work of James Joyce and registers the profound disruption of Irish political history in the early twentieth century. The opening line of the story, 'Snow was falling', recalls the closing paragraph of 'The Dead' in Joyce's *Dubliners*, but the dead in this story are the victims of civil war and their presence persists like a black spot on the snowy landscape.

A strong anti-Revivalist impulse extends to the poetry of the 1920s and 1930s, though few writers manage to equal either the visionary brilliance or the fierce grasp of events that the work of W. B. Yeats displays in these decades. While not entirely neglecting ancient Ireland, the poetry written by Yeats's contemporaries tends to eschew romantic ideals and settle for a more modest set of images, often based on close attachment to local ways and customs, as can be seen in the poems of F. R. Higgins and Seumas O'Sullivan. It is Patrick Kavanagh, however, who best illustrates the poetic virtue of fidelity to place and time. The title of his 'Inniskeen Road: July Evening' aptly illustrates this point, but it also shows how Kavanagh takes that most prestigious of European literary forms—the sonnet— and makes it his own.

The partition of Ireland in 1921 meant that twenty-six counties now constituted the Irish Free State (not designated the Republic of

Ireland until 1949), while the six counties of Northern Ireland remained under British rule. Kavanagh's County Monaghan, historically part of Ulster, was not among the six designated counties of Northern Ireland. Geographically, however, Kavanagh was well positioned to influence poets both north and south of the border. Seamus Heaney was among a later generation of poets to be moved by 'something new, authentic and liberating' in Kavanagh's poetry.[40] That later generation also looked to the example of John Hewitt, whose poems seek to reconcile the national and regional imperatives of his imagination in the Ulster landscapes of his childhood. Hewitt was a socialist who admired the egalitarian principles of James Connolly, as well as an Ulsterman who was deeply attached to his region. His little-known early poems are aptly represented here by a critique of Revivalist glamour, a lyric reflection on the events of Easter 1916 and a eulogy on the Mourne Mountains.

It might be said that the Irish Literary Revival came to a final halt with the death of W. B. Yeats in 1939. In his great elegy, 'In Memory of W. B. Yeats', W. H. Auden famously declared of his fellow poet, 'mad Ireland hurt you into poetry'.[41] In different ways, Ireland also hurt into poetry the dazzling imagination of Louis MacNeice. MacNeice's *Autumn Journal*, published in 1939, is ample evidence that the sway of the Literary Revival is at an end. In earlier poems like 'Belfast' and 'Carrickfergus', MacNeice gives voice to the cultural distinctiveness of the north, associating it with particular historical, archaeological, and industrial images. In *Autumn Journal*, that other Ireland of romantic myth is sharply rebuked:

> Kathaleen ni Houlihan! Why
> Must a country, like a ship or a car, be always female,
> Mother or sweetheart?

It is not just MacNeice's ironic detachment that gives his work its special appeal. The verbal and visual excitement of poems like 'Snow' was to inspire later poets such as Michael Longley, Derek Mahon, Paul Muldoon, and Ciaran Carson.

1939 is a year in which modern Irish literature reaches new

---

[40] Seamus Heaney, 'From Monaghan to the Grand Canal: The Poetry of Patrick Kavanagh', in *Preoccupations: Selected Prose 1968–1978* (London: Faber and Faber, 1980), 116.

[41] *The English Auden: Poems, Essays and Dramatic Writings 1927–1939*, ed. Edward Mendelson (London: Faber and Faber, 1977; rev. 1978), 242.

heights of achievement. As well as seeing the publication of Yeats's *Last Poems*, MacNeice's *Autumn Journal*, and O'Brien's *At Swim-Two-Birds*, it also marks the appearance of James Joyce's *Finnegans Wake*, a novel of extraordinary linguistic exuberance. One obvious sign of the growing self-confidence of Irish literature at this time is its striking capacity for dialogue with earlier literary works, repeating and revising familiar themes and stylistic gestures. Across the period from 1789 to 1939, the writings included here enter into strange and unexpected constellations with each other, challenging and renewing the various ways in which Ireland has been imagined and defined. In this respect, these writings are not so much relics of cultural antiquity as glimpses of an imagined future, always waiting to be read and always ready to be newly understood. What they leave us with is a generous conception of possibilities: not just settled reflections of Ireland as it was, but vivid imaginings of a better, more peaceful Ireland in the coming times.

NOTE ON THE ANTHOLOGY

For ease of reference, the anthology is in two parts. Part One includes works written between 1789 and 1890, and Part Two includes works written between 1890 and 1939. The mid-point of 1890 is usually associated with the emergence of the Irish Literary Revival and the beginnings of Irish modernism. W. B. Yeats and others saw the death of Parnell in 1891 as the most significant event in the decade, marking a loss of faith in parliamentary politics and a turning to a cultural nationalism that would culminate in the Easter Rising of 1916. The chronological arrangement of the anthology provides a valuable correspondence between works of literature and moments of historical crisis. There are writings that emerge from, and respond to, the revolutionary spirit of the 1790s, the aspiring Catholic nationalism of the 1820s and 1830s, the Young Ireland Movement of the 1840s, the Fenian Movement of the 1860s, and the struggle for independence in the early decades of the twentieth century. History refuses to be relegated to some subordinate role as 'background' or 'context' to the literary works included here.

The purpose of the anthology, however, is not simply to illustrate the course of Irish history, but to encourage readers to discover for themselves the strange and unexpected ways in which works of literature engage with their times. The anthology highlights the formal and linguistic complexity of Irish literature in the period 1789 to 1939 and shows how stylistic attributes correspond to certain ways of seeing and organizing the world. The works included here are diverse in form: there are letters, speeches, memoirs, and travel writings, as well as novels, stories, songs, poems, and plays. The emphasis is on 'writing' rather than 'literature' in its conventional and sometimes limiting sense. The arrangement of texts is chronological but also generic, and it is hoped that this will draw attention to significant developments of a formal, discursive kind. If these texts relate to the world in particular ways, they also relate to each other, replaying and renewing familiar rhetorical devices and stylistic resources.

The anthology concentrates, nevertheless, on fiction, poetry, and drama. There are potent connections between the novels of

1789–1890 and those of 1890–1939. From *Castle Rackrent* onwards, there is a persistent concern with Irish character, Irish landscape, and Irish speech, and also with the conventions through which these might be effectively realized in fiction. Certain preoccupations can be traced across the scope of the anthology: a curious interest in Gothic motifs and situations, for instance, or an anxious dwelling on the fate of the Protestant Ascendancy and its 'Big House' culture. Extracts from novels can give a misleading impression of an author's work and sometimes there is a limited usefulness in detaching a particular episode or sequence from a larger narrative structure. A better strategy perhaps is to introduce a novel through its opening pages, giving readers an incentive to pursue the rest of the narrative outside the anthology. Several novels are introduced in this way, including *Castle Rackrent, Melmoth the Wanderer*, and *Hurrish*. Happily, it has been possible to include the whole of the opening episode of James Joyce's *Ulysses*. The short story is a form in which Irish writers have excelled and four stories (by James Joyce, Seán O'Faoláin, Liam O'Flaherty, and Frank O'Connor) are printed in their entirety.

If there is a personal indulgence in this anthology, it is in the broad selection of poetry offered to readers. With the obvious exception of Yeats, Irish poetry has not received the critical attention it deserves. As well as situating Yeats in relation to his acknowledged predecessors—Davis, Mangan, Ferguson—the anthology also considers some less well-known influences such as William Allingham, along with a fair selection of work by some of Yeats's contemporaries, including Ethna Carbery, Seumas O'Sullivan, and Francis Ledwidge. An anthology like this cannot hope to do justice to the wealth of poetry that has been made available through translations and versions of Gaelic originals. However, some indication of that rich resource can be found in the translations and near-translations undertaken by Charlotte Brooke, Thomas Furlong, James Clarence Mangan, Samuel Ferguson, Douglas Hyde, and Augusta Gregory.

Drama, unfortunately, fares less well than poetry. There are obvious problems in trying to extract a single scene or episode from a play text and in trying to convey the dramatic potential of the larger work. In the end, it is probably better to have a small number of plays in their entirety than a large number of plays in extracted form. Three prominent plays of the Literary Revival by W. B. Yeats,

Augusta Gregory, and J. M. Synge are presented here in full, along with extracts from well-known plays by Oscar Wilde and Seán O'Casey. Inevitably, copyright restrictions impinged upon the selection of materials in the anthology and had a greater impact on fiction and drama than on poetry.

In most cases, the texts presented here are those of the earliest printing in book form. For most of the novels, including *Ulysses*, the first edition has been chosen as the copytext. *Castle Rackrent* is an important exception, as the first edition of 1800 is generally considered inferior to that which appears in the 1832 collected edition of Maria Edgeworth's works. As well as removing minor errors and making some brief amendments, the 1832 edition introduces modern conventions of punctuation. Poems and stories are generally taken from collected editions of individual authors' works. If poems and stories have previously appeared in journals, there will be an accompanying explanatory note to this effect. The dates given in brackets in the contents pages generally refer to the first book publication. Plays are dated according to their first production. The dates provided for speeches *in extremis* by Robert Emmett and Roger Casement, for Daniel O'Connell's speech at Tara, and also for Wolfe Tone's autobiography, refer to the immediate circumstances of their composition and delivery. In a few other cases, as the explanatory notes make clear, the dates given are those of composition rather than publication. It is helpful, for instance, to know that W. B. Yeats's 'Easter 1916' was written in the year of the Rising and not in 1921 when it appeared in the book titled *Michael Robartes and the Dancer*.

In selecting the materials for this anthology and in preparing the editorial notes, I have turned for guidance to a good number of books on modern Irish history and literature, all of which are listed in the Select Bibliography. Over the past few years, however, some of these books have stayed with me and have been a continuing source of information and illumination. I have returned many times to Seamus Deane's *Strange Country: Modernity and Nationhood in Irish Writing Since 1790*, which I first encountered as the Clarendon Lectures in Oxford in 1995. *The Field Day Anthology of Irish Writing* has been an immensely valuable resource as well as a pleasure to read and re-read. I have also been inspired by Declan Kiberd's lucid and stimulating criticism, most recently in his *Irish Classics*. Terry Eagleton's

Irish trilogy—*Heathcliff and the Great Hunger, Crazy John and the Bishop*, and *Rebels and Scholars in Nineteenth-Century Ireland*—has made a massive contribution to the study of modern Irish culture, both offering new theoretical inroads and reclaiming some forgotten figures. Two other books have been especially helpful. David Pierce's *Irish Writing in the Twentieth Century: A Reader* has provided an excellent model of editorial endeavour and Robert Welch's *Oxford Companion to Irish Literature* has more than justified its title. Without the support and guidance of Judith Luna at Oxford University Press, I might have taken Yeats to heart and thrown poor words away. As well as putting her trust in this anthology from the outset, she has gently shaped it and brought it into being.

SELECT BIBLIOGRAPHY

Reference

B. Arnold, *A Concise History of Irish Art* (London: Thames and Hudson, 1969; rev. edn. 1977).

Henry Boylan, *A Dictionary of Irish Biography*, 3rd edn. (Dublin: Gill and Macmillan, 1999).

Anne M. Brady and Brian Cleeve, *A Biographical Dictionary of Irish Writers* (Mullingar: Lilliput Press, 1985).

S. J. Connolly (ed.), *The Oxford Companion to Irish History* (Oxford: Oxford University Press, 1998).

E. E. Evans, *Irish Folkways* (London: Routledge and Kegan Paul, 1957).

Alexander G. Gonzalez (ed.), *Modern Irish Writers: A Bio-Critical Sourcebook* (London: Aldwych Press; Westport, Conn.: Greenwood Press, 1997).

Robert Hogan (ed.), *The Macmillan Dictionary of Irish Literature* (London: Macmillan, 1980).

—— (ed.), *Dictionary of Irish Literature*, 2 vols. (Westport, Conn.: Greenwood, 1996).

W. J. McCormack (ed.), *The Blackwell Companion to Modern Irish Culture* (Oxford: Blackwell, 1999).

Sean McMahon and Jo O'Donoghue, *The Mercier Companion to Irish Literature* (Cork: Mercier Press, 1998).

Victor Meally (ed.), *Encyclopaedia of Ireland* (Dublin: Allen Figgis; New York and Toronto: McGraw Hill, 1971).

G. F. Mitchell, *The Irish Landscape* (London: Collins, 1976).

Bernard O'Donoghue (ed.), *Irish Quotations* (Oxford: Oxford University Press, 1999).

Sean Sheehan (ed.), *Dictionary of Irish Quotations* (Cork: Mercier Press, 1993).

Richard Wall, *A Dictionary and Glossary for the Irish Literary Revival* (Gerrards Cross: Colin Smythe, 1995).

Robert Welch (ed.), *The Oxford Companion to Irish Literature* (Oxford: Clarendon, 1996).

Anthologies

Dermot Bolger (ed.), *The New Picador Book of Irish Fiction* (London: Picador, 2000).

Angela Bourke *et al.* (eds.), *The Field Day Anthology of Irish Writing*, iv–v (Cork: Cork University Press, 2002).

Patricia Craig (ed.), *The Oxford Book of Ireland* (Oxford: Oxford University Press, 1998).

Seamus Deane (ed.), *The Field Day Anthology of Irish Writing*, i–iii (Derry: Field Day Publications, 1991).

Noel Duffy and Theo Dorgan (eds.), *Watching the River Flow: A Century in Irish Poetry* (Dublin: Poetry Ireland, 1999).

Henry Glassie (ed.), *Irish Folk Tales* (Harmondsworth: Penguin, 1987).

David H. Greene (ed.), *An Anthology of Irish Literature* (New York: Modern Library, 1954).

John P. Harrington (ed.), *Modern Irish Drama* (New York and London: W. W. Norton, 1991).

Marie Heaney (ed.), *Over Nine Waves: A Book of Irish Legends* (London: Faber, 1994).

Brendan Kennelly (ed.), *The Penguin Book of Irish Verse* (Harmondsworth: Penguin, 1979).

Thomas Kinsella (ed.), *The New Oxford Book of Irish Verse* (Oxford and New York: Oxford University Press, 1986).

Michael Longley (ed.), *20th-Century Irish Poems* (London: Faber and Faber, 2002).

Ferdia MacAnna (ed.), *An Anthology of Irish Comic Writing* (London: Michael Joseph, 1995).

Donagh MacDonagh and Lennox Robinson (eds.), *The Oxford Book of Irish Verse, XVIIth Century–XXth Century* (Oxford: Clarendon Press, 1958).

John Montague (ed.), *The Faber Book of Irish Verse* (London: Faber and Faber, 1978).

Paul Muldoon (ed.), *The Faber Book of Contemporary Irish Poetry* (London: Faber and Faber, 1986).

Frank O'Connor (ed.), *A Book of Ireland* (London: Collins, 1959).

—— *Classic Irish Short Stories* (Oxford and New York: Oxford University Press, 1985).

Maureen O'Rourke Murphy and James MacKillop (eds.), *Irish Literature: A Reader* (Syracuse, NY: Syracuse University Press, 1987).

David Pierce (ed.), *Irish Writing in the Twentieth Century: A Reader* (Cork: Cork University Press, 2000).

Lennox Robinson (ed.), *A Golden Treasury of Irish Verse* (London: Macmillan, 1925).

Desmond Ryan (ed.), *The 1916 Poets* (Westport, Conn.: Greenwood Press, 1963).

Colm Toibin, *The Penguin Book of Irish Fiction* (London: Viking, 2000).

William Trevor (ed.), *The Oxford Book of Irish Short Stories* (Oxford and New York: Oxford University Press, 1991).

History

J. C. Beckett, *The Making of Modern Ireland 1603–1923* (London: Faber and Faber, 1966).

—— *Confrontations: Studies in Irish History* (London: Faber and Faber, 1972).

—— *The Anglo-Irish Tradition* (London: Faber and Faber, 1976).

J. B. Bell, *The Secret Army: A History of the IRA 1916–79* (London: Blond, 1970; Dublin: Academy Press, 1979).

Paul Bew, *Land and the National Question in Ireland 1858–82* (Dublin: Gill and Macmillan, 1978).

—— *Conflict and Conciliation in Ireland 1890–1910: Parnellites and Radical Agrarians* (Oxford: Clarendon Press, 1987).

—— *Ideology and the Irish Question: Ulster Unionism and Irish Nationalism 1912–1916* (Oxford: Clarendon Press, 1994).

S. Clark and J. Donnelly (eds.), *Irish Peasants: Violence and Political Unrest 1780–1914* (Manchester: Manchester University Press, 1983).

P. J. Corish, *The Irish Catholic Experience: A Historical Survey* (Dublin: Gill and Macmillan, 1985).

Ruth Dudley Edwards, *An Atlas of Irish History*, 2nd edn. (London: Methuen, 1981).

Marianne Elliott, *Partners in Revolution: The United Irishmen and France* (London and New Haven: Yale University Press, 1978).

R. F. Foster, *Modern Ireland 1600–1972* (London: Allen Lane, Penguin Books, 1988).

—— (ed.), *The Oxford Illustrated History of Modern Ireland* (London: Oxford University Press, 1989).

T. Garvin, *Nationalist Revolutionaries in Ireland 1858–1928* (Oxford: Clarendon Press, 1987).

H. Gough and D. Dickson (eds.), *Ireland and the French Revolution* (Dublin: Irish Academic Press, 1990).

Alvin Jackson, *Ireland 1798–1998* (Oxford: Blackwell, 1999).

R. Kee, *The Green Flag: A History of Irish Nationalism* (London: Weidenfeld and Nicolson, 1972).

Desmond J. Keenan, *The Catholic Church in Nineteenth-Century Ireland* (Dublin: Gill and Macmillan, 1993).

Dáire Keogh, *The French Disease: The Catholic Church and Radicalism in Ireland 1790–1800* (Dublin: Four Courts Press, 1993).

Joseph J. Lee, *The Modernisation of Irish Society 1848–1918* (Dublin: Gill and Macmillan, 1973).

—— *Ireland 1912–85: Politics and Society* (Cambridge: Cambridge University Press, 1990).

C. D. A. Leighton, *Catholicism in a Protestant Kingdom: A Study of the Irish Ancien Régime* (Dublin: Gill and Macmillan, 1994).

F. S. L. Lyons, *Ireland Since the Famine* (London: Fontana, 1973).

—— *Culture and Anarchy in Ireland 1890–1939* (Oxford: Oxford University Press, 1979).

Ian McBride (ed.), *History and Memory in Modern Ireland* (Cambridge: Cambridge University Press, 2001).

T. W. Moody (ed.), *The Fenian Movement* (Cork and Dublin: Mercier Press, 1968).

C. H. E. Philpin (ed.), *Nationalism and Popular Protest in Ireland* (Cambridge: Cambridge University Press, 1987).

T. P. Power and K. Whelan (eds.), *Endurance and Emergence: Catholics in Ireland in the Eighteenth Century* (Dublin: Irish Academic Press, 1990).

Hugh Kearney, *The British Isles: A History of Four Nations* (Cambridge: Cambridge University Press, 1989).

Kevin Whelan, *The Tree of Liberty: Radicalism, Catholicism and the Construction of Irish Identity 1760–1830* (Notre Dame, Ind.: Notre Dame University Press, 1997).

—— *Fellowship of Freedom: The United Irishmen and 1798* (Cork: Cork University Press, 1998).

Literary and Cultural Criticism

Michael Allen and Angela Wilcox (eds.), *Critical Approaches to Anglo-Irish Literature* (Gerrards Cross: Colin Smythe, 1989).

E. A. Boyd, *Ireland's Literary Renaissance* (Dublin and London: Maunsel, 1916; rev. edn., New York: Barnes and Noble, 1968).

Malcolm Brown, *The Politics of Irish Literature: From Thomas Davis to W. B. Yeats* (London: Allen and Unwin, 1972).

Terence Brown, *Ireland: A Social and Cultural History 1922–1985* (London: Fontana, 1985).

—— *Ireland's Literature: Selected Essays* (Mullingar, Co. Westmeath: The Lilliput Press; Totowa, NJ: Barnes and Noble, 1988).

James M. Cahalan, *Great Hatred, Little Room. The Irish Historical Novel* (Syracuse, NY: Syracuse University Press, 1983).

—— *The Irish Novel: A Critical History* (Dublin: Gill and Macmillan, 1988).

—— *Modern Irish Literature and Culture: A Chronology* (New York: G. K. Hall; Toronto: Maxwell Macmillan, 1993).

David Cairns and Shaun Richards, *Writing Ireland: Colonialism, Nationalism and Culture* (Manchester: Manchester University Press; New York: St Martin's Press, 1988).

Andrew Carpenter (ed.), *Place, Personality and the Irish Writer* (Gerrards Cross: Colin Smythe, 1977).

Neil Corcoran, *After Yeats and Joyce: Reading Modern Irish Literature* (Oxford and New York: Oxford University Press, 1997).

Daniel Corkery, *The Hidden Ireland: A Study of Gaelic Munster in the Eighteenth Century* (Dublin: Gill, 1925; reprinted Gill and Macmillan, 1975).

—— *Synge and Anglo-Irish Literature* (Cork: Cork University Press, 1931).

Peter Costello, *The Heart Grown Brutal: The Irish Revolution in Literature from Parnell to the Death of Yeats, 1891–1939* (Dublin: Gill and Macmillan, 1977).

John Cronin, *Irish Fiction 1900–1940* (Belfast: Appletree Press, 1992).

Michael Cronin, *Translating Ireland: Translation, Languages, Cultures* (Cork: Cork University Press, 1996).

R. Davis, *The Young Ireland Movement* (Dublin: Gill and Macmillan, 1987).

Gerald Dawe and Edna Longley (eds.), *Across a Roaring Hill: The Protestant Imagination in Modern Ireland* (Belfast: Blackstaff Press, 1985).

Seamus Deane, *Celtic Revivals: Essays in Modern Irish Literature 1880–1980* (London: Faber and Faber, 1985).

—— *A Short History of Irish Literature* (London: Hutchinson, 1986).

—— (ed.), *Nationalism, Colonialism and Literature* (Minneapolis: Field Day Company and University of Minnesota Press, 1990).

—— *Strange Country: Modernity and Nationhood in Irish Writing Since 1790* (Oxford: Clarendon Press, 1997).

Denis Donoghue, *We Irish: The Selected Essays of Denis Donoghue* (London: Harvester Press, 1986).

Terry Eagleton, *Heathcliff and the Great Hunger: Studies in Irish Culture* (London: Verso, 1995).

—— *Crazy John and the Bishop* (Cork: Cork University Press, in association with Field Day, 1998).

—— *Scholars and Rebels in Nineteenth-Century Ireland* (Oxford: Blackwell, 1999).

Una Ellis-Fermor, *The Irish Dramatic Movement* (London: Methuen, 1939; revised edition 1954).

Richard Fallis, *The Irish Renaissance* (Syracuse, NY: Syracuse University Press, 1977).

Field Day Theatre Company, *Ireland's Field Day* (London: Hutchinson, 1985; Notre Dame, Ind.: University of Notre Dame Press, 1986).

Thomas Flanagan, *The Irish Novelists 1800–1850* (New York: Columbia University Press, 1959).

John Wilson Foster, *Fictions of the Irish Revival* (Dublin: Gill and Macmillan, 1987).

—— *Colonial Consequences: Essays in Irish Literature and Culture* (Dublin: Lilliput Press, 1991).

R. F. Foster, *Paddy and Mr Punch: Connections in Irish and British History* (London: Allen Lane, 1993).

—— *The Irish Story: Telling Tales and Making it Up in Ireland* (London: Allen Lane, 2001).

Robert F. Garratt, *Modern Irish Poetry: Tradition and Community from Yeats to Heaney* (Berkeley: University of California Press, 1986).

Luke Gibbons, *Transformations in Irish Culture* (Cork: Cork University Press, 1996).

Colin Graham and Richard Kirkland (eds.), *Ireland and Cultural Theory: The Mechanics of Authenticity* (Basingstoke: Macmillan, 1999).

Colin Graham, *Deconstructing Ireland: Identity, Theory, Culture* (Edinburgh: Edinburgh University Press, 2001).

Nicholas Grene, *The Politics of Irish Drama: Plays in Context from Boucicault to Friel* (Cambridge: Cambridge University Press, 1999).

W. E. Hall, *Shadowy Heroes: Irish Literature of the 1890s* (Syracuse, NY: Syracuse University Press, 1980).

Maurice Harmon (ed.), *Image and Illusion: Anglo-Irish Literature and its Contexts* (Dublin: Wolfhound Press, 1979).

—— *The Irish Writer and the City* (Gerrards Cross: Colin Smythe; Totowa, NJ.: Barnes and Noble, 1984).

Seamus Heaney, *Preoccupations: Selected Prose 1968–1978* (London: Faber and Faber, 1980).

—— *The Government of the Tongue* (London: Faber and Faber, 1988).

—— *The Redress of Poetry* (London: Faber and Faber, 1995).

—— *Finders Keepers: Selected Prose 1971–2001* (London: Faber and Faber, 2002).

Mark Patrick Hederman and Richard Kearney (eds.), *The Crane Bag Book of Irish Studies 1977–1981* (Dublin: Blackwater Press, 1982).

—— *The Crane Bag Book of Irish Studies 1982–1985* (Dublin: Blackwater Press, 1986).

Herbert Howarth, *The Irish Writers 1880–1940: Literature Under Parnell's Star* (London: Rockliff, 1958).

Stephen Howe, *Ireland and Empire: Colonial Legacies in Irish History and Culture* (Oxford: Oxford University Press, 2000).

Hugh Hunt, *The Abbey, Ireland's National Theatre 1904–1979* (Dublin: Gill and Macmillan, 1979).

J. Hutchinson, *The Dynamics of Cultural Nationalism: The Gaelic Revival and the Creation of the Irish Nation State* (London: Allen and Unwin, 1987).

Paul Hyland and Neil Sammells (eds.), *Irish Writing: Exile and Subversion* (Basingstoke: Macmillan; New York: St Martin's Press, 1991).

C. L. Innes, *Woman and Nation in Irish Literature and Society 1880–1935* (London: Harvester Wheatsheaf, 1993).

A. N. Jeffares, *Anglo-Irish Literature* (London: Macmillan, 1982).

Dillon Johnston, *Irish Poetry After Joyce* (Notre Dame, Ind.: University of Notre Dame Press, 1985).

Hugh Kenner, *A Colder Eye: The Modern Irish Writers* (London: Allen Lane, 1983).

Ben Levitas, *The Theatre of Nation: Irish Drama and Cultural Nationalism 1890–1916* (Oxford: Oxford University Press, 2003).

Toni O'Brien Johnson and David Cairns, *Gender in Irish Writing* (Milton Keynes: Open University Press, 1991).

Richard Kearney, *Transitions: Narratives in Modern Irish Culture* (Manchester: Manchester University Press, 1988).

—— *Postnationalist Ireland: Politics, Culture, Philosophy* (London and New York: Routledge, 1997).

Michael Kenneally (ed.), *Irish Literature and Culture* (Gerrards Cross: Colin Smythe, 1992).

Declan Kiberd, *Inventing Ireland: The Literature of the Modern Nation* (London: Jonathan Cape, 1995).

—— *Irish Classics* (London: Granta; Cambridge, Mass.: Harvard University Press, 2000).

Benedict Kiely, *Modern Irish Fiction: A Critique* (Dublin: Golden Eagle Books, 1950).

—— *A Raid into Dark Corners and Other Essays* (Cork: Cork University Press, 1999).

James F. Kilroy (ed.), *The Irish Short Story: A Critical History* (Boston: Twayne, 1984).

Joep T. Leersen, *Mere Irish and Fíor-Ghael: Studies in the Idea of Irish Nationality, its Development and Literary Expression Prior to the Nineteenth Century* (Amsterdam and Philadelphia: John Benjamins, 1988).

—— *Remembrance and Imagination: Patterns in the Historical and Literary Representation of Ireland in the Nineteenth Century* (Cork: Cork University Press, 1996).

David Lloyd, *Nationalism and Minor Literature: James Clarence Mangan and the Emergence of Irish Cultural Nationalism* (Berkeley: University of California Press, 1987).

—— *Irish Writing and the Post-Colonial Moment* (Dublin: Lilliput Press, 1993).

—— *Ireland After History* (Cork: Cork University Press, 1999).

Richard Loftus, *Nationalism in Modern Anglo-Irish Poetry* (Madison and Milwaukee: University of Wisconsin Press, 1969).

Edna Longley, *Poetry in the Wars* (Newcastle: Bloodaxe Books, 1986).

—— *The Living Stream: Literature and Revisionism in Ireland* (Newcastle: Bloodaxe Books, 1994).

Alan Marshall and Neil Sammells (eds.), *Irish Encounters: Poetry, Politics and Prose since 1880* (Bath: Sulis Press, 1998).

Augustine Martin, *The Genius of Irish Prose* (Dublin and Cork: Mercier Press, 1984).

W. J. McCormack, *Ascendancy and Tradition in Anglo-Irish Literature 1789–1939* (Oxford: Oxford University Press, 1985).

—— *From Burke to Beckett: Ascendancy, Tradition and Betrayal in Literary History* (Cork: Cork University Press, 1994).

Ronan McDonald, *Tragedy and Irish Literature* (Basingstoke: Palgrave, 2002).

D. E. S. Maxwell, *A Critical History of Modern Irish Drama 1891–1980* (Cambridge: Cambridge University Press, 1985).

Vivian Mercier, *The Irish Comic Tradition* (Oxford: Clarendon Press, 1962).

Julian Moynahan, *Anglo-Irish: The Literary Imagination in a Hyphenated Culture* (Princeton: Princeton University Press, 1995).

Paul Muldoon, *To Ireland, I* (Oxford: Oxford University Press, 2000).

James H. Murphy, *Catholic Fiction and Social Reality in Ireland, 1873–1922* (Westport, Conn.: Greenwood, 1997).

Christopher Murray, *Twentieth-Century Irish Drama: Mirror Up to Nature* (Manchester: Manchester University Press, 1997).

Ulick O'Connor, *Celtic Dawn: A Portrait of the Irish Literary Renaissance* (London: Hamilton, 1984).

Philip O'Leary, *The Prose Literature of the Gaelic Revival 1881–1921: Ideology and Innovation* (University Park, Pa.: Pennsylvania State University Press, 1994).

Tom Paulin, *Ireland and the English Crisis* (Newcastle: Bloodaxe Books, 1984).

—— *Writing to the Moment: Selected Critical Essays 1980–1996* (London: Faber, 1996).

Lionel Pilkington, *Theatre and State in Twentieth-Century Ireland: Cultivating the People* (London: Routledge, 2001).

Patrick Rafroidi and Terence Brown (eds.), *The Irish Short Story* (Gerrards Cross: Colin Smythe, 1979).

Shaun Richards, *The Drama of Modern Ireland: An Infinite Rehearsal* (Basingstoke: Macmillan, 2001).

Ray Ryan, *Ireland and Scotland: Literature and Culture, State and Nation, 1966–2000* (Oxford: Oxford University Press, 2000).

Gerry Smyth, *Decolonisation and Criticism: The Construction of Irish Literature* (London: Pluto, 1998).

Mark Storey, *Poetry and Ireland Since 1800: A Source Book* (London: Croom Helm, 1988).

Loreto Todd, *The Language of Irish Literature* (Basingstoke: Macmillan, 1989).

Robert Tracy, *The Unappeasable Host: Studies in Irish Identities* (Dublin: UCD Press, 1998).

William Trevor, *A Writer's Ireland: Landscape in Literature* (London: Thames and Hudson, 1984).

Norman Vance, *Irish Literature: A Social History* (Oxford: Blackwell, 1990).

—— *Irish Literature Since 1800* (Harlow: Longman, 2002).

Éibhear Walshe (ed.), *Sex, Nation and Dissent in Irish Writing* (Cork: Cork University Press, 1997).

G. J. Watson, *Irish Identity and the Literary Revival* (London: Croom Helm, 1979; 2nd edn., Washington: The Catholic University Press of America, 1994).

Robert Welch, *Irish Poetry from Moore to Yeats* (Gerrards Cross: Colin Smythe, 1980).

—— *A History of Verse Translation from the Irish 1789–1897* (Gerrards Cross: Colin Smythe, 1988).

—— *Changing States: Transformations in Modern Irish Writing* (London and New York: Routledge, 1993).

Katharine Worth, *The Irish Drama of Europe from Yeats to Beckett* (London: Athlone Press, 1978).

Studies of Individual Authors

Sue Asbee, *Flann O'Brien* (Boston: Twayne Publishers, 1991).

Derek Attridge (ed.), *The Cambridge Companion to James Joyce* (Cambridge: Cambridge University Press, 1990).

Malcolm Brown, *Sir Samuel Ferguson* (Lewisburg, Pa.: Bucknell University Press, 1973).

Terence Brown, *Louis MacNeice: Sceptical Vision* (Dublin: Gill and Macmillan, 1975).

Marilyn Butler, *Maria Edgeworth: A Literary Biography* (Oxford: Clarendon Press, 1972).

J. E. Chamberlin, *Ripe Was the Drowsy Hour: The Age of Oscar Wilde* (New York: Seabury Press, 1977).

Vincent Cheng, *Joyce, Race and Empire* (Cambridge: Cambridge University Press, 1995).

Anne Clissmann, *Flann O'Brien: A Critical Introduction to his Writings* (Dublin: Gill and Macmillan, 1975).

Elizabeth Butler Cullingford, *Yeats, Ireland and Fascism* (New York and London: New York University Press, 1981).

—— *Gender and History in Yeats's Love Poetry* (Cambridge: Cambridge University Press, 1993).

Alice Curtayne, *Francis Ledwidge: A Life of the Poet* (Dublin: New Island Books, 1998).

Peter Denman, *Samuel Ferguson: The Literary Achievement* (Gerrards Cross: Colin Smythe, 1990).

Tom Dunne, *Maria Edgeworth and the Colonial Mind* (Cork: Cork University Press, 1984).

Marianne Elliott, *Wolfe Tone: Prophet of Irish Independence* (London and New Haven: Yale University Press, 1989).

Richard Ellmann, *The Identity of Yeats* (London: Faber and Faber; New York: Oxford University Press, 1954).

—— *Eminent Domain: Yeats Among Wilde, Joyce, Pound, Eliot, and Auden* (New York: Oxford University Press, 1967).

—— *James Joyce* (1959; rev. edn. 1982; corr. New York: Oxford University Press, 1983).

—— *Yeats: The Man and the Masks* (rev. edn., New York: W. W. Norton, 1979).

—— *Oscar Wilde* (London: Hamish Hamilton, 1987).

James Fairhall, *James Joyce and the Question of History* (Cambridge: Cambridge University Press, 1993).

Richard Finneran (ed.), *Yeats Annual*, 1–2 (London: Macmillan, 1982).

R. F. Foster, *W. B. Yeats: A Life*, i: *The Apprentice Mage* (Oxford: Oxford University Press, 1997).

—— *W. B. Yeats: A Life*, ii: *The Arch-Poet* (Oxford: Oxford University Press, 2003).

Tom Furniss, *Edmund Burke's Aesthetic Ideology: Language, Gender and Political Economy in Revolution* (Cambridge: Cambridge University Press, 1993).

Andrew Gibson, *Joyce's Revenge: History, Politics, and Aesthetics in Ulysses* (Oxford: Oxford University Press, 2003).

Victoria Glendinning, *Elizabeth Bowen* (New York: Knopf, 1978).

Warwick Gould (ed.), *Yeats Annual* (London: Macmillan, 1985–).

Maurice Harmon, *Seán O'Faoláin: A Critical Introduction* (Notre Dame, Ind., and London: University of Notre Dame Press, 1966).

Keith Hopper, *Flann O'Brien: A Portrait of the Artist as a Young Post-modernist* (Cork: Cork University Press, 1995).

Marjorie Howes, *Yeats's Nations: Gender, Class and Irishness* (Cambridge: Cambridge University Press, 1996).

Michael Hurst, *Maria Edgeworth and the Public Scene: Intellect, Fine Feeling and Landlordism in the Age of Reform* (London: Macmillan, 1969).

A. Norman Jeffares, *A New Commentary on the Poems of W. B. Yeats* (Stanford Calif.: Stanford University Press, 1984).

Declan Kiberd, *Synge and the Irish Language* (London: Macmillan, 1979; 2nd edn. 1993).

Edward Larrissy, *Yeats the Poet: The Measures of Difference* (London: Harvester, 1994).

—— *W. B. Yeats* (Plymouth: Northcote House, 1999).

Hermione Lee, *Elizabeth Bowen: An Estimation* (Totowa, NJ: Barnes and Noble, 1981).

Edna Longley, *Louis MacNeice: A Study* (London: Faber and Faber, 1988).

Maud Gonne MacBride, *A Servant of the Queen* (1938), ed. A. N. Jeffares and Anna MacBride White (Gerrards Cross: Colin Smythe, 1994).

Colin MacCabe, *James Joyce and the Revolution of the Word* (London: Macmillan, 1978; 2nd edn., Palgrave, 2002).

—— (ed.), *James Joyce: New Perspectives* (Brighton: Harvester Press, 1982).

Jerusha McCormack (ed.), *Wilde the Irishman* (New Haven and London: Yale University Press, 1998).

W. J. McCormack, *Sheridan Le Fanu and Victorian Ireland* (Oxford: Clarendon Press, 1980).

—— *Dissolute Characters: Irish Literary History through Balzac, Sheridan Le Fanu, Yeats and Bowen* (Manchester: Manchester University Press, 1993).

—— *Fool of the Family: A Life of J. M. Synge* (London: Weidenfeld and Nicolson, 2000).

Oliver MacDonagh, *O'Connell: The Life of Daniel O'Connell 1775–1847* (London: Weidenfeld and Nicolson, 1991).

Peter McDonald, *Louis MacNeice: The Poet in his Contexts* (Oxford: Oxford University Press, 1991).

Dominic Manganiello, *Joyce's Politics* (London: Routledge and Kegan Paul, 1980).

Katherine Mullin, *James Joyce, Sexuality and Social Purity* (Cambridge: Cambridge University Press, 2003).

Sean Mythen, *Thomas Furlong: The Forgotten Wexford Poet* (Ferns, Co. Wexford: Clone Publications, 1998).

Emer Nolan, *James Joyce and Nationalism* (London and New York: Routledge, 1995).

Johann Norstedt, *Thomas MacDonagh: A Critical Biography* (Charlottesville, Va.: University of Virginia Press, 1980).

David Pierce, *James Joyce's Ireland* (New Haven and London: Yale University Press, 1992).

—— *Yeats's Worlds: Ireland, England and the Poetic Imagination* (New Haven and London: Yale University Press, 1995).

Hilary Robinson, *Somerville and Ross: A Critical Appreciation* (Dublin: Gill and Macmillan, 1980).

Ellen Shannon-Mangan, *James Clarence Mangan: A Biography* (Dublin: Irish Academic Press, 1996).

Jon Stallworthy, *Louis MacNeice* (London: Faber and Faber, 1995).

Michael Steinman, *Yeats's Heroic Figures: Wilde, Parnell, Swift, Casement* (London: Macmillan, 1983).

John Stokes, *Oscar Wilde* (London: Longman, 1978).

—— *Oscar Wilde: Myths, Miracles, and Intentions* (Cambridge: Cambridge University Press, 1996).

Mary Helen Thuente, *W. B. Yeats and Irish Folklore* (Dublin: Gill and Macmillan, 1980).

Deirdre Toomey (ed.), *Yeats and Women* (Basingstoke: Macmillan, 1997).

Joseph Valente, *James Joyce and the Problem of Justice* (Cambridge: Cambridge University Press, 1995).

Anne Varty, *A Preface to Oscar Wilde* (London: Addison-Wesley, 1998).

Katie Wales, *The Language of James Joyce* (Basingstoke: Macmillan, 1992).

Thomas R. Whitaker, *Swan and Shadow: Yeats's Dialogue with History* (Chapel Hill, NC: University of North Carolina Press, 1964).

Further Reading in Oxford World's Classics

Edmund Burke, *A Philosophical Enquiry into the Origin of our Idea of the Sublime and Beautiful*, ed. Adam Phillips.

—— *Reflections on the Revolution in France*, ed. L. G. Mitchell.

Maria Edgeworth, *The Absentee*, ed. W. J. McCormack and Kim Walker.

—— *Belinda*, ed. Kathryn Kirkpatrick.

—— *Castle Rackrent*, ed. George Watson.

Empire Writing: An Anthology of Colonial Literature 1870–1918, ed. Elleke Boehmer.

—— *Dubliners*, ed. Jeri Johnson.

James Joyce, *Occasional, Critical, and Political Writing*, ed. Kevin Barry.

James Joyce, *A Portrait of the Artist as a Young Man*, ed. Jeri Johnson.

—— *Ulysses: The 1922 Text*, ed. Jeri Johnson.

Sheridan Le Fanu, *In a Glass Darkly*, ed. Robert Tracy.

Charles Maturin, *Melmoth the Wanderer*, ed. Douglas Grant.

Sydney Owenson (Lady Morgan), *The Wild Irish Girl*, ed. Kathryn Kirkpatrick.

Bram Stoker, *Dracula*, ed. Maud Ellmann.

J. M. Synge, *The Playboy of the Western World and Other Plays*, ed. Ann Saddlemyer.

Oscar Wilde, *The Major Works*, ed. Isobel Murray.

W. B. Yeats, *The Major Works*, ed. Edward Larrissy.

CHRONOLOGY OF KEY EVENTS

1789   *Reliques of Irish Poetry* by Charlotte Brooke.

1790   *Reflections on the Revolution in France* by Edmund Burke.

1791   Wolfe Tone's *Argument on behalf of the Catholics of Ireland* and the foundation of United Irishmen. Catholic Committee petitions for civil rights.

1792   Relief Act allows Catholics to practise law. Belfast Harp Festival.

1793   Relief Act admits Catholics to parliamentary franchise. Irish Militia established.

1794   Dublin United Irishmen suppressed. Birth of William Carleton.

1795   Catholic seminary established at Maynooth. Orange Order founded.

1796   Insurrection Act and suspension of habeas corpus. French invasion attempted at Bantry Bay in support of United Irishmen.

1797   Death of Edmund Burke.

1798   Martial law imposed. Rebellion in Wexford (May). French fleet under General Humbert lands in Killala (Aug.). Wolfe Tone arrested and dies by his own hand (Nov.).

1800   Act of Union between Great Britain and Ireland receives royal assent. Ireland to be governed by Westminster. *Castle Rackrent* by Maria Edgeworth.

1801   Act of Union effective.

1803   Robert Emmet's rising, trial, and execution. Birth of James Clarence Mangan.

1806   *The Wild Irish Girl* by Sydney Owenson (Lady Morgan).

1808   Foundation of the Christian Brothers.

1810   Birth of Samuel Ferguson.

1812   *The Absentee* by Maria Edgeworth.

1814   Birth of Sheridan Le Fanu and Thomas Davis.

1820   *Melmoth the Wanderer* by Charles Maturin.

1821   Theatre Royal, Dublin, opened.

1822   Irish Constabulary Act, establishing county police forces and a salaried magistracy.

1823   Catholic Association founded, led by Daniel O'Connell.

1824   Free Trade in manufactured articles established between Britain and Ireland.

1825   Catholic Emancipation bill rejected by House of Lords.

1828   O'Connell elected for County Clare.

1829   Catholic Emancipation Act allows Catholics to sit in parliament.

1830   *Traits and Stories of the Irish Peasantry* by William Carleton (2nd series, 1833).

1831   Introduction of national system of elementary education. Foundation of the Sisters of Mercy.

1832   Irish Reform Act passed.

1833   Irish Church Temporalities Act. *Dublin University Magazine* founded.

1834   O'Connell introduces a parliamentary debate on repeal of the Union. First steam-powered train in Ireland. *Reliques of Father Prout* by Francis Sylvester Mahony.

1837   Accession of Queen Victoria.

1838   Irish Poor Law enacted. Foundation of Father Mathew's temperance movement.

1840   O'Connell's Repeal Association founded. Irish Municipal Reform Act.

1841   First reliable census of the population (8,175,124 people recorded). *Cork Examiner* founded. O'Connell elected Lord Mayor of Dublin.

1842   *The Nation* newspaper founded by Thomas Davis.

1843   'Monster' repeal meeting held at Tara, Co. Meath. Repeal meeting at Clontarf prohibited.

1845   Colleges Act: Queen's Colleges established in Belfast, Cork, and Galway. Blight in the potato harvest. Beginning of the Great Famine (1845–9). Death of Thomas Davis.

1846   Repeal of the Corn Laws. Total failure of potato harvest. First deaths from starvation (Oct.). Posthumous publication of *Poems* and *Literary and Historical Essays* by Thomas Davis.

1847   Foundation of Irish Confederation. Peak of fever academic. Death of Daniel O'Connell.

1848   Foundation of the *United Irishman* journal by John Mitchel. Rising of Young Irelanders in Ballingarry, Co. Tipperary.

1849   Encumbered Estates Act, facilitating sale of land. Opening of the Queen's Colleges. *The Poets and Poetry of Munster* by James Clarence Mangan. Death of Mangan. Death of Maria Edgeworth.

1850   Irish Reform Act trebles county electorate and reduces borough electorate. Establishment of the Irish Tenant League.

1851 Census taken (6,552,385 people recorded).

1852 Birth of George Moore. Birth of Isabella Augusta Persse (Lady Gregory). Death of Thomas Moore.

1854 Catholic University of Ireland founded under the rectorship of John Henry Newman. Birth of Oscar Wilde.

1856 Phoenix Society (forerunner of the Fenian movement) founded in Skibbereen. Birth of George Bernard Shaw.

1858 James Stephens returns from France and establishes the Irish Republican Brotherhood.

1859 Fenian Brotherhood founded in the USA. First number of the *Irish Times*.

1860 *Collected Works* by William Carleton. Birth of Douglas Hyde.

1861 Census taken (5,798,967 people recorded).

1863 *The House by the Church-yard* by Sheridan Le Fanu.

1865 John O'Leary arrested. Birth of W. B. Yeats. *Lays of the Western Gael* by Samuel Ferguson.

1866 Archbishop Paul Cullen becomes the first Irish Cardinal.

1867 Fenian rising suppressed. Execution of the 'Manchester Martyrs'. Birth of George Russell (AE). *On the Study of Celtic Literature* by Matthew Arnold.

1868 Foundation of the Amnesty campaign for Fenian prisoners.

1869 Disestablishment of the Church of Ireland by W. E. Gladstone. Death of William Carleton. Birth of John Millington Synge.

1870 Gladstone's first Irish Land Act, acknowledging tenant rights. Foundation of the Home Rule movement by Isaac Butt.

1871 Census taken (5,412,377 people recorded).

1873 Home Rule League founded. Defeat of Gladstone's Irish University Bill. Death of Sheridan Le Fanu.

1874 UK General election: 60 Home Rulers elected. Home Rule Parliamentary Party created.

1875 Charles Stewart Parnell elected MP for County Meath.

1876 Society for the Preservation of the Irish Language established.

1877 Parnell elected president of Home Rule Confederation of Great Britain.

1878 *History of Ireland: Heroic Period* by Standish O'Grady (Vol. II in 1880). Birth of Oliver St John Gogarty.

1879 Irish National Land League founded. Beginning of land agitation at Irishtown, Co. Mayo. Birth of Patrick Pearse.

1880 Parnell elected chairman of Irish Parliamentary Party. Parnell visits the USA. Birth of Seán O'Casey. Birth of James Stephens.

1881 Gladstone's second Land Act. Ladies' Land League founded. Royal University of Ireland established. Census taken (5,174,836 people recorded). Birth of Padraic Colum. *Poems* by Oscar Wilde.

1882 Irish National League replaces Land League. Kilmainham 'treaty' marks end of land war. Phoenix Park murders of Chief Secretary of Ireland, Lord Frederick Cavendish, and his Under-Secretary, T. H. Burke. Gaelic League founded. University College, Dublin, founded. Birth of James Joyce.

1884 Franchise extended by Representation of the People Act. Gaelic Athletic Association founded.

1885 Irish Loyal and Patriotic Union founded. Irish Parliamentary Party under Parnell wins 86 seats at Westminster.

1886 Government of Ireland (Home Rule) bill defeated in Commons. Death of Samuel Ferguson. *Hurrish* by Emily Lawless.

1887 National Library of Ireland established.

1888 *Confessions of a Young Man* by George Moore. *The Happy Prince and Other Tales* by Oscar Wilde. *Fairy and Folk Tales of the Irish Peasantry* by W. B. Yeats.

1889 O'Shea names Parnell as co-respondent in divorce petition. *The Wanderings of Oisin and Other Poems* by W. B. Yeats.

1890 Gladstone threatens to resign if Parnell remains as leader. Parnell denounced by own party. *Beside the Fire: A Collection of Irish Gaelic Folk Stories* by Douglas Hyde.

1891 Parnell's death (Oct.). Irish Literary Society founded in London by W. B. Yeats and others. *The Quintessence of Ibsenism* by George Bernard Shaw. *The Picture of Dorian Gray* by Oscar Wilde.

1892 *The Countess Kathleen and Various Legends and Lyrics* by W. B. Yeats. *Lady Windermere's Fan* by Oscar Wilde.

1893 Second Government of Ireland (Home Rule) bill defeated in Lords. Gaelic League founded, with Douglas Hyde as president. *Love Songs of Connacht* by Douglas Hyde. *The Celtic Twilight* by W. B. Yeats. *Salomé* by Oscar Wilde.

1894 Foundation of Irish Agricultural Organisation Society and Irish Trades Union Congress. *Esther Waters* by George Moore. *The Real Charlotte* by Edith Somerville and Martin Ross.

1895 *The Story of Early Gaelic Literature* by Douglas Hyde. *The Importance of Being Earnest* and *An Ideal Husband* by Oscar Wilde. Trial and imprisonment of Oscar Wilde.

1896   Foundation of the Irish Socialist Republican Party. Birth of Liam O'Flaherty.

1897   *Bards of the Gael and Gall* by George Sigerson. *Dracula* by Bram Stoker. *The Secret Rose* by W. B. Yeats.

1898   United Irish League founded. Local government reform applies parliamentary franchise to local elections, extending vote to some women. *The Ballad of Reading Gaol* by Oscar Wilde.

1899   *United Irishman* founded by Arthur Griffith. Irish Literary Theatre founded. *A Literary History of Ireland* by Douglas Hyde. *The Heather Field* by Edward Martyn. *Some Experiences of an Irish R. M.* by Edith Somerville and Martin Ross. *The Wind Among the Reeds* by W. B. Yeats.

1900   John Redmond elected Chairman of Irish Parliamentary Party and United Irish League. *The Leader* begun by D. P. Moran. 'The Necessity for De-Anglicising Ireland' (lecture) by Douglas Hyde. Death of Oscar Wilde. Birth of Seán O'Faoláin.

1901   Death of Queen Victoria and accession of Edward VII. Census taken (4,458,775 people recorded).

1902   Land conference brings together landlords and tenants. Maud Gonne in first performance of *Cathleen ni Houlihan* by W. B. Yeats and Lady Augusta Gregory. *Cuchulain of Muirthemne* by Lady Gregory.

1903   Land Act: comprehensive scheme of land purchase launched. Formation of Arthur Griffith's National Council and Sloan's Independent Orange Order. *Poets and Dreamers* by Lady Gregory. *The Untilled Field* by George Moore. Birth of Frank O'Connor (Michael Francis O'Donovan).

1904   Irish Reform Association founded. Abbey Theatre, Dublin, opened. Irish Folk Song Society formed. *John Bull's Other Island* by George Bernard Shaw. *Riders to the Sea* by J. M. Synge. *In the Seven Woods* by W. B. Yeats. Birth of Patrick Kavanagh. James Joyce leaves Ireland.

1905   Formation of Ulster Unionist Council and Irish Industrial Development Association. Sinn Féin established. *The Philosophy of Irish Ireland* by D. P. Moran. *In the Shadow of the Glen* and *The Well of the Saints* by J. M. Synge. *De Profundis* by Oscar Wilde.

1906   *Religious Songs of Connacht* by Douglas Hyde. Birth of Samuel Beckett.

1907   Dockers' strike and riots in Belfast. Rioting at opening performances of *The Playboy of the Western World* by J. M. Synge. *The*

Rising of the Moon by Lady Gregory. *Deirdre* by W. B. Yeats. *The Aran Isles* by J. M. Synge. Birth of Louis MacNeice.

1908 National University of Ireland established. *The Tinker's Wedding* by J. M. Synge. Irish Women's Franchise League founded by Hannah and Francis Sheehy-Skeffington.

1909 Foundation of Irish Transport and General Workers' Union by James Larkin. First compulsory powers of land purchase enacted.

1910 Edward Carson becomes leader of Ulster Unionist Party. *Deirdre of the Sorrows* by J. M. Synge. *The Green Helmet and Other Poems* by W. B. Yeats.

1911 SS *Titanic* launched by Harland and Wolff in Belfast. Census taken (4,381,951 people recorded). *Hail and Farewell* by George Moore. Birth of Flann O'Brien.

1912 Asquith's introduction of third Government of Ireland (Home Rule) bill. Irish Labour Party begun by James Connolly and James Larkin. Catholic workers expelled from Belfast shipyards. Ulster Covenants signed on 'Ulster Day' (28 Sept.) in opposition to Home Rule. *Titanic* disaster. *The Crock of Gold* by James Stephens.

1913 Formation of Ulster Volunteer Force, Irish Citizens' Army, and Irish (National) Volunteers. Dublin strikes and lock-out. Death of Emily Lawless. *Collected Poems* by AE (George Russell).

1914 Illegal importation of arms by Ulster Volunteers and Irish Volunteers. Buckingham Palace conference fails to reach agreement on exclusion of Ulster from Home Rule. Outbreak of war between Britain and Germany. Home Rule enacted but suspended. *Responsibilities* by W. B. Yeats. *Dubliners* by James Joyce.

1915 Reorganization of the Irish Republican Brotherhood. Military Council formed. Gaelic League votes to take a more overtly political line and Douglas Hyde resigns from the presidency. *Lusitania* sunk by U-boat (Sir Hugh Lane among passengers lost).

1916 Easter Rising. Irish Republic proclaimed in Dublin (24 Apr.). Martial law imposed, rebels surrender (29 Apr.) and face imprisonment and execution. Lloyd George attempts to implement Home Rule with exclusion of six counties. W. B. Yeats composes 'Easter 1916'. Sir Roger Casement hanged. *Songs of the Fields* by Francis Ledwidge. *Literature in Ireland, Studies Irish and Anglo-Irish* by Thomas MacDonagh. *A Portrait of the Artist as a Young Man* by James Joyce.

1917 Sinn Féin and Irish Volunteers reorganize under Eamon de Valera's leadership. *The Wild Swans at Coole* by W. B. Yeats.

1918   Sinn Féin success (73 seats) in general election (Dec.). *Exiles* by James Joyce.

1919   Anglo-Irish War (War of Independence), 1919–21. Formation of Dáil Éireann. De Valera seeks recognition of Irish claim through Peace Conference and embarks on tour of USA.

1920   Better Government of Ireland Act introduces partition between two Home Rule states. Riots in Derry and Belfast. Revival of Ulster Volunteers, expulsion of Catholic shipyard workers, and Republican 'Belfast Boycott'. Reorganization of police and imposition of limited martial law. Terence MacSwiney, Mayor of Cork, dies on hunger strike in Brixton Prison.

1921   Truce in Anglo-Irish War. Meetings of Lloyd George and de Valera followed by peace conference and Anglo-Irish Treaty (6 Dec.). *Michael Robartes and the Dancer* by W. B. Yeats.

1922   Formation of provisional government under Michael Collins (Jan.). Convention of anti-Treaty Irish Republican Army. Arrest of anti-Treaty leaders and outbreak of Civil War (June). National Army given emergency powers. Assassination of Michael Collins. Inauguration of Irish Free State. *Ulysses* by James Joyce.

1923   End of Civil War. Irish Free State government led by W. T. Cosgrave. Free State admitted to League of Nations. W. B. Yeats awarded Nobel Prize for poetry. *The Shadow of a Gunman* by Seán O'Casey.

1924   Reorganization of National Army. Death of Edward Martyn. *The Hidden Ireland* by Daniel Corkery. *Juno and the Paycock* by Seán O'Casey.

1925   Partition confirmed by tripartite agreement. *A Vision* by W. B. Yeats. *The Informer* by Liam O'Flaherty.

1926   De Valera founds Fianna Fáil. Radio Eireann begins broadcasting. Rioting at opening of *The Plough and the Stars* by Seán O'Casey. Census taken (2,971,992 people recorded in Irish Free State and Northern Ireland).

1927   Kevin O'Higgins, Minister of Justice, assassinated. Fianna Fáil enters Dáil. General election, Irish Free State. *Pomes Penyeach* by James Joyce.

1928   Gate Theatre, Dublin, opened. *The Tower* by W. B. Yeats.

1929   General election, Northern Ireland. Opening of the Shannon hydro–electric scheme. Proportional Representation abolished in Northern Ireland. Censorship of Publications Act. *The Last September* by Elizabeth Bowen. *The Silver Tassie* by Seán O'Casey.

1930   Irish Free State elected to the Council of the League of Nations. Irish Labour Party and Trades Union Congress separate.

1931   Banning of the IRA in Free State. *The Moon in the Yellow River* by Denis Johnston. *Guests of the Nation* by Frank O'Connor.

1932   Fianna Fáil success in general election. De Valera replaces Cosgrave as president of Executive Council. Opening of the Stormont parliament building in Northern Ireland. Death of Lady Gregory. *Midsummer Madness* by Seán O'Faoláin. *Words for Music Perhaps* by W. B. Yeats.

1933   National Guard (Blueshirts) formed. United Ireland Party (Fine Gael) formed under O'Duffy (Blueshirts leader). Death of George Moore. *A Nest of Simple Folk* by Seán O'Faoláin. *The Winding Stair and Other Poems* and *Collected Poems* by W. B. Yeats.

1934   Cosgrave reinstated as O'Duffy resigns. *Collected Plays* by W. B. Yeats.

1935   Irish Folklore Commission established. Public Dance Halls Act. Rioting in Belfast during celebrations of George V's Jubilee. Death of Edward Carson. Death of George Russell (AE). *Poems* by Louis MacNeice. *A Full Moon in March* by W. B. Yeats.

1936   Free State Senate abolished. IRA proscribed. First Aer Lingus flight from Dublin to London. *Ploughman and Other Poems* by Patrick Kavanagh. *Bird Alone* by Seán O'Faoláin.

1937   General election and constitutional referendum. Constitution of Éire replaces Free State. *Famine* by Liam O'Flaherty. *As I Was Going Down Sackville Street* by Oliver St John Gogarty.

1938   Anglo-Irish Agreement: settlement of economic war. New Irish Senate established. Douglas Hyde elected first President of Éire. *Murphy* by Samuel Beckett. *The Death of the Heart* by Elizabeth Bowen. *The Green Fool* by Patrick Kavanagh. *New Poems* by W. B. Yeats.

1939   IRA bombing campaign in Britain. Éire's declaration of neutrality implemented after outbreak of Second World War (Sept.). Death of W. B. Yeats. *Last Poems and Two Plays* by W. B. Yeats. *Finnegans Wake* by James Joyce. *Call My Brother Back* by Michael McLaverty. *Autumn Journal* by Louis MacNeice. *At Swim-Two-Birds* by Flann O'Brien.

WRITINGS 1789–1890

1. POLITICAL WRITINGS AND SPEECHES

EDMUND BURKE
(1729–1797)

from *Reflections on the Revolution in France* (1790)

It is now sixteen or seventeen years since I saw the queen of France, then the dauphiness, at Versailles; and surely never lighted on this orb, which she hardly seemed to touch, a more delightful vision. I saw her just above the horizon, decorating and cheering the elevated sphere she just began to move in,—glittering like the morning-star, full of life, and splendor, and joy. Oh! what a revolution! and what an heart must I have, to contemplate without emotion that elevation and that fall! Little did I dream when she added titles of veneration to those of enthusiastic, distant, respectful love, that she should ever be obliged to carry the sharp antidote against disgrace concealed in that bosom; little did I dream that I should have lived to see such disasters fallen upon her in a nation of gallant men, in a nation of men of honour and of cavaliers. I thought ten thousand swords must have leaped from their scabbards to avenge even a look that threatened her with insult.—But the age of chivalry is gone.—That of sophisters, oeconomists, and calculators, has succeeded; and the glory of Europe is extinguished for ever. Never, never more, shall we behold that generous loyalty to rank and sex, that proud submission, that dignified obedience, that subordination of the heart, which kept alive, even in servitude itself, the spirit of an exalted freedom. The unbought grace of life, the cheap defence of nations, the nurse of manly sentiment and heroic enterprize is gone! It is gone, that sensibility of principle, that chastity of honour, which felt a stain like a wound, which inspired courage whilst it mitigated ferocity, which ennobled whatever it touched, and under which vice itself lost half its evil, by losing all its grossness.

This mixed system of opinion and sentiment had its origin in the antient chivalry; and the principle, though varied in its appearance by the varying state of human affairs, subsisted and influenced through a long succession of generations, even to the time we live in. If it should ever be totally extinguished, the loss I fear will be great. It is this which has given its character to modern Europe. It is this which has distinguished it under all its forms of government, and distinguished it to its advantage, from the states of Asia, and possibly from those states which flourished in the most brilliant periods of the antique world. It was this, which, without confounding ranks, had produced a noble equality, and handed it down through all the gradations of social life. It was this opinion which mitigated kings into companions, and raised private men to be fellows with kings. Without force, or opposition, it subdued the fierceness of pride and power; it obliged sovereigns to submit to the soft collar of social esteem, compelled stern authority to submit to elegance, and gave a domination vanquisher of laws, to be subdued by manners.

But now all is to be changed. All the pleasing illusions, which made power gentle, and obedience liberal, which harmonized the different shades of life, and which, by a bland assimilation, incorporated into politics the sentiments which beautify and soften private society, are to be dissolved by this new conquering empire of light and reason. All the decent drapery of life is to be rudely torn off. All the superadded ideas, furnished from the wardrobe of a moral imagination, which the heart owns, and the understanding ratifies, as necessary to cover the defects of our naked shivering nature, and to raise it to dignity in our own estimation, are to be exploded as a ridiculous, absurd, and antiquated fashion.

On this scheme of things, a king is but a man; a queen is but a woman; a woman is but an animal; and an animal not of the highest order. All homage paid to the sex in general as such, and without distinct views, is to be regarded as romance and folly. Regicide, and patricide, and sacrilege, are but fictions of superstition, corrupting jurisprudence by destroying its simplicity. The murder of a king, or a queen, or a bishop, or a father, are only common homicide; and if the people are by any chance, or in any way gainers by it, a sort of homicide much the most pardonable, and into which we ought not to make too severe a scrutiny.

On the scheme of this barbarous philosophy, which is the off-spring of cold hearts and muddy understandings, and which is as void of solid wisdom, as it is destitute of all taste and elegance, laws are to be supported only by their own terrors, and by the concern, which each individual may find in them, from his own private speculations, or can spare to them from his own private interests. In the groves of *their* academy, at the end of every visto, you see nothing but the gallows. Nothing is left which engages the affections on the part of the commonwealth. On the principles of this mechanic philosophy, our institutions can never be embodied, if I may use the expression, in persons; so as to create in us love, veneration, admiration, or attachment. But that sort of reason which banishes the affections is incapable of filling their place. These public affections, combined with manners, are required sometimes as supplements, sometimes as correctives, always as aids to law. The precept given by a wise man, as well as a great critic, for the construction of poems, is equally true as to states. *Non satis est pulchra esse poemata, dulcia sunto.** There ought to be a system of manners in every nation which a well-formed mind would be disposed to relish. To make us love our country, our country ought to be lovely.

But power, of some kind or other, will survive the shock in which manners and opinions perish; and it will find other and worse means for its support. The usurpation which, in order to subvert antient institutions, has destroyed antient principles, will hold power by arts similar to those by which it has acquired it. When the old feudal and chivalrous spirit of *Fealty*, which, by freeing kings from fear, freed both kings and subjects from the precautions of tyranny, shall be extinct in the minds of men, plots and assassinations will be anticipated by preventive murder and preventive confiscation, and that long roll of grim and bloody maxims, which form the political code of all power, not standing on its own honour, and the honour of those who are to obey it. Kings will be tyrants from policy when subjects are rebels from principle.

When antient opinions and rules of life are taken away, the loss cannot possibly be estimated. From that moment we have no compass to govern us; nor can we know distinctly to what port we steer. Europe undoubtedly, taken in a mass, was in a flourishing condition the day on which your Revolution was compleated. How much of that prosperous state was owing to the spirit of our old manners and opinions is not easy to say; but as such causes cannot be indifferent in their operation, we must presume, that, on the whole, their operation was beneficial.

We are but too apt to consider things in the state in which we find them, without sufficiently adverting to the causes by which they have been produced, and possibly may be upheld. Nothing is more certain, than that our manners, our civilization, and all the good things which are connected with manners, and with civilization, have, in this European world of ours, depended for ages upon two principles; and were indeed the result of both combined; I mean the spirit of a gentleman, and the spirit of religion. The nobility and the clergy, the one by profession, the other by patronage, kept learning in existence, even in the midst of arms and confusions, and whilst governments were rather in their causes than formed. Learning paid back what it received to nobility and to priesthood; and paid it with usury, by enlarging their ideas and by furnishing their minds. Happy if they had all continued to know their indissoluble union, and their proper place! Happy if learning, not debauched by ambition, had been satisfied to continue the instructor, and not aspired to be the master! Along with its natural protectors and guardians, learning will be cast into the mire, and trodden down under the hoofs of a swinish multitude.*

If, as I suspect, modern letters owe more than they are always willing to own to antient manners, so do other interests which we value full as much as they are worth. Even commerce, and trade, and manufacture, the gods of our oeconomical politicians, are themselves perhaps but creatures; are themselves but effects, which, as first causes, we choose to worship. They certainly grew under the same shade in which learning flourished. They too may decay with their natural protecting principles. With you, for the present at least, they all threaten to disappear together. Where trade and manufactures are wanting to a people, and the spirit of nobility and religion remains, sentiment supplies, and not always ill supplies their place; but if commerce and the arts should be lost in an experiment to try how well a state may stand without these old fundamental principles, what sort of a thing must be a nation of gross, stupid, ferocious, and at the same time, poor and sordid barbarians, destitute of religion, honour, or manly pride, possessing nothing at present, and hoping for nothing hereafter?

I wish you may not be going fast, and by the shortest cut, to that horrible and disgustful situation. Already there appears a poverty of conception, a coarseness and vulgarity in all the proceedings of the assembly and of all their instructors. Their liberty is not liberal. Their science is presumptuous ignorance. Their humanity is savage and brutal.

It is not clear, whether in England we learned those grand and decorous principles, and manners, of which considerable traces yet remain, from you, or whether you took them from us. But to you, I think, we trace them best. You seem to me to be—*gentis incunabula nostrae*.* France has always more or less influenced manners in England; and when your fountain is choaked up and polluted, the stream will not run long, or not run clear with us, or perhaps with any nation. This gives all Europe, in my opinion, but too close and connected a concern in what is done in France. Excuse me, therefore, if I have dwelt too long on the atrocious spectacle of the sixth of October 1789, or have given too much scope to the reflections which have arisen in my mind on occasion of the most important of all revolutions, which may be dated from that day, I mean a revolution in sentiments, manners, and moral opinions. As things now stand, with every thing respectable destroyed without us, and an attempt to destroy within us every principle of respect, one is almost forced to apologize for harbouring the common feelings of men.

from *Letter to Richard Burke* (1792)

MY DEAR SON,

We are all again assembled in Town, to finish the last, but the most laborious of the tasks which have been imposed upon me during my Parliamentary service. We are as well as, at our time of life, we can expect to be. We have indeed some moments of anxiety about you. You are engaged in an undertaking similar in its principle to mine. You are engaged in the relief of an oppressed people. In that service you must necessarily excite the same sort of passions in those who have exercised, and who wish to continue that oppression, that I have had to struggle with in this long labour. As your Father has done, you must make enemies of many of the rich, of the proud, and of the powerful. I and you began in the same way. I must confess, that if our place was of our choice, I could wish it had been your lot to begin the career of your life with an endeavour to render some more moderate, and less invidious service to the publick. But being engaged in a great and critical work, I have not the least hesitation about your having hitherto done your duty as becomes you. If I had not an assurance not to be shaken, from the character of your mind I should be satisfied on that point, by the cry that is raised against you. If you had behaved as they call it discreetly, that is, faintly and treacherously, in the execution of your trust, you would have had for a while, the good word of all sorts of men; even of many of those whose cause you had betrayed; and whilst your favour lasted, you might have coined that false reputation into a true and solid interest to yourself. This you are well apprized of; and you do not refuse to travel that beaten road from an ignorance, but from a contempt of the objects it leads to.

When you choose an arduous and slippery path, God forbid that any weak feelings of my declining age, which calls for soothings and supports, and which can have none but from you, should make me wish that you should abandon what you are about, or should trifle with it. In this House we submit, though with troubled minds, to that order, which has connected all great duties with toils and with perils, which has conducted the road to glory through the regions of obloquy and reproach, and which will never suffer the disparaging alliance of spurious, false, and fugitive praise, with genuine and permanent reputation. We know, that the Power which has settled that order, and subjected you to it by placing you in the situation you are in, is able to bring you out of it, with credit, and with safety. His will be done. All must come right. You may open the way with pain, and under reproach. Others will pursue it with ease and with applause.

I am sorry to find that pride and passion, and that sort of zeal for religion, which never shews any wonderful heat but when it afflicts and mortifies our neighbour, will not let the ruling description perceive that the privilege for which your clients contend, is very nearly as much for the benefit of those who refuse it, as those who ask it. I am not to examine into the charges that are daily made on the Administration of Ireland. I am not qualified to say how much in them is cold truth, and how much rhetorical exaggeration. Allowing some foundation to the complaint, it is to no purpose that these people alledge that their Government is a job in its administration. I am sure it is a job in its constitution; nor is it possible, a scheme of polity which, in total exclusion of the body of the community, confines (with little or no regard to their rank or condition in life) to a certain set of favoured citizens the rights which formerly belonged to the whole, should not, by the operation of the same selfish and narrow principles, teach the persons who administer in that Government, to prefer their own particular, but well understood private interest, to the false and ill calculated private interest of the monopolizing Company they belong to. Eminent characters, to be sure, overrule places and circumstances. I have nothing to say to that virtue which shoots up in full force by the native vigour of the seminal principle, in spite of the adverse soil and climate that it grows in. But speaking of things in their ordinary course, in a Country of monopoly there *can* be no patriotism. There may be a party spirit—but public spirit there can be none. As to a spirit of liberty, still less can it exist, or any thing like it. A liberty made up of penalties! a liberty made up of incapacities! a liberty made up of exclusion and proscription, continued for ages of four-fifths, perhaps, of the inhabitants of all ranks and fortunes! In what does such liberty differ from the description of the most shocking kind of servitude?

But it will be said, in that Country, some people are free—why this is the very description of despotism. *Partial freedom is privilege and prerogative, and not liberty*. Liberty, such as deserves the name, is an honest, equitable, diffusive, and impartial principle. It is a great and enlarged virtue, and not a sordid, selfish, and illiberal vice. It is the portion of the mass of the citizens; and not the haughty licence of some potent individual, or some predominant faction.

If any thing ought to be despotick in a Country, it is its Government; because there is no cause, of constant operation, to make its yoke unequal. But the dominion of a party must continually, steadily, and by its very essence, lean upon the prostrate description. A Constitution formed so as to enable a party to overrule its very Government, and to overpower the people too, answers the purposes neither of Government nor of freedom. It compels that power, which ought, and often would be, disposed *equally* to protect the Subjects, to fail in its trust, to counteract its purposes, and to become no better than the instrument of the wrongs of a faction. Some degree of influence must exist in all Governments. But a Government, which has no interest to please the body of the people, and can neither support

them, nor with safety call for their support, nor is of power to sway
the domineering faction, can only exist by corruption; and taught by
that monopolizing party which usurps the title and qualities of the
publick, to consider the body of the people as out of the Constitution, they will consider those who are in it in the light in which they
choose to consider themselves. The whole relation of Government
and of freedom, will be a battle, or a traffick.

This system in its real nature, and under its proper appellations, is
odious and unnatural, especially when a Constitution is admitted,
which not only, as all Constitutions do profess, has a regard to the
good of the multitude, but in its theory makes profession of their
power also. But of late, this scheme of theirs has been new christened—*honestum nomen imponitur vitio.** A word has been lately
struck in the mint of the Castle of Dublin; thence it was conveyed to
the Tholsel, or City-hall, where having passed the touch of the Corporation,*—so respectably stamped and vouched, it soon became
current in Parliament, and was carried back by the Speaker of the
House of Commons* in great pomp, as an offering of homage from
whence it came. The word is *ascendancy*. It is not absolutely new. But
the sense in which I have hitherto seen it used, was to signify an
influence obtained over the minds of some other person by love and
reverence, or by superior management and dexterity. It had therefore, to this its promotion, no more than a moral, not a civil or
political use. But I admit it is capable of being so applied; and if the
Lord Mayor of Dublin,* and the Speaker of the Irish Parliament,
who recommend the preservation of the Protestant ascendancy,
mean to employ the word in that sense, that is, if they understand by
it the preservation of the influence of that description of gentlemen
over the Catholicks, by means of an authority derived from their
wisdom and virtue, and from an opinion they raise in that people of a
pious regard and affection for their freedom and happiness, it is
impossible not to commend their adoption of so apt a term into the
family of politicks. It may be truly said to enrich the language. Even
if the Lord Mayor and Speaker mean to insinuate that this influence
is to be obtained and held by flattering their people, by managing
them by skilfully adapting themselves to the humours and passions
of those whom they would govern, he must be a very untoward
critick who would cavil even at this use of the word, though such
cajoleries would perhaps be more prudently practised than pro-

fessed. These are all meanings laudable, or at least tolerable. But when we look a little more narrowly, and compare it with the plan to which it owes its present technical application, I find it has strayed far from its original sense. It goes much further than the privilege allowed by Horace. It is more than *parce detorsum*.* This Protestant ascendancy means nothing less than an influence obtained by virtue, by love, or even by artifice and seduction; full as little an influence derived from the means by which Ministers have obtained an influence, which might be called, without straining, an *ascendancy* in publick Assemblies in England, that is, by a liberal distribution of places and pensions and other graces of Government. This last is wide indeed of the signification of the word. New *ascendancy* is the old mastership. It is neither more nor less than the resolution of one set of people in Ireland, to consider themselves as the sole citizens in the commonwealth; and to keep a dominion over the rest by reducing them to absolute slavery, under a military power; and thus fortified in their power, to divide the publick estate, which is the result of general contribution, as a military booty, solely amongst themselves.

The poor word ascendancy, so soft and melodious in its sound, so lenitive and emollient in its first usage, is now employed to cover to the world, the most rigid and perhaps not the most wise of all plans of policy. The word is large enough in its comprehension. I cannot conceive what mode of oppression in civil life, or what mode of religious persecution, may not come within the methods of preserving an *ascendancy*. In plain old English, as they apply it, it signifies *pride and dominion* on the one part of the relation, and on the other *subserviency and contempt*—and it signifies nothing else. The old words are as fit to be set to musick as the new; but use has long since affixed to them their true signification, and they sound, as the other will, harshly and odiously to the moral and intelligent ears of mankind.

This ascendancy, by being a *Protestant* ascendancy, does not better it from the combination of a note or two more in this anti-harmonick scale. If Protestant ascendancy means the proscription from citizenship of by far the major part of the people of any Country, then Protestant ascendancy is a bad thing; and it ought to have no existence. But there is a deeper evil. By the use that is so frequently made of the term, and the policy which is engrafted on it, the name

Protestant becomes nothing more or better than the name of a persecuting faction, with a relation of some sort of theological hostility to others, but without any sort of ascertained tenets of its own, upon the ground of which it persecutes other men; for the patrons of this Protestant ascendancy neither do nor can, by any thing positive, define or describe what they mean by the word Protestant. . . .

A very great part of the mischiefs that vex the world, arises from words. People soon forget the meaning, but the impression and the passion remain. The word Protestant is the charm that locks up in the dungeon of servitude three millions of your people. It is not amiss to consider this spell of potency, this abracadabra that is hung about the necks of the unhappy, not to heal, but to communicate disease. We sometimes hear of a Protestant *Religion*, frequently of a Protestant *interest*. We hear of the latter the most frequently, because it has a positive meaning. The other has none. We hear of it the most frequently, because it has a word in the phrase, which, well or ill understood, has animated to persecution and oppression at all times infinitely more than all the dogmas in dispute between religious factions. These are indeed well formed to perplex and torment the intellect; but not half so well calculated to inflame the passions and animosities of men.

I do readily admit, that a great deal of the wars, seditions and troubles of the world, did formerly turn upon the contention between *interests* that went by the names of Protestant and Catholick. But I imagined that at this time no one was weak enough to believe, or impudent enough to pretend, that questions of Popish and Protestant opinions or interest are the things by which men are at present menaced with crusades by foreign invasion, or with seditions which shake the foundations of the State at home. It is long since all this combination of things has vanished from the view of intelligent observers. The existence of quite another system of opinions and interests is now plain to the grossest sense. Are these the questions that raise a flame in the minds of men at this day? If ever the Church and the Constitution of England should fall in these Islands (and they will fall together) it is not Presbyterian discipline, nor Popish hierarchy, that will rise upon their ruins. It will not be the Church of Rome, nor the Church of Scotland—not the Church of Luther, nor the Church of Calvin. On the contrary, all these Churches are menaced, and menaced alike. It is the new fanatical Religion, now in the heat of its first ferment, of the Rights of Man, which rejects all Establishments, all discipline, all Ecclesiastical, and in truth all Civil order, which will triumph, and which will lay prostrate your Church; which will destroy your distinctions, and which will put all your properties to auction, and disperse you over the Earth. If the present Establishment should fall, it is this Religion which will triumph in Ireland and in England, as it has triumphed in France. This Religion, which laughs at creeds and dogmas and confessions of faith, may be fomented equally amongst all descriptions, and all sects; amongst nominal Catholicks, and amongst nominal Churchmen; and amongst those Dissenters who know little, and care less, about a Presbytery, or any of its discipline, or any of its doctrine.

Against this new, this growing, this exterminatory system, all these Churches have a common concern to defend themselves. How the enthusiasts of this rising sect rejoice to see you of the old Churches play their game, and stir and rake the cinders of animosities sunk in their ashes, in order to keep up the execution of their plan for your common ruin!

WOLFE TONE
(1763–1798)

from *The Life of Theobald Wolfe Tone* (1797)

The French Revolution had now been above a twelvemonth in its progress; at its commencement, as the first emotions are generally honest, every one was in its favour; but, after some time, the probable consequences to monarchy and aristocracy began to be foreseen, and the partisans of both to retrench considerably in their admiration.

In England, Burke had the triumph completely to decide the public; fascinated by an eloquent publication,* which flattered so many of their prejudices, and animated by their unconquerable hatred of France, which no change of circumstances could alter, the whole English nation, it may be said, retracted from their first decision in favour of the glorious and successful efforts of the French people; they sickened at the prospect of the approaching liberty and happiness of that mighty nation: they calculated, as merchants, the probable effects which the energy of regenerated France might have on their commerce; they rejoiced when they saw the combination of despots formed to restore the ancient system, and perhaps to dismember the monarchy; and they waited with impatience for an occasion, which, happily for mankind, they soon found, when they might, with some appearance of decency, engage in person in the infamous contest.

But matters were very different in Ireland, an oppressed, insulted, and plundered nation. As we well knew, experimentally, what it was to be enslaved, we sympathized most sincerely with the French people, and watched their progress to freedom with the utmost anxiety; we had not, like England, a prejudice rooted in our very nature against France. As the Revolution advanced, and as events expanded themselves, the public spirit of Ireland rose with a rapid acceleration. The fears and animosities of the aristocracy rose in the same, or a still higher proportion. In a little time the French Revolution became the test of every man's political creed, and the nation was fairly divided into two great parties, the Aristocrats and the Democrats (epithets borrowed from France), who have ever since been measuring each other's strength, and carrying on a kind of smothered war, which the course of events, it is highly probable, may soon call into energy and action.

It is needless, I believe, to say that I was a Democrat from the very commencement, and, as all the retainers of Government, including the sages and judges of the law, were, of course, on the other side, this gave the *coup de grâce** to any expectations, if any such I had, of my succeeding at the Bar, for I soon became pretty notorious; but, in fact, I had for some time renounced all hope, and, I may say, all desire, of succeeding in a profession which I alway disliked, and which the political prostitution of its members (though otherwise men of high honour and of great personal worth) had taught me sincerely to despise. I therefore seldom went near the Four Courts, nor did I adopt any one of the means, and, least of all, the study of the law, which are successfully employed by those young men whose object it is to rise in their profession.

It was pretty much about this time that my connection with the Catholic body commenced in a manner which I am about to relate. I cannot pretend to strict accuracy as to dates, for I write entirely from memory; all my papers being in America.

Russell* had, on his arrival to join his regiment at Belfast, found the people so much to his taste, and in return had rendered himself so agreeable to them, that he was speedily admitted into their confidence, and became a member of several of their clubs. This was an unusual circumstance, as British officers, it may well be supposed, were no great favourites with the Republicans of Belfast.

Russell wrote me an account of all this, and it immediately set me on thinking more seriously than I had yet done upon the state of Ireland. I soon formed my theory, and on that theory I have unvaryingly acted ever since.

To subvert the tyranny of our execrable Government, to break the connection with England, the never-failing source of all our political evils, and to assert the independence of my country—these were my objects. To unite the whole people of Ireland, to abolish the memory of all past dissentions, and to substitute the common name of Irishman in place of the denominations of Protestant, Catholic, and Dissenter—these were my means. To effectuate these great objects, I reviewed the three great sects. The Protestants I despaired of from the outset for obvious reasons. Already in possession by an unjust monopoly of the whole power and patronage of the country, it was not to be supposed they would ever concur in measures the certain tendency of which must be to lessen their influence as a party, how much soever the nation might gain. To the Catholics I thought it unnecessary to address myself, because, that as no change could make their political situation worse, I reckoned upon their support to a certainty; besides, they had already begun to manifest a strong sense of their wrongs and oppressions; and finally, I well knew that, however it might be disguised or suppressed, there existed in the breast of every Irish Catholic an inextirpable abhorrence of the English name and power. There remained only the Dissenters, whom I knew to be patriotic and enlightened; however, the recent events at Belfast had showed me that all prejudice was not yet entirely removed from their minds. I sat down accordingly, and wrote a pamphlet addressed to the Dissenters, and which I entitled, 'An Argument on behalf of the Catholics of Ireland,' the object of which was to convince them that they and the Catholics had but one common interest and one common enemy; that the depression and slavery of Ireland was produced and perpetuated by the divisions existing between them, and that, consequently, to assert the independence of their country, and their own individual liberties, it was necessary to forget all former feuds, to consolidate the entire strength of the whole nation, and to form for the future but one people. These principles I supported by the best arguments which suggested themselves to me, and particularly by demonstrating that the cause of the failure of all former efforts, and more especially of the Volunteer Convention in 1783,* was the unjust neglect of the claims of their Catholic brethren. This pamphlet which appeared in September, 1791, under the signature of A Northern Whig, had a considerable degree of success. As my pamphlet spread more and more, my acquaintance amongst the Catholics extended accordingly. My first friend in the body was John Keogh,* and through him I became acquainted with all the leaders, as Richard McCormick, John Sweetman, Edward Byrne, Thomas Braughall,—in short, the whole sub-committee, and most of the active members of the General Committee. In short, I began to grow into something like reputation, and my company was, in a manner, a requisite all that winter.

The Volunteers of Belfast, of the first or green company, were pleased, in consequence of my pamphlet, to elect me an honorary member of their corps, a favour which they were very delicate in bestowing, as I believe I was the only person, except the great Henry Flood,* who was ever honoured with that mark of their approbation. I was also invited to spend a few days in Belfast, in order to assist in framing the first club of United Irishmen, and to cultivate a personal acquaintance with those men whom, though I highly esteemed, I knew as yet but by reputation. In consequence, about the beginning of October, I went down with my friend Russell, who had, by this time, quit the army, and was in Dublin, on his private affairs. The incidents of that journey, which was by far the most agreeable and interesting one I had ever made, I recorded in a kind of diary, a practice which I then commenced, and have ever since, from time to time, continued, as circumstances of sufficient importance occurred. To that diary I refer.

ROBERT EMMET
(1778–1803)

Speech from the Dock (1803)

I am asked what I have to say why sentence of death should not be pronounced on me, according to law. I have nothing to say that can alter your pre-determination, nor that it will become me to say, with any view to the mitigation of that sentence which you are to pronounce and I must abide by. But I have that to say which interests me more than life and which you have laboured to destroy. I have much to say why my reputation should be rescued from the load of false accusation and calumny which has been cast upon it. I do not imagine that, seated where you are, your minds can be so free from prejudice as to receive the least impression from what I am going to utter. I have no hope that I can anchor my character in the breast of a court constituted and trammeled as this is.

I only wish, and that is the utmost that I can expect, that your lordships may suffer it to float down your memories untainted by the foul breath of prejudice, until it finds some more hospitable harbour to shelter it from the storms by which it is buffeted. Were I only to suffer death, after being adjudged guilty by your tribunal, I should bow in silence, and meet the fate that awaits me without a murmur; but the sentence of the law which delivers my body to the executioner will, through the ministry of the law, labour in its own vindication, to consign my character to obloquy; for there must be guilt somewhere, whether in the sentence of the court or in the catastrophe—time must determine. A man in my situation has not only to encounter the difficulties of fortune, and the force of power over minds which it has corrupted or subjugated, but the difficulties of established prejudice. The man dies, but his memory lives. That mine may not perish, that it may live in the respect of my countrymen, I seize upon this opportunity to vindicate myself from some of the charges alleged against me. When my spirit shall be wafted to a more friendly port, when my shade shall have joined the bands of those martyred heroes who have shed their blood on the scaffold and in the field in defense of their country and of virtue, this is my hope: I wish that my memory and my name may animate those who survive me, while I look down with complacency on the destruction of that perfidious government which upholds its domination by blasphemy of the Most High; which displays its power over man as over the beasts of the forest; which sets man upon his brother, and lifts his hand in the Name of God, against the throat of his fellow who believes or doubts a little more or a little less than the government standard, a government which is steeled to barbarity by the cries of the orphans and the tears of the widows it has made.

Here Lord Norbury interrupted Emmet, saying that 'the mean and wicked enthusiasts who felt as he did, were not equal to the accomplishment of their wild designs.'

I appeal to the immaculate God, I swear by the Throne of Heaven, before which I must shortly appear, by the blood of the murdered patriots who have gone before me, that my conduct has been, through all this peril, and through all my purposes, governed only by the conviction which I have uttered, and by no other view than that of the emancipation of my country from the super-inhuman oppression under which she has so long and too patiently travailed; and I confidently hope that, wild and chimerical as it may appear, there is still union and strength in Ireland to accomplish this noblest of enterprises. Of this I speak with confidence, with intimate knowledge, and with the consolation that appertains to that confidence. Think not, my lords, I say this for the petty gratification of giving you a transitory uneasiness. A man who never yet raised his voice to assert a lie will not hazard his character with posterity by asserting a falsehood on a subject so important to his country, and on an occasion like this. Yes, my lords, a man who does not wish to have his epitaph written until his country is liberated, will not leave a weapon in the power of envy, or a pretense to impeach the probity which he means to preserve, even in the grave to which tyranny consigns him.

Here he was again interrupted by Norbury.

Again I say that what I have spoken was not intended for your lordship, whose situation I commiserate rather than envy—my expressions were for my countrymen. If there is a true Irishman present, let my last words cheer him in the hour of his affliction.

Here he was again interrupted. Lord Norbury said he did not sit there to hear treason.

I have always understood it to be the duty of a judge, when a prisoner has been convicted, to pronounce the sentence of the law. I have also understood that judges sometimes think it their duty to hear with patience, and to speak with humanity; to exhort the victim of the laws, and to offer, with tender benignity, their opinions of the motives by which he was actuated in the crime of which he was adjudged guilty. That a judge has thought it his duty so to have done, I have no doubt; but where is the boasted freedom of your institutions, where is the vaunted impartiality, clemency and mildness of your courts of justice if an unfortunate prisoner, whom your policy and not justice is about to deliver into the hands of the executioner, is not suffered to explain his motives sincerely and truly, and to vindicate the principles by which he was actuated? My lord, it may be a part of the system of angry justice to bow a man's mind by humiliation to the purposed ignominy of the scaffold; but worse to me than the purposed shame of the scaffold's terrors would be the shame of such foul and unfounded imputations as have been laid against me in this court. You, my lord, are a judge; I am the supposed culprit. I am a man; you are a man also. By a revolution of power we might exchange places? Though we never could change characters. If I stand at the bar of this court and dare not vindicate my character, what a farce is your justice! If I stand at this bar and dare not vindicate my character, how dare you calumniate it? Does the sentence of death, which your unhallowed policy inflicts on my body, condemn my tongue to silence and my reputation to reproach? Your executioner may abridge the period of my existence; but while I exist I shall not forebear to vindicate my character and motives from your aspersion; and as a man to whom fame is dearer than life, I will make the last use of that life in doing justice to that reputation which is to live after me, and which is the only legacy I can leave to those I honour and love and for whom I am proud to perish. As men, my lords, we must appear on the great day at one common tribunal; and it will then remain for the Searcher of all hearts to show a collective universe, who was engaged in the most virtuous actions or swayed by the purest motives, my country's oppressor, or—

Here he was interrupted and told to listen to the sentence of the court.

My lords, will a dying man be denied the legal privilege of exculpating himself in the eyes of the community from an undeserved reproach, thrown upon him during his trial, by charging him with ambition and attempting to cast away for paltry consideration the liberties of his country? Why did your lordships insult me? Or rather, why insult justice, in demanding of me why sentence of death should not be pronounced against me? I know my lords, that form prescribes that you should ask the question, the form also presents the right of answering. This, no doubt, may be dispensed with, and so might the whole ceremony of the trial, since sentence was already pronounced at the Castle before the jury was impaneled. Your lordships are but the priests of the oracle, and I insist on the whole of the forms.

I am charged with being an emissary of France. An emissary of France! And for what end? It is alleged that I wished to sell the independence of my country. And for what end? Was this the object of my ambition? And is this the mode by which a tribunal of justice reconciles contradiction? No, I am no emissary; and my ambition was to hold a place among the deliverers of my country, not in power nor in profit, but in the glory of the achievement. Sell my country's independence to France! And for what? Was it a change of masters? No, but for my ambition. O, my country, was it a personal ambition that could influence me? Had it been the soul of my actions, could I not by my education and fortune, by the rank and consideration of my family, have placed myself amongst the proudest of your oppressors. My country was my idol. To it I sacrificed every selfish, every endearing sentiment, and for it I now offer up myself, O God! No, my lords; I acted as an Irishman, determined on delivering my country from the yoke of a foreign and unrelenting tyranny and the more galling yoke of a domestic faction, which is its joint partner and perpetrator in the patricide, from the ignominy existing with an exterior of splendour and a conscious depravity. It was the wish of my heart to extricate my country from this doubly riveted despotism; I wished to place her independence beyond the reach of any power on earth. I wished to exalt her to that proud station in the world. Connection with France was, indeed, intended, but only as far as mutual interest would sanction or require. Were the French to assume any authority inconsistent with the purest independence, it would be the signal for their destruction. We sought their aid and we sought it as we had assurance we should obtain it as auxiliaries in war and allies in peace. Were the French to come as invaders or enemies uninvited by the wishes of the people, I should oppose them to the utmost of my strength. Yes, my countrymen, I should advise you to meet them upon the beach with a sword in one hand and a torch in the other. I would meet them with all the destructive fury of war. I would animate my countrymen to immolate them in their boats, before they had contaminated the soil of my country. If they succeeded in landing, and if forced to retire before superior discipline, I would dispute every inch of the ground, burn every blade of grass, and the last entrenchment of liberty should be my grave. What I could not do myself, if I should fall, I should leave as a last charge to my countrymen to accomplish; because I should feel conscious that life, any more than death, is unprofitable when a foreign nation holds my country in subjection. But it was not as an enemy that the soldiers of France were to land. I looked, indeed, for the assistance of France; but I wished to prove to France and to the world that Irish men deserved to be assisted; that they were indignant at slavery, and ready to assert the independence and liberty of their country. I wished to procure for my country the guarantee which Washington procured for America; to procure an aid which, by its example would be as important as its valour disciplined, gallant, pregnant with science and experience, that of a people who would perceive the good and polish the rough points of our character. They would come to us as strangers and leave us as friends, after sharing in our perils and elevating our destiny. These were my objects; not to receive new task-masters, but to expel old tyrants. It was for these ends I sought aid from France; because France, even as an enemy, could not be more implacable than the enemy already in the bosom of my country.

Here he was interrupted by the court.

I have been charged with that importance in the emancipation of my country as to be considered the keystone of the combination of Irishmen; or, as your lordships expressed it, 'the life and blood of the conspiracy.' You do me honour over much; you have given to the subaltern all the credit of a superior. There are men engaged in this conspiracy who are not only superior to me, but even to your own conceptions of yourself, my lord; men before the splendour of whose genius and virtues I should bow with respectful deference and who would think themselves disgraced by shaking your blood-stained hand.

Here he was interrupted.

What! my lord, shall you tell me on the passage to the scaffold, which that tyranny (of which you are only the intermediary executioner) has erected for my murder, that I am accountable for all the blood that has been shed and will be shed in this struggle of the oppressed against the oppressor; shall thou tell me this, and must I be so very a slave as not to repel it? I do not fear to approach the Omnipotent Judge to answer for the conduct of my whole life; and am I to be appalled and falsified by a mere remnant of mortality here? By you, too, although if it were possible to collect all the innocent blood that you have shed in your unhallowed ministry in one great reservoir, your lordship might swim in it.

Here the judge interrupted.

Let no man dare, when I am dead, to charge me with dishonour; let no man taint my memory by believing that I could have engaged in any cause but that of my country's liberty and independence; or that I could have become the pliant minion of power in the oppression of my country. The Proclamation of the Provisional Government speaks for our views; no inference can be tortured from it to countenance barbarity or debasement at home, or subjection, humiliation or treachery from abroad. I would not have submitted to a foreign oppressor, for the same reason that I would resist the foreign and domestic oppressor. In the dignity of freedom I would have fought upon the threshold of my country, and its enemy would enter only by passing over the lifeless corpse. And am I who lived but for my country, and have subjected myself to the dangers of the jealous and watchful oppressor, and the bondage of the grave, only to give my countrymen their rights and my country her independence, am I to be loaded with calumny and not suffered to resent it? No; God forbid!

Here Norbury told the prisoner that his sentiments and language disgraced his family and education, but more particularly his father, Dr Robert Emmet, who was a man that would, if alive, discountenance such opinions. To which Emmet replied:

If the spirit of the illustrious dead participate in the concerns and cares of those who were dear to them in this transitory life, O, ever dear and venerated shade of my departed father, look down with scrutiny upon the conduct of your suffering son and see if I have even for a moment, deviated from those principles of morality and patriotism which it was your care to instill into my youthful mind, and for which I am now about to offer up my life! My lords, you are impatient for the sacrifice. The blood which you seek is not congealed by the artificial terrors which surround your victim; it circulates warm and unruffled through the channels which God created for noble purpose, but which you are now bent to destroy for purposes so grievous that they cry to heaven. Be yet patient! I have but a few more words to say. I am going to go to my cold and silent grave. My lamp of life is nearly extinguished. My race is run. The grave opens to receive me and I sink into its bosom. I have but one request to ask at my departure from this world. It is the charity of its silence. Let no man write my epitaph; for as no man who knows my motives dare now vindicate them, let not prejudice or ignorance asperse them. Let them and me rest in obscurity and peace; and my tomb remain uninscribed and my memory in oblivion until other times and other men can do justice to my character. When my country takes her place among the nations of the earth, then, and not till then let my epitaph be written. I have done.

DANIEL O'CONNELL
(1775–1847)

Speech at Tara (1843)

It would be the extreme of affectation in me to suggest that I have not some claims to be the leader of this majestic meeting. It would be worse than affectation—it would be drivelling folly, if I were not to feel the awful responsibility of the part I have taken in this majestic movement imposed upon me (*hear, hear*.) I feel responsibility to my country, responsibility to my Creator. Yes, I feel the tremulous nature of that responsibility—Ireland is aroused, is aroused from one end to another. Her multitudinous population have but one expression and one wish, and that is the extinction of the Union, the restoration of her nationality.

Suddenly, someone cried, 'there will be no compromise.'

Who is it that talks of compromise? I am not here for the purpose of making anything like a schoolboy's attempt at declamatory eloquence; I am not here to revive in your recollection any of those poetic imaginings respecting the spot on which we stand, and which have really become as familiar as household words; I am not here to exaggerate the historical importance of the spot on which we are congregated—but it is impossible to deny that Tara has historical recollections that give to it an importance, relatively, to other portions of the land, and deserves to be so considered by every person who comes to it for political purposes, and gives it an elevation and point of impression in the public mind that no other part of Ireland can possibly have. History may be tarnished by exaggeration, but the fact is undoubted that we are at Tara of the Kings. We are on the spot where the monarchs of Ireland were elected, and where the chieftains of Ireland bound themselves by the sacred pledge of honour and the tie of religion to stand by their native land against the Danes or any other stranger [*cheers*]. This is emphatically the spot from which emanated the social power—the legal authority— the right to dominion over the furthest extremes of the island, and the power of concentrating the force of the entire nation for the purpose of national defence. On this important spot I have an important duty to perform. I here protest in the face of my country, in the face of my Creator—in the face of Ireland and her God, I protest against the continuance of the unfounded and unjust Union. My proposition to Ireland is that the Union is not binding upon us; it is not binding, I mean, upon conscience. It is void in principle. It is void as matter of right and it is void in constitutional law. I protest everything that is sacred, without being profane, to the truth of my assertion there is really no union between the two countries.

My proposition is that there was no authority vested in any person to pass the Act of Union. I deny the authority of the Act, I deny the competency of the two legislatures to pass that Act. The English legislature had no such competency—that must be admitted by every person. The Irish legislature had no such competency; and I arraign the Union, therefore, on the ground of the incompetency of the bodies that passed it. No authority could render it binding but the authority of the Irish people, consulted individually through the counties, cities, towns, and villages; and if the people of Ireland called for the Union, then it was binding on them, but there was no other authority that could make it binding. The Irish Parliament had no such authority; they were elected to make laws and not legislatures, and it had no right to the authority which alone belonged to the people of Ireland. The trustee might as well usurp the right of the person who trusts him; the servant might as well usurp the power of the master; the Irish Parliament were elected as our trustees, we were their masters—they were but our servant and they had no right to transfer us to any other power on the face of the earth. This doctrine is manifest, and would be admitted by every person; if it were applied to England, would any person venture to assert that the Parliament of England should have the power to transfer its privileges to make laws from England to the legislative chamber of France? Would any person be so insane as to admit it, and that insanity would not be misstated even if they were allowed to send over their representatives to France? Yes, every person would admit in that case that the Union was void.

I have no higher affection for England than for France. They are both foreign authorities to me. The highest legal authority in England has declared us aliens in blood, aliens in religion, and aliens in language from the English. Let no person groan him—I thank him for the honesty of the expression. I never heard of any other act of honesty on his part, and the fact of his having committed one act of honesty ought to recommend him to your good graces. I can refer you to the principle of constitutional law, and to Locke on government, to show that the Irish Parliament had no power or authority to convey itself away. I will only detain you on that point by citing the words of Lord Chancellor Plunket. He declared in the Irish House of Commons that they had no right to transfer the power of legislation from the country. He called upon them to have his words taken down, and he defied the power of Lord Castlereagh to have him censured for the expression, limiting the authority of Parliament. He said to them that they could not transfer their authority, that the maniacal suicide might as well imagine that the blow by which he destroyed his miserable body could annihilate his immortal soul, as they to imagine they could annihilate the soul of Ireland, her constitutional right. The illustration is a happy one. I am here the representative of the Irish nation, and in the name of that great, that virtuous, that moral, temperate, brave, and religious nation, I proclaim the Union a nullity, for it is a nullity in point of right. Never was any measure carried by such iniquitous means as the Union was carried. The first thing that taints it in its origin, and makes it, even if it were a compact, utterly void, is the fraud committed in fermenting discord in the country, and encouraging the rebellion until it broke out, and in making that rebellion and the necessity for crushing it the means of taking from Ireland her constitution and her liberties. There was this second fraud committed on her, that at the time of the passing of the Act of Union Ireland had no legal protection; the habeas corpus was suspended, martial law was proclaimed, trial by jury was at an end, and the lives and liberties of all the King's subjects in Ireland were at the mercy of the courts martial. Those among you who were old enough at the time remember when the shriek from the triangle was heard from every village and town, and when the troops would march out from Trim and lay desolate the country for nine or ten miles around. The military law was established in all its horrors throughout every district of the country and the people were trampled in the dust under the feet of the yeomanry, army, and fencibles. The next fraudulent device to which England had recourse in order to carry this infamous measure, and to promote her own prosperity on the ruins of Irish nationality, was to take the most effective means in order to prevent the Irish people from meeting to remonstrate against the insult and the injury which was about to be inflicted upon them. The Union was void no less from the utter incompetency of the contracting parties to enter into any such contract than by reason of the fact, that it was carried into operation by measures most iniquitous, atrocious and illegal; the habeas corpus act was suspended, torture, flogging, pitch caps, and imprisonment were the congenial agencies whereby England endeavored to carry her infamous designs, and executions upon the gallows for no other crime than that of being suspected to be suspicious, were of daily occurrence in every part of the kingdom. Thus it was that they endeavored to crush the expression of the people's feelings, whom they resolved to plunder and degrade. The people were not permitted to assemble together for the purpose of remonstrating against the Union. Meetings convened by the officers of justice—by the high sheriffs of counties, were dispersed at the point of the bayonet. The people were not permitted to meet together for remonstrance, but they got up petitions in every direction, to testify their feelings upon the subject, and although no less than seven hundred and seven thousand signatures were signed to petitions against the Union, despite of all the corrupt influence of the Government, more than three thousand wretches could not be found to sign a petition in favour of the measure.

The next impeachment which I bring against the Union is that it was brought about not only by physical force, but by bribery the most unblushing and corruption the most profligate. One million two hundred and seventy-five thousand pounds were expended upon the purchase of rotten boroughs alone, and no less a sum than two millions of money were lavished upon peculation unparalleled, and bribery the most enormous and most palpable that ever yet disgraced the annals of humility. There was not an office, civil, military, or ecclesiastical in the county, which was not flung open to the Unionist as the pence and wages of his political depravity. Six or seven judges bought their seats upon the bench by giving in their adhesion to the Union; and having no claim to wear the ermine other than that which was to be derived from the fact of their being recreants to their country, they continued in right of this during their lives to inflict the effects of their iniquity upon the people whom they betrayed. Twelve bishops obtained their seats by voting for the Union, for the spirit of corruption spared nothing. Men were made prelates, generals, admirals, commissioners for supporting the ministry in this infamous design, and every office in the revenue and customs was placed at the disposal of those who were base enough to sell their country for a mess of pottage.* In fact, corruption was never known to have been carried before or since to such excess in any country of the world, and if such a contract, if contract it could be called, was to be binding on the Irish nation, there was no longer any use for honesty or justice in the world. But strong as was the influence of corruption on the human mind, the victory which the English ministry achieved was slow and by no means easy of accomplishment, for the intimidation to the death upon the one hand, and bribery on the other, were impotent to procure a majority for them in the Irish House of Commons in the first session, when the bill was introduced. On the contrary, when the first attempt was

made to frustrate our liberties, there was a majority of eleven against
the Union Bill. But the despoiler was not easy to be foiled, nor was
he apt to be disheartened by a single failure. The work of corruption
was set on foot with redoubled energy, and the wretches who were
not so utterly abandoned as to suffer themselves to be bribed for the
direct and positive purpose of giving their vote for the Union,
accepted bribes on the condition of withdrawing from the House
altogether, and accordingly they vacated their seats, and in their
place stepped in Englishmen and Scotchmen who knew nothing of
Ireland, and who were not impeded by any conscientious scruples
whatever from giving their unqualified sanction to any plot of the
English, how infamous so ever, to oppress and plunder the country.
By these accumulated means the Union was carried and the fate of
Ireland sealed. But the monster evil of the Union is the financial
robbery which by its means was practiced upon Ireland. A scandalous injustice thus inflicted would be in itself sufficient even in the
absence of other arguments—even if other arguments were wanting—to render the Union void and of no effect. At the passing of
that fatal act—badge of our ruin and disgrace—Ireland owed only
twenty millions, England owed four hundred and forty six millions,
and the equitable terms on which the contract was based, whereby
both countries were to be allied and identified—identified indeed!—
were these, that England was generously to undertake the liability of
one-half of her national debt, on condition that we would undertake
the responsibility of one-half of hers. This is not a befitting time nor
season to enter into minute details relative to the particulars of this
financial swindle, but I may be permitted to direct your attention to
this very obvious fact, that whereas England has only doubled her
debt since the passing of the Union, the increase of the national debt
of Ireland during the same period cannot with justice be estimated
on a different ratio, and that consequently Ireland, at the very highest calculation, cannot in reality and as of her own account, owe a
larger sum than forty millions; and I will tell you, my friends, that
never will we consent to pay one shilling more of a national debt than
that. I say it in the name and on behalf of the Irish nation. But I will
tell you this, as a secret, and you may rely upon it as a truth, that in
point of fact we do not owe one farthing more than thirty millions;
and in proof of the truth of this assertion, I beg leave to refer you to a
work published by a very near and dear relative of mine—my third

son, the member for Kilkenny*—who, by the most accurate statistical calculations, and by a process of argument intelligible to the
humblest intellect, has made the fact apparent to the world, that
according to the terms of honest and equitable dealing, as between
both countries, Ireland's proportion of the national debt cannot be
set down at a larger sum than I state, thirty millions. I am proud that
there is a son of mine who, after the Repeal shall have been carried,
will be able to meet the cleverest English financier of them all, foot to
foot and hand to hand, and prove by arguments most incontestable
how grievous and intolerable is the injustice which was inflicted
upon our country in this respect by the Union. The project of robbing Ireland by joining her legislatively with England was no new
scheme which entered the minds of the English for the first time
about the year, 1800. It was a project which was a favourite theme of
dissertation with all the English essayists for years previous to the
period when it was carried into practical effect, and the policy
towards Ireland, which their literary men were continually urging
upon the English people for their adoption, was similar to that of the
avaricious housewife who killed the goose who laid her golden eggs.
Yes, such was the course they pursued towards Ireland, and you will
deserve the reputation of being the lineal descendants of that goose
if you be such ganders as not to declare in a voice of thunder that no
longer shall this system of plunder be permitted to continue.

My next impeachment of the Union is founded upon the disas-
trous effects which have resulted therefrom to our commercial and
manufacturing interests, as well as to our general national interests.
Previous to the Union, the county Meath was filled with the seats of
noblemen at Semen! What a contrast does its present state present! I,
on Monday read at the Association a list of the deserted mansions
which are now to be found ruined and desolate in your country. Even
the spot where the Duke of Wellington—famed the world over for
his detestation of his country—drew his first breath, instead of bearing a noble castle, or splendid mansion, presented the aspect of ruin
and desolation, and briars and nettles adequately marked the place
that produced him. The county of Meath was at one time studded
thickly with manufactories in every direction, and an enormous sum
was expended yearly in wages, but here, as in every other district of
the country, the eye was continually shocked with sights which evi-
denced with but too great eloquence the lamentable decay which has

been entailed upon our country by the Union. The linen trade at one period kept all Ulster in a state of affluence and prosperity. Kilkenny was for ages celebrated for its extensive blanket manufactures and Cork also—and Carrick-on-Suir, and in a thousand other localities, too numerous to mention, thousands were kept in constant and lucrative employment, at various branches of national industry, from year's end to year's end, before the passing of the Union. But this is no longer the case, and one man is not now kept in employment for a thousand who were employed before the Union. The report of the English commissioners themselves has declared this appalling fact to the world that one-third of our population are in a state of actual destitution; and yet, in the face of all this, men may be found who, claiming to themselves the character of political honesty, stand up and declare themselves in favour of the continuance of the Union. It is no bargain; it was a base swindle. Had it, indeed, been a fair bargain, the Irish would have continued faithful to it to the last, regardless of the injuries which it might have entailed upon them for the Irish people have been invariably faithful to their contracts; whereas England never yet made a promise which she did not violate, nor ever entered into a contract which she did not shamelessly and scandalously outrage. Even the Union itself, beneficial as it is to England, is but a living lie to Ireland. Everybody now admits the mischief that the Union has produced to Ireland. The very fact of its not being a compact is alone sufficient to nullify the Union, and on that ground I here proclaim, in the name of the Irish nation, that it is null and void. It is a union of legislators, but not a union of nations. Are you and I one bit more of Englishmen now than we were twenty or forty years ago? If we had a Union would not Ireland have the same parliamentary franchise that is enjoyed by England? But calling it a Union, could anything be more unjust on the part of England than to give her own people a higher and more extensive grade of franchise? And to the Irish people a more limited and an extinguishing and perishing franchise. She has given to her people an extended municipal reform, and to Ireland a wretched and miserable municipal reform. Even within the last week a plan was brought forward by Lord Elliot and the [*sneers*] Attorney-General Smith, that will have the effect of depriving one-third of those who now enjoy the franchise of its possession. No, the Union is void, but it is more peremptorily void on the ground of the ecclesiastical revenues of the counts being left to support a church of a small portion of the people. In England the ecclesiastical revenues of the country are given to the clergy that the majority of the people believe to teach the truth. In Scotland the ecclesiastical revenues are, or at least were up to a late period, paid to the clergy of the majority of the people; but the Irish people are compelled to pay the clergy of a small minority, not amounting to more than the one-tenth of the people of the entire island. The Union was effected against all constitutional principle by the most atrocious fraud—by the most violent and most iniquitous exercise of force, by the most abominable corruption and bribery, by the shifting of Irish members out of their seats, and the putting of Englishmen and Scotchmen into their places; and that was followed by the destruction of our commerce, by the annihilation of our manufactures, by the depreciation of our farmers—and you know I speak the truth when I talk of the depression of the farming interests by financial robbery, on an extensive scale to be sure, but a robbery on that very account, only the more iniquitous, fiendish, and harsh. I contend, therefore, that the Union is a nullity; but do I, on that account, advise you to turn out against it? No such thing. I advise you to act quietly and peaceably and in no other way.

Then a voice cried, 'any way you like.'

Remember that my doctrine is that 'the man who commits a crime gives strength to the enemy,' and you should not act in any manner that would strengthen the enemies of your country. You should act peaceably and quietly, but firmly and determinedly. You may be certain that your cheers here today will be conveyed to England.

The vast assemblage here commenced cheering in the most deafening and enthusiastic manner, and the distant lines of people on the limits of the assembly were seen waving their hats and handkerchiefs in response.

Yes, the overwhelming majesty of your multitude will be taken to England, and will have its effect there. The Duke of Wellington began by threatening us. He talked of civil war, but he does not say a single word of that now. He is now getting eyelet holes made in the old barracks, and only think of an old general doing such a thing, just as if we were going to break our heads against stone walls. I am glad to find that a great quantity of brandy and biscuits has been latterly imported, and I hope the poor soldiers get some of them. But the

Duke of Wellington is not now talking of attacking us, and I am glad of it; but I tell him this—I mean no disrespect to the brave, the gallant, and the good conducted soldiers that compose the Queen's army; and all of them that we have in this country are exceedingly well conducted. There is not one of you that has a single complaint to make against any of them. They are the bravest army in the world and therefore I do not mean to disparage them at all, but I feel it to be a fact, that Ireland, roused as she is at the present moment, would, if they made war upon us, furnish women enough to beat the entire of the Queen's forces. At the last fight for Ireland, when she was betrayed by having confided in England's honour, but oh! English honour will never again betray our land, for the man will deserve to be betrayed who would confide again in England. I would as soon think of confiding in the cousin-german of a certain personage having two horns and a hoof. At that last battle, the Irish soldiers, after three days fighting, being attacked by fresh troops, faltered and gave way, and 1,500 of the British army entered the breach. The Irish soldiers were fainting and retiring when the women of Limerick threw themselves between the contending forces, and actually stayed the progress of the advancing enemy. I am stating matter of history to you, and the words I use are not mine, but those of Parson Story, the chaplain of King William, who describes the siege, and who admits that the Limerick women drove back the English soldiers from fifteen to thirty paces. Several of the women were killed, when a shriek of horror resounded from the ranks of the Irish. They cried out, 'Let us rather die to the last man than that our women should be injured,' and then they threw themselves forward, and, made doubly valiant by the bravery of the women, they scattered the Saxon and the Dane before them. Yes, I have women enough in Ireland to beat them if necessary; but, my friends, it is idle to imagine that any statesman ever existed who could resist the cry that Ireland makes for justice . . .

We will break no law. See how we have accumulated the people of Ireland for this Repeal Year. When, on the 2nd of January, I ventured to call it the Repeal Year, every person laughed at me. Are they laughing now? It is our turn to laugh at present. Before twelve months more, the Parliament will be in College Green. I said the Union did not take away from the people of Ireland their legal rights. I told you that the Union did not deprive the people of that right, or take away the authority to have self-legislation. It has not less-ened the prerogatives of the Crown, or taken away the rights of the Sovereign, and amongst them is the right to call her Parliament wherever the People are entitled to it, and the people of Ireland are entitled to have it in Ireland. And the Queen has only tomorrow to issue her writs and get the Chancellor to seal them, and if Sir Edward Sugden does not sign them she will soon get an Irishman that will, to revive the Irish Parliament. The towns which sold their birthright have no right to be reckoned amongst the towns sending members to Parliament. King James the First, in one day, created forty boroughs in Ireland, and the Queen has the same right as her predecessor to do so. We have a list of the towns to return members according to their population, and the Queen has only to order writs to issue, and to have honest ministers to advise her to issue those wants, and the Irish Parliament is revived by its own energy, and the force of the Sovereign's prerogative. I will only require the Queen to exercise her perogative, and the Irish people will obtain their nation-ality again. If, at the present moment, the Irish Parliament was in existence, even as it was in 1800, is there a coward amongst you—is there a wretch amongst you so despicable that would not die rather than allow the Union to pass?

Another voice interrupted him, 'Yes, to the last man.'

Let every man who, if we had an Irish Parliament, would rather die than allow the Union to pass lift up his hands. Yes, the Queen will call that Parliament; you may say it is the act of her ministry, if you please. To be sure it would be the act of her ministry, and the people of Ireland are entitled to have their friends appointed to the ministry. The Irish Parliament will then assemble, and I defy all the generals, old and young, and all the old women in pantaloons. Nay, I defy all the chivalry of the earth to take away that Parliament from us again. Well, my friends, may I ask you to obey me in the course of conduct I point out to you, when I dismiss you to-day; when you have heard the resolutions put, I am sure you will go home with the same tranquillity with which you came here, every man of you; and if I wanted you again, would you not come again to Tara Hill for me? Remember me, I lead you into no peril. If danger existed, it would arise from some person who would attack us, for we will attack nobody; and if that danger exists you will not find me in the rear rank. The Queen will be able to restore our Parliament to us. The absentee drains, which caused the impoverishment of the country, will be at an end—the wholesale ejectment of tenants and turning them out on the highway—the murdering of tenants by the landlords will be at an end. The rights of the landlords will be respected, but their duties shall be enforced—an equitable tenure will take the place of the cruel tyranny of the present code of laws, and the protection of the occupying tenants of Ireland be inscribed on the banner of Repeal. Carry home with you my advice. Let there be peace and quiet, law and order, and let every one of you enroll yourselves Repealers—men, women, and children. Give me three millions of Repealers, and I will soon have them. The next step is being taken, and I announce to you from this spot, that all the magistrates that have been deprived of the communion of the peace shall be appointed by the Association to settle all the disputes and differences in their neighbourhood. Keep out of the petty sessions court, and go to them on next Monday. We will submit a plan to choose persons to be arbitrators to settle the differences of the people without expense, and I call upon every man that wishes to be thought the friend of Ireland, to have his disputes settled by the arbitrators, and not again to go to the petty sessions. We shall shortly have the preservative society to arrange the means of procuring from her Majesty the exercise of her prerogative, and I believe I am able to announce to you that twelve months cannot possibly elapse without having a hurrah for our Parliament in College Green. Remember, I pronounce the Union to be null—to be obeyed, as an injustice must be obeyed, when it is supported by law until we have the royal authority to set the matter right, and substitute our own Parliament. I delight at having this day presided over such an assemblage on Tara Hill. Those shouts that burst from you were enough to recall to life the Kings and Chiefs of Ireland. I almost fancy that the spirits of the mighty dead are hovering over us, that the ancient Kings and Chiefs of Ireland are from yonder clouds listening to us. Oh, what a joyous and cheering sound is conveyed in the chirrup for Old Ireland! It is the most beautiful, the most fertile—the most abundant, the most productive country on the face of the earth. It is a lovely land, indented with noble harbours, intersected with transcendent, translucent streams divided by mighty estuaries. Its harbours are open at every hour for every tide, and are sheltered from every storm that can blow from any quarter of Heaven. Oh, yes, it is a lovely land and where is the coward that would not dare to die for it! Yes, our country exhibits the extreme of civilization, and your majestic movement is already the admiration of the civilised world. No other country could produce such an amount of physical force, coupled with so much decorum and propriety of conduct. Many thousands of persons assembled together, and, though they have force sufficient to carry any battle that ever was fought, they separate with the tranquillity of schoolboys breaking up in the afternoon. I wish you could read my heart, to see how deeply the love of Ireland is engraven upon it, and let the people of Ireland, who stood by me so long, stand by me a little longer, and Ireland shall be a nation again.

JAMES FINTAN LALOR
(1807–1849)

Letter to the Irish Felon (1848)

... Without agreement as to our objects we cannot agree on the course we should follow. It is requisite the paper should have but one object and that the public should understand what that object is. Mine is not to repeal the Union, nor restore Eighty-two. This is not the year '82; this is the year '48. For Repeal I never went into 'Agitation' and will not go into insurrection. On that question I refuse to arm, or to act in any mode—and the country refuses. O'Connell made no mistake when he pronounced it to be not worth the price of one drop of blood; and for myself, I regret it was not left in the hands of Conciliation Hall whose lawful property it was and is. Moral force, and Repeal, the means and the purpose, were just fitted to each other, *Arcades ambo*,* balmy Arcadians both. When the means were limited it was only proper and necessary to limit the purpose. When the means were enlarged, the purpose ought to have been enlarged also. Repeal in its vulgar meaning, I look on as utterly impracticable by any mode of action whatever, and the constitution of '82 as absurd, worthless, and worse than worthless. The English government will never concede or surrender to any species of moral force whatsoever; and the country-peasantry will never arm and fight for it—neither will I. If I am to stake life and fame it must assuredly be for something better and greater, more likely to last, more likely to succeed, and better worth success. And a stronger passion, a higher purpose, a nobler and more needful enterprise is fermenting in the hearts of the people. A mightier question moves Ireland today than that of merely repealing the Act of Union. Not the constitution that Tone died to abolish, but the constitution that Tone died to obtain,* independence, full and absolute independence, for this island, and for every man within this island. Into no movement that would leave an enemy's garrison in possession of all our lands, masters of our liberties, our lives and all our means of life and happiness—into no such movement will a single man of the greycoats enter with an armed band, whatever the town population may do. On a wider fighting field, with stronger positions and greater resources than are afforded by the paltry question of Repeal, must we close for our final struggle with England, or sink and surrender. Ireland her own— Ireland her own, and all therein, from the sod to the sky. The soil of Ireland for the people of Ireland, to have and to hold from God alone who gave it—to have and to hold to them and their heirs for ever, without suit or service, faith or fealty, rent or render, to any power under Heaven. From a worse bondage than the bondage of any foreign government, from a dominion more grievous and grinding than the dominion of England in its worst days—from the cruellest tyranny that ever yet laid its vulture clutch on the body and soul of a country, from the robber rights and robber rule that have turned us into slaves and beggars in the land that God gave us for ours.— Deliverance, oh Lord; Deliverance or Death—Deliverance, or this island a desert! This is the one prayer, and terrible need, and real passion of Ireland today, as it has been for ages. Now, at last it begins to shape into defined and desperate purpose; and into it all smaller and meaner purposes must settle and merge. It might have been kept in abeyance, and away from the sight of the sun—aye, till this old native race had been finally conquered out and extinguished *sub silentio*,* without noise or notice. But once propounded and proclaimed as a principle, not in the dusk of remote country districts, but loudly and proudly, in the tribunes of the capital, it must now be accepted and declared, as the first great Article of Association in the National Covenant of organised defence and armed resistance; as the principle to take ground, and stand and fight upon. When a greater and more ennobling enterprise is on foot, every inferior and feebler project or proceeding will soon be left in the hands of old women, of dastards, impostors, swindlers, and imbeciles. All the strength and manhood of the island—all the courage, energies, and ambition—all the passions, heroism, and chivalry—all the strong men, and strong minds—all those things that make revolutions will quickly desert it, and throw themselves into the greater movement, throng into the larger and loftier undertaking and flock round the banner that flies nearest the sky. There go the young and the gallant, the gifted, and the daring, and there too go the wise. For wisdom knows that in national action *littleness* is more fatal than the wildest rashness; that greatness of object is essential to greatness of effort, strength, and success; that a revolution ought never to take its stand on low or narrow ground, but seize on the broadest and highest ground it can lay hands on; and that a petty enterprise seldom succeeds. Had America aimed or declared for less than independence she would probably have failed, and been a fettered slave today.

Not to repeal the Union, then, but to repeal the Conquest—not to disturb or dismantle the empire, but to abolish it forever—not to fall back on '82 but act up to '48—not to resume or restore an old constitution, but to found a new nation, and raise up a free people, and strong as well as free, and secure as well as strong, based on a peasantry rooted like rocks in the soil of the land—this is my object, as I hope it is yours; and this, you may be assured, is the easier, as it is the nobler and more pressing enterprise. For Repeal, all the moral means at our disposal have been used, abused, and abandoned. All the military means it can command will fail as utterly. Compare the two questions. Repeal would require a national organization; a central representative authority, formally convened, formally elected; a regular army, a regulated war of concerted action, and combined movement. When shall we have them? Where is your National Council of Three Hundred? Where is your National Guard of Three Hundred Thousand? On Repeal, Ireland, of necessity, should resolve and act *by the kingdom*, all together, linked and led; and if beaten in the kingdom there would be nothing to fall back upon. She could not possibly act by parishes. To club and arm would not be enough, or rather it would be nothing; and for Repeal alone Ireland will neither club nor arm. The towns only will do so. A Repeal-war would probably be the fight and defeat of a single field-day; or if protracted, it would be a mere game of chess—and England, be assured, would beat you in the game of chess. On the other question all circumstances differ, as I could easily show you. But I have gone into this portion of the subject prematurely and unawares, and here I stop—being reluctant besides to trespass too long on the time of her Majesty's legal and military advisers.

I would regret much to have my meaning, in any degree, misconceived. I do not desire, by any means, to depreciate the value and importance of Repeal, in the valid and vigorous sense of the term, but only in its vulgar acceptation. I do not want to make the tenure question the sole or main topic or purpose of the *Felon*, or to make Repeal only secondary and subservient. I do not wish—far from it—to consider the two questions as antagonistic or distinct. My wish is to combine and cement the two into one; and so, perfect, and reinforce, and carry both. I, too, want to bring about an alliance and 'combination of classes'—an alliance more wanted and better worth, more feasible, effective and honourable, than any treasonable alliance with the enemy's garrison, based on the surrender and sacrifice of the rights and lives of the Irish people. I want to ally the town and country. Repeal is the question of the town population; the land tenure question is that of the country peasantry; both combined, taking each in its full extent and efficacy, form the question of Ireland—her question for the battle-day.

The principle I state, and mean to stand upon, is this, that the entire ownership of Ireland, moral and material, up to the sun, and down to the centre, is vested of right in the people of Ireland; that they, and none but they, are the land-owners and law-makers of this island; that all laws are null and void not made by them; and all titles to land invalid not conferred and confirmed by them; and that this full right of ownership may and ought to be asserted and enforced by any and all means which God has put in the power of man. In other, if not plainer words, I hold and maintain that the entire soil of a country belongs of right to the people of that country, and is the rightful property not of any one class, but of the nation at large, in full effective possession, to let to whom they will on whatever tenures, terms, rents, services, and conditions they will; one condition, however, being unavoidable, and essential, the condition that the tenant shall bear full, true, and undivided fealty, and allegiance to the nation, and the laws of the nation whose lands he holds, and own no allegiance whatsoever to any other prince, power, or people, or any obligation of obedience or respect to their will, orders, or laws. I hold further, and firmly believe, that the enjoyment by the people of this right, of first ownership of the soil, is essential to the vigour and vitality of all other rights; to their validity, efficacy, and value; to their secure possession and safe exercise. For let no people deceive themselves, or be deceived by the words, and colours, and phrases, and forms, of a mock freedom, by constitutions, and charters and articles, and franchises. These things are paper and parchment, waste and worthless. Let laws and institutions say what they will, this fact will be stronger than all laws, and prevail against them—the fact that those who own your land will make your laws, and command your liberties, and your lives. But this is tyranny and slavery—tyranny in its wildest scope, and worst shape; slavery of body and soul from the cradle to the coffin—slavery, with all its horrors, and with none of its physical comforts and security; even as it is in Ireland, where the whole community is made up of tyrants, slaves, and slave-drivers. A people whose lands and lives are thus in the keeping and custody of others, instead of in their own, are not in a position of common safety. The Irish famine of '46 is example and proof. The corn crops were sufficient to feed the island. But the landlords *would* have their rents in spite of famine, and in defiance of fever. They took the whole harvest and left hunger to those who raised it. Had the people of Ireland been the landlords of Ireland, not a single human creature would have died of hunger, nor the failure of the potato been considered a matter of any consequence.

This principle, then, that the property and possession of land, as well as the powers of legislation, belong of right to people who live in the land and under the law—do you assent to it in its full integrity, and to the present necessity of enforcing it? Your *reason* may assent, yet your *feelings* refuse and revolt—or those of others at least may do so. Mercy is for the merciful; and you may think it pity to oust and abolish the present noble race of land-owners, who have ever been pitiful and compassionate themselves.

What! is your sympathy for a class so great, and your sympathy for a whole people so small? For those same land-owners are now treading out the very life and existence of an entire people, and trampling down the liberties and hopes of this island for ever. It is a mere question between a people and a class—between a people of eight millions and a class of eight thousand. They or we must quit this island. It is a people to be saved or lost—it is the island to be kept or surrendered. They have served us with a general writ of ejectment. Wherefore, I say, let them get a notice to quit at once; or we shall oust possession under the law of nature. There are men who claim protection for them, and for all their tyrannous rights and powers, being as 'one class of the Irish people.' I deny the claim. They form no class of the Irish people, or of any other people. Strangers they are in this land they call theirs—strangers here and strangers everywhere, owning no country and owned by none; rejecting Ireland, and rejected by England; tyrants to this island, and slaves to another; here they stand hating and hated—their hand ever against us, as ours against them, an outcast and ruffianly horde, alone in the world, and alone in its history, a class by themselves. They do not know, and never did belong to this island. Tyrants and traitors have they ever been to us and ours since first they set foot on our soil. Their crime it is and not England's that Ireland stands where she does today—or rather it is our own that have borne them so long. Were they a class of the Irish people the Union could be repealed without a life lost. Had they been a class of the Irish people that Union would have never been. But for them we would now be free, prosperous and happy. Until they be removed no people can ever take root, grow up and flourish here. The question between them and us must sooner or later have been brought to a deadly issue. For heaven's sake, and for Ireland's, let us settle it now, and not leave it to our children to settle. Indeed it *must* be settled now—for it is plain to any ordinary sight that they or we are doomed. A cry has gone up to heaven for the living and the dead—to save the living, and avenge the dead.

There are, however, many landlords perhaps, and certainly a few, not fairly chargeable with the crimes of their order; and you may think it hard they should lose their lands. But recollect, the principle I assert would make Ireland *in fact* as she is of *right*, the mistress and queen of all those lands; that she, poor lady, had ever a soft and grateful disposition; and that she may, if she please, in reward of allegiance, confer new titles, or confirm the old. Let us crown her a queen; and then let her do with her lands as a queen may do.

In the case of any existing interest, of what nature soever, I feel assured that no question but one would need to be answered. Does the owner of that interest assent to swear allegiance to the people of

Ireland, and to hold in fee from the Irish nation? If the assent may be assured he will suffer no loss. No eventual or permanent loss, I mean; for some temporary loss he must assuredly suffer. But such loss would be incidental and inevitable to any armed insurrection whatever, no matter on what principle the right of resistance would be resorted to. If he refuse—then I say away with him—out of this land with him—himself and all his robber rights, and all the things himself and his rights have brought into our island—blood, and tears, and famine, and the fever that goes with famine. Between the relative merits and importance of the two rights, the people's right to the land, and their right to legislation, I do not mean or wish to institute any comparison. I am far indeed from desirous to put the two rights in competition, or contrast, for I consider each alike as the natural complement of the other, necessary to its theoretical completeness, and practical efficacy. But, considering them for a moment as distinct, I do mean to assert this—that the land question contains, and the legislative question does *not* contain, the materials from which victory is manufactured; and that, therefore, if we be truly in earnest and determined on success, it is on the former question, and not on the latter that we must take our stand, fling out our banner, and hurl down to England our gage of battle.* Victory follows that banner alone, that and no other. This island is ours, and have it we will, if the leaders be true to the people, and the people be true to themselves.

The rights of property may be pleaded. No one has more respect for the real rights of property than I have; but I do not class among them the robber's right by which the lands of this country are now held in fee for the British crown. I acknowledge no right of property in a small class which goes to abrogate the rights of a numerous people. I acknowledge no right of property in eight thousand persons, be they noble or ignoble, which takes away all rights of property, security, independence, and existence itself, from a population of eight millions, and stands in bar to all the political rights of the island, and all the social rights of its inhabitants. I acknowledge no right of property which takes away the food of millions, and gives them a famine—which denies to the peasant the right of a home, and concedes, in exchange, the right of a workhouse. I deny and challenge all such rights, howsoever founded or enforced. I challenge them, as founded only on the code of the brigand, and enforced only by the sanction of the hangman. Against them I assert the true and indefeasible right of property—the right of our people to live in this land and possess it—to live in it in security, comfort and independence, and to live in it by their own labour, on their own land, as God and nature intended them to do. Against them I shall array, if I can, all the forces that yet remain in this island. And against them I am determined to make war—to their destruction or my own.

These are my principles and views. I shall have other opportunities to develop and defend them. I have some few other requisitions to make, but I choose to defer them for other reasons besides want of time and space. Our first business, before we can advance a step, is to fix our own footing and make good our position. That once done, this contest must, if possible, be brought to a speedy close.

2. REFLECTIONS ON IRISH CULTURE

CHARLOTTE BROOKE
(c.1740–1793)

Preface to Reliques of Irish Poetry (1789)

In a preface to a translation of ancient Irish poetry, the reader will naturally expect to see the subject elucidated and enlarged upon, with the pen of learning and antiquity. I lament that the limited circle of my knowledge does not include the power of answering so just an expectation; but my regret at this circumstance is considerably lessened, when I reflect, that had I been possessed of all the learning requisite for such an undertaking, it would only have qualified me for an unnecessary foil to the names of O'CONOR, O'HALLORAN and VALLANCEY.

My comparatively feeble hand aspires only (like the ladies of ancient Rome) to strew flowers in the paths of these laureled champions of my country. The flowers of earth, the *terrestrial* offspring of Phœbus, were scattered before the steps of victorious WAR; but, for triumphant GENIUS are reserved the *cælestial* children of his beams, the unfading flowers of the Muse. To pluck, and thus to bestow them, is mine, and I hold myself honoured in the task.

'The esteem (says Mr O'HALLORAN) which mankind conceive of nations in general, is always in proportion to the figure they have made in arts and in arms. It is on this account that all civilized countries are eager to display their heroes, legislators, poets and philosophers—and with justice, since every individual participates in the glory of his illustrious countrymen.'—But where, alas, is this thirst for national glory? when a subject of such importance is permitted to a pen like mine! Why does not some *son of Anak* in genius step forward, and boldly throw his gauntlet to Prejudice, the avowed and approved champion of his country's lovely muse?

It is impossible for imagination to conceive too highly of the pitch of excellence to which a science must have soared which was cherished with such enthusiastic regard and cultivation as that of poetry, in this country. It was absolutely, for ages, the vital soul of the nation;[1] and shall we then have no curiosity respecting the productions of genius once so celebrated, and so prized?

True it is, indeed, and much to be lamented, that few of the compositions of those ages that were famed, in Irish annals, for the *light of song*, are now to be obtained by the most diligent research. The greater number of the poetical remains of our Bards, yet extant, were written during the middle ages; periods when the genius of Ireland was in its wane,

——— Yet still, not lost
All its original brightness———.

On the contrary, many of the productions of those times breathe the true spirit of poetry, besides the merit they possess with the Historian and Antiquary, as so many faithful delineations of the manners and ideas of the periods in which they were composed.

With a view to throw some light on the antiquities of this country, to vindicate, in part, its history, and prove its claim to scientific as well as to military fame, I have been induced to undertake the following work. Besides the four different species of composition which it contains, (the HEROIC POEM, the ODE, the ELEGY, and the SONG) others yet remain unattempted by translation:—the ROMANCE, in particular, which unites the fire of Homer with the enchanting wildness of Ariosto. But the limits of my present plan have necessarily excluded many beautiful productions of genius, as little more can be done, within the compass of a single volume, than merely to give a few specimens, in the hope of awakening a just and useful curiosity, on the subject of our poetical compositions.

Unacquainted with the rules of translation, I know not how far those rules may censure, or acquit me. I do not profess to give a merely literal version of my originals, for that I should have found an impossible undertaking.—Besides the spirit which they breathe, and which lifts the imagination far above the tameness, let me say, the *injustice*, of such a task,—there are many complex words that could

---

[1] See the elegant and faithful O'CONOR upon this subject; (*Dissertations on the History of Ireland*, p. 66.) and he is supported by the testimonies of the most authentic of antient and modern historians.

not be translated literally, without great injury to the original,—without being 'false to its sense, and falser to its fame.'

I am aware that in the following poems there will sometimes be found a sameness, and repetition of thought, appearing but too plainly in the English version, though scarcely perceivable in the original Irish, so great is the variety as well as beauty peculiar to that language. The number of synonima[2] in which it abounds, enables it, perhaps beyond any other, to repeat the same thought, without tiring the fancy or the ear.

It is really astonishing of what various and comprehensive powers this neglected language is possessed. In the pathetic, it breathes the most beautiful and affecting simplicity; and in the bolder species of composition, it is distinguished by a force of expression, a sublime dignity, and rapid energy, which it is scarcely possible for any translation fully to convey; as it sometimes fills the mind with ideas altogether new, and which, perhaps, no modern language is entirely prepared to express. One compound epithet must often be translated by two lines of English verse, and, on such occasions, much of the beauty is necessarily lost; the force and effect of the thought being weakened by too slow an introduction on the mind; just as that light which dazzles, when flashing swiftly on the eye, will be gazed at with indifference, if let in by degrees.

But, though I am conscious of having, in many instances, failed in my attempts to do all the justice I wished to my originals, yet still, some of their beauties are, I hope, preserved; and I trust I am doing an acceptable service to my country, while I endeavour to rescue from oblivion a few of the invaluable reliques of her ancient genius; and while I put it in the power of the public to form some idea of them, by clothing the thoughts of our Irish muse in a language with which they are familiar, at the same time that I give the originals, as vouchers for the fidelity of my translation, as far as two idioms so widely different would allow.

However deficient in the powers requisite to so important a task, I may yet be permitted to point out some of the good consequences which might result from it, if it were but performed to my wishes. The productions of our Irish Bards exhibit a glow of cultivated

---

[2] There are upwards of forty names to express a *Ship* in the Irish language, and nearly an equal number for a *House*, &c.

genius,—a spirit of elevated heroism,—sentiments of pure honor,—instances of disinterested patriotism,—and manners of a degree of refinement, totally astonishing, at a period when the rest of Europe was nearly sunk in barbarism: And is not all this very honorable to our countrymen? Will they not be benefited,—will they not be gratified, at the lustre reflected on them by ancestors so very different from what modern prejudice has been studious to represent them? But this is not all.——

As yet, we are too little known to our noble neighbour of Britain; were we better acquainted, we should be better friends. The British muse is not yet informed that she has an elder sister in this isle; let us then introduce them to each other! together let them walk abroad from their bowers, sweet ambassadresses of cordial union between two countries that seem formed by nature to be joined by every bond of interest, and of amity. Let them entreat of Britain to cultivate a nearer acquaintance with her neighbouring isle. Let them conciliate for us her esteem, and her affection will follow of course. Let them tell her, that the portion of her blood which flows in our veins is rather ennobled than disgraced by the mingling tides that descended from our heroic ancestors. Let them come—but will they answer to a voice like mine? Will they not rather depute some favoured pen, to chide me back to the shade whence I have been allured, and where, perhaps, I ought to have remained, in respect to the memory, and superior genius of a Father—it avails not to say how dear!—But my feeble efforts presume not to emulate,—and they cannot injure his fame.

To guard against criticism I am no way prepared, nor do I suppose I shall escape it; nay, indeed, I do not wish to escape the pen of the *candid* critic: And I would willingly believe that an individual capable of no offence, and pretending to no pre-eminence, cannot possibly meet with any severity of criticism, but what the mistakes, or the deficiencies of this performance, may be justly deemed to merit; and what, indeed, could scarcely be avoided by one unskilled in composition, and now, with extreme diffidence, presenting, for the first time, her literary face to the world.

It yet remains to say a few words relative to the TALE which is annexed to this volume: for that I had no original; the story, however, is not my own; it is taken from a revolution in the history of ancient Ireland, Anno Mundi 3649. And no where will the Muse be furnished with nobler subjects than that neglected history affords. The whole reign of CEALLACHAIN is one continued series of heroism, and high-wrought honor, that rises superior to all the flight of ROMANCE, and defies Poetic fable to surpass it. Also, the reign of BRIAN BOIROIMH, and the famous retreat of the glorious tribe of DALGAIS; besides many other instances too numerous for detail; amongst which I selected the story of MAON, as a subject more suited to my limited powers, than those which demand a 'Muse of fire,' to record them.

LE CHEVALIER DE LA TOCNAYE
(*c.*1767–?)

from *A Frenchman's Walk Through Ireland* (1797)

Dublin

Dublin is a very considerable city, about one-fourth the size of London, of which it is the image in little—even the streets bear the same names; the beauty of the buildings may dispute for precedence with those of the capital; one is astonished at their magnificence and number. The Parliament House does honour to the nation's representatives; it is an immense circular building surrounded by a magnificent colonnade.

It is worthy of remark that the place where the deputies or representatives of the greatest nation assemble is commonly an old, irregular, ugly building, for which there is such attachment or affection that nobody thinks of displacing it by a new and more commodious structure.

The Bourse or Royal Exchange is somewhat like the Mansion House in London, but smaller. The Customs House is much too fine for its work, and the new building which they call the Four Courts of Justice* gives Themis* the pleasure to see herself decently lodged, a rare thing in European countries. Her old residence was a frightful place, as much on account of the members as by reason of the lugubrious and sombre appearance of the cave where they practised. I amused myself often by walking among them, and as it was extremely unlikely that I, in my circumstances, should ever have anything to do with them, I could laugh at their big wigs, in which the face is so buried that only a long nose protrudes. They reminded me of hawks dressed to pounce on their prey, with the beaks only visible. If rumour is to be believed, attorneys here yield in nothing to their brethren of our courts; indeed, from certain stories I have heard it would seem that they are even cleverer.

The squares are large and well built, only the port seems to me to be unworthy of the city. There has just been constructed an immense dock, which will make good certain shortcomings when some houses have been built to protect it from wind. It is singular that the inhabitants have never thought of building a beautiful church here: the churches are all old and without the least decoration. Among them all there are but two miserable bell-towers, and this want prevents the city from having the fine appearance it should exhibit from a distance.

As my object is not to give a topographical description of this great city, I shall not attempt to describe the Castle and the beautiful buildings associated. The splendid carriages and the apparent wealth of the principal houses render the more displeasing the sight of the beggars, whose abject poverty is horrible. They may be seen hanging on for hours to the railings of basement stories, forcing charity by depriving those who live in these places of light and air. Some of them are insolent, seeking to get in some fashion, by force, what is not forthcoming by good-will. These disgusting scenes harden the heart little by little, and I never felt less disposed to alms-giving than after having lived some time in Dublin.

I occupied my leisure in the early days of my sojourn as I do ordinarily in such times elsewhere, by moving from one place to another, and mixing as much as possible with the crowd. I joined one which seemed, on a certain day, to be expecting something with impatience, and found myself among them in front of a large building which had something of the look of an old castle. There was a little platform at the level of a window in the second storey; two men of somewhat disagreeable look made their appearance on it, and I thought I was about to witness some peculiar ceremony. But I was promptly disabused of this idea, for one of them passed a loop of rope round the neck of the other and fastened the cord to a bar of iron above him. I turned to get away, but the crowd was too dense for movement; the poor wretch stood for a moment, alone, in view of the people, then a bolt slipped, and the little platform on which he stood fell against the wall. The Irish have, perhaps, got the better of their neighbours in the matter of hanging people with grace, but to me it appears a great cruelty to make a sort of parade of the death of a man, and in diminishing the horror of the punishment crime is increased and executions multiplied. I think I am not far wrong in assigning this as the reason why there are more people hung in Great Britain and Ireland than in all the rest of Europe.

The crowd seemed to move steadily in one direction, and I followed again—this time to be led to Phœnix Park, where there was a horse race. I really could not say which of the two—execution or race—gave the greater pleasure to the hundred-headed monster.

Although the part of the city where the well-to-do people live is perhaps as beautiful as anything similar in Europe, nothing anywhere can compare with the dirt and misery of the quarters where the lower classes vegetate. They call these quarters 'The Liberties'* of Dublin, and this made me think often of 'liberties' of France under Robespierre, than which there was nothing more disgusting in the universe. . . .

Cork

The climate of Cork is rainy in the extreme. It rains every day in life, and the temperature of the air has perhaps influenced the character of the inhabitants. It would not be incorrect to call this country 'The Land of Whim and Spleen.' There are a great number of people here who are called 'characters,' and who have all sorts of strange whims and crotchets. One will never sit down to table for fear of being suffocated by the odour of the viands, and takes his meals alone in the vestibule; another spends his income on favourite animals, or 'pets,' as they are called; a third, after having enchanted you by a beautiful voice and charming music, finishes up by boxing you. There is one with a red cap who gallops through the streets and enters shops on horseback, when he wants to buy anything. There is one who plays the bagpipes and who is willing to be disinherited from nearly two thousand pounds sterling per annum, rather than give up his pipes, which are at present his sole source of income. There is a man who believes that everybody wishes to poison him. He watches for the entry of any person into a baker's shop, follows him, and when the stranger has bought a loaf he seizes it and runs off with it, believing that the bakers are not anxious to poison anybody but himself. He acts the same way in butchers' shops. Another has constituted himself children's nurse, and washes, rubs, combs, and wipes them. I could mention many other examples of these 'characters,' but have said enough.

There is no place of shelter for the weak-minded of Cork—it is a hideous spectacle to see them in the streets. For the greater part, it is true, they are quiet, but it is so cruel and humiliating to see human nature degraded that an effort should be made to separate them from society.

Yet it must be admitted that the city of Cork has recently made great progress in commerce, in increase of houses, and of inhabitants, and, to some degree, in their amelioration. The city stands on several little marshy islands in the middle of the river, and it is from this circumstance that it takes its name, for Cork means 'muddy' in Irish, and it is passably well named. The narrow canals which separate the islands are only filled with water at high tide, and so destroy considerably the salubrity of the air.

It would seem to be absolutely necessary for the prosperity of the town that the principal magistrates, for a dozen years, should be strong and prudent men, whose judgment would not be narrowed to the dust of their offices, and who would not be so much accustomed to count halfpennies and farthings, or to think of interest at four, five or six per cent. In the whole of Great Britain, the Mayor or Provost is always elected from amongst the merchants and general traders, the inhabitants justly confiding their interests to one who has a commercial career. This arrangement works very well in towns that are much frequented, where the opinion of the merchant is enlightened by that of a large public, and of strangers who may visit the place; but in towns where the merchant can have no ideas other than his own, or where, being a foreigner, his sole aim is to gather as much money as possible, and quit the country afterwards, it must be evident that the embellishments and amelioration of the city, of which he is a principal magistrate for a year, will not interest him very much.

I believe that what I have said may explain the little progress which Cork has made in the arts and in matters of public welfare and interest. I imagine that if a man of character generally esteemed (Lord Shannon, for instance) would consent, during several years, to clean this Augean stable,* he would be actuated by a desire for the public good, instead of by self-interest, and he would not be found to retard the construction of establishments required by the mass of the inhabitants because the revenues of the city might diminish by a few shillings or pounds.

Since I have extended my remarks on this subject so much, the reader will perhaps want to know what are the ameliorations of which I speak, and what I think the public-spirited Mayor might do. I shall mention a few of the principal, and in a manner most concise. First of all, demolish the two hideous prisons which are at the end of the bridges joining this muddy island with the banks of the river and build new, outside the town, in an airy position. Clean the streets— don't permit the inhabitants to allow their pigs to roam wherever they may seek pasture, and don't let these pigs be seen after their throats have been cut. Build a grain market in a suitable position. Establish public schools and hospitals where the people may be sure that their children are instructed in the religion they wish to follow, and not in that which others wish them to follow. Build an asylum for the insane. Furnish the city with public fountains. Clear the quays of the sheds which disfigure them. Encourage, as far as possible, manufactures of all kinds, and establish a House of Industry, so as to get rid of the beggars which dishonour the streets. Have public works in which every man wanting bread may find the means to earn it, &c.

I am convinced that if these plans could be carried out during fifty years, Cork would become more important than Dublin itself, on account of the safety and fine situation of its port. The principal exportation is at present of salted meat; beasts are killed in the season by thousands, and the season over, there is nothing to do. I have known a merchant who, from what I am told, kills every year between twenty and twenty-five thousand pigs, which statement gave me occasion to say to him that he was the greatest murderer of hogs I ever knew. This digression is a little long, and may perhaps appear fastidious to some who do not take much interest in Cork, but it is more for the Irish than the foreigner that I write, and I hope that the purity of my motive will be taken as excuse. . . .

Armagh

This country is entirely occupied in the manufacture of linen, but the late troubles have made trade to languish. The mills, however, are still going, and it is hoped that a year of peace will restore order and prosperity. Military law was rigorously enforced here on the inhabitants; they were not permitted to have lights in their houses after nine o'clock, and any person found in the streets after that hour was in danger of being arrested. A fair was held during the time I stayed in this little town, and it passed over quite peacefully; the soldiers promenaded through the market-place and obliged women who wore anything green, ribbon or otherwise,* to take it off. Had one-fourth of the precaution taken here been observed in France, there would certainly have been no Revolution. I was much struck here by the thought of the different results which different characters in government may produce. It is remarkable how in France a weak government and foolish ministers have led a people entirely Royalist to slay a King they loved, and whose good qualities they respected, and to destroy a flourishing monarchy for whose prosperity they had been enthusiastic; while here, surrounded by enemies, a vigorous government in Ireland has been able to repress, and hold in the path of duty, a people discontented and seduced by the success of the French innovations.

The boldness of the United Irishmen increased each day as long as the Government did not interfere; many who had joined them had done so out of fear, and there were with them a number of weak, undecided people ready to range themselves on the winning side, and so immediately on the Government's determination to act vigorously, it was only necessary to let the soldiers appear upon the scene, and the difficulties disappeared.

The poor peasant on this occasion, as in so many others, was the dupe of rogues, who put him in the front, and were very careful themselves to stay behind the curtain. The troops went through the country, burning the houses of those who were suspected of having taken the 'Union' oath, or of having arms, and on many occasions they acted with great severity.

On the way to Armagh I passed through a superb country; there is a charming valley, and well-wooded, near Tandragee. Between this town and Armagh I met a company of Orangemen,* as they are called, wearing orange cockades, and some of them having ties of the same colour. The peasantry seemed very much afraid of them. I went into one or two cabins to rest myself, and was offered, certainly, hospitality in the ordinary way, but it did not seem to be with the same air as before, and at last, near the town, a good woman said to me, 'You seem to have come from far, my dear Sir, I hope that your umbrella or the string of it will not bring you into trouble.' I laughed at the good woman's fears, but, on reflection, I felt that since she had remarked that my umbrella was greenish, and the cord of a bright green, soldiers might make the same observation, and that in any case it would be very disagreeable to have any trouble over such a silly thing, and I cut the green cord off my umbrella.

Arriving in the town of St Patrick, I went immediately to pay my duty to his metropolitan church. The foundations of this, they say, were laid by the Saint himself on the ruins of a Druidic establishment. History relates that there was here a lively passage at arms between the Saint and the Druids in presence of the great monarch who was then King of Ulster, and the Saint, having convinced his Majesty, baptised him and all his court, and afterwards sent missionaries into the other kingdoms of Ireland. The old cathedral has been destroyed and burned several times, and has been rebuilt always on the same spot.

The city had been reduced to the miserable state of a little country town, but the last Archbishop, the Rev. —— Robertson, being a man of learning and friend of the public welfare, liberal, and without family, set himself to improve and increase it, so that at present it is really a very handsome little city. The cathedral is situated on a rocky height (as the name Ard indicates), and here, a few years ago, among some ruins was found an ancient cross of stone in one piece, with strange looking figures thereon carved, and appearing to be a representation of a man baptising converts. It has been erected in the market-place.

Primate Robertson has built at his own charges an observatory, and has furnished funds to give it an annual income of £300 sterling, which is paid to the person in charge. He has also established, at great cost, a well-furnished library, which is open to the public four hours every day. He has erected a hospital and several other edifices, and certainly merits as much gratitude from the inhabitants of the diocese as may be considered due to St Patrick himself.

The revenues of the Archbishop amount to eight or nine thousand pounds sterling per annum, but it is known that the estates belonging to the seat bring in to those who have farmed them £150,000 (3,750,000 francs). If the Archbishop had such an income, it might well excite the jealousy of the Government, as well as the discontent of the rent-farmers, who regard these estates as heritages belonging to their families, thus, prudently, the leases are renewed every year at the same price, plus a considerable *pot-de-vin.** The demesne of the Archbishop is superb; the Palace, although very large and well built, does not seem too magnificent for the embellishments of the park surrounding. There is in it a chapel, brilliant in architecture, in which there is some very fine stained glass.

There are four Archbishops in Ireland, who all take the title of Primate. He of Armagh is called Primate of All Ireland, the Dublin Archbishop is called Primate of Ireland, that of Cashel, Primate of Munster, and that of Tuam, Primate of Connaught. This is pretty well for Primates. In England there are only two: the Archbishop of Canterbury, Primate of All England, and that of York, Primate of England. I am sorry I cannot remember how many there were in France; but perhaps the reader is pleased to be without the information.

The country in the neighbourhood of Armagh is charming, full of little hills and plains and pretty little lakes. Among the places I saw I remarked, especially, Castle Dillon and Drumilly, where I was received by Colonel Spencer, whose acquaintance I had made at Westport in the summer. Certainly there could not be a more agreeable quarter; the country is a little paradise, it is impossible to conceive anything better cultivated or more romantic. What a pity then, that the spirit of discord and fury has laid hold of the inhabitants to a point that might well make one fear to live among them. Every morning there is news of crimes committed during the night. Not a day passes without murders or the burning of houses. For the sake of a walk I accompanied one of the officers who was going to verify information by visiting a man who had been beaten. We found the man with one eye punched in, it is true, but I thought the injury might just as well have been the result of a private dispute with which politics had nothing to do. The house of one good woman had certainly been 'wrecked,' as they say, by some armed men, but that was all we were able to learn.

I think it my duty to give here a little information on the subject of the troubles, which for so long have desolated this beautiful country. The quarrel between Catholics and Protestants of this county began with a private dispute between two peasants at a fair. The one was Catholic and the other Protestant. During the fight ill-advised words passed from one side to the other, and these had the effect, as is unfortunately the custom at most fairs, of ranging the friends of the two combatants into parties who fought each other with sticks. That day the Protestants were beaten, but at another fair they took their revenge, falling, armed, on the Catholics, and a number were killed. The animosity between the parties manifested itself for a long time before the Government appeared to take any notice; in the end, however, the magistrates, although not very energetically, took certain proceedings, and put into execution a part of the law which at that time forbade Catholics to have possession of arms. It followed that, as there was no power to disarm the other side, the former were entirely at the mercy of the latter.

I have been assured that there were certain persons who thought it their duty to take the Protestant side in order not to lose their votes in the parliamentary elections. This unfortunate partisanship increased the audacity of the triumphant side, who formed a military corps, to which they gave the name of 'Orange Boys,' in memory of the Prince of Orange (King William) and of the Revolution. The other side took, correctly enough, the name of 'Defenders,' for it is true that, at first, they only thought of defence. The Orange Boys had the advantage over their adversaries, seeing that they were armed, and the others were not. Matters came to such a point that Defenders, who were obnoxious, received letters in these terms:

'Peter —— or James ——, you have —— time to sell your things and go to Connaught, or you will go to Hell.'

Some disdained to submit to these barbarous orders, and during the night their cabins would be overturned or demolished over their heads, or a dozen of shots would be sent into a bedroom. These horrors started the Defenders to commit excesses no less cruel. The atrocities were not repressed with the necessary vigour to put an end to them, in fact it seemed as if very little attention was given to them. Peaceful families of both religions, frightened at these disorders, hastened to sell their effects at loss, and retired to the province of

Connaught, where I have seen a number of them welcomed by Colonel Martin and Lord Altamont.

While, here, matters were in this distressing state, it is very singular that troubles of a totally different character appeared in the neighbouring counties. Those of Armagh really belonged to a religious war, those of the Counties of Down, Antrim, and Londonderry had, for pretext, the reform of Parliament, and the discontented affected to speak with indifference of all religions. I have known cases of men who, having practised the most barbarous cruelties on their compatriots on religious pretexts, affected, in the name of United Irishmen, to say that all religions were equal, while they appeared not to believe in any.

They assembled, appointed chiefs, announced republican opinions, and declared that they only waited the arrival of the French to join them.

It is certain that this new spirit of dissension by throwing ridicule at, and treating with contempt, the troubles of Armagh succeeded in settling these to a great extent. But the new ideas, by their immediate connection with the revolution in France, were likely to become much more dangerous than the first. It is well known to what indefensible excesses the United Irishmen proceeded. I have mentioned some of them which happened before I reached Scotland. I was convinced then, by the knowledge I had of the people of this country, that this frenzy would calm down, and that unless there were really an invasion on a large scale, there was absolutely no fear about the surety of the Government. Such was the situation of the country at the time I started for Scotland. Perhaps on my return I would have found things in the same state, if the arrival of the French Fleet in the bay of Bantry had not opened the eyes of the Government as to the dangers they ran, and convinced them of the necessity for rigorous methods in dealing with the dissatisfaction.

JOHN GAMBLE
(1770–1831)

An Irish Wake (1826)

An Irish wake has been often described, and often ridiculed; I saw nothing ridiculous in the present one: though every apartment in the house was crowded, the most perfect order and decorum prevailed; the kitchen was filled with servants and labourers, to whom tea and tobacco were liberally given; in the parlour were assembled the neighbouring farmers and shopkeepers; wine and punch were on the table; but they were taken sparingly, and several did not take them at all; these were Catholics: of late years, they are not permitted to drink at wakes: this is a regulation of their clergy,—a most laudable one, as disgusting scenes of drunkenness, doubtless, often occurred: nothing more forcibly marks the influence the Catholic clergy possess over the middle and lower classes of their own order than this circumstance; if they gave up whiskey, they would give up any thing.

Two large candles were placed on a table in the room where the corpse lay: they gave a gloomy and sepulchral kind of light, as superstition does not allow them to be snuffed: the bed was hung round with white; the body was dressed in a shroud and a cap with black riband; a plate of salt was laid on the breast, not, as has been supposed, in the expectation of its keeping the dead from corruption, but on account of its preserving the living from infection; possibly, likewise, from some fanciful analogy between corporeal and spiritual corruption.

I approached the dead body and uncovered the face: I contemplated it long: I scarcely know a more sublime object than the face of a dead man: the passions that distorted it are fled; there is no longer either joy or sorrow; all is silent as the dark mansion in which it is to be enclosed.

I have witnessed the last struggles of many dying persons: in general, I am happy to state (for in the last struggles of poor human nature we are all interested), they seemed to suffer much less than would be supposed: convulsions passed over, but seldom much distorted, the face; a smile, even, would often play upon the lips while they stood quivering on the cheeks and temples; a celestial expression would shine in their eyes, as they imitated, with their hands on the bed-clothes, the pretty movements of gathering flowers, and talked in broken and indistinct language of green fields and falling waters: who can tell but at those moments they had lofty glimpses of thought, more sublime than ever entered into the conception of a poet? who can tell but at those moments they had a bright foretaste of the happiness of Heaven in the verdant meadows, the shady bowers, and cooling streams, in which, in fancy, they were wandering?

They gradually sank down lower and lower in the bed; a slight heaving of the shoulders, and drawing up of the limbs, were almost immediately followed by their stretching themselves out to everlasting quietness. Cæsar, when he found his fate inevitable, drew his robes around him, that he might fall with dignity; in falling so, he did no more than is done by the commonest man: the attitude of death is ever a graceful one.

The company in this apartment were relations of the deceased, and mostly women; for where sorrow is, women are mostly to be found.

In England, relations generally keep away on such occasions; I suppose, because it is not accounted wise to indulge in unavailing sorrow: it *is wise* to indulge in it; for, 'by the sadness of the countenance, the heart is made better:' it is wise to contemplate, often to contemplate, what we must one day be ourselves: we may run away from our friend's funeral, we cannot run away from our own.

The conversation was carried on in an under voice, and turned on death and judgment, and ghosts and apparitions: more stories were told of these latter than I can remember: I was as forcibly struck with the look and tone of terror and affright, with which they were told and listened to, as I was with the importance they showed man is of to himself, who cannot die but that hundreds of imaginary beings are conjured up to bewail his dissolution, and give warning of it.

The Banshee (a spiritual being who foretels death by the most plaintive cries), a cousin of the deceased related, was heard wailing the live-long night of his death, and, just before it happened, vanished, clapping her hands, and crying, 'Oh, Katty Galbraith (the young man's mother)! Katty Galbraith! but you are going to get a sore heart.'

The sudden death, a short time before, of a young lady in the neighbourhood, was talked of, and lamented, as a most unexpected and unaccountable circumstance. 'Dear heart! dear heart!' said an old woman, 'I might have told of it weeks and weeks before. Didn't I see, with my own eyes, her *wraith* going up the bank of the river, behind her father's house, with a water-bottle in her hand?'

A wraith is such a shadowy representation of a living person, as a ghost is of a dead one: whenever it is seen, it is a sure sign that the person, man or woman, to whom it belongs, is shortly to die.

From death, I know not by what transition, they came to talk of marriage. In marriage, as well as in hanging, there has always been supposed a destiny, and fate was powerful in these marriages. It is an article of popular belief in Ireland, as well as in Scotland, that if certain ceremonies are performed at midnight on Allhallows eve,* the person who performs them shall see the figure of his or her future wife or husband: the beautiful poem of Halloween, by Robert Burns, contains a faithful and amusing account of these lingering superstitions of other days: to those, if there be any, who have not read it, the following will give a faint idea of them.

Two girls went out at the dark of the moon, and washed their shifts* in south running water, in the devil's name; they hung them before the fire in the room where they lay, keeping awake and silent, as the charm requires. Towards morning, two apparitions came in and turned them: the one was that of a man with a rope about his neck, the other was that of a man in a coffin. Shortly afterwards, the two girls were married to men bearing the forms in question: one of these was hanged for horse-stealing, and the other died the day after his marriage.

A comely servant maid of a neighbouring farmer went out, in a similar manner, to wash her shift in the devil's name: the apparition of her master passed; as she had left him asleep in bed, she was in a terrible fright: she came in, and told the circumstance to her mistress, who persuaded her to go out a second time, and to take with her a pair of scissors: the apparition once again slowly passed; she, unobserved, cut off a piece from the skirt of its coat, and returned with it to her mistress. 'Well!' said the good woman, 'what must be must; you will be his second wife; and be kind to my children, for I have but a short time to live.' The servant maid, however, forgot this injunction; and when married to her master, which she was about twelve months afterwards, proved a very step-mother.

At the dawn of day, the whole company, with one voice, uttered a wild and sudden shriek: this is an ancient custom, and appears to me a natural one: the first rays of new-born day break dismally on the brilliant halls of rejoicing, and give the gay figures, who glide over their figured floors, a sad and livid hue; they may well be supposed to make death more ghastly, and its apartment more sorrowful.

At eight o'clock the funeral went out: the frantic sorrow of the mother and sisters, as the coffin was removing, it would be impossible to describe; they hung round it, tore their hair, which they flung in handfuls on it, clasped it in their arms, beat on it with their hands, called on the deceased by his name, by a thousand tender, by a thousand almost reproachful names, to hear, to answer, to come forth: they called on their Saviour, who had raised Lazarus from the grave, to burst the bands of death, and bid him come forth—in his winding-sheet, in putrefaction, in corruption, to come forth: the mother flung herself across the head of the little stairs to block up the passage, and it was only by stepping over her, that the body could at length be brought down.

I felt as if the weight of a mountain were taken off my breast, when I got out of hearing (which was not for a long time) of her, and of her daughters' cries.

The priest stopped at a field near the church: the coffin was laid at his feet, and the people ranged themselves round, while he read the funeral service of the church of Rome in a solemn and impressive manner. Fondly attached to their ancient burying-places, which they regard as holy ground, the Catholics still bear their dead to them, though they are mostly now Protestant churchyards. It is almost superfluous to say, that they are not allowed to perform there the ceremonies of their religion, and that the body is laid in the clay, and that the earth falls lumbering upon it, with no solemn mass said or dirge sung. This, to the eye of reason that resides in a large town, will appear a slight evil, but to the heart of sensibility that dwells in the country it is a great one. The more, indeed, I reflect on the evils of the people of Ireland, I am the more disposed to refer a portion of them to feeling, as much as to condition, and to believe that, had they people of feeling to deal with (which statesmen rarely are), they might be got rid of.

The service was succeeded by the mournful cry of death, which continued until we reached the churchyard. To my ears—perhaps attuned to it by the lamentations they just had heard—it seemed a sadly pleasing strain, such as sorrow well might utter, and pensiveness might love to hear. Many who will not allow the Irish cry to be musical, have admitted that it is melancholy; and have thereby admitted their own want of knowledge of music. No concourse of sounds can be melancholy without being musical, nor, paradoxical as it may appear, can any, I think, be fully musical without being melancholy. Music, as well as poetry, issues from heaven, and never can reside in its perfection with noisy mirth or broad-faced laughter.

WILLIAM CARLETON
(1794–1869)

from *The Lough Derg Pilgrim* (1828)

The next morning, when I awoke, I joined with all haste the aggregate crowd that proceeded in masses towards the lake—or Purgatory*—which lies amongst the hills that extend to the north-east of Petigo.* While ascending the bleak, hideous mountain range, whose ridge commands a full view of this celebrated scene of superstition, the manner and appearance of the pilgrims were deeply interesting. Such groupings as pressed forward around me would have made fine studies either for him who wished to deplore or to ridicule the degradations and absurdities of human nature; indeed there was an intense interest in the scene. I look back at this moment with awe towards the tremulous and high-strained vibrations of my mind, as it responded to the excitement. Reader, have you ever approached the Eternal City? have you ever, from the dreary solitudes of the Campagna, seen the dome of St Peter's for the first time? and have the monuments of the greatest men and the mightiest deeds that ever the earth witnessed—have the names of the Cæsars, and the Catos, and the Scipios, excited a curiosity amounting to a sensation almost too intense to be borne? I think I can venture to measure the expansion of your mind, as it enlarged itself before the crowding visions of the past, as the dim grandeur of ages rose up and developed itself from amidst the shadows of time; and entranced amidst the magic of your own associations, you desired to stop—you were almost content to go no farther—your *own* Rome, you were in the midst of—Rome free—Rome triumphant—Rome classical. And perhaps it is well you awoke in good time from your shadowy dream, to escape from the unvaried desolation and the wasting *malaria* that brooded all around. Reader, I can fancy that such might have been your sensations when the domes and the spires of the world's capital first met your vision: and I can assure you, that while ascending the ridge that was to give me a view of Patrick's Purgatory, my sensations were as impressively, as powerfully excited. For I desire you to recollect, that the welfare of your immortal soul was not connected with your imaginings, your magnificent visions did not penetrate into the soul's doom. You were not submitted to the agency of a transcendental power. You were, in a word, a poet, but not a fanatic. What comparison, then, could there be between the exercise of your free, manly, cultivated understanding, and my feelings on this occasion, with my thick-coming visions of immortality, that almost lifted me from the mountain-path I was ascending, and brought me, as it were, into contact with the invisible world? I repeat it, then, that such were my feelings, when all the faculties which exist in the mind were aroused and concentrated upon one object. In such a case, the pilgrim stands, as it were, between life and death; and as it was superstition that placed him there, she certainly conjures up to his heated fancy those dark, fleeting, and indistinct images which are best adapted to that gloom which she has already cast over his mind. Although there could not be less than two hundred people, young and old, boys and girls, men and women, the hale and the sickly, the blind and the lame, all climbing to gain the top with as little delay as possible, yet was there scarcely a sound, certainly not a word, to be heard among them. For my part, I plainly heard the palpitations of my heart, both loud and quick. Had I been told that the veil of eternity was about to be raised before me at that moment, I could scarcely have felt more intensely. Several females were obliged to rest for some time, in order to gain both physical and moral strength—one fainted; and several old men were obliged to sit down. All were praying, every crucifix was out, every bead in requisition; and nothing broke a silence so solemn but a low, monotonous murmur of deep devotion.

As soon as we ascended the hill, the whole scene was instantly before us: a large lake, surrounded by an amphitheatre of mountains, bleak, uncomfortable, and desolate. In the lake itself, about half a mile from the edge next us, was to be seen the 'Island,' with two or three slated houses on it, naked and unplastered, as desolate-looking almost as the mountains. A little range of exceeding low hovels, which a dwarf could scarcely enter without stooping, appeared to the left; and the eye could rest on nothing more, except a living mass of human beings crawling slowly about. The first thing the pilgrim does when he gets a sight of the lake, is to prostrate himself, kiss the earth, and then on his knees *offer up* three *Paters* and *Aves*, and a *Creed** for the favour of being permitted to see this blessed place. When this is over, he descends to the lake, and after paying tenpence to the ferryman, is rowed over to the Purgatory.

When the whole view was presented to me, I stood for some time to contemplate it; and I cannot better illustrate the reaction which took place in my mind, than by saying that it resembles that awkward inversion which a man's proper body experiences when, on going to pull something from which he expects a marvellous resistance, it comes with him at a touch, and the natural consequence is, that he finds his head down and his heels up. That which dashed the whole scene from the dark elevation in which the romance of devotion had placed it was the appearance of slated houses, and of the smoke that curled from the hovels and the prior's residence. This at once brought me back to humanity; and the idea of roasting meat, boiling pots, and dressing dinners, dispossessed every fine and fearful image which had floated through my imagination for the last twelve hours. In fact, allowing for the difference of situation, it nearly resembled John's Well, or James's Fair, when beheld at a distance, turning the slated houses into inns, and the hovels into tents. A certain idea, slight, untraceable, and involuntary, went over my brain on that occasion, which, though it did not *then* cost me a single effort of reflection, I think was revived and developed at a future period of my life, and became, perhaps to a certain extent, the means of opening a wider range of thought to my mind, and of giving a new tone to my existence. Still, however, nothing except my idea of its external appearance disappointed me; I accordingly descended with the rest, and in a short time found myself among the living mass upon the island.

The first thing I did was to hand over my three cakes of oaten bread which I had got made in Petigo, tied up in a handkerchief, as well as my hat and second shirt, to the care of the owner of one of the huts: having first, by the way, undergone a second prostration on touching the island, and greeted it with fifteen holy kisses, and another string of prayers. I then, according to the regulations, should commence the *stations*,* lacerated as my feet were after so long a journey; so that I had not a moment to rest. Think, therefore, what I must have suffered, on surrounding a large chapel, in the direction of from east to west, over a pavement of stone spikes, every one of them making its way along my nerves and muscles to my unfortunate brain. I was absolutely stupid and dizzy with the pain, the praying, the jostling, the elbowing, the scrambling and the uncomfortable penitential murmurs of the whole crowd. I knew not what I was about, but went through the forms in the same mechanical spirit which pervaded all present. As for that solemn, humble, and heart-felt sense of God's presence, which Christian prayer demands, its existence in the mind would not only be a moral but a physical impossibility in Lough Derg. I verily think that if mortification of the body, without conversion of the life or heart—if penance and not repentance *could* save the soul, no wretch who performed a pilgrim-age here could with a good grace be damned. Out of hell the place is matchless, and if there *be* a purgatory in the other world, it may very well be said there is a fair rehearsal of it in the county of Donegal in Ireland!

When I commenced my station, I started from what is called the 'Beds,' and God help St Patrick if he lay upon them: they are sharp stones placed circularly in the earth, with the spike ends of them up, one circle within another; and the manner in which the pilgrim gets as far as the innermost, resembles precisely that in which school-boys enter the 'Walls of Troy' upon their slates. I moved away from these upon the sharp stones with which the whole island is surfaced, keeping the chapel, or 'Prison,' as it is called, upon my right; then turning, I came round again, with a *circumbendibus*,* to the spot from which I set out. During this circuit, as well as I can remember, I *repeated* fifty-five *paters* and *aves*, and five creeds, or five decades; and be it known, that the fifty prayers were *offered up* to the Virgin Mary, and the odd five to God! I then commenced getting round the external beds, during which I *repeated*, I think, fifteen *paters* and *aves* more; and as the beds decreased in circumference, the prayers decreased in length, until a short circuit and three *paters* and *aves* finished the last and innermost of these blessed couches. I really forget how many times each day the prison and these beds are to be surrounded, and how many hundred prayers are to be *repeated* during the circuit, though each circuit is in fact making the grand tour of the island; but I never shall forget that I was the best part of a July day at it, when the soles of my feet were flayed, and the stones hot enough to broil a beef-steak! When the first day's station was over, is it necessary to say that a little rest would have been agreeable? But no, this would not suit the policy of the place: here it may be truly said that there is no rest for the wicked. The only luxury allowed me was the privilege of feasting upon one of my cakes (having not tasted food that blessed day until then); upon one of my cakes, I say, and a copious supply of the water of the lake, which, to render the repast more agreeable, was made lukewarm! This was to keep my spirits up after the delicate day's labour I had gone through, and to cheer me against the pleasant prospect of a hard night's praying without sleep, which lay in the back ground! But when I saw every one at this refreshing meal with a good, thick, substantial *bannock*,* and then looked at the immateriality of my own, I could not help reverting to the woman who made them for me, with a degree of vivacity not altogether in unison with the charity of a Christian. The knavish creature defrauded me of one half of the oatmeal, although I had purchased it myself in Petigo for the occasion; being determined that as I was only to get two meals in the three days, they should be such as a person could fast upon. Never was there a man more bitterly disappointed; for they were not thicker than crown-pieces, and I searched for them in my mouth to no purpose—the only thing like substance I could feel there was the warm water. At last, night came; but here to describe the horrors of what I suffered I hold myself utterly inadequate. I was wedged in a shake-down bed with seven others, one of whom was a Scotch Papist—another a man with a shrunk leg, who wore a crutch—all afflicted with that disease which northern men that feed on oatmeal are liable to; and then the swarms that fell upon my poor young skin, and probed, and stung, and fed on me! it was pressure and persecution almost insupportable, and yet such was my fatigue that sleep even here began to weigh down my eyelids.

I was just on the point of enjoying a little rest, when a man ringing a large hand-bell, came round, crying out in a low, supernatural growl, which could be heard double the distance of the loudest shout—'Waken up, waken up, and come to prison!' The words were no sooner out of his mouth, than there was a sudden start, and a general scramble in the dark for our respective garments. When we got dressed, we proceeded to the waters of the lake, in which we washed our face and hands, repeating prayers during the ablution. This to me was the most impressive and agreeable part of the whole station. The night while we were in bed, or rather in torture, had become quite stormy, and the waves of the lake beat against the shore with the violence of an agitated sea. There was just sufficient moon to make the 'darkness visible,' and to show the black clouds drifting with rapid confusion, in broken masses, over our heads. This, joined to the tossing of the billows against the shore—the dark silent groups that came, like shadows, stooping for a moment over the surface of the waters, and retreating again in a manner which the severity of the night rendered necessarily quick, raising thereby in the mind the idea of gliding spirits—then the pre-conceived desolation of the surrounding scenery—the indistinct shadowy chain of dreary mountains which, faintly relieved by the lurid sky, hemmed in the lake—the silence of the forms, contrasted with the tumult of the elements about us—the loneliness of the place—its isolation and remoteness from the habitations of men—all this put together, joined to the feeling of deep devotion in which I was wrapped, had really a sublime effect upon me. Upon the generality of those who were there, blind to the natural beauty and effect of the hour and the place, and viewing it only through the medium of superstitious awe, it was indeed calculated to produce the notion of something not belonging to the circumstances and reality of human life.

From this scene we passed to one, which, though not characterised by its dark awful beauty, was scarcely inferior to it in effect. It was called the 'Prison,' and it is necessary to observe here, that every pilgrim must pass twenty-four hours in this place, kneeling, without food or sleep, although one meal of bread and warm water, and whatever sleep he could get in Petigo with seven in a bed, were his allowance of food and sleep during the twenty-four hours previous. I must here beg the good reader's attention for a moment, with reference to our penance in the 'Prison.' Let us consider now the nature of this pilgrimage: it must be performed on foot, no matter what the distance of residence (allowing for voyages)—the condition of life— the age or the sex of the pilgrim may be. Individuals, from France, from America, England, and Scotland visit it—as voluntary devotees, or to perform an act of penance for some great crime, or perhaps to atone for a bad life in general. It is performed, too, in the dead heat of summer, when labour is slack, and the lower orders have sufficient leisure to undertake it; and, I may add, when travelling on foot is most fatiguing: they arrive, therefore, without a single exception, blown and jaded almost to death. The first thing they do, notwithstanding this, is to commence the fresh rigours of the station, which occupies them several hours. This consists in what I have already described, viz. the pleasant promenade upon the stony spikes around the prison and the 'beds;' that over, they take their first and only meal for the day; after which, as in my own case just related, they must huddle themselves in clusters, on what is barefacedly called a bed, but which is nothing more nor less than a beggarman's shake-down, where the smell, the heat, the filth, and above all, the vermin, are intolerable to the very farthest stretch of the superlative degree. As soon as their eyes begin to close here, they are roused by the bellman, and summoned at the hour of twelve—first washing themselves as aforesaid, in the lake, and then adjourning to the prison, which I am about to describe. There is not on earth, with the exception of pagan rites,—and it is melancholy to be compelled to compare any institution of the Christian religion with a Juggernaut,*—there is not on earth, I say, a regulation of a religious nature, more barbarous and inhuman than this. It has destroyed thousands since its establishment—has left children without parents, and parents childless. It has made wives widows, and torn from the disconsolate husband the mother of his children; and is itself the monster which St Patrick is said to have destroyed in the place—a monster, which is a complete and significant allegory of this great and destructive superstition. But what is even worse than death, by stretching the powers of human sufferance until the mind cracks under them, it is said sometimes to return these pitiable creatures maniacs—exulting in the laugh of madness, or sunk for ever in the incurable apathy of religious melancholy. I mention this now, to exhibit the purpose for which these calamities are turned to account, and the dishonesty which is exercised over these poor, unsuspecting people, in consequence of their occurrence. The pilgrims, being thus aroused at midnight, are sent to prison; and what think you is the impression under which they enter it? one indeed, which, when we consider their bodily weakness and mental excitement, must do its work with success. It is this: that as soon as they enter the prison, a *supernatural* tendency to sleep will come over them, which, they say, is peculiar to the place; that this is an emblem of the influence of sin over the soul, and a type of their future fate; that if they resist this they will be saved; but that if they yield to it, they will not only be damned in the next world, but will go mad, or incur some immediate and dreadful calamity in this. Is it any wonder that a weak mind and exhausted body, wrought upon by these bugbears, should induce upon by itself, by its own terrors, the malady of derangement? We know that nothing acts so strongly and so fatally upon reason, as an imagination diseased by religious terrors: and I regret to say, that I had upon that night an opportunity of witnessing a fatal instance of it.

After having washed ourselves in the dark waters of the lake, we entered this famous 'prison,' which is only a naked, unplastered chapel, with an altar against one of the side-walls, and two galleries. On entering this place, a scene presented itself altogether unparalleled on the earth, and in every point of view capable to sustain the feelings raised in the mind by the midnight scenery of the lake as seen during the ablutions. The prison was full, but not crowded; for had it been crowded, we would have been happy. It was, however, just sufficiently filled to give every individual the pleasure of sustaining himself, without having it in his power to recline for a moment in an attitude of rest, or to change that most insupportable of all bodily suffering, uniformity of position. There we knelt upon a hard ground floor, and commenced praying; and again I must advert to the policy which prevails in this island. During the period of imprisonment, there are no prescribed prayers nor ceremonies whatever to be performed, and this is the more strange, as every other stage of the station has its proper devotions. But these are suspended here, lest the attention of the prisoners might be fixed on any particular object, and the supernatural character of drowsiness imputed to the place be thus doubted—they are, therefore, turned in without anything to excite them to attention, or to resist the propensity to sleep occasioned by their fatigue and want of rest. Having thus nothing to do, nothing to sustain, nothing to stimulate them, it is very natural that they should, even if unexhausted by previous lassitude, be inclined to sleep; but everything that can weigh them down is laid upon them in this heavy and oppressive superstition, that the strong delusion may be kept up.

On entering the prison, I was struck with the dim religious twilight of the place. Two candles gleamed faintly from the altar, and there was something I thought of a deadly light about them, as they burned feebly and stilly against the darkness which hung over the other part of the building. Two priests, facing the congregation, stood upon the altar in silence, with pale spectral visages, their eyes catching an unearthly glare from the sepulchral light of the slender tapers. But that which was strangest of all, and, as I said before, without parallel in this world, was the impression and effect produced by the deep, drowsy, hollow, hoarse, guttural, ceaseless, and monotonous *hum*, which proceeded from about four hundred individuals, half asleep and at prayer; for their cadences were blended and slurred into each other, as they repeated, in an awe-struck and earnest undertone, the prayers in which they were engaged. It was certainly the strangest sound I ever heard, and resembled a thousand subterraneous groans, uttered in a kind of low, deep, unvaried chant. Nothing could produce a sense of gloomy alarm in a weak superstitious mind equal to this; and it derived much of its wild and singular character, as well as of its lethargic influence, from its continuity; for it still—still rung lowly and supernaturally on my ear. Perhaps the deep, wavy prolongation of the bass of a large cathedral bell, or that low, continuous sound, which is distinct from its higher and louder intonations, would give a faint notion of it, yet only a faint one; for the body of hoarse monotony here was immense. Indeed, such a noise had something so powerfully lulling, that human nature, even excited by the terrible suggestions of superstitious fear, was scarcely able to withstand it.

Now the poor pilgrims forget, that this strong disposition to sleep arises from the weariness produced by their long journeys—by the exhausting penance of the station, performed without giving them time to rest—by the other still more natural consequence of not giving them time to sleep—by the drowsy darkness of the chapel—and by the heaviness caught from the low peculiar murmur of the pilgrims, which would of itself overcome the lightest spirit. I was here but a very short time when I began to doze, and just as my chin was sinking placidly on my breast, and the words of an *Ave Maria* dying upon my lips, I felt the charm all at once broken by a well-meant rap upon the occiput, conferred through the instrumentality of a little angry-looking squat urchin of sixty years, and a remarkably good black-thorn cudgel, with which he was engaged in thwacking the heads of such sinners as, not having the dread of insanity and the regulations of the place before their eyes, were inclined to sleep. I declare the knock I received told to such purpose on my head, that nothing occurred during the pilgrimage that vexed me so much.

After all, I really slept the better half of the night; yet so indescribably powerful was the apprehension of derangement, that my hypocritical tongue wagged aloud at the prayers, during these furtive naps. Nay, I not only slept but dreamed. I experienced also that singular state of being, in which, while the senses are accessible to the influence of surrounding objects, the process of thought is suspended, the man seems to enjoy an inverted existence, in which the soul sleeps, and the body remains awake and susceptible of external impressions. I once thought I was washing myself in the lake, and that the dashing noise of its waters rang in my ears: I also fancied myself at home in conversation with my friends; yet, in neither case, did I altogether forget where I was. Still in struggling to bring my mind back, so paramount was the dread of awaking deranged should I fall asleep, that these occasional visions—associating themselves with this terror—and this again broken in upon by the hoarse murmurs about me, throwing their dark shade on every object that passed my imagination, the force of reason being too vague at the moment; these occasional visions, I say, and this jumbling together of broken images and disjointed thoughts, had such an effect upon me, that I imagined several times that the awful penalty was exacted, and that my reason was gone for ever. I frequently started, and on seeing two dim lights upon the altar, and on hearing the ceaseless and eternal murmurs going on—going on—around me, without being immediately able to ascribe them to their proper cause, I set myself down as a lost man; for on that terror I was provokingly clear during the whole night. I more than once gave an involuntary groan or shriek, on finding myself in this singular state; so did many others, and these groans and shrieks were wildly and fearfully contrasted with the never-ending hum, which, like the ceaseless noise of a distant waterfall, went on during the night. The perspiration occasioned by this inconceivable distress, by the heat of the place, and by the unchangeableness of my position, flowed profusely from every pore. About two o'clock in the morning an unhappy young man, either in a state of lethargic indifference, or under the influence of these sudden paroxysms, threw himself, or fell from one of the galleries, and was so shattered by the fall, that he died next day at twelve o'clock,—and, what was not much to the credit of the clergyman on the island,—without the benefit of the clergy; for I saw a priest with his stole and box of chrism* finishing off his extreme unction* when he was quite dead. This is frequently done in the Church of Rome, under a hope that life may not be utterly extinct, and that consequently the final separation of the soul and body may not have taken place.

In this prison, during the night, several persons go about with rods and staves, rapping those on the head whom they see heavy; snuff-boxes also go round very freely, elbows are jogged, chins chucked, and ears twitched, for the purpose of keeping each other awake. The rods and staves are frequently changed from hand to hand, and I thought it would be a lucky job if I could get one for a little, to enable me to change my position. I accordingly asked a man who had been a long time banging in this manner, if he would allow me to take his place for some time, and he was civil enough to do so. I therefore set out on my travels through the prison, rapping about me at a great rate, and with remarkable effect; for, whatever was the cause of it, I perceived that not a soul seemed the least inclined to doze after a visit from me; on the contrary, I observed several to scratch their heads, giving me at the same time significant looks of very sincere thankfulness.

But what I am convinced was the most meritorious act of my whole pilgrimage, as it was certainly the most zealously performed, was a remembrance I gave the squat fellow, who visited me in the early part of the night. He was engaged, tooth and nail, with another man, at a *De profundis*,* and although not asleep at the time, yet on the principle that prevention is better than cure, I thought it more prudent to let him have his rap before the occasion for it might come on: he accordingly got full payment, at compound interest, for the villanous knock he had *lent* me before.

This employment stirred my blood a little, and I got much lighter. I could now pay some attention to the scene about me, and the first object that engaged it was a fellow with a hare-lip, who had completely taken the lead at prayer. The organs of speech seemed to have been transferred from his mouth to his nose, and, although Irish was his vernacular language, either some fool or knave had taught him to *say his prayers* in English: and you may take this as an observation founded on fact, that the language which a Roman Catholic of the lower class does *not* understand, is the one in which he is disposed to pray. As for him he had lots of English prayers, though he was totally ignorant of that language. The twang from the nose, the loud and rapid tone in which he spoke, and the *malapro- prian** happiness with which he travestied every prayer he uttered, would have compelled any man to smile. The priests laughed out- right before the whole congregation, particularly one of them, whom I well knew; the other turned his face towards the altar, and leaning over a silver pix, in which, according to their own tenets, the Redeemer of the world must have been at that moment, as it con- tained the consecrated wafers, gave full vent to his risibility. Now it is remarkable that no one present attached the slightest impropriety to this—I for one did not; although it certainly occurred to me with full force at a subsequent period.

When morning came, the blessed light of the sun broke the leaden charm of the prison, and infused into us a wonderful portion of fresh vigour. This day being the second from our arrival, we had our second station to perform, and consequently all the sharp spikes to re-traverse. We were not permitted at all to taste food during these twenty-four hours, so that our weakness was really very great. I beg leave, however, to return my special acknowledgements for the truly hospitable allowance of *wine* with which I, in common with every other pilgrim, was treated. This wine is made by filling a large pot with the lake water, and making it lukewarm. It is then handed round in jugs and wooden noggins—to their credit be it recorded—in the greatest possible abundance. On this alone I breakfasted, dined, and supped, during the second or prison day of my pilgrimage

At twelve o'clock that night we left prison, and made room for another squadron, who gave us their kennels. Such a luxury was sleep to me, however, that I felt not the slightest inconvenience from the vermin, though I certainly made a point to avoid the Scotchman and the cripple. On the following day, I confessed; and never was an unfortunate soul so grievously afflicted with a bad memory as I was on that occasion—the whole thing altogether, but particularly the prison scene, had knocked me up, I could not therefore remember a tithe of my sins; and the priest, poor man, had really so much to do, and was in such a hurry, that he had me clean absolved before I had got half through the preface, or knew what I was about. I then went with a fresh batch to receive the sacrament, which I did from the hands of the good-humoured gentleman who enjoyed so richly the praying talents of the hare-lipped devotee in the prison.

I cannot avoid mentioning here a practice peculiar to Roman Catholics, which consists in an exchange of one or more prayers, by a stipulation between two persons: *I offer up a pater* and *ave* for you, and you again for me. It is called *swapping* or exchanging *prayers*. After I had received the sacrament, I observed a thin, sallow little man, with a pair of beads, as long as himself, moving from knot to knot, but never remaining long in the same place. At last he glided up to me, and in a whisper asked me if I knew him. I answered in the negative. 'Oh, then, a lanna,* ye war never here before?' 'Never.' 'Oh, I see that, a cushla,* you would a-known me if you had: well then, did ye never hear of Sol Donnel, the pilgrim?'

'I never did,' I replied, 'but are we not all pilgrims while here?'

'To be sure, aroon,* but I'm a pilgrim every place else, you see, as well as here, my darlin' sweet young man.'

'Then you're a pilgrim by profession?' 'That's it, astore machree;* everybody that comes here the second time, sure, knows Sol Donnel, the blessed pilgrim.'

THOMAS DAVIS
(1814–1845)

from *Ballad Poetry of Ireland* (1845)

How slow we have all been in coming to understand the meaning of Irish Nationality!

Some, dazzled by visions of pagan splendour, and the pretensions of pedigree, and won by the passions and romance of the olden races, continued to speak in the nineteenth century of an Irish nation as they might have done in the tenth. They forgot the English Pale, the Ulster Settlement,* and the filtered colonization of men and ideas. A Celtic kingdom with the old names and the old language, without the old quarrels, was their hope; and, though they would not repeat O'Neill's comment, as he passed Barrett's castle on his march to Kinsale,* and heard it belonged to a Strongbownian,* that 'he hated the Norman churl as if he came yesterday;' yet they quietly assumed that the Norman and Saxon elements would disappear under the Gaelic genius like the tracks of cavalry under a fresh crop.

The Nationality of Swift and Grattan* was equally partial. They saw that the Government and laws of the settlers had extended to the island—that Donegal and Kerry were in the Pale; they heard the English tongue in Dublin, and London opinions in Dublin—they mistook Ireland for a colony wronged, and great enough to be a nation.

A lower form of nationhood was before the minds of those who saw in it nothing but a parliament in College Green. They had not erred in judging, for they had not tried to estimate the moral elements and tendencies of the country. They were as narrow bigots to the omnipotency of an institution as any Cockney Radical. Could they, by any accummulation of English stupidity and Irish laziness, have got possession of an Irish government, they would soon have distressed every one by their laws whom they had not provoked by their administration, or disgusted by their dulness.

Far healthier with all its defects, was the idea of those who saw in Scotland a perfect model—who longed for a literary and artistic nationality—who prized the oratory of Grattan and Curran, the novels of Griffin and Carleton, the pictures of Maclise and Burton,* the ancient music, as much as any, and far more than most, of the political nationalists, but who regarded political independence as a dangerous dream. Unknowingly they fostered it. Their writings, their patronage, their talk was of Ireland; yet it hardly occurred to them that the ideal would flow into the practical, or that they, with their dread of agitation, were forwarding a revolution.

At last we are beginning to see what we are, and what is our destiny. Our duty arises where our knowledge begins. The elements of Irish nationality are not only combining—in fact, they are growing confluent in our minds. Such nationality as merits a good man's help, and wakens a true man's ambition—such nationality as could stand against internal faction and foreign intrigue, such nationality, as would make the Irish hearth happy and the Irish name illustrious, is becoming understood. It must contain and represent the races of

Ireland. It must not be Celtic, it must not be Saxon—it must be Irish. The Brehon law, and the maxims of Westminster, the cloudy and lightning genius of the Gael, the placid strength of the Sasanach, the marshalling insight of the Norman—a literature which shall exhibit in combination the passions and idioms of all, and which shall equally express our mind in its romantic, its religious, its forensic, and its practical tendencies—finally, a native government, which shall know and rule by the might and right of all; yet yield to the arrogance of none—these are components of *such* a nationality.

But what have these things to do with the 'Ballad Poetry of Ireland?' Much every way. It is the result of the elements we have named—it is compounded of all; and never was there a book fitter to advance that perfect nationality to which Ireland begins to aspire. That a country is without national poetry proves its hopeless dulness or its utter provincialism. National poetry is the very flowering of the soul—the greatest evidence of its health, the greatest excellence of its beauty. Its melody is balsam to the senses. It is the playfellow of childhood, ripens into the companion of his manhood, consoles his age. It presents the most dramatic events, the largest characters, the most impressive scenes, and the deepest passions in the language most familiar to us. It shows us magnified, and ennobles our hearts, our intellects, our country and our countrymen—binds us to the land by its condensed and gem-like history, to the future by examples and by aspirations. It solaces us in travel, fires us in action, prompts our invention, sheds a grace beyond the power of luxury round our homes, is the recognised envoy of our minds among all mankind and to all time.

In possessing the powers and elements of a glorious nationality, we owned the sources of a national poetry. In the combination and joint development of the latter, we find a pledge and a help to that of the former.

from *The History of Ireland* (1845)

Something has been done to rescue Ireland from the reproach that she was a wailing and ignorant slave.

Brag as we like, the reproach was not undeserved, nor is it quite removed.

She is still a serf-nation, but she is struggling wisely and patiently, and is ready to struggle with all the energy her advisers think politic, for liberty. She has ceased to wail—she is beginning to make up a record of English crime and Irish suffering, in order to explain the past, to justify the present, and caution the future. She begins to study the past—not to acquire a beggar's eloquence in petition, but a hero's wrath in strife. She no longer tears and parades her wounds, to win her smiter's mercy; and now she should look upon her breast and say—'That wound makes me distrust, and this makes me guard, and they all will make me steadier to resist, or, if all else fails, fiercer to avenge.'

Thus will Ireland do naturally and honourably. Our spirit has increased—our liberty is not far off.

But to make our spirit lasting and wise as it is bold—to make our liberty an inheritance for our children, and a charter for our posterity, we must study as well as strive, and learn as well as feel.

If we attempt to govern ourselves without statesmanship—to be a nation without a knowledge of the country's history, and of the propensities to good and ill of the people—or to fight without generalship, we will fail in policy, society, and war. These—all these things—we, people of Ireland, must know if we would be a free, strong nation. A mockery of Irish independence is not what we want. The bauble of a powerless parliament does not lure us. We are not children. The office of supplying England with recruits, artizans, and corn, under the benign interpositions of an Irish Grand Jury, *shall* not be our destiny. By our deep conviction—by the power of mind over the people, we say, No!

We are true to our colour, 'the green,' and true to our watchword, 'Ireland for the Irish.' We want to win Ireland and keep it. If we win it, we will not lose it, nor give it away to a bribing, a bullying, or a flattering minister. But, to be able to keep it, and use it, and govern it, the men of Ireland must know what it is, what it was, and what it can be made. They must study her history, perfectly know her present state, physical and moral—and train themselves up by science, poetry, music, industry, skill, and by all the studies and accomplishments of peace and war.

If Ireland were in national health, her history would be familiar by books, pictures, statuary, and music to every cabin and shop in the land—her resources as an agricultural, manufacturing, and trading people, would be equally known—and every young man would be trained, and every grown man able, to defend her coast, her plains, her towns, and her hills—not with his right arm merely, but by his disciplined habits and military accomplishments. These are the pillars of independence.

Academies of art, institutes of science, colleges of literature, schools and camps of war, are a nation's means for teaching itself strength, and winning safety and honour; and when we are a nation, please God, we shall have them all. Till then, we must work for ourselves. So far as we can study music in societies, art in schools, literature in institutes, science in our colleges, or soldiership in theory, we are bound as good citizens to learn. Where these are denied by power, or unattainable by clubbing the resources of neighbours, we must try and study for ourselves. We must visit museums and antiquities, and study, and buy, and assist books of history, to know what the country and people were, how they fell, how they suffered, and how they rose again. We must read books of statistics—and let us pause to regret that there is no work on the statistics of Ireland, except the scarce lithograph of Moreau,* the papers in the second Report of the Railway Commission, and the chapters, in McCulloch's '*Statistics of the British Empire*'—the Repeal Association ought to have a handbook first, and then an elaborate and vast account of Ireland's statistics brought out.

To resume, we must read such statistics as we have, and try and get better; and we must get the best maps of the country—the Ordnance and County Index Maps, price 2s. 6d. each, and the Railway Map, price £1—into our Mechanics' Institutes, Temperance Reading-rooms, and schools. We must, in making our journeys of business and pleasure, observe and ask for the nature and amount of the agriculture, commerce, and manufactures of the place we are in, and its shape, population, scenery, antiquities, arts, music, dress, and capabilities for improvement. A large portion of our people travel a greal deal within Ireland, and often return with no knowledge, save of the inn they slept in, and the traders they dealt with.

We must give our children in schools the best knowledge of science, art, and literary elements possible. And at home they should see and hear as much of national pictures, music, poetry, and military science as possible.

And finally, we must keep our own souls, and try, by teaching and example, to lift up the souls of all our family and neighbours to that pitch of industry, courage, information, and wisdom necessary to enable an enslaved, dark, and starving people to become free, and rich, and rational.

We sat down intending to write a paragraph on 'The National History of Ireland,' and were moved by the glorious prospect which a late survey of the literary projects in hand affords, to write generally upon Irishmen's duties, as students of the past and present.

3. FICTION

MARIA EDGEWORTH
(1767–1849)

from *Castle Rackrent* (1800)

Monday morning.^G

Having, out of friendship for the family, upon whose estate, praised be Heaven! I and mine have lived rent-free, time out of mind, voluntarily undertaken to publish the MEMOIRS of the RACKRENT FAMILY, I think it my duty to say a few words, in the first place, concerning myself. My real name is Thady Quirk, though in the family I have always been known by no other than '*honest Thady*',— afterwards, in the time of Sir Murtagh, deceased, I remember to hear them calling me '*old Thady*', and now I'm come to 'poor Thady'; for I wear a long great coat[1] winter and summer, which is very handy, as I

---

[1] The cloak, or mantle, as described by Thady, is of high antiquity. Spencer,* in his 'View of the State of Ireland', proves that it is not, as some have imagined, peculiarly derived from the Scythians, but that 'most nations of the world anciently used the mantle; for the Jews used it, as you may read of Elias's mantle, &c.; the Chaldees also used it, as you may read in Diodorus; the Egyptians likewise used it, as you may read in Herodotus, and may be gathered by the description of Berenice, in the Greek Commentary upon Callimachus; the Greeks also used it anciently, as appeared by Venus's mantle lined with stars, though afterwards they changed the form thereof into their cloaks, called Pallai, as some of the Irish also use: and the ancient Latins and Romans used it, as you may read in Virgil, who was a very great antiquary, that Evander, when Æneas came to him at his feast, did entertain and feast him sitting on the ground, and lying on mantles: insomuch that he useth the very word mantile for a mantle,

'—Humi mantilia sternunt':

so that it seemeth that the mantle was a general habit to most nations, and not proper to the Scythians only.'

Spencer knew the convenience of the said mantle, as housing, bedding, and clothing.

'*Iren.* Because the commodity doth not countervail the discommodity; for the inconveniences which thereby do arise are much more many; for it is a fit house for an outlaw, a meet bed for a rebel, and an apt cloak for a thief. First, the outlaw being for his many crimes and villanies, banished from the towns and houses of honest men, and wandering in wastes places, far from danger of law, maketh his mantle his house, and never put my arms into the sleeves; they are as good as new, though come Holantide* next I've had it these seven years; it holds on by a single button round my neck, cloak fashion. To look at me, you would hardly think 'poor Thady' was the father of attorney Quirk; he is a high gentleman, and never minds what poor Thady says, and having better than fifteen hundred a year, landed estate, looks down upon honest Thady; but I wash my hands of his doings, and as I have lived so will I die, true and loyal to the family. The family of the Rackrents is, I am proud to say, one of the most ancient in the kingdom. Every body knows this is not the old family name, which was O'Shaughlin, related to the kings of Ireland—but that was before my time. My grandfather was driver to the great Sir Patrick O'Shaughlin, and I heard him, when I was a boy, telling how the Castle Rackrent estate came to Sir Patrick; Sir Tallyhoo Rackrent was cousin-german* to him, and had a fine estate of his own, only never a gate upon it, it being his maxim that a car* was the best gate. Poor gentleman! he lost a fine hunter and his life, at last, by it, all in one day's hunt. But I ought to bless that day, for the estate came straight into *the* family, upon one condition, which Sir Patrick O'Shaughlin at the time took sadly to heart, they say, but thought better of it afterwards, seeing how large a stake depended upon it, that he should by act of parliament, take and bear the surname and arms of Rackrent.

Now it was that the world was to see what was *in* Sir Patrick. On coming into the estate, he gave the finest entertainment ever was heard of in the country: not a man could stand after supper but Sir Patrick himself, who could sit out the best man in Ireland, let alone the three kingdoms itself.[G]* He had his house, from one year's end to another, as full of company as ever it could hold, and fuller; for rather than be left out of the parties at Castle Rackrent, many gentlemen, and those men of the first consequence and landed estates in the country, such as the O'Neils of Ballynagrotty, and the Money-gawls of Mount Juliet's Town, and O'Shannons of New

under it covereth himself from the wrath of Heaven, from the offence of the earth, and from the sight of men. When it raineth, it is his pent-house; when it bloweth, it is his tent; when it freezeth it is his tabernacle. In summer he can wear it loose; in winter he can wrap it close; at all times he can use it; never heavy, never cumbersome. Likewise for a rebel it is as serviceable; for in this war that he maketh (if at least it deserves the name of war), when he still flieth from his foe, and lurketh in the *thick woods* (*this should be black bogs*) and straight passages waiting for advantages, it is his bed, yea, and almost his household stuff.'

Town Tullyhog, made it their choice, often and often, when there was no room to be had for love nor money, in long winter nights, to sleep in the chicken-house, which Sir Patrick had fitted up for the purpose of accommodating his friends and the public in general, who honoured him with their company unexpectedly at Castle Rackrent; and this went on, I can't tell you how long—the whole country rang with his praises!—Long life to him! I'm sure I love to look upon his picture, now opposite to me; though I never saw him, he must have been a portly gentleman—his neck something short, and remarkable for the largest pimple on his nose, which, by his particular desire, is still extant in his picture, said to be a striking likeness, though taken when young. He is said also to be the inventor of raspberry whiskey, which is very likely, as nobody has ever appeared to dispute it with him, and as there still exists a broken punch-bowl at Castle Rackrent, in the garret, with an inscription to that effect—a great curiosity. A few days before his death he was very merry; it being his honour's birth-day, he called my grandfather in, God bless him! to drink the company's health, and filled a bumper himself, but could not carry it to his head, on account of the great shake in his hand; on this he cast his joke, saying 'What would my poor father say to me if he was to pop out of the grave, and see me now? I remember when I was a little boy, the first bumper of claret he gave me after dinner, how he praised me for carrying it so steady to my mouth. Here's my thanks to him—a bumper toast.' Then he fell to singing the favourite song he learned from his father—for the last time, poor gentleman—he sung it that night as loud and as hearty as ever with a chorus:

'He that goes to bed, and goes to bed sober,
Falls as the leaves do, falls as the leaves do, and dies in October;
But he that goes to bed, and goes to bed mellow,
Lives as he ought to do, lives as he ought to do, and dies an
   honest fellow.'*

Sir Patrick died that night: just as the company rose to drink his health with three cheers, he fell down in a sort of fit, and was carried off; they sat it out, and were surprised, on inquiry, in the morning, to find that it was all over with poor Sir Patrick. Never did any gentleman live and die more beloved in the country by rich and poor. His funeral was such a one as was never known before or since in the

county! All the gentlemen in the three counties were at it; far and
near, how they flocked: my great grandfather said, that to see all the
women even in their red cloaks, you would have taken them for the
army drawn out. Then such a fine whillaluh!^G you might have heard
it to the farthest end of the county, and happy the man who could get
but a sight of the hearse! But who'd have thought it? just as all was
going on right, through his own town they were passing, when the
body was seized for debt—a rescue was apprehended from the mob;
but the heir who attended the funeral was against that, for fear of
consequences, seeing that those villains who came to serve acted
under the disguise of the law: so, to be sure, the law must take its
course, and little gain had the creditors for their pains. First and
foremost, they had the curses of the country: and Sir Murtagh
Rackrent, the new heir, in the next place, on account of this affront
to the body, refused to pay a shilling of the debts, in which he was
countenanced by all the best gentlemen of property, and others of his
acquaintance; Sir Murtagh alleging in all companies, that he all
along meant to pay his father's debts of honour, but the moment the
law was taken of him, there was an end of honour to be sure. It was
whispered (but none but the enemies of the family believe it), that
this was all a sham seizure to get quit of the debts, which he had
bound himself to pay in honour.

It's a long time ago, there's no saying how it was, but this for
certain, the new man did not take at all after the old gentleman; the
cellars were never filled after his death, and no open house, or any
thing as it used to be; the tenants even were sent away without their
whiskey.^G I was ashamed myself, and knew not what to say for the
honour of the family; but I made the best of a bad case, and laid it all
at my lady's door, for I did not like her any how, nor any body else;
she was of the family of the Skinflints, and a widow; it was a strange
match for Sir Murtagh; the people in the country thought he
demeaned himself greatly,^G but I said nothing: I knew how it was;
Sir Murtagh was a great lawyer, and looked to the great Skinflint
estate; there, however, he overshot himself; for though one of the co-
heiresses, he was never the better for her, for she outlived him
many's the long day—he could not see that to be sure when he
married her. I must say for her, she made him the best of wives,
being a very notable stirring woman, and looking close to every
thing. But I always suspected she had Scotch blood in her veins; any

thing else I could have looked over in her from a regard to the family. She was a strict observer for self and servants of Lent, and all fast days, but not holidays. One of the maids having fainted three times the last day of Lent, to keep soul and body together, we put a morsel of roast beef into her mouth, which came from Sir Murtagh's dinner, who never fasted, not he; but somehow or other it unfortunately reached my lady's ears, and the priest of the parish had a complaint made of it the next day, and the poor girl was forced as soon as she could walk to do penance for it, before she could get any peace or absolution, in the house or out of it. However, my lady was very charitable in her own way. She had a charity school for poor children, where they were taught to read and write gratis, and where they were kept well to spinning gratis for my lady in return; for she had always heaps of duty yarn from the tenants, and got all her household linen out of the estate from first to last; for after the spinning, the weavers on the estate took it in hand for nothing, because of the looms my lady's interest could get from the Linen Board to distribute gratis.* Then there was a bleach-yard near us, and the tenant dare refuse my lady nothing, for fear of a lawsuit Sir Murtagh kept hanging over him about the water-course. With these ways of managing, 'tis surprising how cheap my lady got things done, and how proud she was of it. Her table the same way, kept for next to nothing; duty fowls, and duty turkies, and duty geese,^G came as fast as we could eat 'em, for my lady kept a sharp look-out, and knew to a tub of butter every thing the tenants had, all round. They knew her way, and what with fear of driving for rent and Sir Murtagh's lawsuits, they were kept in such good order, they never thought of coming near Castle Rackrent without a present of something or other—nothing too much or too little for my lady—eggs, honey, butter, meal, fish, game, grouse, and herrings, fresh or salt, all went for something. As for their young pigs, we had them, and the best bacon and hams they could make up, with all young chickens in spring; but they were a set of poor wretches, and we had nothing but misfortunes with them, always breaking and running away. This, Sir Murtagh and my lady said, was all their former landlord Sir Patrick's fault, who let 'em get the half year's rent into arrear; there was something in that to be sure. But Sir Murtagh was as much the contrary way; for let alone making English tenants^G of them, every soul, he was always driving and driving, and pounding and pounding, and canting and canting,[G] and replevying and replevying,* and he made a good living of trespassing cattle; there was always some tenant's pig, or horse, or cow, or calf, or goose, trespassing, which was so great a gain to Sir Murtagh, that he did not like to hear me talk of repairing fences. Then his heriots* and duty work[G] brought him in something, his turf was cut, his potatoes set and dug, his hay brought home, and, in short, all the work about his house done for nothing; for in all our leases there were strict clauses heavy with penalties, which Sir Murtagh knew well how to enforce; so many days' duty work of man and horse, from every tenant, he was to have, and had, every year; and when a man vexed him, why the finest day he could pitch on, when the cratur was getting in his own harvest, or thatching his cabin, Sir Murtagh made it a principle to call upon him and his horse; so he taught 'em all, as he said, to know the law of landlord and tenant. As for law, I believe no man, dead or alive, ever loved it so well as Sir Murtagh. He had once sixteen suits pending at a time, and I never saw him so much himself; roads, lanes, bogs, wells, ponds, eel-wires, orchards, trees, tithes, vagrants, gravelpits, sandpits, dunghills, and nuisances, every thing upon the face of the earth furnished him good matter for a suit. He used to boast that he had a lawsuit for every letter in the alphabet. How I used to wonder to see Sir Murtagh in the midst of the papers in his office! Why he could hardly turn about for them. I made bold to shrug my shoulders once in his presence, and thanked my stars I was not born a gentleman to so much toil and trouble; but Sir Murtagh took me up short with his old proverb, 'learning is better than house or land'.* Out of forty-nine suits which he had, he never lost one but seventeen;[G] the rest he gained with costs, double costs, treble costs sometimes; but even that did not pay. He was a very learned man in the law, and had the character of it; but how it was I can't tell, these suits that he carried cost him a power of money; in the end he sold some hundreds a year of the family estate; but he was a very learned man in the law, and I know nothing of the matter, except having a great regard for the family; and I could not help grieving when he sent me to post up notices of the sale of the fee-simple* of the lands and appurtenances of Timoleague. 'I know, honest Thady,' says he, to comfort me, 'what I'm about better than you do; I'm only selling to get the ready money wanting to carry on my suit with spirit with the Nugents of Carrickashaughlin.'

He was very sanguine about that suit with the Nugents of Carrickashaughlin. He could have gained it, they say, for certain, had it pleased Heaven to have spared him to us, and it would have been at the least a plump two thousand a year in his way; but things were ordered otherwise, for the best to be sure. He dug up a fairy-mount[2G] against my advice, and had no luck afterwards. Though a learned man in the law, he was a little too incredulous in other matters. I warned him that I heard the very Banshee[3] that my grandfather heard under Sir Patrick's window a few days before his death. But Sir Murtagh thought nothing of the Banshee, nor of his cough with a spitting of blood, brought on, I understand, by catching cold in attending the courts, and overstraining his chest with making himself heard in one of his favourite causes. He was a great speaker with a powerful voice; but his last speech was not in the courts at all. He and my lady, though both of the same way of thinking in some things, and though she was as good a wife and great economist as you could see, and he the best of husbands, as to looking into his affairs, and making money for his family; yet I don't know how it was, they had a great deal of sparring and jarring between them. My lady had her privy purse—and she had her weed ashes,[G] and her sealing money[G] upon the signing of all the leases, with something to buy gloves besides; and besides again often took money from the tenants, if offered properly, to speak for them to Sir Murtagh about abatements* and renewals. Now the weed ashes and the glove money he allowed her clear perquisites; though once when he saw her in a new gown saved out of the weed ashes, he told her to my face (for he could say a sharp thing), that she should not put on her weeds before her husband's death. But in a dispute about an abatement, my lady would have the last word, and Sir Murtagh grew mad;[G] I was within hearing of the door, and now I wish I had made bold to step in. He

---

[2] These fairy-mounts are called ant-hills in England. They are held in high reverence by the common people in Ireland. A gentleman, who in laying out his lawn had occasion to level one of these hillocks, could not prevail upon any of his labourers to begin the ominous work. He was obliged to take a *loy** from one of their reluctant hands, and began the attack himself. The labourers agreed, that the vengeance of the fairies would fall upon the head of the presumptuous mortal, who first disturbed them in their retreat.

[3] The Banshee is a species of aristocratic fairy, who, in the shape of a little hideous old woman, has been known to appear, and heard to sing in a mournful supernatural voice under the windows of great houses, to warn the family that some of them are soon to die. In the last century every great family in Ireland had a Banshee, who attended regularly; but latterly their visits and songs have been discontinued.

spoke so loud, the whole kitchen was out on the stairs.[G] All of a sudden he stopped and my lady too. Something has surely happened, thought I—and so it was, for Sir Murtagh in his passion broke a blood-vessel, and all the law in the land could do nothing in that case. My lady sent for five physicians, but Sir Murtagh died, and was buried. She had a fine jointure settled upon her, and took herself away to the great joy of the tenantry. I never said any thing one way or the other, whilst she was part of the family, but got up to see her go at three o'clock in the morning. 'It's a fine morning, honest Thady,' said she; 'good bye to ye,' and into the carriage she stept, without a word more, good or bad, or even half a crown; but I made my bow, and stood to see her safe out of sight for the sake of the family.

GLOSSARY

Some friends, who have seen Thady's history since it has been printed, have suggested to the Editor that many of the terms and idiomatic phrases, with which it abounds, could not be intelligible to the English reader without further explanation. The Editor has therefore furnished the following Glossary.

[Page 79] *Monday morning.*—Thady begins his memoirs of the Rackrent Family by dating *Monday morning*, because no great undertaking can be auspiciously commenced in Ireland on any morning but *Monday morning*. 'O, please God we live till Monday morning, we'll set the slater to mend the roof of the house. On Monday morning we'll fall to, and cut the turf. On Monday morning we'll see and begin mowing. On Monday morning, please your honour, we'll begin and dig the potatoes,' &c.

All the intermediate days, between the making of such speeches and the ensuing Monday, are wasted: and when Monday morning comes, it is ten to one that the business is deferred to *the next* Monday morning. The Editor knew a gentleman, who, to counteract this prejudice, made his workmen and labourers begin all new pieces of work upon a Saturday.

[Page 80] *Let alone the three kingdoms itself.*—*Let alone*, in this sentence, means *put out of consideration*. The phrase, *let alone*, which is now used as the imperative of a verb, may in time become a conjunction, and may exercise the ingenuity of some future etymologist.

The celebrated Horne Tooke has proved most satisfactorily, that the conjunction *but* comes from the imperative of the Anglo-Saxon verb (*bouant*) *to be out;* also that *if* comes from *gift*, the imperative of the Anglo-Saxon verb which signifies *to give*, &c.

[Page 82] *Whillaluh.*—Ullaloo, Gol, or lamentation over the dead—

'Magnoque ululante tumultu.'—VIRGIL.

'Ululatibus omne
Implevere nemus.'—OVID.

A full account of the Irish Gol, or Ullaloo, and of the Caoinan or Irish funeral song, with its first semichorus, second semichorus, full chorus of sighs and groans, together with the Irish words and music, may be found in the fourth volume of the transactions of the Royal Irish Academy. For the advantage of *lazy* readers, who would rather read a page than walk a yard, and from compassion, not to say sympathy, with their infirmity, the Editor transcribes the following passages:

'The Irish have been always remarkable for their funeral lamentations, and this peculiarity has been noticed by almost every traveller who visited them; and it seems derived from their Celtic ancestors, the primæval inhabitants of this isle . . .

'It has been affirmed of the Irish, that to cry was more natural to them than to any other nation, and at length the Irish cry became proverbial . . .

'Cambrensis in the twelfth century says, the Irish then musically expressed their griefs; that is, they applied the musical art, in which they excelled all others, to the orderly celebration of funeral obsequies, by dividing the mourners into two bodies, each alternately singing their part, and the whole at times joining in full chorus . . . The body of the deceased, dressed in grave clothes, and ornamented with flowers, was placed on a bier, or some elevated spot. The relations and keepers (*singing mourners*) ranged themselves in two divisions, one at the head, and the other at the feet of the corpse. The bards and croteries had before prepared the funeral Caoinan. The chief bard of the head chorus began by singing the first stanza in a low, doleful tone, which was softly accompanied by the harp; at the conclusion, the foot semichorus began the lamentation, or Ullaloo, from the final note of the preceding stanza, in which they were answered by the head semichorus; then both united in one general chorus. The chorus of the first stanza being ended, the chief bard of the foot semichorus began the second Gol or lamentation, in which he was answered by that of the head; and then, as before, both united in the general full chorus. Thus alternately were the song and choruses performed during the night. The genealogy, rank, possessions, the virtues and vices of the dead were rehearsed, and a number of interrogations were addressed to the deceased; as, Why did he die? If married, whether his wife was faithful to him, his sons dutiful, or good hunters or warriors? If a woman, whether her daughters were fair or chaste? If a young man, whether he had been crossed in love; or if the blue-eyed maids of Erin treated him with scorn?'

We are told, that formerly the feet (the metrical feet) of the Caoinan were much attended to; but on the decline of the Irish bards these feet were gradually neglected, and the Caoinan fell into a sort of slipshod metre amongst women. Each province had different Caoinans, or at least different imitations of the original. There was the Munster cry, the Ulster cry, &c. It became an extempore performance, and every set of keepers varied the melody according to their own fancy.

It is curious to observe how customs and ceremonies degenerate. The present Irish cry, or howl, cannot boast of such melody, nor is the funeral procession conducted with much dignity. The crowd of people who assemble at these funerals sometimes amounts to a thousand, often to four or five hundred. They gather as the bearers of the hearse proceed on their way, and when they pass through any village, or when they come near any houses, they begin to cry—Oh! Oh! Oh! Oh! Oh! Agh! Agh! raising their notes from the first *Oh!* to the last *Agh!* in a kind of mournful howl. This gives notice to the inhabitants of the village that a *funeral is passing*, and immediately they flock out to follow it. In the province of Munster it is a common thing for the women to follow a funeral, to join in the universal cry with all their might and main for some time, and then to turn and ask—'Arrah! who is it that's dead?—who is it we're crying for?' Even the poorest people have their own burying-places, that is, spots of ground in the church-yards, where they say that their ancestors have been buried ever since the wars of Ireland; and if these burial-places are ten miles from the place where a man dies, his friends and neighbours take care to carry his corpse thither. Always one priest, often five or six priests, attend these funerals; each priest repeats a mass, for which he is paid, sometimes a shilling, sometimes half-a-crown, sometimes half-a-guinea, or a guinea, according to their circumstances, or, as they say, according to the *ability* of the deceased. After the burial of any very poor man, who has left a widow or children, the priest makes what is called a *collection* for the widow; he goes round to every person present, and each contributes sixpence or a shilling, or what they please. The reader will find in the note upon the word *Wake* ... more particulars respecting the conclusion of the Irish funerals.

Certain old women, who cry particularly loud and well, are in great request, and, as a man said to the Editor, 'Every one would wish and be proud to have such at his funeral, or at that of his friends.' The lower Irish are wonderfully eager to attend the funerals of their friends and relations, and they make their relationships branch out to a great extent. The proof that a poor man has been well beloved during his life is his having a crowded funeral. To attend a neighbour's funeral is a cheap proof of humanity, but it does not, as some imagine, cost nothing. The time spent in attending funerals may be safely valued at half a million to the Irish nation; the Editor thinks that double that sum would not be too high an estimate. The habits of profligacy and drunkenness, which are acquired at *wakes*, are here put out of the question. When a labourer, a carpenter, or a smith, is not at his work, which frequently happens, ask where he is gone, and ten to one the answer is—'Oh faith, please your honour, he couldn't do a stroke to-day, for he's gone to *the* funeral.'

Even beggars, when they grow old, go about begging *for their own funerals*; that is, begging for money to buy a coffin, candles, pipes and tobacco. For the use of the candles, pipes, and tobacco, see *Wake*.

Those who value customs in proportion to their antiquity, and nations in proportion to their adherence to ancient customs, will, doubtless, admire the Irish *Ullaloo*, and the Irish nation, for persevering in this usage from time immemorial. The Editor, however, has observed some alarming symptoms, which seem to prognosticate the declining taste for the Ullaloo in Ireland. In a comic theatrical entertainment, represented not long since on the Dublin stage, a chorus of old women was introduced, who set up the Irish howl round the relics of a physician, who is supposed to have fallen under the wooden sword of Harlequin. After the old women have continued their Ullaloo for a decent time, with all the necessary accompaniments of wringing their hands, wiping or rubbing their eyes with the corners of their gowns or aprons, &c. one of the mourners suddenly suspends her lamentable cries, and, turning to her neighbour, asks, 'Arrah now, honey, who is it we're crying for?'

[Page 82] *The tenants even were sent away without their whiskey.*—It is usual with some landlords to give their inferior tenants a glass of whiskey when they pay their rents. Thady calls it *their* whiskey; not that the whiskey is actually the property of the tenants, but that it becomes their *right* after it has been often given to them. In this general mode of reasoning respecting *rights* the lower Irish are not singular, but they are peculiarly quick and tenacious in claiming these rights. 'Last year your honour gave me some straw for the roof of my house, and I *expect* your honour will be after doing the same this year.' In this manner gifts are frequently turned into tributes. The high and low are not always dissimilar in their habits. It is said, that the Sublime Ottoman Porte is very apt to claim gifts as tributes: thus it is dangerous to send the Grand Seignor a fine horse on his birthday one year, lest on his next birthday he should expect a similar present, and should proceed to demonstrate the reasonableness of his expectations.

[Page 82] *He demeaned himself greatly*—means, he lowered or disgraced himself much.

[Page 83] *Duty fowls, and duty turkies, and duty geese.*—In many leases in Ireland, tenants were *formerly* bound to supply an inordinate quantity of poultry to their landlords. The Editor knew of thirty turkies being reserved in one lease of a small farm.

[Page 83] *English tenants.*—An English tenant does not mean a tenant who is an Englishman, but a tenant who pays his rent the day that it is due. It is a common prejudice in Ireland, amongst the poorer classes of people, to believe that all tenants in England pay their rents on the very day when they become due. An Irishman, when he goes to take a farm, if he wants to prove to his landlord that he is a substantial man, offers to become an *English tenant*. If a tenant disobliges his landlord by voting against him, or against his opinion, at an election, the tenant is immediately informed by the agent, that he must become an *English tenant*. This threat does not imply that he is to change his language or his country, but that he must pay all the arrear of rent which he owes, and that he must thenceforward pay his rent on that day when it becomes due.

[Page 84] *Canting*—does not mean talking or writing hypocritical nonsense, but selling substantially by auction.

[Page 84] *Duty work*.—It was formerly common in Ireland to insert clauses in leases, binding tenants to furnish their landlords with labourers and horses for several days in the year. Much petty tyranny and oppression have resulted from this feudal custom. Whenever a poor man disobliged his landlord, the agent sent to him for his duty work, and Thady does not exaggerate when he says, that the tenants were often called from their own work to do that of their landlord. Thus the very means of earning their rent were taken from them: whilst they were getting home their landlord's harvest, their own was often ruined, and yet their rents were expected to be paid as punctually as if their time had been at their own disposal. This appears the height of absurd injustice.

In Esthonia, amongst the poor Sclavonian race of peasant slaves, they pay tributes to their lords, not under the name of duty work, duty geese, duty turkies, &c., but under the name of *righteousnesses*. The following ballad is a curious specimen of Esthonian poetry:—

> This is the cause that the country is ruined,
> And the straw of the thatch is eaten away,
> The gentry are come to live in the land—
> Chimneys between the village,
> And the proprietor upon the white floor!
> The sheep brings forth a lamb with a white forehead,
>> This is paid to the lord for a *righteousness sheep*.
>> The sow farrows pigs,
>> They go to the spit of the lord.
>> The hen lays eggs,
>> They go into the lord's frying-pan.
>> The cow drops a male calf,

That goes into the lord's herd as a bull.
The mare foals a horse foal,
That must be for my lord's nag.
The boor's wife has sons,
They must go to look after my lord's poultry.

[Page 84] *Out of forty-nine suits which he had, he never lost one but seventeen.*—Thady's language in this instance is a specimen of a mode of rhetoric common in Ireland. An astonishing assertion is made in the beginning of a sentence, which ceases to be in the least surprising, when you hear the qualifying explanation that follows. Thus a man who is in the last stage of staggering drunkenness will, if he can articulate, swear to you—'Upon his conscience now, and may he never stir from the spot alive if he is telling a lie, upon his conscience he has not tasted a drop of any thing, good or bad, since morning at-all-at-all, but half a pint of whiskey, please your honour.'

[Page 85] *Fairy mounts*—Barrows. It is said that these high mounts were of great service to the natives of Ireland when Ireland was invaded by the Danes. Watch was always kept on them, and upon the approach of an enemy a fire was lighted to give notice to the next watch, and thus the intelligence was quickly communicated through the country. *Some years ago*, the common people believed that these barrows were inhabited by fairies, or, as they called them, by the *good people*. 'O troth, to the best of my belief, and to the best of my judgement and opinion,' said an elderly man to the Editor, 'it was only the old people that had nothing to do, and got together, and were telling stories about them fairies, but to the best of my judgement there's nothing in it. Only this I heard myself not very many years back from a decent kind of a man, a grazier, that as he was coming just *fair and easy* (*quietly*) from the fair, with some cattle and sheep, that he had not sold, just at the church of—, at an angle of the road like, he was met by a good-looking man, who asked him where he was going? And he answered, "Oh, far enough, I must be going all night." "No that you mustn't nor won't (says the man), you'll sleep with me the night, and you'll want for nothing, nor your cattle nor sheep neither, nor your *beast* (*horse*); so come along with me." With that the grazier *lit* (*alighted*) from his horse, and it was dark night; but presently he finds himself, he does not know in the wide world how, in a fine house, and plenty of every thing to eat and drink; nothing at all wanting that he could wish for or think of. And he does not *mind* (*recollect* or *know*) how at last he falls asleep; and in the morning he finds himself lying, not in ever a bed or a house at all, but just in the angle of the road where first he met the strange man: there he finds himself lying on his back on the grass, and all his sheep feeding as quiet as ever all round about him, and his horse the same way, and the bridle of the beast over his wrist. And I asked him what he thought of it; and from first to last he could think of nothing, but for certain sure it must have been the fairies that entertained him so well. For there was no house to see any where nigh hand, or any building, or barn, or place at all, but only the church and the *mole* (*barrow*). There's another odd thing enough that they tell about this same church, that if any person's corpse, that had not a right to be buried in that church-yard, went to be burying there in it, no, not all the men, women, or childer in all Ireland could get the corpse any way into the church-yard; but as they would be trying to go into the church-yard, their feet would seem to be going backwards instead of forwards; ay, continually backwards the whole funeral would seem to go; and they would never set foot with the corpse in the church-yard. Now they say that it is the fairies do all this; but it is my opinion it is all idle talk, and people are after being wiser now.'

The country people in Ireland certainly *had* great admiration mixed with reverence, if not dread, of fairies. They believed that beneath these fairy-mounts were spacious subterraneous palaces, inhabited by *the good people*, who must not on any account be disturbed. When the wind raises a little eddy of dust upon the road, the poor people believe that it is raised by the fairies, that it is a sign that they are journeying from one of the fairies' mounts to another, and they say to the fairies, or to the dust as it passes, 'God speed ye, gentlemen; God speed ye.' This averts any evil that *the good people* might be inclined to do them. There are innumerable stories told of the friendly and unfriendly feats of these busy fairies; some of these tales are ludicrous, and some romantic enough for poetry. It is a pity that poets should lose such convenient, though diminutive machinery. By-the-bye, Parnel, who showed himself so deeply 'skilled in faerie lore', was an Irishman; and though he has presented his faeries to the world in the ancient English dress of 'Britain's isle, and Arthur's days', it is probable that his first acquaintance with them began in his native country.

Some remote origin for the most superstitious or romantic popular illusions or vulgar errors may often be discovered. In Ireland, the old churches and church-yards have been usually fixed upon as the scenes of wonders. Now the antiquarians tell us, that near the ancient churches in that kingdom caves of various constructions have from time to time been discovered, which were formerly used as granaries or magazines by the ancient inhabitants, and as places to which they retreated in time of danger. There is (p. 84 of the R.I.A. Transactions for 1789) a particular account of a number of these artificial caves at the west end of the church of Killossy, in the county of Kildare. Under a rising ground, in a dry sandy soil, these subterraneous dwellings were found: they have pediment roofs, and they communicate with each other by small apertures. In the Brehon laws these are mentioned, and there are fines inflicted by those laws upon persons who steal from the subterraneous granaries. All these things show that there was a real foundation for the stories which were told of the appearance of lights, and of the sounds of voices near these places. The persons who had property concealed there very willingly countenanced every wonderful relation that tended to make these places objects of sacred awe or superstitious terror.

[Page 85] *Weed ashes.*—By ancient usage in Ireland, all the weeds on a farm belonged to the farmer's wife, or to the wife of the squire who holds the ground in his own hands. The great demand for alkaline salts in bleaching rendered these ashes no inconsiderable perquisite.

[Page 85] *Sealing money.*—Formerly it was the custom in Ireland for tenants to give the squire's lady from two to fifty guineas as a perquisite upon the sealing of their leases. The Editor not very long since knew of a baronet's lady accepting fifty guineas as sealing money, upon closing a bargain for a considerable farm.

[Page 85] *Sir Murtagh grew mad.*—Sir Murtagh grew angry.

[Page 86] *The whole kitchen was out on the stairs*—means that all the inhabitants of the kitchen came out of the kitchen, and stood upon the stairs. These, and similar expressions, show how much the Irish are disposed to metaphor and amplification.

SYDNEY OWENSON (LADY MORGAN)
(1776–1859)

from *The Wild Irish Girl* (1806)

LETTER V

TO J. D. ESQ. M.P.

Castle of Inismore, Barony of ——

Ay, 'tis even so—point your glass, and rub your eyes, 'tis all one, here I am, and here I am likely to remain for some time. But, whether a prisoner of war, or taken up on a suspicion of espionage, or to be offered as an appeasing sacrifice to the *manes** of the old Prince of Inismore, you must for awhile suspend your patience to learn.

According to the *carte du pays** laid out for me by the fisherman, I left the shore and crossed the summit of a mountain, which, after an hour's ascension, I found sloped almost perpendicularly down to a bold and rocky coast, its base terminating in a peninsula, that advanced for near half a mile into the ocean. Towards the extreme western point of this peninsula, which was wildly romantic beyond all description, arose a vast and grotesque pile of rocks, at once forming the scite and fortifications of the noblest mass of ruins on which my eye ever rested. Grand even in desolation, and magnificent in decay—it was the Castle of Inismore! The setting sun shone brightly on its mouldering turrets, and the waves, which bathed its rocky basis, reflected on their swelling bosoms the dark outlines of its awful ruins.[1]

As I descended the mountain's brow, I observed that the little isthmus, which joined the peninsula to the main-land, had been cut away, and a curious danger-threatening bridge was rudely thrown across the intervening gulf, flung from the rocks on one side to an angle of the mountain on the other, leaving a yawning chasm of some fathoms deep beneath the foot of the wary passenger. This

---

[1] Those who have visited the Castle of Dunluce, near the Giants'-Causeway, may, perhaps, trace some of its striking features in this rude draught of the Castle of Inismore.

must have been a very perilous pass in days of civil warfare; and in the intrepidity of my daring ancestor, I almost forgot his crime. Amidst the interstices of the rocks which skirted the shores of this interesting peninsula, patches of the richest vegetation were to be seen, and the trees, which sprung wildly among its venerable ruins, were bursting into all the vernal luxuriancy of spring. In the course of my descent, several cabins, of a better description than I had yet seen, appeared scattered beneath the shelter of the mountain's innumerable projections; while, in the air and dress of their inhabitants (whom the sound of my horse's feet brought to their respective doors), I evidently perceived an original and primitive something, which I had never before noticed here in this class of persons.

They appeared to me, I know not why, to be in their holiday garb, and their dress, though grotesque and coarse, was cleanly and characteristic. I observed that round the heads of the elderly dames were folded several wreaths of white or coloured linen,[2] that others had handkerchiefs[3] lightly folded round their brows and curiously fastened under the chin; while the young wore their hair fastened up with wooden bodkins. They were all enveloped in large shapeless mantles of blue frieze, and most of them had a rosary hanging on the arm, whence I inferred they were on the point of attending vespers at the chapel of Inismore. I alighted at the door of a cabin a few paces distant from the Alpine bridge, and entreated a shed for my horse, while I performed my devotions. The man to whom I addressed myself seemed the only one of several who surrounded me, that understood English, and appeared much edified by my pious intention, saying, 'that God would prosper my honour's journey, and that I was welcome to a shed for my horse, and a night's lodging for myself into the bargain.' He then offered to be my guide, and, as we crossed the drawbridge, he told me I was out of luck by not coming earlier, for that high mass had been celebrated that morning for the repose of the soul of a Prince of

---

[2] 'The women's ancient head-dress so perfectly resembles that of the Egyptian Isis, that it cannot be doubted but that the modes of Egypt were preserved among the Irish.'—*Walker on the Ancient Irish Dress*, p. 62.

The author's father, who lived in the early part of his life in a remote skirt of the province of Connaught, remembers to have seen the heads of the female peasantry encircled with folds of linen in the form of a turban.

[3] These handkerchiefs they call *Binnogues:* it is a remnant of a very ancient mode.

Inismore, who had been murdered on this very day of the month. 'And when this day comes round,' he added, 'we all attend dressed in our best; for my part, I never wear my poor old grandfather's *berrad* but on the like occasion;' taking off a curious cap of a conical form, which he twirled round his hand, and regarded with much satisfaction.[4]

By heavens! as I breathed this region of superstition, so strongly was I infected, that my usual scepticism was scarcely proof against my inclination to mount my horse and gallop off, as I shudderingly pronounced—

'I am then entering the Castle of Inismore, on the anniversary of that day on which my ancestors took the life of its venerable prince!'

You see, my good friend, how much we are the creatures of situation and circumstance, and with what pliant servility the mind resigns itself to the impressions of the senses, or the illusions of the imagination.

We had now reached the ruined cloisters of the chapel; I had paused to examine their curious but dilapidated architecture, when my guide, hurrying me on, said, 'if I did not quicken my pace, I should miss getting a good view of the Prince,' who was just entering by a door opposite to that we had passed through. Behold me, then, mingling among a group of peasantry, and, like them, straining my eyes to that magnet which fascinated every glance.

And surely, Fancy, in her boldest flight, never gave to the fairy vision of poetic dreams, a combination of images more poetically fine, more strikingly picturesque, or more impressively touching. Nearly one half of the chapel of Inismore has fallen into decay, and the ocean breeze, as it rushed through the fractured roof, wafted the torn banners of the family which hung along its dismantled walls. The red beams of the sinking sun shone on the glittering tabernacle which stood on the altar, and touched with their golden light the sacerdotal vestments of the two officiating priests, who ascended its broken steps at the moment that the prince and his family entered.

The first of this most singular and interesting group was the venerable Father John, the chaplain. Religious enthusiasm never gave to

---

[4] A few years back, Hugh Dugan, a peasant of the county of Kilkenny, who affected the ancient Irish dress, seldom appeared without his *berrad*.

the fancied form of the first of the patriarchs a countenance of more holy expression, or divine resignation; a figure more touching by its dignified simplicity, or an air more beneficently mild—more meekly good. He was dressed in his pontificals,* and, with his eyes bent to earth, his hands spread upon his breast, he joined his coadjutors.

What a contrast to this saintly being now struck my view; a form almost gigantic in stature, yet gently thrown forward by evident infirmity; limbs of Herculean mould, and a countenance rather furrowed by the inroads of vehement passions, than the deep trace of years; eyes, still emanating the ferocity of an unsubdued spirit, yet tempered by a strong trait of benevolence; which, like a glory* irradiated a broad expansive brow; a mouth, on which even yet the spirit of convivial enjoyment seemed to hover, though shaded by two large whiskers on the upper lip,[5] that still preserved their ebon hue; while time or grief had bleached the scattered hairs, which hung their snows upon the manly temple. The drapery which covered this striking figure was singularly appropriate, and as I have since been told, strictly conformable to the ancient costume of the Irish nobles.[6]

The only part of the under-garment visible, was the ancient Irish *truis*, which, closely adhering to the limbs from the waist to the ankle, includes the pantaloon and hose, and terminates in a kind of buskin, not dissimilar to the Roman *perones*. A triangular mantle of bright *scarlet* cloth, embroidered and fringed round the edges, fell from his shoulders to the ground, and was fastened at the breast with a large circular golden brooch,[7] of a workmanship most curiously

[5] 'I have been confidently assured that the grandfather of the present Right Hon. John O'Neil (great grandfather to the present Lord O'Neile, the elegant and accomplished owner of Shanes Castle, wore his beard after the *prohibited* Irish mode.'—*Walker*, p. 62.

[6] The Irish mantle, with the fringed or shagged borders sewed down the edges of it, was not always made of frieze and such coarse materials, which was the dress of the lower sort of people, but, according to the rank and quality of the wearer, was sometimes made of the finest cloth, bordered with silken fringe of scarlet, and various colours.—*Ware*, vol. ii. p. 75.

[7] Several of these useful ornaments (in Irish *dealg fallain*), some gold, some silver, have been found in various parts of the kingdom, and are to be seen in the cabinets of our national *virtuosi*. Joseph Cooper Walker, Esq., to whose genius, learning, and exertions, Ireland stands so deeply indebted, speaking of a broach he had seen in the possession of R. Ousley, Esq., says, 'Neither my pen or pencil can give an adequate idea of the elegant gold filigree work with which it is composed.'

beautiful; round his neck hung a golden collar, which seemed to denote the wearer of some order of knighthood, probably hereditary in his family; a dagger, called a *skiene* (for my guide explained every article of the dress to me,) was sheathed in his girdle, and was discerned by the sun-beam, that played on its brilliant haft. As he entered the chapel, he removed from his venerable head a cap, or berrad, of the same form as that I had noticed with my guide, but made of velvet, richly embroidered.

The chieftain moved with dignity—yet with difficulty—and his colossal but infirm frame appeared to claim support from a form so almost impalpably delicate, that, as it floated on the gaze, it seemed like the incarnation of some pure ethereal spirit, which a sigh too roughly breathed would dissolve into its kindred air; yet to this sylphid elegance of spheral beauty was united all that symmetrical contour which constitutes the luxury of human loveliness. This scarcely 'mortal mixture of earth's mould' was vested in a robe of vestal white, which was folded beneath the bosom with a narrow girdle embossed with precious stones.

From the shoulder fell a crimson mantle, fastened at the neck with a silver bodkin, while the finely turned head was enveloped in a veil of point-lace, bound round the brow with a band, or diadem, ornamented with the same description of jewels which encircled her arms.[8]

Such was the *figure* of the Princess of Inismore! But, oh! not once was the face turned round towards that side where I stood; and, when I shifted my position, the envious veil intercepted the ardent glance which eagerly sought the fancied charms it concealed: for, was it possible to doubt the face would not 'keep the promise which the form had made?'

The group that followed was grotesque beyond all powers of description. The ancient bard, whose long white beard

        'Descending swept his aged breast'—

---

[8] This was, with little variation, the general costume of the female *noblesse* of Ireland from a very early period. In the fifteenth century the veil was very prevalent, and was termed fillag, or scarf; the Irish ladies, like those of ancient or modern Greece, seldom appearing unveiled. As the veil made no part of the Celtic costume, its origin was probably merely oriental.

The great love of ornaments betrayed by the Irish ladies of other times, 'the beauties of the heroes of old,' are thus described by a quaint and ancient author:—'Their necks are hung with chains and carkanets—their arms wreathed with many bracelets.'

the incongruous constume—half modern, half antique—of the bare-footed domestics; the ostensible air of the steward, who closed the procession;—and, above all, the dignified importance of the *nurse*, who took the lead in it immediately after her young lady: her air, form, countenance, and dress, were indeed so singularly fantastic and *outré*,* that the genius of masquerade might have adopted her figure as the finest model of grotesque caricature.

Conceive for a moment a form, whose longitude bore no degree of proportion to her latitude, dressed in a short jacket of brown cloth, with loose sleeves from the elbow to the wrist, made of red camlet, striped with green, and turned up with a broad cuff—a petticoat of scarlet frieze, covered by an apron of green serge, longitudinally striped with scarlet tape, and sufficiently short to betray an ancle that sanctioned all the libels ever uttered against the ancles of the Irish fair. True national brogues set off her blue worsted stockings, and her yellow hair, dragging over a high roll, was covered on the summit with a little coif, over which was flung a scarlet handkerchief, fastened in a large bow under her rubicund chin.[9]

As this singular and interesting group advanced up the centre aisle of the chapel, reverence and affection were evidently blended in the looks of the multitude, which hung upon their steps; and, though the Prince and his daughter seemed to lose in the meekness of true religion all sense of temporal inequality, and promiscuously mingled with the congregation, yet *that* distinction they humbly avoided was reverentially forced on them by the affectionate crowd, which drew back on either side as they advanced, until the chieftain and his child stood alone in the centre of the ruined choir—the winds of heaven playing freely amidst their garments—the sun's setting beam enriching their beautiful figures with its orient tints, while he, like Milton's ruined angel,*

> 'Above the rest,
> In shape and feature proudly eminent
> Stood like a tow'r;'

---

[9] Such was the dress of Mary Morgan, a poor peasant in the neighbourhood of Drogheda, in 1786.—'In the close of the last century Mrs Power, of Waterford, vulgarly called the *Queen of Credan*, appeared constantly in this dress, with the exception of ornaments being gold, silver, and fine Brussels lace.'—See *Walker's Essay on Ancient Irish Dress*, p. 73.

and she, like the personified spirit of Mercy, hovered round him, or supported, more by her tenderness than her strength, him from whom she could no longer claim support.

Those grey-headed domestics too—those faithful though but nominal vassals, who offered that voluntary reverence with their looks which is repaid with fatherly affection, while the anguish of a suffering heart hung on his pensive smile, sustained by the firmness of that indignant pride which lowered on his ample brow!

What a picture!

As soon as the first flush of interest, curiosity, and amazement, had subsided, my attention was carried towards the altar; and then I thought, as I watched the impressive avocation of father John, that had I been the Prince, I would have been the *Caiphas** too.

What a religion is this! How finely does it harmonize with the weakness of our nature; how seducingly it speaks to the senses; how forcibly it works on the passions; how strongly it seizes on the imagination; how interesting its forms; how graceful its ceremonies; how awful its rites. What a captivating, what a *picturesque*, faith! Who would not become its proselyte, were it not for the stern opposition of reason—the cold suggestions of philosophy!

The concluding strain of the vesper hymn died on the air as the sun's last beam faded on the casements of the chapel; when the Prince and his daughter, to avoid the intrusion of the crowd, withdrew through a private door, which communicated by a ruinous arcade with the castle.

I was the first to leave the chapel, and followed them at a distance as they moved slowly along, their fine figures sometimes concealed behind a pillar, and again emerging from the transient shade, flushed with the deep suffusion of the crimsoned firmament.

Once they paused, as if to admire the beautiful effect of the retreating light, as it faded on the ocean's swelling bosom; and once the Princess raised her hand and pointed to the evening star, which rose brilliantly on the deep cerulean blue* of a cloudless atmosphere, and shed its fairy beams on the mossy summit of a mouldering turret.

Such were the sublime objects which seemed to engage their attention, and added their *sensible* inspiration to the fervour of those more abstracted devotions in which they were so recently engaged. At last they reached the portals of the castle, and I lost sight of them.

Yet still, spell-bound, I stood transfixed to the spot whence I had caught a last view of their receding figures.

While I felt like the victim of superstitious terror when the spectre of its distempered fancy vanishes from its strained and eager gaze, all I had lately seen revolved in my mind like some pictured story of romantic fiction. I cast my eyes around; all still seemed the vision of awakened imagination—surrounded by a scenery, grand even to the boldest majesty of nature, and wild even to desolation—the day's dying splendors awfully involving in the gloomy haze of deepening twilight—the grey mists of stealing night gathering on the still-faintly illuminated surface of the ocean, which, awfully spreading to infinitude, seemed to the limited gaze of human vision to incorporate with the heaven, whose last glow it reflected—the rocks, which on every side rose to Alpine elevation, exhibiting, amidst the soft obscurity, forms savagely bold, or grotesquely wild; and those finely interesting ruins, which spread grandly desolate in the rear, and added a moral interest to the emotions excited by this view of nature in her most awful, most touching aspect.

Thus, suddenly withdrawn from the world's busiest haunts, its hackneyed modes, its vicious pursuits, and unimportant avocations—dropt as it were amidst scenes of mysterious sublimity—alone—on the wildest shores of the greatest ocean of the universe—immersed amidst the decaying monuments of past ages—still viewing in recollection such forms, such manners, such habits, (as I had lately beheld,) which to the worldly mind may be well supposed to belong to a race long passed beyond the barrier of existence, with 'the years beyond the flood'—I felt like the being of some other sphere, newly alighted on a distant orb. While the novel train of thought which stole on my mind seemed to seize its tone from the awful tranquillity by which I was surrounded, and I remained leaning on the fragment of a rock, as the waves dashed idly against its base, until their dark heads were silvered by the rising moon, and while my eyes dwelt on her silent progress, the castle-clock struck nine. Thus warned, I arose to depart, yet not without reluctance. My soul, for the first time, had there held commune with herself: the 'lying vanities' of life no longer intoxicating my senses, appeared to me for the first time in their genuine aspect, and my heart still fondly loitered over those scenes of solemn interest, where some of its best feelings had been called into existence.

Slowly departing, I raised my eyes to the Castle of Inismore, sighed, and almost wished I had been born the lord of these beautiful ruins, the prince of this isolated little territory, the adored chieftain of these affectionate and natural people. At that moment a strain of music stole by me, as if the breeze of midnight had expired in a murmur on the Eolian lyre.* Emotion, indefinite emotion, thrilled on every nerve. I listened—I trembled. The breathless silence of the region gave me every note. Was it the illusion of my now all awakened fancy, or the professional exertions of the bard of Inismore? Oh, no! for the voice it symphonized—the low, wild, tremulous voice, which sweetly sighed its soul of melody over the harp's responsive chords, was the voice of *a woman!*

Directed by the witching strain, I approached an angle of the building whence it seemed to proceed; and, perceiving a light streaming through an open casement, I climbed, with some difficulty, the ruins of a parapet wall, which encircled this wing of the castle, and which rising immediately under the casement, gave me, when I stood on it, a perfect view of the interior of that apartment to which it belonged.

Two tapers burned on a marble slab, at the remotest extremity of this vast and gloomy chamber, and shed their dim blue light on the saintly countenance of Father John, who, with a large folio open before him, seemed wholly wrapt in studious meditation; while the Prince, reclined on an immense gothic couch, with his robe thrown over the arm that supported his head, betrayed, by the expression of his countenance, those emotions which agitated his soul, as he listened to those strains which at once spoke to the heart of the father, the patriot, and the man—breathed from the chords of his country's emblem—breathed in the pathos of his country's music—breathed from the lips of his apparently inspired daughter! The 'white rising of her hands upon the harp;' the half-drawn veil, that imperfectly discovered the countenance of a seraph; the moonlight that played round her fine form, and partially touched her drapery with its silver beam—her attitude! her air!—But how cold—how inanimate—how imperfect this description! Oh! could I but seize the touching features—could I but realize the vivid tints of this enchanting picture, as they then glowed on my fancy! You would still think the mimic copy fabulous; the 'celestial visitant' of an over-heated imagination. Yet, as if the independent witchery of the lovely minstrel was not in itself all, all-sufficient, at the back of her chair stood the grotesque figure of her antiquated nurse. O the precious contrast!—and yet it heightened, it finished the picture.

While thus entranced in breathless observation, endeavouring to support my precarious tenement, and to prolong this rich feast of the senses and the soul, the loose stones on which I tottered, gave way under my feet; and, impulsively clinging to the wood-work of the casement, it mouldered in my grasp. I fell—but, before I reached the earth, I was bereft of sense. With its return I found myself in a large apartment, stretched on a bed, and supported in the arms of the Prince of Inismore! His hand was pressed to my bleeding temple; while the priest applied a styptic to the wound it had received; and the nurse was engaged in binding up my arm, which had been dreadfully bruised and fractured a little above the wrist. Some domestics, with an air of mingled concern and curiosity, surrounded my couch; and at her father's side stood the Lady Glorvina, her looks pale and disordered, and her trembling hands busily employed in preparing bandages, for which my skilful doctress impatiently called.

While my mind almost doubted the evidence of my senses, and a physical conviction alone *painfully* proved to me the reality of all I beheld, my wandering, wondering eyes met those of the Prince of Inismore! A volume of pity and benevolence was registered in their glance; nor were mine, I suppose, inexpressive of my feelings, for he thus replied to them:—

'Be of good cheer, young stranger; you are in no danger; be composed, be confident; conceive yourself in the midst of friends; for you are surrounded by those who would wish to be considered as such.'

I attempted to speak, but my voice faltered, my tongue was nerveless, my mouth dry and parched. A trembling hand presented a cordial to my lips. I quaffed the philter, and fixed my eyes on the face of my ministering angel—that angel was Glorvina!—I closed them, and sunk on the bosom of her father.

'Oh, he faints again!' cried a sweet and plaintive voice.

'On the contrary,' replied the priest, 'the weariness of acute pain, something subsided, is lulling him into a soft repose! for, see, the colour re-animates his cheek, and his pulse quickens.'

'It indeed beats most wildly,' returned the sweet physician—for the pulse, which responded to her finger's thrilling pressure, moved with no languid throb.

'Let us retire,' added the priest; 'all danger is now, thank Heaven, over; and repose and quiet are the most salutary requisites for our patient.'

At these words he arose from my bedside; and the Prince, gently withdrawing his supporting arms, laid my head upon the pillow. In a moment all was deathlike stillness, and, stealing a glance from under my half-closed eyes, I found myself alone with my skilful doctress, the nurse; who shading the taper's light from the bed, had taken her distaff, and seated herself on a little stool at some distance.

This was a golden respite to feelings wound up to that vehement excess which forbade all expression, which left my tongue powerless, while my heart overflowed with emotion the most powerful.

Good God! I, the son of Lord M——, the hereditary object of hereditary detestation, beneath the roof of my implacable enemy! Supported in his arms, relieved from anguish by his charitable attention, honoured by the solicitude of his lovely daughter, overwhelmed by the charitable exertions of his whole family, and reduced to that bodily infirmity that would of necessity oblige me to continue for some time the object of their beneficent attentions!

What a series of emotions did this conviction awaken in my heart! Emotions of a character, an energy, long unknown to my apathized feelings; while gratitude to those who had drawn them into existence, combined with the interest, the curiosity, the admiration, they had awakened, tended to confirm my irresistible desire of perpetuating the immunities I enjoyed, as the guest and patient of the Prince and his daughter. And while the touch of this Wild Irish Girl's hand thrilled on every sense—while her voice of tenderest pity murmured on my ear, and I secretly triumphed over the prejudices of her father, I would not have exchanged my broken arm and wounded temple for the strongest limb and soundest head in the kingdom; but the same chance which threw me into the supporting arms of the irascible Prince, might betray to him, in the person of his patient, the son of his hereditary enemy; it was at least probable he would make some inquiries relative to the object of his benevolence, and the singular cause which rendered him such; it was therefore a necessary policy in me to be provided against this scrutiny.

Already deep in adventure, a thousand seducing reasons were suggested by my newly-awakened heart, to proceed with the romance, and to secure for my future residence in the castle, that interest, which, if known to be the son of Lord M——, I must eventually have forfeited for the cold aversion of irreclaimable prejudice. The imposition was at least innocent, and might tend to future and mutual advantage; and, after the ideal assumption of a thousand fictitious characters, I at last fixed on that of an itinerant artist, as consonant to my most cultivated talent, and to the testimony of those witnesses which I had fortunately brought with me; namely, my drawing-book, pencils, &c. &c.—self-nominated *Henry Mortimer*, to answer the initials on my linen, the only proofs against me, for I had not even a letter with me.

I was now armed at all points for inspection; and as the Prince lived in a perfect state of isolation, and I was unknown in the country, I entertained no apprehensions of discovery, during the time I should remain at the castle; and full of hope, strong in confidence, but wearied by incessant cogitation, and something exhausted by pain, I fell into that profound slumber I did before but feign.

CHARLES ROBERT MATURIN
(1780–1824)

from *Melmoth the Wanderer* (1820)

> Alive again? Then show me where he is;
> I'll give a thousand pounds to look upon him.
>
> SHAKESPEARE*

In the autumn of 1816, John Melmoth, a student in Trinity College, Dublin, quitted it to attend a dying uncle on whom his hopes for independence chiefly rested. John was the orphan son of a younger brother, whose small property scarce could pay John's college expences; but the uncle was rich, unmarried, and old; and John, from his infancy, had been brought up to look on him with that mingled sensation of awe, and of the wish, without the means to conciliate, (that sensation at once attractive and repulsive), with which we regard a being who (as nurse, domestic, and parent have tutored us to believe) holds the very threads of our existence in his hands, and may prolong or snap them when he pleases.

On receiving this summons, John set immediately out to attend his uncle.

The beauty of the country through which he travelled (it was the county Wicklow) could not prevent his mind from dwelling on many painful thoughts, some borrowed from the past, and more from the future. His uncle's caprice and moroseness,—the strange reports concerning the cause of the secluded life he had led for many years,—his own dependent state,—fell like blows fast and heavy on his mind. He roused himself to repel them,—sat up in the mail,* in which he was a solitary passenger,—looked out on the prospect,— consulted his watch;—then he thought they receded for a moment,—but there was nothing to fill their place, and he was forced to invite them back for company. When the mind is thus active in calling over invaders, no wonder the conquest is soon completed. As the carriage drew near the Lodge, (the name of old Melmoth's seat), John's heart grew heavier every moment.

The recollection of this awful uncle from infancy,—when he was never permitted to approach him without innumerable lectures,— *not to be troublesome*,—not to go too near his uncle,—not to ask him any questions,—on no account to disturb the inviolable arrangement of his snuff-box, hand-bell, and spectacles, nor to suffer the glittering of the gold-headed cane to tempt him to the mortal sin of handling it,—and, finally, to pilot himself aright through his perilous course in and out of the apartment without striking against the piles of books, globes, old newspapers, wig-blocks,* tobacco-pipes, and snuff-cannisters, not to mention certain hidden rocks of rat-traps and mouldy books beneath the chairs,—together with the final reverential bow at the door, which was to be closed with cautious gentleness, and the stairs to be descended as if he were 'shod with felt.'*—This recollection was carried on to his school-boy years, when at Christmas and Easter, the ragged poney, the jest of the school, was dispatched to bring the reluctant visitor to the Lodge,— where his pastime was to sit vis-a-vis to his uncle, without speaking or moving, till the pair resembled Don Raymond and the ghost of Beatrice in the Monk,*—then watching him, as he picked the bones of lean mutton out of his mess of weak broth, the latter of which he handed to his nephew with a needless caution not to 'take more than he liked,'—then hurried to bed by daylight, even in winter, to save the expence of an inch of candle, where he lay awake and restless from hunger, till his uncle's retiring at eight o'clock gave signal to the governante of the meagre household to steal up to him with some fragments of her own scanty meal, administering between every mouthful a whispered caution not to tell his uncle. Then his college life, passed in an attic in the second square, uncheered by an invitation to the country; the gloomy summer wasted in walking up and down the deserted streets, as his uncle would not defray the expences of his journey;—the only intimation of his existence, received in quarterly epistles, containing, with the scanty but punctual remittance, complaints of the expences of his education, cautions against extravagance, and lamentations for the failure of tenants and the fall of the value of lands. All these recollections came over him, and along with them the remembrance of that last scene, where his dependence on his uncle was impressed on him by the dying lips of his father.

'John, I must leave you, my poor boy; it has pleased God to take your father from you before he could do for you what would have made this hour less painful to him. You must look up, John, to your uncle for every thing. He has oddities and infirmities, but you must learn to bear with them, and with many other things too, as you will learn too soon. And now, my poor boy, may He who is the father of the fatherless look on your desolate state, and give you favour in the eyes of your uncle.' As this scene rose to John's memory, his eyes filled fast with tears, which he hastened to wipe away as the carriage stopt to let him out at his uncle's gate.

He alighted, and with a change of linen in a handkerchief, (his only travelling equipment), he approached his uncle's gate. The lodge was in ruins, and a barefooted boy from an adjacent cabin ran to lift on its single hinge what had once been a gate, but was now a few planks so villainously put together, that they clattered like a sign in a high wind. The stubborn post of the gate, yielding at last to the united strength of John and his barefooted assistant, grated heavily through the mud and gravel stones, in which it left a deep and sloughy furrow, and the entrance lay open. John, after searching his pocket in vain for a trifle to reward his assistant, pursued his way, while the lad, on his return, cleared the road at a hop step and jump, plunging through the mud with all the dabbling and amphibious delight of a duck, and scarce less proud of his agility than of his 'starving a gentleman.' As John slowly trod the miry road which had once been the approach, he could discover, by the dim light of an autumnal evening, signs of increasing desolation since he had last visited the spot,—signs that penury had been aggravated and sharpened into downright misery. There was not a fence or a hedge round the domain: an uncemented wall of loose stones, whose numerous gaps were filled with furze or thorns, supplied their place. There was not a tree or shrub on the lawn; the lawn itself was turned into pasture-ground, and a few sheep were picking their scanty food amid the pebblestones, thistles, and hard mould, through which a few blades of grass made their rare and squalid appearance.

The house itself stood strongly defined even amid the darkness of the evening sky; for there were neither wings, or offices, or shrubbery, or tree, to shade or support it, and soften its strong harsh outline. John, after a melancholy gaze at the grass-grown steps and boarded windows, 'addressed himself' to knock at the door; but knocker there was none: loose stones, however, there were in plenty; and John was making vigorous application to the door with one of them, till the furious barking of a mastiff, who threatened at every bound to break his chain, and whose yell and growl, accompanied by 'eyes that glow and fangs that grin',* savoured as much of hunger as of rage, made the assailant raise the siege on the door, and betake himself to a well-known passage that led to the kitchen. A light glimmered in the window as he approached: he raised the latch with a doubtful hand; but, when he saw the party within, he advanced with the step of a man no longer doubtful of his welcome.

Round a turf-fire, whose well-replenished fuel gave testimony to the 'master's' indisposition, who would probably as soon have been placed on the fire himself as seen the whole *kish** emptied on it once, were seated the old housekeeper, two or three *followers*, (*i.e.* people who ate, drank, and lounged about in any kitchen that was open in the neighbourhood, on an occasion of grief or joy, all for his honor's sake, and for the great rispict they bore the family), and an old woman, whom John immediately recognized as the doctress of the neighbourhood,—a withered Sybil, who prolonged her squalid existence by practising on the fears, the ignorance, and the sufferings of beings as miserable as herself. Among the better sort, to whom she sometimes had access by the influence of servants, she tried the effects of some simples, her skill in which was sometimes productive of success. Among the lower orders she talked much of the effects of the 'evil eye,' against which she boasted a counter-spell, of unfailing efficacy; and while she spoke, she shook her grizzled locks with such witch-like eagerness, that she never failed to communicate to her half-terrified, half-believing audience, some portion of that enthusiasm which, amid all her consciousness of imposture, she herself probably felt a large share of; still, when the case at last became desperate, when credulity itself lost all patience, and hope and life were departing together, she urged the miserable patient to confess '*there was something about his heart*;' and when his confession was extorted from the weariness of pain and the ignorance of poverty, she nodded and muttered so mysteriously, as to convey to the bystanders, that she had had difficulties to contend with which were invincible by human power. When there was no pretext, from indisposition, for her visiting either 'his honor's' kitchen, or the cottar's hut,*—when the stubborn and persevering convalescence of the whole country threatened her with starvation,—she still had a resource:—if there were no lives to be shortened, there were fortunes to be told;—she worked 'by spells, and by such daubry as is beyond our element.'* No one twined so well* as she the mystic yarn to be dropt into the lime-kiln pit, on the edge of which stood the shivering inquirer into futurity, doubtful whether the answer to her question of 'who holds?' was to be uttered by the voice of demon or lover.

No one knew so well as she to find where the four streams met, in which, on the same portentous season, the chemise was to be immersed, and then displayed before the fire, (in the name of one whom we dare not mention to 'ears polite'*), to be turned by the figure of the destined husband before morning. No one but herself (she said) knew the hand in which the comb was to be held, while the other was employed in conveying the apple to the mouth,—while, during the joint operation, the shadow of the phantom-spouse was to pass across the mirror before which it was performed. No one was more skilful or active in removing every iron implement from the kitchen where these ceremonies were usually performed by the credulous and terrified dupes of her wizardry, lest, instead of the form of a comely youth exhibiting a ring on his white finger, an headless figure should stalk to the rack, (*Anglicè*,* dresser), take down a long spit, or, in default of that, snatch a poker from the fire-side, and mercilessly take measure with its iron length of the sleeper for a coffin. No one, in short, knew better how to torment or terrify her victims into a belief of that power which may and has reduced the strongest minds to the level of the weakest; and under the influence of which the cultivated sceptic, Lord Lyttleton;* yelled and gnashed and writhed in his last hours, like the poor girl who, in the belief of the horrible visitation of the vampire, shrieked aloud, that her grandfather was sucking her vital blood while she slept, and expired under the influence of imaginary horror. Such was the being to whom old Melmoth had committed his life, half from credulity, and (*Hibernicè* speaking) *more than half* from avarice. Among this groupe John advanced,—recognising some,—disliking more,—distrusting all. The old housekeeper received him with cordiality;—he was always her 'white-headed boy,' she said,—(*imprimis,** his hair was as black as jet), and she tried to lift her withered hand to his head with an action between a benediction and a caress, till the difficulty of the attempt forced on her the conviction that that head was fourteen inches higher than her reach since she had last patted it. The men, with the national deference of the Irish to a person of superior rank, all rose at his approach, (their stools chattering on the broken flags), and wished his honor 'a thousand years, and long life to the back of that; and would not his honour take something to keep the grief out of his heart;' and so saying, five or six red and bony hands tendered him glasses of whiskey all at once. All this time the Sybil sat silent in the ample chimney-corner, sending redoubled whiffs out of her pipe. John gently declined the offer of spirits, received the attentions of the old housekeeper cordially, looked askance at the withered crone who occupied the chimney corner, and then glanced at the table, which displayed other cheer than he had been accustomed to see in his 'honor's time.' There was a wooden dish of potatoes, which old Melmoth would have considered enough for a week's subsistence. There was the salted salmon, (a luxury unknown even in London. *Vide* Miss Edgeworth's Tales,* 'The Absentee').

There was the *slink-veal,** flanked with tripe; and, finally, there were lobsters and *fried* turbot enough to justify what the author of the tale asserts, 'suo periculo,'* that when his great grandfather, the Dean of Killala,* hired servants at the deanery, they stipulated that they should not be required to eat turbot or lobster more than twice a-week. There were also bottles of Wicklow ale, long and surreptitiously borrowed from his 'honor's' cellar, and which now made their first appearance on the kitchen hearth, and manifested their impatience of further constraint, by hissing, spitting, and bouncing in the face of the fire that provoked its animosity. But the whiskey (genuine illegitimate potsheen, smelling strongly of weed and smoke, and breathing defiance to excisemen) appeared, the 'veritable Amphitryon' of the feast;* every one praised, and drank as deeply as he praised.

John, as he looked round the circle, and thought of his dying uncle, was forcibly reminded of the scene at Don Quixote's departure, where, in spite of the grief caused by the dissolution of the worthy knight, we are informed that 'nevertheless the niece eat her victuals, the housekeeper drank to the repose of his soul, and even Sancho cherished his little carcase.'* After returning, 'as he might,' the courtesies of the party, John asked how his uncle was. 'As bad as he can be;'—'Much better, and many thanks to your honor,' was uttered in such rapid and discordant unison by the party, that John turned from one to the other, not knowing which or what to believe. 'They say his honor has had a fright,' said a fellow, upwards of six feet high, approaching by way of whispering, and then bellowing the sound six inches above John's head. 'But then his honor has had *a cool* since,' said a man who was quietly swallowing the spirits that John had refused. At these words the Sybil who sat in the chimney corner slowly drew her pipe from her mouth, and turned towards the party: The oracular movements of a Pythoness on her tripod* never excited more awe, or impressed for the moment a deeper silence. 'It's not *here*,' said she, pressing her withered finger on her wrinkled forehead, 'nor *here*,—nor *here*;' and she extended her hand to the foreheads of those who were near her, who all bowed as if they were receiving a benediction, but had immediate recourse to the spirits afterwards, as if to ensure its effects.—'It's all *here*—it's all *about the heart*;' and as she spoke she spread and pressed her fingers on her hollow bosom with a force of action that thrilled her hearers.—'It's all *here*,' she added, repeating the action, (probably excited by the effect she had produced), and then sunk on her seat, resumed her pipe, and spoke no more. At this moment of involuntary awe on the part of John, and of terrified silence on that of the rest, an unusual sound was heard in the house, and the whole company started as if a musket had been discharged among them:—it was the unwonted sound of old Melmoth's bell. His domestics were so few, and so constantly near him, that the sound of his bell startled them as much as if he had been ringing the knell for his own interment. 'He used always to *rap down* for me,' said the old housekeeper, hurrying out of the kitchen; 'he said pulling the bells wore out the ropes.'

The sound of the bell produced its full effect. The housekeeper rushed into the room, followed by a number of women, (the Irish præficæ*); all ready to prescribe for the dying or weep for the dead,— all clapping their hard hands, or wiping their dry eyes. These hags all surrounded the bed; and to witness their loud, wild, and desperate grief, their cries of 'Oh! he's going, his honor's going, his honor's going,' one would have imagined their lives were bound up in his, like those of the wives in the story of Sinbad the Sailor* who were to be interred alive with their deceased husbands.

Four of them wrung their hands and howled round the bed, while one, with all the adroitness of a Mrs Quickly, felt his honor's feet, and 'upward and upward,' and 'all was cold as any stone.'*

Old Melmoth withdrew his feet from the grasp of the hag,— counted with his keen eye (keen amid the approaching dimness of death) the number assembled round his bed,—raised himself on his sharp elbow, and pushing away the housekeeper, (who attempted to settle his nightcap, that had been shoved on one side in the struggle, and gave his haggard, dying face, a kind of grotesque fierceness), bellowed out in tones that made the company start,—'What the devil brought ye all here?' The question scattered the whole party for a moment; but rallying instantly, they communed among themselves in whispers, and frequently using the sign of the cross, muttered 'The devil,—Christ save us, the devil in his mouth the first word he spoke.' 'Aye,' roared the invalid, 'and the devil in my eye the first sight I see.' 'Where,—where?' cried the terrified housekeeper, cling-ing close to the invalid in her terror, and half-hiding herself in the blanket, which she snatched without mercy from his struggling and exposed limbs. 'There, there,' he repeated, (during the battle of the blanket), pointing to the huddled and terrified women, who stood aghast at hearing themselves arointed as the very demons they came to banish. 'Oh! Lord keep your honor's head,' said the housekeeper in a more soothing tone, when her fright was over; 'and sure your honor knows them all, is'n't *her* name,—and *her* name,—and *her* name,'—and she pointed respectively to each of them, adding their names, which we shall spare the English reader the torture of reciting, (as a proof of our lenity, adding the last only, Cotchleen

O'Mulligan), 'Ye lie, ye b——h,' growled old Melmoth; 'their name is Legion,* for they are many,—turn them all out of the room,—turn them all out of doors,—if they howl at my death, they shall howl in earnest,—not for my death, for they would see me dead and damned too with dry eyes, but for want of the whiskey that they would have stolen if they could have got at it,' (and here old Melmoth grasped a key which lay under his pillow, and shook it in vain triumph at the old housekeeper, who had long possessed the means of getting at the spirits unknown to his 'honor'), 'and for want of the victuals you have pampered them with.' '*Pampered*, oh Ch—st!' ejaculated the housekeeper. 'Aye, and what are there so many candles for, all *fours*, and the same below I warrant. Ah! you—you—worthless, wasteful old devil.' 'Indeed, your honor, they are all *sixes*'.* Sixes,—and what the devil are you burning sixes for, d'ye think it's *the wake* already? Ha?' 'Oh! not yet, your honor, not yet,' chorussed the beldams; 'but in God's good time, your honor knows,' in a tone that spoke ill suppressed impatience for the event. 'Oh! that your honor would think of making your soul.' 'That's the first sensible word you have said,' said the dying man, 'fetch me the prayer-book,—you'll find it there under that old boot-jack,—blow off the cobwebs;—it has not been opened this many a year.' It was handed to him by the old governante, on whom he turned a reproaching eye. 'What made you burn sixes in the kitchen, you extravagant jade? How many years have you lived in this house?' 'I don't know, your honor.' 'Did you ever see any extravagance or waste in it?' 'Oh never, never, your honor.' 'Was any thing but a farthing candle ever burned in the kitchen?' 'Never, never, your honor.' 'Were not you kept as tight as hand and head and heart could keep you, were you not? answer me that.' 'Oh yes, sure, your honor; every *sowl* about us knows that,—every one does your honor justice, that you kept the closest house and closest hand in the country,—your honor was always a good warrant for it.' 'And how dare you unlock my hold before death has unlocked it,' said the dying miser, shaking his meagre hand at her. 'I smelt meat in the house,—I heard voices in the house,—I heard the key turn in the door over and over. Oh that I was up,' he added, rolling in impatient agony in his bed, 'Oh that I was up, to see the waste and ruin that is going on. But it would kill me,' he continued, sinking back on the bolster, for he never allowed himself a pillow; 'it would kill me,—the very thought of it is killing me now.' The women, discomfited and defeated, after sundry winks and whispers, were huddling out of the room, till recalled by the sharp eager tones of old Melmoth.—'Where are ye trooping to now? back to the kitchen to gormandize and guzzle? Won't one of ye stay and listen while there's a prayer read for me? Ye may want it one day for yourselves, ye hags.' Awed by this expostulation and menace, the train silently returned, and placed themselves round the bed, while the housekeeper, though a Catholic, asked if his honor would not have a clergyman to give him *the rights*, (rites) of his church. The eyes of the dying man sparkled with vexation at the proposal. 'What for,—just to have him expect a scarf and hat-band at the funeral. Read the prayers yourself, you old ——; that will save something.' The housekeeper made the attempt, but soon declined it, alleging, as her reason, that her eyes had been watery ever since his honor took ill. 'That's because you had always a drop in them,' said the invalid, with a spiteful sneer, which the contraction of approaching death stiffened into a hideous grin.—'Here,—is not there one of you that's gnashing and howling there, that can get up a prayer to keep me from it?' So abjured, one of the women offered her services; and of her it might truly be said, as of the 'most desartless man of the watch' in Dogberry's time, that 'her reading and writing came by nature;'* for she never had been at school, and had never before seen or opened a Protestant prayer book in her life; nevertheless, on she went, and with more emphasis than good discretion, read nearly through the service for the 'churching of women;'* which in our prayer-books following that of the burial of the dead, she perhaps imagined was someway connected with the state of the invalid.

She read with great solemnity,—it was a pity that two interruptions occurred during the performance, one from old Melmoth, who, shortly after the commencement of the prayers, turned towards the old housekeeper, and said, in a tone scandalously audible, 'Go down and draw the niggers* of the kitchen fire closer, and lock the door, and let me *hear it locked*. I can't mind any thing till that's done.' The other was from John Melmoth gliding into the room, hearing the inappropriate words uttered by the ignorant woman, taking quietly as he knelt beside her the prayer-book from her hands, and reading in a suppressed voice part of that solemn service which, by the forms of the Church of England, is intended for the consolation of the departing.

'That is John's voice,' said the dying man; and the little kindness he had ever shewed this unfortunate lad rushed on his hard heart at this moment, and touched it. He saw himself, too, surrounded by heartless and rapacious menials; and slight as must have been his dependence on a relative whom he had always treated as a stranger, he felt at this hour he was no stranger, and grasped at his support like a straw amid his wreck. 'John, my good boy, you are there.—I kept you far from me when living, and now you are nearest me when dying.—John, *read on.*' John, affected deeply by the situation in which he beheld this *poor man,* amid all his wealth, as well as by the solemn request to impart consolation to his dying moments, read on;—but in a short time his voice became indistinct, from the horror with which he listened to the increasing hiccup of the patient, which, however, he struggled with from time to time, to ask the housekeeper if *the niggers were closed.* John, who was a lad of feeling, rose from his knees in some degree of agitation. 'What, are you leaving me like the rest?' said old Melmoth, trying to raise himself in the bed. 'No, Sir,' said John; 'but,' observing the altered looks of the dying man, 'I think you want some refreshment, some support, Sir.' 'Aye, I do, I do, but whom can I trust to get it for me. *They,* (and his haggard eye wandered round the groupe), *they* would poison me.' 'Trust me, Sir,' said John; 'I will go to the apothecary's, or whoever you may employ.' The old man grasped his hand, drew him close to his bed, cast a threatening yet fearful eye round the party, and then whispered in a voice of agonized constraint, 'I want a glass of wine, it would keep me alive for some hours, but there is not one I can trust to get it for me,—*they'd steal a bottle, and ruin me.*' John was greatly shocked. 'Sir, for God's sake, let *me* get a glass of wine for you.' 'Do you know where?' said the old man, with an expression in his face John could not understand. 'No, Sir; you know I have been rather a stranger here, Sir.' 'Take this key,' said old Melmoth, after a violent spasm; 'take this key, there is wine in that closet,—*Madeira.* I always told them there was nothing there, but they did not believe me, or I should not have been robbed as I have been. At one time I said it was whiskey, and then I fared worse than ever, for they drank twice as much of it.'

John took the key from his uncle's hand; the dying man pressed it as he did so, and John, interpreting this as a mark of kindness, returned the pressure. He was undeceived by the whisper that followed,—'John, my lad, don't drink any of that wine while you are there.' 'Good God!' said John, indignantly throwing the key on the bed; then, recollecting that the miserable being before him was no object of resentment, he gave the promise required, and entered the closet, which no foot but that of old Melmoth had entered for nearly sixty years. He had some difficulty in finding out the wine, and indeed staid long enough to justify his uncle's suspicions,—but his mind was agitated, and his hand unsteady. He could not but remark his uncle's extraordinary look, that had the ghastliness of fear super-added to that of death, as he gave him permission to enter his closet. He could not but see the looks of horror which the women exchanged as he approached it. And, finally, when he was in it, his memory was malicious enough to suggest some faint traces of a story, too horrible for imagination, connected with it. He remembered in one moment most distinctly, that no one but his uncle had ever been known to enter it for many years.

Before he quitted it, he held up the dim light, and looked around him with a mixture of terror and curiosity. There was a great deal of decayed and useless lumber, such as might be supposed to be heaped up to rot in a miser's closet; but John's eyes were in a moment, and as if by magic, rivetted on a portrait that hung on the wall, and appeared, even to his untaught eye, far superior to the tribe of family pictures that are left to moulder on the walls of a family mansion. It represented a man of middle age. There was nothing remarkable in the costume, or in the countenance, but *the eyes*, John felt, were such as one feels they wish they had never seen, and feels they can never forget. Had he been acquainted with the poetry of Southey, he might have often exclaimed in his after-life,

> 'Only the eyes had life,
> They gleamed with demon light.'—THALABA.*

From an impulse equally resistless and painful, he approached the portrait, held the candle towards it, and could distinguish the words on the border of the painting,—Jno. Melmoth, anno 1646. John was neither timid by nature, or nervous by constitution, or superstitious from habit, yet he continued to gaze in stupid horror on this singular picture, till, aroused by his uncle's cough, he hurried into his room. The old man swallowed the wine. He appeared a little revived; it was long since he had tasted such a cordial,—his heart appeared to expand to a momentary confidence. 'John, what did you see in that room?' 'Nothing, Sir.' 'That's a lie; every one wants to cheat or to rob me.' 'Sir, I don't want to do either.' 'Well, what did you see that you—you took notice of?' 'Only a picture, Sir.' 'A picture, Sir!—the original is still alive.' John, though under the impression of his recent feelings, could not but look incredulous. 'John,' whispered his uncle;—'John, they say I am dying of this and that; and one says it is for want of nourishment, and one says it is for want of medicine,— but, John,' and his face looked hideously ghastly, 'I am dying of a fright. That man,' and he extended his meagre arm toward the closet, as if he was pointing to a living being; 'that man, I have good reason to know, is alive still.' 'How is that possible, Sir?' said John involuntarily, 'the date on the picture is 1646.' 'You have seen it,— you have noticed it,' said his uncle. 'Well,'—he rocked and nodded on his bolster for a moment, then, grasping John's hand with an unutterable look, he exclaimed, 'You will see him again, he is alive.' Then, sinking back on his bolster, he fell into a kind of sleep or stupor, his eyes still open, and fixed on John.

The house was now perfectly silent, and John had time and space for reflection. More thoughts came crowding on him than he wished to welcome, but they would not be repulsed. He thought of his uncle's habits and character, turned the matter over and over again in his mind, and he said to himself, 'The last man on earth to be superstitious. He never thought of any thing but the price of stocks, and the rate of exchange, and my college expences, that hung heavier at his heart than all; and such a man to die of a fright,—a ridiculous fright, that a man living 150 years ago is alive still, and yet—he is dying.' John paused, for facts will confute the most stubborn logician. 'With all his hardness of mind, and of heart, he is dying of a fright. I heard it in the kitchen, I have heard it from himself,—he could not be deceived. If I had ever heard he was nervous, or fanciful, or superstitious, but a character so contrary to all these impressions;—a man that, as poor Butler* says, in his Remains, of the Antiquarian, would have "sold Christ over again for the numerical piece of silver which Judas got for him,"—such a man to die of fear! Yet he *is* dying,' said John, glancing his fearful eye on the contracted nostril, the glazed eye, the dropping jaw, the whole horrible apparatus of the *facies Hippocratica** displayed, and soon to cease its display.

Old Melmoth at this moment seemed to be in a deep stupor; his eyes lost that little expression they had before, and his hands, that had convulsively been catching at the blankets, let go their short and quivering grasp, and lay extended on the bed like the claws of some bird that had died of hunger,—so meagre, so yellow, so spread. John, unaccustomed to the sight of death, believed this to be only a sign that he was going to sleep; and, urged by an impulse for which he did not attempt to account to himself, caught up the miserable light, and once more ventured into the forbidden room,—the *blue chamber* of the dwelling.* The motion roused the dying man;—he sat bolt upright in his bed. This John could not see, for he was now in the closet; but he heard the groan, or rather the choaked and guggling rattle of the throat, that announces the horrible conflict between muscular and mental convulsion. He started, turned away; but, as he turned away, he thought he saw the eyes of the portrait, on which his own was fixed, *move*, and hurried back to his uncle's bedside.

Old Melmoth died in the course of that night, and died as he had lived, in a kind of avaricious delirium. John could not have imagined a scene so horrible as his last hours presented. He cursed and blasphemed about three half-pence, missing, as he said, some weeks before, in an account of change with his groom, about hay to a starving horse that he kept. Then he grasped John's hand, and asked him to give him the sacrament. 'If I send to the clergyman, he will charge me something for it, which I cannot pay,—I cannot. They say I am rich,—look at this blanket;—but I would not mind that, if I could save my soul.' And, raving, he added, 'Indeed, Doctor, I am a very poor man. I never troubled a clergyman before, and all I want is, that you will grant me two trifling requests, very little matters in your way,—save my soul, and (whispering) make interest to get me a parish coffin,—I have not enough left to bury me. I always told every one I was poor, but the more I told them so, the less they believed me.'

John, greatly shocked, retired from the bed-side, and sat down in a distant corner of the room. The women were again in the room, which was very dark. Melmoth was silent from exhaustion, and there was a death-like pause for some time. At this moment John saw the door open, and a figure appear at it, who looked round the room, and then quietly and deliberately retired, but not before John had discovered in his face the living original of the portrait. His first impulse was to utter an exclamation of terror, but his breath felt stopped. He was then rising to pursue the figure, but a moment's reflection checked him. What could be more absurd, than to be alarmed or amazed at a resemblance between a living man and the portrait of a dead one! The likeness was doubtless strong enough to strike him even in that darkened room, but it was doubtless only a likeness; and though it might be imposing enough to terrify an old man of gloomy and retired habits, and with a broken constitution, John resolved it should not produce the same effect on him.

But while he was applauding himself for this resolution, the door opened, and the figure appeared at it, beckoning and nodding to him, with a familiarity somewhat terrifying. John now started up, determined to pursue it; but the pursuit was stopped by the weak but shrill cries of his uncle, who was struggling at once with the agonies of death and his housekeeper. The poor woman, anxious for her master's reputation and her own, was trying to put on him a clean shirt and nightcap, and Melmoth, who had just sensation enough to perceive they were taking something from him, continued exclaiming feebly, 'They are robbing me,—robbing me in my last moments,—robbing a dying man. John, won't you assist me,—I shall die a beggar; they are taking my last shirt,—I shall die a beggar.'——And the miser died.

JOSEPH SHERIDAN LE FANU
(1814–1873)

from *The House by the Church-yard* (1863)

XXXIV

IN WHICH A CERTAIN TROUBLED SPIRIT WALKS

Mr Dangerfield was at the Club that night, and was rather in spirits than otherwise, except, indeed, when poor Charles Nutter was talked of. Then he looked grave, and shrugged, and shook his head, and said—

'A bad business, sir; and where's his poor wife?'

'Spending the night with us, poor soul,' said Major O'Neill, mildly, 'and hasn't an idaya, poor thing; and indeed, I hope, she mayn't hear it.'

'Pooh! sir, she must hear it; but you know she might have heard worse sir, eh?' rejoined Dangerfield.

'True for you, sir,' said the Major, suspending the filling of his pipe to direct a quiet glance of significance at Dangerfield, and then closing his eyes with a nod.

And just at this point in came Spaight.

'Well, Spaight!'

'Well, sir.'

'You saw the body, eh?' and a dozen other interrogatories followed, as, cold and wet with melting snow, dishevelled, and stormbeaten—for it was a plaguey rough night—the young fellow, with a general greeting to the company, made his way to the fire.

' 'Tis a tremendious night, gentlemen, so by your leave I'll stir the fire—and, yes, I seen him, poor Nutter—and, paugh, an ugly sight he is, I can tell you; here, Larry, bring me a rummer-glass* of punch—his right ear's gone, and a'most all his right hand—and screeching hot, do you mind—an', phiew—altogether 'tis sickening—them fishes, you know—I'm a'most sorry I went in—you remember Dogherty's whiskey shop in Ringsend*—he lies in the back parlour, and wondherful little changed in appearance.'

And so Mr Spaight with a little round table at his elbow, and his heels over the fender, sipped his steaming punch, and thawed inwardly and outwardly, as he answered their questions and mixed in their speculations.

Up at the Mills, which had heard the awful news, first from the Widow Macan, and afterwards from Pat Moran, the maids sat over their tea in the kitchen in high excitement and thrilling chat—'The poor master;' 'oh, the poor man;' 'oh, la, what's that,' with a start and a peep over the shoulders; 'and oh, dear, and how in the world will the poor little misthress ever live over the news,' and so forth, made a principal part of their talk. There was a good accompaniment of wind outside, and a soft pelting of snow on the window panes, 'and oh, my dear life, but wasn't it dark!'

Up went Moggy, with her thick-wick'd kitchen candle, to seek repose; and Betty, resolving not to be long behind, waited only 'to wash up her plates' and slack down the fire,* having made up her mind, for she grew more nervous in solitude, to share Moggy's bed for that night.

Moggy had not been twenty minutes gone, and her task was nearly ended, when—'Oh, blessed saints!' murmurs Betty, with staring eyes, and dropping the sweeping-brush on the flags,* she heard, or thought she heard, her master's step, which was peculiar, crossing the floor overhead.

She listened, herself as pale as a corpse, and nearly as breathless; but there was nothing now but the muffled gusts of the storm, and the close soft beat of the snow, so she listened and listened, but nothing came of it.

' 'Tis only the vapours,'* said Betty, drawing a long breath, and doing her best to be cheerful; and so she finished her labours, stopping every now and then to listen, and humming tunes very loud, in fits and starts. Then it came to her turn to take her candle and go up stairs; she was a good half hour later than Moggy—all was quiet within the house—only the sound of the storm—the creak and rattle of its strain, and the hurly-burly of the gusts over the roof and chimneys.

Over her shoulder she peered jealously this way and that, as with flaring candle she climbed the stairs. How black the window looked on the lobby, with its white patterns of snow flakes in perpetual succession sliding down the panes. Who could tell what horrid face might be looking in close to her as she passed, secure in the darkness and that drifting white lace veil of snow? So nimbly and lightly up the stairs climbed Betty, the cook.

If listeners seldom hear good of themselves, it is also true that peepers sometimes see more than they like; and Betty, the cook, as she reached the landing, glancing askance with ominous curiosity, beheld a spectacle, the sight of which nearly bereft her of her senses.

Crouching in the deep doorway on the right of the lobby, the cook, I say, saw something—a figure—or a deep shadow—only a deep shadow—or maybe a dog. She lifted the candle—she peeped under the candlestick: 'twas no shadow, as I live, 'twas a well-defined figure!

He was draped in black, cowering down low, with the face turned up. It was Charles Nutter's face, fixed and stealthy. It was only while the fascination lasted—while you might count one, two, three, deliberately—that the horrid gaze met mutually. But there was no mistake there. She saw the stern dark picture as plainly as ever she did. The light glimmered on his white eyeballs.

Starting up, he struck at the candle with his hat. She uttered a loud scream, and flinging stick and all at the figure, with a great clang against the door behind, all was swallowed in instantaneous darkness; she whirled into the opposite bed-room she knew not how, and locked the door within, and plunged head-foremost under the bed-clothes, half mad with terror.

The squall was heard of course. Moggy heard it, but she heeded not; for Betty was known to scream at mice, and even moths. And as her door was heard to slam, as was usual in panics of the sort, and as she returned no answer, Moggy was quite sure there was nothing in it.

But Moggy's turn was to come. When spirits 'walk,' I've heard they make the most of their time, and sometimes pay a little round of visits on the same evening.

This is certain; Moggy was by no means so great a fool as Betty in respect of Hobgoblins, witches, banshees, pookas, and the world of spirits in general. She eat heartily, and slept soundly, and as yet had never seen the devil. Therefore, such terrors as she that night experienced were new to her, and I can't reasonably doubt the truth of her narrative. Awaking suddenly in the night, she saw a light in the room, and heard a quiet rustling going on in the corner, where the old white-painted press* showed its front from the wall. So Moggy popped her head through her thin curtains at the side, and—blessed hour!—there she saw the shape of a man looking into the press, the doors being wide open, and the appearance of a key in the lock, though she well knew the mistress had taken it away with her.

The shape was very like her master. The saints between us and harm! The glow was reflected back from the interior of the press, and showed the front part of the figure in profile with a sharp line of light. She said he had some sort of thick slippers over his boots, a dark coat, with the cape buttoned, and a hat flapping over his face; coat and hat, and all, sprinkled over with snow.

As if he heard the rustle of the curtain, he turned toward the bed, and with an awful ejaculation she cried, ' 'Tis you, sir!'

'Don't stir, and you'll meet no harm,' he said, and over he posts to the bedside, and he laid his cold hand on her wrist, and told her again to be quiet, and for her life to tell no one what she had seen, and with that she supposed she swooned away; for the next thing she remembered was listening in mortal fear, the room being all dark, and she heard a sound at the press again, and then steps crossing the floor, and she gave herself up for lost; but he did not come to the bedside any more, and the tread passed out at the door, and so, as she thought went down stairs.

In the morning the press was locked and the door shut, and the hall-door and back-door locked, and the keys on the hall table, where they had left them the night before.

You may be sure these two ladies were thankful to behold the gray light, and hear the cheerful sounds of returning day; and it would be no easy matter to describe which of the two looked most pallid, scared, and jaded that morning, as they drank a hysterical dish of tea together in the kitchen, close up to the window, and with the door shut, discoursing, and crying, and praying over their tea-pot in miserable rivalry.

EMILY LAWLESS
(1845–1913)

from *Hurrish* (1886)

I

AN IRON LAND

Wilder regions there are few to be found, even in the wildest west of Ireland, than that portion of north Clare known to its inhabitants as 'The Burren.' Seen from the Atlantic, which washes its western base, it presents to the eye a succession of low hills, singularly grey in tone,—deepening often, towards evening, into violet or dull reddish plum colour—sometimes, after sunset, to a pale ghostly iridescence. They are quite low these hills—not above a thousand feet at their highest point, and for the most part considerably less. Hills of this height, whatever their other merits, seldom attain to the distinction of being spoken of as 'grand.' Their character is essentially 'mutton-suggesting.' You picture them dotted over with flocks of sheep, which nibble the short sweet grass, and frisk in their idle youth over the little declivities. If here and there like that most unaccountable of little animals, they, too, sprang into the waves and were lost. Little change has taken place in the aspect of the region since those unknown races passed away. Their great stone-duns are even still in many places the largest buildings to be seen,—the little oratories and churches which succeeded them having become in their turn, with hardly an exception, ruins like themselves, their very sites forgotten, melted into the surrounding stoniness. The Burren is not—in all probability never will be—a tourist-haunt, but for the few who know it, it has a place apart, a distinct personality—strange, remote, indescribable. Everything that the eye rests on tells us that we are on one of the last standpoints of an old world, worn out with its own profusion, and reduced here to the barest elements. Mother Earth, once young, buxom, frolicsome, is here a wrinkled woman, sitting alone in the evening of her days, and looking with melancholy eyes at the sunset.

The valley of Gortnacoppin is a sort of embodiment of the Burren. Standing in it you might fairly believe yourself in the heart of some alpine region, high above the haunts of men, where only the eagle or the marmot make their homes. All the suggestions are alpine, some of them almost arctic. The white stream cutting its way through the heaped-up drift; the water churning and frothing hither and thither in its impatience, and leaving a white deposit upon all the reeds and stones; the pallid greyish-green vegetation, with here and there a bit of dazzling red or orange; the chips and flakes of rock which lie strewn about; the larger stones and boulders toppled down from the cliff above, and lying heaped one over the other in the bed of the stream,—many of the latter, you may perceive, have not long fallen, for their edges are still unweathered. Here and there over the top and sides of the drift a little thin grass has spread itself, through which trenches have been torn, showing the earth and stones below. Truly a grim scene!—suggestive of nothing so much as one of those ugly little early German prints, where every stick and stone seems to be grimacing with unpleasant intention. Only look hard enough at any of the rocks, and you will assuredly see a gnome appear!

Towards the bottom, where it approaches the sea, this valley, however, expands, and becomes an irregular lake-like circle, mapped out into small fields, separated from one another by tottering lace-work walls. After following the downward course of the upper valley, you would have been surprised at the sudden fertility of this little space, the greenness of the grass, the promising look of the small crops of bottle-green potatoes. If something of a geologist, however, you would have suspected that the mass of detritus, borne down from the hills, and spread abroad here at their feet, had something to say to that satisfactory result.

Between five and six years ago the greater part of this little fertile oasis was rented by Horatio, or, as he was less classically called by his neighbours, Hurrish O'Brien, one of the countless O'Briens of Clare. His cabin—a rather large one, built of stone and thatched—stood upon the summit of a little ridge, conspicuous, like a small fly upon a large window-pane, in the absence of any other building; rendered still more so by a good-sized ash-tree, which stood upon the ridge beside it—a noticeable distinction in so leafless a district.

It was a warm morning late in May, and even the stony Burren had begun to feel a touch of spring, its ferns and little delicate-petalled blossoms to reach out inquiring heads over their stony prisons. Hurrish had just returned to breakfast. He had been down early to the sea, to set some fishing-lines—for, like most of the inhabitants of that amphibious part of the island, he was part farmer and part fisherman,—perhaps it would be more accurate in his case to say three-parts farmer to one-part fisherman, the latter vocation being, in fact, rather a matter of 'intertainmint' than profit.

The door of the cabin was open, and the window unshuttered (the latter for an excellent reason, there were no shutters), yet the cabin itself was lit by its fire. The light, spreading from the blazing turf, broke in red flakes upon the bare rafters of the roof, upon the roughly plastered walls, upon a quantity of highly coloured pious prints upon the walls, upon others of a less pious character pinned beside them, upon a rough white terrier, two solemn black pigs, and three children scattered over the mud floor, upon an *omnium gatherum** of tags and rags, stray fragments of furniture, tools, cloth-ing, straw, bedding, sacks, heaps of potatoes,—an indescribable and incalculable collection of long accumulated rubbish, huddled, in more or less picturesque confusion, one on top of another—the sort of picturesqueness which fastidious people prefer in its painted rather than in its actual form!

Hurrish sat upon a low 'creepy' stool,* with a huge mug of stir-about (known to the ignorant as porridge) upon his knees, which he was shovelling down his throat by the aid of a large iron spoon. A broad-shouldered, loose-limbed, genial-faced giant* was Hurrish, such as these western Irish counties occasionally breed. Irish in every feature, look, and gesture, there was yet a smack of something foreign about him, to be accounted for possibly by that oft-quoted admixture of Spanish blood, the result of bygone centuries of more or less continuous intercourse. His hair was black as a cormorant's wing, and curly under the old felt hat, half of whose brim had vanished in some distant engagement; his beard was curly too, and black, yet his eyes were grey, his skin evidently originally fair, and his expression open, good-humoured, irresolute, with a spice of native fun and jollity about it. Despite the jollity which was its prevailing expression, he did not seem to be altogether a contented giant. There were lines of perplexity and disturbance here and there discernible. Yet Hurrish O'Brien was a well-to-do man. He had a good stock of cows and calves; he held his farm on a moderate rental; his wife had brought him fifty gold sovereigns tied up in a pocket-handkerchief; his children were strong and healthy; and he was regarded by his neighbours generally as one of the 'warmest' men between Black-head and the mouth of the Shannon.

Opposite, upon another low creepy-stool, sat his mother, Bridget O'Brien, engaged in stirring a steaming black pot—an employment which would have given a sensitive looker-on a delightful thrill, so appropriate was the operation to the operator. In Bridget O'Brien the Southern type was also strongly visible. Women like her—as gaunt, as wrinkled, as black-browed, as witch-like—may be seen seated upon thousands of doorsteps all over the Spanish peninsula. It is not a very comfortable type, one would think, for everyday domestic use; too suggestive of an elderly bird of prey—a vulture, old, yet with claws ever upon the watch to tear, and a beak which yearns to plunge itself into the still palpitating flesh. Her eyes were black—a wicked black—and bright still amid the multiplicity of wrinkles which surrounded them, as cracks a half-dried pool. Her hair, too, was dark, and hung in heavy hanks about her forehead, reaching nearly to the grizzled eyebrows, projecting like unclipped eaves over her eyes.

Bridget O'Brien was an ardent patriot! The latest tide of revolutionary sentiment had begun to spread its waves even to the heart of remotest Burren, and she was the chief recipient of it in the O'Brien household. It was she who knew when, where, how, and why the latest agrarian outrage had been committed, and was the first to raise the war-cry of triumph and exultation upon these joyful occasions. Not that the rest of the family were backward in their degree. Hurrish had called himself a Fenian almost ever since he could remember, and nothing but his distance from the seat of war had prevented him from striking a blow when that ill-starred apology for a rebellion* came to its final and melancholy close. Animosity against England was a creed with him, a sort of shibboleth— something like the middle-class English hatred of France some three-quarters of a century ago. His belief in its wickedness and atrocities was a belief that knew absolutely no misgivings. Had he been assured that, like Herod of old, an order had just been issued by its Government for all infants under two years of age to be slaughtered, I doubt if it would have struck him as at all incredible, or even out of character with what he supposed to be the normal nature of its proceedings.

Hurrish's patriotic potations, however, were mild and diluted compared with those quaffed to the very dregs by his mother. He was not a man easily roused to bitterness, and would hardly, I think, have cared to kill even an Englishman, unless some very good purpose could have been served by so doing. When Bridget brought back tales of vengeance, executed upon the latest enemies of their country he listened, but rarely found himself warmed to the point of emulation; the details of those gallant achievements being apt, in fact, to have rather a chilling and discouraging effect upon his imagination. What he enjoyed was what may be called the frivolous side of patriotism,—the mere noise, the crowd, the excitement, the waving flags, the new tin-pikes, the thrilling, delightful, inexhaustible oratory of his chosen leaders. All this was meat, drink, and clothing to him, and he would have walked thirty miles any day of his life to enjoy it. On the other hand, the detailed projects of vengeance were apt to pass over his head. He admitted their necessity, but blinked the details. When Ned Clancy, for instance, with his wife and four small children, were turned out of their cabin in the dead of a January night, because Clancy had taken Lynch's farm, contrary to well-known if unwritten local laws, Hurrish had been disposed to feel sorry for the more juvenile of the criminals. Not so his mother. 'What ailed he to be pityin' of thim? wasn't it known they wouldn't have been sarved so if they hadn't been desarvin'?' that thoroughgoing woman asked fiercely. Hideous prints, of still more hideous significance, disfigured a considerable portion of the cabin walls.

There was one cheerful design in particular, representing the roasting alive of men in swallow-tail coats, tall hats, and white neck-cloths, presumably landlords and their myrmidons.* The intention was allegorical, probably, but to Bridget it was literal enough, and it was upon such pabulum* she feasted her eyes with all the relish of a petticoated vampire.

4. POETRY

ANTOINE RAFTERY
(c. 1784–1835)

I Am Raftery (c. 1830)

I am Raftery the poet,
   Full of hope and love,
With eyes that have no light,
   With gentleness that has no misery.

Going west upon my pilgrimage
   Guided by the light of my heart,
Feeble and tired,
   To the end of my road.

Behold me now,
   And my face to a wall,
A-playing music
   Unto empty pockets.

CHARLOTTE BROOKE
(c. 1740–1793)

Elegy on the Death of Carolan (1789)

I came, with friendship's face, to glad my heart,
But sad, and sorrowful my steps depart!
In my friend's stead—a spot of earth was shown,
And on his grave my woe-struck eyes were thrown!
No more to their distracted sight remain'd,
But the cold clay that all they lov'd contain'd:

And there his last and narrow bed was made,
And the drear tomb-stone for its covering laid!

Alas!—for this my aged heart is wrung!
Grief chokes my voice, and trembles on my tongue.
Lonely and desolate, I mourn the dead,
The friend with whom my every comfort fled!
There is no anguish can with this compare!
No pains, diseases, suffering, or despair,
Like that I feel, while such a loss I mourn,
My heart's companion from its fondness torn!
Oh insupportable, distracting grief!
Woe, that through life, can never hope relief!
Sweet-singing harp!—thy melody is o'er!
Sweet friendship's voice!—I hear thy sound no more!
My bliss,—my wealth of poetry is fled.
And every joy, with him I lov'd, is dead!
Alas! what wonder, (while my heart drops blood
Upon the woes that drain its vital flood,)
If maddening grief no longer can be borne,
And frenzy fill the breast, with anguish torn!

THOMAS MOORE
(1779–1852)

*Oh! breathe not his name** (1807)

Oh! breathe not his name, let it sleep in the shade,
Where cold and unhonour'd his relics are laid:
Sad, silent, and dark, be the tears that we shed,
As the night-dew that falls on the grass o'er his head.

But the night-dew that falls, though in silence it weeps,
Shall brighten with verdure the grave where he sleeps;
And the tear that we shed, though in secret it rolls,
Shall long keep his memory green in our souls.

*She is far from the land** (1811)

She is far from the land where her young hero sleeps,
    And lovers are round her, sighing:
But coldly she turns from their gaze, and weeps,
    For her heart in his grave is lying.

She sings the wild song of her dear native plains,
    Every note which he lov'd awaking;—
Ah! little they think who delight in her strains,
    How the heart of the Minstrel is breaking.

He had liv'd for his love, for his country he died,
    They were all that to life had entwin'd him;
Nor soon shall the tears of his country be dried,
    Nor long will his love stay behind him.

Oh! make her a grave where the sunbeams rest,
    When they promise a glorious morrow;
They'll shine o'er her sleep, like a smile from the West,
    From her own lov'd island of sorrow.

Dear Harp of my Country (1815)

Dear Harp of my Country! in darkness I found thee,
    The cold chain of silence had hung o'er thee long,
When proudly, my own Island Harp, I unbound thee,
    And gave all thy chords to light, freedom, and song!

The warm lay of love and the light note of gladness
    Have waken'd thy fondest, thy liveliest thrill;
But, so oft hast thou echo'd the deep sigh of sadness,
    That ev'n in thy mirth it will steal from thee still.

Dear Harp of my Country! farewell to thy numbers,
    This sweet wreath of song is the last we shall twine!
Go, sleep with the sunshine of Fame on thy slumbers,
    Till touch'd by some hand less unworthy than mine;

If the pulse of the patriot, soldier, or lover,
    Have throbb'd at our lay, 'tis thy glory alone;
I was *but* as the wind, passing heedlessly over,
    And all the wild sweetness I wak'd was thy own.

The harp that once through Tara's halls* (1807)

The harp that once through Tara's halls
    The soul of music shed,
Now hangs as mute on Tara's walls
    As if that soul were fled.
So sleeps the pride of former days,
    So glory's thrill is o'er,
And hearts, that once beat high for praise,
    Now feel that pulse no more.

No more to chiefs and ladies bright
    The harp of Tara swells;
The chord alone, that breaks at night,
    Its tale of ruin tells.
Thus freedom now so seldom wakes,
    The only throb she gives,
Is when some heart indignant breaks,
    To show that still she lives.

Oft, in the stilly night (1818)

Oft, in the stilly night,
    Ere Slumber's chain has bound me,
Fond Memory brings the light
    Of other days around me;
      The smiles, the tears
        Of boyhood's years,
    The words of love then spoken;
      The eyes that shone,
        Now dimm'd and gone,
    The cheerful hearts now broken!
Thus, in the stilly night,

Ere Slumber's chain has bound me,
Sad Memory brings the light
    Of other days around me.

When I remember all
    The friends, so link'd together,
I've seen around me fall
    Like leaves in wintry weather;
        I feel like one
        Who treads alone
Some banquet-hall deserted,
        Whose lights are fled,
        Whose garlands dead,
    And all but he departed!
Thus, in the stilly night,
    Ere Slumber's chain has bound me,
Sad Memory brings the light
    Of other days around me.

The Minstrel Boy (1813)

The Minstrel Boy to the war is gone,
    In the ranks of death you'll find him;
His father's sword he has girded on,
    And his wild harp slung behind him.—
'Land of song!' said the warrior-bard,
    'Though all the world betray thee,
One sword, at least, thy rights shall guard,
    One faithful harp shall praise thee!'

The Minstrel fell!—but the foeman's chain
    Could not bring his proud soul under;
The harp he loved ne'er spoke again,
    For he tore its cords asunder;
And said, 'No chains shall sully thee,
    Thou soul of love and bravery!
Thy songs were made for the brave and free,
    They shall never sound in slavery!'

MARY TIGHE
(1772–1810)

Written at the Eagle's Nest, Killarney (1800)

Here let us rest, while with meridan blaze
    The sun rides glorious 'mid the cloudless sky,
    While o'er the lake no cooling Zephyrs fly,
But on the liquid glass we dazzled gaze,
And fainting ask for shade: lo! where his nest
    The bird of Jove has fixed: the lofty brow,
With arbutus and fragrant wild shrubs drest,
    Impendent frowns, nor will approach allow:
Here the soft turf invites; here magic sounds
    Celestially respondent shall enchant,
While Melody from you steep wood rebounds
    In thrilling cadence sweet. Sure, life can grant
No brighter hours than this; and memory oft
Shall paint this happiest scene with pencil soft.

Written at Killarney (1800)

How soft the pause! the notes melodious cease,
    Which from each feeling could an echo call;
    Rest on your oars; that not a sound may fall
To interrupt the stillness of our peace:
The fanning west-wind breathes upon our cheeks
    Yet glowing with the sun's departed beams.
    Through the blue heavens the cloudless moon pours streams
Of pure resplendent light, in silver streaks
Reflected on the still, unruffled lake.
    The Alpine hills in solemn silence frown,
    While the dark woods night's deepest shades embrown.
And now once more that soothing strain awake!
Oh, ever to my heart, with magic power,
Shall those sweet sounds recal this rapturous hour!

On Leaving Killarney (1800)

Farewel, sweet scenes! pensive once more I turn
    Those pointed hills, and wood-fringed lakes to view
    With fond regret; while in this last adieu
A silent tear those brilliant hours shall mourn
For ever past. So from the pleasant shore,
    Borne with the struggling bark against the wind,
    The trembling pennant fluttering looks behind
With vain reluctance! 'Mid those woods no more
For me the voice of pleasure shall resound,
    Nor soft flutes warbling o'er the placid lake
    Aërial music shall for me awake,
And wrap my charmed soul in peace profound!
Though lost to me, here still may Taste delight
To dwell, nor the rude axe the trembling Dryads fright!

Address to my Harp (1811)

Oh, my loved Harp! companion dear!
    Sweet soother of my secret grief,
No more thy sounds my soul must cheer,
    No more afford a soft relief.

When anxious cares my heart oppressed,
    When doubts distracting tore my soul,
The pains which heaved my swelling breast
    Thy gentle sway could oft control.

Each well remembered, practised strain,
    The cheerful dance, the tender song,
Recalled with pensive, pleasing pain
    Some image loved and cherished long.

Where joy sat smiling o'er my fate,
    And marked each bright and happy day,
When partial friends around me sat,
    And taught my lips the simple lay;

And when by disappointment grieved
   I saw some darling hope o'erthrown,
Thou hast my secret pain relieved;
   O'er thee I wept, unseen, alone.

Oh! must I leave thee, must we part,
   Dear partner of my happiest days?
I may forget thy much-loved art,
   Unused thy melody to raise,

But ne'er can memory cease to love
   Those scenes where I thy charms have felt,
Though I no more thy power may prove,
   Which taught my softened heart to melt.

Forced to forego with thee this spot,
   Endeared by many a tender tie,
When rosy pleasure blessed my lot,
   And sparkled in my cheated eye.

Yet still thy strings, in Fancy's ear,
   With soothing melody shall play;
Thy silver sounds I oft shall hear,
   To pensive gloom a silent prey.

THOMAS FURLONG
(1794–1827)

Roisin Dubh (1831)

Oh! My sweet little rose, cease to pine for the past,
For the friends that come eastward shall see thee at last;
They bring blessings—they bring favors which the past never knew,
To pour forth in gladness on my Roisin Dubh.

Long, long with my dearest, thro' strange scenes I've gone.
O'er mountains and broad valleys I have still toil'd on;

O'er the Erne I have sail'd as the rough gales blew,
While the harp pour'd its music for my Roisin Dubh.

Tho' wearied oh! My fair one! Do not slight my song,
For my heart dearly loves thee, and hath lov'd thee long;
In sadness and in sorrow I shall still be true,
And cling with wild fondness round my Roisin Dubh.

There's no flower that e'er bloom'd can my rose excel,
There's no tongue that e'er moved half my love can tell;
Had I strength, had I skill the wide world to subdue,
Oh! The queen of that wide world should be Roisin Dubh.

Had I power, oh! My lov'd one, but to plead thy right,
I should speak out in boldness for my heart's delight;
I would tell to all around me how my fondness grew,
And bid them bless the beauty of my Roisin Dubh.

The mountains, high and misty, thro' the moors must go,
The rivers shall run backward, and the lakes overflow;
And the wild waves of old ocean wear a crimson hue,
Ere the world sees the ruin of my Roisin Dubh.

Eileen a Roon (1831)

I'll love thee evermore,
Eileen a Roon!
I'll bless thee o'er and o'er,
Eileen a Roon!
Oh! For thy sake I'll tread,
Where the plains of Mayo spread;
My hope still fondly led,
Eileen a Roon!

Oh! How may I gain thee?
Eileen a Roon!
Shall feasting entertain thee?
Eileen a Roon!
I would range the world wide,

With love alone to guide,
To win thee for my bride,
Eileen a Roon!

Then wilt thou come away?
Eileen a Roon!
Oh! Wilt thou come or stay?
Eileen a Roon!
Oh yes! oh yes! with thee
I will wander far and free,
And thy only love shall be,
Eileen a Roon!

A hundred thousand welcomes,
Eileen a Roon!
A hundred thousand welcomes,
Eileen a Roon!
Oh! Welcome evermore,
With welcomes yet in store,
Till love and life are o'er,
Eileen a Roon!

The Spirit of Irish Song (1827)

Lov'd land of the Bards, and Saints! to me
There's nought so dear as thy minstrelsy;
Bright is Nature in every dress,
Rich in unborrow'd loveliness;
Winning is every shape she wears,
Winning she is in thine own sweet airs;
What to the spirit more cheering can be
Than the lay whose ling'ring notes recall
The thoughts of the holy-the fair-the free
Belov'd in life or deplor'd in their fall?
Fling, fling the forms of art aside,
Dull is the ear that these forms enthral;
Let the simple songs of our sires be tried,
They go to the heart—and the heart is all.

Give me the full responsive sigh,
The glowing cheek and the moisten'd eye;
Let these the minstrel's might attest,
And the vain and the idle—may share the rest.

JAMES CLARENCE MANGAN
(1803–1849)

To My Native Land (1832)

Awake! arise! shake off thy dreams!
  Thou art not what thou wert of yore:
Of all those rich, those dazzling beams,
  That once illum'd thine aspect o'er
Show me a solitary one
Whose glory is not quenched and gone.

The harp remaineth where it fell,*
  With mouldering frame and broken chord;
Around the song there hangs no spell—
  No laurel wreath entwines the sword;
And startlingly the footstep falls
Along thy dim and dreary halls.

When other men in future years,
  In wonder ask, how this could be?
Then answer only by thy tears,
  That ruin fell on thine and thee,
Because thyself wouldst have it so—
Because thou welcomedst the blow!

To stamp dishonour on thy brow
  Was not within the power of earth;
And art thou agonised, when now
  The hour that lost thee all thy worth
And turned thee to the thing thou art,
Rushes upon thy bleeding heart?

Weep, weep, degraded one—the deed,
    The desperate deed was all thine own:
Thou madest more than maniac speed
    To hurl thine honours from their throne.
Thine honours fell, and when they fell
The nations rang thy funeral knell.

Well may thy sons be seared in soul,
    Their groans be deep by night and day;
Till day and night forget to roll,
    Their noblest hopes shall mourn decay—
Their freshest flowers shall die by blight—
Their brightest suns shall set in night.

The stranger, as he treads thy sod,
    And views thy universal wreck,
May execrate the foot that trod
    Triumphant on a prostrate neck;
But what is that to thee? Thy woes
May hope in vain for pause or close.

Awake! arise! shake off thy dreams!
    'Tis idle all to talk of power,
And fame and glory—these are themes
    Befitting ill so dark an hour;
Till miracles be wrought for thee,
Nor fame, nor glory, shalt thou see.

Thou art forsaken by the earth,
    Which makes a by-word of thy name:
Nations, and thrones, and powers, whose birth
    As yet is not, shall rise to fame,
Shall flourish and may fall—but thou
Shalt linger as thou lingerest now.

And till all earthly powers shall wane,
    And Time's grey pillars, groaning, fall,
Thus shall it be, and still in vain
    Thou shalt essay to burst the thrall

Which binds, in fetters forged by fate,
The wreck and ruin of what once was great.

The Woman of Three Cows (1840)

(From the Irish)

O Woman of Three Cows, agragh!* don't let your tongue thus rattle!
O, don't be saucy, don't be stiff, because you may have cattle.
I have seen—and, here's my hand to you, I only say what's true—
A many a one with twice your stock not half so proud as you.

Good luck to you, don't scorn the poor, and don't be their despiser,
For worldly wealth soon melts away, and cheats the very miser,
And Death soon strips the proudest wreath from haughty human
    brows;
Then don't be stiff, and don't be proud, good Woman of Three
    Cows!

See where Momonia's* heroes lie, proud Owen More's descendants,
'Tis they that won the glorious name, and had the grand attendants!
If *they* were forced to bow to Fate, as every mortal bows,
Can *you* be proud, can *you* be stiff, my Woman of Three Cows!

The brave sons of the Lord of Clare,* they left the land to mourning;
*Movrone!** for they were banished, with no hope of their returning—
Who knows in what abodes of want those youths were driven to
    house?
Yet *you* can give yourself these airs, O Woman of Three Cows!

O, think of Donnell of the Ships,* the Chief whom nothing
    daunted—
See how he fell in distant Spain, unchronicled, unchanted!
He sleeps, the great O'Sullivan, where thunder cannot rouse—
Then ask yourself, should *you* be proud, good Woman of Three
    Cows!

O'Ruark, Maguire, those souls of fire,* whose names are shrined in
    story—

Think how their high achievements once made Erin's highest
    glory—
Yet now their bones lie mouldering under weeds and cypress
    boughs,
And so, for all your pride, will yours, O Woman of Three Cows!

The O'Carrolls,* also, famed when Fame was only for the boldest,
Rest in forgotten sepulchres with Erin's best and oldest;
Yet who so great as they of yore in battle or carouse?
Just think of that, and hide your head, good Woman of Three
    Cows!

Your neighbour's poor, and you, it seems, are big with vain ideas,
Because, *inagh!** you've got three cows—one more, I see, than *she*
    has.
That tongue of yours wags more at times than Charity allows,
But if you're strong, be merciful, great Woman of Three Cows!

The Summing Up

Now, there you go! You still, of course, keep up your scornful
    bearing,
And I'm too poor to hinder you; but, by the cloak I'm wearing,
If I had but *four* cows myself, even though you were my spouse,
I'd thwack you well to cure your pride, my Woman of Three Cows!

Lamentation of Mac Liag for Kincora (1841)

(From the Irish)

Oh, where Kincora! is Brian the Great?
And where is the beauty that once was thine?
Oh, where are the princes and nobles that sate
At the feast in thy halls, and drank the red wine?
              Where, oh, Kincora?

Oh, where, Kincora! are thy valorous lords?
Oh, whither, thou Hospitable! are they gone?

Oh, where are the Dalcassians* of the Golden Swords?
And where are the warriors Brian led on?
                    Where, oh, Kincora?

And where is Morogh,* the descendant of kings—
The defeater of a hundred—the daringly brave—
Who set but slight store by jewels and rings—
Who swam down the torrent and laughed at its wave?
                    Where, oh, Kincora?

And where is Donagh,* King Brian's worthy son?
And where is Conaing,* the Beautiful Chief?
And Kian,* and Corc?* Alas! they are gone—
They have left me this night alone with my grief,
                    Left me, Kincora!

And where are the chiefs with whom Brian went forth,
The ne'er vanquished son of Erin the Brave,*
The great King of Onaght,* renowned for his worth,
And the hosts of Baskinn,* from the western wave?
                    Where, oh, Kincora?

Oh, where is Duvlann* of the swift-footed Steeds?
And where is Kian, who was son of Molloy?
And where is King Lonergan,* the fame of whose deeds
In the red battle-field no time can destroy?
                    Where, oh, Kincora?

And where is that youth of majestic height,
The faith-keeping Prince of the Scots?*—Even he,
As wide as his fame was, as great as was his might,
Was tributary, oh, Kincora, to thee!
                    Thee, oh, Kincora!

They are gone, those heroes of royal birth,
Who plundered no churches, and broke no trust,
'Tis weary for me to be living on earth
When they, oh, Kincora, lie low in the dust!
                    Low, oh, Kincora!

Oh, never again will Princes appear,
To rival the Dalcassians of the Cleaving Swords!
I can never dream of meeting afar or anear,
In the east or the west, such heroes and lords!
     Never, Kincora!

Oh, dear are the images my memory calls up
Of Brian Boru!—how he never would miss
To give me at the banquet the first bright cup!
Ah! why did he heap on me honour like this?
     Why, oh, Kincora?

I am Mac Liag, and my home is on the Lake;
Thither often, to that palace whose beauty is fled
Came Brian to ask me, and I went for his sake
Oh, my grief! that I should live, and Brian be dead!
     Dead, oh, Kincora!

Kathaleen Ny-Houlahan (1841)

(*From the Irish*)

Long they pine in weary woe, the nobles of our land,
Long they wander to and fro, proscribed, alas! and banned;
Feastless, houseless, altarless, they bear the exile's brand,
 But their hope is in the coming-to of Kathaleen Ny-Houlahan!

Think her not a ghastly hag, too hideous to be seen,
Call her not unseemly names, our matchless Kathaleen;
Young she is, and fair she is, and would be crowned a queen,
 Were the king's son at home here with Kathaleen Ny-Houlahan!

Sweet and mild would look her face, O, none so sweet and mild,
Could she crush the foes by whom her beauty is reviled;
Woollen plaids would grace herself and robes of silk her child,
 If the king's son were living here with Kathaleen Ny-Houlahan!

Sore disgrace it is to see the Arbitress of thrones,
Vassal to a *Saxoneen** of cold and sapless bones!

Bitter anguish wrings our souls—with heavy sighs and groans
　　We wait the Young Deliverer* of Kathaleen Ny-Houlahan!

Let us pray to Him* who holds Life's issues in His hands—
Him who formed the mighty globe, with all its thousand lands;
Girding them with seas and mountains, rivers deep, and strands,
　　To cast a look of pity upon Kathaleen Ny-Houlahan!

He, who over sands and waves led Israël along—
He, who fed, with heavenly bread, that chosen tribe and throng—
He, who stood by Moses, when his foes were fierce and strong—
　　May He show forth His might in saving Kathaleen Ny-Houlahan.

Dark Rosaleen (1846)

(*From the Irish*)

O my Dark Rosaleen,
　　Do not sigh, do not weep!
The priests are on the ocean green,
　　They march along the Deep.
There's wine . . . from the royal Pope
　　Upon the ocean green;
And Spanish ale shall give you hope,*
　　My Dark Rosaleen!
　　My own Rosaleen!
Shall glad your heart, shall give you hope,
Shall give you health, and help, and hope,
　　My Dark Rosaleen.

Over hills and through dales,
　　Have I roamed for your sake;
All yesterday I sailed with sails
　　On river and on lake.
The Erne . . . at its highest flood*
　　I dashed across unseen,
For there was lightning in my blood,
　　My Dark Rosaleen!
　　My own Rosaleen!

Oh! there was lightning in my blood,
Red lightning lightened through my blood,
  My Dark Rosaleen!

All day long in unrest
  To and fro do I move,
The very soul within my breast
  Is wasted for you, love!
The heart . . . in my bosom faints
  To think of you, my Queen,
My life of life, my saint of saints,
  My Dark Rosaleen!
  My own Rosaleen!
To hear your sweet and sad complaints,
My life, my love, my saint of saints,
  My Dark Rosaleen!

Woe and pain, pain and woe,
  Are my lot night and noon,
To see your bright face clouded so,
  Like to the mournful moon.
But yet . . . will I rear your throne
  Again in golden sheen;
'Tis you shall reign, shall reign alone,
  My Dark Rosaleen!
  My own Rosaleen!
'Tis you shall have the golden throne,
'Tis you shall reign, and reign alone,
  My Dark Rosaleen!

Over dews, over sands
  Will I fly for your weal;
Your holy delicate white hands
  Shall girdle me with steel.
At home . . . in your emerald bowers,
  From morning's dawn till e'en,
You'll pray for me, my flower of flowers,
  My Dark Rosaleen!
  My fond Rosaleen!

You'll think of me through daylight's hours,
My virgin flower, my flower of flowers,
   My Dark Rosaleen!

I could scale the blue air,
   I could plough the high hills,
Oh, I could kneel all night in prayer,
   To heal your many ills!
And one . . . beamy smile from you
   Would float like light between
My toils and me, my own, my true,
   My Dark Rosaleen!
   My fond Rosaleen!
Would give me life and soul anew,
A second life, a soul anew,
   My Dark Rosaleen!

O! the Erne shall run red
   With redundance of blood,
The earth shall rock beneath our tread,
   And flames wrap hill and wood,
And gun-peal, and slogan cry,
   Wake many a glen serene,
Ere you shall fade, ere you shall die,
   My Dark Rosaleen!
   My own Rosaleen!
The Judgement Hour must first be nigh,
Ere you can fade, ere you can die,
   My Dark Rosaleen!

Roisin Dubh (Black-Haired Fair Rose) (1849)

Since last night's star, afar, afar
   Heaven saw my speed,
I seem'd to fly o'er mountains high,
   On magic steed,
I dashed though Erne!* the world may learn
   The cause from Love

For, light or sun shone on me none,
    But *Roisin Dubh*!

O, Roisin mine! droop not nor pine;
    Look not so dull!
The Pope from Rome hath sent thee home
    A pardon full;
The priests are near: O! never fear!
    From Heaven above
They come to thee—they come to free
    My *Roisin Dubh*!

Thee have I loved—for thee have roved
    O'er land and sea:
My heart was sore—it evermore
    Beat but for thee;
I could but weep—I could not sleep—
    I could not move;
For, night or day, I dreamt alway
    Of *Roisin Dubh*!

Through Munsters lands, by shores and strands,
    Far could I roam,
If I might get my loved one yet,
    And bring her home.
O, sweetest flower, that blooms in bower,
    Or dell, or grove,
Thou lovest me, and I love thee,
My *Roisin Dubh*!

The sea shall burn, the earth shall mourn,
    The skies rain blood—
The world shall rise in dread surprise
    And warful mood—
And hill and lake in Eirè shake,
    And hawk turn dove—
Ere you shall pine, ere you decline,
    My *Roisin Dubh*!

The Nameless One (1849)

Ballad

Roll forth, my song, like the rushing river,
    That sweeps along to the mighty sea;
God will inspire me while I deliver
        My soul of thee!

Tell thou the world, when my bones lie whitening
    Amid the last homes of youth and eld,*
That there was once one whose veins ran lightning
        No eye beheld.

Tell how his boyhood was one drear night-hour,
    How shone for *him*, through his griefs and gloom,
No star of all heaven sends to light our
        Path to the tomb.

Roll on, my song, and to after ages
    Tell how, disdaining all earth can give,
He would have taught men, from wisdom's pages,
        The way to live.

And tell how trampled, derided, hated,
    And worn by weakness, disease, and wrong,
He fled for shelter to God, who mated
        His soul with song—

With song which alway, sublime or vapid,
    Flowed like a rill in the morning beam,
Perchance not deep, but intense and rapid—
        A mountain stream.

Tell how this Nameless, condemned for years long
    To herd with demons from hell beneath,
Saw things that made him, with groans and tears, long
        For even death.

Go on to tell how, with genius wasted,
    Betrayed in friendship, befooled in love,
With spirit shipwrecked, and young hopes blasted,
        He still, still strove.

Till, spent with toil, dreeing* death for others,
    And some whose hands should have wrought for *him*
(If children live not for sires and mothers),
        His mind grew dim.

And he fell far through that pit abysmal
    The gulf and grave of Maginn and Burns,
And pawned his soul for the devil's dismal
        Stock of returns.

But yet redeemed it in days of darkness,
    And shapes and signs of the final wrath,
When death, in hideous and ghastly starkness,
        Stood on his path.

And tell how now, amid wreck and sorrow,
    And want, and sickness, and houseless nights,
He bides in calmness the silent morrow,
        That no ray lights.

And lives he still, then? Yes! Old and hoary
    At thirty-nine, from despair and woe,
He lives enduring what future story
        Will never know.

Him grant a grave to, ye pitying noble,
    Deep in your bosoms! There let him dwell!
He, too, had tears for all souls in trouble,
        Here and in hell.

FRANCIS SYLVESTER MAHONY
(1804–1866)

The Bells of Shandon (1836)

'Sabbata pango,
Funera plango,
Solemnia clango'

Inscrip. on an old Bell*

With deep affection
And recollection
I often think of
   Those Shandon bells,
Whose sounds so wild would
In the days of childhood
Fling round my cradle
   Their magic spells.
On this I ponder
Where'er I wander,
And thus grow fonder
   Sweet Cork, of thee;
With thy bells of Shandon,
That sound so grand on
The pleasant waters
   Of the river Lee.

I've heard bells chiming
Full many a clime in,
Tolling sublime in
   Cathedral shrine,
While at a glib rate
Brass tongues would vibrate—
But all their music
   Spoke naught like thine;
For memory dwelling
On each proud swelling
Of the belfry knelling

Its bold notes free,
Made the bells of Shandon
Sound far more grand on
The pleasant waters
    Of the river Lee.

I've heard bells tolling
Old 'Adrian's Mole' in,
Their thunder rolling
    From the Vatican,
And cymbals glorious
Swinging uproarious
In the gorgeous turrets
    Of Notre Dame;
But thy sounds were sweeter
Than the dome of Peter
Flings o'er the Tiber,
    Pealing solemnly;—
O! the bells of Shandon
Sound far more grand on
The pleasant waters
    Of the river Lee.

There's a bell in Moscow,
While on tower and kiosk, O!
In Saint Sophia
    The Turkman gets,
And loud in air
Calls men to prayer
From the tapering summit
    Of tall minarets.
Such empty phantom
I freely grant them;
But there is an anthem
    More dear to me,—
'Tis the bells of Shandon
That sound so grand on
The pleasant waters
    Of the river Lee.

Samuel Ferguson

SAMUEL FERGUSON
(1810–1886)

Lament for the Death of Thomas Davis (1847)

I walked through Ballinderry in the springtime,
    When the bud was on the tree,
And I said, in every fresh-ploughed field beholding
    The sowers striding free,
Scattering broadcast forth the corn in golden plenty,
    On the quick, seed-clasping soil,
'Even such this day, among the fresh-stirred hearts of Erin,
    Thomas Davis, is thy toil!'

I sat by Ballyshannon in the summer,
    And saw the salmon leap,
And I said, as I beheld the gallant creatures
    Spring glittering from the deep,
Through the spray and through the prone heaps striving onward
    To the calm clear streams above,
'So seekest thou thy native founts of freedom, Thomas Davis,
    In thy brightness of strength and love!'

I stood in Derrybawn in the autumn,
    I heard the eagle call,
With a clangorous cry of wrath and lamentation
    That filled the wide mountain hall,
O'er the bare, deserted place of his plundered eyrie,
    And I said, as he screamed and soared,
'So callest thou, thou wrathful-soaring Thomas Davis,
    For a nation's rights restored.'

And Alas! to think but now that thou art lying,
    Dear Davis, dead at thy mother's knee,
And I, no mother near, on my own sick-bed,
    That face on earth shall never see;
I may lie and try to feel that I am dreaming,
    I may lie and try to say, 'Thy Will be done'—

But a hundred such as I will never comfort Erin
    For the loss of that noble son.

Young husbandman of Erin's fruitful seed-time,
    In the fresh track of danger's plough!
Who will walk the heavy, toilsome, perilous furrow,
    Girt with freedom's seed-sheets now?
Who will vanish with the wholesome crop of knowledge,
    The flaunting weed and the bitter thorn,
Now that thou thyself art but a seed for hopeful planting
    Against the resurrection morn?

Young salmon of the flood-time of freedom
    That swells round Erin's shore,
Thou wilt leap against their loud, oppressive torrent
    Of bigotry and hate no more!
Drawn downward by their prone material instinct,
    Let them thunder on their rocks, and foam;
Thou hast leaped, aspiring soul, to founts beyond their raging,
    Where troubled waters never come.

But I grieve not, eagle of the empty eyrie,
    That thy wrathful cry is still,
And that the songs alone of peaceful mourners
    Are heard to-day on Erin's hill.
Better far if brothers' war be destined for us—
    God avert that horrid day, I pray!—
That ere our hands be stained with slaughter fratricidal,
    Thy warm heart should be cold in clay.

But my trust is strong in God who made us brothers,
    That He will not suffer these right hands,
Which thou hast joined in holier rites than wedlock,
    To draw opposing brands.
O many a tuneful tongue that thou madest vocal,
    Would lie cold and silent then,
And songless long once more should often-widowed Erin
    Mourn the loss of her brave young men.

O brave young men, my love, my pride, my promise,
    'Tis on you my hopes are set,
In manliness, in kindliness, in justice,
    To make Erin a nation yet;
Self-respecting, self-relying, self-advancing,
    In union or in severance, free and strong,
And if God grant this, then, under God, to Thomas Davis,
    Let the greater praise belong!

Cashel of Munster (1867)

(From the Irish)

I'd wed you without herds, without money, or rich array,
And I'd wed you on a dewy morning at day-dawn grey;
My bitter woe it is, love, that we are not far away
In Cashel town, though the bare deal board were our marriage bed
    this day!

Oh, fair maid, remember the green hillside,
Remember how I hunted about the valleys wide;
Time now has worn me; my locks are turned to grey,
The year is scarce and I am poor, but send me not, love, away!

Oh, deem not my blood is of base strain, my girl,
Oh, deem not my birth was as the birth of the churl;
Marry me, and prove me, and say soon you will,
That noble blood is written on my right side still!

My purse holds no red gold, no coin of the silver white,
No herds are mine to drive through the long twilight!
But the pretty girl that would take me, all bare though I be and lone,
Oh, I'd take her with me kindly to the county Tyrone.

Oh, my girl, I can see 'tis in trouble you are,
And, oh, my girl, I see 'tis your people's reproach you bear:
'I am a girl in trouble for his sake with whom I fly,
And, oh, may no other maiden know such reproach as I!'

The Coolun (1867)

(From the Irish)

O had you seen the Coolun
    Walking down by the cuckoo's street,
With the dew of the meadow shining
    On her milk-white twinkling feet!
My love she is, and my coleen oge,*
    And she dwells in Bal'nagar;
And she bears the palm of beauty bright
    From the fairest that in Erin are.

In Bal'nagar is the Coolun,
    Like the berry on the bough her cheek;
Bright beauty dwells for ever
    On her fair neck and ringlets sleek;
Oh, sweeter is her mouth's soft music
    Than the lark or thrush at dawn,
Or the blackbird in the greenwood singing
    Farewell to the setting sun.

Rise up, my boy! make ready
    My horse, for I forth would ride,
To follow the modest damsel,
    Where she walks on the green hillside:
For ever since our youth were we plighted
    In faith, troth, and wedlock true—
She is sweeter to me nine times over,
    Than organ or cuckoo!

For, ever since my Childhood
    I've loved the fair and darling child;
But our people came between us,
    And with lucre our pure love defiled:
Ah, my woe it is, and my bitter pain,
    And I weep it night and day,
That the coleen bawn* of my early love
    Is torn from my heart away.

Sweetheart and faithful treasure,
  Be constant still, and true;
Nor for want of herds and houses
  Leave one who would ne'er leave you.
I'll pledge you the blessèd Bible,
  Without and eke within,
That the faithful God will provide for us,
  Without thanks to kith or kin.

Oh, love, do you remember
  When we lay all night alone,
Beneath the ash in the winter storm,
  When the oak wood round did groan?
No shelter then from the blast had we,
  The bitter blast or sleet,
But your gown to wrap about our heads,
  And my coat around our feet.

Dear Dark Head (1867)

(*From the Irish*)

Put your head, darling, darling, darling,
  Your darling black head my heart above;
Oh, mouth of honey, with the thyme for fragrance,
  Who, with heart in breast, could deny you love?

Oh, many and many a young girl for me is pining,
  Letting her locks of gold to the cold wind free,
For me, the foremost of our gay young fellows;
  But I'd leave a hundred, pure love, for thee!

Then put your head, darling, darling, darling,
  Your darling black head my heart above;
Oh, mouth of honey, with the thyme for fragrance,
  Who, with heart in breast, could deny you love?

THOMAS DAVIS
(1814–1845)

A Nation Once Again (1845)

When boyhood's fire was in my blood,
   I read of ancient freemen,
For Greece and Rome who bravely stood,
   Three Hundred men and Three men.
And then I prayed I yet might see
   Our fetters rent in twain,
And Ireland, long a province, be
   A Nation once again.

And, from that time, through wildest woe,
   That hope has shone, a far light;
Nor could love's brightest summer glow
   Outshine that solemn starlight:
It seemed to watch above my head
   In forum, field, and fane,
Its angel voice sang round my bed,
   'A Nation once again'.

It whispered, too, that 'freedom's ark
   And service high and holy,
Would be profaned by feelings dark,
   And passions vain or lowly;
For freedom comes from God's right hand,
   And needs a godly train;
And righteous men must make our land
   A Nation once again.'

So, as I grew from boy to man,
   I bent me to that bidding—
My spirit of each selfish plan
   And cruel passion ridding;
For, thus I hoped some day to aid—
   Oh! can such hope be vain?

When my dear country shall be made
~~A Nation once again.~~

The West's Asleep (1845)

When all beside a vigil keep,
The West's asleep, the West's asleep—
Alas! and well may Erin weep,
When Connaught lies in slumber deep.
There lake and plain smile fair and free,
'Mid rocks—their guardian chivalry—
Sing oh! let man learn liberty
From crashing wind and lashing sea.

That chainless wave and lovely land
Freedom and Nationhood demand—
Be sure, the great God never plann'd,
For slumbering slaves, a home so grand.
And, long, a brave and haughty race
Honoured and sentinelled the place—
Sing oh! not even their sons' disgrace
Can quite destroy their glory's trace.

For often, in O'Connor's van,
To triumph dash'd each Connaught clan—
And fleet as deer the Normans ran
Through Coirrslabh Pass and Ard Rathain.*
And later times saw deeds as brave;
And glory guards Clanricarde's grave—
Sing, oh! they died their land to save,
At Aughrim's slopes and Shannon's wave.*

And if, when all a vigil keep,
The West's asleep, the West's asleep—
Alas! and well may Erin weep,
That Connaught lies in slumber deep.
But—hark!—some voice like thunder spake:
'The West's awake, the West's awake'—.

Sing, oh! hurra! let England quake,
We'll watch till death for Erin's sake!

AUBREY DE VERE
(1814–1902)

The Little Black Rose (1861)

The Little Black Rose shall be red at last;
  What made it black but the March wind dry,
And the tear of the widow that fell on it fast?
  It shall redden the hills when June is nigh.

The Silk of the Kine* shall rest at last;
  What drove her forth but the dragon-fly?
In the golden vale she shall feed full fast,
  With her mild gold horn and her slow, dark eye.

The wounded wood-dove lies dead at last!
  The pine long bleeding, it shall not die!
This song is secret. Mine ear it passed
  In a wind o'er the plains at Athenry.*

Florence MacCarthy's Farewell to His English Love (1855)

I

England's fair child, Evangeline!
In that far-distant land of mine
  There stands a Yew-tree among tombs!
For ages there that tree hath stood,
A black pall dash'd with drops of blood;
  O'er all my world it breathes its glooms.

II

Evangeline! Evangeline!
Because my Yew-tree is not thine,
  Because thy Gods on mine wage war,

Farewell! Back fall the gates of brass;
The exile to his own must pass:
   I seek the land of tombs once more.

JOHN KELLS INGRAM (1823–1907)

The Memory of the Dead (1843)

Who fears to speak of Ninety-eight?
Who blushes at the name?
When cowards mock the patriot's fate,
Who hangs his head for shame?
He's all a knave, or half a slave,
Who slights his country thus;
But a true man, like you, man,
Will fill your glass with us.

We drink the memory of the brave,
The faithful and the few;
Some lie far off beyond the wave,
Some sleep in Ireland, too;
All, all are gone; but still lives on
The fame of those who died;
All true men, like you, men,
Remember them with pride.

Some on the shores of distant lands
Their weary hearts have laid,
And by the stranger's heedless hands
Their lonely graves were made;
But though their clay be far away
Beyond the Atlantic foam,
In true men, like you, men,
Their spirit's still at home.

The dust of some is Irish earth,
Among their own they rest,
And the same land that gave them birth
Has caught them to her breast;

And we will pray that from their clay
Full many a race may start
Of true men, like you, men,
To act as brave a part.

They rose in dark and evil days
To right their native land;
They kindled here a living blaze
That nothing shall withstand.
Alas! that might can vanquish right—
They fell and passed away;
But true men, like you, men,
Are plenty here to-day.

Then here's their memory—may it be
For us a guiding light,
To cheer our strife for liberty,
And teach us to unite—
Through good and ill, be Ireland's still,
Though sad as theirs your fate,
And true men be you, men,
Like those of Ninety-eight.

WILLIAM ALLINGHAM
(1824–1889)

The Fairies (1849)

(*A Child's Song*)

Up the airy mountain,
    Down the rushy glen,
We daren't go a-hunting
    For fear of little men;
Wee folk, good folk,
    Trooping all together;
Green jacket, red cap,
    And white owl's feather!

Down along the rocky shore
  Some make their home—
They live on crispy pancakes
  Of yellow tide-foam;
Some in the reeds
  Of the black mountain lake,
With frogs for their watch-dogs,
  All night awake.

High on the hill-top
  The old King sits;
He is now so old and grey
  He's nigh lost his wits.
With a bridge of white mist
  Columbkill he crosses,
On his stately journeys
  From Slieveleague to Rosses;
Or going up with music
  On cold starry nights,
To sup with the Queen
  Of the gay Northern Lights.

They stole little Bridget
  For seven years long;
When she came down again
  Her friends were all gone.
They took her lightly back,
  Between the night and morrow;
They thought that she was fast asleep,
  But she was dead with sorrow.
They have kept her ever since
  Deep within the lake,
On a bed of flag-leaves,
  Watching till she wake.

By the craggy hill-side,
  Through the mosses bare,
They have planted thorn-trees
  For pleasure here and there.

Is any man so daring
   As dig one up in spite,
He shall find their sharpest thorns
   In his bed at night.

Up the airy mountain,
   Down the rushy glen,
We daren't go a-hunting
   For fear of little men;
Wee folk, good folk,
   Trooping all together;
Green jacket, red cap,
   And white owl's feather!

The Maids of Elfin-Mere (1850)

'Twas when the spinning-room was here.
Came Three Damsels clothed in white,
With their spindles every night;
Two and one, and Three fair Maidens,
Spinning to a pulsing cadence,
Singing songs of Elfin-Mere;
Till the eleventh hour was toll'd,
Then departed through the wold.
   Years ago, and years ago;
   And the tall reeds sigh as the wind doth blow.

Three white Lilies, calm and clear,
And they were loved by every one;
Most of all, the Pastor's Son,
Listening to their gentle singing,
Felt his heart go from him, clinging
Round these Maids of Elfin-Mere;
Sued each night to make them stay,
Sadden'd when they went away.
   Years ago, and years ago;
   And the tall reeds sigh as the wind doth blow.

Hands that shook with love and fear
Dared put back the village clock,—
Flew the spindle, turn'd the rock,
Flow'd the song with subtle rounding,
Till the false 'eleven' was sounding;
Then these Maids of Elfin-Mere
Swiftly, softly, left the room,
Like three doves on snowy plume.
   Years ago, and years ago;
   And the tall reeds sigh as the wind doth blow.

One that night who wander'd near
Heard lamentings by the shore,
Saw at dawn three stains of gore
In the waters fade and dwindle.
Nevermore with song and spindle
Saw we Maids of Elfin-Mere.
The Pastor's Son did pine and die;
Because true love should never lie.
   Years ago, and years ago;
   And the tall reeds sigh as the wind doth blow.

A Dream (1850)

I heard the dogs howl in the moonlight night;
I went to the window to see the sight;
All the Dead that ever I knew
Going one by one and two by two.

On they pass'd, and on they pass'd;
Townsfellows all, from first to last;
Born in the moonlight of the lane,
Quench'd in the heavy shadow again.

Schoolmates, marching as when we play'd
At soldiers once—but now more staid;
Those were the strangest sight to me
Who were drown'd, I knew, in the awful sea.

Straight and handsome folk; bent and weak too;
Some that I loved, and gasp'd to speak to;
Some but a day in their churchyard bed;
Some that I had not known were dead.

A long, long crowd—where each seem'd lonely,
Yet of them all there was one, one only,
Raised a head or look'd my way;
She linger'd a moment,—she might not stay.

How long since I saw that fair pale face!
Ah! Mother dear! might I only place
My head on thy breast, a moment to rest,
While thy hand on my tearful cheek were prest.

On, on a moving bridge they made
Across the moon-stream from shade to shade,
Young and old, women and men;
Many long forgot, but remember'd then.

And first there came a bitter laughter;
A sound of tears the moment after;
And then a music so lofty and gay,
That every morning, day by day,
I strive to recall it if I may.

The Winding Banks of Erne (1865)

(A Local Ballad)

Adieu to Ballyshanny! where I was bred and born;
Go where I may, I'll think of you, as sure as night and morn,
The kindly spot, the friendly town, where every one
   is known,
And not a face in all the place but partly seems my own;
There's not a house or window, there's not a field or hill,
But, east or west, in foreign lands, I'll recollect them still.

I leave my warm heart with you, though my back I'm forced to
    turn—
So adieu to Ballyshanny, and the winding banks of Erne!

No more on pleasant evenings we'll saunter down the Mall,
When the trout is rising to the fly, the salmon to the fall.
The boat comes straining on her net, and heavily she creeps,
Cast off, cast off!—she feels the oars, and to her berth she sweeps;
Now fore and aft keep hauling, and gathering up the clew,
Till a silver wave of salmon rolls in among the crew.
Then they may sit, with pipes a-lit, and many a joke and
    'yarn';—
Adieu to Ballyshanny, and the winding banks of Erne!

The music of the waterfall, the mirror of the tide,
When all the green-hill'd harbour is full from side to side—
From Portnasun to Bulliebawns, and round the Abbey Bay,
From rocky Inis Saimer to Coolnargit sandhills gray
While far upon the southern line, to guard it like a wall,
The Leitrim mountains clothed in blue gaze calmly over all,
And watch the ship sail up or down, the red flag at her stern;—
Adieu to these, adieu to all the winding banks of Erne!

Farewell to you, Kildoney lads, and them that pull an oar,
A lug-sail set, or haul a net, from the Point to Mullaghmore;
From Killybegs to bold Slieve-League, that ocean mountain steep,
Six hundred yards in air aloft, six hundred in the deep;
From Dooran to the Fairy Bridge, and round by Tullen strand,
Level and long, and white with waves, where gull and curlew stand;
Head out to sea when on your lee the breakers you discern!—
Adieu to all the billowy coast, and winding banks of Erne!

Farewell Coolmore,—Bundoran! and your summer crowds that
    run
From inland homes to see with joy th' Atlantic-setting sun;
To breathe the buoyant salted air, and sport among the waves;
To gather shells on sandy beach, and tempt the gloomy caves;
To watch the flowing, ebbing tide, the boats, the crabs, the fish;
Young men and maids to meet and smile, and form a tender wish;

The sick and old in search of health, for all things have their turn—
And I must quit my native shore, and the winding banks of Erne!

Farewell to every white cascade from the Harbour to Belleek,
And every pool where fins may rest, and ivy-shaded creek;
The sloping fields, the lofty rocks, where ash and holly grow,
The one split yew-tree gazing on the curving flood below;
The Lough, that winds through islands under Turaw mountain
    green;
And Castle Caldwell's stretching woods, with tranquil bays between;
And Breesie Hill, and many a pond among the heath and fern,—
For I must say adieu—adieu to the winding banks of Erne!

The thrush will call through Camlin groves the live-long summer
    day;
The waters run by mossy cliff, and banks with wild flowers gay;
The girls will bring their work and sing beneath a twisted thorn,
Or stray with sweethearts down the path among the growing corn;
Along the river side they go, where I have often been,—
O, never shall I see again the days that I have seen!
A thousand chances are to one I never may return,—
Adieu to Ballyshanny, and the winding banks of Erne!

Adieu to evening dances, when merry neighbours meet,
And the fiddle says to boys and girls, 'Get up and shake your feet!'
To 'shanachus'* and wise old talk of Erin's days gone by—
Who trench'd the rath* on such a hill, and where the bones may lie
Of saint, or king, or warrior chief; with tales of fairy power,
And tender ditties sweetly sung to pass the twilight hour.
The mournful song of exile is now for me to learn—
Adieu, my dear companions on the winding banks of Erne!

Now measure from the Commons down to each end of the Purt,
Round the Abbey, Moy, and Knather,—I wish no one any hurt;
The Main Street, Back Street, College Lane, the Mall, and
    Portnasun,
If any foes of mine are there, I pardon every one.
I hope that man and womankind will do the same by me;
For my heart is sore and heavy at voyaging the sea.

My loving friends I'll bear in mind, and often fondly turn
To think of Ballyshanny, and the winding banks of Erne.

If ever I'm a money'd man, I mean, please God, to cast
My golden anchor in the place where youthful years were
    pass'd;
Though heads that now are black and brown must meanwhile gather
    gray,
New faces rise by every hearth, and old ones drop away—
Yet dearer still that Irish hill than all the world beside;
It's home, sweet home, where'er I roam, through lands and waters
    wide.
And if the Lord allows me, I surely will return
To my native Ballyshanny, and the winding banks of Erne.

from *Laurence Bloomfield in Ireland* (1864)

In early morning twilight, raw and chill,
Damp vapours brooding on the barren hill,
Through miles of mire in steady grave array
Threescore well-arm'd police pursue their way;
Each tall and bearded man a rifle swings,
And under each greatcoat a bayonet clings;
The Sheriff on his sturdy cob astride
Talks with the chief, who marches by their side,
And, creeping on behind them, Paudeen Dhu
Pretends his needful duty much to rue.
Six big-boned labourers, clad in common frieze,
Walk in the midst, the Sheriff's staunch allies;
Six crowbar men, from distant county brought,—
Orange, and glorying in their work, 'tis thought,
But wrongly,—churls of Catholics are they,
And merely hired at half-a-crown a day.

The Hamlet clustering on its hill is seen,
A score of petty homesteads, dark and mean;
Poor always, not despairing until now;
Long used, as well as poverty knows how,

With life's oppressive trifles to contend.
This day will bring its history to an end.
Moveless and grim against the cottage walls
Lean a few silent men: but someone calls
Far off; and then a child 'without a stitch'
Runs out of doors, flies back with piercing screech,
And soon from house to house is heard the cry
Of female sorrow, swelling loud and high,
Which makes the men blaspheme between their teeth.
Meanwhile, o'er fence and watery field beneath,
The little army moves through drizzling rain;
A 'Crowbar' leads the Sheriff's nag; the lane
Is enter'd, and their plashing tramp draws near:
One instant, outcry holds its breath to hear;
'Halt!'—at the doors they form in double line,
And ranks of polish'd rifles wetly shine.

The Sheriff's painful duty must be done;
He begs for quiet—and the work's begun.
The strong stand ready; now appear the rest,
Girl, matron, grandsire, baby on the breast,
And Rosy's thin face on a pallet borne;
A motley concourse, feeble and forlorn.
One old man, tears upon his wrinkled cheek,
Stands trembling on a threshold, tries to speak,
But, in defect of any word for this,
Mutely upon the doorpost prints a kiss,
Then passes out for ever. Through the crowd
The children run bewilder'd, wailing loud;
Where needed most, the men combine their aid;
And, last of all, is Oona forth convey'd,
Reclined in her accustom'd strawen chair,
Her aged eyelids closed, her thick white hair
Escaping from her cap; she feels the chill,
Looks round and murmurs, then again is still.

Now bring the remnants of each household fire.
On the wet ground the hissing coals expire;
And Paudeen Dhu, with meekly dismal face,
Receives the full possession of the place.

Whereon the Sheriff, 'We have legal hold.
Return to shelter with the sick and old.
Time shall be given; and there are carts below
If any to the workhouse choose to go.'
A young man makes him answer, grave and clear,
'We're thankful to you! but there's no one here
Goin' back into them houses: do your part.
Nor we won't trouble Pigot's horse and cart.'
At which name, rushing into th' open space,
A woman flings her hood from off her face,
Falls on her knees upon the miry ground,
Lifts hands and eyes, and voice of thrilling sound,—
'Vengeance of God Almighty fall on you,
James Pigot!—may the poor man's curse pursue,
The widow's and the orphan's curse, I pray,
Hang heavy round you at your dying day!'
Breathless and fix'd one moment stands the crowd
To hear this malediction fierce and loud.

Meanwhile (our neighbour Neal is busy there)
On steady poles be lifted Oona's chair,
Well-heap'd with borrow'd mantles; gently bear
The sick girl in her litter, bed and all;
Whilst others hug the children weak and small
In careful arms, or hoist them pick-a-back;
And, 'midst the unrelenting clink and thwack
Of iron bar on stone, let creep away
The sad procession from that hill-side grey,
Through the slow-falling rain. In three hours more
You find, where Ballytullagh stood before,
Mere shatter'd walls, and doors with useless latch,
And firesides buried under fallen thatch.

5. POPULAR SONGS AND BALLADS

Boulavogue (1898)

At Boulavogue, as the sun was setting
  O'er the green May meadows of Shelmalier,
A rebel band set the heather blazing,
  And brought the neighbours from far and near.
Then Father Murphy, of old Kilcormack,
  Spurred up the rocks with a warring cry—
'Arm! Arm!' he cried, 'for I've come to lead you—
  Now priest and people must fight or die!'

He led us on 'gainst the coming soldiers,
  And the cowardly Yeomen we put to flight;
Down at the Harrow, the Boys of Wexford
  Showed Bookey's regiment how men could fight!
Look out for hirelings, King George of England,
  Search every kingdom that breeds a slave!
For Father Murphy, of the County Wexford,
  Sweeps o'er the earth like a mighty wave!

We took Camolin and Enniscorthy,
  And Wexford storming, drove out our foes;
'Twas at Slieve Kiltha our pikes were reeking
  With the crimson stream of the beaten Yeos.
At Tubberneering and Ballyellis
  Full many a Hessian* lay in his gore!
Ah, Father Murphy, had aid come over,
  A green flag floated from shore to shore!

At Vinegar Hill, o'er the pleasant Slaney,
  Our heroes vainly stood back to back,
And the Yeos at Tullow took Father Murphy,
  And burned his body upon the rack.

God give you glory, brave Father Murphy,
  And open heaven to all your men;
The cause that called you may call tomorrow
  In another war for the Green again.

The Shan Van Vocht (1842)

Oh! the French are on the sea,
  Says the *Shan Van vocht*;
The French are on the sea,
  Says the *Shan Van vocht*;
Oh! the French are in the bay,
They'll be here without delay,
And the Orange* will decay,
  Says the *Shan Van vocht*.

Chorus

Oh! the French are in the bay,
They'll be here by break of day,
And the Orange will decay,
  Says the *Shan Van vocht*.

And where will they have their camp?
  Says the *Shan Van vocht*;
Where will they have their camp?
  Says the *Shan Van vocht*;
On the Currach of Kildare,*
The boys they will be there
With their pikes in good repair,
  Says the *Shan Van vocht*.

To the Currach of Kildare
The boys they will repair,
And Lord Edward* will be there,
  Says the *Shan Van vocht*.

Then what will the yeomen do?
  Says the *Shan Van vocht*;

What *will* the yeomen do?
  Says the *Shan Van vocht*;
What *should* the yeomen do,
But throw off the red and blue,
And swear that they'll be true
    To the *Shan Van vocht*.

What *should* the yeomen do
But throw off the red and blue,
And swear that they'll be true
    To the *Shan Van vocht*.

And what colour will they wear?
  Says the *Shan Van vocht*;
What colour will they wear?
  Says the *Shan Van vocht*;
What colour should be seen
Where our fathers' homes have been,
But their own immortal Green?
  Says the *Shan Van vocht*.

What colour should be seen
Where our fathers' homes have been,
But their own immortal Green?
  Says the *Shan Van vocht*.

And will Ireland then be free?
  Says the *Shan Van vocht*;
Will Ireland then be free?
  Says the *Shan Van vocht*;
Yes! Ireland SHALL be free,
From the centre to the sea;
Then hurra for Liberty!
  Says the *Shan Van vocht*.

Yes! Ireland SHALL be free,
From the centre to the sea;
Then hurra for Liberty!
  Says the *Shan Van vocht*.

The Wearin' o' the Green (c.1798)

Oh, Paddy dear! and did ye hear the news that's goin' round?
The shamrock is forbid by law to grow on Irish ground!
No more St Patrick's day we'll keep; his colour can't be seen,
For there's a cruel law ag'in' the Wearin' o' the Green!

I met with Napper Tandy,* and he took me by the hand,
And he said, 'How's poor ould Ireland, and how does she stand?'
'She's the most distressful country that ever yet was seen,
For they're hanging men and women for the Wearin' o' the Green.'

An' if the colour we must wear is England's cruel red,
Let it remind us of the blood that Ireland has shed;
Then pull the shamrock from your hat, and throw it on the sod,
An' never fear, 'twill take root there, though under foot 'tis trod.

When law can stop the blades of grass from growin' as they grow,
An' when the leaves in summer time their colour dare not show,
Then I will change the colour, too, I wear in my caubeen;*
But till that day, plaise God, I'll stick to the Wearin' o' the Green.

The Croppy Boy (c.1798)

It was early, early in the spring,
The birds did whistle and sweetly sing,
Changing their notes from tree to tree
And the song they sang was 'Old Ireland Free'.

It was early, early in the night,
The Yeoman cavalry gave me a fright,
The Yeoman cavalry was my downfall
And I was taken by Lord Cornwall.

It was in the coach house that I was laid
And in the parlour that I was tried.
My sentence passed and my courage low
As to Duncannon I was forced to go.

As I was going up Wexford Street
My own first cousin I chanced to meet.
My own first cousin did me betray
And for one bare guinea swore my life away.

As I was passing my father's door
My brother William stood in the door.
My aged father stood there before
And my own dear mother her hair she tore.

As I was going up Wexford Hill
Oh who would blame me to cry my fill?
I looked behind and I looked before
And my own dear mother I shall ne'er see more.

As I was standing on the scaffold high
My own dear father was standing nigh.
My own dear father did me deny
And the name he gave me was 'The Croppy Boy'.

It was in Duncannon this young man died
And in Duncannon his body was laid.
Now all good people that do pass by
O spare a tear for 'The Croppy Boy'.

The Rising of the Moon (1866)

Tell me, tell me, Shawn O'Farrell,
    Why it is you hurry so?
Hush *ma bouchal*,* hush and listen,
    And his cheeks were in a glow.
I bear orders from the captain,
    Get you ready quick and soon,
For our pikes must be together
    By the rising of the moon.

Tell me, tell me, Shawn O'Farrell,
    Where the gathering is to be.

At the old spot by the river
   That's well known to you and me.
One word more, our signal token,
   Whistle up the marching tune,
Hurrah, my boys, for Ireland's freedom,
   By the rising of the moon.

Down by the lonely river,
   A dark mass of men were seen,
Far above the starry banner
   Hung our own immortal green.
Death to every foe and traitor,
   Forward on the marching tune,
And a million pikes were shining
   By the rising of the moon.

Out of every mud wall cabin
   Eyes were watching all the night,
Many a manly breast was throbbing
   For the blessed morning light.
Murmurs passed along the valley
   Like the banshee's lonely croon,
And a million pikes were shining
   By the rising of the moon.

Well they fought for poor old Ireland,
   And bitter was their fate,
What a feeling of pride and sorrow
   Fills the name of Ninety-Eight.
But yet we have in poor old Ireland
   Hearts that beat as firm and true,
We will follow in their footsteps
   By the rising of the moon.

Granuaile (*c.* 1798)

All through the north as I walked forth to view the shamrock plain
I stood a while where nature smiled amid the rocks and streams

On a matron mild I fixed my eyes beneath a fertile vale
As she sang her song it was on the wrongs of poor old Granuaile.

Her head was bare and her grey hair over her eyes hung down
Her waist and neck, her hands and feet, with iron chains were bound
Her pensive strain and plaintive wail mingled with the evening gale
And the song she sung with mournful tongue was Poor Old
    Granuaile.

The gown she wore was stained with gore all by a ruffian band
Her lips so sweet that monarchs kissed are now grown pale and wan
The tears of grief fell from her eyes each tear as large as hail
None could express the deep distress of poor old Granuaile.

On her harp she leaned and thus exclaimed My royal Brian* is gone
Who in his day did drive away the tyrants every one
On Clontarf's plains against the Danes his faction did prepare
Brave Brian Boru cut their lines in two and freed old Granuaile.

But now, alas, I must confess, avengers I have none
There's no brave Lord to wave his sword in my defence—not one
My enemies just when they please with blows they do assail
The flesh they tore clean off the bones of poor old Granuaile.

Six hundred years the briny tears have flowed down from my eyes
I curse the day that Henry made of me proud Albion's prize
From that day down with chains I'm bound no wonder I look pale
The blood they drained from every vein of poor old Granuaile.

There was a lord came from the south he wore a laurel crown
Saying 'Grania dear, be of good cheer, no longer you'll be bound
I am the man they call great Dan, who never yet did fail
I have got the bill for to fulfil your wishes Granuaile.'

With blood besmeared and bathed in tears her harp she sweetly
    strung
And oh the change, her mournful air from one last chord she wrung
Her voice so clear fell on my ear, at length my strength did fail
I went away and thus did say, 'God help you, Granuaile'.

PART TWO
WRITINGS 1890–1939

1. NATIONALIST WRITINGS AND THE EASTER RISING

MAUD GONNE
(1866–1953)

The Famine Queen (1900)

'The Queen's visit to Ireland is in no way political,' proclaims the Lord Lieutenant, and the English ministers. 'The Queen's visit has no political signification, and the Irish nation must receive her Majesty with the generous hospitality for which it is celebrated,' hastens to repeat Mr John Redmond, and our servile Irish members whose nationality has been corrupted by a too lengthy sojourn in the enemy's country.

'The Queen's visit to Ireland has nothing at all to do with politics,' cries the fishmonger, Pile, whose ambitious soul is not satisfied by the position of Lord Mayor and who hankers after an English title.

'Let us to our knees, and present the keys of the city to her Most Gracious Majesty, and compose an address in her honour.'

'Nothing political! nothing political! Let us present an address to this virtuous lady,' echo 30 town councillors, who when they sought the votes of the Dublin people called themselves Irishmen and Nationalists, but who are overcome by royal glamour. Poor citizens of Dublin! your thoughtlessness in giving your votes to these miserable creatures will cost you dear. It has already cost the arrests of sixteen good and true men, and many broken heads and bruised limbs from police batons, for you have realised—if somewhat late—the responsibility of Ireland's capital, and, aghast at the sight of the men elected by you betraying and dishonouring Ireland, you have, with a courage which makes us all proud of you, raised a protest, and cried aloud, 'The visit of the Queen of England is a political action, and if we accord her a welcome we shall stand shamed before the nations. The world will no longer believe in the sincerity of our demand for National Freedom!'

And in truth, for Victoria, in the decrepitude of her eighty-one years, to have decided after an absence of half-a-century to revisit the country she hates and whose inhabitants are the victims of the criminal policy of her reign, the survivors of sixty years of organised famine, the political necessity must have been terribly strong; for after all she is a woman, and however vile and selfish and pitiless her soul may be, she must sometimes tremble as death approaches when she thinks of the countless Irish mothers who, shelterless under the cloudy Irish sky, watching their starving little ones, have cursed her before they died.

Every eviction during sixty-three years has been carried out in Victoria's name, and if there is a Justice in Heaven the shame of those poor Irish emigrant girls whose very innocence renders them an easy prey and who have been overcome in the terrible struggle for existence on a foreign shore, will fall on this woman, whose bourgeoise virtue is so boasted and in whose name their homes were destroyed. If she comes to Ireland again before her death to contemplate the ruin she has made it is surely because her ministers and advisors think that England's situation is dangerous and that her journey will have a deep political importance. England has lived for years on a prestige which has had no solid foundation. She has hypnotised the world with the falsehood of her greatness; she has made great nations and small nations alike, believe in her power. It required the dauntless courage and energy of the Boers to destroy for ever this illusion and rescue Europe from the fatal enchantment. Today no one fears the British Empire, her prestige has gone down before the rifles of a few thousand heroic peasants.

If the British Empire means to exist she will have to rely on real strength, and real strength she has not got. England is in decadence. She has sacrificed all to getting money, and money cannot create men, nor give courage to her weakly soldiers. The men who formerly made her greatness, the men from the country districts have disappeared; they have been swallowed up by the great black manufacturing cities; they have been flung into the crucible where gold is made. Today the giants of England are the giants of finance and of the Stock Exchange, who have risen to power on the backs of a struggling mass of pale, exhausted slaves. The storm approaches; the gold which the English have made out of the blood and tears of millions of human beings attracts the covetousness of the world. Who will aid the pirates to keep their spoils? In their terror they turn to Victoria, their Queen. She has succeeded in amassing more gold than any of her subjects; she has always been ready to cover with her royal mantle the crimes and turpitude of her Empire, and now, trembling on the brink of the grave, she rises once more at their call. Soldiers are needed to protect the vampires. The Queen issues an appeal in England, the struggling mass of slaves cry 'Hurrah'; but there is no blood in their veins, no strength in their arms. Soldiers must be found, so Victoria will go herself to fetch them; she will go over to Ireland—to this people who have despised gold, and who, in spite of persecutions and threats, have persisted in their dream of Freedom and idealism, and who, though reduced in numbers, have maintained all the beauty and strength and vitality of their race.

Taking the Shamrock in her withered hand she dares to ask Ireland for soldiers—for soldiers to protect the exterminators of their race! And the reply of Ireland comes sadly but proudly, not through the lips of the miserable little politicians who are touched by the English canker but through the lips of the Irish people:

'Queen, return to your own land; you will find no more Irishmen ready to wear the red shame of your livery. In the past they have done so from ignorance, and because it is hard to die of hunger when one is young and strong and the sun shines, but they shall do so no longer; see! your recruiting agents return unsuccessful and alone from my green hills and plains, because once more hope has revived, and it will be in the ranks of your enemies that my children will find employment and honour! As to those who today enter your service to help in your criminal wars, I deny them! If they die, if they live, it matters not to me, they are no longer Irishmen.'

PATRICK PEARSE
(1879–1916)

The Coming Revolution (1913)

I have come to the conclusion that the Gaelic League, as the Gaelic League, is a spent force; and I am glad of it. I do not mean that no work remains for the Gaelic League, or that the Gaelic League is no longer equal to work; I mean that the vital work to be done in the new Ireland will be done not so much by the Gaelic League itself as by men and movements that have sprung from the Gaelic League or have received from the Gaelic League a new baptism and a new life of grace. The Gaelic League was no reed shaken by the wind, no mere *vox clamantis*:* it was a prophet and more than a prophet. But it was not the Messiah. I do not know if the Messiah has yet come, and I am not sure that there will be any visible and personal Messiah in this redemption: the people itself will perhaps be its own Messiah, the people labouring, scourged, crowned with thorns, agonising and dying, to rise again immortal and impassible. For peoples are divine and are the only things that can properly be spoken of under figures drawn from the divine epos.

If we do not believe in the divinity of our people we have had no business, or very little, all these years in the Gaelic League. In fact, if we had not believed in the divinity of our people, we should in all probability not have gone into the Gaelic League at all. We should have made our peace with the devil, and perhaps might have found him a very decent sort; for he liberally rewards with attorney-generalships, bank balances, villa residences, and so forth, the great and the little who serve him well. Now, we did not turn our backs upon all these desirable things for the sake of *is* and *tá*.* We did it for the sake of Ireland. In other words, we had one and all of us (at least, I had, and I hope that all you had) an ulterior motive in joining the Gaelic League. We never meant to be Gaelic Leaguers and nothing more than Gaelic Leaguers. We meant to do something for Ireland, each in his own way. Our Gaelic League time was to be our tutelage: we had first to learn to know Ireland, to read the lineaments of her face, to understand the accents of her voice; to re-possess ourselves, disinherited as we were, of her spirit and mind, re-enter into our mystical birthright. For this we went to school to the Gaelic League. It was a good school, and we love its name and will champion its fame throughout all the days of our later fighting and striving. But we do not propose to remain schoolboys for ever.

I have often said (quoting, I think, Herbert Spencer)* that education should be a preparation for complete living; and I say now that our Gaelic League education ought to have been a preparation for our complete living as Irish Nationalists. In proportion as we have been faithful and diligent Gaelic Leaguers, our work as Irish

Nationalists (by which term I mean people who accept the ideal of, and work for, the realisation of an Irish Nation, by whatever means) will be earnest and thorough, a valiant and worthy fighting, not the mere carrying out of a ritual. As to what your work as an Irish Nationalist is to be, I cannot conjecture; I know what mine is to be, and would have you know yours and buckle yourself to it. And it may be (nay, it is) that yours and mine will lead us to a common meeting-place, and that on a certain day we shall stand together, with many more beside us, ready for a greater adventure than any of us has yet had, a trial and a triumph to be endured and achieved in common.

This is what I meant when I said that our work henceforward must be done less and less through the Gaelic League and more and more through the groups and the individuals that have arisen, or are arising, out of the Gaelic League. There will be in the Ireland of the next few years a multitudinous activity of Freedom Clubs, Young Republican Parties, Labour Organisations, Socialist Groups, and what not; bewildering enterprises undertaken by sane persons and insane persons, by good men and bad men, many of them seemingly contradictory, some mutually destructive, yet all tending towards a common objective, and that objective: the Irish Revolution.

For if there is one thing that has become plainer than another it is that when the seven men met in O'Connell Street to found the Gaelic League,* they were commencing, had there been a Lian-court* there to make the epigram, not a revolt, but a revolution. The work of the Gaelic League, its appointed work, was that: and the work is done. To every generation its deed. The deed of the generation that has now reached middle life was the Gaelic League: the beginning of the Irish Revolution. Let our generation not shirk *its* deed, which is to accomplish the revolution.

I believe that the national movement of which the Gaelic League has been the soul has reached the point which O'Connell's movement had reached at the close of the series of monster meetings. Indeed, I believe that our movement reached that point a few years ago—say, at the conclusion of the fight for Essential Irish; and I said so at the time. The moment was ripe then for a new Young Ireland Party, with a forward policy; and we have lost much by our hesitation. I propose in all seriousness that we hesitate no longer—that we push on. I propose that we leave Conciliation Hall behind us and go into the Irish Confederation.

Whenever Dr Hyde,* at a meeting at which I have had a chance of speaking after him, has produced his dove of peace, I have always been careful to produce my sword; and to tantalise him by saying that the Gaelic League has brought into Ireland 'Not Peace, but a Sword.' But this does not show any fundamental difference of outlook between my leader and me; for while he is thinking of peace between brother-Irishmen, I am thinking of the sword-point between banded Irishmen and the foreign force that occupies Ireland: and his peace is necessary to my war. It is evident that there can be no peace between the body politic and a foreign substance that has intruded itself into its system: between them war only until the foreign substance is expelled or assimilated.

Whether Home Rule means a loosening or a tightening of England's grip upon Ireland remains yet to be seen. But the coming of Home Rule, if come it does, will make no material difference in the nature of the work that lies before us: it will affect only the means we are to employ, our plan of campaign. There remains, under Home Rule as in its absence, the substantial task of achieving the Irish Nation. I do not think it is going to be achieved without stress and trial, without suffering and bloodshed; at any rate, it is not going to be achieved without *work*. Our business here and now is to get ourselves into harness for such work as has to be done.

I hold that before we can do any work, any *men's* work, we must first realise ourselves as men. Whatever comes to Ireland she needs men. And we of this generation are not in any real sense men, for we suffer things that men do not suffer, and we seek to redress griev-ances by means which men do not employ. We have, for instance, allowed ourselves to be disarmed; and, now that we have the chance of re-arming, we are not seizing it. Professor Eoin Mac Neill* pointed out last week that we have at this moment an opportunity of rectifying the capital error we made when we allowed ourselves to be disarmed; and such opportunities, he reminds us, do not always come back to nations.

A thing that stands demonstrable is that nationhood is not achieved otherwise than in arms: in one or two instances there may have been no actual bloodshed, but the arms were there and the ability to use them. Ireland unarmed will attain just as much freedom as it is convenient for England to give her; Ireland armed will attain ultimately just as much freedom as she wants. These are matters which may not concern the Gaelic League, as a body; but they concern every member of the Gaelic League, and every man and woman of Ireland. I urged much of this five or six years ago in addresses to the Ard-Chraobh:* but the League was too busy with resolutions to think of revolution, and the only resolution that a member of the League could not come to was the resolution to be a man. My fellow-Leaguers had not (and have not) apprehended that the thing which cannot defend itself, even though it may wear trousers, is no man.

I am glad, then, that the North has 'begun.'* I am glad that the Orangemen have armed, for it is a goodly thing to see arms in Irish hands. I should like to see the A. O. H.* armed. I should like to see the Transport Workers* armed. I should like to see any and every body of Irish citizens armed. We must accustom ourselves to the thought of arms, to the sight of arms, to the use of arms. We may make mistakes in the beginning and shoot the wrong people; but bloodshed is a cleansing and a sanctifying thing, and the nation which regards it as the final horror has lost its manhood. There are many things more horrible than bloodshed; and slavery is one of them.

JAMES CONNOLLY
(1868–1916)

The Irish Flag (1916)

The Council of the Irish Citizen Army has resolved, after grave and earnest deliberation, to hoist the green flag of Ireland over Liberty Hall, as over a fortress held for Ireland by the arms of Irishmen.

This is a momentous decision in the most serious crisis Ireland has witnessed in our day and generation. It will, we are sure, send a thrill through the hearts of every true Irish man and woman, and send the red blood coursing fiercely along the veins of every lover of the race.

It means that in the midst of and despite the treasons and back-slidings of leaders and guides, in the midst of and despite all the weaknesses, corruption and moral cowardice of a section of the people, in the midst of and despite all this there still remains in Ireland a spot where a body of true men and women are ready to hoist, gather round, and to defend the flag made sacred by all the sufferings of all the martyrs of the past.

Since this unholy war first started we have seen every symbol of Irish freedom desecrated to the purposes of the enemy, we have witnessed the prostitution of every holy Irish tradition. That the young men of Ireland might be seduced into the service of the nation that denies every national power to their country, we have seen appeals made to our love of freedom, to our religious instincts, to our sympathy for the oppressed, to our kinship with suffering.

The power that for seven hundred years has waged bitter and unrelenting war upon the freedom of Ireland, and that still declares that the rights of Ireland must forever remain subordinate to the interests of the British Empire, hypocritically appealed to our young men to enlist under her banner and shed their blood 'in the interests of freedom'.

The power whose reign in Ireland has been one long carnival of corruption and debauchery of civic virtue, and which has rioted in the debasement and degradation of everything Irish men and women hold sacred, appealed to us in the name of religion to fight for her as the champion of christendom.

The power which holds in subjection more of the world's population than any other power on the globe, and holds them in subjection as slaves without any guarantee of freedom or power of self-government, this power that sets Catholic against Protestant, the Hindu against the Mohammedan, the yellow man against the brown, and keeps them quarrelling with each other whilst she robs and murders them all—this power appeals to Ireland to send her sons to fight under England's banner for the cause of the oppressed. The power whose rule in Ireland has made of Ireland a desert, and made the history of our race read like the records of a shambles, as she plans for the annihilation of another race appeals to our manhood to fight for her because of our sympathy for the suffering, and of our hatred of oppression.

For generations the shamrock was banned as a national emblem of Ireland, but in her extremity England uses the shamrock as a means for exciting in foolish Irishmen loyalty to England. For centuries the green flag of Ireland was a thing accurst and hated by the English garrison in Ireland, as it is still in their inmost hearts. But in India, in Egypt, in Flanders, in Gallipoli, the green flag is used by our rulers to encourage Irish soldiers of England to give up their lives for the power that denies their country the right of nationhood. Green flags wave over recruiting offices in Ireland and England as a bait to lure on poor fools to dishonourable deaths in England's uniform.

The national press of Ireland, the true national press, uncorrupted and unterrified, has largely succeeded in turning back the tide of demoralization, and opening up the minds of the Irish public to a realization of the truth about the position of their country in the war. The national press of Ireland is a real flag of freedom flying for Ireland despite the enemy, but it is well that also there should fly in Dublin the green flag of this country as a rallying point of our forces and embodiment of all our hopes. Where better could that flag fly than over the unconquered citadel of the Irish working class, Liberty Hall, the fortress of the militant working class of Ireland.

We are out for Ireland for the Irish. But who are the Irish? Not the rack-renting, slum-owning landlord; not the sweating, profit-grinding capitalist; not the sleek and oily lawyer; not the prostitute pressman—the hired liars of the enemy. Not these are the Irish upon whom the future depends. Not these, but the Irish working class, the only secure foundation upon which a free nation can be reared.

The cause of labour is the cause of Ireland, the cause of Ireland is the cause of labour. They cannot be dissevered. Ireland seeks freedom. Labour seeks that an Ireland free should be the sole mistress of her own destiny, supreme owner of all material things within and upon her soil. Labour seeks to make the free Irish nation the guardian of the interests of the people of Ireland, and to secure that end would vest in that free Irish nation all property rights as against the claims of the individual, with the end in view that the individual may be enriched by the nation, and not by the spoiling of his fellows.

Having in view such a high and holy function for the nation to perform, is it not well and fitting that we of the working class should fight for the freedom of the nation from foreign rule, as the first requisite for the free development of the national powers needed for our class? It is so fitting. Therefore on Sunday, 16 April 1916, the green flag of Ireland will be solemnly hoisted over Liberty Hall as the symbol of our faith in freedom, and as a token to all the world that the working class of Dublin stands for the cause of Ireland, and the cause of Ireland is the cause of a separate and distinct nationality.

In these days of doubt, despair, and resurgent hope we fling our banner to the breeze, the flag of our fathers, the symbol of our national redemption, the sunburst shining over an Ireland re-born.

JAMES STEPHENS
(1880–1950)

from *The Insurrection in Dublin* (1916)

III

WEDNESDAY

It was three o'clock before I got to sleep last night, and during the hours machine guns and rifle firing had been continuous.

This morning the sun is shining brilliantly, and the movement in the streets possesses more of animation than it has done. The movement ends always in a knot of people, and folk go from group to group vainly seeking information, and quite content if the rumour they presently gather differs even a little from the one they have just communicated.

The first statement I heard was that the Green had been taken by the military; the second that it had been re-taken; the third that it had not been taken at all. The facts at last emerged that the Green had not been occupied by the soldiers, but that the Volunteers had retreated from it into a house which commanded it. This was found to be the College of Surgeons, and from the windows and roof of this College they were sniping. A machine gun was mounted on the roof; other machine guns, however, opposed them from the roofs of the Shelbourne Hotel, the United Service Club, and the Alexandra Club. Thus a triangular duel opened between these positions across the trees of the Park.

Through the railings of the Green some rifles and bandoliers could be seen lying on the ground, as also the deserted trenches and snipers' holes. Small boys bolted in to see these sights and bolted out again with bullets quickening their feet. Small boys do not believe that people will really kill them, but small boys were killed.

The dead horse was still lying stiff and lamentable on the footpath.

This morning a gunboat came up the Liffey and helped to bombard Liberty Hall. The Hall is breeched and useless. Rumour says that it was empty at the time, and that Connolly with his men had marched long before to the Post Office and the Green. The same source of information relates that three thousand Volunteers came from Belfast on an excursion train and that they marched into the Post Office.

On this day only one of my men came in. He said that he had gone on the roof and had been shot at, consequently that the Volunteers held some of the covering houses. I went to the roof and remained there for half an hour. There were no shots, but the firing from the direction of Sackville Street was continuous and at times exceedingly heavy.

To-day the *Irish Times* was published. It contained a new military proclamation, and a statement that the country was peaceful, and told that in Sackville Street some houses were burned to the ground.

On the outside railings a bill proclaiming Martial Law was posted.

Into the newspaper statement that peace reigned in the country one was inclined to read more of disquietude than of truth, and one said is the country so extraordinarily peaceful that it can be dismissed in three lines. There is too much peace or too much reticence, but it will be some time before we hear from outside of Dublin.

Meanwhile the sun was shining. It was a delightful day, and the streets outside and around the areas of fire were animated and even gay. In the streets of Dublin there were no morose faces to be seen. Almost everyone was smiling and attentive, and a democratic feeling was abroad, to which our City is very much a stranger; for while in private we are a sociable and talkative people we have no street manners or public ease whatever. Every person spoke to every other person, and men and women mixed and talked without constraint.

Was the City for or against the Volunteers? Was it for the Volunteers, and yet against the rising? It is considered now (writing a day or two afterwards) that Dublin was entirely against the Volunteers, but on the day of which I write no such certainty could be put forward. There was a singular reticence on the subject. Men met and talked volubly, but they said nothing that indicated a personal desire or belief. They asked for and exchanged the latest news, or, rather, rumour, and while expressions were frequent of astonishment at the suddenness and completeness of the occurrence, no expression of opinion for or against was anywhere formulated.

Sometimes a man said, 'They will be beaten of course,' and, as he prophesied, the neighbour might surmise if he did so with a sad heart or a merry one, but they knew nothing and asked nothing of his views, and themselves advanced no flag.

This was among the men.

The women were less guarded, or, perhaps, knew they had less to fear. Most of the female opinion I heard was not alone unfavourable but actively and viciously hostile to the rising. This was noticeable among the best dressed class of our population; the worst dressed, indeed the female dregs of Dublin life, expressed a like antagonism, and almost in similar language. The view expressed was—

'I hope every man of them will be shot.'

And—

'They ought to be all shot.'

Shooting, indeed, was proceeding everywhere. During daylight, at least, the sound is not sinister nor depressing, and the thought that perhaps a life had exploded with that crack is not depressing either.

In the last two years of world-war our ideas on death have undergone a change. It is not now the furtive thing that crawled into your bed and which you fought with pill-boxes and medicine bottles. It has become again a rider of the wind whom you may go coursing with through the fields and open places. All the morbidity is gone, and the sickness, and what remains to Death is now health and excitement. So Dublin laughed at the noise of its own bombardment, and made no moan about its dead—in the sunlight. Afterwards—in the rooms, when the night fell, and instead of silence that mechanical barking of the maxims and the whistle and screams of the rifles, the solemn roar of the heavier guns, and the red glare covering the sky. It is possible that in the night Dublin did not laugh, and that she was gay in the sunlight for no other reason than that the night was past.

On this day fighting was incessant at Mount Street Bridge. A party of Volunteers had seized three houses covering the bridge and converted these into forts. It is reported that military casualties at this point were very heavy. The Volunteers are said also to hold the South Dublin Union. The soldiers have seized Guinness's Brewery, while their opponents have seized another brewery in the neighbourhood, and between these two there is a continual fusilade.

Fighting is brisk about Ringsend and along the Canal. Dame Street was said to be held in many places by the Volunteers. I went down Dame Street, but saw no Volunteers, and did not observe any sniping from the houses. Further, as Dame Street is entirely commanded by the roofs and windows of Trinity College, it is unlikely that they should be here.

It was curious to observe this, at other times, so animated street, broad and deserted, with at the corners of side streets small knots of people watching. Seen from behind, Grattan's Statue in College Green seemed almost alive, and he had the air of addressing warnings and reproaches to Trinity College.

The Proclamation issued to-day warns all people to remain within doors until five o'clock in the morning, and after seven o'clock at night.

It is still early. There is no news of any kind, and the rumours begin to catch quickly on each other and to cancel one another out. Dublin is entirely cut off from England, and from the outside world. It is, just as entirely cut off from the rest of Ireland; no news of any kind filters in to us. We are land-locked and sea-locked, but, as yet, it does not much matter.

Meantime the belief grows that the Volunteers may be able to hold out much longer than had been imagined. The idea at first among the people had been that the insurrection would be ended the morning after it had begun. But to-day, the insurrection having lasted three days, people are ready to conceive that it may last for ever. There is almost a feeling of gratitude towards the Volunteers because they are holding out for a little while, for had they been beaten the first or second day the City would have been humiliated to the soul.

People say: 'Of course, they will be beaten.' The statement is almost a query, and they continue, 'but they are putting up a decent fight.' For being beaten does not greatly matter in Ireland, but not fighting does matter. 'They went forth always to the battle; and they always fell,' Indeed, the history of the Irish race is in that phrase.

The firing from the roofs of Trinity College became violent. I crossed Dame Street some distance up, struck down the Quays, and went along these until I reached the Ballast Office. Further than this it was not possible to go, for a step beyond the Ballast Office would have brought one into the unending stream of lead that was pouring from Trinity and other places. I was looking on O'Connell Bridge and Sackville Street, and the house facing me was Kelly's—a red-brick fishing tackle shop, one half of which was on the Quay and the other half in Sackville Street. This house was being bombarded.

I counted the report of six different machine guns which played on it. Rifles innumerable and from every sort of place were potting its windows, and at intervals of about half a minute the shells from a heavy gun lobbed in through its windows or thumped mightily against its walls.

For three hours that bombardment continued, and the walls stood in a cloud of red dust and smoke. Rifle and machine gun bullets pattered over every inch of it, and, unfailingly the heavy gun pounded its shells through the windows.

One's heart melted at the idea that human beings were crouching inside that volcano of death, and I said to myself, 'Not even a fly can be alive in that house.'

No head showed at any window, no rifle cracked from window or roof in reply. The house was dumb, lifeless, and I thought every one of those men are dead.

It was then, and quite suddenly, that the possibilities of street fighting flashed on me, and I knew there was no person in the house, and said to myself, 'They have smashed through the walls with a hatchet and are sitting in the next house, or they have long ago climbed out by the skylight and are on a roof half a block away.' Then the thought came to me—they have and hold the entire of Sackville Street down to the Post Office. Later on this proved to be the case, and I knew at this moment that Sackville Street was doomed.

I continued to watch the bombardment, but no longer with the anguish which had before torn me. Near by there were four men, and a few yards away, clustered in a laneway, there were a dozen others. An agitated girl was striding from the farther group to the one in which I was, and she addressed the men in the most obscene language which I have ever heard. She addressed them man by man, and she continued to speak and cry and scream at them with all that obstinate, angry patience of which only a woman is capable.

She cursed us all. She called down diseases on every human being in the world excepting only the men who were being bombarded.

She demanded of the folk in the laneway that they should march at least into the roadway and prove that they were proud men and were not afraid of bullets. She had been herself into the danger zone. Had stood herself in the track of the guns, and had there cursed her fill for half an hour, and she desired that the men should do at least what she had done.

This girl was quite young—about nineteen years of age—and was dressed in the customary shawl and apron of her class. Her face was rather pretty, or it had that pretty slenderness and softness of outline which belong to youth. But every sentence she spoke contained half a dozen indecent words. Alas, it was only that her vocabulary was not equal to her emotions, and she did not know how to be emphatic without being obscene—it is the cause of most of the meaningless swearing one hears every day. She spoke to me for a minute, and her eyes were as soft as those of a kitten and her language was as gentle as her eyes. She wanted a match to light a cigarette, but I had none, and said that I also wanted one. In a few minutes she brought me a match, and then she recommenced her tireless weaving of six vile words into hundreds of stupid sentences.

About five o'clock the guns eased off of Kelly's.

To inexperienced eyes they did not seem to have done very much damage, but afterwards one found that although the walls were standing and apparently solid there was no inside to the house. From roof to basement the building was bare as a dog kennel. There were no floors inside, there was nothing there but blank space; and on the ground within was the tumble and rubbish that had been roof and floors and furniture. Everything inside was smashed and pulverised into scrap and dust, and the only objects that had consistency and their ancient shape were the bricks that fell when the shells struck them.

Rifle shots had begun to strike the house on the further side of the street, a jewellers' shop called Hopkins & Hopkins. The impact of these balls on the bricks was louder than the sound of the shot which immediately succeeded, and each bullet that struck brought down a shower of fine red dust from the walls. Perhaps thirty or forty shots in all were fired at Hopkins', and then, except for an odd crack, firing ceased.

During all this time there had been no reply from the Volunteers, and I thought they must be husbanding their ammunition, and so must be short of it, and that it would be only a matter of a few days before the end. All this, I said to myself, will be finished in a few days, and they will be finished; life here will recommence exactly where it left off, and except for some newly-filled graves, all will be as it had been until they become a tradition and enter the imagination of their race.

I spoke to several of the people about me, and found the same willingness to exchange news that I had found elsewhere in the City, and the same reticences as regarded their private opinions. Two of them, indeed, and they were the only two I met with during the insurrection, expressed, although in measured terms, admiration for the Volunteers, and while they did not side with them they did not say anything against them. One was a labouring man, the other a gentleman. The remark of the latter was:

'I am an Irishman, and (pointing to the shells that were bursting through the windows in front of us) I hate to see that being done to other Irishmen.'

He had come from some part of the country to spend the Easter Holidays in Dublin, and was unable to leave town again.

The labouring man—he was about fifty-six years of age—spoke very quietly and collectedly about the insurrection. He was a type with whom I had come very little in contact, and I was surprised to find how simple and good his speech was, and how calm his ideas. He thought labour was in this movement to a greater extent than was imagined. I mentioned that Liberty Hall had been blown up, and that the garrison had either surrendered or been killed. He replied that a gunboat had that morning come up the river and had blown Liberty Hall into smash, but, he added, there were no men in it. All the Labour Volunteers had marched with Connolly into the Post Office.

He said the Labour Volunteers might possibly number about one thousand men, but that it would be quite safe to say eight hundred, and he held that the Labour Volunteers, or the Citizens' Army, as they called themselves, had always been careful not to reveal their numbers. They had always announced that they possessed about two hundred and fifty men, and had never paraded any more than that number at any one time. Workingmen, he continued, knew that the men who marched were always different men. The police knew it, too, but they thought that the Citizens Army was the *most deserted-from force* in the world.

The men, however, were not deserters—you don't, he said, desert a man like Connolly, and they were merely taking their turn at being drilled and disciplined. They were raised against the police who, in the big strike of two years ago, had acted towards them with unparalleled savagery, and the men had determined that the police would never again find them thus disorganised.

This man believed that every member of the Citizen Army had marched with their leader.

'The men, I know,' said he, 'would not be afraid of anything, and,' he continued, 'they are in the Post Office now.'

'What chance have they?'

'None,' he replied, 'and they never said they had, and they never thought they would have any.'

'How long do you think they'll be able to hold out?'

He nodded towards the house that had been bombarded by heavy guns.

'That will root them out of it quick enough,' was his reply.

'I'm going home,' said he then, 'the people will be wondering if I'm dead or alive,' and he walked away from that sad street, as I did myself a few minutes afterwards.

CONSTANCE MARKIEWICZ
(1868–1927)

Stephen's Green (1926)

I am afraid I can only give you a little account of those who were enrolled like me in the Irish Citizen Army, and those who were with me or whom I met during the week. Some were members of Cumann na mBan, and others just women who were ready to die for Ireland.

My activities were confined to a very limited area. I was mobilised for Liberty Hall and was sent from there via the City Hall, to Stephen's Green, where I remained.

On Easter Monday there was a great hosting of disciplined and armed men and women at Liberty Hall. Padraig Pearse and James Connolly addressed us and told us that from now on the

Volunteers and the ICA were not two forces, but two wings of the Irish Republican Army.

There were a considerable number of ICA women. These were absolutely on the same footing as the men. They took part in all marches, and even in the manoeuvres that lasted all night. Moreover, Connolly made it quite clear to us that unless we women took our share in the drudgery of training and preparing, we should not be allowed to take any share at all in the fight. You may judge how fit we were when I tell you that sixteen miles was the length of the average route march.

Connolly had appointed two staff officers—Commandant Mallin and myself. I held a commission, giving me the rank of Staff Lieutenant. I was accepted by Tom Clarke and the members of the Provisional Government as the second of Connolly's 'ghosts'. Ghosts was the name we gave to those who stood secretly behind the leaders, and who were entrusted with enough of the plans of the Rising to enable them to carry on that leader's work should anything happen to himself. Commandant Mallin was over me and next in command to Connolly. Dr Kathleen Lynn was our medical officer, holding the rank of Captain.

We watched the little bodies of men and women march off— Pearse and Connolly to the GPO, Sean Connolly to the City Hall. I went with the Doctor in her car. We carried a huge store of first aid necessities and drove off through the quiet, dusty streets and across the river, reaching the City Hall just at the very moment Commandant Sean Connolly and his little troop of men and women swung round the corner and he raised his gun and shot the policeman who barred the way. A wild excitement ensued, people running from every side to see what was up. The Doctor got out, and I remember Mrs Barrett—sister of Scan Connolly—and others helping to carry in the Doctor's bundle. I did not meet Dr Lynn again till my release, when her car met me, and she welcomed me to her house where she cared for me and fed me up and looked after me till I had recovered from the evil effects of the English prison system.

When I reported with the car to Commandant Mallin in Stephen's Green he told me that he must keep me. He said that, owing to MacNeill's call-off of the Volunteers, a lot of the men who should have been under him had had to be distributed round other posts and that few of those left him were trained to shoot, so I must stay and be ready to take up the work of a sniper. He took me round the Green and showed me how the barricading of the gates and digging trenches had begun, and left me in charge of this work while he went to superintend the erection of barricades in the street and arrange other work. About two hours later he definitely promoted me to be his second-in-command. This work was very exciting when the fighting began. I continued to go round and round the Green, reporting back if anything was wanted or tackling any sniper who was particularly objectionable.

Madeleine ffrench-Mullen was in charge of the Red Cross and the commissariat in the Green. Some of the girls had revolvers and with these they sallied forth and held up bread-vans.

This was necessary, because the first prisoner we took was a British officer, and Commandant Mallin treated him as such. He took his parole as 'an officer and a gentleman' not to escape and he left him at large in the Green before the gates were shut. This English gentleman walked around and found out all he could and then 'bunked.'

We had a couple of sick men and prisoners in the band-stand, the Red Cross flag flying to protect them. The English in the Shelbourne turned a machine-gun on to them. A big group of our girls were attending to the sick, making tea for the prisoners, or resting themselves. I never saw anything like their courage. Madeleine ffrench-Mullen brought them, with the sick and the prisoners, out and into a safer place. It was all done slowly and in perfect order. More than one girl said to me: 'What is there to be afraid of? Won't I go straight to heaven if I die for Ireland.' However it was, they came out unscathed from under a shower of shrapnel.

On Tuesday we began to be short of food. There were no bread carts on the streets. We retired into the College of Surgeons that evening and were joined by some of our men, who had been in other places, and by quite a large squad of Volunteers, and with this increase in our numbers the problem of food became very serious.

Nellie Gifford was put in charge of one large classroom with a big grate; but alas! there was nothing to cook. When we were all starving she produced a quantity of oatmeal from somewhere and made pot after potful of the most delicious porridge, which kept us going. But, all the same, on Tuesday and Wednesday we absolutely starved. There seemed to be no bread in the town.

Later on Mary Hyland was given charge of a little kitchen somewhere down through the houses, near where the Eithne Workroom now is.

We had only one woman casualty—Margaret Skinnider. She, like myself, was in uniform and carried an army rifle. She had enlisted as a private in the ICA. She was one of a party who went out to set fire to a house just behind Russell's Hotel. The English opened fire on them from the ground floor of a house just opposite. Poor Freddy Ryan was killed and Margaret was very badly wounded. She owes her life to William Partridge. He carried her away under fire and back to the College.

God rest his noble soul! Brilliant orator and labour leader, comrade and friend of Connolly's, he was content to serve as a private in the ICA. He was never strong and the privations he suffered in an English jail left him a dying man.

Margaret's only regret was her bad luck in being disabled so early in the day, though she must have suffered terribly; but the end was nearer than we thought, for it was only a few days later that we had her carried over to Vincent's Hospital, so that she would not fall wounded into the hands of the English.

The memory of Easter Week with its heroic dead is sacred to us who survived. Many of us could almost wish we had died in the moment of ecstasy when, with the Tricolour over our heads we went out and proclaimed the Irish Republic and with guns in our hands tried to establish it. We failed, but not until we had seen regiment after regiment run from our few guns. Our effort will inspire the people who come after us and will give them hope and courage. If we failed to win, so did the English. They slaughtered and imprisoned, only to rouse the nation to a passion of love and loyalty—loyalty to Ireland and hatred of foreign rule. Once they see clearly that the English rule us still, only with a new personnel of traitors and new uniforms, they will finish the work begun by the men and women of Easter Week.

ROGER CASEMENT
(1864–1916)

Speech from the Dock (1916)

I may say at once, my lord, that I protest against that jurisdiction of this court in my case on this charge and the argument that I am now going to read is addressed not to this court, but to my own countrymen. There is an objection, possibly not good in law, but surely good on moral grounds, against the application to me here of this old English statute, 565 years old, that seeks to deprive an Irishman to-day of life and honour, not for adhering to the king's enemies, but for adhering to his own people. When this statute was passed in 1351, what was the state of men's minds on the question of a far higher allegiance—that of a man to God and his kingdom? The law of that day did not permit a man to forsake his Church, or deny his God, save with his life. The 'heretic' then had the same doom as the 'traitor'. Today, a man may forswear God and his heavenly kingdom without fear or penalty—all earlier statutes having gone the way of Nero's edicts against the Christians; but that Constitutional phantom, 'the King', can still dig up from the dungeons and torture-chambers of the Dark Ages a law that takes a man's life and limb for an exercise of conscience.

If true religion rests on love, it is equally true that loyalty rests on love. The law I am charged under has no parentage in love, and claims the allegiance of to-day on the ignorance and blindness of the past. I am being tried, in truth, not by my peers of the live present, but by the fears of the dead past; not by the civilization of the twentieth century, but by the brutality of the fourteenth; not even by a statute framed in the language of the land that tries me, but emitted in the language of an enemy-land—so antiquated is the law that must be sought to-day to slay an Irishman, whose offence is that he puts Ireland first! Loyalty is a sentiment, not a law. It rests on love, not on restraint. The government of Ireland by England rests on restraint, and not on law; and, since it demands no love, it can evoke no loyalty.

But this statute is more absurd even than it is antiquated; and if it be potent to hang even one Irishman, it is still more potent to gibbet all Englishmen. Edward III was king, not only of the realm of England, but also of the realm of France, and he was not king of Ireland. Yet his dead hand to-day may pull the noose around the Irishman's neck, whose sovereign he was not, but it can strain no strand around the Frenchman's throat, whose sovereign he was. For centuries, the successors of Edward III claimed to be kings of France, and quartered the arms of France on their royal shield down to the Union with Ireland on January 1st, 1801. Throughout these hundreds of years, these 'kings of France' were constantly at war with their realm of France and their French subjects, who should have gone from birth to death with an obvious fear of treason before their eyes. But did they? Did the 'kings of France' resident here at Windsor or in the Tower of London hang, draw and quarter as a traitor every Frenchman for four hundred years who fell into their power with arms in his hands? On the contrary, they received embassies of these traitors, presents from these traitors, even knighthood itself at the hands of these traitors, feasted with them, tilted with them, fought with them—but did not assassinate them by law.

Judicial assassination to-day is reserved only for one race of the king's subjects—for Irishmen, for those who cannot forget their allegiance to the realm of Ireland. The kings of England as such had no rights in Ireland up to the time of Henry VIII, save such as rested on compact and mutual obligation entered into between them and certain princes, chiefs and lords of Ireland. This form of legal right, such as it was, gave no king of England lawful power to impeach an Irishman for his high treason under this statute of King Edward III of England until an Irish Act, known as Poyning's Law, the tenth of Henry VII, was passed in 1494 at Drogheda by the Parliament of the Pale in Ireland and enacted as law *in that part of Ireland*. But if by Poyning's Law an Irishman of the Pale could be indicted for high treason under this Act, he could be indicted only in one way, and before one tribunal—by the law of the realm of Ireland, and in Ireland. The very law of Poyning, which, I believe, applies this statute of Edward III to Ireland, enacted also for the Irishman's defence 'all those laws by which England claims her liberty'. And what is the fundamental charter of an Englishman's liberty? That he shall be tried by his peers. With all respect, I assert this court is to me, an Irishman, not a jury of my peers to try me in this vital issue; for it is patent to every man of conscience that I have an indefeasible right, if tried at all under this statute of high treason, to be tried in Ireland, before an Irish Court and by an Irish jury. This court, this jury, the public opinion of this country, England, cannot but be prejudiced in varying degrees against me, most of all in time of war. I did not land in England. I landed in Ireland. It was to Ireland I came; to Ireland I wanted to come; and the last place I desired to land in was England.

But, for the Attorney-General of England there is only England; there is no Ireland; there is only the law of England, no right of Ireland; the liberty of Ireland and of Irishmen is to be judged by the power of England. Yet for me, the Irish outlaw, there is a land of Ireland, a right of Ireland, and a charter for all Irishmen to appeal to, in the last resort, a charter that even the very statutes of England itself cannot deprive us of—nay more, a charter that Englishmen themselves assert as the fundamental bond of law that connects the two kingdoms. This charge of high treason involves a moral responsibility, as the very terms of the indictment against myself recite, inasmuch as I committed the acts I am charged with to 'the evil example of others in the like case'. What was the evil example I set to others in the like case, and who were these others? The 'evil example' charge is that I asserted the right of my own country, and 'the others' to whom I appealed to aid my endeavour were my own countrymen. The example was given not to Englishmen, but to Irishmen, and 'the like case' can never arise in England, but only in Ireland. To Englishmen, I set no evil example, for I make no appeal to them. I asked no Englishman to help me. I asked Irishmen to fight for their rights. The 'evil example' was only to other Irishmen, who might come after me and in 'like case' seek to do as I did. How, then, since neither my example nor my appeal was addressed to Englishmen, can I be rightly tried by them?

If I did wrong in making that appeal to Irishmen to join with me in an effort to fight for Ireland, it is by Irishmen, and by them alone, I can be rightfully judged. From this court and its jurisdiction I appeal to those I am alleged to have wronged and injured by my 'evil example' and claim that they alone are competent to decide my guilt or innocence. If they find me guilty, the statute may affix the penalty; but the statute does not override or annul my right to seek judgement at their hands. This is so fundamental a right, so natural, so obvious, that it is clear the Crown were aware of it when they brought me by force and by stealth from Ireland to this country. It was not I who landed in England, but the Crown that dragged me here, away from my own country, to which I had returned with a price upon my head; away from my own countrymen, whose loyalty is not in doubt, and safe from the judgement of my peers, whose judgement I do not shrink from. I admit no other judgement but theirs. I accept no verdict save at their hands.

I assert from this dock that I am being tried here, not because it is just, but because it is unjust. Place me before a jury of my countrymen, be it Protestant or Catholic, Unionist or Nationalist, Sinn Féineach or Orange, and I shall accept the verdict, and bow to the statute and all its penalties. But I shall accept no meaner finding against me than that of those whose loyalty I endangered by my example and to whom alone I made appeal. If they adjudge me guilty, then guilty I am. It is not I who am afraid of their verdict—it is the Crown. If this is not so, why fear the test? I fear it not. I demand it as my right. This is the condemnation of English rule, of English-made law, of English government in Ireland, that it dare not rest on the will of the Irish people, but exists in defiance of their will; that it is a rule derived not from right, but from conquest. But conquest, my lord, gives no title; and, if it exists over the body, it fails over the mind. It can exert no empire over men's reason and judgement and affections; and it is from this law of conquest that I appeal. I would add that the generous expressions of sympathy extended to me from many quarters, particularly from America, have touched me very much. In that country, as in my own, I am sure my motives are understood, and not misjudged,—for the achievement of their liberty has been an abiding inspiration to Irishmen, and to all men elsewhere, rightly struggling to be free.

Let me pass from myself and my own fate to a more pressing, as it is a far more urgent theme—not the fate of the individual Irishman who may have tried and failed, but the claims and the fate of the country that has not failed. Ireland has not failed. Ireland has outlived the failure of all her hopes—and she still hopes. Ireland has seen her sons—aye, and her daughters, too!—suffer from generation to generation, always for the same cause, meeting always the same fate, and always at the hands of the same power. Still, always a fresh generation has passed on to withstand the same oppression. For if English authority be omnipotent—a power, as Mr Gladstone phrased it, that reaches to the very ends of the earth—Irish hope exceeds the dimensions of that power, excels its authority, and renews with each generation the claims of the last. The cause that begets this indomitable persistency, the faculty of preserving through centuries of misery the remembrance of lost liberty—this surely is the noblest cause ever man strove for, ever lived for, ever died for. If this be the cause I stand here to-day indicted for and convicted of sustaining, then I stand in a goodly company and a right noble succession.

My counsel has referred to the Ulster Volunteer movement, and I will not touch at length upon that ground, save only to say this: that neither I nor any of the leaders of the Irish Volunteers, who were founded in Dublin in November 1913, had any quarrel with the Ulster Volunteers as such, who were born a year earlier. Our movement was not directed against them, but against the men who misused and misdirected the courage, the sincerity and the local patriotism of the men of the North of Ireland. On the contrary, we welcomed the coming of the Ulster Volunteers, even while we deprecated the aims and intentions of those Englishmen who sought to pervert to an English party use—to the mean purposes of their own bid for place and power in England—the armed activity of simple Irishmen. We aimed at winning the Ulster Volunteers to the cause of a United Ireland. We aimed at uniting all Irishmen in a natural and national bond of cohesion based on mutual self-respect. Our hope was a natural one and, were we left to ourselves, not hard to accomplish. If internal influences of disintegration would but leave us alone, we were sure that nature itself must bring us together. It was not we, the Irish Volunteers, who broke the law, but a British party. The Government had permitted the Ulster Volunteers to be armed by Englishmen, to threaten not merely an English party in its hold on office, but to threaten that party through the lives and blood of Irishmen.

The battle was to be fought in Ireland in order that the political 'outs' of to-day should be the 'ins' of to-morrow in Great Britain. A law designed for the benefit of Ireland was to be met, not on the floor of Parliament, where the fight had indeed been won, but on the field of battle much nearer home, where the armies would be composed of Irishmen slaying each other for some English party gain; and the British Navy would be the chartered 'transports' that were to bring to our shores a numerous assemblage of military and ex-military experts in the congenial and profitable exercise of holding down subject populations abroad. Our choice lay in submitting to foreign lawlessness or resisting it, and we did not hesitate to choose. But while the law-breakers had armed their would-be agents openly, and had been permitted to arm them openly, we were met within a few days of founding of our movement—that aimed at a United Ireland from within—by Government action from without, directed against our obtaining any arms at all.

The Manifesto of the Irish Volunteers, promulgated at a public meeting in Dublin, November 25th 1913, stated with certainty the aims of the organization, as I have outlined them. If the aims set out in that manifesto were a threat to the unity of the British Empire, then so much the worse for the Empire. An Empire that can only be held together by one section of its governing population perpetually holding down and sowing dissension among a smaller but none-the-less governing section, must have some canker at its heart, some ruin at its root. The Government that permitted the arming of those whose leaders declared that Irish national unity was a thing that should be opposed by force of arms, within nine days of the issue of our manifesto of good-will to Irishmen of every creed and class, took steps to nullify our efforts by prohibiting the import of all arms into Ireland as if it had been a hostile and blockaded coast. And this Proclamation of the 4th December 1913, known as the Arms Proclamation, was itself based on an illegal interpretation of the law, as the Chief Secretary* has now publicly confessed. The Proclamation was met by the loyalists of Great Britain with an act of still more lawless defiance—an act of widespread gun-running into Ulster, that was denounced by the Lord Chancellor of England as 'grossly illegal and utterly unconstitutional'.* How did the Irish Volunteers meet the incitements to civil war that were uttered by the party of law and order in England?

I can answer for my own acts and speeches. While one English party was responsible for preaching a doctrine of hatred, designed to bring about civil war in Ireland, the other—and that the party in power—took no active steps to restrain a propaganda that found its advocates in the Army, Navy and Privy Council—in the Houses of Parliament and in the State Church—a propaganda the methods of whose expression were so 'grossly illegal and utterly unconstitutional' that even the Lord Chancellor of England could find only words and no repressive action to apply them. Since lawlessness sat in high places in England and laughed at the law as at the custodians of the law, what wonder was it that Irishmen should refuse to accept the verbal protestations of an English Lord Chancellor as a sufficient safeguard for their liberties. I know not how all my colleagues on the Volunteer Committee in Dublin received the growing menace, but those with whom I was in closest co-operation re-doubled, in face of these threats from without, our efforts to unite all Irishmen from within. Our appeals were made to Protestant and Unionist as much almost as to Catholic and Nationalist Irishmen. We hoped that by the exhibition of affection and good-will on our part towards our political opponents in Ireland, we should yet succeed in winning them from the side of an English party, whose sole interest in our country lay in its oppression in the past, and in the present in its degradation to the mean and narrow needs of their political animosities.

It is true that they based their actions—so they averred—on 'fears for the Empire' and on a very diffuse loyalty that took in all the peoples of the Empire, save only the Irish. That blessed word *Empire*, that bears so paradoxical resemblance to charity! For if charity begins at home, *Empire* begins in other men's homes, and both may cover a multitude of sins. I, for one, was determined that Ireland was much more to me than *Empire*, and that, if charity begins at home, so must loyalty. Since arms were so necessary to make our organization a reality, and to give to the minds of Irishmen, menaced with the most outrageous threats, a sense of security, it was our bounden duty to get arms before all else. I decided, with this end in view, to go to America, with surely, a better right to appeal to Irishmen there for help in an hour of great national trial than those envoys of Empire could assert for their week-end descents on Ireland, or their appeals to Germany. If, as the right honourable gentleman, the present Attorney-General,* asserted in a speech at Manchester, Nationalists would neither fight for Home Rule nor pay for it, it was our duty to show him that *we* knew how to do both. Within a few weeks of my arrival in the United States, the fund that had been opened to secure arms for the Volunteers of Ireland amounted to many thousands of pounds. In every case the money subscribed, whether it came from the purse of the wealthy man or the still readier pocket of the poor man, was Irish gold.

Then came the war!—which, as Mr Birrell said, 'upset all calculations'. It upset mine no less than Mr Birrell's, and put an end to my
peaceful effort in America. A constitutional movement in Ireland is
never very far from a breach of the constitution, as the loyalists of
Ulster have been so eager to show us. A constitution, to be maintained intact, must be the achievement and the pride of the people
themselves, must rest on their own free will and on their own
determination to maintain it, instead of being something resident in
another land, whose chief representative is an armed force—armed
not to protect the population, but to hold it down. We had seen the
workings of 'the Irish Constitution' in the refusal of the Army of
Occupation at the Curragh to obey the orders of the Crown.* And
now that we were told the first duty of an Irishman was to enter that
army, in return for a promissory note, payable after death—a scrap
of paper that might or might not be redeemed—I felt, over there, in
America, that my first duty was to keep Irishmen at home in the only
army that could safeguard our national existence. If small nation-
alities were to be the pawns in this game of embattled giants, I saw no
reason why Ireland should shed her blood in any cause but her own,
and, if that be treason beyond the seas, I am not ashamed to avow it,
or to answer for it here with my life. And when we had the doctrine
of Unionist loyalty at last—'Mausers* and Kaisers, and any king
you like', and I have heard that at Hamburg, not far from Limburg
on the Lahn—I felt that I needed no other than that these words
conveyed, to go forth and do likewise.

The difference between us was that the Unionist champions chose
a path which they felt would lead to the woolsack, while I went a
road I knew must lead to the dock. The difference between us was
that my 'treason' was based on a ruthless sincerity that forced me to
attempt in time and season to carry out in action what I said in
words, whereas their treason lay in verbal incitements that they knew
would never be made good in their bodies. And so I am prouder to
stand here to-day, in the traitor's dock, to answer this impeachment,
than to fill the place of my right honourable accusers.

We have been told, have been asked to hope, that after this war
Ireland will get Home Rule as a reward for the life-blood shed in a
cause which, whomever else its success may benefit, can surely not
benefit Ireland. And what will Home Rule be in return for what its
vague promise has taken, and still hopes to take, from Ireland? It is

not necessary to climb the painful stairs of Irish history—to review the long list of British promises, made only to be broken; of Irish hopes, raised only to be dashed to the ground. Home Rule, when it comes, if come it does, will find an Ireland drained of all that is vital to its very existence, unless it be that unquenchable hope that we build on the graves of the dead. We are told that if Irishmen go by the thousand to die *not* for Ireland, but for Flanders, for Belgium, for a patch of sand on the deserts of Mesopotamia, or a rocky trench on the heights of Gallipoli, they are winning self-government for Ireland. But if they dare to lay down their lives on their native soil, if they dare to dream even that freedom can be won only at home by men resolved to fight for it there, then they are traitors to their country.

But history is not so recorded in other lands. In Ireland alone, in this twentieth century, is loyalty held to be a crime. If loyalty be something less than love and more than law, then we have had enough of such loyalty for Ireland or Irishmen. Self-government is our right, a thing born in us at birth, a thing no more to be doled out to us or withheld from us by another people than the right to life itself—the right to feel the sun or smell the flowers, or love our kind. It is only from the convict these things are withheld, for crime committed and proven—and Ireland, that has wronged no man, that has injured no land, that has sought no dominion over others—Ireland is being treated to-day among the nations of the world as if she were a convicted criminal. If it be treason to fight against such an unnatural fate as this, then I am proud to be a rebel, and shall cling to my 'rebellion', with the last drop of my blood. If there be no right of rebellion against this state of things that no savage tribe would endure without resistance, then I am sure that it is better for men to fight and to die without right than to live in such a state of right as this. Where all your rights have become only an accumulated wrong, where men must beg with bated breath for leave to subsist in their own land, to think their own thoughts, to sing their own songs, to garner the fruits of their own labours, and, even while they beg, to see things inexorably withdrawn from them—then, surely, it is a braver, a saner and a truer thing to be a rebel in act and deed against such circumstances than tamely to accept them as the natural lot of men.

My lord, I have done. Gentlemen of the jury, I wish to thank you for your verdict. I hope you will not take amiss what I said, or think that I made any imputation upon your truthfulness or your integrity when I spoke and said that this was not a trial by my peers. I maintain that I have a natural right to be tried in that natural jurisdiction, Ireland, my own country; and I would put it to you, how would you feel in the converse case—rather, how would all men here feel in the converse case—if an Englishman had landed here in England, and the Crown or the Government, for its own purposes, had conveyed him secretly from England to Ireland under a false name, committed him to prison under a false name, and brought him before a tribunal in Ireland under a statute which they knew involved a trial before an Irish jury? How would you feel, yourselves, as Englishmen if that Englishman was to be submitted to trial by jury in a land inflamed against him, and believing him to be a criminal, when his only crime was that he had cared for England more than for Ireland?

THOMAS MACDONAGH
(1878–1916)

from *Literature in Ireland* (1916)

In Ireland a period intervened between the last days of the Gaelic literature that mattered and the beginning of the new literature in the English tongue, between the hope and admiration that captured the imagination of the people in the days of Hugh O'Neill and Hugh O'Donnell,* then of Eoghan Ruadh O'Neill,* then of the Jacobites, and the new hope and anticipation that dawned in the last century and is widened to morning in this. The old Gaelic polity and culture having lost their force and their integrity, Gaelic literature became decadent in the time of the Penal Laws.* Whatever the fate of the Gaelic language and literature now may be—whether its long sickness end now in death without issue, or, as some of us confidently hope, in revival and vigorous life, with renewal of the same personality, a second youth, or in the birth of a new language to utter a new literature, destined to take after its Gaelic mother only in some parts, and for the rest to bear the name of bastard in its childhood and of true-born heir in its age, a well of Irish undefiled—whatever is to be in the unknown future, it would be folly to deny the sickness, the decadence, of the immediate past. And while Irish was decadent, English was not yet able either to carry on the tradition or to syllable anew for itself here. The English-speaking population in Ireland had none of the qualities—social cohesion and integrity, culture, enthusiasm, joy, high and brave emotion—to stammer and then to utter clearly the new word. That word came to the call of the country. It came in the new language and was heard in the new day. The Renaissance that stirred England to its greatest literature brought the mingling of the cosmopolitan with the national. Here the waters have been stirred by the breath of freedom: the alien language has stirred to expression on the lips of the native people.

The revival of nationalism among the Irish subject majority following the days of the Irish Volunteers, the United Irishmen, the independent Parliament; this nationalism, strengthened by O'Connell* with Catholic Emancipation and the franchise; this nationalism, hardened by the austere independence of Parnell,* by the land war and its victorious close; this, brought to full manhood by the renewed struggle for legislative freedom and the certainty of triumph and responsibility; this, free from alien hope and fear, craving no ease, hearing always the supreme song of victory on the dying lips of martyrs; this produced the unrest, the impetuous, intrepid adventure that shouts the song of joy for the sad things and for the glad things of life. The song in the new language demanded an intellectual effort that gave it a worth apart. English had to be broken and re-made to serve that song. The language that had been brought to perfection for English use, and then worn by that use, that had had the fixing of the printing press and had set the printer's word above the spoken, that language, in order to serve the different purpose of the new people, had to go back to the forge of the living speech. King Alfred, in the first days of English prose, wrote long, awkward strings of words for sentences, with little syntactical order. The modern English author writes well-balanced, well-ordered sentences. But the Saxon King expressed more truly his thought; in him the word order imaged more truly the thought order. The modern writer uses counters where he used coin. The modern writer cannot distinguish between his idea and the set phrase that does duty for its expression, though its terms have other meanings. He alludes to things. His prose is a hint, perfectly understood no doubt by others who know the code, but not for all that a true language. Almost perfectly it does duty for a true language to the people with whom it has grown; better than perfectly in its poetry, which gains in suggestiveness more than its loss in concreteness. Compare the prose of this language with the superior prose of French. Compare its poetry with the far inferior poetry of French. It was, in a word, the English language, good for the English people, redolent of English history, even of the vagaries and absurdities of the history of the English people, with practical jokes and puns and stupid grammatical blunders smelling sweet with the aroma of some splendid verse—with golden lads and girls that come to dust, as chimney sweepers, and with deeds of derring-do. This language, now a courser of ethereal race, now a hack between the shafts of commercialism, serving Shakespeare and the stenographer, used efficiently in William Blake's lyrics and in telegrams; this differed in many of the ways of linguistic difference from the language of the Gael. In it the ideas of the Gael did not find easy expression.

But I have been led on a little too far. The language that was brought face to face with Irish in the eighteenth and nineteenth centuries was not the language of English commerce. The Gaelic people had for English tutors the descendants of the old English settlers, in whose mouths the language was still the language of Shakespeare. The transplanted slip of a language does not develop as does the parent tree. By comparison it rather ceases to develop. The descendants of the earliest English colonists here were found, by a new Englishman of Elizabeth's time, using 'the dregs of the old ancient Chaucer English.' So in our day we find in the mouths of the people what such a progressive might call the dregs of the old ancient Shakespeare English. And this was the English that had to be knit into a different complication from the modern complication of the central English language. For the rest, it is not only in Ireland that the phenomenon has occurred: analogous is the use of English by the American booster and by the mystic who has to express in terms of sense and wit the things of God that are made known to him in no language. . . .

The Gaelic Renaissance means to us not only the revival of interest in this old Irish literature, the revival of interest in the civilization, the culture and the history of ancient Ireland, the enthusiasm, the adventure, the pride, the satisfaction, the emotion that are quickened by the discovery of the old monuments, but, added to these, the study of modern Irish as a language capable of literature, the interest in the fragments and traditions that have survived, the reconstruction of our new state on some of the old foundations, and so, patriotism. A recent writer has lamented that instead of the Classic there did not take place in the fourteenth century a Gaelic Renaissance. Of course, the lament and all discussion of it is futile. I listen dreamily to it. To the speakers of the Romance languages, to the readers of Romance literatures, the Classic Renaissance was such as to a strange people, who had seen only the statues of men of our race, would be the sight of the living models. The remarkable thing about the coming of the Classic Renaissance is not its coming in the fourteenth century, but its not coming earlier. The coming was inevitable. It was long prepared for. And when we use the same word, Renaissance, for the Gaelic revival, springing from the rediscovery of the ancient language and literature, and branching now into a double literature in two languages, we do not claim that it is quite the counterpart of the Classic. The old literature that was to be discovered, the ancient Irish art, were not in such consonance even with what of literature and art we still held, as were Classic literature and art with those of mediaeval Europe, with the culture that still held allegiance to Rome and had memories of ancient Greece. Still at the heart of that lament for a Gaelic Renaissance five hundred years ago is this truth, that if history had been different the ancient culture and the ancient literature of our people might have had a more powerful influence on the culture and literature of Europe. The Celtic peoples had kindred memories with ours though they had changed their speech. Of Gaelic influence in literature, in art, in music, there have always been the sure marks and the sure effects, as has been pointed out by Dr Sigerson* and others; but only during the last century has it come home and thriven.

This is not the place to attempt a history of the Revival. I propose here rapidly to survey portions of the literature of ancient Ireland and to come thence to the literature and the prospects of to-day. The poems of Old Irish are from eight to fourteen centuries old. There has been in the intervening period a steady enough stream of literature in Middle and Modern Irish; but my ignorance of all but a small amount of this and my sympathy with the way of the old time send me back to the beginning and then draw me home to the new age opening now.

The themes of Early Irish Literature are many of them the themes of modern romantic literature—in lyric poetry, nature and humanity:—nature: the joy of natural things; the joy of the earth's beauty, the woods and the birds in the woods; the delight of summer, season surpassing, grateful to dwellers in a northern land; the terror of the white winter when not a bell is heard and no crane talks, when shapes are all gone; the joy of the sea, the plain of Ler, with its witching song, the delightful home of ships, the image of Hell with its dread tempest:—humanity: men and women, love and destiny: humanity at odds with life: a king and a hermit; a girl who died for love; a warrior who kept his tryst after death; Deirdre, the pre-destined of sorrow, winning some joy from life before her fate falls; an old woman who has seen the passing away of her famous beauty, who sees the ebb tide carrying away her years, who sees the flood-wave foaming in for others. Later, after the English are settled in the land, not humanity but the nation, Kathleen ni Houlihan, is our heroic theme. The manifestations of nationality are symbolised by man and nature. The silk of the kine* goes lurking in the woods, weeping down tears, while her foe has wine on his table. The little shining rose is black. Ned of the Hill beats on the bolted door of the Nation; he is out under the snow, under the frost, under the rain, without comradeship, hunted with hail of bullets, desolate most of all at the thought that he must go east over the sea because it is there he has no kindred. No wonder that those who, lured by the felicity of gracious words, have learned to read with satisfaction in Shakespeare the easy hideous history of the English Wars of the Roses, half won to sympathy with ravening lust and barbarity, are perplexed by Gaelic Literature of the middle period. And so all Irish Literature is set down as vague, mysterious, obscure. Nothing could be more clear, more direct, more gem-like, hard and delicate and bright, than the earlier lyric poetry, nothing more surely true to nature, full of natural piety, nothing of another kind greater in suggestion, however brief in form. Not till the advent of Wordsworth comes there any-thing like this intimacy with nature into other modern literature. Not till we listen to the voice of Shelley do we hear in other lyric poetry such prophecy of song as has come down through folk poetry in Irish, a lyric poetry which, as Mr John Eglinton* said some years ago, 'has far more in common with the later developments of English poetry—with poems, for example, like Shelley's *When the Lamp is Shattered* or George Meredith's *Love in a Valley*—than anything produced by the wits of the London coffee houses.'

The themes of the old sagas have been used by many in our day as the story of the Trojan war has been used by many nations that read Greek. Deirdre is to us

> 'the morning star of loveliness,
> Unhappy Helen of a western land.'[1]

They have not been used as successfully as the Greek models. They are not the inheritance of this alien civilization. They require different standards. To quote Mr John Eglinton again: 'These subjects, much as we may admire them and regret that we have nothing equivalent to them in the modern world, obstinately refuse to be taken up out of their old environment, and be transplanted into the world of modern sympathies. The proper mode of treating them is a secret lost with the subjects themselves.' It is possible, of course that, while I write, these *dicta* are being disproved. It would be vain, even if unluckily we wished it or could do it, to set bounds to literary genius, which is always breaking new soil, or rather always coming in a new manifestation. It is at its best and highest a new epiphany. Some in our day or after our day may make a great new literature in the tradition of this old world of Early Irish Literature. But I rather expect that the literature of to-morrow will be in terms of the life of to-morrow, and that the old world is too different, too far apart, too much wronged now, I fear, by misrepresentation, by false praise that would make it good of another kind than of its way of goodness, by false blame that would call its culture barbarism, its strength brutality or impropriety, its mysticism magic, its austere sincerity in literature a defect of power and richness, its power and richness, when it has such, exaggeration. We may admit that we cannot now feel those old emotions at first heart, so to put it. We have not reverence for the same things. We cannot pray to the old gods. We could not blaspheme the old gods. We are of a different day; a different light shines upon us. History is between us and our heroes. We cannot rid our memories of the glories and the calamities of our story, of the mighty things, of the futile things. Our thought is woven of the stuff of memory and elder thought and of a knowledge that has gained on this side and lost on that like an island in the sea. Our dreams are children dreams and parent dreams. A part of the old world lives in

---

[1] *The Three Sorrows of Story-Telling: Deirdre*, by Douglas Hyde.

us; to a large part we are alien not in speech only but in feeling, in sense, in instinct, in vision. We are true to the best of the old literature when we are true to that part of it which we inherit now in the twentieth century, when we discover in ourselves something of its good tradition, something that has remained true by the changing standards and measures. . . .

My race has survived the wiles of the foreigner here. It has refused to yield even to defeat, and emerges strong to-day, full of hope and of love, with new strength in its arms to work its new destiny, with a new song on its lips and the word of the new language, which is the ancient language, still calling from age to age. The adorable delicacy, the shrinking sensibility, the paralysing diffidence which has its root in charity, the qualities which make for temporary defeat and yet, being of their nature joined with the unwavering conviction of truth and right, for ultimate victory,—these live on. Now with them, in the same breasts with them, lives this too: its day is come. This arrogance is a sign of energy, of vitality, and so here is good. The Gaelic movement is a revival. Though, through changes of methods and modes of advance, the exhaustion of old methods and the need for new movements, it may seem to-day that the central movement has lost force, it still goes forward. Of a tide of thought, drawn by the inspiration of an ancient cause, there is no ebb. This will have a voice, a literature, tomorrow, the voice of a people new to such a way of speech, the literature of a fresh people. To be a poet one must look with fresh eyes on life; to produce poets a nation must be fresh. Ireland has already produced a great literature of old: the fragments that remain prove that. But, as we are now, we are a fresh people, fresh to literature. We have begun to produce a literature in English, a foreign tongue. This will not injure or delay the progress of Gaelic literature, which must be the work of other writers. Most of the Anglo-Irish poets—and it is almost all poetry still—have spent in attaining their knowledge and mastery of their craft all the resources of learning and acquirement in them. In the matter of technique— and this is all but supremely necessary in modern poetry—one language only will one poet master. Whether our people go forward in Anglo-Irish literature or not, some of our poets and writers of the next generation will certainly continue the production of a new literature in Irish. As I have said, we are fresh in other senses too— fresh from the natural home of man, the fields and the country. We have not all grown up in streets amid the artificialities of civilization, with traditional memories of brick and plaster. The influences of nature will be felt by us as by the true poets of all tongues. Our nature poetry will owe nothing to the botanical observations of city dwellers; it will be no sham pastoral imitation; it will be natural and spontaneous, and our own. But above all we are fresh in language, which the most city-hating English lover of nature cannot be. We are the children of a race that, through need or choice, turned from Irish to English. We have now so well mastered this language of our adoption that we use it with a freshness and power that the English of these days rarely have. But now also we have begun to turn back to the old language, not old to us. The future poets of the country will probably be the sons and daughters of a generation that learned Irish as a strange tongue; the words and phrases of Irish will have a new wonder for them; the figures of speech will have all their first poetry. Carlyle says of Imagination:* 'Metaphors are her stuff; examine language—what, if you except some primitive elements, what is it but metaphors, recognised as such or no longer recognised, still fluid and florid, or now solid-grown and colourless?' The metaphors of Irish will not be colourless to the fresh eyes of the next generation, though the language be their native idiom. Perhaps the temporary abandonment of Irish has not been an unmitigated disaster, now that its revival is assured. A language that transmits its literature mainly by oral tradition cannot, if spoken only by thousands, bequeath as much to posterity as if spoken by millions. The loss of idiom and of literature is a disaster. But, on the other hand, the abandonment has broken a tradition of pedantry and barren conventions; and sincerity gains thereby. The *aisling** is now at last dead; the simple beautiful folk-songs in which recent Irish literature is richer perhaps than any other, are more likely to serve as models than the vain word-weaving of the bards. The writers of the *dán díreach** became at last, to use a mis-translated phrase, mere 'schoolmen of condensed speech,' but their verse at worst had the high virtue of restraint. Their successors became fluent, eloquent craftsmen of skilful word-music. The poets of the next age will learn from the faults of both schools; they will make restraint a canon of their art, not a pedantry; they will know that the too facile use of the adjective is a vice, and verse-music a snare. Let us postulate continuity, but continuity in the true way.

2. MEMOIRS AND AUTOBIOGRAPHIES

JOHN O'LEARY
(1830–1907)

from *Recollections of Fenians and Fenianism* (1896)

It is with a sad heart and a somewhat doubtful mind that I set myself down, on the borders of old age, to say something of what I felt and thought and did in my early youth and mature manhood. Times have changed in Ireland greatly since then, and, no doubt, I have very greatly changed myself—but scarcely with the times. Whether this be my misfortune or my fault, or simply a necessary and inevitable result of the passage of the years, it is impossible for me to tell. I can only recognize the fact, and I feel that my readers will be but too likely to keep it well before their minds. I do not think that I have much of the *laudator temporis acti** in my nature, but I am certainly very little in love with the present, and but for my strong hope of a future other and better than the present, I should have but little pleasure in looking back upon my past or any past.

But to come to that past. Where shall I begin? There is something of a difficulty here, though perhaps not a great one. Nearly all our thoughts and acts have their roots in a past whose distance it is almost impossible to calculate. But then I am not writing of my relation to the universe, but merely of my relation to Fenianism. Here I have little difficulty myself as to where to begin, while feeling that the thing may not be at all so clear to my readers, and especially to such English ones as I may chance to find. I commence my story, then, in what my aforesaid English reader may probably consider a somewhat Irish fashion, by telling how I became a Young Irelander—for here was certainly the root of the matter to me. I have said something of this elsewhere more than once, but here I must go more fully into it.

Sometime in the year 1846, while recovering from a fever, I came across the poems and essays of Thomas Davis,* then recently dead. What Davis has been to more than a generation of Irishmen since his death is well known in his own country, and may in a measure be understood by Englishmen now, since the publication of his prose writings (edited by T. W. Rolleston, in the Camelot series), and of his life, written by his co-labourer and friend, Sir C. G. Duffy.* What he was then to me I feel as if I can only faintly shadow forth at this distance of time. Perhaps it may give some notion of the effect produced on me to say that I then went through a process analogous to what certain classes of Christians call 'conversion.' I can but vaguely remember my unregenerate state. Doubtless (from my surroundings) I was not anti-Irish or West-British:* but then I am confident I was not strongly Irish, and I am sure I was strongly ambitious, and can easily conceive that my ambition, stimulated by much reading of English literature, necessarily either directly or indirectly anti-Irish in spirit, might have led me where it has unfortunately led so many of my countrymen before and since. Now, however, everything was changed. The world was an altered world to me. I felt in quite a new sense that I was an Irishman, and that for weal or woe my fate must be linked with that of my country. I do not think that either then or since I ever had much of that spurious Irishism of Moore's song,* which associates Ireland with virtue and England with guilt; but Irish in a higher and better sense I think I may claim to have at least struggled to be, and, in so far as I have fought the good fight, to Thomas Davis more than to any other, or, indeed more than to all others, is the credit due. I do not like to exaggerate, and do not think I am doing so. I do not, of course, mean in the least to convey that the largest part of my intellectual and moral training does not necessarily come from other and wider regions, but for all that is Irish in me, and, above all, for the inspiration that made me Irish, the fountain and the origin must always be sought in Davis.

But what came out of all this? Little, perhaps, at once—or at least little in the shape of action. What must have followed very soon was the close study of the leading columns, and indeed of many other columns, of the *Nation** newspaper. For what I found there I was, of course, perfectly prepared by the previous reading of Davis; and what was to be found in that paper I must leave the reader to gather from another pen than mine. Something, however, I must say even at this stage as to how the *Nation* affected me; later I shall have more to tell. In leading article, essay, and poem we read, from week to week, the story of Ireland's sufferings under English rule; and now and then we heard of other countries groaning under alien domination, and of their efforts, successful or unsuccessful, to shake it off. At first, perhaps, the teaching of the *Nation* was not directly unconstitutional, though, indirectly, it certainly was so from the beginning. From ceasing to 'fear to speak of '98'* to wishing to imitate the men of that time the transition was very easy indeed to the youthful mind. Many, if not most, of the younger amongst us were Mitchelites before Mitchel, or rather before Mitchel* had put forth his programme. We were told much about the doings of Hugh O'Neill and Owen Roe and Sarsfield,* and led to seek what more we could gather about them elsewhere. But as to the men of '98 there was no difficulty where to search and what to find. We had the fascinating 'Memoirs of Wolfe Tone,'* and the very laborious and full, if somewhat dull and chaotic, book of Madden,* and many a biography and history beside. I may perhaps be mixing up some things in my memory here; but the impression I mean to convey is certainly correct. I may be attributing to the *Nation* other things than I got from it; but that matters little, for Davis was the *Nation* and the *Nation* was Davis; and in saying this I most surely do not in the least mean to detract from the merit of the many able men who with Davis, and without him, made the *Nation*. Anyway, the feeling and sentiment upon which I acted then, and have mainly acted ever since, came from Davis; and what the *Nation* no doubt gave me, or taught me where to get, were such additional facts and fancies as my opinions sought by way of justification of the faith that was in me. . . .

And so the years passed on, leaving Ireland where she was, disgusted, disheartened, and, to all outward appearance, entirely apathetic. The period between the collapse of the Tenant League and the rise of Fenianism was the 'deadest' time in Irish politics within my memory, and perhaps within the memory of any man now living. We were not indeed without our excitements during this period; but they were none of our making, and so left us very much where we were. There was the Crimean War, for instance, which stirred England to the very depths, but which only touched the outer fringe, or, perhaps, I had better call it, the upper crust of Irish Society. The masses were interested, if not moved, but in an adverse sense from that of England. The Czar Nicholas,* who, to the prejudiced and stupid English mind of the time, was simply the incarnation of evil, was to the equally prejudiced, but by no means stupid, Irish mind not in any way a saint or hero, but a being who, whatever might be his nature, must necessarily be beneficent to Ireland in proportion as he was maleficent to England. That was rather a simple way of looking at things, but it has always been our way, is our way still—all pretence of 'union of hearts' notwithstanding—and can only cease to be our way when our relations with England cease to be what they are.

Our feelings during the Crimean War were somewhat complicated by the fact that the French were on the side of England. We did not, any of us, wish them any ill, though many of us wished no good to their scoundrel of an Emperor. But in the next difficulty of England there was no such complication of feeling. Our feelings—that is the feelings of the great mass of Irishmen—were entirely on the side of India during the mutiny. We were altogether untouched by the thrilling stories of Indian cruelty, knowing but too well, from our own history, that England was quite sure to give as good as she got; and all subsequent and authentic accounts of the suppression of the mutiny show that we were quite right in preserving our equanimity, and that England in every sense showed herself quite worthy of her ancient fame, on this occasion.

The Crimean War and the Indian Mutiny came and went, but left us quite as we were before. England's difficulty is proverbially said to be Ireland's opportunity, but opportunities may present themselves to nations, as to individuals, to little effect. Here were opportunities—especially in the case of the Indian Mutiny, when Ireland was nearly entirely denuded of troops—if only we could avail ourselves of them. But, alas! we could not. The country had not yet recovered from the physical collapse of '48, or what may be called the moral collapse of '55. She was without organization, or even the thought of organization, and so such an opportunity as we had not had for long before, have not had since, nor are likely to have soon again, passed away, leaving us no nearer freedom. If Fenianism had been then, things might have been far different now; but the idea still lay more or less dormant in the brain of James Stephens, to wake up into activity, however, very soon after.

OSCAR WILDE
(1854–1900)

from *De Profundis* (1905)

I was a man who stood in symbolic relations to the art and culture of my age. I had realised this for myself at the very dawn of my manhood, and had forced my age to realise it afterwards. Few men hold such a position in their own lifetime and have it so acknowledged. It is usually discerned, if discerned at all, by the historian, or the critic, long after both the man and his age have passed away. With me it was different. I felt it myself, and made others feel it. Byron was a symbolic figure, but his relations were to the passion of his age and its weariness of passion. Mine were to something more noble, more permanent, of more vital issue, of larger scope.

The gods had given me almost everything. I had genius, a distinguished name, high social position, brilliancy, intellectual daring: I made art a philosophy, and philosophy an art: I altered the minds of men and the colours of things: there was nothing I said or did that did not make people wonder: I took the drama, the most objective form known to art, and made it as personal a mode of expression as the lyric or the sonnet, at the same time that I widened its range and enriched its characterisation: drama, novel, poem in rhyme, poem in prose, subtle or fantastic dialogue, whatever I touched I made beautiful in a new mode of beauty: to truth itself I gave what is false no less than what is true as its rightful province, and showed that the false and the true are merely forms of intellectual existence. I treated Art as the supreme reality, and life as a mere mode of fiction: I awoke the imagination of my century so that it created myth and legend around me: I summed up all systems in a phrase, and all existence in an epigram.

Along with these things, I had things that were different. I let myself be lured into long spells of senseless and sensual ease. I amused myself with being a *flâneur*, a dandy, a man of fashion. I surrounded myself with the smaller natures and the meaner minds. I became the spendthrift of my own genius, and to waste an eternal youth gave me a curious joy. Tired of being on the heights I deliberately went to the depths in the search for new sensations. What the paradox was to me in the sphere of thought, perversity became to me in the sphere of passion. Desire, at the end, was a malady, or a madness, or both. I grew careless of the lives of others. I took pleasure where it pleased me and passed on. I forgot that every little action of the common day makes or unmakes character, and that therefore what one has done in the secret chamber one has some day to cry aloud on the housetops. I ceased to be Lord over myself. I was no longer the Captain of my Soul,* and did not know it. I allowed you to dominate me, and your father to frighten me. I ended in horrible disgrace. There is only one thing for me now, absolute Humility also. You had better come down into the dust and learn it beside me.

I have lain in prison for nearly two years. Out of my nature has come wild despair; an abandonment to grief that was piteous even to look at: terrible and impotent rage: bitterness and scorn: anguish that wept aloud: misery that could find no voice: sorrow that was dumb. I have passed through every possible mood of suffering. Better than Wordsworth* himself I know what Wordsworth meant when he said:

> Suffering is permanent, obscure, and dark
> And has the nature of Infinity.

But while there were times when I rejoiced in the idea that my sufferings were to be endless, I could not bear them to be without meaning. Now I find hidden away in my nature something that tells me that nothing in the whole world is meaningless, and suffering least of all. That something hidden away in my nature, like a treasure in a field, is Humility.

It is the last thing left in me, and the best: the ultimate discovery at which I have arrived: the starting-point for a fresh development. It has come to me right out of myself, so I know that it has come at the proper time. It could not have come before, nor later. Had anyone told me of it, I would have rejected it. Had it been brought to me, I would have refused it. As I found it, I want to keep it. I must do so. It is the one thing that has in it the elements of life, of a new life, a *Vita Nuova** for me. Of all things it is the strangest. One cannot give it away, and another may not give it to one. One cannot acquire it, except by surrendering everything that one has. It is only when one has lost all things, that one knows that one possesses it.

Now that I realise that it is in me, I see quite clearly what I have got to do, what, in fact, I must do. And when I use such a phrase as that, I need not tell you that I am not alluding to any external sanction or command. I admit none. I am far more of an individualist than I ever was. Nothing seems to me of the smallest value except what one gets out of oneself. My nature is seeking a fresh mode of self-realisation. That is all I am concerned with. And the first thing that I have got to do is to free myself from any possible bitterness of feeling against you.

I am completely penniless, and absolutely homeless. Yet there are worse things in the world than that. I am quite candid when I tell you that rather than go out from this prison with bitterness in my heart against you or against the world I would gladly and readily beg my bread from door to door. If I got nothing from the house of the rich, I would get something at the house of the poor. Those who have much are often greedy. Those who have little always share. I would not a bit mind sleeping in the cool grass in summer, and when winter came on sheltering myself by the warm close-thatched rick, or under the penthouse of a great barn, provided I had love in my heart. The external things of life seem to me now of no importance at all. You can see to what intensity of individualism I have arrived, or am arriving rather, for the journey is long, and 'where I walk there are thorns.'

Of course I know that to ask for alms on the highway is not to be my lot, and that if ever I lie in the cool grass at night-time it will be to write sonnets to the Moon. When I go out of prison, Robbie* will be waiting for me on the other side of the big iron-studded gate, and he is the symbol not merely of his own affection, but of the affection of many others besides. I believe I am to have enough to live on for about eighteen months at any rate, so that, if I may not write beautiful books, I may at least read beautiful books, and what joy can be greater? After that, I hope to be able to recreate my creative faculty. But were things different: had I not a friend left in the world: were there not a single house open to me even in pity: had I to accept the wallet and ragged cloak of sheer penury: still as long as I remained free from all resentment, hardness, and scorn, I would be able to face life with much more calm and confidence than I would were my body in purple and fine linen, and the soul within it sick with hate. And I shall really have no difficulty in forgiving you. But to make it a pleasure for me you must feel that you want it. When you really want it you will find it waiting for you.

I need not say that my task does not end there. It would be comparatively easy if it did. There is much more before me. I have hills far steeper to climb, valleys much darker to pass through. And I have to get it all out of myself. Neither Religion, Morality, nor Reason can help me at all.

Morality does not help me. I am a born antinomian. I am one of those who are made for exceptions, not for laws. But while I see that there is nothing wrong in what one does, I see that there is something wrong in what one becomes. It is well to have learned that.

Religion does not help me. The faith that others give to what is unseen, I give to what one can touch, and look at. My Gods dwell in temples made with hands, and within the circle of actual experience is my creed made perfect and complete: too complete it may be, for like many or all of those who have placed their Heaven in this earth, I have found in it not merely the beauty of Heaven, but the horror of Hell also. When I think about Religion at all, I feel as if I would like to found an order for those who cannot believe: the Confraternity of the Fatherless one might call it, where on an altar, on which no taper burned, a priest, in whose heart peace had no dwelling, might celebrate with unblessed bread and a chalice empty of wine. Everything to be true must become a religion. And agnosticism should have its ritual no less than faith. It has sown its martyrs, it should reap its saints, and praise God daily for having hidden Himself from man. But whether it be faith or agnosticism, it must be nothing external to me. Its symbols must be of my own creating. Only that is spiritual which makes its own form. If I may not find its secret within myself, I shall never find it. If I have not got it already, it will never come to me.

Reason does not help me. It tells me that the laws under which I am convicted are wrong and unjust laws, and the system under which I have suffered a wrong and unjust system. But, somehow, I have got to make both of these things just and right to me. And exactly as in Art one is only concerned with what a particular thing is at a particular moment to oneself, so it is also in the ethical evolution of one's character. I have got to make everything that has happened to me good for me. The plank-bed, the loathsome food, the hard ropes shredded into oakum till one's finger-tips grow dull with pain, the menial offices with which each day begins and finishes, the harsh orders that routine seems to necessitate, the dreadful dress that makes sorrow grotesque to look at, the silence, the solitude, the shame—each and all of these things I have to transform into a spiritual experience. There is not a single degradation of the body which I must not try and make into a spiritualising of the soul.

I want to get to the point when I shall be able to say, quite simply and without affectation, that the two great turning-points of my life were when my father sent me to Oxford, and when society sent me to prison. I will not say that it is the best thing that could have happened to me, for that phrase would savour of too great bitterness towards myself. I would sooner say, or hear it said of me, that I was so typical a child of my age that in my perversity, and for that perversity's sake, I turned the good things of my life to evil, and the evil things of my life to good. What is said, however, by myself or by others matters little. The important thing, the thing that lies before me, the thing that I have to do, or be for the brief remainder of my days one maimed, marred, and incomplete, is to absorb into my nature all that has been done to me, to make it part of me, to accept it without complaint, fear, or reluctance. The supreme vice is shallowness. Whatever is realised is right. . . .

I hope to live long enough, and to produce work of such a character, that I shall be able at the end of my days to say, 'Yes: this is just where the artistic life leads a man.' Two of the most perfect lives I have come across in my own experience are the lives of Verlaine* and of Prince Kropotkin:* both of them men who passed years in prison: the first, the one Christian poet since Dante, the other a man with the soul of that beautiful white Christ that seems coming out of Russia. And for the last seven or eight months, in spite of a succession of great troubles reaching me from the outside world almost without intermission, I have been placed in direct contact with a new spirit working in this prison through men and things, that has helped me beyond any possibility of expression in words; so that while for the first year of my imprisonment I did nothing else, and can remember doing nothing else, but wring my hands in impotent despair, and say 'What an ending! What an appalling ending!' Now I try to say to myself, and sometimes when I am not torturing myself do really and sincerely say, 'What a beginning! What a wonderful beginning!' It may really be so. It may become so. If it does, I shall owe much to this new personality that has altered every man's life in this place.

Things in themselves are of little importance, have indeed—let us for once thank Metaphysics for something that she has taught us— no real existence. The spirit alone is of importance. Punishment may be inflicted in such a way that it will heal, not make a wound, just as alms may be given in such a manner that the bread changes to a stone in the hands of the giver. What a change there is—not in the regula- tions, for they are fixed by iron rule, but in the spirit that uses them as its expression—you can realise when I tell you that had I been released last May, as I tried to be, I would have left this place loathing it and every official in it with a bitterness of hatred that would have poisoned my life. I have had a year longer of imprisonment, but Humanity has been in the prison along with us all, and now when I go out I shall always remember great kindnesses that I have received here from almost everybody, and on the day of my release will give my thanks to many people and ask to be remembered by them in turn.

The prison-system is absolutely and entirely wrong. I would give anything to be able to alter it when I go out. I intend to try. But there is nothing in the world so wrong but that the spirit of Humanity, which is the spirit of Love, the spirit of the Christ who is not in Churches, may make it, if not right, at least possible to be borne without too much bitterness of heart.

I know also that much is waiting for me outside that is very delightful, from what St Francis of Assisi calls '*my brother the wind*' and '*my sister the rain*,' lovely things both of them, down to the shop- windows and sunsets of great cities. If I made a list of all that still remains to me, I don't know where I should stop: for, indeed, God made the world just as much for me as for anyone else. Perhaps I may go out with something I had not got before. I need not tell you that to me Reformations in Morals are as meaningless and vulgar as Reformations in Theology. But while to propose to be a better man is a piece of unscientific cant, to have become a *deeper* man is the privilege of those who have suffered. And such I think I have become. You can judge for yourself.

If after I go out a friend of mine gave a feast, and did not invite me to it, I shouldn't mind a bit. I can be perfectly happy by myself. With freedom, books, flowers, and the moon, who could not be happy?

Besides, feasts are not for me any more. I have given too many to care about them. That side of life is over for me, very fortunately I dare say. But if, after I go out, a friend of mine had a sorrow, and refused to allow me to share it, I should feel it most bitterly. If he shut the doors of the house of mourning against me I would come back again and again and beg to be admitted, so that I might share in what I was entitled to share in. If he thought me unworthy, unfit to weep with him, I should feel it as the most poignant humiliation, as the most terrible mode in which disgrace could be inflicted on me. But that could not be. I have a right to share in Sorrow, and he who can look at the loveliness of the world, and share its sorrow, and realise something of the wonder of both, is in immediate contact with divine things, and has got as near to God's secret as anyone can get.

Perhaps there may come into my art also, no less than into my life, a still deeper note, one of greater unity of passion, and directness of impulse. Not width but intensity is the true aim of modern Art. We are no longer in Art concerned with the type. It is with the exception we have to do. I cannot put my sufferings into any form they took, I need hardly say. Art only begins where Imitation ends. But something must come into my work, of fuller harmony of words perhaps, of richer cadences, of more curious colour-effects, of simpler architectural-order, of some aesthetic quality at any rate.

When Marsyas* was 'torn from the scabbard of his limbs'—*dalla vagina delle membre sue*, to use one of Dante's most terrible, most Tacitean phrases—he had no more song, the Greeks said. Apollo had been victor. The lyre had vanquished the reed. But perhaps the Greeks were mistaken. I hear in much modern Art the cry of Marsyas. It is bitter in Baudelaire,* sweet and plaintive in Lamartine,* mystic in Verlaine. It is in the deferred resolutions of Chopin's music.* It is in the discontent that haunts the recurrent faces of Burne-Jones's women.* Even Matthew Arnold,* whose song of Callicles tells of 'the triumph of the sweet persuasive lyre,' and the 'famous final victory,' in such a clear note of lyrical beauty—even he, in the troubled undertone of doubt and distress that haunts his verse, had not a little of it. Neither Goethe nor Wordsworth could heal him, though he followed each in turn, and when he seeks to mourn for 'Thyrsis' or to sing of 'the Scholar Gipsy,' it is the reed that he has to take for the rendering of his strain. But whether or not the Phrygian Faun was silent, I cannot be. Expression is as necessary to me as leaf and blossom are to the black branches of the trees that show themselves above the prison wall and are so restless in the wind. Between my art and the world there is now a wide gulf, but between Art and myself there is none. I hope at least that there is none.

To each of us different fates have been meted out. Freedom, pleasure, amusements, a life of ease have been your lot, and you are not worthy of it. My lot has been one of public infamy, of long imprisonment, of misery, of ruin, of disgrace, and I am not worthy of it either—not yet, at any rate. I remember I used to say that I thought I could bear a real tragedy if it came to me with purple pall and a mask of noble sorrow, but that the dreadful thing about modernity was that it put Tragedy into the raiment of Comedy, so that the great realities seemed commonplace or grotesque or lacking in style. It is quite true about modernity. It has probably always been true about actual life. It is said that all martyrdoms seemed mean to the looker-on. The nineteenth century is no exception to the general rule.

Everything about my tragedy has been hideous, mean, repellent, lacking in style. Our very dress makes us grotesques. We are the zanies of sorrow. We are clowns whose hearts are broken. We are specially designed to appeal to the sense of humour. On November 13th 1895 I was brought down here from London. From two o'clock till half-past two on that day I had to stand on the centre platform of Clapham Junction in convict dress and handcuffed, for the world to look at. I had been taken out of the Hospital Ward without a moment's notice being given to me. Of all possible objects I was the most grotesque. When people saw me they laughed. Each train as it came up swelled the audience. Nothing could exceed their amusement. That was of course before they knew who I was. As soon as they had been informed, they laughed still more. For half an hour I stood there in the grey November rain surrounded by a jeering mob.

For a year after that was done to me I wept every day at the same hour and for the same space of time. That is not such a tragic thing as possibly it sounds to you. To those who are in prison, tears are a part of every day's experience. A day in prison on which one does not weep is a day on which one's heart is hard, not a day on which one's heart is happy.

Well, now I am really beginning to feel more regret for the people who laughed than for myself. Of course when they saw me I was not on my pedestal. I was in the pillory. But it is a very unimaginative nature that only cares for people on their pedestals. A pedestal may be a very unreal thing. A pillory is a terrific reality. They should have known also how to interpret sorrow better. I have said that behind Sorrow there is always Sorrow. It were still wiser to say that behind sorrow there is always a soul. And to mock at a soul in pain is a dreadful thing. Unbeautiful are their lives who do it. In the strangely simple economy of the world people only get what they give, and to those who have not enough imagination to penetrate the mere outward of things and feel pity, what pity can be given save that of scorn?

I have told you this account of the mode of my being conveyed here simply that you should realise how hard it has been for me to get anything out of my punishment but bitterness and despair. I have however to do it, and now and then I have moments of submission and acceptance. All the spring may be hidden in a single bud, and the low ground-nest of the lark may hold the joy that is to herald the feet of many rose-red dawns, and so perhaps whatever beauty of life still remains to me is contained in some moment of surrender, abasement and humiliation. I can, at any rate, merely proceed on the lines of my own development, and by accepting all that has happened to me make myself worthy of it.

J. M. SYNGE
(1871–1909)

from *The Aran Islands* (1907)

I am in Aranmor,* sitting over a turf fire, listening to a murmur of Gaelic that is rising from a little public-house under my room.

The steamer which comes to Aran sails according to the tide, and it was six o'clock this morning when we left the quay of Galway in a dense shroud of mist.

A low line of shore was visible at first on the right between the movement of the waves and fog, but when we came further it was lost sight of, and nothing could be seen but the mist curling in the rigging, and a small circle of foam.

There were few passengers; a couple of men going out with young pigs tied loosely in sacking, three or four young girls who sat in the cabin with their heads completely twisted in their shawls, and a builder, on his way to repair the pier at Kilronan, who walked up and down and talked with me.

In about three hours Aran came in sight. A dreary rock appeared at first sloping up from the sea into the fog; then as we drew nearer, a coastguard station and the village.

A little later I was wandering out along the one good roadway of the island, looking over low walls on either side into small flat fields of naked rock. I have seen nothing so desolate. Grey floods of water were sweeping everywhere upon the limestone, making at times a wild torrent of the road, which twined continually over low hills and cavities in the rock or passed between a few small fields of potatoes or grass hidden away in corners that had shelter. Whenever the cloud lifted I could see the edge of the sea below me on the right, and the naked ridge of the island above me on the other side. Occasionally I passed a lonely chapel or schoolhouse, or a line of stone pillars with crosses above them and inscriptions asking a prayer for the soul of the person they commemorated.

I met few people; but here and there a band of tall girls passed me on their way to Kilronan, and called out to me with humorous wonder, speaking English with a slight foreign intonation that differed a good deal from the brogue of Galway. The rain and cold seemed to have no influence on their vitality, and as they hurried past me with eager laughter and great talking in Gaelic, they left the wet masses of rock more desolate than before.

A little after midday when I was coming back one old half-blind man spoke to me in Gaelic, but, in general, I was surprised at the abundance and fluency of the foreign tongue.

In the afternoon the rain continued, so I sat here in the inn looking out through the mist at a few men who were unlading hookers that had come in with turf from Connemara, and at the long-legged pigs that were playing in the surf. As the fishermen came in and out of the public-house underneath my room, I could hear through the broken panes that a number of them still used the Gaelic, though it seems to be falling out of use among the younger people of this village.

The old woman of the house had promised to get me a teacher of the language, and after a while I heard a shuffling on the stairs, and the old dark man I had spoken to in the morning groped his way into the room.

I brought him over to the fire, and we talked for many hours. He told me that he had known Petrie and Sir William Wilde, and many living antiquarians, and had taught Irish to Dr Finck, and Dr Pedersen, and given stories to Mr Curtin* of America. A little after middle age he had fallen over a cliff, and since then he had had little eyesight, and a trembling of his hands and head.

As we talked he sat huddled together over the fire, shaking and blind, yet his face was indescribably pliant, lighting up with an ecstasy of humour when he told me of anything that had a point of wit or malice, and growing sombre and desolate again when he spoke of religion or the fairies.

He had great confidence in his own powers and talent, and in the superiority of his stories over all other stories in the world. When we were speaking of Mr Curtin, he told me that this gentleman had brought out a volume of his Aran stories in America, and made five hundred pounds by the sale of them.

'And what do you think he did then?' he continued; 'he wrote a book of his own stories after making that lot of money with mine. And he brought them out; and the divil a halfpenny did he get for them. Would you believe that?'

Afterwards he told me how one of his children had been taken by the fairies.

One day a neighbour was passing, and she said, when she saw it on the road, 'That's a fine child.'

Its mother tried to say 'God bless it,' but something choked the words in her throat.

A while later they found a wound on its neck, and for three nights the house was filled with noises.

'I never wear a shirt at night,' he said, 'but I got up out of bed, all naked as I was, when I heard the noises in the house, and lighted a light, but there was nothing in it.'

Then a dummy came and made signs of hammering nails in a coffin.

The next day the seed potatoes were full of blood, and the child told his mother that he was going to America.

That night it died, and 'Believe me,' said the old man, 'the fairies were in it.'

(When he went away, a little bare-footed girl was sent up with turf and the bellows to make a fire that would last for the evening.

She was shy, yet eager to talk, and told me that she had good spoken Irish, and was learning to read it in the school, and that she had been twice to Galway, though there are many grown women in the place who have never set a foot upon the mainland.)

The rain has cleared off, and I have had my first real introduction to the island and its people.

I went out through Killeany—the poorest village in Aranmor—to a long neck of sandhill that runs out into the sea towards the south-west. As I lay there on the grass the clouds lifted from the Connemara mountains and, for a moment, the green undulating foreground, backed in the distance by a mass of hills, reminded me of the country near Rome. Then the dun top-sail of a hooker swept above the edge of the sandhill and revealed the presence of the sea.

As I moved on a boy and a man came down from the next village to talk to me, and I found that here, at least, English was imperfectly understood. When I asked them if there were any trees in the island they held a hurried consultation in Gaelic, and then the man asked if 'tree' meant the same thing as 'bush', for if so there were a few in sheltered hollows to the east.

They walked on with me to the sound which separates this island from Inishmaan—the middle island of the group—and showed me the roll from the Atlantic running up between two walls of cliff.

They told me that several men had stayed on Inishmaan to learn Irish, and the boy pointed out a line of hovels where they had lodged running like a belt of straw round the middle of the island. The place looked hardly fit for habitation. There was no green to be seen, and no sign of the people except these beehive-like roofs, and the outline of a Dun that stood out above them against the edge of the sky.

(After a while my companions went away and two other boys came and walked at my heels, till I turned and made them talk to me. They spoke at first of their poverty, and then one of them said—

'I dare say you do have to pay ten shillings a week in the hotel?'

'More,' I answered.

'Twelve?'

'More.'

'Fifteen?'

'More still.'

Then he drew back and did not question me any further, either thinking that I had lied to check his curiosity, or too awed by my riches to continue.)

Repassing Killeany I was joined by a man who had spent twenty years in America, where he had lost his health and then returned, so long ago that he had forgotten English and could hardly make me understand him. He seemed hopeless, dirty, and asthmatic, and after going with me for a few hundred yards he stopped and asked for coppers. I had none left, so I gave him a fill of tobacco, and he went back to his hovel.

When he was gone, two little girls took their place behind me and I drew them in turn into conversation.

They spoke with a delicate exotic intonation that was full of charm, and told me with a sort of chant how they guide 'ladies and gintlemins' in the summer to all that is worth seeing in their neighbourhood, and sell them pampooties and maidenhair ferns, which are common among the rocks.

We were now in Kilronan, and as we parted they showed me holes in their own pampooties, or cowskin sandals, and asked me the price of new ones. I told them that my purse was empty, and then with a few quaint words of blessing they turned away from me and went down to the pier.

All this walk back had been extraordinarily fine. The intense insular clearness one sees only in Ireland, and after rain, was throwing out every ripple in the sea and sky, and every crevice in the hills beyond the bay. . . .*

I am settled at last on Inishmaan in a small cottage with a continual drone of Gaelic coming from the kitchen that opens into my room.

Early this morning the man of the house came over for me with a four-oared curagh—that is, a curagh with four rowers and four oars on either side, as each man uses two—and we set off a little before noon.

It gave me a moment of exquisite satisfaction to find myself moving away from civilisation in this rude canvas canoe of a model that has served primitive races since men first went on the sea.

We had to stop for a moment at a hulk that is anchored in the bay, to make some arrangements for the fish-curing of the middle island, and my crew called out as soon as we were within earshot that they had a man with them who had been in France a month from this day.

When we started again, a small sail was run up in the bow, and we set off across the sound with a leaping oscillation that had no resemblance to the heavy movement of a boat.

The sail is only used as an aid, so the men continued to row after it had gone up, and as they occupied the four cross seats I lay on the canvas at the stern and the frame of slender laths, which bent and quivered as the waves passed under them.

When we set off it was a brilliant morning of April, and the green, glittering waves seemed to toss the canoe among themselves, yet as we drew nearer this island a sudden thunderstorm broke out behind the rocks we were approaching, and lent a momentary tumult to this still vein of the Atlantic.

We landed at a small pier, from which a rude track leads up to the village between small fields and bare sheets of rock like those in Aranmor. The youngest son of my boatman, a boy of about seventeen, who is to be my teacher and guide, was waiting for me at the pier and guided me to his house, while the men settled the curagh and followed slowly with my baggage.

My room is at one end of the cottage, with a boarded floor and ceiling, and two windows opposite each other. Then there is the kitchen with earth floor and open rafters, and two doors opposite each other opening into the open air, but no windows. Beyond it there are two small rooms of half the width of the kitchen with one window apiece.

The kitchen itself, where I will spend most of my time, is full of beauty and distinction. The red dresses of the women who cluster round the fire on their stools give a glow of almost Eastern richness, and the walls have been toned by the turf-smoke to a soft brown that blends with the grey earth-colour of the floor. Many sorts of fishing-tackle, and the nets and oil-skins of the men, are hung upon the walls or among the open rafters; and right overhead, under the thatch, there is a whole cowskin from which they make pampooties.

Every article on these islands has an almost personal character, which gives this simple life, where all art is unknown, something of the artistic beauty of mediæval life. The curaghs and spinning-wheels,

the tiny wooden barrels that are still much used in the place of
earthenware, the home-made cradles, churns, and baskets, are all
full of individuality, and being made from materials that are
common here, yet to some extent peculiar to the island, they seem
to exist as a natural link between the people and the world that is
about them.

The simplicity and unity of the dress increases in another way the
local air of beauty. The women wear red petticoats and jackets of the
island wool stained with madder, to which they usually add a plaid
shawl twisted round their chests and tied at the back. When it rains
they throw another petticoat over their heads with the waistband
round their faces, or, if they are young, they use a heavy shawl like
those worn in Galway. Occasionally other wraps are worn, and during the thunderstorm I arrived in I saw several girls with men's
waistcoats buttoned round their bodies. Their skirts do not come
much below the knee and show their powerful legs in the heavy
indigo stockings with which they are all provided.

The men wear three colours: the natural wool, indigo, and a grey
flannel that is woven of alternate threads of indigo and the natural
wool. In Aranmor many of the younger men have adopted the usual
fisherman's jersey, but I have only seen one on this island.

As flannel is cheap—the women spin the yarn from the wool of
their own sheep, and it is then woven by a weaver in Kilronan for
fourpence a yard—the men seem to wear an indefinite number of
waistcoats and woollen drawers one over the other. They are usually
surprised at the lightness of my own dress, and one old man I spoke
to for a minute on the pier, when I came ashore, asked me if I was not
cold with 'my little clothes.'

As I sat in the kitchen to dry the spray from my coat, several men
who had seen me walking up came in to talk to me, usually murmur-
ing on the threshold, 'The blessing of God on this place,' or some
similar words.

The courtesy of the old woman of the house is singularly attractive, and though I could not understand much of what she said—she
has no English—I could see with how much grace she motioned
each visitor to a chair, or stool, according to his age, and said a few
words to him till he drifted into our English conversation.

For the moment my own arrival is the chief subject of interest,
and the men who come in are eager to talk to me.

Some of them express themselves more correctly than the ordinary peasant, others use the Gaelic idioms continually and substitute 'he' or 'she' for 'it', as the neuter pronoun is not found in modern Irish.

A few of the men have a curiously full vocabulary, others know only the commonest words in English, and are driven to ingenious devices to express their meaning. Of all the subjects we can talk of war seems their favourite, and the conflict between America and Spain is causing a great deal of excitement. Nearly all the families have relations who have had to cross the Atlantic, and all eat the flour and bacon that is brought from the United States, so they have a vague fear that 'if anything happened to America,' their own island would cease to be habitable.

Foreign languages are another favourite topic, and as these men are bilingual they have a fair notion of what it means to speak and think in many different idioms. Most of the strangers they see on the islands are philological students, and the people have been led to conclude that linguistic studies, particularly Gaelic studies, are the chief occupation of the outside world.

'I have seen Frenchmen, and Danes, and Germans,' said one man, 'and there does be a power of Irish books along with them, and they reading them better than ourselves. Believe me there are few rich men now in the world who are not studying the Gaelic.'

They sometimes ask me the French for simple phrases, and when they have listened to the intonation for a moment, most of them are able to reproduce it with admirable precision.

When I was going out this morning to walk round the island with Michael, the boy who is teaching me Irish, I met an old man making his way down to the cottage. He was dressed in miserable black clothes which seemed to have come from the mainland, and was so bent with rheumatism that, at a little distance, he looked more like a spider than a human being.

Michael told me it was Pat Dirane, the story-teller old Mourteen had spoken of on the other island. I wished to turn back, as he appeared to be on his way to visit me, but Michael would not hear of it.

'He will be sitting by the fire when we come in,' he said; 'let you not be afraid, there will be time enough to be talking to him by and by.'

He was right. As I came down into the kitchen some hours later old Pat was still in the chimney-corner, blinking with the turf smoke.

GEORGE MOORE
(1852–1933)

from *Hail and Farewell* (1911)

One of Ireland's many tricks is to fade away to a little speck down on the horizon of our lives, and then to return suddenly in tremendous bulk, frightening us. My words were: In another ten years it will be time enough to think of Ireland again. But Ireland rarely stays away so long. As well as I can reckon, it was about five years after my meditation in the Temple* that W. B. Yeats, the Irish poet, came to see me in my flat in Victoria Street, followed by Edward. My surprise was great at seeing them arrive together, not knowing that they even knew each other; and while staring at them I remembered they had met in my rooms in the King's Bench Walk. But how often had Edward met my friends and liked them, in a way, yet not sufficiently to compel him to hook himself on to them by a letter or a visit? He is one of those self-sufficing men who drift easily into the solitude of a pipe or a book; yet he is cheerful, talkative, and forthcoming when one goes to see him. Our fellowship began in boyhood, and there is affection on his side as well as mine, I am sure of that; all the same he has contributed few visits to the maintenance of our friendship. It is I that go to him, and it was this knowledge of the indolence of his character that caused me to wonder at seeing him arrive with Yeats. Perhaps seeing them together stirred some fugitive jealousy in me, which passed away when the servant brought in the lamp, for, with the light behind them, my visitors appeared a twain as fantastic as anything ever seen in Japanese prints—Edward great in girth as an owl (he is nearly as neckless), blinking behind his glasses, and Yeats lank as a rook, a dream in black silhouette on the flowered wall-paper.

But rooks and owls do not roost together, nor have they a habit or an instinct in common. A mere doorstep casualty, I said, and began to prepare a conversation suitable to both, which was, however, checked by the fateful appearance they presented, sitting side by side, anxious to speak, yet afraid. They had clearly come to me on some great business! But about what, about what? I waited for the servant to leave the room, and as soon as the door was closed they broke forth, telling together that they had decided to found a Literary Theatre in Dublin; so I sat like one confounded, saying to myself: Of course they know nothing of Independent Theatres, and, in view of my own difficulties in gathering sufficient audience for two or three performances, pity began to stir in me for their forlorn project. A forlorn thing it was surely to bring literary plays to Dublin! . . . Dublin of all cities in the world!

It is Yeats, I said, who has persuaded dear Edward, and looking from one to the other, I thought how the cunning rook had enticed the profound owl from his belfry—an owl that has stayed out too late, and is nervous lest he should not be able to find his way back; perplexed, too, by other considerations, lest the Dean and Chapter, having heard of the strange company he is keeping, may have, during his absence, bricked up the entrance to his roost.

As I was thinking these things, Yeats tilted his chair in such dangerous fashion that I had to ask him to desist, and I was sorry to have to do that, so much like a rook did he seem when the chair was on its hind legs. But if ever there was a moment for seriousness, this was one, so I treated them to a full account of the Independent Theatre, begging them not to waste their plays upon Dublin.

It would give me no pleasure whatever to produce my plays in London, Edward said. I have done with London.

Martyn would prefer the applause of our own people, murmured Yeats, and he began to speak of the by-streets, and the lanes, and the alleys, and how one feels at home when one is among one's own people.

Ninety-nine is the beginning of the Celtic Renaissance, said Edward.

I am glad to hear it; the Celt wants a renaissance, and badly; he has been going down in the world for the last two thousand years.

We are thinking, said Yeats, of putting a dialogue in Irish before our play . . . Usheen and Patrick.

Irish spoken on the stage in Dublin! You are not—

Interrupting me, Edward began to blurt out that a change had come, that Dublin was no longer a city of barristers, judges, and officials pursuing a round of mean interests and trivial amusements, but the capital of the Celtic Renaissance.

With all the arts for crown—a new Florence, I said, looking at Edward incredulously, scornfully perhaps, for to give a Literary Theatre to Dublin seemed to me like giving a mule a holiday, and when he pressed me to say if I were with them, I answered with reluctance that I was not; whereupon, and without further entreaty, the twain took up their hats and staves, and they were by the open door before I could beg them not to march away like that, but to give me time to digest what they had been saying to me, and for a moment I walked to and forth, troubled by the temptation, for I am naturally propense to thrust my finger into every literary pie-dish. Something was going on in Ireland for sure, and remembering the literary tone that had crept into a certain Dublin newspaper—somebody sent me the *Express* on Saturdays—I said, I'm with you, but only platonically. You must promise not to ask me to rehearse your plays. I spoke again about the Independent Theatre, and of the misery I had escaped from when I cut the painter.*

But you'll come to Ireland to see our plays, said Edward.

Come to Ireland! and I looked at Edward suspiciously; a still more suspicious glance fell upon Yeats. Come to Ireland! Ireland and I have ever been strangers, without an idea in common. It never does an Irishman any good to return to Ireland . . . and we know it.

One of the oldest of our stories, Yeats began. Whenever he spoke these words a thrill came over me; I knew they would lead me through accounts of strange rites and prophecies, and at that time I believed that Yeats, by some power of divination, or of ancestral memory, understood the hidden meaning of the legends, and whenever he began to tell them I became impatient of interruption. But it was now myself that interrupted, for, however great the legend he was about to tell, and however subtle his interpretation, it would be impossible for me to give him my attention until I had been told how he had met Edward, and all the circumstances of the meeting, and how they had arrived at an agreement to found an Irish Literary Theatre. The story was disappointingly short and simple. When Yeats had said that he had spent the summer at Coole* with Lady Gregory I saw it all; Coole is but three miles from Tillyra: Edward is often at Coole; Lady Gregory and Yeats are often at Tillyra; Yeats and Edward had written plays—the drama brings strange fowls to roost.

So an owl and a rook have agreed to build in Dublin. A strange nest indeed they will put together, one bringing sticks, and the other—with what materials does the owl build? My thoughts hurried on, impatient to speculate on what would happen when the shells began to chip. Would the young owls cast out the young rooks, or would the young rooks cast out the young owls, and what view would the beholders take of this wondrous hatching? And what view would the Church?

So it was in Galway the nest was builded, and Lady Gregory elected to the secretaryship, I said. The introduction of Lady Gregory's name gave me pause . . . And you have come over to find actors, and rehearse your plays. Wonderful, Edward, wonderful! I admire you both, and am with you, but on my conditions. You will remember them? And now tell me, do you think you'll find an audience in Dublin capable of appreciating *The Heather Field?**

Ideas are only appreciated in Ireland, Edward answered, somewhat defiantly.

I begged them to stay to dinner, for I wanted to hear about Ireland, but they went away, speaking of an appointment with Miss Vernon—that name or some other name—a lady who was helping them to collect a cast.

As soon as they had news they would come to me again. And on this I returned to my room deliciously excited, thrilling all over at the thought of an Irish Literary Theatre, and my own participation in the Celtic Renaissance brought about by Yeats. So the drama, I muttered, was not dead but sleeping, and while the hour before dinner was going by, I recalled an evening I had spent about two years ago in the Avenue Theatre. It was there I had seen Yeats for the first time, and it amused me to remember with what eyes I had seen him first, just after the performance of his little one-act play, *The Land of Heart's Desire.** His play neither pleased nor displeased; it struck me as an inoffensive trifle, but himself had provoked in me a violent antipathy, because I judged him from his appearance, and thereby lost two years of his wonderful company. It is true that when I saw him he was on exhibition, striding to and forth at the back of the dress circle, a long black cloak drooping from his shoulders, a soft black sombrero on his head, a voluminous black silk tie flowing from his collar, loose black trousers dragging untidily over his long, heavy feet—a man of such excessive appearance that I could not do otherwise—could I?—than to mistake him for an Irish parody of the poetry that I had seen all my life strutting its rhythmic way in the alleys of the Luxembourg Gardens, preening its rhymes by the fountains, excessive in habit and gait.

As far back as the days when I was a Frenchman,* I had begun to notice that whosoever adorns himself will soon begin to adorn his verses, so robbing them of that intimate sense of life which we admire in Verlaine; his verses proclaim him to have been a man of modest appearance. Never did Hugo or Banville affect any eccentricity of dress—and there are others. But let us be content with the theory, and refrain from collecting facts to support it, for in doing so we shall come upon exceptions, and these will have to be explained away. Suffice it to say, therefore, that Yeats's appearance at the Avenue Theatre confirmed me in the belief that his art could not be anything more than a merely pretty externality, if it were as much, and I declined to allow Nettleship to introduce me to him. No, my good friend, I don't want to know him; he wouldn't interest me, not any more than the Book of Kells*—not so much; Kells has at all events the merit of being archaic, whereas—No, no; to speak to him would make me 'eave—if I may quote a girl whom I heard speaking in the street yesterday.

It was months after, when I had forgotten all about Yeats, that my fingers distractedly picked up a small volume of verse out of the litter in Nettleship's room. Yeats! And after turning over a few pages, I called to Nettleship, who, taking advantage of my liking for the verses, begged again that he might be allowed to arrange a meeting, and, seduced by the strain of genuine music that seemed to whisper through the volume, I consented.

The Cheshire Cheese* was chosen as a tryst, and we started for that tavern one summer afternoon, talking of poetry and painting by turns, stopping at the corner of the street to finish an argument or an anecdote. Oxford Street was all aglow in the sunset, and Nettleship told, as we edged our way through the crowds, how Yeats's great poem was woven out of the legends of the Fianna,* and stopped to recite verses from it so often that when we arrived the poet was seated in front of a large steak, eating abstractedly, I thought, as if he did not know what he was eating—which was indeed the case— for he did not pretend any interest in the remonstrance that I addressed to Nettleship for having failed to choose Friday to dine at the Cheshire Cheese, it being the day when steak-and-kidney pudding was on at that tavern.

In order to help us through the first awkward five minutes, Nettleship informed me that Yeats was writing a work on Blake,* and the moment Blake's name was mentioned Yeats seemed altogether to forget the food before him, and very soon we were deep in a discussion regarding the Book of Thel, which Nettleship said was Blake's most effectual essay in metre. The designs that accompanied Blake's texts were known to me, and when the waiter brought us our steaks, Blake was lost sight of in the interest of the food, and in our interest in Yeats's interpretation of Blake's teaching.

But as the dinner at the Cheshire Cheese was given so that I should make Yeats's acquaintance, Nettleship withdrew from the conversation, leaving me to continue it, expecting, no doubt, that the combat of our wits would provide him with an entertainment as exciting as that of the cock-fights which used to take place a century ago in the adjoining yard. So there was no choice for me but to engage in disputation or to sulk, and the reader will agree with me that I did well to choose the former course, though the ground was all to my disadvantage, my knowledge of Blake being but accidental. There was, however, no dread of combat in me, my adversary not inspiring much belief that he would prove a stout one, and feeling sure that without difficulty I could lay him dead before Nettleship, I rushed at him, all my feathers erect. Yeats parried a blow on which I counted, and he did this so quickly and with so much ease that he threw me on the defensive in a moment. A dialectician, I muttered, of the very first rank; one of a different kind from any I have met before; and a few moments after I began to notice that Yeats was sparring beautifully, avoiding my rushes with great ease, evidently playing to tire me, with the intention of killing me presently with a single spur stroke. In the bout that ensued I was nearly worsted, but at the last moment an answer shot into my mind. Yeats would have discovered its weakness in a moment, and I might have fared ill, so it was a relief to me to notice that he seemed willing to drop our argument about Blake and to talk about something else. He was willing to do this, perhaps because he did not care to humiliate me, or it may have been that he wearied of talking about a literature to one who was imperfectly acquainted with it, or it may have been that I made a better show in argument than I thought for.

EARNÁN O'MALLEY
(1898–1957)

from *On Another Man's Wound* (1936)

I slept out with men from Rosegreen Company at the Centre under a tent which had once been a hayrick cover; some had hammocks which they slung in the hedge from tree branches. I was working in 47 when a scout came to see me. Three men had been captured on the hillside; they were British officers, and the Rosegreen men had them in a dugout lower down. I met the two boys who had captured them. One had a rifle and two rounds of ammunition, the other an empty bandolier, when they saw the three men coming across the fields. The boy with the rifle halted them; the men began to run. He fired. One of the men was wounded slightly, the others came back and all three surrendered. Each had an automatic in his pocket and an identification card. Two were gunner officers from Fethard Artillery Barracks, five miles across the hill. I sent two boys up the hill to find out where the officers had stopped and what they had been doing. Later one came back. The officers had been searching hedges; at a house on the slope they had asked about dug-outs. They had questioned the young man of the house.

I brought them up one by one. They gave me their names, ranks, the name of their commanding officer. They had been out for a walk, they said.

'Any officers we capture in this area are to be shot until such time as you cease shooting your prisoners.'

'We have nothing to do with the shooting of prisoners,' one said.

'This is not a personal question. Our men whom your men may capture and later shoot will have nothing to do with your being shot. My mind is made up about it. You will be shot at dawn tomorrow.'

'Can't you consider the matter?' one asked.

'You will have to consult your officers,' another said; 'you can't do it without authority.'

'I happen to be in command of this area. This is my authority. It would be better to prepare your minds. I will get food ready for you.' I gave them cigarettes. A boy with a rifle lay near the entrance to the dug-out.

A scout rushed down to where I sat. Beside me were six riflemen who had been mobilized in the meantime.

'Soldiers with a machine-gun. They've just come over the brow of the hill and they're searching.'

'Easy,' I said, 'the officers will hear you.'

The scouring soldiers came from Fethard. Other sections of troops would possibly be making their way in our direction.

I blindfolded the officers so that they could not see where they were going. The covering on their eyes made them helpless; their hands were free, but tying a man's hands was not a job we liked. Men held them by the sleeves so that they could walk more easily. One of them limped. He had a slight flesh wound. I put him on a cart.

'If we are surrounded,' I said to the one whose face I liked best, 'I'll let you go. I'm not going to shoot you like dogs.' The guard of riflemen grumbled.

'But you'll shoot them tomorrow, anyhow,' said the Brigade Q.M.* 'Where's the difference?'

The Q.M. was right, but it was tough to have to turn on them suddenly when we were hard put in a fight to shoot them like injured beasts.

One of the officers said, 'We can do first-aid for your wounded if there's a fight.'

A sloe-skin dusk came slowly down on the steep western slopes of Slievenamon* and across the woods there. It blurred the valley of the Suir below the Comeraghs; hedges of tangled hawthorn with fresh leaves, in amongst the neat stems of spruce, stood out against the rise of hills. There was a strong, spicy smell carried across from the bright pink blossoms of a corner hedge of wild crab.

We halted at a gateway. A horse and trap came up. The officers got up into the seats.

A young girl came out from a house. She peered at the men in the half-light. 'Who are they?' she asked.

'English officers,' said a guard.

'Shooting's too good for them,' she said, bitterly; as she looked up at them. They looked down at her with set faces.

'Oh, leave them alone,' I said.

'God help the poor boys,' said a woman beside her, 'perhaps they'd like a sup of milk.' She came back with a large jug and three delph mugs. The officers drank. They thanked her.

We walked into the closing-in darkness, riflemen in front and behind the trap, until we were a distance from where the officers had been captured. I expected a big round-up in which the countryside would be combed by troops from Cahir and Clonmel—both strong military posts. They would probably converge in the triangular area of which Fethard was the apex. We came to a farmhouse up in the fields some way off the main Clonmel road. Sentries were posted. The girls and women of the house got ready supper; they did not ask any questions. A fire was lighted in the room where the officers were. After supper I went into the room. The blinds were drawn so that they could not look out. It was a large room. They were seated at a table. One had his head in his hands.

'Would you like to see a clergyman of your own religion?'

'No,' said one. The others shook their heads.

'Would you like a civilian, an Imperialist, to stay with you?'

'No.' They did not need anyone.

'Here's writing paper and envelopes. You can write to anyone you wish. If you give me your words of honour that you won't mention anything of military importance, you can seal the envelopes yourselves.'

Each gave me his word. There were beds for them to sleep on.

I sat in the kitchen by the fire. The women of the house had gone to bed quietly. None of us spoke for a long time. I was putting myself in the place of the men inside. My turn might come, too, and soon. It seemed easier to face one's own execution than to have to shoot others. 'It's very dark outside,' said the Quartermaster. 'I hope the boys are keeping a good lookout.' He strode into the darkness.

He was an elderly man. Freckles showed through a wintered face. There were thin folds in his neck. He had a long skillet of a jaw, he showed the wide gaps between his teeth when he smiled. His step was as deliberate as a gander's. He would have his say no matter what happened; he was accustomed to jump objections— for that was a quarter-master's offensive. He could advise about a round of ammunition as seriously as we would discuss or draw up a plan of operations. He was the oldest of us, about thirty-five years. He spoke slowly and carefully, toothing his words in a dry humour.

None of us was twenty-four; the youngest officer inside was about that age. One was tall and dark with brown eyes. He had ill-treated prisoners in Tipperary, one of the Rosegreen men said. He had been insulting when on raids. One was stout with a thick neck, his hair was a little thin. He had been more anxious to talk and to remonstrate than the others. The third was quiet and reserved. He had a sensitive face and he did not talk. I liked him best. I was worried about him because he was wounded. It was an accepted convention that a wounded man should not be shot until he was able to walk. I did not bother about the convention, only the presence of the wounded man made its own conditions. I did not see any sense in keeping him for a few days longer. It would be harder on him if his companions went first.

'I wish it were over,' I said to the Q.M. There were two other men seated on chairs making a round of the fire.

'It'll be over soon enough,' he said. He was calm enough about it. I knew that I would continue to shoot their officers. Of that, there would be no doubt, but this kind of work was hard enough. If we shot enough of them, it would make the others think a little. I don't know what we talked about. Odds and rags of conversation about men in other battalions, the relative merits of different kinds of explosives; the making of improvised Stokes guns and the history of this part of Desmond. Two men went out to relieve their comrades. I walked outside in the darkness. The night was misty, the moon shone softly through cloud veils. Sounds carried well; away through the distance came the lonely bray of an ass; it was answered in sardonic harshness nearby. Sheep coughed drily in the shelter of a hedge and a cow chewed loudly.

'It'll soon be dawn,' said the Q.M.

I knocked at the door. They were seated around the table. Their faces looked worn and drawn. None of them had slept.

'Have you written your letters?'

'Yes,' said the thin swarthy one; 'here they are.'

'If you would like to send your money or valuables to your friends or relatives, I will forward them for you.'

'We would like to send them with a note to our C.O., Major Y, in Fethard,' the quiet one said.

I found an empty Fry's chocolate box on a side table. They put their watches, money, and rings inside.

'Would you like some tea? It'll soon be dawn and we'll have to be on our way.'

'No, thanks, we don't want anything.'

We walked down the sloping fields towards the roadway. The sky was clouded with heavy grey. The light was dim, a cold dawn wind blew across the thick hedges. It ruffled the grass which was shiny with dewdrops. Men with rifles formed an extended five-pointed figure. An officer walked on each side of the Q.M. I was behind with the third.

'It's a mistake,' he said. 'It won't do any good. We could be good to prisoners.'

'None of us want to do it,' I said, 'but I must think of our men.' I could not see the ultimate implications of our proposed action. The sky lighted silvery grey, the wind dropped.

We caught up with the three in front. 'Stiff banks those for hunting,' said the tall, swarthy officer. They smiled as if they had thought of horses and the sight of a red-brown fox.

'There's not much hunting now,' I said. We had stopped hunting through the martial law area.

We reached the roadway. There was a wall in front of a church. The three officers were placed on the green grass edge of the dusty road.

'Do you mind?' I said, as I placed their handkerchiefs around their eyes. One handkerchief was of silk and claret-coloured.

'No.'

'This is good-bye,' I said.

They shook hands with the Q.M. and myself. Their hands were cold and limp. They shook hands with each other.

The six men of the firing squad stood near the other side of the road. One of the men fumbled for a while with his magazine. He could not click it into place. An officer pulled down his handkerchief and looked at us, then he put it back over his eyes. Perhaps he thought we were trying to frighten and test them and that we did not intend to shoot.

'Ram in the magazine,' I whispered to the Q.M.

'Are you ready?' asked the Q.M.

One of the officers nodded. They joined hands. 'Good-bye, old boy,' they said, inclining their heads.

'Squad' . . . 'Ready' . . . 'Fire.'

The volley crashed sharply. The three fell to the ground; their arms twitched. The Q.M. put his revolver to each of their foreheads in turn and fired. The bodies lay still on the green grass. We stood to attention. Then slowly we went up the hill across country making for the Centre. None of us spoke till we had crossed a good many fields where wind had snaked the rye grass.

3. SHORT FICTION

JAMES JOYCE
(1882–1941)

A Painful Case (1905)

Mr James Duffy* lived in Chapelizod* because he wished to live as far as possible from the city of which he was a citizen and because he found all the other suburbs of Dublin mean, modern and pretentious. He lived in an old sombre house and from his windows he could look into the disused distillery or upwards along the shallow river on which Dublin is built. The lofty walls of his uncarpeted room were free from pictures. He had himself bought every article of furniture in the room: a black iron bedstead, an iron washstand, four cane chairs, a clothes-rack, a coal-scuttle, a fender and irons and a square table on which lay a double desk.* A bookcase had been made in an alcove by means of shelves of white wood. The bed was clothed with white bed-clothes and a black and scarlet rug covered the foot. A little hand-mirror hung above the washstand and during the day a white-shaded lamp stood as the sole ornament of the mantelpiece. The books on the white wooden shelves were arranged from below upwards according to bulk. A complete Wordsworth stood at one end of the lowest shelf and a copy of the *Maynooth Catechism*,* sewn into the cloth cover of a notebook, stood at one end of the top shelf. Writing materials were always on the desk. In the desk lay a manuscript translation of Hauptmann's *Michael Kramer*,* the stage directions of which were written in purple ink, and a little sheaf of papers held together by a brass pin. In these sheets a sentence was inscribed from time to time and, in an ironical moment, the headline of an advertisement for *Bile Beans** had been pasted on to the first sheet. On lifting the lid of the desk a faint fragrance escaped—the fragrance of new cedarwood pencils or of a bottle of gum or of an over-ripe apple which might have been left there and forgotten.

Mr Duffy abhorred anything which betokened physical or mental disorder. A mediæval doctor would have called him saturnine. His face, which carried the entire tale of his years, was of the brown tint of Dublin streets. On his long and rather large head grew dry black hair and a tawny moustache did not quite cover an unamiable mouth. His cheekbones also gave his face a harsh character; but there was no harshness in the eyes which, looking at the world from under their tawny eyebrows, gave the impression of a man ever alert to greet a redeeming instinct in others but often disappointed. He lived at a little distance from his body, regarding his own acts with doubtful side-glances. He had an odd autobiographical habit which led him to compose in his mind from time to time a short sentence about himself containing a subject in the third person and a predicate in the past tense. He never gave alms to beggars and walked firmly, carrying a stout hazel.

He had been for many years cashier of a private bank in Baggot Street. Every morning he came in from Chapelizod by tram. At midday he went to Dan Burke's and took his lunch—a bottle of lager beer and a small trayful of arrowroot biscuits. At four o'clock he was set free. He dined in an eating-house in George's Street where he felt himself safe from the society of Dublin's gilded youth and where there was a certain plain honesty in the bill of fare. His evenings were spent either before his landlady's piano or roaming about the outskirts of the city. His liking for Mozart's music brought him sometimes to an opera or a concert: these were the only dissipations of his life.

He had neither companions nor friends, church nor creed. He lived his spiritual life without any communion with others, visiting his relatives at Christmas and escorting them to the cemetery when they died. He performed these two social duties for old dignity's sake but conceded nothing further to the conventions which regulate the civic life. He allowed himself to think that in certain circumstances he would rob his bank but, as these circumstances never arose, his life rolled out evenly—an adventureless tale.

One evening he found himself sitting beside two ladies in the Rotunda.* The house, thinly peopled and silent, gave distressing prophecy of failure. The lady who sat next him looked round at the deserted house once or twice and then said:

—What a pity there is such a poor house to-night! It's so hard on people to have to sing to empty benches.

He took the remark as an invitation to talk. He was surprised that she seemed so little awkward. While they talked he tried to fix her permanently in his memory. When he learned that the young girl beside her was her daughter he judged her to be a year or so younger than himself. Her face, which must have been handsome, had remained intelligent. It was an oval face with strongly marked features. The eyes were very dark blue and steady. Their gaze began with a defiant note but was confused by what seemed a deliberate swoon of the pupil into the iris, revealing for an instant a temperament of great sensibility. The pupil reasserted itself quickly, this half-disclosed nature fell again under the reign of prudence, and her astrakhan jacket, moulding a bosom of a certain fulness, struck the note of defiance more definitely.

He met her again a few weeks afterwards at a concert in Earlsfort Terrace and seized the moments when her daughter's attention was diverted to become intimate. She alluded once or twice to her husband but her tone was not such as to make the allusion a warning. Her name was Mrs Sinico. Her husband's great-great-grandfather had come from Leghorn.* Her husband was captain of a mercantile boat plying between Dublin and Holland; and they had one child.

Meeting her a third time by accident he found courage to make an appointment. She came. This was the first of many meetings; they met always in the evening and chose the most quiet quarters for their walks together. Mr Duffy, however, had a distaste for underhand ways and, finding that they were compelled to meet stealthily, he forced her to ask him to her house. Captain Sinico encouraged his visits, thinking that his daughter's hand was in question. He had dismissed his wife so sincerely from his gallery of pleasures that he did not suspect that anyone else would take an interest in her. As the husband was often away and the daughter out giving music lessons Mr Duffy had many opportunities of enjoying the lady's society. Neither he nor she had had any such adventure before and neither was conscious of any incongruity. Little by little he entangled his thoughts with hers. He lent her books, provided her with ideas, shared his intellectual life with her. She listened to all.

Sometimes in return for his theories she gave out some fact of her own life. With almost maternal solicitude she urged him to let his nature open to the full; she became his confessor. He told her that for some time he had assisted at the meetings of an Irish Socialist Party where he had felt himself a unique figure amidst a score of sober workmen in a garret lit by an inefficient oil-lamp. When the party had divided into three sections, each under its own leader and in its own garret, he had discontinued his attendances. The workmen's discussions, he said, were too timorous; the interest they took in the question of wages was inordinate. He felt that they were hard-featured realists and that they resented an exactitude which was the product of a leisure not within their reach. No social revolution, he told her, would be likely to strike Dublin for some centuries.

She asked him why did he not write out his thoughts. For what, he asked her, with careful scorn. To compete with phrasemongers, incapable of thinking consecutively for sixty seconds? To submit himself to the criticisms of an obtuse middle class which entrusted its morality to policemen and its fine arts to impresarios?

He went often to her little cottage outside Dublin; often they spent their evenings alone. Little by little, as their thoughts entangled, they spoke of subjects less remote. Her companionship was like a warm soil about an exotic. Many times she allowed the dark to fall upon them, refraining from lighting the lamp. The dark discreet room, their isolation, the music that still vibrated in their ears united them. This union exalted him, wore away the rough edges of his character, emotionalized his mental life. Sometimes he caught himself listening to the sound of his own voice. He thought that in her eyes he would ascend to an angelical stature; and, as he attached the fervent nature of his companion more and more closely to him, he heard the strange impersonal voice which he recognized as his own, insisting on the soul's incurable loneliness. We cannot give ourselves, it said: we are our own. The end of these discourses was that one night during which she had shown every sign of unusual excitement, Mrs Sinico caught up his hand passionately and pressed it to her cheek.

Mr Duffy was very much surprised. Her interpretation of his words disillusioned him. He did not visit her for a week; then he wrote to her asking her to meet him. As he did not wish their last interview to be troubled by the influence of their ruined confessional they met in a little cakeshop near the Parkgate.* It was cold autumn weather but in spite of the cold they wandered up and down the roads of the Park for nearly three hours. They agreed to break off their intercourse: every bond, he said, is a bond to sorrow. When they came out of the Park they walked in silence towards the tram; but here she began to tremble so violently that, fearing another collapse on her part, he bade her good-bye quickly and left her. A few days later he received a parcel containing his books and music.

Four years passed. Mr Duffy returned to his even way of life. His room still bore witness of the orderliness of his mind. Some new pieces of music encumbered the music-stand in the lower room and on his shelves stood two volumes by Nietzsche: *Thus Spake Zarathustra* and *The Gay Science*. He wrote seldom in the sheaf of papers which lay in his desk. One of his sentences, written two months after his last interview with Mrs Sinico, read: Love between man and man is impossible because there must not be sexual inter-course and friendship between man and woman is impossible because there must be sexual intercourse. He kept away from con-certs lest he should meet her. His father died; the junior partner of the bank retired. And still every morning he went into the city by tram and every evening walked home from the city after having dined moderately in George's Street and read the evening paper for dessert.

One evening as he was about to put a morsel of corned beef and cabbage into his mouth his hand stopped. His eyes fixed themselves on a paragraph in the evening paper which he had propped against the water-carafe. He replaced the morsel of food on his plate and read the paragraph attentively. Then he drank a glass of water, pushed his plate to one side, doubled the paper down before him between his elbows and read the paragraph over and over again. The cabbage began to deposit a cold white grease on his plate. The girl came over to him to ask was his dinner not properly cooked. He said it was very good and ate a few mouthfuls of it with difficulty. Then he paid his bill and went out.

He walked along quickly through the November twilight, his stout hazel stick striking the ground regularly, the fringe of the buff *Mail** peeping out of a side-pocket of his tight reefer overcoat. On the lonely road which leads from the Parkgate to Chapelizod he slackened his pace. His stick struck the ground less emphatically and his breath, issuing irregularly, almost with a sighing sound, con-densed in the wintry air. When he reached his house he went up at once to his bedroom and, taking the paper from his pocket, read the paragraph again by the failing light of the window. He read it not aloud, but moving his lips as a priest does when he reads the prayers *Secreto*.* This was the paragraph:

DEATH OF A LADY AT SYDNEY PARADE

A PAINFUL CASE

To-day at the City of Dublin Hospital the Deputy Coroner (in the absence of Mr Leverett) held an inquest on the body of Mrs Emily Sinico, aged forty-three years, who was killed at Sydney Parade Station yesterday evening. The evidence showed that the deceased lady, while attempting to cross the line, was knocked down by the engine of the ten o'clock slow train from Kingstown, thereby sustaining injuries of the head and right side which led to her death.

James Lennon, driver of the engine, stated that he had been in the employment of the railway company for fifteen years. On hearing the guard's whistle he set the train in motion and a second or two afterwards brought it to rest in response to loud cries. The train was going slowly.

P. Dunne, railway porter, stated that as the train was about to start he observed a woman attempting to cross the lines. He ran towards her and shouted but, before he could reach her, she was caught by the buffer of the engine and fell to the ground.

A juror—You saw the lady fall?

Witness—Yes.

Police Sergeant Croly deposed that when he arrived he found the deceased lying on the platform apparently dead. He had the body taken to the waiting-room pending the arrival of the ambulance.

Constable 57E corroborated.

Dr Halpin, assistant house surgeon of the City of Dublin Hospital, stated that the deceased had two lower ribs fractured and had sustained severe contusions of the right shoulder. The right side of the head had been injured in the fall. The injuries were not sufficient to have caused death in a normal person. Death, in his opinion, had been probably due to shock and sudden failure of the heart's action.

Mr H. B. Patterson Finlay, on behalf of the railway company, expressed his deep regret at the accident. The company had always taken every precaution to prevent people crossing the lines except by the bridges, both by placing notices in every station and by the use of patent spring gates at level crossings. The deceased had been in the habit of crossing the lines late at night from platform to platform and, in view of certain other circumstances of the case, he did not think the railway officials were to blame.

Captain Sinico, of Leoville, Sydney Parade, husband of the deceased, also gave evidence. He stated that the deceased was his wife. He was not in Dublin at the time of the accident as he had arrived only that morning from Rotterdam. They had been married for twenty-two years and had lived happily until about two years ago when his wife began to be rather intemperate in her habits.

Miss Mary Sinico said that of late her mother had been in the habit of going out at night to buy spirits. She, witness, had often tried to reason with her mother and had induced her to join a league.* She was not at home until an hour after the accident.

The jury returned a verdict in accordance with the medical evidence and exonerated Lennon from all blame.

The Deputy Coroner said it was a most painful case, and expressed great sympathy with Captain Sinico and his daughter. He urged on the railway company to take strong measures to prevent the possibility of similar accidents in the future. No blame attached to anyone.

Mr Duffy raised his eyes from the paper and gazed out of his window on the cheerless evening landscape. The river lay quiet beside the empty distillery and from time to time a light appeared in some house on the Lucan road. What an end! The whole narrative of her death revolted him and it revolted him to think that he had ever spoken to her of what he held sacred. The threadbare phrases, the inane expressions of sympathy, the cautious words of a reporter won over to conceal the details of a commonplace vulgar death attacked his stomach. Not merely had she degraded herself; she had degraded him. He saw the squalid tract of her vice, miserable and malodorous. His soul's companion! He thought of the hobbling wretches whom he had seen carrying cans and bottles to be filled by the barman. Just God, what an end! Evidently she had been unfit to live, without any strength of purpose, an easy prey to habits, one of the wrecks on which civilisation has been reared. But that she could have sunk so low! Was it possible he had deceived himself so utterly about her? He remembered her outburst of that night and interpreted it in a harsher sense than he had ever done. He had no difficulty now in approving of the course he had taken.

As the light failed and his memory began to wander he thought her hand touched his. The shock which had first attacked his stomach was now attacking his nerves. He put on his over-coat and hat quickly and went out. The cold air met him on the threshold; it crept into the sleeves of his coat. When he came to the public-house at Chapelizod Bridge he went in and ordered a hot punch.

The proprietor served him obsequiously but did not venture to talk. There were five or six working-men in the shop discussing the value of a gentleman's estate in County Kildare. They drank at intervals from their huge pint tumblers and smoked, spitting often on the floor and sometimes dragging the sawdust over their spits with their heavy boots. Mr Duffy sat on his stool and gazed at them, without seeing or hearing them. After a while they went out and he called for another punch. He sat a long time over it. The shop was very quiet. The proprietor sprawled on the counter reading the *Herald** and yawning. Now and again a tram was heard swishing along the lonely road outside.

As he sat there, living over his life with her and evoking alternately the two images in which he now conceived her, he realized that she was dead, that she had ceased to exist, that she had become a memory. He began to feel ill at ease. He asked himself what else could he have done. He could not have carried on a comedy of deception with her; he could not have lived with her openly. He had done what seemed to him best. How was he to blame? Now that she was gone he understood how lonely her life must have been, sitting night after night alone in that room. His life would be lonely too until he, too, died, ceased to exist, became a memory—if anyone remembered him.

It was after nine o'clock when he left the shop. The night was cold and gloomy. He entered the park by the first gate and walked along under the gaunt trees. He walked through the bleak alleys where they had walked four years before. She seemed to be near him in the darkness. At moments he seemed to feel her voice touch his ear, her hand touch his. He stood still to listen. Why had he withheld life from her? Why had he sentenced her to death? He felt his moral nature falling to pieces.

When he gained the crest of the Magazine Hill he halted and looked along the river towards Dublin, the lights of which burned redly and hospitably in the cold night. He looked down the slope and, at the base, in the shadow of the wall of the park, he saw some human figures lying. Those venal and furtive loves filled him with despair. He gnawed the rectitude of his life; he felt that he had been outcast from life's feast. One human being had seemed to love him and he had denied her life and happiness: he had sentenced her to ignominy, a death of shame. He knew that the prostrate creatures down by the wall were watching him and wished him gone. No one wanted him; he was outcast from life's feast. He turned his eyes to the grey gleaming river, winding along towards Dublin. Beyond the river he saw a goods train winding out of Kingsbridge Station, like a worm with a fiery head winding through the darkness, obstinately and laboriously. It passed slowly out of sight; but still he heard in his ears the laborious drone of the engine reiterating the syllables of her name.

He turned back the way he had come, the rhythm of the engine pounding in his ears. He began to doubt the reality of what memory told him. He halted under a tree and allowed the rhythm to die away. He could not feel her near him in the darkness nor her voice touch his ear. He waited for some minutes listening. He could hear nothing: the night was perfectly silent. He listened again: perfectly silent. He felt that he was alone.

SEÁN O'FAOLÁIN
(1900–1991)

Lilliput (1926)

On those nights when curfew came at ten o'clock and people were hastening within doors, locking doors, bolting doors, chaining doors at a full quarter to the hour, the poor alone were leisurely. Shandon* had therefore struck ten before the last of the apple-sellers began to drag her basket after her into the lanes, but once she was gone the bridge was as empty as a plain.

There had been a fragrance in the air as long as the apples lay there exposed but the smell of the river was about to conquer again. A light fog had crept up the valley of the Lee* from the harbour mouth and the lamps on the bridges had gathered from it a rich and reddish hue, while their dagger-like reflections trembled but slightly in the cold and glassy river-water. Farther down the quays the lovers were parting in the darker nooks, the men with one eye raised for the coming of the patrols, the women drawing their shawls closer around their lovers for the last embrace. Where the nets were drying there hung an odour of tar, and where they wash the sheep-skins the slips and pavement smelt in the night air. Already in the side-streets where there lie stables and storehouses and an occasional dwelling-house it might have been the first hours of the morning. But in one of these streets which lead from the quaysides to the centre of the city through a middle-class quarter, there stood, and had stood all the day long, a cart surmounted by a black box-like erection—a sort of miserable caravan without windows, without chimney and with-out an animal to support the slanting shafts. It might remind you of the little cart of the Poor Shepherd Nuns, or of a small-scale fever-cart intended to carry away the infected clothes from a condemned house. Inside were three children fast asleep. Clothes and cloths and mere rags filled this box of a house. Straw, a bucket, a board, chains—these with some huge stones at the wheels were scattered around it on the street. The cart carried no lamp. The open doorway facing the shafts was curtained by an old yellow coat, but at this hour the whole was a black mass inviting collision from the last-minute jarvey-cars* careering past with their drunken passengers clinging to the seat.

It was now several minutes past the forbidden hour, and any moment the first lorries would be heard tearing along the quays and through the principal streets. None the less you could hear in the square near-by a war of words and distinguish them if you chose to listen. A woman was answering two or three male voices, young and soft in spite of their jeering tones, and as they parted farther and farther from one another, and the steps of the woman came nearer, and the voices of the other more shrill in the distance you might have heard every swear.

'Aha! The Kerry porther* is the best porther, I can tell ye.'

They answered with a crying call such as a savage might use in battle.

'Go home to yeer mothers,' she responded, and followed with a cry as wild as theirs.

Just then the lorries began to whir in the distance and the boyish feet scampered for safety. Indifferent to them she sang herself back to her cart, sometimes muttering between the lines about her husband, and the police, and her donkey-ass. She sang out,

'O-o-oh!
    Will anybody tell me where the Blarney roses grow?
    Is it over in Kilmurry South, or yonder in Cloghroe?'

and tumbled into her cart, and sank at once into a profound sleep. The people of the quarter, however, sate up in their beds for an hour waiting for the patrols to come and take her, and when she was still there in the morning, they said such ungenerous things as 'The devil always looks after his own'; or, 'Look how a good person wouldn't have been so fortunate'; and went by to church with disapproving eyes.

At the first Angelus* the haze still hung over the city, but the morning broke in sunshine shortly before the second bell rang in the noon. From that onwards there were ding-dongs all over the city at intervals of hours or half-hours. Finally when all the children were returning from their usual Sunday Mass she was arisen and had made some slops of tea. The city children gathered around her in wonderment as she washed the little girls' faces in the water she had borrowed near-by. Unperturbed, she combed their hair, peering at the scalp.

She was a sturdy woman with fresh colour in her cheeks, but her dun-coloured hair hung around her in contrast to the neat little figures that watched her and her cart in wonder. She saw this herself and eventually sate down on the sloping shaft to examine their spotless muslin frocks, their white shoes, their frilly lace, and sky-blue ribbons. She began to tell them disconsolately of her husband who was in Moore's Hotel—they knew Moore's Hotel was a jail—and she spoke pityingly of her three children and of the donkey-ass whom 'Cruelty' had led away when her husband was taken. So, all the day long she sate there, only rising at intervals. Once she picked and plucked at the three children, and went off with them to the jail. But she soon returned like a huge liner with three small tenders on her flanks, and began speaking of their father to some women that had gathered around her. The 'polis' had taken him for beating the donkey-ass 'till he brayed and died.' It was a tree fell on the donkey-ass, she said. They asked her had she come far, and she said from Headford. They said she was a pity, and one of the poorest came to her with a pot of soup and vegetables and potatoes. But her eldest child knocked it over by accident, and her mother called her a jade, and sate down for a spell.

All day long there was a changing little crowd around her. Patiently she told again and again of the donkey-ass and *their* father, and Moore's Hotel. She had once lived in Blarney Street and was four years on the road. Or she had lived in Barrackah and was ten years on the road. Or she had been born on the road and didn't know what a roof-tree meant. She told all her stories with her cheek on her fist, occasionally cocking her eye at her listeners but with a bored air. Each one of her listeners said she and her three children were a pity. She told them of the blackguards who called her low names last night, and they promised to keep guard for her, even to go to the sessions with her, and she answered she must rely on the help of God and her neighbours in all things. Some of the women did not like her and asked her questions that she refused to answer, but the other women said that these things were her own business.

At tea-hour the crowd did not slacken. The children from the streets all around became more noisy and familiar and had to be hunted away by the women. She borrowed water again, and a passing man bought her the last two loaves from the nearest huckster's shop. She gave tea to her three little girls within the cart, she herself eating from the roadway like a photographer behind the curtaining yellow coat, just as if her cart were a huge black camera.

At dusk and dark the people of the district became very nervous, and wondered why the police did not come to move her away, and complained that the whole country was in a shocking state, and feared above all, saying so to one another from door to door and window to window, that she would attract the attention of the Tans* and the patrols to their quiet street and they would have no wink of sleep at all that night. At last the police came, but they had no mind to argue with her, and they merely told her to take her cart to hell out of that street even as she brought it in, and then because they knew she would begin to ask how was she to do that, they went away at once so that they should have the last word.

Then the children around began to enjoy themselves in earnest. They laid themselves under the shafts, and, shouting, began to strain and pull, or they heaved the huge stones from beneath the wheels and cried out for orders from the woman. The hoydens from the lane-ways told her to wheel her cart to this place or that, and the children chimed in that Harper's lane was not at all like this street, but was a small narrow lane, down below there. The women gathered around her again and again, or sank on their haunches before her children and returning, told the mother that they were chatting away to themselves. Amid cries the cart began to move, and the loose chains to swing and ring in the dark as the children dragged it from the kerb. But the woman hailed them, and they ordered one another to wheel it back again, and there it stayed yet another night. She lit a candle and put the little girls to bed and its light shone brightly from the interior of the cart until she drew the yellow coat across it.

It was now almost ten o'clock and the women began to scatter, talking among themselves and asking her if she would be all right there. She walked away with a few of them and the wind blew the candle out and the night moulded the cart into the blackness of the street, and the street became as quiet as early dawn. A man who asked the children who owned the cart, and where she was now, had to chase them because they pelted him with stones and called out ribald answers. Then the street settled down to the night again. But a priest walked down the street from the riverside, showing like a statue in jet under the lamps above him. Three girls clasping one another's waists cried out that he was coming and retired to a corner of the square. He looked around when he reached the cart, and down the street ahead of him, and tapped politely at the side of the cart, and looked to the right and then went home tapping his silver-headed stick on the flags. The girls ran another way to watch him and all was still again until the lorries began to whir in the distance as Shandon struck the hour and the girls raced for their homes.

The woman returned shortly after and crept into the cart on her knees. An old woman shuffled along and asked her if she were there last night also, and asked why was the poor man taken, and prayed God to help us all. The woman within spoke out to her to go away for Virgin Mary's sake and let her sleep—which the old woman did, looking back several times as she padded away on her bare feet, the woman within snoring out loud snores that might be heard by a passer-by long before he distinguished the cart from the darkness around it.

Towards midnight a patrol of military tramped slowly down the
street while the wakeful householders held their breath. The patrol
halted at the cart, and the officer flashed his torch into the interior.
Then he murmured something to his sergeant and the sergeant
ordered his men to move on.

'Blimey!' whispered the sergeant to the corporal, and he passed on
the word to the men. 'Blimey, if it isn't a woman.'

'Oo is it?' asked a stupid private.

'Mary Mac* and the Holy Trinity,' said the corporal, who was an
atheist; and sniggering they all tramped away—quietly and slowly as
if they would not disturb her sleep.

LIAM O'FLAHERTY
(1896–1984)

The Mountain Tavern (1929)

Snow was falling.* The bare, flat, fenceless road had long since
disappeared. Now the white snow fell continuously on virgin land,
all level, all white, all silent, between the surrounding dim peaks of
the mountains. Through the falling snow, on every side, squat
humps were visible. They were the mountain peaks. And between
them, the moorland was as smooth as a ploughed field. And as
silent, oh, as silent as an empty church. Here, the very particles of
the air entered the lungs seemingly as big as pebbles and with the
sweetness of ripe fruit. An outstretched hand could almost feel
the air and the silence. There was absolutely nothing, nothing at
all, but falling flakes of white snow, undeflected, falling silently on
fallen snow.

Up above was the sky and God perhaps, though it was hard to
believe it; hard to believe that there was anything in the whole universe but a flat white stretch of virgin land between squat mountain
peaks and a ceaseless shower of falling snow-flakes.

There came the smell of human breathing from the east. Then
three figures appeared suddenly, dark, although they were covered
with snow. They appeared silently, one by one, stooping forward.
The leading man carried his overcoat like a shawl about his head,

with a rifle, butt upwards, slung on his right shoulder and two cloth ammunition belts slung across his body. He wore black top boots. His grim young eyes gazed wearily into the falling snow and his boots, scarcely lifted, raked the smooth earth, scattering the fallen snow-flakes.

The second man wore a belted leather coat, of which one arm hung loose. With the other hand he gripped his chest and staggered forward, with sagging, doddering head. A pistol, pouched in a loose belt, swung back and forth with his gait. There was blood on his coat, on his hand and congealed on his black leggings, along which the melting snow ran in a muddy stream. There was a forlorn look in his eyes, but his teeth were set. Sometimes he bared them and drew in a deep breath with a hissing sound.

The third man walked erect. He wore no overcoat and his head was bare. His hair curled and among the curls the snow lay in little rows like some statue in winter. He had a proud, fearless face, bronzed, showing no emotion nor weariness. Now and again, he shook his great body and the snow fell with a rustling sound off his clothes and off the heavy pack he carried. He also had two rifles wrapped in a cape under his arm; and in his right hand he carried a small wooden box that hung from a leather strap.

They walked in each other's tracks slowly. Rapidly the falling snow filled up the imprints of their feet. And when they passed there was silence again.

The man in front halted and raised his eyes to look ahead. The second man staggered against him, groaned with pain and gripped the other about the body with his loose hand to steady himself. The third man put the wooden box on the ground and shifted his pack.

'Where are we now?' he said.

His voice rang out, hollow, in the stillness and several puffs of hot air, the words, jerked out, like steam from a starting engine.

'Can't say,' muttered the man in front. 'Steady, Commandant. We can't be far now. We're on the road anyway. It should be there in front. Can't see, though. It's in a hollow. That's why.'

'What's in a hollow, Jack?' muttered the wounded man. 'Let me lie down here. It's bleeding again.'

'Hold on, Commandant,' said the man in front. 'We'll be at the Mountain Tavern in half a minute. Christ!'

'Put him on my back,' said the big man. 'You carry the stuff.'

'Never mind. I'll walk,' said the wounded man. 'I'll get there all right. Any sign of them?'

They peered into the falling snow behind them. There was utter silence. The ghostly white shower made no sound. A falling curtain.

'Lead on then,' said the big man. 'Lean on me, Commandant.'

They moved on. The wounded man was groaning now and his feet began to drag. Shortly he began to rave in a low voice. Then they halted again. Without speaking, the big man hoisted his comrade, crosswise, on his shoulders. The other man carried the kit. They moved on again.

The peak in front became larger. It was no longer a formless mass. Gradually, through the curtain of snow, it seemed to move towards them and upwards. The air became still more thin. As from the summit of a towering cliff, the atmosphere in front became hollow; and soon, through the haze of snow, they caught a glimpse of the distant plains, between two mountain peaks. There below it lay, like the bottom of a sea, in silence. The mountain sides sank down into it, becoming darker; for it did not snow down there. There was something, after all, other than the snow. But the snowless, downland earth looked dour and unapproachable.

'It must be here,' the leading man said again. 'Why can't we see it? It's just under the shelter of that mountain. There is a little clump of pine trees and a barn with a red roof. Sure I often had a drink in it. Where the name of God is it, anyway?'

'Go on. Stop talking,' said the curly-headed man.

'Can't you be easy?' muttered the leading man, moving ahead and peering into the snow that made his eyelids blink and blink. 'Supposing this is the wrong road, after all. They say people go round and round in the snow. Sure ye could see it from the other end, four miles away in clear weather, two storey high and a slate roof with the sun shining on it. It's facing this way too, right on the top of the hill, with a black board, "Licensed to Sell." Man called Galligan owns it. I'd swear by the Cross of Christ we must be up on it.'

'Hurry on,' snapped the curly man. 'There's a gurgle in his throat. Jesus! His blood is going down my neck. Why can't you hurry on, blast it?'

'Hey, what place is that?' cried the leading man, in a frightened voice. 'D'ye see a ruin?'

They halted. A moment ago there had been nothing in front but a curtain of falling snow, beyond which, as in a child's sick dream, the darkening emptiness of the snowless lowland approached, tumbling like a scudding black cloud. Now a crazy blue heap appeared quite close. Suddenly it heaved up out of the snow. It was a ruined house. There was a smell from it too. From its base irregular tufts of smoke curled up spasmodically; dying almost as soon as they appeared and then appearing again.

The two men watched it. There was no emotion in their faces. They just looked, as if without interest. It was too strange. The *Mountain Tavern* was a smoking ruin.

'It's gone west',* murmured the leading man.

'Eh?' shouted the curly man. 'Gone did ye say?'

'Aye. Burned to the ground. See?'

'Well?'

'God knows. We're up the pole.'*

Suddenly the curly man uttered a cry of rage and staggered forward under his load. The other man opened his mouth wide, drew in an enormous breath and dropped his head wearily on his chest. Trailing his rifle in the snow behind him, he reeled forward shaking his head from side to side, with his under lip trembling. Then he began to sing foolishly under his breath. There were people around the ruined house. And as the two men, with their dying comrade, came into view, quite close, these people stopped and gaped at them. There was a woman in front of the house, on the road, sitting on an upturned barrel. She was a thin woman with a long pointed nose and thin black hair that hung in disorder on her thin neck, with hairpins sticking in it. She had a long overcoat buttoned over her dress and a man's overcoat about her shoulders. She held a hat with red feathers on it in her right hand, by the rim. Two children, wrapped in queer clothes, stood beside her, clinging to her, a boy and a girl. They also were thin and they had pointed noses like their mother. One man was pulling something out of a window of the ruined house. Another man, within the window, had his head stuck out. He had been handing out something. Another man was in the act of putting a tin trunk on a cart, to which a horse was harnessed, to the right of the house. All looked, gaping, at the newcomers.

'God save all here,' said the curly man, halting near the woman.

Nobody replied. The other man came up and staggered towards the woman, who was sitting on the upturned barrel. The two children, silent with fear, darted around their mother, away from the man. They clutched at her, muttering something inaudibly.

'Is that you, Mrs Galligan?'

'It is then,' said the woman in a stupid, cold voice. 'And who might you be?'

'We're Republican soldiers,' said the curly man. 'I have a dying man here.'

He lowered the wounded man gently to the ground. Nobody spoke or moved. The snow fell steadily.

'Mummy, mummy,' cried one of the children, 'there's blood on him. Oh! mummy.'

The two children began to howl. The dying man began to throw his hands about and mutter something. A great rush of blood flowed from him.

'In the name of the Lord God of Heaven,' yelled the curly man, 'are ye savages not to move a foot? Eh? Can't ye go for a doctor? Is there nothing in the house?'

He stooped over the dying man and clutching him in his arms, he cried hoarsely:

'Easy now, Commandant. I'm beside ye. Give us a hand with him, Jack. We'll fix the bandage.'

The two of them, almost in a state of delirium, began to fumble with the dying man. The children wept. The dying man suddenly cried out:

'Stand fast. Stand fast boys. Stand . . .'

Then he made a violent effort to sit up. He opened his mouth and did not close it again.

The woman looked on dazed, with her forehead wrinkled and her lips set tight. The three men who had been doing something among the ruin began to come up slowly. They also appeared dazed, terrified.

'He's gone,' murmured the curly man, sitting erect on his knees. 'God have mercy on him.'

He laid the corpse flat on the ground. The blood still flowed out. The other soldier took off his hat and then, just as he was going to cross himself, he burst into tears. The three men came close and looked on. Then they sheepishly took off their hats.

'Is he dead?' said one of them.

The curly man sat back on his heels.

'He's dead,' he said. 'The curse o' God on this country.'

'And what did ye say happened?'

'Ambush back there. Our column got wiped out. Haven't ye got anything in the house?'

The woman laughed shrilly. The children stopped crying.

'Is there nothing in the house, ye daylight robber?' she cried. 'Look at it, curse ye. It's a black ruin. Go in. Take what ye can find, ye robber.'

'Robbers!' cried the soldier who had been weeping. 'Come on, Curly. Stand by me. I'm no robber. God! Give me a drink. Something to eat. Christ! I'm dyin'.'

He got to his feet and took a pace forward like a drunken man. The curly-headed soldier caught him.

'Keep yer hair on, Jack,' he said.

'Look at what ye've done,' cried the woman. 'Ye've blown up the house over me head. Ye've left me homeless and penniless with yer war. Oh! God, why don't ye drop down the dome of Heaven on me?'

'Sure we didn't blow up yer house,' cried the curly soldier. 'An' we lookin' for shelter after trampin' the mountains since morning. Woman, ye might respect the dead that died for ye.'

The woman spat and hissed at him.

'Let them die. They didn't die for me,' she said. 'Amn't I ruined and wrecked for three long years with yer fightin', goin' back and forth, lootin' and turnin' the honest traveller from my door? For three long years have I kept open house for all of ye and now yer turnin' on one another like dogs after a bitch.'

'None o' that now,' cried the hysterical soldier, trying to raise his rifle.

'Hold on, man,' cried one of the other men. 'She has cause. She has cause.'

'He grew excited and waved his hands and addressed his own comrades instead of addressing the soldiers.

'The Republicans came to the house this morning,' he cried. 'So Mr Galligan told me an' he goin' down the road for McGilligan's motor. The Republicans came, he said. And then . . . then the Free Staters* came on top of them and the firing began. Women and children out, they said, under a white flag. So Galligan told me. "They damn near shot me," says he to me, "harbourin' Irregulars* under the new act." Shot at sight, or what's worse, they take ye away on the cars, God knows where. Found in a ditch. None of us, God blast my soul if there is a word of a lie in what I am sayin', none of us here have a hand or part in anything. Three miles I came up in the snow when Mr Galligan told me. Says he to me, "I'll take herself and the kids to aunt Julia's in McGilligan's motor." '

'Where did they go?' said the curly soldier.

'I was comin' to that,' said the man, spitting in the snow and turning towards the woman. 'It's with a bomb they did it, Galligan said to me. Something must have fallen in the fire. They stuck it out, he said. There were six men inside. Not a man came out without a wound. So he said. There were two dead. On a door they took 'em away. They took 'em all off in the cars. And they were goin' to take Mr Galligan too. There you are now. May the Blessed Virgin look down on here. An' many's a man 'll go thirsty from this day over the mountain road.'

'Aye,' said the woman. 'For twenty years in that house, since my father moved from the village, after buyin' it from Johnny Reilly.'

'Twenty years,' she said again.

'Can't ye give us something to eat?' cried the hysterical man, trying to break loose from the curly soldier, who still held him.

'There's nothing here,' muttered a man, 'until Mr Galligan comes in the motor. He should be well on the way now.'

'They were all taken,' said the curly soldier.

'All taken,' said the three men, all together.

'Sit down, Jack,' said the curly soldier.

He pulled his comrade down with him on to the snow. He dropped his head on his chest. The others looked at the soldiers sitting in the snow. The others had a curious, malign look in their eyes. They looked at the dazed, exhausted soldiers and at the corpse with a curious apathy. They looked with hatred. There was no pity in their eyes. They looked steadily without speech or movement, with the serene cruelty of children watching an insect being tortured. They looked patiently, as if calmly watching a monster in its death agony.

The curly-headed soldier suddenly seemed to realize that they were watching him. For he raised his head and peered at them shrewdly through the falling snow. There was utter silence everywhere, except the munching sound made by the horse's jaws as he chewed hay. The snow fell, fell now, in the fading light, mournfully, blotting out the sins of the world.

The soldier's face, that had until then shown neither fear nor weariness, suddenly filled with despair. His lips bulged out. His eyes almost closed. His forehead gathered together and he opened his nostrils wide.

'I'm done,' he said. 'It's no use. Say, men. Send word that we're here. Let them take us. I'm tired fightin'. It's no use.'

No one spoke or stirred. A sound approached. Strange to say, no one paid attention to the sound. And even when a military motor lorry appeared at the brow of the road, nobody moved or spoke. There were Free State soldiers on the lorry. They had their rifles pointed. They drew near slowly. Then, with a rush, they dismounted and came running up.

The two Republican soldiers put up their hands, but they did not rise to their feet.

'Robbers,' screamed the woman. 'I hate ye all. Robbers.'

Her husband was there with them.

'Mary, we're to go in the lorry,' he said to her. 'They're goin' to look after us they said. Fr. Considine went to the barracks.'

'The bloody robbers,' she muttered, getting off the barrel.

'Who's this?' the officer said, roughly handling the corpse.

He raised the head of the corpse.

'Ha!' he said. 'So we got him at last. Eh? Heave him into the lorry, boys. Hurry up. Chuck 'em all in.'

They took away the corpse and the prisoners. There was a big dark spot where the corpse had lain. Snow began to fall on the dark spot.

They took away everybody, including the horse and cart. Everybody went away, down the steep mountain road, into the dark low-land country, where no snow was falling. All was silent again on the flat top of the mountain.

There was nothing in the whole universe again but the black ruin and the black spot where the corpse had lain. Night fell and snow fell, fell like soft soothing white flower petals on the black ruin and on the black spot where the corpse had lain.

FRANK O'CONNOR
(1903–1966)

The Majesty of the Law (1935)

Old Dan Bride was breaking brosna* for the fire when he heard a step up the path. He paused, a bundle of saplings on his knee.

Dan had looked after his mother while the spark of life was in her, and after her death no other woman had crossed the threshold. Signs on it, his house had that look. Almost everything in it he had made with his own hands in his own way. The seats of the chairs were only slices of log, rough and round and thick as the saw had left them, and with the rings still plainly visible through the grime and polish that coarse trouser bottoms had in the course of long years imparted. Into these Dan had rammed stout knotted ash boughs which served alike for legs and back. The deal table, bought in a shop, was an inheritance from his mother, and a great pride and joy to him, though it rocked forward and back whenever he touched it. On the wall, unglazed and flyspotted, hung in mysterious isolation a Marcus Stone print* and beside the door was a calendar representing a racehorse. Over the door hung a gun, old but good and in excellent condition, and before the fire was stretched an old setter who raised his head expectantly whenever Dan rose or even stirred.

He raised it now as the steps came nearer, and when Dan, laying down the bundle of saplings, cleaned his hands thoughtfully in the seat of his trousers, he gave a loud bark, but this expressed no more than a desire to display his own watchfulness. He was half human and knew that people thought he was old and past his prime.

A man's shadow fell across the oblong of dusty light thrown over the half door before Dan looked round.

'Are you alone, Dan?' asked an apologetic voice.

'Oh, come in, come in, sergeant, come in and welcome,' exclaimed the old man, hurrying on rather uncertain feet to the door, which the tall policeman opened and pushed in. He stood there, half in sunlight, half in shadow, and seeing him so, you would have realised how dark was the interior of Dan's house. One side of his red face was turned so as to catch the light, and behind it an ash tree raised its boughs of airy green against the sky. Green fields, broken here and there by clumps of red-brown rock, flowed downhill, and beyond them, stretched all across the horizon was the sea, flooded and almost transparent with light. The sergeant's face was fat and fresh, the old man's face, emerging from the twilight of the kitchen, had the colour of wind and sun, while the features had been so shaped by the struggle with time and the elements that they might as easily have been found impressed upon the surface of a rock.

'Begor,* Dan,' said the sergeant, ' 'tis younger you're getting.'

'Middling I am, sergeant, middling,' agreed the old man in a voice which seemed to accept the remark as a compliment of which politeness would not allow him to take too much advantage. 'No complaints.'

'Faix,* and 'tis as well. No wan but a born idiot would believe them. And th' ould dog don't look a day older.'

The dog gave a low growl as though to show the sergeant that he would remember this unmannerly reference to his age, but indeed he growled every time he was mentioned, under the impression that people could have nothing but ill to say of him.

'And how's yourself, sergeant?'

'Well, now, like that in the story, Dan, neither on the pig's back or at the horse's tail. We have our own little worries, but, thanks be to God, we have our compensations.'

'And the wife and care?'

'Good, glory and praise be to God, good. They were away from me with a month, the lot of them, at the mother-in-law's place in Clare.'

'Ah, do you tell me so?'

'I had a fine, quiet time.'

The old man looked about him, and then retired to the near-by bedroom from which he emerged a moment later with an old shirt. With this he solemnly wiped the seat and back of the log-chair nearest the fire.

'Take your ease, now, take your ease. 'Tis tired you must be after the journey. How did you come?'

'Teigue Leary it was that gave me a lift. Wisha,* now Dan, don't you be putting yourself about. I won't be stopping. I promised them I'd be back inside an hour.'

'What hurry is on you?' asked the old man. 'Look now, your foot was on the path when I rose from putting kindling on the fire.'

'Now! Now! You're not making tea for me.'

'I am not then, but for myself, and very bad I'll take it if you won't join me.'

'Dan, Dan, that I mightn't stir, but 'tisn't an hour since I had a cup at the barracks.'

'Ah, *Dhe*, whisht,* now! Whisht, will you! I have something that'll put an appetite on you.'

The old man swung the heavy kettle on to the chain over the open fire, and the dog sat up, shaking his ears with an expression of the deepest interest. The policeman unbuttoned his tunic, opened his belt, took a pipe and a plug of tobacco from his breast-pocket, and crossing his legs in easy posture, began to cut the tobacco slowly and carefully with his pocket-knife. The old man went to the dresser, and took down two handsomely decorated cups, the only cups he had, which, though chipped and handleless, were used at all only on very rare occasions: for himself, he preferred tea from a basin. Happening to glance into them, he noticed that they bore the trace of disuse and had collected a substantial share of the fine white dust which was constantly circulating within the little smoky cottage. Again he thought of the shirt, and, rolling up his sleeves with a stately gesture, he wiped them inside and out till they shone. Then he bent and opened the cupboard. Inside was a quart bottle of pale liquid, obviously untouched. He removed the cork and smelt the contents, pausing for a moment in the act as though to recollect where exactly he had noticed that particular smoky odour before. Then, reassured, he rose and poured out with a liberal hand.

'Try that now, sergeant,' he said.

The sergeant, concealing whatever qualms he might have felt at the thought of imbibing illegal whiskey, looked carefully into the cup, sniffed, and glanced up at old Dan.

'It looks good,' he commented.

'It should be.'

'It tastes good, too,' he added.

'Ah, sha,'* said Dan, clearly not wishing to praise his own hospitality in his own house, ''tis of no great excellence.'

'You're a good judge, I'd say,' said the sergeant without irony.

'Ever since things became what they are,' said Dan, carefully guarding himself from a too direct reference to the peculiarities of the law administered by his guest, 'liquor is not what it used to be.'

'I have heard that remark made before now,' said the sergeant thoughtfully. 'I have often heard it said by men of wide experience that liquor used to be better in the old days.'

'Liquor,' said the old man, 'is a thing that takes time. There was never a good job done in a hurry.'

' 'Tis an art in itself.'

'Just so.'

'And an art takes time.'

'And knowledge,' added Dan with emphasis. 'Every art has its secrets, and the secrets of distilling are being lost the way the old songs were lost. When I was a boy there wasn't a man in the barony but had a hundred songs in his head, but with people running here, there and everywhere, the songs were lost. . . . Ever since things became what they are,' he repeated on the same guarded note, 'there's so much running about the secrets are lost.'

'There must have been a power of them.'

'There was. Ask any man to-day that makes liquor do he know how to make it of heather.'

'And was it made of heather?' asked the policeman.

'It was.'

'Did you ever drink it yourself?'

'I did not; but I knew men that drank it. And a purer, sweeter, wholesomer drink never tickled a man's gullet. Babies they used to give it to and growing children.'

'Musha,* Dan, I think sometimes 'twas a great mistake of the law to set its hand against it.'

Dan shook his head. His eyes answered for him, but it was not in nature that in his own house a man should criticise the occupation of his guest.

'Maybe so, maybe not,' he said in a non-committal tone.

'But sure, what else have the poor people?'

'Them that makes the laws have their own good reasons.'

'All the same, Dan, all the same, 'tis a hard law.'

The sergeant would not be outdone in generosity. Politeness required him not to yield to the old man's defence of his superiors and their mysterious ways.

'It is the secrets I would be sorry for,' said Dan, summing up. 'Men die, and men are born, and where one man drained another will plough, but a secret lost is lost for ever.'

'True,' said the sergeant mournfully. 'Lost for ever.'

Dan took the policeman's cup, rinsed it in a bucket of clear water beside the door and cleaned it anew with the aid of the shirt. Then he placed it carefully at the sergeant's elbow. From the dresser he took a jug of milk and a blue bag containing sugar: this he followed up with a slab of country butter and—a sign that his visitor was not altogether unexpected—a round cake of home-made bread, fresh and uncut. The kettle sang and spat, and the dog, shaking his ears, barked at it angrily.

'Go 'way, you brute!' growled Dan, kicking him out of his way.

He made the tea and filled the two cups. The sergeant cut himself a large slice of bread and buttered it thickly.

'It is just like medicines,' said the old man, resuming his theme with the imperturbability of age. 'Every secret there was is lost. And leave no one tell me a doctor is the measure of one that has secrets from old times.'

'How could he?' asked the sergeant with his mouth full.

'The proof of that was seen when there were doctors and wise people there together.'

'It wasn't to the doctors the people went, I'll engage.'

'It was not. And why?' . . . With a sweeping gesture the old man took in the whole world outside his cabin. 'Out there on the hillsides is the sure cure for every disease. Because it is written'—he tapped the table with his thumb—'it is written by the poets *"an galar 'san leigheas go bhfaghair le ceile"* ("wherever you find the disease you will find the cure"). But people walk up the hills and down the hills and all they see is flowers. Flowers! As if God Almighty—honour and praise to Him!—had nothing better to do with His time than be making ould flowers!'

'Things no doctor could cure the wise people cured.'

'Ah musha, 'tis I know it,' said Dan bitterly, ' 'tis I know it, not in my mind but in my own four bones.'

'Do you tell me the rheumatics do be at you always?'

'They do. . . . Ah, if you were living, Kitty O'Hara, or you, Nora Malley of the Glen, 'tisn't I would be dreading the mountain wind or the sea wind; 'tisn't I'd be creeping down with me misfortunate red ticket for the blue and pink and yellow dribble-drabble of their ignorant dispensary!'

'Why then, indeed,' said the sergeant with sudden determination, 'I'll get you a bottle for that.'

'Ah, there's no bottle ever made will cure me!'

'There is, there is. Don't talk now till you try it. My own mother's brother, it cured him when he was that bad he wanted the carpenter to cut the two legs off him with a hand-saw.'

'I'd give fifty pounds to be rid of it,' said Dan. 'I would and five hundred!'

The sergeant finished his tea in a gulp, blessed himself and struck a match which he then allowed to go out as he answered some question of the old man's. He did the same with a second and third, as though titillating his appetite with delay. At last he succeeded in getting it alight, and then the two men pulled round their chairs, placed their toes side by side in the ashes, and in deep puffs, lively bursts of conversation and long long silences, enjoyed their pipes.

'I hope I'm not keeping you,' said the sergeant, as though struck by the length of his visit.

'Erra,* what keep?'

'Tell me if I am. The last thing I'd like to do is to waste a man's time.'

'Och, I'd ask nothing better than to have you here all night.'

'I like a little talk myself,' admitted the policeman.

And again they became lost in conversation. The light grew thick and coloured, and wheeling about the kitchen before it disappeared became tinged with gold; the kitchen itself sank into a cool greyness with cold light upon the cups and the basins and plates upon the dresser. From the ash tree a thrush began to sing. The open hearth gathered brightness till its light was a warm, even splash of crimson in the twilight.

Twilight was also descending without when the sergeant rose to go. He fastened his belt and tunic and carefully brushed his clothes. Then he put on his cap, tilted a little to side and back.

'Well,' he said, 'that was a great talk.'

'It's a pleasure,' said Dan, 'a real pleasure, that's what it is.'

'And I won't forget the bottle.'

'Heavy handling from God to you!'

'Good-bye now, Dan.'

'Good-bye and good luck.'

Dan did not offer to accompany the sergeant beyond the door. Then he sat down in his old place by the fire. He took out his pipe once more, blew through it thoughtfully, and just as he leaned forward for a twig to kindle it he heard steps returning to the house. It was the sergeant. He put his head a little way over the half door.

'Oh, Dan,' he called softly.

'Ay, sergeant,' replied Dan, looking round, but with one hand still reaching for the twig. He could not see the sergeant's face, only hear his voice.

'I suppose you're not thinking of paying that little fine, Dan?'

There was a brief silence. Dan pulled out the lighted twig, rose slowly and shambled towards the door, stuffing it down into the almost empty bowl of the pipe. He leaned over the half door, while the sergeant with hands in the pockets of his trousers gazed rather in the direction of the laneway, yet taking in a considerable portion of the sea-line.

'The way it is with me, sergeant,' replied Dan unemotionally, 'I am not.'

'I was thinking that, Dan. I was thinking you wouldn't.'

There was a long silence during which the voice of the thrush grew shriller and merrier. The sunken sun lit up islands of purple cloud moored high above the wind.

'In a way,' said the sergeant, 'that was what brought me.'

'I was just thinking so, sergeant, it struck me and you going out the door.'

'If 'twas only the money, I'm sure there's many would be glad to oblige you.'

'I know that, sergeant. No, 'tisn't the money so much as giving that fellow the satisfaction of paying. Because he angered me, sergeant.'

The sergeant made no comment upon this and another long silence ensued.

'They gave me the warrant,' he said at last in a tone which dissociated him from all connection with the document.

'Ay, begod!'* said Dan, without interest.

'So whenever 'twould be convenient to you—'

'Well, now you mention it,' said Dan, by way of throwing out a suggestion for debate, 'I could go with you now.'

'Oh, tut, tut!' protested the sergeant with a wave of his hand, dismissing the idea as the tone required.

'Or I could go to-morrow,' added Dan, warming up to the issue.

'Just as you like now,' replied the sergeant, scaling up his voice accordingly.

'But as a matter of fact,' said the old man emphatically, 'the day that would be most convenient to me would be Friday after dinner, seeing that I have some messages to do in town, and I wouldn't have me jaunt for nothing.'

'Friday will do grand,' said the sergeant with relief that this delicate matter was now practically disposed of. 'You could just walk in yourself and tell them I told you.'

'I'd rather have yourself, if 'twould be no inconvenience, sergeant. As it is, I'd feel a bit shy.'

'You needn't then. There's a man from my own parish there, a warder; one Whelan. You could say you wanted him, and I'll guarantee when he knows you're a friend of mine he'll make you as comfortable as if you were at home by your own fire.'

'I'd like that fine,' said Dan with satisfaction.

'Well, good-bye again now, Dan. I'll have to hurry.'

'Wait now, wait, till I see you to the road!'

Together the two men strolled down the lane way while Dan explained how it was that he, a respectable old man, had had the grave misfortune to open the head of another old man in such a way as to necessitate his being removed to hospital, and why it was that he could not give the old man in question the satisfaction of paying in cash for an injury brought about through the victim's own unmannerly method of argument.

'You see, sergeant,' he said, 'the way it is, he's there now, and he's looking at us as sure as there's a glimmer of sight in his wake, wandering, wathery eyes, and nothing would give him more gratification than for me to pay. But I'll punish him. I'll lie on bare boards for him. I'll suffer for him, sergeant, till he won't be able to rise his head, nor any of his children after him, for the suffering he put on me.'

On the following Friday he made ready his donkey and butt* and set out. On his way he collected a number of neighbours who wished to bid him farewell. At the top of the hill he stopped to send them back. An old man, sitting in the sunlight, hastily made his way within doors, and a moment later the door of his cottage was quietly closed.

Having shaken all his friends by the hand, Dan lashed the old donkey, shouted 'hup, there!' and set out alone along the road to prison.

4. FICTION

SOMERVILLE AND ROSS
(1858–1949) (1862–1915)

from *The Real Charlotte* (1894)

II

The east wind was crying round a small house in the outskirts of an Irish country town. At nightfall it had stolen across the grey expanse of Lough Moyle, and given its first shudder among the hollies and laurestinas that hid the lower windows of Tally Ho Lodge from the too curious passer-by, and at about two o'clock of the November night it was howling so inconsolably in the great tunnel of the kitchen chimney, that Norry the Boat,* sitting on a heap of turf by the kitchen fire, drew her shawl closer about her shoulders, and thought gruesomely of the Banshee.*

The long trails of the monthly roses tapped and scratched against the window panes, so loudly sometimes that two cats, dozing on the rusty slab of a disused hothearth, opened their eyes and stared, with the expressionless yet wholly alert scrutiny of their race. The objects in the kitchen were scarcely more than visible in the dirty light of a hanging lamp, and the smell of paraffin filled the air. High presses and a dresser lined the walls, and on the top of the dresser, close under the blackened ceiling, it was just possible to make out the ghostly sleeping form of a cockatoo. A door at the end of the kitchen opened into a scullery of the usual prosaic, not to say odorous kind, which was now a cavern of darkness, traversed by twin green stars that moved to and fro as the lights move on a river at night, and looked like anything but what they were, the eyes of cats prowling round a scullery sink.

The tall, yellow-faced clock gave the gurgle with which it was accustomed to mark the half-hour, and the old woman, as if reminded of her weariness, stretched out her arms and yawned loudly and dismally.

She put back the locks of greyish-red hair that hung over her forehead and, crouching over the fireplace, she took out of the embers a broken-nosed teapot, and proceeded to pour from it a mug of tea, black with long stewing. She had taken a few sips of it when a bell rang startlingly in the passage outside, jarring the silence of the house with its sharp outcry. Norry the Boat hastily put down her mug, and scrambled to her feet to answer its summons. She groped her way up two cramped flights of stairs that creaked under her as she went, and advanced noiselessly in her stockinged feet across a landing to where a chink of light came from under a door.

The door was opened as she came to it, and a woman's short thick figure appeared in the doorway.

'The mistress wants to see Susan,' this person said in a rough whisper; 'is he in the house?'

'I think he's below in the scullery,' returned Norry; 'but, my Law! Miss Charlotte, what does she want of him? Is it light in her head she is?'

'What's that to you? Go fetch him at once,' replied Miss Charlotte, with a sudden fierceness. She shut the door, and Norry crept downstairs again, making a kind of groaning and lamenting as she went.

Miss Charlotte walked with a heavy step to the fireplace. A lamp was burning dully on a table at the foot of an old-fashioned bed, and the high foot-board threw a shadow that made it difficult to see the occupant of the bed. It was an ordinary little shabby bedroom, the ceiling, seamed with cracks, bulged down till it nearly touched the canopy of the bed. The wall paper had a pattern of blue flowers on a yellowish background; over the chimney shelf a filmy antique mirror looked strangely refined in the company of the Christmas cards and discoloured photographs that leaned against it. There was no sign of poverty, but everything was dingy, everything was taste-less, from the worn Kidderminster carpet to the illuminated text that was pinned to the wall facing the bed.

Miss Charlotte gave the fire a frugal poke, and lit a candle in the flame provoked from the sulky coals. In doing so some ashes became imbedded in the grease, and taking a hair-pin from the ponderous mass of brown hair that was piled on the back of her head, she began to scrape the candle clean. Probably at no moment of her forty years of life had Miss Charlotte Mullen looked more startlingly plain than now, as she stood, her squat figure draped in a magenta flannel dressing-gown, and the candle light shining upon her face. The night of watching had left its traces upon even her opaque skin. The lines about her prominent mouth and chin were deeper than usual; her broad cheeks had a flabby pallor; only her eyes were bright and untired, and the thick yellow-white hand that manipulated the hair-pin was as deft as it was wont to be.

When the flame burned clearly she took the candle to the bedside, and, bending down, held it close to the face of the old woman who was lying there. The eyes opened and turned towards the overhanging face: small dim, blue eyes, full of the stupor of illness, looking out of the pathetically commonplace little old face with a far-away perplexity.

'Was that Francie that was at the door?' she said in a drowsy voice that had in it the lagging drawl of intense weakness.

Charlotte took the tiny wrist in her hand, and felt the pulse with professional attention. Her broad perceptive finger-tips gauged the forces of the little thread that was jerking in the thin network of tendons, and as she laid the hand down she said to herself, 'She'll not last out the turn of the night.'

'Why doesn't Francie come in?' murmured the old woman again in the fragmentary, uninflected voice that seems hardly spared from the unseen battle with death.

'It wasn't her you asked me for at all,' answered Charlotte. 'You said you wanted to say good-bye to Susan. Here, you'd better have a sip of this.'

The old woman swallowed some brandy and water, and the stimulant presently revived unexpected strength in her.

'Charlotte,' she said, 'it isn't cats we should be thinking of now. God knows the cats are safe with you. But little Francie, Charlotte, we ought to have done more for her. You promised me that if you got the money you'd look after her. Didn't you now, Charlotte? I wish I'd done more for her. She's a good little thing—a good little thing—' she repeated dreamily.

Few people would think it worth their while to dispute the wandering futilities of an old dying woman, but even at this eleventh hour Charlotte could not brook the revolt of a slave.

'Good little thing!' she exclaimed, pushing the brandy bottle noisily in among a crowd of glasses and medicine bottles, 'a strapping big woman of nineteen! You didn't think her so good the time you had her here, and she put Susan's father and mother in the well!'

The old lady did not seem to understand what she had said.

'Susan, Susan!' she called quaveringly, and feebly patted the crochet quilt.

As if in answer, a hand fumbled at the door and opened it softly. Norry was standing there, tall and gaunt, holding in her apron, with both hands, something that looked like an enormous football.

'Miss Charlotte!' she whispered hoarsely, 'here's Susan for ye. He was out in the ashpit, an' I was hard set to get him, he was that wild.'

Even as she spoke there was a furious struggle in the blue apron.

'God in Heaven! ye fool!' ejaculated Charlotte. 'Don't let him go!' She shut the door behind Norry. 'Now, give him to me.'

Norry opened her apron cautiously, and Miss Charlotte lifted out of it a large grey tom-cat.

'Be quiet, my heart's love,' she said, 'be quiet.'

The cat stopped kicking and writhing, and, sprawling up on to the shoulder of the magenta dressing-gown, turned a fierce grey face upon his late captor. Norry crept over to the bed, and put back the dirty chintz curtain that had been drawn forward to keep out the draught of the door. Mrs Mullen was lying very still; she had drawn her knees up in front of her, and the bedclothes hung sharply from the small point that they made. The big living old woman took the hand of the other old woman who was so nearly dead, and pressed her lips to it.

'Ma'am, d'ye know me?'

Her mistress opened her eyes.

'Norry,' she whispered, 'give Miss Francie some jam for her tea to-night, but don't tell Miss Charlotte.'

'What's that she's saying?' said Charlotte, going to the other side of the bed. 'Is she asking for me?'

'No, but for Miss Francie,' Norry answered.

'She knows as well as I do that Miss Francie's in Dublin,' said Charlotte roughly; ' 'twas Susan she was asking for last. Here, a'nt, here's Susan for you.'

She pulled the cat down from her shoulder, and put him on the bed, where he crouched with a twitching tail, prepared for flight at a moment's notice.

He was within reach of the old lady's hand, but she did not seem
to know that he was there. She opened her eyes and looked vacantly
round.

'Where's little Francie? You mustn't send her away, Charlotte; you
promised you'd take care of her; didn't you, Charlotte?'

'Yes, yes,' said Charlotte quickly, pushing the cat towards the old
lady; 'never fear, I'll see after her.'

Old Mrs Mullen's eyes, that had rested with a filmy stare on her
niece's face, closed again, and her head began to move a little from
one side to the other, a low monotonous moan coming from her lips
with each turn. Charlotte took her right hand and laid it on the cat's
brindled back. It rested there, unconscious, for some seconds, while
the two women looked on in silence, and then the fingers drooped
and contracted like a bird's claw, and the moaning ceased. There was
at the same time a spasmodic movement of the gathered-up knees,
and a sudden rigidity fell upon the small insignificant face.

Norry the Boat threw herself upon her knees with a howl, and
began to pray loudly. At the sound the cat leaped to the floor, and the
hand that had been placed upon him in the only farewell his mistress
was to take, dropped stiffly on the bed. Miss Charlotte snatched up
the candle, and held it close to her aunt's face. There was no mistak-
ing what she saw there, and, putting down the candle again, she
plucked a large silk handkerchief from her pocket, and, with some
hideous preliminary heavings of her shoulders, burst into transports
of noisy grief.

BRAM STOKER
(1847–1912)

from *Dracula* (1897)

When I had written my two letters I sat quiet, reading a book whilst
the Count wrote several notes, referring as he wrote them to some
books on his table. Then he took up my two and placed them with
his own, and put by his writing materials, after which, the instant the
door had closed behind him, I leaned over and looked at the letters,
which were face down on the table. I felt no compunction in doing

so, for under the circumstances I felt that I should protect myself in every way I could.

One of the letters was directed to Samuel F. Billington, No. 7, The Crescent, Whitby; another to Herr Leutner, Varna; the third was to Coutts & Co., London, and the fourth to Herren Klopstock & Billreuth, bankers, Buda-Pesth. The second and fourth were unsealed. I was just about to look at them when I saw the door-handle move. I sank back in my seat, having just had time to replace the letters as they had been and to resume my book before the Count, holding still another letter in his hand, entered the room. He took up the letters on the table and stamped them carefully, and then, turning to me, said:—

'I trust you will forgive me, but I have much work to do in private this evening. You will, I hope, find all things as you wish.' At the door he turned, and after a moment's pause said:—

'Let me advise you, my dear young friend—nay, let me warn you with all seriousness, that should you leave these rooms you will not by any chance go to sleep in any other part of the castle. It is old, and has many memories, and there are bad dreams for those who sleep unwisely. Be warned! Should sleep now or ever overcome you, or be like to do, then haste to your own chamber or to these rooms, for your rest will then be safe. But if you be not careful in this respect, then—' He finished his speech in a gruesome way, for he motioned with his hands as if he were washing them. I quite understand; my only doubt was as to whether any dream could be more terrible than the unnatural, horrible net of gloom and mystery which seemed closing round me.

Later.—I endorse the last words written, but this time there is no doubt in question. I shall not fear to sleep in any place where he is not. I have placed the crucifix over the head of my bed—I imagine that my rest is thus freer from dreams; and there it shall remain.

When he left me I went to my room. After a little while, not hearing any sound, I came out and went up the stone stair to where I could look out towards the south. There was some sense of freedom in the vast expanse, inaccessible though it was to me, as compared with the narrow darkness of the courtyard. Looking out on this, I felt that I was indeed in prison, and I seemed to want a breath of fresh air, though it were of the night. I am beginning to feel this nocturnal existence tell on me. It is destroying my nerve. I start at my own shadow, and am full of all sorts of horrible imaginings. God knows that there is ground for any terrible fear in this accursed place! I looked out over the beautiful expanse, bathed in soft yellow moonlight till it was almost as light as day. In the soft light the distant hills became melted, and the shadows in the valleys and gorges of velvety blackness. The mere beauty seemed to cheer me; there was peace and comfort in every breath I drew. As I leaned from the window my eye was caught by something moving a story below me, and somewhat to my left, where I imagined, from the lie of the rooms, that the windows of the Count's own room would look out. The window at which I stood was tall and deep, stone-mullioned, and though weather-worn, was still complete; but it was evidently many a day since the case had been there. I drew back behind the stonework, and looked carefully out.

What I saw was the Count's head coming out from the window. I did not see the face, but I knew the man by the neck and the movement of his back and arms. In any case, I could not mistake the hands which I had had so many opportunities of studying. I was at first interested and somewhat amused, for it is wonderful how small a matter will interest and amuse a man when he is a prisoner. But my very feelings changed to repulsion and terror when I saw the whole man slowly emerge from the window and begin to crawl down the castle wall over that dreadful abyss, *face down*, with his cloak spreading out around him like great wings. At first I could not believe my eyes. I thought it was some trick of the moonlight, some weird effect of shadow; but I kept looking, and it could be no delusion. I saw the fingers and toes grasp the corners of the stones, worn clear of the mortar by the stress of years, and by thus using every projection and inequality move downwards with considerable speed, just as a lizard moves along a wall.

What manner of man is this, or what manner of creature is it in the semblance of man? I feel the dread of this horrible place overpowering me; I am in fear—in awful fear—and there is no escape for me; I am encompassed about with terrors that I dare not think of. . . .

15 May.—Once more have I seen the Count go out in his lizard fashion. He moved downwards in a sidelong way, some hundred feet down, and a good deal to the left. He vanished into some hole or window. When his head had disappeared I leaned out to try and see more, but without avail—the distance was too great to allow a proper angle of sight. I knew he had left the castle now, and thought to use the opportunity to explore more than I had dared to do as yet. I went back to the room, and taking a lamp, tried all the doors. They were all locked as I had expected, and the locks were comparatively new; but I went down the stone stairs to the hall where I had entered originally. I found I could pull back the bolts easily enough and unhook the great chains; but the door was locked, and the key was gone! That key must be in the Count's room; I must watch should his door be unlocked, so that I may get it and escape. I went on to make a thorough examination of the various stairs and passages, and to try the doors that opened from them. One or two small rooms near the hall were open, but there was nothing to see in them except old furniture, dusty with age and moth-eaten. At last, however, I found one door at the top of a stairway which, though it seemed to be locked, gave a little under pressure. I tried it harder, and found it was not really locked, but that the resistance came from the fact that the hinges had fallen somewhat, and the heavy door rested on the floor. Here was an opportunity which I might not have again, so I exerted myself, and with many efforts forced it back so that I could enter. I was now in a wing of the castle further to the right than the rooms I knew and a story lower down. From the windows I could see that the suite of rooms lay along to the south of the castle, the windows of the end room looking out both west and south. On the latter side, as well as to the former, there was a great precipice. The castle was built on the corner of a great rock, so that on three sides it was quite impregnable, and great windows were placed here where sling, or bow, or culverin could not reach, and consequently light and comfort, impossible to a position which had to be guarded, were secured. To the west was a great valley, and then, rising far away, great jagged mountain fastnesses, rising peak on peak, the sheer rock studded with mountain ash and thorn, whose roots clung in cracks and crevices and crannies of the stone. This was evidently the portion of the castle occupied in bygone days, for the furniture had more air of comfort than any I had seen. The windows were curtainless, and the yellow moonlight, flooding in through the diamond panes, enabled one to see even colours, whilst it softened the wealth of dust which lay over all and disguised in some measure the ravages of time and the moth. My lamp seemed to be of little effect in the brilliant moonlight, but I was glad to have it with me, for there was a dread loneliness in the place which chilled my heart and made my nerves tremble. Still, it was better than living alone in the rooms which I had come to hate from the presence of the Count, and after trying a little to school my nerves, I found a soft quietude come over me. Here I am, sitting at a little oak table where in old times possibly some fair lady sat to pen, with much thought and many blushes, her ill-spelt love-letter, and writing in my diary in shorthand all that has happened since I closed it last. It is nineteenth century up-to-date with a vengeance. And yet, unless my senses deceive me, the old centuries had, and have powers of their own which mere 'modernity' cannot kill.

Later: the Morning of 16 May.—God preserve my sanity, for to this I am reduced. Safety and the assurance of safety are things of the past. Whilst I live on here there is but one thing to hope for: that I may not go mad, if, indeed, I be not mad already. If I be sane, then surely it is maddening to think that of all the foul things that lurk in this hateful place the Count is the least dreadful to me; that to him alone I can look for safety, even though this be only whilst I can serve his purpose. Great God! merciful God! Let me be calm, for out of that way lies madness indeed. I begin to get new lights on certain things which have puzzled me. Up to now I never quite knew what Shakespeare meant when he made Hamlet say:—

> 'My tablets! quick, my tablets!
> 'Tis meet that I put it down,' etc.,*

for now, feeling as though my own brain was unhinged or as if the shock had come which must end in its undoing, I turn to my diary for repose. The habit of entering accurately must help to soothe me.

The Count's mysterious warning frightened me at the time; it frightens me more now when I think of it, for in future he has a fearful hold upon me. I shall fear to doubt what he may say!

When I had written in my diary and had fortunately replaced the book and pen in my pocket, I felt sleepy. The Count's warning came into my mind, but I took a pleasure in disobeying it. The sense of sleep was upon me, and with it the obstinacy which sleep brings as outrider. The soft moonlight soothed, and the wide expanse without gave a sense of freedom which refreshed me. I determined not to return to-night to the gloom-haunted rooms, but to sleep here, where of old ladies had sat and sung and lived sweet lives whilst their gentle breasts were sad for their menfolk away in the midst of remorseless wars. I drew a great couch out of its place near the corner, so that, as I lay, I could look at the lovely view to east and south, and unthinking of and uncaring for the dust, composed myself for sleep.

I suppose I must have fallen asleep; I hope so, but I fear, for all that followed was startlingly real—so real that now, sitting here in the broad, full sunlight of the morning, I cannot in the least believe that it was all sleep.

I was not alone. The room was the same, unchanged in any way since I came into it; I could see along the floor, in the brilliant moonlight, my own footsteps marked where I had disturbed the long accumulation of dust. In the moonlight opposite me were three young women, ladies by their dress and manner. I thought at the time that I must be dreaming when I saw them, for, though the moonlight was behind them, they threw no shadow on the floor. They came close to me and looked at me for some time and then whispered together. Two were dark, and had high aquiline noses, like the Count's, and great dark, piercing eyes, that seemed to be almost red when contrasted with the pale yellow moon. The other was fair, as fair as can be, with great, wavy masses of golden hair and eyes like pale sapphires. I seemed somehow to know her face, and to know it in connection with some dreamy fear, but I could not recollect at the moment how or where. All three had brilliant white teeth, that shone like pearls against the ruby of their voluptuous lips. There was something about them that made me uneasy, some longing and at the same time some deadly fear. I felt in my heart a wicked, burning desire that they would kiss me with those red lips. It is not good to note this down, lest some day it should meet Mina's eyes and cause her pain; but it is the truth. They whispered together, and then they all three laughed—such a silvery, musical laugh, but as hard as though the sound never could have come through the softness of human lips. It was like the intolerable, tingling sweetness of water-glasses* when played on by a cunning hand. The fair girl shook her head coquettishly, and the other two urged her on. One said:—

'Go on! You are first, and we shall follow; yours is the right to begin.' The other added:—

'He is young and strong; there are kisses for us all.' I lay quiet, looking out under my eyelashes in an agony of delightful anticipation. The fair girl advanced and bent over me till I could feel the movement of her breath upon me. Sweet it was in one sense, honey-sweet, and sent the same tingling through the nerves as her voice, but with a bitter underlying the sweet, a bitter offensiveness, as one smells in blood.

I was afraid to raise my eyelids, but looked out and saw perfectly under the lashes. The fair girl went on her knees and bent over me, fairly gloating. There was a deliberate voluptuousness which was both thrilling and repulsive, and as she arched her neck she actually licked her lips like an animal, till I could see in the moonlight the moisture shining on the scarlet lips and on the red tongue as it lapped the white sharp teeth. Lower and lower went her head as the lips went below the range of my mouth and chin and seemed about to fasten on my throat. Then she paused, and I could hear the churning sound of her tongue as it licked her teeth and lips, and could feel the hot breath on my neck. Then the skin of my throat began to tingle as one's flesh does when the hand that is to tickle it approaches nearer—nearer. I could feel the soft, shivering touch of the lips on the supersensitive skin of my throat, and the hard dents of two sharp teeth, just touching and pausing there. I closed my eyes in a languorous ecstasy and waited—waited with beating heart.

But at that instant another sensation swept through me as quick as lightning. I was conscious of the presence of the Count, and of his being as if lapped in a storm of fury. As my eyes opened involuntarily I saw his strong hand grasp the slender neck of the fair woman and with giant's power draw it back, the blue eyes transformed with fury, the white teeth champing with rage, and the fair cheeks blazing red with passion. But the Count! Never did I imagine such wrath and fury, even in the demons of the pit. His eyes were positively blazing. The red light in them was lurid, as if the flames of hell-fire blazed behind them. His face was deathly pale, and the lines of it were hard like drawn wires; the thick eyebrows that met over the nose now seemed like a heaving bar of white-hot metal. With a fierce sweep of his arm, he hurled the woman from him, and then motioned to the others, as though he were beating them back; it was the same imperious gesture that I had seen used to the wolves. In a voice which, though low and almost a whisper, seemed to cut through the air and then ring round the room, he exclaimed:—

'How dare you touch him, any of you? How dare you cast eyes on him when I had forbidden it? Back, I tell you all! This man belongs to me! Beware how you meddle with him, or you'll have to deal with me.' The fair girl, with laugh of ribald coquetry, turned to answer him:—

'You yourself never loved; you never love!' On this the other women joined, and such a mirthless, hard, soulless laughter rang through the room that it almost made me faint to hear; it seemed like the pleasure of fiends. Then the Count turned, after looking at my face attentively, and said in a soft whisper:—

'Yes, I too can love; you yourselves can tell it from the past. Is it not so? Well, now I promise you that when I am done with him, you shall kiss him at your will. Now go! go! I must awaken him, for there is work to be done.'

'Are we to have nothing to-night?' said one of them, with a low laugh, as she pointed to the bag which he had thrown upon the floor, and which moved as though there were some living thing within it. For answer he nodded his head. One of the women jumped forward and opened it. If my ears did not deceive me there was a gasp and a low wail, as of a half-smothered child. The women closed round, whilst I was aghast with horror; but as I looked they disappeared, and with them the dreadful bag. There was no door near them, and they could not have passed me without my noticing. They simply seemed to fade into the rays of the moonlight and pass out through the window, for I could see outside the dim, shadowy forms for a moment before they entirely faded away.

Then the horror overcame me, and I sank down unconscious.

JAMES JOYCE
(1882–1941)

from *Ulysses* (1922)

Stately, plump Buck Mulligan came from the stairhead, bearing a bowl of lather on which a mirror and a razor lay crossed. A yellow dressinggown, ungirdled, was sustained gently behind him by the mild morning air. He held the bowl aloft and intoned:

—*Introibo ad altare Dei.**

Halted, he peered down the dark winding stairs and called up coarsely:

—Come up, Kinch. Come up, you fearful Jesuit.

Solemnly he came forward and mounted the round gunrest. He faced about and blessed gravely thrice the tower, the surrounding country and the awaking mountains. Then, catching sight of Stephen Dedalus, he bent towards him and made rapid crosses in the air, gurgling in his throat and shaking his head. Stephen Dedalus, displeased and sleepy, leaned his arms on the top of the staircase and looked coldly at the shaking gurgling face that blessed him, equine in its length, and at the light untonsured hair, grained and hued like pale oak.

Buck Mulligan peeped an instant under the mirror and then covered the bowl smartly.

—Back to barracks, he said sternly.

He added in a preacher's tone:

—For this, O dearly beloved, is the genuine Christine: body and soul and blood and ouns.* Slow music, please. Shut your eyes, gents. One moment. A little trouble about those white corpuscles. Silence, all.

He peered sideways up and gave a long low whistle of call then paused awhile in rapt attention, his even white teeth glistening here and there with gold points. Chrysostomos.* Two strong shrill whistles* answered through the calm.

—Thanks, old chap, he cried briskly. That will do nicely. Switch off the current, will you?

He skipped off the gunrest and looked gravely at his watcher, gathering about his legs the loose folds of his gown. The plump shadowed face and sullen oval jowl recalled a prelate, patron of arts in the middle ages. A pleasant smile broke quietly over his lips.

—The mockery of it, he said gaily. Your absurd name, an ancient Greek.*

He pointed his finger in friendly jest and went over to the parapet, laughing to himself. Stephen Dedalus stepped up, followed him wearily halfway and sat down on the edge of the gunrest, watching him still as he propped his mirror on the parapet, dipped the brush in the bowl and lathered cheeks and neck.

Buck Mulligan's gay voice went on.

—My name is absurd too: Malachi Mulligan, two dactyls. But it has a Hellenic ring, hasn't it? Tripping and sunny like the buck himself. We must go to Athens. Will you come if I can get the aunt to fork out twenty quid?

He laid the brush aside and, laughing with delight, cried:

—Will he come? The jejune jesuit.

Ceasing, he began to shave with care.

—Tell me, Mulligan, Stephen said quietly.

—Yes, my love?

—How long is Haines going to stay in this tower?

Buck Mulligan showed a shaven cheek over his right shoulder.

—God, isn't he dreadful? he said frankly. A ponderous Saxon. He thinks you're not a gentleman. God, these bloody English. Bursting with money and indigestion. Because he comes from Oxford. You know, Dedalus, you have the real Oxford manner. He can't make you out. O, my name for you is the best: Kinch, the knifeblade.

He shaved warily over his chin.

—He was raving all night about a black panther, Stephen said. Where is his guncase?

—A woful lunatic, Mulligan said. Were you in a funk?

—I was, Stephen said with energy and growing fear. Out here in the dark with a man I don't know raving and moaning to himself about shooting a black panther. You saved men from drowning. I'm not a hero, however. If he stays on here I am off.

Buck Mulligan frowned at the lather on his razor blade. He hopped down from his perch and began to search his trouser pockets hastily.

—Scutter, he cried thickly.

He came over to the gunrest and, thrusting a hand into Stephen's upper pocket, said:

—Lend us a loan of your noserag to wipe my razor.

Stephen suffered him to pull out and hold up on show by its corner a dirty crumpled handkerchief. Buck Mulligan wiped the razorblade neatly. Then, gazing over the handkerchief, he said:

—The bard's noserag. A new art colour for our Irish poets: snot-green. You can almost taste it, can't you?

He mounted to the parapet again and gazed out over Dublin bay, his fair oakpale hair stirring slightly.

—God, he said quietly. Isn't the sea what Algy* calls it: a great sweet mother? The snotgreen sea. The scrotumtightening sea. *Epi oinopa ponton.** Ah, Dedalus, the Greeks. I must teach you. You must read them in the original. *Thalatta! Thalatta!** She is our great sweet mother. Come and look.

Stephen stood up and went over to the parapet. Leaning on it he looked down on the water and on the mailboat clearing the harbour mouth of Kingstown.

—Our mighty mother, Buck Mulligan said.

He turned abruptly his great searching eyes from the sea to Stephen's face.

—The aunt thinks you killed your mother, he said. That's why she won't let me have anything to do with you.

—Someone killed her, Stephen said gloomily.

—You could have knelt down, damn it, Kinch, when your dying mother asked you, Buck Mulligan said. I'm hyperborean* as much as you. But to think of your mother begging you with her last breath to kneel down and pray for her. And you refused. There is something sinister in you . . .

He broke off and lathered again lightly his farther cheek. A tolerant smile curled his lips.

—But a lovely mummer, he murmured to himself. Kinch, the loveliest mummer of them all.

He shaved evenly and with care, in silence, seriously.

Stephen, an elbow rested on the jagged granite, leaned his palm against his brow and gazed at the fraying edge of his shiny black coatsleeve. Pain, that was not yet the pain of love, fretted his heart. Silently, in a dream she had come to him after her death, her wasted body within its loose brown graveclothes giving off an odour of wax and rosewood, her breath, that had bent upon him, mute, reproachful, a faint odour of wetted ashes. Across the threadbare cuffedge he saw the sea hailed as a great sweet mother by the wellfed voice beside him. The ring of bay and skyline held a dull green mass of liquid. A bowl of white china had stood beside her deathbed holding the green sluggish bile which she had torn up from her rotting liver by fits of loud groaning vomiting.

Buck Mulligan wiped again his razorblade.

—Ah, poor dogsbody, he said in a kind voice. I must give you a shirt and a few noserags. How are the secondhand breeks?

—They fit well enough, Stephen answered.

Buck Mulligan attacked the hollow beneath his underlip.

—The mockery of it, he said contentedly, secondleg they should be. God knows what poxy bowsy left them off. I have a lovely pair with a hair stripe, grey. You'll look spiffing in them. I'm not joking, Kinch. You look damn well when you're dressed.

—Thanks, Stephen said. I can't wear them if they are grey.

—He can't wear them, Buck Mulligan told his face in the mirror. Etiquette is etiquette. He kills his mother but he can't wear grey trousers.

He folded his razor neatly and with stroking palps of fingers felt the smooth skin.

Stephen turned his gaze from the sea and to the plump face with its smokeblue mobile eyes.

—That fellow I was with in the Ship last night said Buck Mulligan says you have g. p. i. He's up in Dottyville* with Conolly Norman. Genera paralysis of the insane.

He swept the mirror a half circle in the air to flash the tidings abroad in sunlight now radiant on the sea. His curling shaven lips laughed and the edges of his white glittering teeth. Laughter seized all his strong wellknit trunk.

—Look at yourself, he said, you dreadful bard.

Stephen bent forward and peered at the mirror held out to him, cleft by a crooked crack, hair on end. As he and others see me. Who chose this face for me? This dogsbody to rid of vermin. It asks me too.

—I pinched it out of the skivvy's room, Buck Mulligan said. It does her all right. The aunt always keeps plainlooking servants for Malachi. Lead him not into temptation. And her name is Ursula.*

Laughing again, he brought the mirror away from Stephen's peering eyes.

—The rage of Caliban* at not seeing his face in a mirror, he said. If Wilde were only alive to see you.

Drawing back and pointing, Stephen said with bitterness:

—It is a symbol of Irish art. The cracked lookingglass of a servant.*

Buck Mulligan suddenly linked his arm in Stephen's and walked with him round the tower, his razor and mirror clacking in the pocket where he had thrust them.

—It's not fair to tease you like that, Kinch, is it? he said kindly.
God knows you have more spirit than any of them.

Parried again. He fears the lancet of my art as I fear that of his.
The cold steel pen.

—Cracked lookingglass of a servant. Tell that to the oxy chap*
downstairs and touch him for a guinea. He's stinking with money
and thinks you're not a gentleman. His old fellow made his tin by
selling jalap to Zulus or some bloody swindle or other. God, Kinch,
if you and I could only work together we might do something for the
island. Hellenise it.*

Cranly's arm. His arm.

—And to think of your having to beg from these swine. I'm the
only one that knows what you are. Why don't you trust me more?
What have you up your nose against me? Is it Haines? If he makes
any noise here I'll bring down Seymour and we'll give him a ragging
worse than they gave Clive Kempthorpe.

Young shouts of moneyed voices in Clive Kempthorpe's rooms.
Palefaces: they hold their ribs with laughter, one clasping another,
O, I shall expire! Break the news to her gently, Aubrey! I shall die!
With slit ribbons of his shirt whipping the air he hops and hobbles
round the table, with trousers down at heels, chased by Ades of
Magdalen with the tailor's shears. A scared calf's face gilded with
marmalade. I don't want to be debagged! Don't you play the giddy
ox with me!

Shouts from the open window startling evening in the quadrangle.*
A deaf gardener, aproned, masked with Matthew Arnold's face,
pushes his mower on the sombre lawn watching narrowly the
dancing motes of grasshalms.

To ourselves . . . new paganism . . . omphalos.*

—Let him stay, Stephen said. There's nothing wrong with him
except at night.

—Then what is it? Buck Mulligan asked impatiently. Cough it up.
I'm quite frank with you. What have you against me now?

They halted, looking towards the blunt cape of Bray Head that lay
on the water like the snout of a sleeping whale. Stephen freed his
arm quietly.

—Do you wish me to tell you? he asked.

—Yes, what is it? Buck Mulligan answered. I don't remember
anything.

He looked in Stephen's face as he spoke. A light wind passed his brow, fanning softly his fair uncombed hair and stirring silver points of anxiety in his eyes.

Stephen, depressed by his own voice, said:

—Do you remember the first day I went to your house after my mother's death?

Buck Mulligan frowned quickly and said:

—What? Where? I can't remember anything. I remember only ideas and sensations. Why? What happened in the name of God?

—You were making tea, Stephen said, and I went across the landing to get more hot water. Your mother and some visitor came out of the drawing room. She asked you who was in your room.

—Yes? Buck Mulligan said. What did I say? I forget.

—You said, Stephen answered, *O, it's only Dedalus whose mother is beastly dead*.

A flush which made him seem younger and more engaging rose to Buck Mulligan's cheek.

—Did I say that? he asked. Well? What harm is that?

He shook his constraint from him nervously.

—And what is death, he asked, your mother's or yours or my own? You saw only your mother die. I see them pop off every day in the Mater and Richmond and cut up into tripes in the dissecting room. It's a beastly thing and nothing else. It simply doesn't matter. You wouldn't kneel down to pray for your mother on her deathbed when she asked you. Why? Because you have the cursed Jesuit strain in you, only it's injected the wrong way. To me it's all a mockery and beastly. Her cerebral lobes are not functioning. She calls the doctor Sir Peter Teazle* and picks buttercups off the quilt. Humour her till it's over. You crossed her last wish in death and yet you sulk with me because I don't whinge like some hired mute from Lalouette's.* Absurd! I suppose I did say it. I didn't mean to offend the memory of your mother.

He had spoken himself into boldness. Stephen, shielding the gaping wounds which the words had left in his heart, said very coldly:

—I am not thinking of the offence to my mother.

—Of what, then? Buck Mulligan asked.

—Of the offence to me, Stephen answered.

Buck Mulligan swung round on his heel.

—O, an impossible person! he exclaimed.

He walked off quickly round the parapet. Stephen stood at his post, gazing over the calm sea towards the headland. Sea and headland now grew dim. Pulses were beating in his eyes, veiling their sight, and he felt the fever of his cheeks.

A voice within the tower called loudly:

—Are you up there, Mulligan?

—I'm coming, Buck Mulligan answered.

He turned towards Stephen and said:

—Look at the sea. What does it care about offences? Chuck Loyola,* Kinch, and come on down. The Sassenach wants his morning rashers.

His head halted again for a moment at the top of the staircase, level with the roof:

—Don't mope over it all day, he said. I'm inconsequent. Give up the moody brooding.

His head vanished but the drone of his descending voice boomed out of the stairhead:

> *And no more turn aside and brood*
> *Upon love's bitter mystery*
> *For Fergus rules the brazen cars.**

Woodshadows floated silently by through the morning peace from the stairhead seaward where he gazed. Inshore and farther out the mirror of water whitened, spurned by lightshod hurrying feet. White breast of the dim sea. The twining stresses, two by two. A hand plucking the harpstrings merging their twining chords. Wavewhite wedded words shimmering on the dim tide.

A cloud began to cover the sun slowly, shadowing the bay in deeper green. It lay behind him, a bowl of bitter waters. Fergus' song: I sang it above in the house, holding down the long dark chords. Her door was open: she wanted to hear my music. Silent with awe and pity I went to her bedside. She was crying in her wretched bed. For those words, Stephen: love's bitter mystery.

Where now?

Her secrets: old feather fans, tassled dancecards, powdered with musk, a gaud of amber beads in her locked drawer. A birdcage hung in the sunny window of her house when she was a girl. She heard old Royce sing in the pantomine of Turko the terrible* and laughed with others when he sang:

> *I am the boy*
> *That can enjoy*
> *Invisibility.*

Phantasmal mirth, folded away: muskperfumed.

> *And no more turn aside and brood.*

Folded away in the memory of nature with her toys. Memories beset his brooding brain. Her glass of water from the kitchen tap when she had approached the sacrament. A cored apple, filled with brown sugar, roasting for her at the hob on a dark autumn evening. Her shapely fingernails reddened by the blood of squashed lice from the children's shirts.

In a dream, silently, she had come to him, her wasted body within its loose graveclothes giving off an odour of wax and rosewood, her breath bent over him with mute secret words, a faint odour of wetted ashes.

Her glazing eyes, staring out of death, to shake and bend my soul. On me alone. The ghostcandle to light her agony. Ghostly light on the tortured face. Her hoarse loud breath rattling in horror, while all prayed on their knees. Her eyes on me to strike me down. *Liliata rutilantium te confessorum turma circumdet: iubilantium te virginum chorus excipiat.**

Ghoul! Chewer of corpses!

No, mother. Let me be and let me live.

—Kinch ahoy!

Buck Mulligan's voice sang from within the tower. It came nearer up the staircase, calling again. Stephen, still trembling at his soul's cry, heard warm running sunlight and in the air behind him friendly words.

—Dedalus, come down, like a good mosey. Breakfast is ready. Haines is apologising for waking us last night. It's all right.

—I'm coming, Stephen said, turning.

—Do, for Jesus' sake, Buck Mulligan said. For my sake and for all our sakes.

His head disappeared and reappeared.

—I told him your symbol of Irish art. He says it's very clever. Touch him for a quid, will you? A guinea, I mean.

—I get paid this morning, Stephen said.

—The school kip? Buck Mulligan said. How much? Four quid?
Lend us one.

—If you want it, Stephen said.

—Four shining sovereigns, Buck Mulligan cried with delight.
We'll have a glorious drunk to astonish the druidy druids. Four
omnipotent sovereigns.

He flung up his hands and tramped down the stone stairs, singing
out of tune with a Cockney accent:

> *O, won't we have a merry time,*
> *Drinking whisky, beer and wine,*
> *On coronation*
> *Coronation day?*
> *O, won't we have a merry time*
> *On coronation day?**

Warm sunshine merrying over the sea. The nickel shavingbowl
shone, forgotten, on the parapet. Why should I bring it down? Or
leave it there all day, forgotten friendship?

He went over to it, held it in his hands awhile, feeling its coolness,
smelling the clammy slaver of the lather in which the brush was
stuck. So I carried the boat of incense then at Clongowes.* I am
another now and yet the same. A servant too. A server of a servant.*

In the gloomy domed livingroom of the tower Buck Mulligan's
gowned form moved briskly about the hearth to and fro, hiding and
revealing its yellow glow. Two shafts of soft daylight fell across the
flagged floor from the high barbacans: and at the meeting of their
rays a cloud of coalsmoke and fumes of fried grease floated, turning.

—We'll be choked, Buck Mulligan said. Haines, open that door,
will you?

Stephen laid the shavingbowl on the locker. A tall figure rose
from the hammock where it had been sitting, went to the doorway
and pulled open the inner doors.

—Have you the key? a voice asked.

—Dedalus has it, Buck Mulligan said. Janey Mack, I'm choked.

He howled without looking up from the fire:

—Kinch!

—It's in the lock, Stephen said, coming forward.

The key scraped round harshly twice and, when the heavy door
had been set ajar, welcome light and bright air entered. Haines

stood at the doorway, looking out. Stephen haled his upended valise to the table and sat down to wait. Buck Mulligan tossed the fry on to the dish beside him. Then he carried the dish and a large teapot over to the table, set them down heavily and sighed with relief.

—I'm melting, he said, as the candle remarked when . . . But hush. Not a word more on that subject. Kinch, wake up. Bread, butter, honey. Haines, come in. The grub is ready. Bless us, O Lord, and these thy gifts. Where's the sugar? O, jay, there's no milk.

Stephen fetched the loaf and the pot of honey and the buttercooler from the locker. Buck Mulligan sat down in a sudden pet.

—What sort of a kip is this? he said. I told her to come after eight.

—We can drink it black, Stephen said. There's lemon in the locker.

—O, damn you and your Paris fads, Buck Mulligan said. I want Sandycove milk.

Haines came in from the doorway and said quietly:

—That woman is coming up with the milk.

—The blessings of God on you, Buck Mulligan cried, jumping up from his chair. Sit down. Pour out the tea there. The sugar is in the bag. Here, I can't go fumbling at the damned eggs. He hacked through the fry on the dish and slapped it out on three plates, saying:

—*In nomine Patris et Filii et Spiritus Sancti.**

Haines sat down to pour out the tea.

—I'm giving you two lumps each, he said. But, I say, Mulligan, you do make strong tea, don't you?

Buck Mulligan, hewing thick slices from the loaf said in an old woman's wheedling voice:

—When I makes tea I makes tea, as old mother Grogan said. And when I makes water I makes water.

—By Jove, it is tea, Haines said.

Buck Mulligan went on hewing and wheedling:

—*So I do, Mrs Cahill*, says she. *Begob, ma'am*, says Mrs Cahill, *God send you don't make them in the one pot.*

He lunged towards his messmates in turn a thick slice of bread, impaled on his knife.

—That's folk, he said very earnestly, for your book, Haines. Five lines of text and ten pages of notes about the folk and the fishgods of Dundrum. Printed by the weird sisters in the year of the big wind.*

He turned to Stephen and asked in a fine puzzled voice, lifting his brows:

—Can you recall, brother, is mother Grogan's tea and water pot spoken of in the Mabinogion* or is it in the Upanishads?*

—I doubt it, said Stephen gravely.

—Do you now? Buck Mulligan said in the same tone. Your reasons, pray?

—I fancy, Stephen said as he ate, it did not exist in or out of the Mabinogion. Mother Grogan was, one imagines, a kinswoman of Mary Ann.

Buck Mulligan's face smiled with delight.

—Charming, he said in a finical sweet voice, showing his white teeth and blinking his eyes pleasantly. Do you think she was? Quite charming.

Then, suddenly overclouding all his features, he growled in a hoarsened rasping voice as he hewed again vigorously at the loaf:

—*For old Mary Ann*
  She doesn't care a damn.
  But, hising up her petticoats . . .

The doorway was darkened by an entering form.

—The milk, sir.

—Come in, ma'am, Mulligan said, Kinch, get the jug.

An old woman came forward and stood by Stephen's elbow.

—That's a lovely morning, sir, she said. Glory be to God.

—To whom? Mulligan said, glancing at her. Ah, to be sure.

Stephen reached back and took the milkjug from the locker.

The islanders, Mulligan said to Haines casually, speak frequently of the collector of prepuces.*

—How much, sir? asked the old woman.

—A quart, Stephen said.

He watched her pour into the measure and thence into the jug rich white milk, not hers. Old shrunken paps. She poured again a measureful and a tilly.* Old and secret she had entered from a morning world, maybe a messenger. She praised the goodness of the milk, pouring it out. Crouching by a patient cow at daybreak in the lush field, a witch on her toadstool, her wrinkled fingers quick at the squirting dugs. They lowed about her whom they knew, dewsilky cattle. Silk of the kine and poor old woman,* names given her in old times. A wandering crone, lowly form of an immortal serving her conqueror and her gay betrayer, their common cuckquean,* a messenger from the secret morning. To serve or to upbraid, whether he could not tell: but scorned to beg her favour.

—It is indeed, ma'am, Buck Mulligan said, pouring milk into their cups.

—Taste it, sir, she said.

He drank at her bidding.

—If we could only live on good food like that, he said to her somewhat loudly, we wouldn't have the country full of rotten teeth and rotten guts. Living in a bogswamp, eating cheap food and the streets paved with dust, horsedung and consumptives' spits.

—Are you a medical student, sir? the old woman asked.

—I am, ma'am, Buck Mulligan answered.

Stephen listened in scornful silence. She bows her old head to a voice that speaks to her loudly, her bonesetter, her medicineman: me she slights. To the voice that will shrive and oil for the grave all there is of her but her woman's unclean loins, of man's flesh made not in God's likeness the serpent's prey.* And to the loud voice that now bids her be silent with wondering unsteady eyes.

—Do you understand what he says? Stephen asked her.

—Is it French you are talking, sir? the old woman said to Haines.

Haines spoke to her again a longer speech, confidently.

—Irish, Buck Mulligan said. Is there Gaelic on you?

—I thought it was Irish, she said, by the sound of it. Are you from west, sir?

—I am an Englishman, Haines answered.

—He's English, Buck Mulligan said, and he thinks we ought to speak Irish in Ireland.

—Sure we ought to, the old woman said, and I'm ashamed I don't speak the language myself. I'm told it's a grand language by them that knows.

—Grand is no name for it, said Buck Mulligan. Wonderful entirely. Fill us out some more tea, Kinch. Would you like a cup, ma'am?

—No, thank you, sir, the old woman said, slipping the ring of the milkcan on her forearm and about to go.

Hanies said to her:

—Have you your bill? We had better pay her, Mulligan, hadn't we? Stephen filled again the three cups.

—Bill, sir? she said, halting. Well, it's seven mornings a pint at two pence is seven twos is a shilling and twopence over and these three mornings a quart at fourpence is three quarts is a shilling and one and two is two and two, sir.

Buck Mulligan sighed and having filled his mouth with a crust thickly buttered on both sides, stretched forth his legs and began to search his trouser pockets.

—Pay up and look pleasant, Haines said to him smiling.

Stephen filled a third cup, a spoonful of tea colouring faintly the thick rich milk. Buck Mulligan brought up a florin, twisted it round in his fingers and cried:

—A miracle!

He passed it along the table towards the old woman, saying:

—Ask nothing more of me, sweet. All I can give you I give.*

Stephen laid the coin in her uneager hand.

—We'll owe twopence, he said.

—Time enough, sir, she said, taking the coin. Time enough. Good morning, sir.

She curtseyed and went out, followed by Buck Mulligan's tender chant:

—*Heart of my heart, were it more,*
More would be laid at your feet.

He turned to Stephen and said:

—Seriously, Dedalus. I'm stony.* Hurry out to your school kip and bring us back some money. Today the bards must drink and junket. Ireland expects that every man this day will do his duty.*

—That reminds me, Haines said, rising, that I have to visit your national library today.

—Our swim first, Buck Mulligan said.

He turned to Stephen and asked blandly:

—Is this the day for your monthly wash, Kinch?

Then he said to Haines:

—The unclean bard makes a point of washing once a month.

—All Ireland is washed by the gulfstream, Stephen said as he let honey trickle over a slice of the loaf.

Haines from the corner where he was knotting easily a scarf about the loose collar of his tennis shirt spoke:

—I intend to make a collection of your sayings if you will let me.

Speaking to me. They wash and tub and scrub. Agenbite of inwit.* Conscience. Yet here's a spot.

—That one about the cracked lookingglass of a servant being the symbol of Irish art is deuced good.

Buck Mulligan kicked Stephen's foot under the table and said with warmth of tone:

—Wait till you hear him on Hamlet, Haines.

—Well, I mean it, Haines said, still speaking to Stephen. I was just thinking of it when that poor old creature came in.

—Would I make money by it? Stephen asked.

Haines laughed and, as he took his soft grey hat from the holdfast of the hammock, said:

—I don't know, I'm sure.

He strolled out to the doorway. Buck Mulligan bent across to Stephen and said with coarse vigour:

—You put your hoof in it now. What did you say that for?

—Well? Stephen said. The problem is to get money. From whom? From the milkwoman or from him. It's a toss up, I think.

—I blow him out about you, Buck Mulligan said, and then you come along with your lousy leer and your gloomy jesuit jibes.

—I see little hope, Stephen said, from her or from him.

Buck Mulligan sighed tragically and laid his hand on Stephen's arm.

—From me, Kinch, he said.

In a suddenly changed tone he added:

—To tell you the God's truth I think you're right. Damn all else they are good for. Why don't you play them as I do? To hell with them all. Let us get out of the kip.

He stood up, gravely ungirdled and disrobed himself of his gown, saying resignedly:

—Mulligan is stripped of his garments.*

He emptied his pockets on to the table.

—There's your snotrag, he said.

And putting on his stiff collar and rebellious tie, he spoke to them, chiding them, and to his dangling watchchain. His hands plunged and rummaged in his trunk while he called for a clean handkerchief.

Agenbite of inwit. God, we'll simply have to dress the character. I want puce gloves and green boots. Contradiction. Do I contradict myself? Very well then, I contradict myself, Mercurial Malachi.* A limp black missile flew out of his talking hands.

—And there's your Latin quarter hat,* he said.

Stephen picked it up and put it on. Haines called to them from the doorway:

—Are you coming, you fellows?

—I'm ready, Buck Mulligan answered, going towards the door. Come out, Kinch. You have eaten all we left, I suppose. Resigned he passed out with grave words and gait, saying, wellnigh with sorrow:

—And going forth he met Butterly.

Stephen, taking his ashplant from its leaningplace, followed them out and, as they went down the ladder, pulled to the slow iron door and locked it. He put the huge key in his inner pocket.

At the foot of the ladder Buck Mulligan asked:

—Did you bring the key?

—I have it, Stephen said, preceding them.

He walked on. Behind him he heard Buck Mulligan club with his heavy bathtowel the leader shoots of ferns or grasses.

—Down, sir. How dare you, sir.

Haines asked:

—Do you pay rent for this tower?

—Twelve quid, Buck Mulligan said.

—To the secretary of state for war, Stephen added over his shoulder. They halted while Haines surveyed the tower and said at last:

—Rather bleak in wintertime, I should say. Martello you call it?

—Billy Pitt had them built, Buck Mulligan said, when the French were on the sea.* But ours is the *omphalos.*

—What is your idea of Hamlet? Haines asked Stephen.

—No, no, Buck Mulligan shouted in pain. I'm not equal to Thomas Aquinas* and the fiftyfive reasons he has made to prop it up. Wait till I have a few pints in me first.

He turned to Stephen, saying as he pulled down neatly the peaks of his primrose waistcoat:

—You couldn't manage it under three pints, Kinch, could you?

—It has waited so long, Stephen said listlessly, it can wait longer.

—You pique my curiosity, Haines said aimiably. Is it some paradox?

—Pooh! Buck Mulligan said. We have grown out of Wilde and paradoxes. It's quite simple. He proves by algebra that Hamlet's grandson is Shakespeare's grandfather and that he himself is the ghost of his own father.

—What? Haines said, beginning to point at Stephen. He himself?

Buck Mulligan slung his towel stolewise round his neck and, bending in loose laughter, said to Stephen's ear:

—O, shade of Kinch the elder! Japhet in search of a father!*

—We're always tired in the morning, Stephen said to Haines. And it is rather long to tell.

Buck Mulligan, walking forward again, raised his hands.

—The sacred pint alone can unbind the tongue of Dedalus, he said.

—I mean to say, Haines explained to Stephen as they followed, this tower and these cliffs here remind me somehow of Elsinore. *That beetles o'er his base into the sea,** isn't it?

Buck Mulligan turned suddenly for an instant towards Stephen but did not speak. In the bright silent instant Stephen saw his own image in cheap dusty mourning between their gay attires.

—It's a wonderful tale, Haines said, bringing them to halt again.

Eyes, pale as the sea the wind had freshened, paler, firm and prudent. The seas' ruler,* he gazed southward over the bay, empty save for the smokeplume of the mailboat, vague on the bright skyline, and a sail tacking by the Muglins.

—I read a theological interpretation of it somewhere, he said bemused. The Father and the Son idea. The Son striving to be atoned with the Father.

Buck Mulligan at once put on a blithe broadly smiling face. He looked at them, his wellshaped mouth open happily, his eyes, from which he had suddenly withrawn all shrewd sense, blinking with mad gaiety. He moved a doll's head to and fro, the brims of his Panama hat quivering, and began to chant in a quiet happy foolish voice:

—*I'm the queerest young fellow that ever you heard.*
  My mother's a jew, my father's a bird.
  With Joseph the joiner I cannot agree,
  So here's to disciples and Calvary.

He held up a forefinger of warning.

> —*If anyone thinks that I amn't divine*
> *He'll get no free drinks when I'm making the wine*
> *But have to drink water and wish it were plain*
> *That I make when the wine becomes water again.*

He tugged swiftly at Stephen's ashplant in farewell and, running forward to a brow of the cliff, fluttered his hands at his sides like fins or wings of one about to rise in the air, and chanted:

> —*Goodbye, now, goodbye. Write down all I said*
> *And tell Tom, Dick and Harry I rose from the dead.*
> *What's bred in the bone cannot fail me to fly*
> *And Olivet's breezy . . . Goodbye, now, goodbye.**

He capered before them down towards the fortyfoot hole, fluttering his winglike hands, leaping nimbly, Mercury's hat quivering in the fresh wind that bore back to them his brief birdlike cries.

Haines, who had been laughing guardedly, walked on beside Stephen and said:

—We oughtn't to laugh, I suppose. He's rather blasphemous. I'm not a believer myself, that is to say. Still his gaiety takes the harm out of it somehow, doesn't it? What did he call it? Joseph the Joiner?

—The ballad of Joking Jesus, Stephen answered.

—O, Haines said, you have heard it before?

—Three times a day, after meals, Stephen said drily.

—You're not a believer, are you? Haines asked. I mean, a believer in the narrow sense of the word. Creation from nothing and miracles and a personal God.

—There's only one sense of the word, it seems to me, Stephen said.

Haines stopped to take out a smooth silver case in which twinkled a green stone.* He sprang it open with his thumb and offered it.

—Thank you, Stephen said, taking a cigarette.

Haines helped himself and snapped the case to. He put it back in his sidepocket and took from his waistcoatpocket a nickel tinderbox, sprang it open too, and, having lit his cigarette, held the flaming spunk towards Stephen in the shell of his hands.

—Yes, of course, he said, as they went on again. Either you believe or you don't, isn't it? Personally I couldn't stomach that idea of a personal God. You don't stand for that, I suppose?

—You behold in me, Stephen said with grim displeasure, a horrible example of free thought.

He walked on, waiting to be spoken to, trailing his ashplant by his side. Its ferrule followed lightly on the path, squealing at his heels. My familiar, after me, calling Steeeeeeeeeeeephen. A wavering line along the path. They will walk on it tonight, coming here in the dark. He wants that key. It is mine, I paid the rent. Now I eat his salt bread. Give him the key too. All. He will ask for it. That was in his eyes.

—After all, Haines began . . .

Stephen turned and saw that the cold gaze which had measured him was not all unkind.

—After all, I should think you are able to free yourself. You are your own master, it seems to me.

—I am the servant of two masters, Stephen said, an English and an Italian.

—Italian? Haines said.

A crazy queen, old and jealous. Kneel down before me.

—And a third, Stephen said, there is who wants me for odd jobs.

—Italian? Haines said again. What do you mean?

—The imperial British state, Stephen answered, his colour rising, and the holy Roman catholic and apostolic church.

Haines detached from his underlip some fibres of tobacco before he spoke.

—I can quite understand that, he said calmly. An Irishman must think like that, I daresay. We feel in England that we have treated you rather unfairly. It seems history is to blame.

The proud potent titles clanged over Stephen's memory the triumph of their brazen bells: *et unam sanctam catholicam et apostolicam ecclesiam:** the slow growth and change of rite and dogma like his own rare thoughts, a chemistry of stars. Symbol of the apostles in the mass for pope Marcellus,* the voices blended, singing alone loud in affirmation: and behind their chant the vigilant angel* of the church militant disarmed and menaced her heresiarchs. A horde of heresies fleeing with mitres awry: Photius* and the brood of mockers of whom Mulligan was one, and Arius,* warring his life long upon the consubstantiality of the Son with the Father, and Valentine,* spurning Christ's terrene body, and the subtle African heresiarch Sabellius* who held that the Father was Himself His own Son. Words Mulligan had spoken a moment since in mockery to the stranger. Idle mockery. The void awaits surely all them that weave the wind: a menace, a disarming and a worsting from those embattled angels of the church, Michael's host, who defend her ever in the hour of conflict with their lances and their shields.

Hear, hear. Prolonged applause. *Zut! Nom de Dieu!*

—Of course I'm a Britisher, Haine's voice said, and I feel as one. I don't want to see my country fall into the hands of German jews either. That's our national problem, I'm afraid, just now.

Two men stood at the verge of the cliff, watching: businessman, boatman.

—She's making for Bullock harbour.

The boatman nodded towards the north of the bay with some disdain.

—There's five fathoms out there, he said. It'll be swept up that way when the tide comes in about one. It's nine days today.

The man that was drowned. A sail veering about the blank bay waiting for a swollen bundle to bob up, roll over to the sun a puffy face, salt white. Here I am.

They followed the winding path down to the creek. Buck Mulligan stood on a stone, in shirtsleeves, his unclipped tie rippling over his shoulder. A young man clinging to a spur of rock near him, moved slowly frogwise his green legs in the deep jelly of the water.

—Is the brother with you, Malachi?

—Down in Westmeath. With the Bannons.

—Still there? I got a card from Bannon. Says he found a sweet young thing down there. Photo girl he calls her.

—Shapshot, eh? Brief exposure.

Buck Mulligan sat down to unlace his boots. An elderly man shot up near the spur of rock a blowing red face. He scrambled up by the stones, water glistening on his pate and on its garland of grey hair, water rilling over his chest and paunch and spilling jets out of his black sagging loincloth.

Buck Mulligan made way for him to scramble past and, glancing at Haines and Stephen, crossed himself piously with his thumbnail at brow and breastbone.

—Seymour's back in town, the young man said, grasping again his spur of rock. Chucked medicine and going in for the army.

—Ah, go to God, Buck Mulligan said.

—Going over next week to stew. You know that red Carlisle girl, Lily?

—Yes.

—Spooning with him last night on the pier. The father is rotten with money.

—Is she up the pole?

—Better ask Seymour that.

—Seymour a bleeding officer, Buck Mulligan said.

He nodded to himself as he drew off his trousers and stood up, saying tritely:

—Redheaded women buck like goats.

He broke off in alarm, feeling his side under his flapping shirt.

—My twelfth rib is gone, he cried. I'm the *Uebermensch.** Toothless Kinch and I, the supermen.

He struggled out of his shirt and flung it behind him to where his clothes lay.

—Are you going in here, Malachi?

—Yes. Make room in the bed.

The young man shoved himself backward through the water and reached the middle of the creek in two long clean strokes. Haines sat down on a stone, smoking.

—Are you not coming in, Buck Mulligan asked.

—Later on, Haines said. Not on my breakfast.

Stephen turned away.

—I'm going, Mulligan, he said.

—Give us that key, Kinch, Buck Mulligan said, to keep my chemise flat.

Stephen handed him the key. Buck Mulligan laid it across his heaped clothes.

—And twopence, he said, for a pint. Throw it there.

Stephen threw two pennies on the soft heap. Dressing, undressing. Buck Mulligan erect, with joined hands before him, said solemnly:

—He who stealeth from the poor lendeth to the Lord.* Thus spake Zarathustra.

His plump body plunged.

—We'll see you again, Haines said, turning as Stephen walked up the path and smiling at wild Irish.

Horn of a bull, hoof of a horse, smile of a Saxon.*

—The Ship, Buck Mulligan cried. Half twelve.

—Good, Stephen said.

He walked along the upwardcurving path.

> *Liliata rutilantium.*
> *Turma circumdet.*
> *Jubilantium te virginum.*

The priest's grey nimbus in a niche where he dressed discreetly. I will not sleep here tonight. Home also I cannot go.

A voice, sweettoned and sustained, called to him from the sea. Turning the curve he waved his hand. It called again. A sleek brown head, a seal's, far out on the water, round.

Usurper.

ELIZABETH BOWEN
(1899–1973)

from *The Last September* (1929)

IV

Lois was sent upstairs for the shawls; it appeared that a touch of dew on the bare skin might be fatal to Lady Naylor or Mrs Montmorency.* On the stairs, her feet found their evening echoes; she dawdled, listening. When she came down everybody was on the steps—at the top, on the wide stone plateau—the parlourmaid looking for somewhere to put the coffee tray. Mrs Montmorency sat in the long chair; her husband was tucking a carriage rug round her knees. 'If you do that,' Lois could not help saying, 'she won't be able to walk about, which is the best part of sitting out.'

No one took any notice: Mr Montmorency went on tucking.

'Haven't you got a wrap for yourself?' said Lady Naylor. Lois took a cushion and sat on the top step with her arms crossed, stroking her elbows. 'I shouldn't sit there,' her aunt continued; 'at this time of night stone will strike up through anything.'

'If you don't get rheumatism now,' added Francie, 'you will be storing up rheumatism.'

'It will be my rheumatism,' said Lois as gently as possible, but added inwardly: 'After you're both dead.' A thought that fifty years hence she might well, if she wished, be sitting here on the steps,—with or without rheumatism—having penetrated thirty years deeper ahead into Time than they could, gave her a feeling of mysteriousness and destination. And she was fitted for this by being twice as complex as their generation—for she must be: double as many people having gone to the making of her.

Laurence, looking resentfully round for somewhere to sit—she had taken the only cushion—said: 'I suppose you think ants cannot run up your legs if you cannot see them?'

Mr Montmorency surprised her by offering a cigarette. He had a theory, he said, that ants did not like cigarette smoke. The air was so quiet now, the flame ran up his match without a tremble. 'The ants are asleep,' she said, 'they disappear into the cracks of the steps. They don't bite, either; but the idea is horrid.'

'Don't you want a chair?' When she said she didn't, he settled back in his own. Creaks ran through the wicker, discussing him, then all was quiet. He was not due to leave the ship in which they were all rushing out into Time till ten years after the others, though it was to the others that he belonged. Turning half round, she watched light breathe at the tips of the cigarettes; it seemed as though everybody were waiting. Night now held the trees with a toneless finality. The sky shone, whiter than glass, fainting down to the fretted leaf-line, but was being steadily drained by the dark below, to which the grey of the lawns, like smoke, as steadily mounted. The house was highest of all with toppling immanence, like a cliff.

'I don't think,' said Francie, 'I remember anything so—so quiet as evenings here.'

'Trees,' said Laurence, shifting his pipe. His shirt-front was high above them, he stood by the door with his foot on the scraper.

'This time to-morrow,' said Lady Naylor, 'we shall want to be quiet—after the tennis party.' She let out a sigh that hung in the silence, like breath in cold air.

'Oh yes, the party! The tennis party . . .'

'Francie, did I tell you who were coming?'

'You told her,' said Laurence. 'I heard you.'

'It is the people who don't play tennis who make it so tiring.'

Something about the way, the resigned way, Francie's hands lay out on the rug gave her the look of an invalid. 'It is a good thing,' said Sir Richard, 'you two never went out to Canada. I never liked the idea myself; I was very much against it at the time, if you remember.'

'I was divided about it myself,' said Hugo. 'It seemed worth trying, and yet there was so much against it. I don't know that I should have done very much good—I wonder.'

They wondered with him, with degrees of indifference. Lois stroked her dress—the feel of the stuff was like cobwebs, sticky and damp. There must be dew falling.

'Oh!' cried Francie. '*Listen!*'

She had so given herself to the silence that the birth of sound, after which the others were still straining, had shocked her nerves like a blow. They looked, from the steps, over a bay of fields, between the plantations, that gave on a sea of space. Far east, beyond the demesne: a motor, straining cautiously out of the silence. A grind, an anguish of sound as it took the hill.

'Patrols,' said Laurence.

Hugo reached out and pressed a hand on to Francie's rug. 'Patrols,' he told her, translating the information.

Sir Richard explained severely: 'Out every night—not always in this direction.'

'They're early; it's half-past nine. Now I wonder . . .'

The sound paused, for a moment a pale light showed up the sky in darkness. Then behind the screen of trees at the skyline, demesne boundary, the sound moved shakily, stoopingly, like some one running and crouching behind a hedge. The jarring echoed down the spines of the listeners. They heard with a sense of complicity.

'A furtive lorry is a sinister thing.'

'Laurence, it isn't furtive!' said Lady Naylor. 'Can't you be ordinary? If it wouldn't be taken in some absurd kind of way as a demonstration, I should ask the poor fellows in to have coffee.'

'They're careful enough,' said Hugo impatiently. It seemed that the lorry took pleasure in crawling with such a menace along the boundary, marking the scope of peace of this silly island, undermining solitude. In the still night sound had a breathlessness, as of intention.

'The roads are so rough,' said Lois: she could see the wary load lurching into the hedges. 'I wonder now,' she added, 'who is with the patrol to-night?'

'Some one you know?' cried Francie. But Sir Richard, who did not like his friends to be distracted from him by lorries any more than by introspection or headaches or the observation of nature, bore this down with one of his major chords:

'The lower tennis court, Hugo'—waving sideways into the darkness—'is not what it used to be. Some cattle got on to it after the rain and destroyed it. It's had rolling enough to level a mountain, but it won't be the same for a long time. D'you remember the fours we had on that court that summer—wasn't it nineteen-six—you and I and O'Donnell and poor John Trent?'

'I do. Now was it James O'Donnell or Peter that went to Ceylon?'

'That was a great summer; I never remember a summer like it. We had the hay in by the end of June.'

The lorry ground off east towards Ballyhinch; silence sifting down on its tracks like sand. Their world was clear of it and a pressure lightened. Once more they could have heard a leaf turn in the trees or a bird shifting along a branch. But they found it was now very dark. Francie shivered, and Lady Naylor, rising formally, said she thought they should go in. 'Poor John Trent,' she added, gathering up her cushions, 'never got over that trouble he had with the Sheehans over the Madder* fishing. It went into court, you know, and of course he lost. We always told him to keep it out of court. He was very obstinate.'

'He was indeed,' said Sir Richard. 'He made an enemy of Sheehan and it's not a good thing to have made an enemy. Though of course he's dead nowadays, so it may not matter.'

'It may to the Archie Trents. . . . Laurence, help Uncle Richard in with the long chair, and remember to bring in your own chair afterwards.'

'I never had a chair.'

'Oh, they haven't lighted the lamp in the hall. That is too bad! I am lost without Sarah—do you remember Sarah, Francie? She died, you know.'

Lois, sitting still among rising, passing and vaguely searching figures, cried: 'But it's only just beginning! You're missing the whole point. I shall walk up the avenue.'

Francie went in, groping; trailing her rug. The three men, carrying wicker chairs, converged at the door: the chairs jostled. They all put them down and apologized. Lois repeated: '*I* shall walk up the avenue.' But having arranged an order of procedure they all passed on into the house, creaking and bumping. She walked down the steps alone: she had wanted to be alone, but to be regretted.

'Mind you don't get locked out!' her uncle shouted after her. The glass doors shut with a rattle.

Lois walked alone up the avenue, where she had danced with Gerald. She thought what a happy night that had been, and how foolish Mr Montmorency now thought them. He had seemed annoyed at her being young when he wasn't. She could not hope to explain that her youth seemed to her also rather theatrical and that she was only young in that way because people expected it. She had never refused a rôle. She could not forgo that intensification, that kindling of her personality at being considered very happy and reckless, even if she were not. She could not hope to assure him she was not enjoying anything he had missed, that she was now unconvinced and anxious but intended to be quite certain, by the time she was his age, that she had once been happy. For to explain this—were explanation possible to so courteous, ironical and unfriendly a listener—would, she felt, be disloyal to herself, to Gerald, to an illusion both were called upon to maintain.

Just by the lime, in that dancing night, she had missed a step and sagged on his arm, which tightened. His hand slid up between her shoulders; then, as she steadied back to the rhythm, down again. They had set out laughing, noisy and conscious, but soon had to save their breath. Gerald's cheek, within an inch of her own, was too near to see. All the way up, he had not missed a step; he was most dependable. And remembering how the family had just now gone into the house—so flatly, so unregrettingly, slamming the glass doors—she felt *that* was what she now wanted most—his eagerness and constancy. She felt, like a steady look from him, the perfectness of their being together.

'Oh, I do want you!'

But he was very musical, he conducted a jazz band they had at the barracks: while reaching out in her thoughts she remembered, the band would be practising now. She was disappointed. To a line of tune the thought flung her, she danced on the avenue.

A shrubbery path was solid with darkness, she pressed down it. Laurels breathed coldly and close: on her bare arms the tips of leaves were timid and dank, like tongues of dead animals. Her fear of the shrubberies tugged at its chain, fear behind reason, fear before her birth; fear like the earliest germ of her life that had stirred in Laura. She went forward eagerly, daring a snap of the chain, singing; a hand to the thump of her heart, dramatic with terror. She thought of herself as forcing a pass. In her life—deprived as she saw it—there was no occasion for courage, which like an unused muscle slackened and slept.

High up a bird shrieked and stumbled down through dark, tearing the leaves. Silence healed, but kept a scar of horror. The shuttered-in drawing-room, the family sealed in lamplight, secure and bright like flowers in a paper-weight—were desirable, worth much of this to regain. Fear curled back from the carpet-border. . . . Now, on the path: grey patches worse than the dark: they slipped up her dress knee-high. The laurels deserted her groping arm. She had come to the holly, where two paths crossed.

First, she did not hear footsteps coming, and as she began to notice the displaced darkness thought what she dreaded was coming, was there within her—she was indeed clairvoyant, exposed to horror and going to see a ghost. Then steps, hard on the smooth earth; branches slipping against a trench-coat. The trench-coat rustled across the path ahead, to the swing of a steady walker. She stood by the holly immovable, blotted out in her black, and there passed within reach of her hand, with the rise and fall of a stride, a resolute profile, powerful as a thought. In gratitude for its fleshliness, she felt prompted to make some contact: not to be known seemed like a doom: extinction.

'It's a fine night,' she would have liked to observe; or, to engage his sympathies: 'Up Dublin!' or even—since it was in her uncle's demesne she was straining under a holly—boldly—'What do you want?'

It must be because of Ireland he was in such a hurry; down from the mountains, making a short cut through their demesne. Here was something else that she could not share. She could not conceive of her country emotionally: it was a way of living, an abstract of several landscapes, or an oblique frayed island, moored at the north but with an air of being detached and washed out west from the British coast.

Quite still, she let him go past in contemptuous unawareness. His intentions burnt on the dark an almost visible trail; he might well have been a murderer he seemed so inspired. The crowd of trees, straining up from the passive disputed earth, each sucking up and exhaling the country's essence—swallowed him finally. She thought: 'Has he come for the guns?'* A man in a trench-coat had passed without seeing her: that was what it amounted to.

She ran back to tell, in excitement. Below, the house waited; vast on its west side, with thin yellow lines round the downstairs shutters. It had that excluded, sad, irrelevant look outsides of houses take in the dark. Inside, they would all be drawing up closer to one another, tricked by the half-revelation of lamplight. 'Compassed about,' thought Lois, 'by so great a cloud of witnesses. . . .'* Chairs standing round dejectedly; upstairs, the confidently waiting beds; mirrors vacant and startling; books read and forgotten, contributing no more to life; dinner-table certain of its regular compulsion; the procession of elephants that throughout uncertain years had not broken file.

But as Lois went up the steps breathlessly, her adventure began to diminish. It held ground for a moment as she saw the rug dropped in the hall by Mrs Montmorency sprawl like a body across the polish. Then confidence disappeared, in a waver of shadow, among the furniture. Conceivably, she had just surprised life at a significant angle in the shrubbery. But it was impossible to speak of this. At a touch from Aunt Myra adventure became literary, to Uncle Richard it suggested an inconvenience; a glance from Mr Montmorency or Laurence would make her encounter sterile.

But what seemed most probable was that they would not listen. . . . She lighted her candle and went up to bed—uncivilly, without saying good night to anyone. Her Uncle Richard, she afterwards heard, was obliged to sit up till twelve o'clock. He had not been told she was in, so did not think it right to lock up the house.

SAMUEL BECKETT
(1906–1989)

from *Murphy* (1938)

I

The sun shone, having no alternative, on the nothing new.* Murphy sat out of it, as though he were free, in a mew in West Brompton. Here for what might have been six months he had eaten, drunk, slept, and put his clothes on and off, in a medium-sized cage of north-western aspect commanding an unbroken view of medium-sized cages of south-eastern aspect. Soon he would have to make other arrangements, for the mew had been condemned. Soon he would have to buckle to and start eating, drinking, sleeping, and putting his clothes on and off, in quite alien surroundings.

He sat naked in his rocking-chair of undressed teak, guaranteed not to crack, warp, shrink, corrode, or creak at night. It was his own, it never left him. The corner in which he sat was curtained off from the sun, the poor old sun in the Virgin* again for the billionth time. Seven scarves held him in position. Two fastened his shins to the rockers, one his thighs to the seat, two his breast and belly to the back, one his wrists to the strut behind. Only the most local movements were possible. Sweat poured off him, tightened the thongs. The breath was not perceptible. The eyes, cold and unwavering as a gull's, stared up at an iridescence splashed over the cornice moulding, shrinking and fading. Somewhere a cuckoo-clock, having struck between twenty and thirty, became the echo of a street-cry, which now entering the mew gave *Quid pro quo! Quid pro quo!* directly.

These were sights and sounds that he did not like. They detained him in the world to which they belonged, but not he, as he fondly hoped. He wondered dimly what was breaking up his sunlight, what wares were being cried. Dimly, very dimly.

He sat in his chair in this way because it gave him pleasure! First it gave his body pleasure, it appeased his body. Then it set him free in his mind. For it was not until his body was appeased that he could come alive in his mind, as described in section six. And life in his mind gave him pleasure, such pleasure that pleasure was not the word.

Murphy had lately studied under a man in Cork called Neary.* This man, at that time, could stop his heart more or less whenever he liked and keep it stopped, within reasonable limits, for as long as he liked. This rare faculty, acquired after years of application somewhere north of the Nerbudda,* he exercised frugally, reserving it for situations irksome beyond endurance, as when he wanted a drink and could not get one, or fell among Gaels and could not escape, or felt the pangs of hopeless sexual inclination.

Murphy's purpose in going to sit at Neary's feet was not to develop the Neary heart, which he thought would quickly prove fatal to a man of his temper, but simply to invest his own with a little of what Neary, at that time a Pythagorean, called the Apmonia.* For Murphy had such an irrational heart that no physician could get to the root of it. Inspected, palpated, auscultated, percussed, radio-graphed and cardiographed, it was all that a heart should be. Buttoned up and left to perform, it was like Petrouchka* in his box. One moment in such labour that it seemed on the point of seizing, the next in such ebullition that it seemed on the point of bursting. It was the mediation between these extremes that Neary called the Apmonia. When he got tired of calling it the Apmonia he called it the Isonomy. When he got sick of the sound of Isonomy he called it the Attunement. But he might call it what he liked, into Murphy's heart it would not enter. Neary could not blend the opposites in Murphy's heart . . .

4

In Dublin a week later, that would be September 19th, Neary minus his whiskers was recognised by a former pupil called Wylie, in the General Post Office contemplating from behind the statue of Cuchulain.* Neary had bared his head, as though the holy ground meant something to him. Suddenly he flung aside his hat, sprang forward, seized the dying hero by the thighs and began to dash his head against his buttocks, such as they are. The Civic Guard on duty in the building, roused from a tender reverie by the sound of blows, took in the situation at his leisure, disentangled his baton and advanced with measured tread, thinking he had caught a vandal in the act. Happily Wylie, whose reactions as a street bookmaker's stand were as rapid as a zebra's, had already seized Neary round the waist, torn him back from the sacrifice and smuggled him half-way to the exit.

'Howlt on there, youze,' said the C.G.

Wylie turned back, tapped his forehead and said, as one sane man to another:

'John o' God's. Hundred per cent harmless.'

'Come back in here owwathat,' said the C.G.

Wylie, a tiny man, stood at a loss. Neary, almost as large as the C.G. though not of course so nobly proportioned, rocked blissfully on the right arm of his rescuer. It was not in the C.G.'s nature to bandy words, nor had it come into any branch of his training. He resumed his steady advance.

'Stillorgan,' said Wylie. 'Not Dundrum.'

The C.G. laid his monstrous hand on Wylie's left arm and exerted a strong pull along the line he had mapped out in his mind. They all moved off in the desired direction, Neary shod with orange-peel.

'John o' God's,' said Wylie. 'As quiet as a child.'

They drew up behind the statue. A crowd gathered behind them. The C.G. leaned forward and scrutinised the pillar and draperies.

'Not a feather out of her,' said Wylie. 'No blood, no brains, nothing.'

The C.G. straightened up and let go Wylie's arm.

'Move on,' he said to the crowd, 'before yer moved on.'

The crowd obeyed, with the single diastolesystole which is all the law requires. Feeling amply repaid by this superb symbol for the trouble and risk he had taken in issuing an order, the C.G. inflected his attention to Wylie and said more kindly:

'Take my advice, mister——' He stopped. To devise words of advice was going to tax his ability to the utmost. When would he learn not to plunge into the labyrinths of an opinion when he had not the slightest idea of how he was to emerge? And before a hostile audience! His embarrassment was if possible increased by the expression of strained attention on Wylie's face, clamped there by the promise of advice.

'Yes, sergeant,' said Wylie, and held his breath.

'Run him back to Stillorgan,' said the C.G. Done it!

Wylie's face came asunder in gratification.

'Never fear, sergeant,' he said, urging Neary towards the exit, 'back to the cell, blood heat, next best thing to never being born, no heroes, no fisc, no——'

Neary had been steadily recovering all this time and now gave such a jerk to Wylie's arm that that poor little man was nearly pulled off his feet.

'Where am I?' said Neary. 'If and when.'

Wylie rushed him into the street and into a Dalkey* tram that had just come in. The crowd dispersed, the better to gather elsewhere. The C.G. dismissed the whole sordid episode from his mind, the better to brood on a theme very near to his heart.

'Is it the saloon,' said Neary, 'or the jugs and bottles?'

Wylie wet his handkerchief and applied it tenderly to the breaches of surface, a ministration immediately poleaxed by Neary, who now saw his saviour for the first time. Punctured by those sharp little features of the fury that had sustained him, he collapsed in a tempest of sobbing on that sharp little shoulder.

'Come, come,' said Wylie, patting the large heaving back. 'Needle is at hand.'

Neary checked his sobs, raised a face purged of all passion, seized Wylie by the shoulders, held him out at arm's length and exclaimed:

'Is it little Needle Wylie, my scholar that was. What will you have?'

'How do you feel?' said Wylie.

It dawned on Neary that he was not where he thought. He rose.

'What is the finest tram in Europe,' he said, 'to a man consumed with sobriety?' He made the street under his own power with Wylie close behind him.

'But by Mooney's clock,' said Wylie, 'the sad news is two–thirty-three.'

Neary leaned against the Pillar railings and cursed, first the day in which he was born, then—in a bold flash-back—the night in which he was conceived.

'There, there,' said Wylie. 'Needle knows no holy hour.'

He led the way to an underground café close by, steered Neary into an alcove and called for Cathleen. Cathleen came.

'My friend Professor Neary,' said Wylie, 'my friend Miss Cathleen na Hennessey.'*

'Pleased,' said Cathleen.

'Why the ——,' said Neary, 'is light given to a man whose way is hid.'

'Pardon,' said Cathleen.

'Two large coffees,' said Wylie. 'Three star.'

One gulp of this and Neary's way was clearer.

'Now tell us all about it,' said Wylie. 'Keep back nothing.'

'The limit of Cork endurance had been reached,' said Neary. 'That Red Branch bum* was the camel's back.'

'Drink a little more of your coffee,' said Wylie.

Neary drank a little more.

'What are you doing in this kip at all?' said Wylie. 'Why aren't you in Cork?'

'My grove on Grand Parade,' said Neary, 'is wiped as a man wipeth a plate, wiping it and turning it upside down.'

'And your whiskers?' said Wylie.

'Suppressed without pity,' said Neary, 'in discharge of a vow, never again to ventilate a virility denied discharge into its predestined channel.'

'These are dark sayings,' said Wylie.

Neary turned his cup upside down.

'Needle,' he said, 'as it is with the love of the body, so with the friendship of the mind, the full is only reached by admittance to the most retired places. Here are the pudenda of my psyche.'

FLANN O'BRIEN
(1911–1966)

from *At Swim-Two-Birds* (1939)

For seven years, to relate precisely, was Sweeny at the air travel of all Erin, returning always to his tree in charming Glen Bolcain, for that was his fortress and his haven, it was his house there in the glen. It was to this place that his foster-brother Linchehaun came for tidings concerning him, for he carried always a deep affection for Sweeny and had retrieved him three times from madness before that. Linchehaun went seeking him in the glen with shouts and found toe-tracks by the stream-mud where the madman was wont to appease himself by the eating of cresses. But track or trace of Sweeny he did not attain for that day and he sat down in an old deserted house in the glen till the labour and weariness of his pursuit brought about his sleep. And Sweeny, hearing his snore from his tree-clump in the glen, uttered this lay in the pitch darkness.

> The man by the wall snores
> a snore-sleep that's beyond me,
> for seven years from that Tuesday at Magh Rath
> I have not slept a wink.
>
> O God that I had not gone
> to the hard battle!

thereafter my name was Mad—
Mad Sweeny in the bush.

Watercress from the well at Cirb
is my lot at terce,
its colour is my mouth,
green on the mouth of Sweeny.

Chill chill is my body
when away from ivy,
the rain torrent hurts it
and the thunder.

I am in summer with the herons of Cuailgne
with wolves in winter,
at other times I am hidden in a copse—
not so the man by the wall.

And thereafter he met Linchehaun who came visiting to his tree
and they parleyed there the two of them together and the one of
them talkative and unseen in branches and prickle-briars. And
Sweeny bade Linchehaun to depart and not to pursue or annoy him
further because the curse of Ronan stopped him from putting his
trust or his mad faith in any man.

Thereafter he travelled in distant places till he came at the black
fall of a night to Ros Bearaigh and lodged himself in a hunched
huddle in the middle of the yew-tree of the church in that place. But
being besieged with nets and hog-harried by the caretaker of the
church and his false wife, he hurried nimbly to the old tree at Ros
Eareain where he remained hidden and unnoticed the length of a full
fortnight, till the time when Linchehaun came and perceived the
murk of his shadow in the sparse branches and saw the other
branches he had broken and bent in his movements and in changing
trees. And the two of them parleyed together until they had said
between them these fine words following.

Sad it is Sweeny, said Linchehaun, that your last extremity should
be thus, without food or drink or raiment like a fowl, the same man
that had cloth of silk and of satin and the foreign steed of the peer-
less bridle, also comely generous women and boys and hounds and

princely people of every refinement; hosts and tenants and men-at-arms, arms, and mugs and goblets and embellished buffalohorns for the savouring of pleasant tasted fine liquors. Sad it is to see the same man as a hapless air-fowl.

Cease now, Linchehaun, said Sweeny, and give me tidings.

Your father is dead, said Linchehaun.

That has seized me with a blind agony, said Sweeny.

Your mother is likewise dead.

Now all the pity in me is at an end.

Dead is your brother.

Gaping open is my side on account of that.

She has died too your sister.

A needle for the heart is an only sister.

Ah, dumb dead is the little son that called you pop.

Truly, said Sweeny, that is the last blow that brings a man to the ground.

When Sweeny heard the sorry word of his small son still and without life, he fell with a crap from the middle of the yew to the ground and Linchehaun hastened to his thornpacked flank with fetters and handcuffs and manacles and locks and black-iron chains and he did not achieve a resting until the lot were about the madman, and through him and above him and over him, round-wise and about. Thereafter there was a concourse of hospitallers and knights and warriors around the trunk of the yew, and after melodious talk they entrusted the mad one to the care of Linchehaun till he would take him away to a quiet place for a fortnight and a month, to the quiet of a certain room where his senses returned to him, the one after the other, with no one near him but the old mill-hag.

O hag, said Sweeny, searing are the tribulations I have suffered; many a terrible leap have I leaped from hill to hill, from fort to fort, from land to land, from valley to valley.

For the sake of God, said the hag, leap for us now a leap such as you leaped in the days of your madness.

And thereupon Sweeny gave a bound over the top of the bedrail till he reached the extremity of the bench.

My conscience indeed, said the hag, I could leap the same leap myself.

And the hag gave a like jump.

Sweeny then gathered himself together in the extremity of his jealousy and threw a leap right out through the skylight of the hostel.

I could vault that vault too, said the hag and straightway she vaulted the same vault. And the short of it is this, that Sweeny travelled the length of five cantreds of leaps until he had penetrated to Glenn na nEachtach in Fiodh Gaibhle with the hag at her hag's leaps behind him; and when Sweeny rested there in a huddle at the top of a tall ivy-branch, the hag was perched there on another tree beside him. He heard there the voice of a stag and he thereupon made a lay eulogizing aloud the trees and the stags of Erin, and he did not cease or sleep until he had achieved these staves.

Bleating one, little antlers,
O lamenter we like
delightful the clamouring
from your glen you make.

O leafy-oak, clumpy-leaved,
you are high above trees,
O hazlet, little clumpy-branch—
the nut-smell of hazels.

O alder, O alder-friend,
delightful your colour,
you don't prickle me or tear
in the place you are.

O blackthorn, little thorny-one,
O little dark sloe-tree;
O watercress, O green-crowned,
at the well-brink.

O holly, holly-shelter,
O door against the wind,
O ash-tree inimical,
you spearshaft of warrior.

O birch clean and blessed,
O melodious, O proud,

delightful the tangle
of your head-rods.

What I like least in woodlands
from none I conceal it—
stirk of a leafy-oak,
as its swaying.

O faun, little long-legs,
I caught you with grips,
I rode you upon your back
from peak to peak.

Glen Bolcain my home ever,
it was my haven,
many a night have I tried
a race against the peak.

I beg your pardon for interrupting, said Shanahan, but you're
after reminding me of something, brought the thing into my head in
a rush.

He swallowed a draught of vesper-milk, restoring the cloudy glass
swiftly to his knee and collecting little belated flavourings from the
corners of his mouth.

That thing you were saying reminds me of something bloody
good. I beg your pardon for interrupting, Mr Storybook.

In the yesterday, said Finn, the man who mixed his utterance with
the honeywords of Finn was the first day put naked into the tree of
Coill Boirche with nothing to his bare hand but a stick of hazel. On
the morning of the second day thereafter. . . .

Now listen for a minute till I tell you something, said Shanahan,
did any man here ever hear of the poet Casey?

Who did you say? said Furriskey.

Casey. Jem Casey.

On the morning of the second day thereafter, he was taken and
bound and rammed as regards his head into a black hole so that his
white body was upside down and upright in Erin for the gazing
thereon of man and beast.

Now give us a chance, Mister Storybook, yourself and your black
hole, said Shanahan fingering his tie-knot with a long memory-frown

across his brow. Come here for a minute. Come here till I tell you about Casey. Do you mean to tell me you never heard of the poet Casey, Mr Furriskey?

Never heard of him, said Furriskey in a solicitous manner.

I can't say, said Lamont, that I ever heard of him either.

He was a poet of the people, said Shanahan.

I see, said Furriskey.

Now do you understand, said Shanahan. A plain upstanding labouring man, Mr Furriskey, the same as you or me. A black hat or a bloody ribbon, no by God, not on Jem Casey. A hard-working well-made block of a working man, Mr. Lamont, with the handle of a pick in his hand like the rest of us. Now say there was a crowd of men with a ganger all working there laying a length of gas-pipe on the road. All right. The men pull off their coats and start shovelling and working there for further orders. Here at one end of the hole you have your men crowded up together in a lump and them working away and smoking their butts and talking about the horses and one thing and another. Now do you understand what I'm telling you. Do you follow me?

I see that.

But take a look at the other end of the hole and here is my brave Casey digging away there on his own. Do you understand what I mean, Mr Furriskey?

Oh I see it all right, said Furriskey.

Right. None of your horses or your bloody blather for him. Not a bit of it. Here is my nabs saying nothing to nobody but working away at a pome in his head with a pick in his hand and the sweat pouring down off his face from the force of his work and his bloody exertions. That's a quare one!

Do you mind that now, said Lamont.

It's a quare one and one that takes a lot of beating. Not a word to nobody, not a look to left or right but the brain-box going there all the time. Just Jem Casey, a poor ignorant labouring man but head and shoulders above the whole bloody lot of them, not a man in the whole country to beat him when it comes to getting together a bloody pome—not a poet in the whole world that could hold a candle to Jem Casey, not a man of them fit to stand beside him. By God I'd back him to win by a canter against the whole bloody lot of them give him his due.

Is that a fact, Mr Shanahan, said Lamont. It's not every day in the week you come across a man like that.

Do you know what I'm going to tell you, Mr Lamont, he was a man that could give the lot of them a good start, pickaxe and all. He was a man that could meet them . . . and meet the best . . . and beat them at their own game, now I'm telling you.

I suppose he could, said Furriskey.

Now I know what I'm talking about. Give a man his due. If a man's station is high or low he is all the same to the God I know. Take the bloody black hats off the whole bunch of them and where are you?

That's the way to look at it, of course, said Furriskey.

Give them a bloody pick, I mean, Mr Furriskey, give them the shaft of a shovel into their hand and tell them to dig a hole and have the length of a page of poetry off by heart in their heads before the five o'clock whistle. What will you get? By God you could take off your hat to what you'd get at five o'clock from that crowd and that's a sure sharkey.

You'd be wasting your time if you waited till five o'clock if you ask me, said Furriskey with a nod of complete agreement.

You're right there, said Shanahan, you'd be waiting around for bloody nothing. Oh I know them and I know my hard Casey too. By Janey he'd be up at the whistle with a pome a yard long, a bloody lovely thing that would send my nice men home in a hurry, home with their bloody tails between their legs. Yes, I've seen his pomes and read them and . . . do you know what I'm going to tell you, I have loved them. I'm not ashamed to sit here and say it, Mr Furriskey. I've known the man and I've known his pomes and by God I have loved the two of them and loved them well, too. Do you understand what I'm saying, Mr Lamont? You, Mr Furriskey?

Oh that's right.

Do you know what it is, I've met the others, the whole lot of them. I've met them all and know them all. I have seen them and I have read their pomes. I have heard them recited by men that know how to use their tongues, men that couldn't be beaten at their own game. I have seen whole books filled up with their stuff, books as thick as that table there and I'm telling you no lie. But by God, at the heel of the hunt, there was only one poet for me.

On the morning of the third day thereafter, said Finn, he was flogged until he bled water.

Only the one, Mr Shanahan? said Lamont.

Only the one. And that one poet was a man . . . by the name . . . of Jem Casey. No 'Sir', no 'Mister', no nothing. Jem Casey, Poet of the Pick, that's all. A labouring man, Mr Lamont, but as sweet a singer in his own way as you'll find in the bloody trees there of a spring day, and that's a fact. Jem Casey, an ignorant God-fearing upstanding labouring man, a bloody navvy. Do you know what I'm going to tell you, I don't believe he ever lifted the latch of a school door. Would you believe that now?

I'd believe it of Casey, said Furriskey, and

I'd believe plenty more of the same man, said Lamont. You haven't any of his pomes on you, have you, Mr Shanahan?

Now take that stuff your man was giving us a while ago, said Shanahan without heed, about the green hills and the bloody swords and the bird giving out the pay from the top of the tree. Now that's good stuff, it's bloody nice. Do you know what it is, I liked it and liked it well. I enjoyed that certainly.

It wasn't bad at all, said Furriskey, I have heard worse, by God, often. It was all right now.

Do you see what I'm getting at, do you understand me, said Shanahan. It's good, very good. But by Christopher it's not every man could see it, I'm bloody sure of that, one in a thousand.

Oh that's right too, said Lamont.

You can't beat it, of course, said Shanahan with a reddening of the features, the real old stuff of the native land, you know, stuff that brought scholars to our shore when your men on the other side were on the flat of their bellies before the calf of gold with a sheepskin around their man. It's the stuff that put our country where she stands to-day, Mr Furriskey, and I'd have my tongue out of my head by the bloody roots before I'd be heard saying a word against it. But the man in the street, where does he come in? By God he doesn't come in at all as far as I can see.

What do my brave men in the black hats care whether he's in or out, asked Furriskey. What do they care? It's a short jump for the man in the street, I'm thinking, if he's waiting for that crowd to do anything for him. They're a nice crowd, now, I'm telling you.

Oh that's the truth, said Lamont.

Another thing, said Shanahan, you can get too much of that stuff. Feed yourself up with that tack once and you won't want more for a long time.

There's no doubt about it, said Furriskey.

Try it once, said Shanahan, and you won't want it a second time.

Do you know what it is, said Lamont, there are people who read that . . . and keep reading it . . . and read damn the bloody thing else. Now that's a mistake.

A big mistake, said Furriskey.

But there's one man, said Shanahan, there's one man that can write pomes that you can read all day and all night and keep reading them to your heart's content, stuff you'd never tire of. Pomes written by a man that is one of ourselves and written down for ourselves to read. The name of that man . . .

Now that's what you want, said Furriskey.

The name of that man, said Shanahan, is a name that could be christianed on you or me, a name that won't shame us. And that name, said Shanahan, is Jem Casey.

And a very good man, said Lamont.

Jem Casey, said Furriskey.

Do you understand what I mean, said Shanahan.

You haven't any of his pomes on you, have you, said Lamont. If there's one thing I'd like. . . .

I haven't one *on* me if that's what you mean, Mr Lamont, said Shanahan, but I could give one out as quick as I'd say my prayers. By God it's not for nothing that I call myself a pal of Jem Casey.

I'm glad to hear it, said Lamont.

Stand up there and recite it man, said Furriskey, don't keep us waiting. What's the name of it now?

The name or title of the pome I am about to recite, gentlemen, said Shanahan with leisure priest-like in character, is a pome by the name of the 'Workman's Friend'. By God you can't beat it. I've heard it praised by the highest. It's a pome about a thing that's known to all of us. It's about a drink of porter.

Porter!

Porter.

Up on your legs man, said Furriskey. Mr Lamont and myself are waiting and listening. Up you get now.

Come on, off you go, said Lamont.

Now listen, said Shanahan clearing the way with small coughs. Listen now.

He arose holding out his hand and bending his knee beneath him on the chair.

> When things go wrong and will not come right,
> Though you do the best you can,
> When life looks black as the hour of night—
> A PINT OF PLAIN IS YOUR ONLY MAN.

By God there's a lilt in that, said Lamont.

Very good indeed, said Furriskey. Very nice.

I'm telling you it's the business, said Shanahan. Listen now.

> When money's tight and is hard to get
> And your horse has also ran,
> When all you have is a heap of debt—
> A PINT OF PLAIN IS YOUR ONLY MAN.

> When health is bad and your heart feels strange,
> And your face is pale and wan,
> When doctors say that you need a change,
> A PINT OF PLAIN IS YOUR ONLY MAN.

There are things in that pome that make for what you call *permanence*. Do you know what I mean, Mr Furriskey?

There's no doubt about it, it's a grand thing, said Furriskey. Come on, Mr Shanahan, give us another verse. Don't tell me that is the end of it.

Can't you listen? said Shanahan.

> When food is scarce and your larder bare
> And no rashers grease your pan,
> When hunger grows as your meals are rare—
> A PINT OF PLAIN IS YOUR ONLY MAN.

What do you think of that now?

It's a pome that'll live, called Lamont, a pome that'll be heard and clapped when plenty more . . .

But wait till you hear the last verse, man, the last polish-off, said Shanahan. He frowned and waved his hand.

Oh it's good, it's good, said Furriskey.

> In time of trouble and lousy strife,
> You have still got a darlint plan,
> You still can turn to a brighter life—
> A PINT OF PLAIN IS YOUR ONLY MAN!

Did you ever hear anything like it in your life, said Furriskey. A pint of plain, by God, what! Oh I'm telling you, Casey was a man in twenty thousand, there's no doubt about that. He knew what he was at, too true he did. If he knew nothing else, he knew how to write a pome. A pint of plain is your only man.

Didn't I tell you he was good? said Shanahan. Oh by Gorrah you can't cod me.

There's one thing in that pome, *permanence*, if you know what I mean. That pome, I mean to say, is a pome that'll be heard wherever the Irish race is wont to gather, it'll live as long as there's a hard root of an Irishman left by the Almighty on this planet, mark my words. What do you think, Mr Shanahan?

It'll live, Mr Lamont, it'll live.

I'm bloody sure it will, said Lamont.

A pint of plain, by God, eh? said Furriskey.

5. POETRY

AUGUSTA GREGORY
(1852–1932)

Grief of a Girl's Heart (1901)

(*From the Irish*)

O Donal Oge, if you go across the sea,
Bring myself with you and do not forget it;
And you will have a sweetheart for fair days and market days,
And the daughter of the King of Greece beside you at night.

It is late last night the dog was speaking of you;
The snipe was speaking of you in her deep marsh.
It is you are the lonely bird through the woods;
And that you may be without a mate until you find me.

You promised me, and you said a lie to me,
That you would be before me where the sheep are flocked;
I gave a whistle and three hundred cries to you,
And I found nothing there but a bleating lamb.

You promised me a thing that was hard for you,
A ship of gold under a silver mast;
Twelve towns with a market in all of them,
And a fine white court by the side of the sea.

You promised me a thing that is not possible,
That you would give me gloves of the skin of a fish;
That you would give me shoes of the skin of a bird;
And a suit of the dearest silk in Ireland.

O Donal Oge, it is I would be better to you
Than a high, proud, spendthrift lady:

I would milk the cow; I would bring help to you;
And if you were hard pressed, I would strike a blow for you.

O, ochone,* and it's not with hunger
Or with wanting food, or drink, or sleep,
That I am growing thin, and my life is shortened;
But it is the love of a young man has withered me away.

It is early in the morning that I saw him coming,
Going along the road on the back of a horse;
He did not come to me; he made nothing of me;
And it is on my way home that I cried my fill.

When I go by myself to the Well of Loneliness,
I sit down and I go through my trouble;
When I see the world and do not see my boy,
He that has an amber shade in his hair.

It was on that Sunday I gave my love to you;
The Sunday that is last before Easter Sunday.
And myself on my knees reading the Passion;
And my two eyes giving love to you for ever.

O, aya!* my mother, give myself to him;
And give him all that you have in the world;
Get out yourself to ask for alms,
And do not come back and forward looking for me.

My mother said to me not to be talking with you, to-day,
Or to-morrow, or on Sunday;
It was a bad time she took for telling me that;
It was shutting the door after the house was robbed.

My heart is as black as the blackness of the sloe,
Or as the black coal that is on the smith's forge;
Or as the sole of a shoe left in white halls;
It was you put that darkness over my life.

You have taken the east from me; you have taken the west from me,
You have taken what is before me and what is behind me;

You have taken the moon, you have taken the sun from me,
And my fear is great that you have taken God from me!

OSCAR WILDE
(1854–1900)

Requiescat (1881)

Tread lightly, she is near
    Under the snow,
Speak gently, she can hear
    The daisies grow.

All her bright golden hair
    Tarnished with rust,
She that was young and fair
    Fallen to dust.

Lily-like, white as snow,
    She hardly knew
She was a woman, so
    Sweetly she grew.

Coffin-board, heavy stone,
    Lie on her breast,
I vex my heart alone,
    She is at rest.

Peace, Peace, she cannot hear
    Lyre or sonnet,
All my life's buried here,
    Heap earth upon it.

Avignon.

Impression du Matin (1881)

The Thames nocturne of blue and gold
   Changed to a Harmony in grey:
   A barge with ochre-coloured hay
Dropt from the wharf: and chill and cold

The yellow fog came creeping down
   The bridges, till the houses' walls
   Seemed changed to shadows, and S. Paul's
Loomed like a bubble o'er the town.

Then suddenly arose the clang
   Of waking life; the streets were stirred
   With country waggons: and a bird
Flew to the glistening roofs and sang.

But one pale woman all alone,
   The daylight kissing her wan hair,
   Loitered beneath the gas lamps' flare,
With lips of flame and heart of stone.

Helas! (1881)

To drift with every passion till my soul
Is a stringed lute on which all winds can play,*
Is it for this that I have given away
Mine ancient wisdom, and austere control?
Methinks my life is a twice-written scroll
Scrawled over on some boyish holiday
With idle songs for pipe and virelay,*
Which do but mar the secret of the whole.
Surely there was a time I might have trod
The sunlit heights, and from life's dissonance
Struck one clear chord to reach the ears of God:
Is that time dead? lo! with a little rod*
I did but touch the honey of romance—
And must I lose a soul's inheritance?

The Harlot's House (1885)

We caught the tread of dancing feet,
We loitered down the moonlit street,
And stopped beneath the Harlot's house.

Inside, above the din and fray,
We heard the loud musicians play
The 'Treues Liebes Herz'* of Strauss.

Like strange mechanical grotesques,
Making fantastic arabesques,
The shadows raced across the blind.

We watched the ghostly dancers spin
To sound of horn and violin,
Like black leaves wheeling in the wind.

Like wire-pulled automatons,
Slim silhouetted skeletons
Went sidling through the slow quadrille,*

Then took each other by the hand,
And danced a stately saraband;
Their laughter echoed thin and shrill.

Sometimes a clock-work puppet pressed
A phantom lover to her breast,
Sometimes they seemed to try and sing,

Sometimes a horrible Marionette
Came out, and smoked its cigarette
Upon the steps like a live thing.

Then turning to my love I said,
'The dead are dancing with the dead,
The dust is whirling with the dust.'

But she, she heard the violin,
And left my side, and entered in;
Love passed into the house of Lust.

Then suddenly the tune went false,
The dancers wearied of the waltz,
The shadows ceased to wheel and whirl,

And down the long and silent street,
The dawn with silver-sandalled feet,
Crept like a frightened girl.

Sonnet. On the Sale by Auction of Keats' Love Letters (1885)

These are the letters which Endymion* wrote
    To one he loved in secret, and apart.
    And now the brawlers of the auction mart
Bargain and bid for each poor blotted note,
Ay! for each separate pulse of passion quote
    The merchant's price: I think they love not Art
    Who break the crystal of a poet's heart
That small and sickly eyes may glare and gloat.

Is it not said that many years ago,
    In a far Eastern town, some soldiers ran
    With torches through the midnight, and began
To wrangle for mean raiment, and to throw
    Dice for the garments of a wretched man,
Not knowing the God's wonder, or his woe?

Symphony in Yellow (1889)

An omnibus across the bridge
    Crawls like a yellow butterfly,
    And, here and there, a passer-by
Shows like a little restless midge.

Big barges full of yellow hay
    Are moored against the shadowy wharf,

And, like a yellow silken scarf,
The thick fog hangs along the quay.

The yellow leaves begin to fade
  And flutter from the Temple* elms,
  And at my feet the pale green Thames
Lies like a rod of rippled jade.

DOUGLAS HYDE
(1860–1949)

My Grief on the Sea (1893)

(*From the Irish*)

My grief on the sea,
  How the waves of it roll!
For they heave between me
  And the love of my soul!

Abandoned, forsaken,
  To grief and to care,
Will the sea ever waken
  Relief from despair?

My grief, and my trouble!
  Would he and I were
In the province of Leinster,
  Or county of Clare.

Were I and my darling—
  Oh, heart-bitter wound!—
On board of the ship
  For America bound.

On a green bed of rushes
  All last night I lay,
And I flung it abroad
  With the heat of the day.

And my love came behind me—
He came from the south;
His breast to my bosom,
His mouth to my mouth.

W. B. YEATS
(1865–1939)

The Lake Isle of Innisfree (1888)

I will arise and go now, and go to Innisfree,
And a small cabin build there, of clay and wattles made:
Nine bean-rows will I have there, a hive for the honey-bee,
And live alone in the bee-loud glade.

And I shall have some peace there, for peace comes dropping slow,
Dropping from the veils of the morning to where the cricket sings;
There midnight's all a glimmer, and noon a purple glow,
And evening full of the linnet's wings.

I will arise and go now, for always night and day
I hear lake water lapping with low sounds by the shore;
While I stand on the roadway, or on the pavements grey,
I hear it in the deep heart's core.

To Ireland in the Coming Times (1892)

Know, that I would accounted be
True brother of a company
That sang, to sweeten Ireland's wrong,
Ballad and story, rann* and song;
Nor be I any less of them,
Because the red-rose-bordered hem*
Of her, whose history began
Before God made the angelic clan,
Trails all about the written page.
When Time began to rant and rage

The measure of her flying feet
Made Ireland's heart begin to beat;
And Time bade all his candles flare
To light a measure here and there;
And may the thoughts of Ireland brood
Upon a measured quietude.

Nor may I less be counted one
With Davis, Mangan, Ferguson,*
Because, to him who ponders well,
My rhymes more than their rhyming tell
Of things discovered in the deep,
Where only body's laid asleep.
For the elemental creatures go
About my table to and fro,
That hurry from unmeasured mind
To rant and rage in flood and wind;
Yet he who treads in measured ways
May surely barter gaze for gaze.
Man ever journeys on with them
After the red-rose-bordered hem.
Ah, faeries, dancing under the moon,
A Druid land, a Druid tune!

While still I may, I write for you
The love I lived, the dream I knew.
From our birthday, until we die,
Is but the winking of an eye;
And we, our singing and our love,
What measurer Time has lit above,
And all benighted things that go
About my table to and fro,
Are passing on to where may be,
In truth's consuming ecstasy,
No place for love and dream at all;
For God goes by with white footfall.
I cast my heart into my rhymes,
That you, in the dim coming times,
May know how my heart went with them
After the red-rose-bordered hem.

The Song of Wandering Aengus (1897)

I went out to the hazel wood,
Because a fire was in my head,
And cut and peeled a hazel wand,*
And hooked a berry to a thread;
And when white moths were on the wing,
And moth-like stars were flickering out,
I dropped the berry in a stream
And caught a little silver trout.

When I had laid it on the floor
I went to blow the fire aflame,
But something rustled on the floor,
And some one called me by my name:
It had become a glimmering girl
With apple blossom in her hair
Who called me by my name and ran
And faded through the brightening air.

Though I am old with wandering
Through hollow lands and hilly lands,
I will find out where she has gone,
And kiss her lips and take her hands;
And walk among long dappled grass,
And pluck till time and times are done
The silver apples of the moon,
The golden apples of the sun.

To a Shade (1913)

If you have revisited the town, thin Shade,
Whether to look upon your monument
(I wonder if the builder has been paid)
Or happier-thoughted when the day is spent
To drink of that salt breath out of the sea
When grey gulls flit about instead of men,
And the gaunt houses put on majesty:

Let these content you and be gone again;
For they are at their old tricks yet.
                              A man*
Of your own passionate serving kind who had brought
In his full hands what, had they only known,
Had given their children's children loftier thought,
Sweeter emotion, working in their veins
Like gentle blood, has been driven from the place,
And insult heaped upon him for his pains,
And for his open-handedness, disgrace;
Your enemy, an old foul mouth,* had set
The pack upon him.
                              Go, unquiet wanderer,
And gather the Glasnevin coverlet*
About your head till the dust stops your ear,
The time for you to taste of that salt breath
And listen at the corners has not come;
You had enough of sorrow before death—
Away, away! You are safer in the tomb.

September 29, 1913

September 1913 (1913)

What need you, being come to sense,
But fumble in a greasy till
And add the halfpence to the pence
And prayer to shivering prayer, until
You have dried the marrow from the bone;
For men were born to pray and save:
Romantic Ireland's dead and gone,
It's with O'Leary* in the grave.

Yet they were of a different kind,
The names that stilled your childish play,
They have gone about the world like wind,
But little time had they to pray
For whom the hangman's rope was spun,

And what, God help us, could they save?
Romantic Ireland's dead and gone,
It's with O'Leary in the grave.

Was it for this the wild geese* spread
The grey wing upon every tide;
For this that all that blood was shed,
For this Edward Fitzgerald* died,
And Robert Emmet and Wolfe Tone,
All that delirium of the brave?
Romantic Ireland's dead and gone,
It's with O'Leary in the grave.

Yet could we turn the years again,
And call those exiles as they were
In all their loneliness and pain,
You'd cry, 'Some woman's yellow hair
Has maddened every mother's son':*
They weighed so lightly what they gave.
But let them be, they're dead and gone,
They're with O'Leary in the grave.

Easter 1916 (1916)

I have met them at close of day
Coming with vivid faces
From counter or desk among grey
Eighteenth-century houses.
I have passed with a nod of the head
Or polite meaningless words,
Or have lingered awhile and said
Polite meaningless words,
And thought before I had done
Of a mocking tale or a gibe
To please a companion
Around the fire at the club,
Being certain that they and I
But lived where motley is worn:
All changed, changed utterly:
A terrible beauty is born.

That woman's days* were spent
In ignorant good-will,
Her nights in argument
Until her voice grew shrill.
What voice more sweet than hers
When, young and beautiful,
She rode to harriers?
This man had kept a school
And rode our wingèd horse;*
This other* his helper and friend
Was coming into his force;
He might have won fame in the end,
So sensitive his nature seemed,
So daring and sweet his thought.
This other man* I had dreamed
A drunken, vainglorious lout.
He had done most bitter wrong
To some who are near my heart,
Yet I number him in the song;
He, too, has resigned his part
In the casual comedy;
He, too, has been changed in his turn,
Transformed utterly:
A terrible beauty is born.

Hearts with one purpose alone
Through summer and winter seem
Enchanted to a stone
To trouble the living stream.
The horse that comes from the road,
The rider, the birds that range
From cloud to tumbling cloud,
Minute by minute they change;
A shadow of cloud on the stream
Changes minute by minute;
A horse-hoof slides on the brim,
And a horse plashes within it;
The long-legged moor-hens dive,
And hens to moor-cocks call;

Minute by minute they live:
The stone's in the midst of all.

Too long a sacrifice
Can make a stone of the heart.
O when may it suffice?
That is Heaven's part, our part
To murmur name upon name,
As a mother names her child
When sleep at last has come
On limbs that had run wild.
What is it but nightfall?
No, no, not night but death;
Was it needless death after all?
For England may keep faith*
For all that is done and said.
We know their dream; enough
To know they dreamed and are dead;
And what if excess of love
Bewildered them till they died?
I write it out in a verse—
MacDonagh and MacBride
And Connolly* and Pearse
Now and in time to be,
Wherever green is worn,
Are changed, changed utterly:
A terrible beauty is born.

September 25, 1916

The Wild Swans at Coole (1916)

The trees are in their autumn beauty,
The woodland paths are dry,
Under the October twilight the water
Mirrors a still sky;
Upon the brimming water among the stones
Are nine-and-fifty swans.

The nineteenth autumn has come upon me
Since I first made my count;
I saw, before I had well finished,
All suddenly mount
And scatter wheeling in great broken rings
Upon their clamorous wings.

I have looked upon those brilliant creatures,
And now my heart is sore.
All's changed since I, hearing at twilight,
The first time on this shore,
The bell-beat of their wings above my head,
Trod with a lighter tread.

Unwearied still, lover by lover,
They paddle in the cold
Companionable streams or climb the air;
Their hearts have not grown old;
Passion or conquest, wander where they will,
Attend upon them still.

But now they drift on the still water,
Mysterious, beautiful;
Among what rushes will they build,
By what lake's edge or pool
Delight men's eyes when I awake some day
To find they have flown away?

Meditations in Time of Civil War (1921–1923)

I

Ancestral Houses

Surely among a rich man's flowering lawns,
Amid the rustle of his planted hills,
Life overflows without ambitious pains;
And rains down life until the basin spills,
And mounts more dizzy high the more it rains

As though to choose whatever shape it wills
And never stoop to a mechanical
Or servile shape, at others' beck and call.

Mere dreams, mere dreams! Yet Homer had not sung
Had he not found it certain beyond dreams
That out of life's own self-delight had sprung
The abounding glittering jet; though now it seems
As if some marvellous empty sea-shell flung
Out of the obscure dark of the rich streams,
And not a fountain, were the symbol which
Shadows the inherited glory of the rich.

Some violent bitter man, some powerful man
Called architect and artist in, that they,
Bitter and violent men, might rear in stone
The sweetness that all longed for night and day,
The gentleness none there had ever known;
But when the master's buried mice can play,
And maybe the great-grandson of that house,
For all its bronze and marble, 's but a mouse.

O what if gardens where the peacock strays
With delicate feet upon old terraces,
Or else all Juno* from an urn displays
Before the indifferent garden deities;
O what if levelled lawns and gravelled ways
Where slippered Contemplation finds his ease
And Childhood a delight for every sense,
But take our greatness with our violence?

What if the glory of escutcheoned doors,
And buildings that a haughtier age designed,
The pacing to and fro on polished floors
Amid great chambers and long galleries, lined
With famous portraits of our ancestors;
What if those things the greatest of mankind
Consider most to magnify, or to bless,
But take our greatness with our bitterness?

II

My House

An ancient bridge, and a more ancient tower,
A farmhouse that is sheltered by its wall,
An acre of stony ground,
Where the symbolic rose can break in flower,
Old ragged elms, old thorns innumerable,
The sound of the rain or sound
Of every wind that blows;
The stilted water-hen
Crossing stream again
Scared by the splashing of a dozen cows;

A winding stair, a chamber arched with stone,
A grey stone fireplace with an open hearth,
A candle and written page.
Il Penseroso's Platonist* toiled on
In some like chamber, shadowing forth
How the daemonic rage
Imagined everything.
Benighted travellers
From markets and from fairs
Have seen his midnight candle glimmering.

Two men have founded here. A man-at-arms
Gathered a score of horse and spent his days
In this tumultuous spot,
Where through long wars and sudden night alarms
His dwindling score and he seemed castaways
Forgetting and forgot;
And I, that after me
My bodily heirs may find,
To exalt a lonely mind,
Befitting emblems of adversity.

III

My Table

Two heavy trestles, and a board
Where Sato's gift, a changeless sword,*

By pen and paper lies,
That it may moralise
My days out of their aimlessness.
A bit of an embroidered dress
Covers its wooden sheath.
Chaucer had not drawn breath
When it was forged. In Sato's house,
Curved like new moon, moon-luminous,
It lay five hundred years.
Yet if no change appears
No moon; only an aching heart
Conceives a changeless work of art.
Our learned men have urged
That when and where 'twas forged
A marvellous accomplishment,
In painting or in pottery, went
From father unto son
And through the centuries ran
And seemed unchanging like the sword.
Soul's beauty being most adored,
Men and their business took
The soul's unchanging look;
For the most rich inheritor,
Knowing that none could pass Heaven's door
That loved inferior art,
Had such an aching heart
That he, although a country's talk
For silken clothes and stately walk,
Had waking wits; it seemed
Juno's peacock screamed.

IV

My Descendants

Having inherited a vigorous mind
From my old fathers, I must nourish dreams
And leave a woman and a man behind
As vigorous of mind, and yet it seems
Life scarce can cast a fragrance on the wind,
Scarce spread a glory to the morning beams,

But the torn petals strew the garden plot;
And there's but common greenness after that.

And what if my descendants lose the flower
Through natural declension of the soul,
Through too much business with the passing hour,
Through too much play, or marriage with a fool?
May this laborious stair and this stark tower
Become a roofless ruin that the owl
May build in the cracked masonry and cry
Her desolation to the desolate sky.

The Primum Mobile* that fashioned us
Has made the very owls in circles move;
And I, that count myself most prosperous,
Seeing that love and friendship are enough,
For an old neighbour's friendship chose the house
And decked and altered it for a girl's love,
And know whatever flourish and decline
These stones remain their monument and mine.

V

The Road at my Door

An affable Irregular,*
A heavily-built Falstaffian man,*
Comes cracking jokes of civil war
As though to die by gunshot were
The finest play under the sun.

A brown Lieutenant and his men,
Half dressed in national uniform,*
Stand at my door, and I complain
Of the foul weather, hail and rain,
A pear tree broken by the storm.

I count those feathered balls of soot
The moor-hen guides upon the stream,
To silence the envy in my thought;
And turn towards my chamber, caught
In the cold snows of a dream.

VI

The Stare's Nest by my Window

The bees build in the crevices
Of loosening masonry, and there
The mother birds bring grubs and flies.
My wall is loosening; honey-bees,
Come build in the empty house of the stare.*

We are closed in, and the key is turned
On our uncertainty; somewhere
A man is killed, or a house burned,
Yet no clear fact to be discerned:
Come build in the empty house of the stare.

A barricade of stone or of wood;
Some fourteen days of civil war;
Last night they trundled down the road
That dead young soldier in his blood:
Come build in the empty house of the stare.

We had fed the heart on fantasies,
The heart's grown brutal from the fare;
More substance in our enmities
Than in our love; O honey-bees,
Come build in the empty house of the stare.

VII

*I see Phantoms of Hatred and of the Heart's Fullness
and of the Coming Emptiness*

I climb to the tower-top and lean upon broken stone,
A mist that is like blown snow is sweeping over all,
Valley, river, and elms, under the light of a moon
That seems unlike itself, that seems unchangeable,
A glittering sword out of the east. A puff of wind
And those white glimmering fragments of the mist sweep by.
Frenzies bewilder, reveries perturb the mind;
Monstrous familiar images swim to the mind's eye.

'Vengeance upon the murderers,' the cry goes up,
'Vengeance for Jacques Molay.'* In cloud-pale rags, or in lace,
The rage-driven, rage-tormented, and rage-hungry troop,
Trooper belabouring trooper, biting at arm or at face,
Plunges towards nothing, arms and fingers spreading wide
For the embrace of nothing; and I, my wits-astray
Because of all that senseless tumult, all but cried
For vengeance on the murderers of Jacques Molay.

Their legs long, delicate and slender, aquamarine their eyes,
Magical unicorns bear ladies on their backs.
The ladies close their musing eyes. No prophecies,
Remembered out of Babylonian almanacs,*
Have closed the ladies' eyes, their minds are but a pool
Where even longing drowns under its own excess;
Nothing but stillness can remain when hearts are full
Of their own sweetness, bodies of their loveliness.

The cloud-pale unicorns, the eyes of aquamarine,
The quivering half-closed eyelids, the rags of cloud or of lace,
Or eyes that rage has brightened, arms it has made lean,
Give place to an indifferent multitude, give place
To brazen hawks. Nor self-delighting reverie,
Nor hate of what's to come, nor pity for what's gone,
Nothing but grip of claw, and the eye's complacency,
The innumerable clanging wings that have put out the moon.

I turn away and shut the door, and on the stair
Wonder how many times I could have proved my worth
In something that all others understand or share;
But O! ambitious heart, had such a proof drawn forth
A company of friends, a conscience set at ease,
It had but made us pine the more. The abstract joy,
The half-read wisdom of daemonic images,
Suffice the ageing man as once the growing boy.

1923

The Tower (1925)

I

What shall I do with this absurdity—
O heart, O troubled heart—this caricature,
Decrepit age that has been tied to me
As to a dog's tail?

                Never had I more
Excited, passionate, fantastical
Imagination, nor an ear and eye
That more expected the impossible—
No, not in boyhood when with rod and fly,
Or the humbler worm, I climbed Ben Bulben's back*
And had the livelong summer day to spend.
It seems that I must bid the Muse go pack,
Choose Plato and Plotinus* for a friend
Until imagination, ear and eye,
Can be content with argument and deal
In abstract things; or be derided by
A sort of battered kettle at the heel.

II

I pace upon the battlements and stare
On the foundations of a house, or where
Tree, like a sooty finger, starts from the earth;
And send imagination forth
Under the day's declining beam, and call
Images and memories
From ruin or from ancient trees,
For I would ask a question of them all.

Beyond that ridge lived Mrs French, and once
When every silver candlestick or sconce
Lit up the dark mahogany and the wine,
A serving-man, that could divine
That most respected lady's every wish,
Ran and with the garden shears
Clipped an insolent farmer's ears
And brought them in a little covered dish.

W. B. Yeats

Some few remembered still when I was young
A peasant girl commended by a song,
Who'd lived somewhere upon that rocky place,
And praised the colour of her face,
And had the greater joy in praising her,
Remembering that, if walked she there,
Farmers jostled at the fair
So great a glory did the song confer.

And certain men, being maddened by those rhymes,
Or else by toasting her a score of times,
Rose from the table and declared it right
To test their fancy by their sight;
But they mistook the brightness of the moon
For the prosaic light of day—
Music had driven their wits astray—
And one was drowned in the great bog of Cloone.*

Strange, but the man who made the song was blind;*
Yet, now I have considered it, I find
That nothing strange; the tragedy began
With Homer that was a blind man,
And Helen has all living hearts betrayed.*
O may the moon and sunlight seem
One inextricable beam,
For if I triumph I must make men mad.

And I myself created Hanrahan*
And drove him drunk or sober through the dawn
From somewhere in the neighbouring cottages.
Caught by an old man's juggleries
He stumbled, tumbled, fumbled to and fro
And had but broken knees for hire
And horrible splendour of desire;
I thought it all out twenty years ago:

Good fellows shuffled cards in an old bawn;
And when that ancient ruffian's turn was on
He so bewitched the cards under his thumb

That all but the one card became
A pack of hounds and not a pack of cards,
And that he changed into a hare.
Hanrahan rose in frenzy there
And followed up those baying creatures towards—

O towards I have forgotten what—enough!
I must recall a man that neither love
Nor music nor an enemy's clipped ear
Could, he was so harried, cheer;
A figure that has grown so fabulous
There's not a neighbour left to say
When he finished his dog's day:
An ancient bankrupt master of this house.

Before that ruin came, for centuries,
Rough men-at-arms, cross-gartered to the knees
Or shod in iron, climbed the narrow stairs,
And certain men-at-arms there were
Whose images, in the Great Memory* stored,
Come with loud cry and panting breast
To break upon a sleeper's rest
While their great wooden dice beat on the board.

As I would question all, come all who can;
Come old, necessitous, half-mounted man;
And bring beauty's blind rambling celebrant;
The red man the juggler sent
Through God-forsaken meadows; Mrs French,
Gifted with so fine an ear;
The man drowned in a bog's mire,
When mocking muses chose the country wench.

Did all old men and women, rich and poor,
Who trod upon these rocks or passed this door,
Whether in public or in secret rage
As I do now against old age?
But I have found an answer in those eyes
That are impatient to be gone;

Go therefore; but leave Hanrahan,
For I need all his mighty memories.

Old lecher with a love on every wind,
Bring up out of that deep considering mind
All that you have discovered in the grave,
For it is certain that you have
Reckoned up every unforeknown, unseeing
Plunge, lured by a softening eye,
Or by a touch or a sigh,
Into the labyrinth of another's being;

Does the imagination dwell the most
Upon a woman won or woman lost?
If on the lost, admit you turned aside
From a great labyrinth out of pride,
Cowardice, some silly over-subtle thought
Or anything called conscience once;
And that if memory recur, the sun's
Under eclipse and the day blotted out.

III

It is time that I wrote my will;
I choose upstanding men
That climb the streams until
The fountain leap, and at dawn
Drop their cast at the side
Of dripping stone; I declare
They shall inherit my pride,
The pride of people that were
Bound neither to Cause nor to State,
Neither to slaves that were spat on,
Nor to the tyrants that spat,
The people of Burke and of Grattan*
That gave, though free to refuse—
Pride, like that of the morn,
When the headlong light is loose,
Or that of the fabulous horn,*
Or that of the sudden shower

When all streams are dry,
Or that of the hour
When the swan must fix his eye
Upon a fading gleam,
Float out upon a long
Last reach of glittering stream
And there sing his last song.
And I declare my faith:
I mock Plotinus' thought
And cry in Plato's teeth,
Death and life were not
Till man made up the whole,
Made lock, stock and barrel
Out of his bitter soul,
Aye, sun and moon and star, all,
And further add to that
That, being dead, we rise,
Dream and so create
Translunar Paradise.
I have prepared my peace
With learned Italian things
And the proud stones of Greece,
Poet's imaginings
And memories of love,
Memories of the words of women,
All those things whereof
Man makes a superhuman
Mirror-resembling dream.

As at the loophole there
The daws* chatter and scream,
And drop twigs layer upon layer.
When they have mounted up,
The mother bird will rest
On their hollow top,
And so warm her wild nest.

I leave both faith and pride
To young upstanding men

Climbing the mountain side,
That under bursting dawn
They may drop a fly;
Being of that metal made
Till it was broken by
This sedentary trade.

Now shall I make my soul,
Compelling it to study
In a learned school
Till the wreck of body,
Slow decay of blood,
Testy delirium
Or dull decrepitude,
Or what worse evil come—
The death of friends, or death
Of every brilliant eye
That made a catch in the breath—
Seem but the clouds of the sky
When the horizon fades;
Or a bird's sleepy cry
Among the deepening shades.

Sailing to Byzantium (1926)

I

That is no country* for old men. The young
In one another's arms, birds in the trees,
—Those dying generations—at their song,
The salmon-falls, the mackerel-crowded seas,
Fish, flesh, or fowl, commend all summer long
Whatever is begotten, born, and dies.
Caught in that sensual music all neglect
Monuments of unageing intellect.

II

An aged man is but a paltry thing,
A tattered coat upon a stick, unless

Soul clap its hands and sing, and louder sing
For every tatter in its mortal dress,
Nor is there singing school but studying
Monuments of its own magnificence;
And therefore I have sailed the seas and come
To the holy city of Byzantium.

III

O sages standing in God's holy fire
As in the gold mosaic of a wall,*
Come from the holy fire, perne in a gyre,*
And be the singing-masters of my soul.
Consume my heart away; sick with desire
And fastened to a dying animal
It knows not what it is; and gather me
Into the artifice of eternity.

IV

Once out of nature I shall never take
My bodily form from any natural thing,
But such a form as Grecian goldsmiths make
Of hammered gold and gold enamelling
To keep a drowsy Emperor awake;
Or set upon a golden bough* to sing
To lords and ladies of Byzantium
Of what is past, or passing, or to come.

The Circus Animals' Desertion (1937–1938)

I

I sought a theme and sought for it in vain,
I sought it daily for six weeks or so.
Maybe at last being but a broken man
I must be satisfied with my heart, although
Winter and summer till old age began
My circus animals were all on show,
Those stilted boys, that burnished chariot,
Lion and woman and the Lord knows what.

II

What can I but enumerate old themes,
First that sea-rider Oisin led by the nose
Through three enchanted islands, allegorical dreams,
Vain gaiety, vain battle, vain repose,
Themes of the embittered heart, or so it seems,
That might adorn old songs or courtly shows;
But what cared I that set him on to ride,
I, starved for the bosom of his fairy bride.*

And then a counter-truth filled out its play,
'The Countess Cathleen'* was the name I gave it,
She, pity-crazed, had given her soul away
But masterful Heaven had intervened to save it.
I thought my dear* must her own soul destroy
So did fanaticism and hate enslave it,
And this brought forth a dream and soon enough
This dream itself had all my thought and love.

And when the Fool and Blind Man stole the bread
Cuchulain fought the ungovernable sea;*
Heart mysteries there, and yet when all is said
It was the dream itself enchanted me:
Character isolated by a deed
To engross the present and dominate memory.
Players and painted stage took all my love
And not those things that they were emblems of.

III

Those masterful images because complete
Grew in pure mind but out of what began?
A mound of refuse or the sweepings of a street,
Old kettles, old bottles, and a broken can,
Old iron, old bones, old rags, that raving slut
Who keeps the till. Now that my ladder's gone
I must lie down where all the ladders start
In the foul rag and bone shop of the heart.

ETHNA CARBERY
(1866–1902)

The Love-Talker (1902)

I met the Love-Talker one eve in the glen,
He was handsomer than any of our handsome young men,
His eyes were blacker than the sloe, his voice sweeter far
Than the crooning of old Kevin's pipes beyond in Coolnagar.

I was bound for the milking with a heart fair and free—
My grief! my grief! that bitter hour drained the life from me;
I thought him human lover, though his lips on mine were cold,
And the breath of death blew keen on me within his hold.

I know not what way he came, no shadow fell behind,
But all the sighing rushes swayed beneath a fairy wind;
The thrush ceased its singing, a mist crept about,
We two clung together—with the world shut out.

Beyond the ghostly mist I could hear my cattle low,
The little cow from Ballina, clean as driven snow,
The dun cow from Kerry, the roan from Inisheer,
Oh, pitiful their calling—and his whispers in my ear!

His eyes were a fire; his words were a snare;
I cried my mother's name, but no help was there;
I made the blessed Sign: then he gave a dreary moan,
A wisp of cloud went floating by, and I stood alone.

Running ever thro' my head is an old-time rune—
'Who meets the Love-Talker must weave her shroud soon.'
My mother's face is furrowed with the salt tears that fall,
But the kind eyes of my father are the saddest sight of all.

I have spun the fleecy lint and now my wheel is still,
The linen length is woven for my shroud fine and chill,

I shall stretch me on the bed where a happy maid I lay—
Pray for the soul of Máire Óg at dawning of the day!

The Brown Wind of Connaught (1902)

The brown wind of Connaught—
    Across the bogland blown,
(*The brown wind of Connaught*),
    Turns my heart to a stone;
For it cries my name at twilight,
    And cries it at the noon—
O, Mairgread Bán! O, Mairgread Bán!
    Just like a fairy tune.

The brown wind of Connaught,
    When Dermot came to woo,
(*The brown wind of Connaught*),
    It heard his whispers too;
And while my wheel goes whirring,
    It taps on my window-pane,
Till I open wide to the Dead outside,
    And the sea-salt misty rain.

The brown wind of Connaught
    With women wailed one day
(*The brown wind of Connaught*),
    For a wreck in Galway Bay;
And many the dark-faced fishers
    That gathered their nets in fear,
But one sank straight to the Ghostly Gate—
    And he was my Dermot Dear.

The brown wind of Connaught
    Still keening in the dawn,
(*The brown wind of Connaught*),
    For my true love long gone.

Oh, cold green wave of danger,
   Drift him a restful sleep
O'er his young black head on its lowly bed,
   While his weary wake I keep.

Rody McCorley (1902)

Ho! see the fleet-foot hosts of men
Who speed with faces wan,
From farmstead and from fisher's cot
Upon the banks of Bann!*
They come with vengeance in their eyes—
Too late, too late are they—
For Rody McCorley goes to die
On the Bridge of Toome to-day.

Oh Ireland, Mother Ireland,
You love them still the best,
The fearless brave who fighting fall
Upon your hapless breast;
But never a one of all your dead
More bravely fell in fray,
Than he who marches to his fate
On the Bridge of Toome to-day.

Up the narrow street he stepped,
Smiling and proud and young;
About the hemp-rope on his neck
The golden ringlets clung.
There's never a tear in the blue, blue eyes,
Both glad and bright are they—
As Rody McCorley goes to die
On the Bridge of Toome to-day.

Ah! When he last stepped up that street,
His shining pike in hand,
Behind him marched in grim array
A stalwart earnest band!

For Antrim town! for Antrim town!
He led them to the fray—
And Rody McCorley goes to die
On the Bridge of Toome to-day.

The gray coat and its sash of green*
Were brave and stainless then;
A banner flashed beneath the sun
Over the marching men—
The coat hath many a rent this noon,
The sash is torn away,
And Rody McCorley goes to die
On the Bridge of Toome to-day.

Oh, how his pike flashed to the sun!
Then found a foeman's heart!
Through furious fight, and heavy odds,
He bore a true man's part;
And many a red-coat bit the dust
Before his keen pike-play—
But Rody McCorley goes to die
On the Bridge of Toome to-day.

Because he loved the Motherland,
Because he loved the Green,
He goes to meet the martyr's fate
With proud and joyous mien,
True to the last, true to the last,
He treads the upward way—
Young Rody McCorley goes to die
On the Bridge of Toome to-day.

The Passing of the Gael (1902)

They are going, going, going from the valleys and the hills,
They are leaving far behind them heathery moor and mountain rills,
All the wealth of hawthorn hedges where the brown thrush sways
    and trills.

They are going, shy-eyed colleens and lads so straight and tall,
From the purple peaks of Kerry, from the crags of wild Imaal,
From the greening plains of Mayo and the glens of Donegal.

They are leaving pleasant places, shores with snowy sands
    outspread;
Blue and lonely lakes a-stirring when the wind stirs overhead;
Tender living hearts that love them, and the graves of kindred dead.

They shall carry to the distant land a tear-drop in the eye
And some shall go uncomforted—their days an endless sigh
For Kathaleen Ní Houlihan's sad face, until they die.

Oh, Kathaleen Ní Houlihan, your road's a thorny way,
And 'tis a faithful soul would walk the flints with you for aye,
Would walk the sharp and cruel flints until his locks grew gray.

So some must wander to the East, and some must wander West;
Some seek the white wastes of the North, and some a Southern
    nest;
Yet never shall they sleep so sweet as on your mother breast.

The whip of hunger scourged them from the glens and quiet
    moors,
But there's a hunger of the heart that plenty never cures;
And they shall pine to walk again the rough road that is yours.

Within the city streets, hot, hurried, full of care,
A sudden dream shall bring them a whiff of Irish air—
A cool air, faintly-scented, blown soft from otherwhere.

Oh, the cabins long-deserted!—Olden memories awake—
Oh, the pleasant, pleasant places!—Hush! the blackbird in the brake!
Oh, the dear and kindly voices!—Now their hearts are fain to ache.

They may win a golden store—sure the whins were golden too;
And no foreign skies hold beauty like the rainy skies they knew;
Nor any night-wind cool the brow as did the foggy dew.

They are going, going, going, and we cannot bid them stay;
The fields are now the strangers' where the strangers' cattle stray.
Oh! Kathaleen Ní Houlihan, your way's a thorny way!

Beannacht Leat (1902)

Beannacht leat!
   I hold your hand in mine, I say
   The parting words this parting day—
   And if a sob be stifled, Dear,
   I pray you turn aside, nor hear—
   I would be brave, and yet, and yet,
   Can we two sunder without regret?

Beannacht leat!
   May every vagrant wind a-stir
   Between us be a messenger,
   Each falling wild-rose petal blow
   A haunting perfume where you go,
   And all the brown birds in the blue
   Sing memories of me to you.

Beannacht leat!
   Thank God! 'tis not a long good-bye
   We give each other, you and I—
   Sure in my heart the hope is fain
   To whisper, You will come again
   With the kind eyes, the same kind smile—
   Then for a little lonely while,
        Beannacht leat!

LIONEL JOHNSON
(1867–1902)

By the Statue of King Charles at Charing Cross (1889)

Sombre and rich, the skies;
Great glooms, and starry plains.
Gently the night wind sighs;
Else a vast silence reigns.

The splendid silence clings
Around me: and around
The saddest of all kings
Crowned, and again discrowned.

Comely and calm, he rides
Hard by his own Whitehall:
Only the night wind glides:
No crowds, nor rebels, brawl.

Gone, too, his Court: and yet,
The stars his courtiers are:
Stars in their stations set;
And every wandering star.

Alone he rides, alone,
The fair and fatal king:
Dark night is all his own,
That strange and solemn thing.

Which are more full of fate:
The stars; or those sad eyes?
Which are more still and great:
Those brows; or the dark skies?

Although his whole heart yearn
In passionate tragedy:

Never was face so stern
With sweet austerity.

Vanquished in life, his death
By beauty made amends:
The passing of his breath
Won his defeated ends.

Brief life, and hapless? Nay:
Through death, life grew sublime.
Speak after sentence? Yea:*
And to the end of time.

Armoured he rides, his head
Bare to the stars of doom:
He triumphs now, the dead,
Beholding London's gloom.

Our wearier spirit faints,
Vexed in the world's employ:
His soul was of the saints;
And art to him was joy.

King, tired in fires of woe!
Men hunger for thy grace:
And through the night I go,
Loving thy mournful face.

Yet, when the city sleeps;
When all the cries are still:
The stars and heavenly deeps
Work out a perfect will.

Mystic and Cavalier (1889)

Go from me: I am one of those, who fall.
What! hath no cold wind swept your heart at all,
In my sad company? Before the end,
   Go from me, dear my friend!

Yours are the victories of light: your feet
Rest from good toil, where rest is brave and sweet.
But after warfare in a mourning gloom,
   I rest in clouds of doom.

Have you not read so, looking in these eyes?
Is it the common light of the pure skies,
Lights up their shadowy depths? The end is set:
   Though the end be not yet.

When gracious music stirs, and all is bright,
And beauty triumphs through a courtly night;
When I too joy, a man like other men:
   Yet, am I like them, then?

And in the battle, when the horsemen sweep
Against a thousand deaths, and fall on sleep:
Who ever sought that sudden calm, if I
   Sought not? Yet, could not die.

Seek with thine eyes to pierce this crystal sphere:
Canst read a fate there, prosperous and clear?
Only the mists, only the weeping clouds:
   Dimness, and airy shrouds.

Beneath, what angels are at work? What powers
Prepare the secret of the fatal hours?
See! the mists tremble, and the clouds are stirred:
   When comes the calling word?

The clouds are breaking from the crystal ball,
Breaking and clearing: and I look to fall.
When the cold winds and airs of portent sweep,
   My spirit may have sleep.

O rich and sounding voices of the air!
Interpreters and prophets of despair:
Priests of a fearful sacrament! I come,
   To make with you mine home.

The Dark Angel (1893)

Dark Angel, with thine aching lust
To rid the world of penitence:
Malicious Angel, who still dost
My soul such subtile violence!

Because of thee, no thought, no thing,
Abides for me undesecrate:
Dark Angel, ever on the wing,
Who never reachest me too late!

When music sounds, then changest thou
Its silvery to a sultry fire:
Nor will thine envious heart allow
Delight untortured by desire.

Through thee, the gracious Muses turn
To Furies,* O mine Enemy!
And all the things of beauty burn
With flames of evil ecstasy.

Because of thee, the land of dreams
Becomes a gathering place of fears:
Until tormented slumber seems
One vehemence of useless tears.

When sunlight glows upon the flowers,
Or ripples down the dancing sea:
Thou, with thy troop of passionate powers,
Beleaguerest, bewilderest, me.

Within the breath of autumn woods,
Within the winter silences:
Thy venomous spirit stirs and broods,
O Master of impieties!

The ardour of red flame is thine,
And thine the steely soul of ice:

Thou poisonest the fair design
Of nature, with unfair device.

Apples of ashes,* golden bright;
Waters of bitterness, how sweet!
O banquet of a foul delight,
Prepared by thee, dark Paraclete!*

Thou art the whisper in the gloom,
The hinting tone, the haunting laugh:
Thou art the adorner of my tomb,
The minstrel of mine epitaph.

I fight thee, in the Holy Name!
Yet, what thou dost, is what God saith:
Temper! should I escape thy flame,
Thou wilt have helped my soul from Death:

The second Death, that never dies,
That cannot die, when time is dead:
Live Death, wherein the lost soul cries,
Eternally uncomforted.

Dark Angel, with thine aching lust!
Of two defeats, of two despairs:
Less dread, a change to drifting dust,
Than thine eternity of cares.

Do what thou wilt, thou shalt not so,
Dark Angel! triumph over me:
Lonely, unto the Lone I go;
Divine, to the Divinity.

Ninety-Eight (1893)

Who fears to speak of ninety-eight?
He, who despairs of Ireland still:

Whose paltry soul finds nothing great
In honest failure: he, whose will,
Feeble and faint in days of gloom,
Takes old defeat for final doom.

Who fears to speak of ninety-eight?
The man, who fears to speak of death:
Who clings and clasps the knees of fate,
And whimpers with his latest breath:
Who hugs his comfort to his heart,
And dares not play a Christian's part.

Who fears to speak of ninety-eight?
The renegade, who sells his trust:
Whose love has rottened into hate,
Whose hopes have withered into dust:
He, who denies, and deems it mad,
The faith his nobler boyhood had.

Who fears to speak of ninety-eight?
The enemy of Ireland fears!
For Ireland undegenerate
Keeps yet the spirit of old years:
He sees, in visions of the night,
A nation arming for the right.

Who fears to speak of ninety-eight?
Not he, who hates a poisonous peace:
For, while the days of triumph wait,
And till the days of sorrow cease,
He, with the Lord of Hosts his friend,
Will fight for Ireland to the end.

Let sword cross sword, or thought meet thought:
One fire of battle thrills them both.
Deliverance only can be wrought
By warfare without stay or sloth:
And by your prayers at Heaven's high gate.
True hearts, that beat in Ninety-Eight.

Parnell (1893)

The wail of Irish winds,
The cry of Irish seas:
Eternal sorrow finds
Eternal voice in these.

I cannot praise our dead,
Whom Ireland weeps so well:
Her morning light, that fled;
Her morning star, that fell.

She of the mournful eyes
Waits, and no dark clouds break:
Waits, and her strong son lies
Dead, for her holy sake.

Her heart is sorrow's home,
And hath been from of old:
An host of griefs hath come,
To make that heart their fold.

Ah, the sad autumn day,
When the last sad troop came
Swift down the ancient way,
Keening a chieftain's name!

Gray hope was there, and dread;
Anger, and love in tears:
They mourned the dear and dead,
Dirge of the ruined years.

Home to her heart she drew
The mourning company:
Old sorrows met the new,
In sad fraternity.

A mother, and forget!
Nay! all her children's fate
Ireland remembers yet,
With love insatiate.

She hears the heavy bells:
Hears, and with passionate breath
Eternally she tells
A rosary of death.

Faithful and true is she,
The mother of us all:
Faithful and true! may we
Fail her not, though we fall.

Her son, our brother, lies
Dead, for her holy sake:
But from the dead arise
Voices, that bid us wake.

Not his, to hail the dawn:
His but the herald's part.
Be ours to see withdrawn
Night from our mother's heart.

GEORGE RUSSELL (AE)
(1867–1935)

Carrowmore (1913)

It's a lonely road through bogland to the lake at
    Carrowmore,
And a sleeper there lies dreaming where the water laps
    the shore;
Though the moth-wings of the twilight in their purples are
    unfurled,
Yet his sleep is filled with music by the masters of the world.

There's a hand as white as silver that is fondling with his hair.
There are glimmering feet of sunshine that are dancing by him
    there:
And half-open lips of faery that were dyed a faery red
In their revels where the Hazel Tree its holy clusters shed.

'Come away,' the red lips whisper, 'all the world is weary now;
'Tis the twilight of the ages and it's time to quit the plough.
Oh, the very sunlight's weary ere it lightens up the dew,
And its gold is changed and faded before it falls to you.

'Though your colleen's* heart be tender, a tenderer heart is near.
What's the starlight in her glances when the stars are shining clear?
Who would kiss the fading shadow when the flower-face glows
    above?
'Tis the beauty of all Beauty that is calling for your love.'

Oh, the great gates of the mountain have opened once again,
And the sound of song and dancing falls upon the ears of men,
And the Land of Youth lies gleaming, flushed with rainbow light and
    mirth,
And the old enchantment lingers in the honey-heart of earth.

EVA GORE-BOOTH
(1870–1926)

The Little Waves of Breffny (1904)

The grand road from the mountain goes shining to the sea,
And there is traffic in it and many a horse and cart,
But the little roads of Cloonagh are dearer far to me,
And the little roads of Cloonagh go rambling through my heart.

A great storm from the ocean goes shouting o'er the hill,
And there is glory in it and terror on the wind,
But the haunted air of twilight is very strange and still,
And the little winds of twilight are dearer to my mind.

The great waves of the Atlantic sweep storming on their way,
Shining green and silver with the hidden herring shoal,
But the Little Waves of Breffny have drenched my heart
   in spray,
And the Little Waves of Breffny go stumbling through
   my soul.

The Land to a Landlord (1904)

You hug to your soul a handful of dust,
And you think the round world your sacred trust—
But the sun shines, and the wind blows,
And nobody cares and nobody knows.

O the bracken waves and the foxgloves flame,
And none of them ever has heard your name—
Near and dear is the curlew's cry,
You are merely a stranger* passing by.

Sheer up through the shadows the mountain towers
And dreams wander free in this world of ours,—
Though you may turn the grass to gold,
The twilight has left you out in the cold.

Though you are king of the rose and the wheat,
Not for you, not for you is the bog-myrtle sweet,
Though you are lord of the long grass,
The hemlock bows not her head as you pass.

The poppies would flutter amongst the corn
Even if you had never been born,
With your will or without your will
The ragweed can wander over the hill.

Down there in the bog where the plovers call
You are but an outcast after all,
Over your head the sky gleams blue—
Not a cloud or a star belongs to you.

Women's Rights (1906)

Down by Glencar* Waterfall
There's no winter left at all.

Every little flower that blows
Cold and darkness overthrows.

Every little thrush that sings
Quells the wild air with brave wings.

Every little stream that runs
Holds the light of brighter suns.

But where men in office sit
Winter holds the human wit.

In the dark and dreary town
Summer's green is trampled down.

Frozen, frozen everywhere
Are the springs of thought and prayer.

Rise with us and let us go
To where the living waters flow.

Oh, whatever men may say
Ours is the wide and open way.

Oh, whatever men may dream
We have the blue air and the stream.

Men have got their towers and walls,
We have cliffs and waterfalls.

Oh, whatever men may do
Ours is the gold air and the blue.

Men have got their pomp and pride—
All the green world is on our side.

J. M. SYNGE
(1871–1909)

Prelude (1909)

Still south I went and west and south again,
Through Wicklow* from the morning till the night,
And far from cities, and the sites of men,
Lived with the sunshine and the moon's delight.

I knew the stars, the flowers, and the birds,
The grey and wintry sides of many glens,
And did but half remember human words,
In converse with the mountains, moors, and fens.

Beg-Innish (1909)

Bring Kateen-Beag and Maurya Jude
To dance in Beg-Innish,
And when the lads (they're in Dunquin)
Have sold their crabs and fish,
Wave fawney shawls and call them in,
And call the little girls who spin,
And seven weavers from Dunquin,
To dance in Beg-Innish.

I'll play you jigs, and Maurice Kean,
Where nets are laid to dry,
I've silken strings would draw a dance
From girls are lame or shy;
Four strings I've brought from Spain and France
To make your long men skip and prance,
Till stars look out to see the dance
Where nets are laid to dry.

We'll have no priest or peeler* in
To dance at Beg-Innish;
But we'll have drink from M'riarty Jim
Rowed round while gannets fish,
A keg with porter* to the brim,
That every lad may have his whim,
Till we up with sails with M'riarty Jim
And sail from Beg-Innish.

To the Oaks of Glencree (1909)

My arms are round you, and I lean
Against you, while the lark
Sings over us, and golden lights and green
Shadows are on your bark.

There'll come a season when you'll stretch
Black boards to cover me;
Then in Mount Jerome I'll lie, poor wretch,
With worms eternally.

A Question (1909)

I asked if I got sick and died, would you
With my black funeral go walking too,
If you'd stand close to hear them talk or pray
While I'm let down in that steep bank of clay.

And, No, you said, for if you saw a crew
Of living idiots pressing round that new
Oak coffin—they alive, I dead beneath
That board—you'd rave and rend them with your teeth.

In Glencullen (1909)

Thrush, linnet, stare, and wren,
Brown lark beside the sun,
Take thought of kestrel, sparrow-hawk,
Birdlime and roving gun.

You great-great-grandchildren
Of birds I've listened to,
I think I robbed your ancestors
When I was young as you.

OLIVER ST JOHN GOGARTY
(1878–1957)

To the Liffey with the Swans (1923)

Keep you these calm and lovely things,
    And float them on your clearest water;
For one would not disgrace a King's
    Transformed beloved and buoyant daughter.

And with her goes this sprightly swan,
    A bird of more than royal feather,
With alban* beauty clothed upon:
    O keep them fair and well together!

As fair as was that doubled Bird,*
    By love of Leda so besotten,
That she was all with wonder stirred,
    And the Twin Sportsmen* were begotten!

THOMAS MACDONAGH
(1878–1916)

John-John (1910)

I dreamt last night of you, John-John,
    And thought you called to me;
And when I woke this morning, John,
    Yourself I hoped to see;

But I was all alone, John-John,
    Though still I heard your call:
I put my boots and bonnet on,
    And took my Sunday shawl,
And went, full sure to find you, John,
                    To Nenagh fair.

The fair was just the same as then,
    Five years ago to-day,
When first you left the thimble men
    And came with me away;
For there again were thimble men
    And shooting galleries,
And card-trick men and Maggie men
    Of all sorts and degrees—
But not a sight of you, John-John,
                    Was anywhere.

I turned my face to home again,
    And called myself a fool
To think you'd leave the thimble men
    And live again by rule,
And go to Mass and keep the fast
    And till the little patch:
My wish to have you home was past
    Before I raised the latch
And pushed the door and saw you, John,
                    Sitting down there.

How cool you came in here, begad,
    As if you owned the place!
But rest yourself there now, my lad,
    'Tis good to see your face;
My dream is out, and now by it
    I think I know my mind:
At six o'clock this house you'll quit,
    And leave no grief behind;—

But until six o'clock, John-John,
   My bit you'll share.

The neighbours' shame of me began
 When first I brought you in:
To wed and keep a tinker man
 They thought a kind of sin;
But now this three year since you're gone
 'Tis pity me they do,
And that I'd rather have, John-John,
 Than that they'd pity you.
Pity for me and you, John-John,
    I could not bear.

Oh, you're my husband right enough,
 But what's the good of that?
You know you never were the stuff
 To be the cottage cat,
To watch the fire and hear me lock
 The door and put out Shep—
But there now, it is six o'clock
 And time for you to step.
God bless and keep you far, John-John!
   And that's my prayer.

Of a Poet Patriot (1913)

His songs were a little phrase
 Of eternal song,
Drowned in the harping of lays
 More loud and long.

His deed was a single word,
 Called out alone
In a night when no echo stirred
 To laughter or moan.

But his songs new souls shall thrill,
 The loud harps dumb,

And his deed the echoes fill
  When the dawn is come.

The Yellow Bittern (1913)

(*From the Irish*)

The yellow bittern that never broke out
  In a drinking bout, might as well have drunk;
His bones are thrown on a naked stone
  Where he lived alone like a hermit monk.
O yellow bittern! I pity your lot,
  Though they say that a sot like myself is curst—
I was sober a while, but I'll drink and be wise
  For I fear I should die in the end of thirst.

It's not for the common birds that I'd mourn,
  The black-bird, the corn-crake, or the crane,
But for the bittern that's shy and apart
  And drinks in the marsh from the lone bog-drain.
Oh! if I had known you were near your death,
  While my breath held out I'd have run to you,
Till a splash from the Lake of the Son of the Bird
  Your soul would have stirred and waked anew.

My darling told me to drink no more
  Or my life would be o'er in a little short while;
But I told her 'tis drink gives me health and strength
  And will lengthen my road by many a mile.
You see how the bird of the long smooth neck
  Could get his death from the thirst at last—
Come, son of my soul, and drain your cup,
  You'll get no sup when your life is past.

In a wintering island by Constantine's halls*
  A bittern calls from a wineless place,
And tells me that hither he cannot come
  Till the summer is here and the sunny days.

When he crosses the stream there and wings o'er the sea
    Then a fear comes to me he may fail in his flight—
Well, the milk and the ale are drunk every drop,
    And a dram won't stop our thirst this night.

The Night Hunt (1913)

In the morning, in the dark,
When the stars begin to blunt,
By the wall of Barna Park
Dogs I heard and saw them hunt.
All the parish dogs were there,
All the dogs for miles around,
Teeming up behind a hare,
In the dark, without a sound.

How I heard I scarce can tell—
'Twas a patter in the grass—
And I did not see them well
Come across the dark and pass;
Yet I saw them and I knew
Spearman's dog and Spellman's dog
And, beside my own dog too,
Leamy's from the Island Bog.

In the morning when the sun
Burnished all the green to gorse,
I went out to take a run
Round the bog upon my horse;
And my dog that had been sleeping
In the heat beside the door
Left his yawning and went leaping
On a hundred yards before.

Through the village street we passed—
Not a dog there raised a snout—
Through the street and out at last
On the white bog road and out

Over Barna Park full pace,
Over to the Silver Stream,
Horse and dog in happy race,
Rider between thought and dream.

By the stream at Leamy's house,
Lay a dog—my pace I curbed—
But our coming did not rouse
Him from drowsing undisturbed;
And my dog, as unaware
Of the other, dropped beside
And went running by me there
With my horse's slackened stride.

Yet by something, by a twitch
Of the sleeper's eye, a look
From the runner, something which
Little chords of feeling shook,
I was conscious that a thought
Shuddered through the silent deep
Of a secret—I had caught
Something I had known in sleep.

JOSEPH CAMPBELL
(1879–1944)

My Lagan Love (1904)

Where Lagan stream sings lullaby,
There blows a lily fair;
The twilight gleam is in her eye,
The night is on her hair.
But like a love-sick leanannsidhe,*
She has my heart in thrall.
No life I own nor liberty,
For love is lord of all.

And often when the beetle's horn
Has lulled the eve to sleep;
I steal up to her sheiling lorn
And through the dooring peep;
There by the cricket's singing-stone*
She spares* the bogwood fire,
And sings in sad sweet undertone,
The song of heart's desire.

SEUMAS O'SULLIVAN
(1879–1958)

The Lamplighter (1929)

Here to the leisured side of life,
Remote from traffic, free from strife,
A cul-de-sac, a sanctuary
Where old quaint customs creep to die
And only ancient memories stir,
At evening comes the lamplighter;
With measured steps, without a sound,
He treads the unalterable round,
Soundlessly touching one by one
The waiting posts that stand to take
The faint blue bubbles in his wake;
And when the night begins to wane
He comes to take them back again,
Before the chilly dawn can blight
The delicate frail buds of light.

Geese (1939)

My blessing on the gentle geese,
My blessing, and a lasting peace,
For on a day in fierce July
When not a cloud was in the sky,

Upon a day without a breeze
They looked like snow beneath the trees.

PATRICK PEARSE
(1879–1916)

A Rann I Made (1917)

A rann I made within my heart
To the rider, to the high king,
A rann I made to my love,
To the king of kings, ancient death.

Brighter to me than light of day
The dark of thy house, tho' black clay;
Sweeter to me than the music of trumpets
The quiet of thy house and its eternal silence.

I am Ireland (1917)

I am Ireland:
I am older than the Old Woman of Beare.

Great my glory:
I that bore Cuchulainn* the valiant.

Great my shame:
My own children that sold their mother.

I am Ireland:
I am lonelier than the Old Woman of Beare.

On the Strand of Howth (1917)

On the strand of Howth
Breaks a sounding wave;

A lone sea-gull screams
Above the bay.

In the middle of the meadow
Beside Glasnevin
The corncrake speaks
All night long.

There is minstrelsy of birds
In Glenasmole,
The blackbird and thrush
Chanting music.

There is shining of sun
On the side of Slieverua,
And the wind blowing
Down over its brow.

On the harbour of Dunleary
Are boat and ship
With sails set
Ploughing the waves.

Here in Ireland,
Am I, my brother,
And you far from me
In gallant Paris,

I beholding
Hill and harbour,
The strand of Howth
And Slieverua's side,

And you victorious
In mighty Paris
Of the limewhite palaces
And the surging hosts;

And what I ask
Of you, beloved,

Far away
Is to think at times

Of the corncrake's tune
Beside Glasnevin
In the middle of the meadow,
Speaking in the night;

Of the voice of the birds
In Glenasmole
Happily, with melody,
Chanting music;

Of the strand of Howth
Where a wave breaks,
And the harbour of Dunleary,
Where a ship rocks;

On the sun that shines
On the side of Slieverua,
And the wind that blows
Down over its brow.

The Mother (1915)

I do not grudge them: Lord, I do not grudge
My two strong sons that I have seen go out
To break their strength and die, they and a few,
In bloody protest for a glorious thing,
They shall be spoken of among their people,
The generations shall remember them,
And call them blessed;
But I will speak their names to my own heart
In the long nights;
The little names that were familiar once
Round my dead hearth.
Lord, thou art hard on mothers:
We suffer in their coming and their going;

And tho' I grudge them not, I weary, weary
Of the long sorrow—And yet I have my joy:
My sons were faithful, and they fought.

Christmas 1915 (1915)

O King that was born
To set bondsmen free,
In the coming battle,
Help the Gael!

The Wayfarer (1916)

The beauty of the world hath made me sad,
This beauty that will pass;
Sometimes my heart hath shaken with great joy
To see a leaping squirrel in a tree,
Or a red lady-bird upon a stalk,
Or little rabbits in a field at evening,
Lit by a slanting sun,
Or some green hill where shadows drifted by
Some quiet hill where mountainy man hath sown
And soon would reap; near to the gate of Heaven;
Or children with bare feet upon the sands
Of some ebbed sea, or playing on the streets
Of little towns in Connacht,
Things young and happy.
And then my heart hath told me:
These will pass,
Will pass and change, will die and be no more,
Things bright and green, things young and happy;
And I have gone upon my way
Sorrowful.

PADRAIC COLUM
(1881–1972)

She Moved Through the Fair (1916)

My young love said to me, 'My brothers won't mind,
And my parents won't slight you for your lack of kind.'
Then she stepped away from me, and this she did say,
'It will not be long, love, till our wedding day.'

She stepped away from me and she moved through the fair,
And fondly I watched her go here and go there,
Then she went her way homeward with one star awake,
As the swan in the evening moves over the lake.

The people were saying no two were e'er wed
But one had a sorrow that never was said,
And I smiled as she passed with her goods and her gear,
And that was the last that I saw of my dear.

I dreamt it last night that my young love came in,
So softly she entered, her feet made no din;
She came close beside me, and this she did say,
'It will not be long, love, till our wedding day.'

FRANCIS LEDWIDGE
(1891–1917)

A Twilight in Middle March (1914)

Within the oak a throb of pigeon wings
Fell silent, and grey twilight hushed the fold,
And spiders' hammocks swung on half-oped things
That shook like foreigners upon our cold.
A gipsy lit a fire and made a sound
Of moving tins, and from an oblong moon

The river seemed to gush across the ground
To the cracked metre of a marching tune.

And then three syllables of melody
Dropped from a blackbird's flute, and died apart
Far in the dewy dark. No more but three,
Yet sweeter music never touched a heart
Neath the blue domes of London. Flute and reed
Suggesting feelings of the solitude
When will was all the Delphi* I would heed,
Lost like a wind within a summer wood
From little knowledge where great sorrows brood.

June (1914)

Broom out the floor now, lay the fender by,
And plant this bee-sucked bough of woodbine there,
And let the window down. The butterfly
Floats in upon the sunbeam, and the fair
Tanned face of June, the nomad gipsy, laughs
Above her widespread wares, the while she tells
The farmers' fortunes in the fields, and quaffs
The water from the spider-peopled wells.

The hedges are all drowned in green grass seas,
And bobbing poppies flare like Elmo's light,*
While siren-like the pollen-stainèd bees
Drone in the clover depths. And up the height
The cuckoo's voice is hoarse and broke with joy.
And on the lowland crops the crows make raid,
Nor fear the clappers of the farmer's boy,
Who sleeps, like drunken Noah,* in the shade.

And loop this red rose in that hazel ring
That snares your little ear, for June is short
And we must joy in it and dance and sing,
And from her bounty draw her rosy worth.
Ay! soon the swallows will be flying south,
The wind wheel north to gather in the snow,

Even the roses spilt on youth's red mouth
Will soon blow down the road all roses go.

August (1914)

She'll come at dusky first of day,
White over yellow harvest's song.
Upon her dewy rainbow way
She shall be beautiful and strong.
The lidless eye of noon shall spray
Tan on her ankles in the hay,
Shall kiss her brown the whole day long.

I'll know her in the windrows, tall
Above the crickets of the hay.
I'll know her when her odd eyes fall,
One May-blue, one November-grey.
I'll watch her from the red barn wall
Take down her rusty scythe, and call,
And I will follow her away.

Thomas MacDonagh (1916)

He shall not hear the bittern cry
In the wild sky, where he is lain,
Nor voices of the sweeter birds
Above the wailing of the rain.

Nor shall he know when loud March blows
Through slanting snows her fanfare shrill,
Blowing to flame the golden cup
Of many an upset daffodil.

But when the Dark Cow leaves the moor,
And pastures poor with greedy weeds,
Perhaps he'll hear her low at morn
Lifting her horn in pleasant meads.

The Wedding Morning (1916)

Spread the feast, and let there be
Such music heard as best beseems
A king's son coming from the sea
To wed a maiden of the streams.

Poets, pale for long ago,
Bring sweet sounds from rock and flood,
You by echo's accent know
Where the water is and wood.

Harpers whom the moths of Time
Bent and wrinkled dusty brown,
Her chains are falling with a chime,
Sweet as bells in Heaven town.

But, harpers, leave your harps aside,
And, poets, leave awhile your dreams.
The storm has come upon the tide
And Cathleen weeps among her streams.

The Blackbirds (1916)

I heard the Poor Old Woman say:
'At break of day the fowler came,
And took my blackbirds from their songs
Who loved me well thro' shame and blame.

No more from lovely distances
Their songs shall bless me mile by mile,
Nor to white Ashbourne call me down
To wear my crown another while.

With bended flowers the angels mark
For the skylark the place they lie,
From there its little family
Shall dip their wings first in the sky.

And when the first surprise of flight
Sweet songs excite, from the far dawn
Shall there come blackbirds loud with love,
Sweet echoes of the singers gone.

But in the lonely hush of eve
Weeping I grieve the silent bills.'
I heard the Poor Old Woman say
In Derry of the little hills.

The Herons (1916)

As I was climbing Ardán Mór
From the shore of Sheelin lake
I met the herons coming down
Before the water's wake.

And they were talking in their flight
Of dreamy ways the herons go
When all the hills are withered up
Nor any waters flow.

F. R. HIGGINS
(1896–1941)

Father and Son (1923)

Only last week, walking the hushed fields
Of our most lovely Meath, now thinned by November,
I came to where the road from Laracor leads
To the Boyne river—that seemed more lake than river,
Stretched in uneasy light and stript of reeds.

And walking longside an old weir
Of my people's, where nothing stirs—only the shadowed
Leaden flight of a heron up the lean air—

I went unmanly with grief, knowing how my father,
Happy though captive in years, walked last with me there.

Yes, happy in Meath with me for a day
He walked, taking stock of herds hid in their own breathing;
And naming colts, gusty as wind, once steered by his hand,
Lightnings winked in the eyes that were half shy in greeting
Old friends—the wild blades, when he gallivanted the land.

For that proud, wayward man now my heart breaks—
Breaks for that man whose mind was a secret eyrie,
Whose kind hand was sole signet of his race,
Who curbed me, scorned my green ways, yet increasingly loved me
Till Death drew its grey blind down his face.

And yet I am pleased that even my reckless ways
Are living shades of his rich calms and passions—
Witnesses for him and for those faint namesakes
With whom now he is one, under yew branches,
Yes, one in a graven silence no bird breaks.

To My Blackthorn Stick (1923)

When sap ebbed low and your green days were over—
Hedging a gap to rugged land,
Bare skinned and straight you were; and there I broke you
To champion my right hand.

Well shod in bronze and lithe with hillside breeding,
Yet, like a snarl, you dogged my side,
Mailed in your tridents and flaunting out the fierceness
That bristled through your hide.

So armed as one, have we not shared each journey
On noiseless path or road of stone;
O exiled brother of the flowering sloe tree,
Your past ways are my own.

Lonesome, like me, and song-bred on Mount Nephin,
You, also, found that in your might
You broke in bloom before the time of leafing
And shocked a world with light.

But you grew shy,—eyed through by glowering twilights—
Sharing the still of night's grey brew,
Secret and shy, while things unseen were sighing
Their grass tunes under you.

Manured with earth's own sweat you stretched in saplings;
Seasoned, you cored your fruit with stone;
Then stript in fight, your strength came out of wrestling
All winds by winter blown.

I took that strength: my axe blow was your trumpet,
You rose from earth, god-cleaned and strong;
And here, as in green days you were the perch,
You're now the prop of song.

PATRICK KAVANAGH
(1904–1967)

To a Blackbird (1930)

O pagan poet you
And I are one
In this—we lose our god
At set of sun.

And we are kindred when
The hill wind shakes
Sweet song like blossoms on
The calm green lakes.

We dream while Earth's sad children
Go slowly by

Pleading for our conversion
With the Most High.

Shancoduff (1934)

My black hills have never seen the sun rising,
Eternally they look north towards Armagh.
Lot's wife would not be salt if she had been
Incurious as my black hills that are happy
When dawn whitens Glassdrummond chapel.

My hills hoard the bright shillings of March
While the sun searches in every pocket.
They are my Alps and I have climbed the Matterhorn
With a sheaf of hay for three perishing calves
In the field under the Big Forth of Rocksavage.

The sleety winds fondle the rushy beards of Shancoduff
While the cattle-drovers sheltering in the Featherna Bush
Look up and say: 'Who owns them hungry hills
That the water-hen and snipe must have forsaken?
A poet? Then by heavens he must be poor.'
I hear and is my heart not badly shaken?

Monaghan 1934

Inniskeen Road: July Evening (1935)

The bicycles go by in twos and threes—
There's a dance in Billy Brennan's* barn tonight,
And there's the half-talk code of mysteries
And the wink-and-elbow language of delight.
Half-past eight and there is not a spot
Upon a mile of road, no shadow thrown
That might turn out a man or woman, not
A footfall tapping secrecies of stone.

I have what every poet hates in spite
Of all the solemn talk of contemplation.
Oh, Alexander Selkirk* knew the plight
Of being king and government and nation.
A road, a mile of kingdom, I am king
Of banks and stones and every blooming thing.

JOHN HEWITT
(1907–1987)

To a Modern Irish Poet (1927)

You drowsed my senses by your misty kings,
 dream-drunken ladies languid as the noon,
until I deemed no other songbird sings,
 save nightingale in twilight to the moon.

You came with your strange, wistful, trembling verse,
 beguiled me for a while in quaint deceit;
and I forgot th'oppressor's blow and curse,
 the muffled tread of workless in the street.

A silver trumpet, or a golden thong,
 these are the harmonies loved of thy muse.
'Tis better done to beat from bitter wrong
 a flaming slogan's challenge, fit for use!

Easter Tuesday (1931)

I carefully let Easter pass this year
 Without a thought of Calvary's bare hill,
 being intent on bird and daffodil,
and April skies with one cold star and clear,
I watched the red-tipped daisies peep and peer
 out of the fresh thick grass, and skylarks fill
 the air with fluttered chorusing until
I felt myself a similar sonneteer.

But yesterday a man went up the street
 singing a rebel song of Easter Week.
  and the old unquiet woke within my head.
I saw again the blood bedabbled feet,
 and all the horror that I dared not speak,
  and knew that Christ and Connolly were dead.

Mourne Mountains (1937)

But these are not my hills, they are too high:
they have not been, since ice ground slowly over,
abased to any force beneath the sky;
they are too harsh for me to be their lover.
The broad stone winking with the flattened stream,
the sheer cliff barren and the timeless peak:
not even sharp against the sun's last gleam
can I find comfort in them I may speak:
for they are from a world beyond my reach,
not the warm human world of broken earth,
the hand-chipped flints along the gravel beach,
the tilted dolmen and the baked clay hearth.
I do not fear a bare land but a high:
the curlew-whistling moors have no affright:
the bog-brown trout stream twisting hurriedly
can flash no terror in the failing light.
But the cold summit harried by the rain,
smothered in cloud or bannered far with snow,
has all the high sublimities of pain
I leave for braver hearts than mine to know.

LOUIS MACNEICE
(1907–1963)

Belfast (1931)

The hard cold fire of the northerner
Frozen into his blood from the fire in his basalt*
Glares from behind the mica* of his eyes
And the salt carrion water* brings him wealth.

Down there at the end of the melancholy lough
Against the lurid sky over the stained water
Where hammers clang murderously on the girders
Like crucifixes the gantries stand.

And in the marble stores rubber gloves like polyps
Cluster; celluloid, painted ware, glaring
Metal patents, parchment lampshades, harsh
Attempts at buyable beauty.

In the porch of the chapel before the garish Virgin
A shawled factory-woman as if shipwrecked there
Lies a bunch of limbs glimpsed in the cave of gloom
By us who walk in the street so buoyantly and glib.

Over which country of cowled and haunted faces
The sun goes down with a banging of Orange drums*
While the male kind murders each its woman
To whose prayer for oblivion answers no Madonna.

Snow (1935)

The room was suddenly rich and the great bay-window was
Spawning snow and pink roses against it
Soundlessly collateral and incompatible:
World is suddener than we fancy it.

World is crazier and more of it than we think,
Incorrigibly plural. I peel and portion
A tangerine and spit the pips and feel
The drunkenness of things being various.

And the fire flames with a bubbling sound for world
Is more spiteful and gay than one supposes—
On the tongue on the eyes on the ears in the palms of
    one's hands—
There is more than glass between the snow and the huge roses.

Carrickfergus (1937)

I was born in Belfast between the mountain and the gantries
    To the hooting of lost sirens and the clang of trams:
Thence to Smoky Carrick in County Antrim
    Where the bottle-neck harbour collects the mud which jams

The little boats beneath the Norman castle,
    The pier shining with lumps of crystal salt;
The Scotch Quarter was a line of residential houses
    But the Irish Quarter was a slum for the blind and halt.

The brook ran yellow from the factory stinking of chlorine,
    The yarn-mill called its funeral cry at noon;
Our lights looked over the lough to the lights of Bangor
    Under the peacock aura of a drowning moon.

The Norman walled this town against the country
    To stop his ears to the yelping of his slave
And built a church in the form of a cross but denoting
    The list of Christ on the cross* in the angle of the nave.

I was the rector's son, born to the anglican order,
    Banned for ever from the candles of the Irish poor;
The Chichesters knelt in marble* at the end of a transept
    With ruffs about their necks, their portion sure.

The war came and a huge camp of soldiers
   Grew from the ground in sight of our house with long
Dummies hanging from gibbets for bayonet practice
   And the sentry's challenge echoing all day long;

A Yorkshire terrier ran in and out by the gate-lodge
   Barred to civilians, yapping as if taking affront:
Marching at ease and singing 'Who Killed Cock Robin?'
   The troops* went out by the lodge and off to the Front.

The steamer was camouflaged that took me to England—
   Sweat and khaki in the Carlisle train;
I thought that the war would last for ever and sugar
   Be always rationed and that never again

Would the weekly papers not have photos of sandbags
   And my governess not make bandages from moss
And people not have maps above the fireplace
   With flags on pins moving across and across—

Across the hawthorn hedge the noise of bugles,
   Flares across the night,
Somewhere on the lough was a prison ship for Germans,
   A cage across their sight.

I went to school in Dorset,* the world of parents
   Contracted into a puppet world of sons
Far from the mill girls, the smell of porter, the salt-mines
   And the soldiers with their guns.

Autumn Journal (1939)

XVI

   Nightmare leaves fatigue:
     We envy men of action
  Who sleep and wake, murder and intrigue

Without being doubtful, without being haunted.
And I envy the intransigence of my own
     Countrymen who shoot to kill and never
See the victim's face become their own
     Or find his motive sabotage their motives.
So reading the memoirs of Maud Gonne,*
     Daughter of an English mother and a soldier father,
I note how a single purpose can be founded on
     A jumble of opposites:
Dublin Castle, the vice-regal ball,
     The embassies of Europe,
Hatred scribbled on a wall,
     Gaols and revolvers.
And I remember, when I was little, the fear
     Bandied among the servants
That Casement* would land at the pier
     With a sword and a horde of rebels;
And how we used to expect, at a later date,
     When the wind blew from the west, the noise of shooting
Starting in the evening at eight
     In Belfast in the York Street district;
And the voodoo of the Orange bands*
     Drawing an iron net through darkest Ulster,
Flailing the limbo lands—
     The linen mills, the long wet grass, the ragged hawthorn.
And one read black where the other read white, his hope
     The other man's damnation:
Up the Rebels, To Hell with the Pope,
     And God Save—as you prefer—the King or Ireland.
The land of scholars and saints:
     Scholars and saints my eye, the land of ambush,
Purblind manifestoes, never-ending complaints,
     The born martyr and the gallant ninny;
The grocer drunk with the drum,
     The land-owner shot in his bed, the angry voices
Piercing the broken fanlight in the slum,
     The shawled woman weeping at the garish altar.
Kathaleen ni Houlihan!* Why
     Must a country, like a ship or a car, be always female,

Mother or sweetheart? A woman passing by,
 We did but see her passing.
Passing like a patch of sun on the rainy hill
 And yet we love her for ever and hate our neighbour
And each one in his will
 Binds his heirs to continuance of hatred.
Drums on the haycock, drums on the harvest, black
 Drums in the night shaking the windows:
King William is riding his white horse back
 To the Boyne* on a banner.
Thousands of banners, thousands of white
 Horses, thousands of Williams
Waving thousands of swords and ready to fight
 Till the blue sea turns to orange.
Such was my country and I thought I was well
 Out of it, educated and domiciled in England,
Though yet her name keeps ringing like a bell
 In an under-water belfry.
Why do we like being Irish? Partly because
 It gives us a hold on the sentimental English
As members of a world that never was,
 Baptised with fairy water;
And partly because Ireland is small enough
 To be still thought of with a family feeling,
And because the waves are rough
 That split her from a more commercial culture;
And because one feels that here at least one can
 Do local work which is not at the world's mercy
And that on this tiny stage with luck a man
 Might see the end of one particular action.
It is self-deception of course;
 There is no immunity in this island either;
A cart that is drawn by somebody else's horse
 And carrying goods to somebody else's market.
The bombs in the turnip sack, the sniper from the roof,
 Griffith, Connolly, Collins,* where have they brought us?
Ourselves alone!* Let the round tower stand aloof
 In a world of bursting mortar!
Let the school-children fumble their sums

In a half-dead language;
Let the censor be busy on the books; pull down the Georgian slums;
 Let the games be played in Gaelic.
Let them grow beet-sugar; let them build
 A factory in every hamlet;
Let them pigeon-hole the souls of the killed
 Into sheep and goats, patriots and traitors.
And the North, where I was a boy,
 Is still the North, veneered with the grime of Glasgow,
Thousands of men whom nobody will employ
 Standing at the corners, coughing.
And the street-children play on the wet
 Pavement—hopscotch or marbles;
And each rich family boasts a sagging tennis-net
 On a spongy lawn beside a dripping shrubbery.
The smoking chimneys hint
 At prosperity round the corner
But they make their Ulster linen from foreign lint
 And the money that comes in goes out to make more money.
A city built upon mud;
 A culture built upon profit;
Free speech nipped in the bud,
 The minority always guilty.
Why should I want to go back
 To you, Ireland, my Ireland*
The blots on the page are so black
 That they cannot be covered with shamrock.
I hate your grandiose airs,
 Your sob-stuff, your laugh and your swagger,
Your assumption that everyone cares
 Who is the king of your castle.
Castles are out of date,
 The tide flows round the children's sandy fancy;
Put up what flag you like, it is too late
 To save your soul with bunting.
Odi atque amo:
 Shall we cut this name on trees with a rusty dagger?
Her mountains are still blue, her rivers flow
 Bubbling over the boulders.

She is both a bore and a bitch;
    Better close the horizon,
Send her no more fantasy, no more longings which
    Are under a fatal tariff.
For common sense is the vogue
    And she gives her children neither sense nor money
Who slouch around the world with a gesture and a brogue
    And a faggot of useless memories.

6. DRAMA

OSCAR WILDE
(1854–1900)

from *The Importance of Being Earnest* (1895)

FIRST ACT

SCENE: *Morning-room in* ALGERNON'*s flat in Half Moon Street. The room is luxuriously and artistically furnished. The sound of a piano is heard in the adjoining room.*

LANE *is arranging afternoon tea on the table, and after the music has ceased,* ALGERNON *enters.*

Algernon. Did you hear what I was playing, Lane?

Lane. I didn't think it polite to listen, sir.

Algernon. I'm sorry for that, for your sake. I don't play accurately—anyone can play accurately—but I play with wonderful expression. As far as the piano is concerned, sentiment is my forte. I keep science for Life.

Lane. Yes, sir.

Algernon. And, speaking of the science of Life, have you got the cucumber sandwiches cut for Lady Bracknell?

Lane. Yes, sir. (*Hands them on a salver.*)

Algernon (*inspects them, takes two, and sits down on the sofa*). Oh! . . . by the way, Lane, I see from your book that on Thursday night, when Lord Shoreham and Mr Worthing were dining with me, eight bottles of champagne are entered as having been consumed.

Lane. Yes, sir; eight bottles and a pint.

Algernon. Why is it that at a bachelor's establishment the servants invariably drink the champagne? I ask merely for information.

Lane. I attribute it to the superior quality of the wine, sir. I have often observed that in married households the champagne is rarely of a first-rate brand.

Algernon. Good Heavens! Is marriage so demoralizing as that?

Lane. I believe it *is* a very pleasant state, sir. I have had very little experience of it myself up to the present. I have only been married once. That was in consequence of a misunderstanding between myself and a young person.

Algernon (*languidly*). I don't know that I am much interested in your family life, Lane.

Lane. No, sir; it is not a very interesting subject. I never think of it myself.

Algernon. Very natural, I am sure. That will do, Lane, thank you.

Lane. Thank you, sir.

[LANE *goes out.*

Algernon. Lane's views on marriage seem somewhat lax. Really, if the lower orders don't set us a good example, what on earth is the use of them? They seem, as a class, to have absolutely no sense of moral responsibility.

Enter LANE.

Lane. Mr Ernest Worthing.

Enter JACK.

[LANE *goes out.*

Algernon. How are you, my dear Ernest? What brings you up to town?

Jack. Oh, pleasure, pleasure! What else should bring one anywhere? Eating as usual, I see, Algy!

Algernon (*stiffly*). I believe it is customary in good society to take some slight refreshment at five o'clock. Where have you been since last Thursday?

Jack (*sitting down on the sofa*). In the country.

Algernon. What on earth do you do there?

Jack (*pulling off his gloves*). When one is in town one amuses oneself. When one is in the country one amuses other people. It is excessively boring.

Algernon. And who are the people you amuse?

Jack (*airily*). Oh, neighbours, neighbours.

Algernon. Got nice neighbours in your part of Shropshire?

Jack. Perfectly horrid! Never speak to one of them.

Algernon. How immensely you must amuse them! (*Goes over and takes sandwich.*) By the way, Shropshire is your county, is it not?

Jack. Eh? Shropshire? Yes, of course. Hallo! Why all these cups? Why cucumber sandwiches? Why such reckless extravagance in one so young? Who is coming to tea?

Algernon. Oh! merely Aunt Augusta and Gwendolen.

Jack. How perfectly delightful!

Algernon. Yes, that is all very well; but I am afraid Aunt Augusta won't quite approve of your being here.

Jack. May I ask why?

Algernon. My dear fellow, the way you flirt with Gwendolen is perfectly disgraceful. It is almost as bad as the way Gwendolen flirts with you.

Jack. I am in love with Gwendolen. I have come up to town expressly to propose to her.

Algernon. I thought you had come up for pleasure? . . . I call that business. -

Jack. How utterly unromantic you are!

Algernon. I really don't see anything romantic in proposing. It is very romantic to be in love. But there is nothing romantic about a definite proposal. Why, one may be accepted. One usually is, I believe. Then the excitement is all over. The very essence of romance is uncertainty. If ever I get married, I'll certainly try to forget the fact.

Jack. I have no doubt about that, dear Algy. The Divorce Court* was specially invented for people whose memories are so curiously constituted.

Algernon. Oh! there is no use speculating on that subject. Divorces are made in Heaven—(JACK *puts out his hand to take a sandwich.* ALGERNON *at once interferes.*) Please don't touch the cucumber sandwiches. They are ordered specially for Aunt Augusta. (*Takes one and eats it.*)

Jack. Well, you have been eating them all the time.

Algernon. That is quite a different matter. She is my aunt. (*Takes plate from below.*) Have some bread and butter. The bread and butter is for Gwendolen. Gwendolen is devoted to bread and butter.

Jack (*advancing to table and helping himself*). And very good bread and butter it is too.

Algernon. Well, my dear fellow, you need not eat as if you were going to eat it all. You behave as if you were married to her already. You are not married to her already, and I don't think you ever will be.

Jack. Why on earth do you say that?

Algernon. Well, in the first place girls never marry the men they flirt with. Girls don't think it right.

Jack. Oh, that is nonsense!

Algernon. It isn't. It is a great truth. It accounts for the extraordinary number of bachelors that one sees all over the place. In the second place, I don't give my consent.

Jack. Your consent!

Algernon. My dear fellow, Gwendolen is my first cousin. And before I allow you to marry her, you will have to clear up the whole question of Cecily. (*Rings bell.*)

Jack. Cecily! What on earth do you mean? What do you mean, Algy, by Cecily? I don't know anyone of the name of Cecily.

Enter LANE.

Algernon. Bring me that cigarette case Mr Worthing left in the smoking-room the last time he dined here.

Lane. Yes, sir.

[LANE *goes out.*

Jack. Do you mean to say you have had my cigarette case all this time? I wish to goodness you had let me know. I have been writing frantic letters to Scotland Yard* about it. I was very nearly offering a large reward.

Algernon. Well, I wish you would offer one. I happen to be more than usually hard up.

Jack. There is no good offering a large reward now that the thing is found.

Enter LANE *with the cigarette case on a salver.* ALGERNON *takes it at once.* LANE *goes out.*

Algernon. I think that is rather mean of you, Ernest, I must say. (*Opens case and examines it.*) However, it makes no matter, for, now that I look at the inscription inside, I find that the thing isn't yours after all.

Jack. Of course it's mine. (*Moving to him.*) You have seen me with it a hundred times, and you have no right whatsoever to read what is written inside. It is a very ungentlemanly thing to read a private cigarette case.

Algernon. Oh! it is absurd to have a hard-and-fast rule about what one should read and what one shouldn't. More than half of modern culture depends on what one shouldn't read.

Jack. I am quite aware of the fact, and I don't propose to discuss modern culture. It isn't the sort of thing one should talk of in private. I simply want my cigarette case back.

Algernon. Yes; but this isn't your cigarette case. This cigarette case is a present from someone of the name of Cecily, and you said you didn't know anyone of that name.

Jack. Well, if you want to know, Cecily happens to be my aunt.

Algernon. Your aunt!

Jack. Yes. Charming old lady she is, too. Lives at Tunbridge Wells. Just give it back to me, Algy.

Algernon (*retreating to back of sofa*). But why does she call herself little Cecily if she is your aunt and lives at Tunbridge Wells? (*Reading.*) 'From little Cecily with her fondest love'.

Jack (*moving to sofa and kneeling upon it*). My dear fellow, what on earth is there in that? Some aunts are tall, some aunts are not tall. That is a matter that surely an aunt may be allowed to decide for herself. You seem to think that every aunt should be exactly like your aunt! That is absurd! For Heaven's sake give me back my cigarette case. (*Follows* ALGERNON *round the room.*)

Algernon. Yes. But why does your aunt call you her uncle? 'From little Cecily, with her fondest love to her dear Uncle Jack.' There is no objection, I admit, to an aunt being a small aunt, but why an aunt, no matter what her size may be, should call her own nephew her uncle, I can't quite make out. Besides, your name isn't Jack at all; it is Ernest.

Jack. It isn't Ernest; it's Jack.

Algernon. You have always told me it was Ernest. I have introduced you to everyone as Ernest. You answer to the name of Ernest. You look as if your name was Ernest. You are the most earnest looking person I ever saw in my life. It is perfectly absurd your saying that your name isn't Ernest. It's on your cards. Here is one of them. (*Taking it from case.*) 'Mr Ernest Worthing, B. 4, The Albany.' I'll keep this as a proof that your name is Ernest if ever you attempt to deny it to me, or to Gwendolen, or to anyone else. (*Puts the card in his pocket.*)

Jack. Well, my name is Ernest in town and Jack in the country, and the cigarette case was given to me in the country.

Algernon. Yes, but that does not account for the fact that your small Aunt Cecily, who lives at Tunbridge Wells, calls you her dear uncle. Come, old boy, you had much better have the thing out at once.

Jack. My dear Algy, you talk exactly as if you were a dentist. It is very vulgar to talk like a dentist when one isn't a dentist. It produces a false impression.

Algernon. Well, that is exactly what dentists always do. Now, go on! Tell me the whole thing. I may mention that I have always suspected you of being a confirmed and secret Bunburyist, and I am quite sure of it now.

Jack. Bunburyist? What on earth do you mean by a Bunburyist?

Algernon. I'll reveal to you the meaning of that incomparable expression as soon as you are kind enough to inform me why you are Ernest in town and Jack in the country.

Jack. Well, produce my cigarette case first.

Algernon. Here it is. (*Hands cigarette case.*) Now produce your explanation, and pray make it improbable. (*Sits on sofa.*)

Jack. My dear fellow, there is nothing improbable about my explanation at all. In fact it's perfectly ordinary. Old Mr Thomas Cardew, who adopted me when I was a little boy, made me in his will guardian to his grand-daughter, Miss Cecily Cardew. Cecily who addresses me as her uncle from motives of respect that you could not possibly appreciate, lives at my place in the country under the charge of her admirable governess, Miss Prism.

Algernon. Where is that place in the country, by the way?

Jack. That is nothing to you, dear boy. You are not going to be invited. . . . I may tell you candidly that the place is not in Shropshire.

Algernon. I suspected that, my dear fellow! I have Bunburyed all over Shropshire on two separate occasions. Now, go on. Why are you Ernest in town and Jack in the country?

Jack. My dear Algy, I don't know whether you will be able to understand my real motives. You are hardly serious enough. When one is placed in the position of guardian, one has to adopt a very high moral tone on all subjects. It's one's duty to do so. And as a high moral tone can hardly be said to conduce very much to either one's health or one's happiness, in order to get up to town I have always pretended to have a younger brother of the name of Ernest, who lives in the Albany, and gets into the most dreadful scrapes. That, my dear Algy, is the whole truth pure and simple.

Algernon. The truth is rarely pure and never simple. Modern life would be very tedious if it were either, and modern literature a complete impossibility!

Jack. That wouldn't be at all a bad thing.

Algernon. Literary criticism is not your forte, my dear fellow. Don't try it. You should leave that to people who haven't been at a University. They do it so well in the daily papers. What you really are is a Bunburyist. I was quite right in saying you were a Bunburyist. You are one of the most advanced Bunburyists I know.

Jack. What on earth do you mean?

Algernon. You have invented a very useful younger brother called Ernest, in order that you may be able to come up to town as often as you like. I have invented an invaluable permanent invalid called Bunbury, in order that I may be able to go down into the country whenever I choose. Bunbury is perfectly invaluable. If it wasn't for Bunbury's extraordinary bad health, for instance, I wouldn't be able to dine with you at Willis's* tonight, for I have been really engaged to Aunt Augusta for more than a week.

Jack. I haven't asked you to dine with me anywhere tonight.

Algernon. I know. You are absurdly careless about sending out invitations. It is very foolish of you. Nothing annoys people so much as not receiving invitations.

Jack. You had much better dine with your Aunt Augusta.

Algernon. I haven't the smallest intention of doing anything of the kind. To begin with, I dined there on Monday, and once a week is quite enough to dine with one's own relations. In the second place, whenever I do dine there I am always treated as a member of the family, and sent down* with either no woman at all, or two. In the third place, I know perfectly well whom she will place me next to, tonight. She will place me next Mary Farquhar, who always flirts with her own husband across the dinner-table. That is not very pleasant. Indeed, it is not even decent . . . and that sort of thing is enormously on the increase. The amount of women in London who flirt with their own husbands is perfectly scandalous. It looks so bad. It is simply washing one's clean linen in public. Besides, now that I know you to be a confirmed Bunburyist I naturally want to talk to you about Bunburying. I want to tell you the rules.

Jack. I'm not a Bunburyist at all. If Gwendolen accepts me, I am going to kill my brother, indeed I think I'll kill him in any case. Cecily is a little too much interested in him. It is rather a bore. So I am going to get rid of Ernest. And I strongly advise you to do the same with Mr . . . with your invalid friend who has the absurd name.

Algernon. Nothing will induce me to part with Bunbury, and if you ever get married, which seems to me extremely problematic, you will be very glad to know Bunbury. A man who marries without knowing Bunbury has a very tedious time of it.

Jack. That is nonsense. If I marry a charming girl like Gwendolen, and she is the only girl I ever saw in my life that I would marry, I certainly won't want to know Bunbury.

Algernon. Then your wife will. You don't seem to realize, that in married life three is company and two is none.

Jack (*sententiously*). That, my dear young friend, is the theory that the corrupt French Drama has been propounding for the last fifty years.

Algernon. Yes; and that the happy English home has proved in half the time.

Jack. For heaven's sake, don't try to be cynical. It's perfectly easy to be cynical.

Algernon. My dear fellow, it isn't easy to be anything nowadays. There's such a lot of beastly competition about. (*The sound of an electric bell is heard.*) Ah! that must be Aunt Augusta. Only relatives, or creditors, ever ring in that Wagnerian manner.* Now, if I get her out of the way for ten minutes, so that you can have an opportunity for proposing to Gwendolen, may I dine with you tonight at Willis's?

Jack. I suppose so, if you want to.

Algernon. Yes, but you must be serious about it. I hate people who are not serious about meals. It is so shallow of them.

Enter LANE.

Lane. Lady Bracknell and Miss Fairfax.

ALGERNON *goes forward to meet them. Enter* LADY BRACKNELL *and* GWENDOLEN.

Lady Bracknell. Good afternoon, dear Algernon, I hope you are behaving very well.

Algernon. I'm feeling very well, Aunt Augusta.

Lady Bracknell. That's not quite the same thing. In fact the two things rarely go together. (*Sees* JACK *and bows to him with icy coldness.*)

Algernon (*to* GWENDOLEN). Dear me, you are smart!

Gwendolen. I am always smart! Aren't I, Mr Worthing?

Jack. You're quite perfect, Miss Fairfax.

Gwendolen. Oh! I hope I am not that. It would leave no room for developments, and I intend to develop in many directions. (GWENDOLEN *and* JACK *sit down together in the corner.*)

Lady Bracknell. I'm sorry if we are a little late, Algernon, but I was obliged to call on dear Lady Harbury. I hadn't been there since her poor husband's death. I never saw a woman so altered; she looks quite twenty years younger. And now I'll have a cup of tea, and one of those nice cucumber sandwiches you promised me.

Algernon. Certainly, Aunt Augusta. (*Goes over to tea-table.*)

Lady Bracknell. Won't you come and sit here, Gwendolen?

Gwendolen. Thanks, mamma, I'm quite comfortable where I am.

Algernon (*picking up empty plate in horror*). Good heavens! Lane! Why are there no cucumber sandwiches? I ordered them specially.

Lane (*gravely*). There were no cucumbers in the market this morning, sir. I went down twice.

Algernon. No cucumbers!

Lane. No, sir. Not even for ready money.

Algernon. That will do, Lane, thank you.

Lane. Thank you, sir.

[*Goes out.*

W. B. YEATS AND AUGUSTA GREGORY
(1865–1939) (1852–1932)

Cathleen ni Houlihan (1902)

PERSONS IN THE PLAY

Peter Gillane

Michael Gillane, his son, going to
  be married

Patrick Gillane, a lad of twelve,
  Michael's brother

Bridget Gillane, Peter's wife

Delia Cahel, engaged to Michael

The Poor Old Woman

Neighbours

Interior of a cottage close to Killala, in 1798. BRIDGET *is standing at a table undoing a parcel.* PETER *is sitting at one side of the fire,* PATRICK *at the other.*

Peter. What is that sound I hear?

Patrick. I don't hear anything. (*He listens.*) I hear it now. It's like cheering. (*He goes to the window and looks out.*) I wonder what they are cheering about. I don't see anybody.

Peter. It might be a hurling.*

Patrick. There's no hurling to-day. It must be down in the town the cheering is.

Bridget. I suppose the boys must be having some sport of their own. Come over here, Peter, and look at Michael's wedding clothes.

Peter (*shifts his chair to table*). Those are grand clothes, indeed.

Bridget. You hadn't clothes like that when you married me, and no coat to put on of a Sunday more than any other day.

Peter. That is true, indeed. We never thought a son of our own would be wearing a suit of that sort for his wedding, or have so good a place to bring a wife to.

Patrick (*who is still at the window*). There's an old woman coming down the road. I don't know is it here she is coming.

Bridget. It will be a neighbour coming to hear about Michael's wedding. Can you see who it is?

Patrick. I think it is a stranger, but she's not coming to the house. She's turned into the gap that goes down where Maurteen and his sons are shearing sheep. (*He turns towards* BRIDGET.) Do you remember what Winny of the Cross Roads was saying the other night about the strange woman that goes through the country whatever time there's war or trouble coming?

Bridget. Don't be bothering us about Winny's talk, but go and open the door for your brother. I hear him coming up the path.

Peter. I hope he has brought Delia's fortune with him safe, for fear the people might go back on the bargain and I after making it. Trouble enough I had making it.

PATRICK *opens the door and* MICHAEL *comes in.*

Bridget. What kept you, Michael? We were looking out for you this long time.

Michael. I went round by the priest's house to bid him be ready to marry us to-morrow.

Bridget. Did he say anything?

Michael. He said it was a very nice match, and that he was never better pleased to marry any two in his parish than myself and Delia Cahel.

Peter. Have you got the fortune, Michael?

Michael. Here it is.

MICHAEL *puts bag on table and goes over and leans against chimney-jamb.* BRIDGET, *who has been all this time examining the clothes, pulling the seams and trying the lining of the pockets, etc., puts the clothes on the dresser.*

Peter (getting up and taking the bag in his hand and turning out the money). Yes, I made the bargain well for you, Michael. Old John Cahel would sooner have kept a share of this a while longer. 'Let me keep the half of it until the first boy is born,' says he. 'You will not,' says I. 'Whether there is or is not a boy, the whole hundred pounds must be in Michael's hands before he brings your daughter to the house.' The wife spoke to him then, and he gave in at the end.

Bridget. You seem well pleased to be handling the money, Peter.

Peter. Indeed, I wish I had had the luck to get a hundred pounds, or twenty pounds itself, with the wife I married.

Bridget. Well, if I didn't bring much I didn't get much. What had you the day I married you but a flock of hens and you feeding them, and a few lambs and you driving them to the market at Ballina?* (*She is vexed and bangs a jug on the dresser.*) If I brought no fortune I worked it out in my bones, laying down the baby, Michael that is standing there now, on a stook of straw, while I dug the potatoes, and never asking big dresses or anything but to be working.

Peter. That is true, indeed.

[*He pats her arm.*

Bridget. Leave me alone now till I ready the house for the woman that is to come into it.

Peter. You are the best woman in Ireland, but money is good, too. (*He begins handling the money again and sits down.*) I never thought to see so much money within my four walls. We can do great things now we have it. We can take the ten acres of land we have the chance of since Jamsie Dempsey died, and stock it. We will go to the fair at Ballina to buy the stock. Did Delia ask any of the money for her own use, Michael?

Michael. She did not, indeed. She did not seem to take much notice of it, or to look at it at all.

Bridget. That's no wonder. Why would she look at it when she had yourself to look at, a fine, strong young man? It is proud she must be to get you; a good steady boy that will make use of the money, and not be running through it or spending it on drink like another.

Peter. It's likely Michael himself was not thinking much of the fortune either, but of what sort the girl was to look at.

Michael (*coming over towards the table*). Well, you would like a nice comely girl to be beside you, and to go walking with you. The fortune only lasts for a while, but the woman will be there always.

Patrick (*turning round from the window*). They are cheering again down in the town. Maybe they are landing horses from Enniscrone.* They do be cheering when the horses take the water well.

Michael. There are no horses in it. Where would they be going and no fair at hand? Go down to the town, Patrick, and see what is going on.

Patrick (*opens the door to go out, but stops for a moment on the threshold*). Will Delia remember, do you think, to bring the greyhound pup she promised me when she would be coming to the house?

Michael. She will surely.

[PATRICK *goes out, leaving the door open.*

Peter. It will be Patrick's turn next to be looking for a fortune, but he won't find it so easy to get it and he with no place of his own.

Bridget. I do be thinking sometimes, now things are going so well with us, and the Cahels such a good back to us in the district, and Delia's own uncle a priest, we might be put in the way of making Patrick a priest some day, and he so good at his books.

Peter. Time enough, time enough. You have always your head full of plans, Bridget.

Bridget. We will be well able to give him learning, and not to send him tramping the country like a poor scholar that lives on charity.

Michael. They're not done cheering yet.

He goes over to the door and stands there for a moment, putting up his hand to shade his eyes.

Bridget. Do you see anything?

Michael. I see an old woman coming up the path.

Bridget. Who is it, I wonder? It must be the strange woman Patrick saw a while ago.

Michael. I don't think it's one of the neighbours anyway, but she has her cloak over her face.

Bridget. It might be some poor woman heard we were making ready for the wedding and came to look for her share.

Peter. I may as well put the money out of sight. There is no use leaving it out for every stranger to look at.

He goes over to a large box in the corner, opens it and puts the bag in and fumbles at the lock.

Michael. There she is, father! (*An* OLD WOMAN *passes the window slowly. She looks at* MICHAEL *as she passes.*) I'd sooner a stranger not to come to the house the night before my wedding.

Bridget. Open the door, Michael; don't keep the poor woman waiting.

The OLD WOMAN *comes in.* MICHAEL *stands aside to make way for her.*

Old Woman. God save all here!

Peter. God save you kindly!

Old Woman. You have good shelter here.

Peter. You are welcome to whatever shelter we have.

Bridget. Sit down there by the fire and welcome.

Old Woman (*warming her hands*). There is a hard wind outside.

MICHAEL *watches her curiously from the door.* PETER *comes over to the table.*

Peter. Have you travelled far to-day?

Old Woman. I have travelled far, very far; there are few have travelled so far as myself, and there's many a one that doesn't make me welcome. There was one that had strong sons I thought were friends of mine, but they were shearing their sheep, and they wouldn't listen to me.

Peter. It's a pity indeed for any person to have no place of their own.

Old Woman. That's true for you indeed, and it's long I'm on the roads since I first went wandering.

Bridget. It is a wonder you are not worn out with so much wandering.

Old Woman. Sometimes my feet are tired and my hands are quiet, but there is no quiet in my heart. When the people see me quiet, they think old age has come on me and that all the stir has gone out of me. But when the trouble is on me I must be talking to my friends.

Bridget. What was it put you wandering?

Old Woman. Too many strangers in the house.*

Bridget. Indeed you look as if you'd had your share of trouble.

Old Woman. I have had trouble indeed.

Bridget. What was it put the trouble on you?

Old Woman. My land that was taken from me.

Peter. Was it much land they took from you?

Old Woman. My four beautiful green fields.*

Peter (*aside to* BRIDGET). Do you think could she be the widow Casey that was put out of her holding at Kilglass* a while ago?

Bridget. She is not. I saw the widow Casey one time at the market in Ballina, a stout fresh woman.

Peter (*to* OLD WOMAN). Did you hear a noise of cheering, and you coming up the hill?

Old Woman. I thought I heard the noise I used to hear when my friends came to visit me.

She begins singing half to herself.

> I will go cry with the woman,
> For yellow-haired Donough is dead,*
> With a hempen rope for a neckcloth,
> And a white cloth on his head,——

Michael (*coming from the door*). What is it that you are singing, ma'am?

Old Woman. Singing I am about a man I knew one time, yellow-haired Donough that was hanged in Galway.

She goes on singing, much louder.

> I am come to cry with you, woman,
> My hair is unwound and unbound;
> I remember him ploughing his field,
> Turning up the red side of the ground,
> And building his barn on the hill
> With the good mortared stone;
> O! we'd have pulled down the gallows
> Had it happened in Enniscrone!

Michael. What was it brought him to his death?

Old Woman. He died for love of me: many a man has died for love of me.

Peter (aside to BRIDGET*).* Her trouble has put her wits astray.

Michael. Is it long since that song was made? Is it long since he got his death?

Old Woman. Not long, not long. But there were others that died for love of me a long time ago.

Michael. Were they neighbours of your own, ma'am?

Old Woman. Come here beside me and I'll tell you about them. (MICHAEL *sits down beside her on the hearth.*) There was a red man of the O'Donnells from the north, and a man of the O'Sullivans from the south, and there was one Brian that lost his life at Clontarf* by the sea, and there were a great many in the west, some that died hundreds of years ago, and there are some that will die to-morrow.

Michael. Is it in the west that men will die to-morrow?

Old Woman. Come nearer, nearer to me.

Bridget. Is she right, do you think? Or is she a woman from beyond the world?

Peter. She doesn't know well what she's talking about, with the want and the trouble she has gone through.

Bridget. The poor thing, we should treat her well.

Peter. Give her a drink of milk and a bit of the oaten cake.

Bridget. Maybe we should give her something along with that, to bring her on her way. A few pence or a shilling itself, and we with so much money in the house.

Peter. Indeed I'd not begrudge it to her if we had it to spare, but if we go running through what we have, we'll soon have to break the hundred pounds, and that would be a pity.

Bridget. Shame on you, Peter. Give her the shilling and your blessing with it, or our own luck will go from us.

PETER *goes to the box and takes out a shilling.*

Bridget (*to the* OLD WOMAN). Will you have a drink of milk, ma'am?

Old Woman. It is not food or drink that I want.

Peter (*offering the shilling*). Here is something for you.

Old Woman. This is not what I want. It is not silver I want.

Peter. What is it you would be asking for?

Old Woman. If anyone would give me help he must give me himself, he must give me all.

PETER *goes over to the table staring at the shilling in his hand in a bewildered way, and stands whispering to* BRIDGET.

Michael. Have you no one to care you in your age, ma'am?

Old Woman. I have not. With all the lovers that brought me their love I never set out the bed for any.

Michael. Are you lonely going the roads, ma'am?

Old Woman. I have my thoughts and I have my hopes.

Michael. What hopes have you to hold to?

Old Woman. The hope of getting my beautiful fields back again; the hope of putting the strangers out of my house.

Michael. What way will you do that, ma'am?

Old Woman. I have good friends that will help me. They are gathering to help me now. I am not afraid. If they are put down to-day they will get the upper hand to-morrow. (*She gets up.*) I must be going to meet my friends. They are coming to help me and I must be there to welcome them. I must call the neighbours together to welcome them.

Michael. I will go with you.

Bridget. It is not her friends you have to go and welcome, Michael; it is the girl coming into the house you have to welcome. You have plenty to do; it is food and drink you have to bring to the house. The woman that is coming home is not coming with empty hands; you would not have an empty house before her. (*To the* OLD WOMAN.) Maybe you don't know, ma'am that my son is going to be married to-morrow.

Old Woman. It is not a man going to his marriage that I look to for help.

Peter (*to* BRIDGET). Who is she, do you think, at all?

Bridget. You did not tell us your name yet, ma'am.

Old Woman. Some call me the Poor Old Woman, and there are some that call me Cathleen, the daughter of Houlihan.*

Peter. I think I knew some one of that name, once. Who was it, I wonder? It must have been some one I knew when I was a boy. No, no; I remember, I heard it in a song.

Old Woman (*who is standing in the doorway*). They are wondering that there were songs made for me; there have been many songs made for me, I heard one on the wind this morning.

Sings

> Do not make a great keening*
> When the graves have been dug to-morrow.
> Do not call the white-scarfed riders*
> To the burying that shall be to-morrow.
>
> Do not spread food to call strangers
> To the wakes that shall be to-morrow;
> Do not give money for prayers
> For the dead that shall die to-morrow . . .

They will have no need of prayers, they will have no need of prayers.

Michael. I do not know what that song means, but tell me something I can do for you.

Peter. Come over to me, Michael.

Michael. Hush, father, listen to her.

Old Woman. It is a hard service they take that help me. Many that are red-cheeked now will be pale-cheeked; many that have been free to walk the hills and the bogs and the rushes will be sent to walk hard streets in far countries; many a good plan will be broken; many that have gathered money will not stay to spend it; many a child will be born and there will be no father at its christening to give it a name. They that have red cheeks will have pale cheeks for my sake, and for all that, they will think they are well paid.

[*She goes out; her voice is heard outside singing.*]

> They shall be remembered for ever,
> They shall be alive for ever,
> They shall be speaking for ever,
> The people shall hear them for ever.

Bridget (to PETER). Look at him, Peter; he has the look of a man that has got the touch.* (*Raising her voice.*) Look here, Michael, at the wedding clothes. Such grand clothes as these are! You have a right to fit them on now; it would be a pity to-morrow if they did not fit. The boys would be laughing at you. Take them, Michael, and go into the room and fit them on.

She puts them on his arm.

Michael. What wedding are you talking of? What clothes will I be wearing to-morrow?

Bridget. These are the clothes you are going to wear when you marry Delia Cahel to-morrow.

Michael. I had forgotten that.

He looks at the clothes and turns towards the inner room, but stops at the sound of cheering outside.

Peter. There is the shouting come to our own door. What is it has happened?

Neighbours come crowding in, PATRICK *and* DELIA *with them.*

Patrick. There are ships in the Bay; the French are landing at Killala!

PETER *takes his pipe from his mouth and his hat off, and stands up. The clothes slip from* MICHAEL's *arm.*

Delia. Michael! (*He takes no notice*.) Michael! (*He turns towards her*.) Why do you look at me like a stranger?

> *She drops his arm.* BRIDGET *goes over towards her.*

Patrick. The boys are all hurrying down the hillside to join the French.

Delia. Michael won't be going to join the French.

Bridget (*to* PETER). Tell him not to go, Peter.

Peter. It's no use. He doesn't hear a word we're saying.

Bridget. Try and coax him over to the fire.

Delia. Michael, Michael! You won't leave me! You won't join the French, and we going to be married!

> *She puts her arms about him, he turns towards her as if about to yield.*
> OLD WOMAN's *voice outside.*

They shall be speaking for ever,
The people shall hear them for ever.

> MICHAEL *breaks away from* DELIA, *stands for a second at the door, then rushes out, following the* OLD WOMAN's *voice.* BRIDGET *takes* DELIA, *who is crying silently, into her arms.*

Peter (*to* PATRICK, *laying a hand on his arm*). Did you see an old woman going down the path?

Patrick. I did not, but I saw a young girl, and she had the walk of a queen.

THE END

AUGUSTA GREGORY
(1852–1932)

The Rising of the Moon (1907)

PERSONS

Sergeant   Policeman B
Policeman X   A Ragged Man

SCENE: *Side of a quay in a seaport town. Some posts and chains. A large barrel. Enter three policemen. Moonlight.*

SERGEANT, *who is older than the others, crosses the stage to right and looks down steps. The others put down a pastepot and unroll a bundle of placards.*

Policeman B. I think this would be a good place to put up a notice.

[*He points to barrel.*

Policeman X. Better ask him. (*Calls to* SERGEANT.) Will this be a good place for a placard?   [*No answer.*

Policeman B. Will we put up a notice here on the barrel?

[*No answer.*

Sergeant. There's a flight of steps here that leads to the water. This is a place that should be minded well. If he got down here, his friends might have a boat to meet him; they might send it in here from outside.

Policeman B. Would the barrel be a good place to put a notice up?

Sergeant. It might; you can put it there. [*They paste the notice up.*

Sergeant (*reading it*). Dark hair—dark eyes, smooth face, height five feet five—there's not much to take hold of in that—It's a pity I had no chance of seeing him before he broke out of gaol. They say he's a wonder, that it's he makes all the plans for the whole organisation. There isn't another man in Ireland would have broken gaol the way he did. He must have some friends among the gaolers.

Policeman B. A hundred pounds is little enough for the Government to offer for him. You may be sure any man in the force that takes him will get promotion.

Sergeant. I'll mind this place myself. I wouldn't wonder at all if he came this way. He might come slipping along there (*points to side of quay*), and his friends might be waiting for him there (*points down steps*), and once he got away it's little chance we'd have of finding him; it's maybe under a load of kelp he'd be in a fishing boat, and not one to help a married man that wants it to the reward.

Policeman X. And if we get him itself, nothing but abuse on our heads for it from the people, and maybe from our own relations.

Sergeant. Well, we have to do our duty in the force. Haven't we the whole country depending on us to keep law and order? It's those that are down would be up and those that are up would be down, if it wasn't for us. Well, hurry on, you have plenty of other places to placard yet, and come back here then to me. You can take the lantern. Don't be too long now. It's very lonesome here with nothing but the moon.

Policeman B. It's a pity we can't stop with you. The Government should have brought more police into the town, with *him* in gaol, and at assize time too.* Well, good luck to your watch.   [*They go out.*

Sergeant (*walks up and down once or twice and looks at placard*). A hundred pounds and promotion sure. There must be a great deal of spending in a hundred pounds. It's a pity some honest man not to be the better of that.

A ragged MAN *appears at left and tries to slip past.* SERGEANT
suddenly turns.

Sergeant. Where are you going?

Man. I'm a poor ballad-singer, your honour. I thought to sell some of these (*holds out bundle of ballads*) to the sailors. [*He goes on.*

Sergeant. Stop! Didn't I tell you to stop? You can't go on there.

Man. Oh, very well. It's a hard thing to be poor. All the world's against the poor.

Sergeant. Who are you?

Man. You'd be as wise as myself if I told you, but I don't mind. I'm one Jimmy Walsh, a ballad-singer.

Sergeant. Jimmy Walsh? I don't know that name.

Man. Ah, sure, they know it well enough in Ennis. Were you ever in Ennis, sergeant?

Sergeant. What brought you here?

Man. Sure, it's to the assizes I came, thinking I might make a few shillings here or there. It's in the one train with the judges I came.

Sergeant. Well, if you came so far, you may as well go farther, for you'll walk out of this.

Man. I will, I will; I'll just go on where I was going.

[*Goes towards steps.*

Sergeant. Come back from those steps; no one has leave to pass down them to-night.

Man. I'll just sit on the top of the steps till I see will some sailor buy a ballad off me that would give me my supper. They do be late going back to the ship. It's often I saw them in Cork carried down the quay in a hand-cart.

Sergeant. Move on, I tell you. I won't have anyone lingering about the quay to-night.

Man. Well, I'll go. It's the poor have the hard life! Maybe yourself might like one, sergeant. Here's a good sheet now. (*Turns one over.*) 'Content and a pipe'—that's not much. 'The Peeler and the goat'—you wouldn't like that. 'Johnny Hart'—that's a lovely song.

Sergeant. Move on.

Man. Ah, wait till you hear it. (*Sings*)—

There was a rich farmer's daughter lived near the town of Ross;
She courted a Highland soldier, his name was Johnny Hart;
Says the mother to her daughter, 'I'll go distracted mad
If you marry that Highland soldier dressed up in Highland plaid.'

Sergeant. Stop that noise.

MAN *wraps up his ballads and shuffles towards the steps.*

Sergeant. Where are you going?

Man. Sure you told me to be going, and I am going.

Sergeant. Don't be a fool. I didn't tell you to go that way; I told you to go back to the town.

Man. Back to the town, is it?

Sergeant (taking him by the shoulder and shoving him before him). Here, I'll show you the way. Be off with you. What are you stopping for?

Man (who has been keeping his eye on the notice, points to it). I think I know what you're waiting for, sergeant.

Sergeant. What's that to you?

Man. And I know well the man you're waiting for—I know him well—I'll be going.

[*He shuffles on.*

Sergeant. You know him? Come back here. What sort is he?

Man. Come back is it, sergeant? Do you want to have me killed?

Sergeant. Why do you say that?

Man. Never mind. I'm going. I wouldn't be in your shoes if the reward was ten times as much. (*Goes on off stage to left.*) Not if it was ten times as much.

Sergeant (rushing after him). Come back here, come back. (*Drags him back.*) What sort is he? Where did you see him?

Man. I saw him in my own place, in the County Clare. I tell you you wouldn't like to be looking at him. You'd be afraid to be in the one place with him. There isn't a weapon he doesn't know the use of, and as to strength, his muscles are as hard as that board (*slaps barrel*).

Sergeant. Is he as bad as that?

Man. He is then.

Sergeant. Do you tell me so?

Man. There was a poor man in our place, a sergeant from Bally-vaughan.—It was with a lump of stone he did it.

Sergeant. I never heard of that.

Man. And you wouldn't, sergeant. It's not everything that happens gets into the papers. And there was a policeman in plain clothes, too . . . It is in Limerick he was. . . . It was after the time of the attack on the police barrack at Kilmallock. . . . Moonlight . . . just like this . . . waterside . . . Nothing was known for certain.

Sergeant. Do you say so? It's a terrible county to belong to.

Man. That's so, indeed! You might be standing there, looking out that way, thinking you saw him coming up this side of the quay (*points*), and he might be coming up this other side (*points*), and he'd be on you before you knew where you were.

Sergeant. It's a whole troop of police they ought to put here to stop a man like that.

Man. But if you'd like me to stop with you, I could be looking down this side. I could be sitting up here on this barrel.

Sergeant. And you know him well, too?

Man. I'd know him a mile off, sergeant.

Sergeant. But you wouldn't want to share the reward?

Man. Is it a poor man like me, that has to be going the roads and singing in fairs, to have the name on him that he took a reward? But you don't want me. I'll be safer in the town.

Sergeant. Well, you can stop.

Man (*getting up on barrel*). All right, sergeant. I wonder, now, you're not tired out, sergeant, walking up and down the way you are.

Sergeant. If I'm tired I'm used to it.

Man. You might have hard work before you to-night yet. Take it easy while you can. There's plenty of room up here on the barrel, and you see farther when you're higher up.

Sergeant. Maybe so. (*Gets up beside him on barrel, facing right. They sit back to back, looking different ways.*) You made me feel a bit queer with the way you talked.

Man. Give me a match, sergeant (*he gives it, and Man lights pipe*); take a draw yourself? It'll quiet you. Wait now till I give you a light, but you needn't turn round. Don't take your eye off the quay for the life of you.

Sergeant. Never fear, I won't. (*Lights pipe. They both smoke.*) Indeed it's a hard thing to be in the force, out at night and no thanks for it, for all the danger we're in. And it's little we get but abuse from the people, and no choice but to obey our orders, and never asked when a man is sent into danger, if you are a married man with a family.

Man (*sings*)—

As through the hills I walked to view the hills and shamrock plain,

I stood awhile where nature smiles to view the rocks and streams,
On a matron fair I fixed my eyes beneath a fertile vale,
As she sang her song it was on the wrong of poor old Granuaile.*

Sergeant. Stop that; that's no song to be singing in these times.

Man. Ah, sergeant, I was only singing to keep my heart up. It sinks when I think of him. To think of us two sitting here, and he creeping up the quay, maybe, to get to us.

Sergeant. Are you keeping a good lookout?

Man. I am; and for no reward too. Amn't I the foolish man? But when I saw a man in trouble, I never could help trying to get him out of it. What's that? Did something hit me?   [*Rubs his heart.*

Sergeant (*patting him on the shoulder*). You will get your reward in heaven.

Man. I know that, I know that, sergeant, but life is precious.

Sergeant. Well, you can sing if it gives you more courage.

Man (*sings*)—

Her head was bare, her hands and feet with iron bands were
    bound,
Her pensive strain and plaintive wail mingles with the evening gale,
And the song she sang with mournful air, I am old Granuaile.
Her lips so sweet that monarchs kissed . . .

Sergeant. That's not it. . . . 'Her gown she wore was stained with gore.' . . . That's it—you missed that.

Man. You're right, sergeant, so it is; I missed it. (*Repeats line.*) But to think of a man like you knowing a song like that.

Sergeant. There's many a thing a man might know and might not have any wish for.

Man. Now, I daresay, sergeant, in your youth, you used to be sitting up on a wall, the way you are sitting up on this barrel now, and the other lads beside you, and you singing 'Granuaile'? . . .

Sergeant. I did then.

Man. And the 'Shan Bhean Bhocht'? . . . *

Sergeant. I did then.

Man. And the 'Green on the Cape'?*

Sergeant. That was one of them.

Man. And maybe the man you are watching for to-night used to be sitting on the wall, when he was young, and singing those same songs. . . . It's a queer world. . . .

Sergeant. Whisht! . . . I think I see something coming. . . . It's only a dog.

Man. And isn't it a queer world? . . . Maybe it's one of the boys you used to be singing with that time you will be arresting to–day or to–morrow, and sending into the dock. . . .

Sergeant. That's true indeed.

Man. And maybe one night, after you had been singing, if the other boys had told you some plan they had, some plan to free the country, you might have joined with them. . . . and maybe it is you might be in trouble now.

Sergeant. Well, who knows but I might? I had a great spirit in those days.

Man. It's a queer world, sergeant, and it's little any mother knows when she sees her child creeping on the floor what might happen to it before it has gone through its life, or who will be who in the end.

Sergeant. That's a queer thought now, and a true thought. Wait now till I think it out . . . If it wasn't for the sense I have, and for my wife and family, and for me joining the force the time I did, it might be myself now would be after breaking gaol and hiding in the dark, and it might be him that's hiding in the dark and that got out of gaol would be sitting up where I am on this barrel. . . . And it might be myself would be creeping up trying to make my escape from himself, and it might be himself would be keeping the law, and myself would be breaking it, and myself would be trying maybe to put a bullet in his head, or to take up a lump of a stone the way you said he did . . . no, that myself did . . . Oh! (*Gasps. After a pause.*) What's that? (*Grasps* MAN's *arm.*)

Man (*jumps off barrel and listens, looking out over water.*) It's nothing, sergeant.

Sergeant. I thought it might be a boat. I had a notion there might be friends of his coming about the quays with a boat.

Man. Sergeant, I am thinking it was with the people you were, and not with the law you were when you were a young man.

Sergeant. Well, if I was foolish then, that time's gone.

Man. Maybe, sergeant, it comes into your head sometimes, in spite of your belt and your tunic, that it might have been as well for you to have followed Granuaile.

Sergeant. It's no business of yours what I think.

Man. Maybe, sergeant, you'll be on the side of the country yet.

Sergeant (*gets off barrel*). Don't talk to me like that. I have my duties and I know them. (*Looks round.*) That was a boat; I hear the oars.

> [*Goes to the steps and looks down.*

Man (*sings*)—

> O, then, tell me, Shawn O'Farrell,
>   Where the gathering is to be.
> In the old spot by the river
>   Right well known to you and me!

Sergeant. Stop that! Stop that, I tell you!

Man (*sings louder*).

> One word more, for signal token,
>   Whistle up the marching tune,
> With your pike upon your shoulder,
>   At the Rising of the Moon.*

Sergeant. If you don't stop that, I'll arrest you.

A whistle from below answers, repeating the air.

Sergeant. That's a signal (*stands between him and steps.*) You must not pass this way . . . Step farther back . . . Who are you? You are no ballad-singer.

Man. You needn't ask who I am; that placard will tell you (*points to placard.*)

Sergeant. You are the man I am looking for.

Man (*takes off hat and wig.* SERGEANT *seizes them.*) I am. There's a hundred pounds on my head. There is a friend of mine below in a boat. He knows a safe place to bring me to.

Sergeant (*looking still at hat and wig*). It's a pity! it's a pity. You deceived me. You deceived me well.

Man. I am a friend of Granuaile. There is a hundred pounds on my head.

Sergeant. It's a pity, it's a pity!

Man. Will you let me pass, or must I make you let me?

Sergeant. I am in the force. I will not let you pass.

Man. I thought to do it with my tongue (*puts hand in breast*). What is that?

(*Voice of* POLICEMAN X *outside.*) Here, this is where we left him.

Sergeant. It's my comrades coming.

Man. You won't betray me ... the friend of Granuaile (*slips behind barrel*).

(*Voice of* POLICEMAN B.) That was the last of the placards.

Policeman X (*as they come in*). If he makes his escape it won't be unknown he'll make it.

SERGEANT *puts hat and wig behind his back.*

Policeman B. Did anyone come this way?

Sergeant (*after a pause*). No one.

Policeman B. No one at all?

Sergeant. No one at all.

Policeman B. We had no orders to go back to the station; we can stop along with you.

Sergeant. I don't want you. There is nothing for you to do here.

Policeman B. You bade us to come back here and keep watch with you.

Sergeant. I'd sooner be alone. Would any man come this way and you making all that talk? It is better the place to be quiet.

Policeman B. Well, we'll leave you the lantern anyhow.

[*Hands it to him.*

Sergeant. I don't want it. Bring it with you.

Policeman B. You might want it. There are clouds coming up and you have the darkness of the night before you yet. I'll leave it over here on the barrel.

[Goes to barrel.

Sergeant. Bring it with you I tell you. No more talk.

Policeman B. Well, I thought it might be a comfort to you. I often think when I have it in my hand and can be flashing it about into every dark corner (*doing so*) that it's the same as being beside the fire at home, and the bits of bog-wood blazing up now and again.

Flashes it about, now on the barrel, now on SERGEANT.

Sergeant (*furious*). Be off the two of you, yourselves and your lantern!

They go out. MAN *comes from behind barrel. He and* SERGEANT *stand looking at one another.*

Sergeant. What are you waiting for?

Man. For my hat, of course, and my wig. You wouldn't wish me to get my death of cold?

*[*SERGEANT *gives them.*

Man (*going towards steps*). Well, good-night, comrade, and thank you. You did me a good turn to-night, and I'm obliged to you. Maybe I'll be able to do as much for you when the small rise up and the big fall down . . . when we all change places at the Rising (*waves his hand and disappears*) of the Moon.

Sergeant (*turning his back to audience and reading placard*). A hundred pounds reward! A hundred pounds! (*Turns towards audience.*) I wonder now, am I as great a fool as I think I am?

Curtain.

J. M. SYNGE
(1871–1909)

Riders to the Sea (1904)

PERSONS

Maurya, an old woman
Bartley, her son
Cathleen, her daughter
Nora, a younger daughter
Men and Women

SCENE

An Island off the West of Ireland

FIRST PRODUCTION
(Dublin, 25 February 1904)

Cottage kitchen, with nets, oil-skins, spinning wheel, some new boards standing by the wall, etc. CATHLEEN, *a girl of about twenty, finishes kneading cake, and puts it down in the pot-oven* by the fire; then wipes her hands, and begins to spin at the wheel.* NORA, *a young girl, puts her head in at the door.*

Nora (in a low voice). Where is she?

Cathleen. She's lying down, God help her, and maybe sleeping, if she's able.

NORA *comes in softly, and takes a bundle from under her shawl.*

Cathleen (spinning the wheel rapidly). What is it you have?

Nora. The young priest is after bringing them. It's a shirt and a plain stocking were got off a drowned man in Donegal.

CATHLEEN *stops her wheel with a sudden movement, and leans out to listen.*

Nora. We're to find out if it's Michael's they are, some time herself will be down looking by the sea.

Cathleen. How would they be Michael's, Nora. How would he go the length of that way to the far north?

Nora. The young priest says he's known the like of it. 'If it's Michael's they are,' says he, 'you can tell herself he's got a clean burial by the grace of God, and if they're not his, let no one say a word about them, for she'll be getting her death,' says he, 'with crying and lamenting.'

The door which NORA *half closed behind her is blown open by a gust of wind.*

Cathleen (*looking out anxiously*). Did you ask him would he stop Bartley going this day with the horses to the Galway fair?

Nora. 'I won't stop him,' says he, 'but let you not be afraid. Herself does be saying prayers half through the night, and the Almighty God won't leave her destitute,' says he, 'with no son living.'

Cathleen. Is the sea bad by the white rocks, Nora?

Nora. Middling bad, God help us. There's a great roaring in the west, and it's worse it'll be getting when the tide's turned to the wind. (*She goes over to the table with the bundle.*) Shall I open it now?

Cathleen. Maybe she'd wake up on us, and come in before we'd done (*coming to the table*). It's a long time we'll be, and the two of us crying.

Nora (*goes to the inner door and listens*). She's moving about on the bed. She'll be coming in a minute.

Cathleen. Give me the ladder, and I'll put them up in the turf-loft,* the way she won't know of them at all, and maybe when the tide turns she'll be going down to see would he be floating from the east.

They put the ladder against the gable of the chimney; CATHLEEN *goes up a few steps and hides the bundle in the turf-loft.* MAURYA *comes from the inner room.*

Maurya (*looking up at* CATHLEEN *and speaking querulously*). Isn't it turf enough you have for this day and evening?

Cathleen. There's a cake baking at the fire for a short space (*throwing down the turf*), and Bartley will want it when the tide turns if he goes to Connemara.

NORA *picks up the turf and puts it round the pot-oven.*

Maurya (*sitting down on a stool at the fire*). He won't go this day with the wind rising from the south and west. He won't go this day, for the young priest will stop him surely.

Nora. He'll not stop him, mother, and I heard Eamon Simon and Stephen Pheety and Colum Shawn saying he would go.

Maurya. Where is he itself?

Nora. He went down to see would there be another boat sailing in the week, and I'm thinking it won't be long till he's here now, for the tide's turning at the green head,* and the hooker's tacking from the east.*

Cathleen. I hear some one passing the big stones.

Nora (*looking out*). He's coming now, and he in a hurry.

Bartley (*comes in and looks round the room; speaking sadly and quietly*). Where is the bit of new rope, Cathleen, was bought in Connemara?

Cathleen (*coming down*). Give it to him, Nora; it's on a nail by the white boards. I hung it up this morning, for the pig with the black feet* was eating it.

Nora (*giving him a rope*). Is that it, Bartley?

Maurya (*as before*). You'd do right to leave that rope, Bartley, hanging by the boards. (BARTLEY *takes the rope.*) It will be wanting in this place, I'm telling you, if Michael is washed up tomorrow morning, or the next morning, or any morning in the week, for it's a deep grave we'll make him by the grace of God.

Bartley (*beginning to work with the rope*). I've no halter the way I can ride down on the mare, and I must go now quickly. This is the one boat going for two weeks or beyond it, and the fair will be a good fair for horses I heard them saying below.

Maurya. It's a hard thing they'll be saying below if the body is washed up and there's no man in it to make the coffin, and I after giving a big price for the finest white boards you'd find in Connemara. (*She looks round at the boards.*)

Bartley. How would it be washed up, and we after looking each day for nine days, and a strong wind blowing a while back from the west and south?

Maurya. If it isn't found itself, that wind is raising the sea, and there was a star up against the moon, and it rising in the night. If it was a hundred horses, or a thousand horses you had itself, what is the price of a thousand horses against a son where there is one son only?

Bartley (*working at the halter, to* CATHLEEN). Let you go down each day, and see the sheep aren't jumping in on the rye, and if the jobber* comes you can sell the pig with the black feet if there is a good price going.

Maurya. How would the like of her get a good price for a pig?

Bartley (*to* CATHLEEN). If the west wind holds with the last bit of the moon let you and Nora get up weed enough for another cock for the kelp.* It's hard set we'll be from this day with no one in it but one man to work.

Maurya. It's hard set we'll be surely the day you're drown'd with the rest. What way will I live and the girls with me, and I an old woman looking for the grave?

BARTLEY *lays down the halter, takes off his old coat, and puts on a newer one of the same flannel.*

Bartley (*to* NORA). Is she coming to the pier?

Nora (*looking out*). She's passing the green head and letting fall her sails.

Bartley (*getting his purse and tobacco*). I'll have half an hour to go down, and you'll see me coming again in two days, or in three days, or maybe in four days if the wind is bad.

Maurya (*turning round to the fire, and putting her shawl over her head*). Isn't it a hard and cruel man won't hear a word from an old woman, and she holding him from the sea?

Cathleen. It's the life of a young man to be going on the sea, and who would listen to an old woman with one thing and she saying it over?

Bartley (*taking the halter*). I must go now quickly. I'll ride down on the red mare, and the grey pony'll run behind me. . . . The blessing of God on you.

[*He goes out.*

Maurya (*crying out as he is in the door way*). He's gone now, God spare us, and we'll not see him again. He's gone now, and when the black night is falling I'll have no son left me in the world.

Cathleen. Why wouldn't you give him your blessing and he looking round in the door? Isn't it sorrow enough is on every one in this house without your sending him out with an unlucky word behind him, and a hard word in his ear?

MAURYA *takes up the tongs and begins raking the fire aimlessly without looking round.*

Nora (*turning towards her*). You're taking away the turf from the cake.

Cathleen (*crying out*). The Son of God forgive us, Nora, we're after forgetting his bit of bread.

She comes over to the fire.

Nora. And it's destroyed* he'll be going till dark night, and he after eating nothing since the sun went up.

Cathleen (*turning the cake out of the oven*). It's destroyed he'll be, surely. There's no sense left on any person in a house where an old woman will be talking forever.

MAURYA *sways herself on her stool.*

Cathleen (*cutting off some of the bread and rolling it in a cloth, to* MAURYA). Let you go down now to the spring well and give him this and he passing. You'll see him then and the dark word will be broken, and you can say 'God speed you', the way he'll be easy in his mind.

Maurya (*taking the bread*). Will I be in it as soon as himself?

Cathleen. If you go now quickly.

Maurya (*standing up unsteadily*). It's hard set I am to walk.

Cathleen (*looking at her anxiously*). Give her the stick, Nora, or maybe she'll slip on the big stones.

Nora. What stick?

Cathleen. The stick Michael brought from Connemara.

Maurya (*taking a stick* NORA *gives her*). In the big world the old people do be leaving things after them for their sons and children, but in this place it is the young men do be leaving things behind for them that do be old.

> [*She goes out slowly.*
> NORA *goes over to the ladder.*

Cathleen. Wait, Nora, maybe she'd turn back quickly. She's that sorry, God help her, you wouldn't know the thing she'd do.

Nora. Is she gone round by the bush?

Cathleen (*looking out*). She's gone now. Throw it down quickly, for the Lord knows when she'll be out of it again.

Nora (*getting the bundle from the loft*). The young priest said he'd be passing tomorrow, and we might go down and speak to him below if it's Michael's they are surely.

Cathleen (*taking the bundle from* NORA). Did he say what way they were found?

Nora (*coming down*). 'There were two men,' says he, 'and they rowing round with poteen* before the cocks crowed, and the oar of one of them caught the body, and they passing the black cliffs of the north.'

Cathleen (*trying to open the bundle*). Give me a knife, Nora, the string's perished with the salt water, and there's a black knot on it* you wouldn't loosen in a week.

Nora (*giving her a knife*). I've heard tell it was a long way to Donegal.

Cathleen (*cutting the string*). It is surely. There was a man in here a while ago—the man sold us that knife—and he said if you set off walking from the rocks beyond, it would be in seven days you'd be in Donegal.

Nora. And what time would a man take, and he floating?

> CATHLEEN *opens the bundle and takes out a bit of a shirt and a stocking. They look at them eagerly.*

Cathleen (*in a low voice*). The Lord spare us, Nora! Isn't it a queer hard thing to say if it's his they are surely?

Nora. I'll get his shirt off the hook the way we can put the one flannel on the other. (*She looks through some clothes hanging in the corner.*) It's not with them, Cathleen, and where will it be?

Cathleen. I'm thinking Bartley put it on him in the morning, for his own shirt was heavy with the salt in it. (*Pointing to the corner.*) There's a bit of a sleeve was of the same stuff. Give me that and it will do.

NORA *brings it to her and they compare the flannel.*

Cathleen. It's the same stuff, Nora; but if it is itself aren't there great rolls of it in the shops of Galway, and isn't it many another man may have a shirt of it as well as Michael himself?

Nora (*who has taken up the stocking and counted the stitches, crying out*). It's Michael, Cathleen, it's Michael; God spare his soul, and what will herself say when she hears this story, and Bartley on the sea?

Cathleen (*taking the stocking*). It's a plain stocking.

Nora. It's the second one of the third pair I knitted, and I put up three score stitches, and I dropped four of them.

Cathleen (*counts the stitches*). It's that number is in it. (*Crying out.*) Ah, Nora, isn't it a bitter thing to think of him floating that way to the far north, and no one to keen him but the black hags* that do be flying on the sea?

Nora (*swinging herself round and throwing out her arms on the clothes*). And isn't it a pitiful thing when there is nothing left of a man who was a great rower and fisher, but a bit of an old shirt and a plain stocking?

Cathleen (*after an instant*). Tell me is herself coming, Nora? I hear a little sound on the path.

Nora (*looking out*). She is, Cathleen. She's coming up to the door.

Cathleen. Put these things away before she'll come in. Maybe it's easier she'll be after giving her blessing to Bartley, and we won't let on we've heard anything the time he's on the sea.

Nora (*helping* CATHLEEN *to close the bundle*). We'll put them here in the corner.

They put them into a hole in the chimney corner. CATHLEEN *goes back to the spinning-wheel.*

Nora. Will she see it was crying I was?

Cathleen. Keep your back to the door the way the light'll not be on you.

NORA *sits down at the chimney corner, with her back to the door.*
MAURYA *comes in very slowly, without looking at the girls, and goes
over to her stool at the other side of the fire. The cloth with the bread
is still in her hand. The girls look at each other, and* NORA *points
to the bundle of bread.*

Cathleen (after spinning for a moment). You didn't give him his bit of bread?

MAURYA *begins to keen softly, without turning round.*

Cathleen. Did you see him riding down?

MAURYA *goes on keening.*

Cathleen (a little impatiently). God forgive you; isn't it a better thing to raise your voice and tell what you seen, than to be making lamentation for a thing that's done? Did you see Bartley, I'm saying to you.

Maurya (with a weak voice). My heart's broken from this day.

Cathleen (as before). Did you see Bartley?

Maurya. I seen the fearfullest thing.

Cathleen (leaves her wheel and looks out). God forgive you; he's riding the mare now over the green head, and the grey pony behind him.

*Maurya (starts, so that her shawl falls back from her head and shows
her white tossed hair. With a frightened voice).* The grey pony behind him . . .

Cathleen (coming to the fire). What is it ails you, at all?

Maurya (speaking very slowly). I've seen the fearfullest thing any person has seen, since the day Bride Dara seen the dead man with the child in his arms.

Cathleen and Nora. Uah.

They crouch down in front of the old woman at the fire.

Nora. Tell us what it is you seen.

Maurya. I went down to the spring well, and I stood there saying a prayer to myself. Then Bartley came along, and he riding on the red mare with the grey pony behind him (*she puts up her hands, as if to hide something from her eyes*). The Son of God spare us, Nora!

Cathleen. What is it you seen?

Maurya. I seen Michael himself.

Cathleen (*speaking softly*). You did not, mother; it wasn't Michael you seen, for his body is after being found in the far north, and he's got a clean burial by the grace of God.

Maurya (*a little defiantly*). I'm after seeing him this day, and he riding and galloping. Bartley came first on the red mare; and I tried to say 'God speed you,' but something choked the words in my throat. He went by quickly; and 'the blessing of God on you,' says he, and I could say nothing. I looked up then, and I crying, at the grey pony, and there was Michael upon it—with fine clothes on him, and new shoes on his feet.

Cathleen (*begins to keen*). It's destroyed we are from this day. It's destroyed, surely.

Nora. Didn't the young priest say the Almighty God won't leave her destitute with no son living?

Maurya (*in a low voice, but clearly*). It's little the like of him knows of the sea. . . . Bartley will be lost now, and let you call in Eamon and make me a good coffin out of the white boards, for I won't live after them. I've had a husband, and a husband's father, and six sons in this house—six fine men, though it was a hard birth I had with every one of them and they coming to the world—and some of them were found and some of them were not found, but they're gone now the lot of them. . . . There were Stephen, and Shawn, were lost in the great wind, and found after in the Bay of Gregory of the Golden Mouth,* and carried up the two of them on one plank, and in by that door.

> *She pauses for a moment; the girls start as if they heard something through the door that is half open behind them.*

Nora (*in a whisper*). Did you hear that, Cathleen? Did you hear a noise in the north-east?

Cathleen (*in a whisper*). There's some one after crying out by the seashore.

Maurya (continues without hearing anything). There was Sheamus and his father, and his own father again, were lost in a dark night, and not a stick or sign was seen of them when the sun went up. There was Patch after was drowned out of a curagh* that turned over. I was sitting here with Bartley, and he a baby, lying on my two knees, and I seen two women, and three women, and four women coming in, and they crossing themselves, and not saying a word. I looked out then, and there were men coming after them, and they holding a thing in the half of a red sail, and water dripping out of it—it was a dry day, Nora—and leaving a track to the door.

*She pauses again with her hand stretched out towards the door. It opens softly and old women begin to come in, crossing themselves on the threshold, and kneeling down in front of the stage with red petticoats over their heads.**

Maurya (half in a dream, to CATHLEEN*).* Is it Patch, or Michael, or what is it at all?

Cathleen. Michael is after being found in the far north, and when he is found there how could he be here in this place?

Maurya. There does be a power of young men floating round in the sea, and what way would they know if it was Michael they had, or another man like him, for when a man is nine days in the sea, and the wind blowing, it's hard set his own mother would be to say what man was in it.

Cathleen. It's Michael, God spare him, for they're after sending us a bit of his clothes from the far north.

She reaches out and hands MAURYA *the clothes that belonged to* MICHAEL. MAURYA *stands up slowly, and takes them in her hands.* NORA *looks out.*

Nora. They're carrying a thing among them and there's water dripping out of it and leaving a track by the big stones.

Cathleen (in a whisper to the women who have come in). Is it Bartley it is?

One of the women. It is surely, God rest his soul.

Two younger women come in and pull out the table. Then men carry in the body of BARTLEY, *laid on a plank, with a bit of a sail over it, and lay it on the table.*

Cathleen (*to the women, as they are doing so*). What way was he drowned?

One of the women. The grey pony knocked him over into the sea, and he was washed out where there is a great surf on the white rocks.

MAURYA *has gone over and knelt down at the head of the table. The women are keening softly and swaying themselves with a slow movement.* CATHLEEN *and* NORA *kneel at the other end of the table. The men kneel near the door.*

Maurya (*raising her head and speaking as if she did not see the people around her*). They're all gone now, and there isn't anything more the sea can do to me. . . . I'll have no call now to be up crying and praying when the wind breaks from the south, and you can hear the surf is in the east, and the surf is in the west, making a great stir with the two noises, and they hitting one on the other. I'll have no call now to be going down and getting Holy Water in the dark nights after Samhain,* and I won't care what way the sea is when the other women will be keening. (*To* NORA.) Give me the Holy Water, Nora, there's a small sup still on the dresser. (NORA *gives it to her.* MAURYA *drops* MICHAEL's *clothes across* BARTLEY's *feet, and sprinkles the Holy Water over him.*) . . . It isn't that I haven't prayed for you, Bartley, to the Almighty God. It isn't that I haven't said prayers in the dark night till you wouldn't know what I'd be saying; but it's a great rest I'll have now, and it's time surely. It's a great rest I'll have now, and great sleeping in the long nights after Samhain, if it's only a bit of wet flour we do have to eat, and maybe a fish that would be stinking. (*She kneels down again, crossing herself, and saying prayers under her breath.*)

Cathleen (*to an old man kneeling near her*). Maybe yourself and Eamon would make a coffin when the sun rises. We have fine white boards herself bought, God help her, thinking Michael would be found, and I have a new cake you can eat while you'll be working.

The old man (*looking at the boards*). Are there nails with them?

Cathleen. There are not, Colum; we didn't think of the nails.

Another man. It's a great wonder she wouldn't think of the nails, and all the coffins she's seen made already.

Cathleen. It's getting old she is, and broken.

MAURYA *stands up again very slowly and spreads out the pieces of* MICHAEL's *clothes beside the body, sprinkling them with the last of the Holy Water.*

Nora (*in a whisper to* CATHLEEN). She's quiet now and easy; but the day Michael was drowned you could hear her crying out from this to the spring well. It's fonder she was of Michael, and would any one have thought that?

Cathleen (*slowly and clearly*). An old woman will soon be tired with anything she will do, and isn't it nine days herself is after crying, and keening, and making great sorrow in the house?

Maurya (*puts the empty cup mouth downwards on the table, and lays her hands together on* BARTLEY's *feet*). They're all together this time, and the end is come. May the Almighty God have mercy on Bartley's soul, and on Michael's soul, and on the souls of Sheamus and Patch, and Stephen and Shawn (*bending her head*) . . . and may He have mercy on my soul, Nora, and on the soul of everyone is left living in the world. (*She pauses, and the keen rises a little more loudly from the women, then sinks away. Continuing.*) Michael has a clean burial in the far north, by the grace of the Almighty God. Bartley will have a fine coffin out of the white boards, and a deep grave surely. . . . What more can we want than that? . . . No man at all can be living for ever, and we must be satisfied.

She kneels down again and the curtain falls slowly.

THE END

SEÁN O'CASEY
(1880–1964)

from *Juno and the Paycock* (1924)

ACT I

The living room of a two-room tenancy occupied by the BOYLE *family in a tenement house in Dublin. Left, a door leading to another part of the house; left of door a window looking into the street; at back a dresser; farther to right at back, a window looking into the back of the house. Between the window and the dresser is a picture of the Virgin; below the picture, on a bracket, is a crimson bowl in which a floating votive light is burning. Farther to the right is a small bed partly concealed by cretonne hangings strung on a twine. To the right is the fireplace; near the fireplace is a door leading to the other room. Beside the fireplace is a box containing coal. On the mantelshelf is an alarm clock lying on its face. In a corner near the window looking into the back is a galvanized bath. A table and some chairs. On the table are breakfast things for one. A teapot is on the hob and a frying-pan stands inside the fender. There are a few books on the dresser and one on the table. Leaning against the dresser is a long-handled shovel—the kind invariably used by labourers when turning concrete or mixing mortar.* JOHNNY BOYLE *is sitting crouched beside the fire.* MARY *with her jumper off—it is lying on the back of a chair—is arranging her hair before a tiny mirror perched on the table. Beside the mirror is stretched out the morning paper which she looks at when she isn't gazing into the mirror. She is a well-made and good-looking girl of twenty-two. Two forces are working in her mind—one, through the circumstances of her life, pulling her back; the other, through the influence of books she has read, pushing her forward. The opposing forces are apparent in her speech and her manners, both of which are degraded by her environment, and improved by her acquaintance—slight though it be—with literature. The time is early forenoon.*

Mary (*looking at the paper*). On a little bye-road, out beyant Finglas, he was found.

MRS BOYLE *enters by door on right; she has been shopping and carries a small parcel in her hand. She is forty-five years of age, and twenty years ago she must have been a pretty woman; but her face has now assumed that look which ultimately settles down upon the faces of the women of the working-class; a look of listless monotony and harassed anxiety, blending with an expression of mechanical resistance. Were circumstances favourable, she would probably be a handsome, active and clever woman.*

Mrs Boyle. Isn't he come in yet?

Mary. No, mother.

Mrs Boyle. Oh, he'll come in when he likes; struttin' about the town like a paycock with Joxer, I suppose. I hear all about Mrs Tancred's son is in this mornin's paper.

Mary. The full details are in it this mornin'; seven wounds he had—one entherin' the neck, with an exit wound beneath the left shoulder-blade; another in the left breast penethratin' the heart, an' . . .

Johnny (*springing up from the fire*). Oh, quit that readin', for God's sake! Are yous losin' all your feelins? It'll soon be that none of yous'll read anythin' that's not about butcherin'!

[*He goes quickly into the room on left.*

Mary. He's gettin' very sensitive, all of a sudden!

Mrs Boyle. I'll read it myself, Mary, by an' by, when I come home. Everybody's sayin' that he was a Die-hard*—thanks be to God that Johnny had nothin' to do with him this long time. . . . (*Opening the parcel and taking out some sausages, which she places on a plate.*) Ah, then, if that father o' yours doesn't come in soon for his breakfast, he may go without any; I'll not wait much longer for him.

Mary. Can't you let him get it himself when he comes in?

Mrs Boyle. Yes, an' let him bring in Joxer Daly along with him? Ay, that's what he'd like, an' that's what he's waitin' for—till he thinks I'm gone to work, an' then sail in with the boul' Joxer, to burn all the coal an' dhrink all the tea in the place, to show them what a good Samaritan he is! But I'll stop here till he comes in, if I have to wait till to-morrow mornin'.

Voice of Johnny inside. Mother!

Mrs. Boyle. Yis?

Voice of Johnny. Bring us in a dhrink o' wather.

Mrs Boyle. Bring in that fella a dhrink o' wather, for God's sake, Mary.

Mary. Isn't he big an' able enough to come out an' get it himself?

Mrs Boyle. If you weren't well yourself you'd like somebody to bring you in a dhrink o' wather.

[*She brings in drink and returns.*

Mrs Boyle. Isn't it terrible to have to be waitin' this way! You'd think he was bringin' twenty pouns a week into the house the way he's going on. He wore out the Health Insurance long ago, he's afther wearin' out the unemployment dole, an', now, he's thryin' to wear out me! An' constantly singin', no less, when he ought always to be on his knees offerin' up a Novena for a job!

Mary (*tying a ribbon, fillet wise around her head*). I don't like this ribbon, ma; I think I'll wear the green—it looks betther than the blue.

Mrs Boyle. Ah, wear whatever ribbon you like, girl, only don't be botherin' me. I don't know what a girl on strike wants to be wearin' a ribbon round her head for or silk stockins on her legs either; its wearin' them things that make the employers think they're givin' yous too much money.

Mary. The hour is past now when we'll ask the employers' permission to wear what we like.

Mrs Boyle. I don't know why you wanted to walk out for Jennie Claffey; up to this you never had a good word for her.

Mary. What's the use of belongin' to a Trades Union if you won't stand up for your principles? Why did they sack her? It was a clear case of victimization. We couldn't let her walk the streets, could we?

Mrs Boyle. No, of course yous couldn't—yous wanted to keep her company. Wan victim wasn't enough. When the employers sacrifice wan victim, the Trades Unions go wan betther be sacrificin' a hundred.

Mary. It doesn't matther what you say, ma—a principle's a principle.

Mrs Boyle. Yis; an' when I go into oul' Murphy's to-morrow, an' he gets to know that, instead o' payin' all, I'm goin' to borry more, what'll he say when I tell him a principle's a principle? What'll we do if he refuses to give us any more on tick?

Mary. He daren't refuse—if he does, can't you tell him he's paid?

Mrs Boyle. It's lookin' as if he was paid, whether he refuses or no.

JOHNNY *appears at the door on left. He can be plainly seen now; he is a thin delicate fellow, something younger than* MARY. *He has evidently gone through a rough time. His face is pale and drawn; there is a tremulous look of indefinite fear in his eyes. The left sleeve of his coat is empty, and he walks with a slight halt.*

Johnny. I was lyin' down; I thought yous were gone. Oul' Simon Mackay is thrampin' about like a horse over me head, an' I can't sleep with him—they're like thunder-claps in me brain! The curse o'—God forgive me for goin' to curse!

Mrs Boyle. There, now; go back an' lie down agen, an I'll bring you in a nice cup o' tay.

Johnny. Tay, tay, tay! You're always thinkin' o' tay. If a man was dyin', you'd thry to make him swally a cup o' tay!

[*He goes back.*

Mrs Boyle. I don't know what's goin' to be done with him. The bullet he got in the hip in Easter Week was bad enough, but the bomb that shatthered his arm in the fight in O'Connell Street put the finishin' touch on him. I knew he was makin' a fool of himself. God knows I went down on me bended knees to him not to go agen the Free State.*

Mary. He stuck to his principles, an', no matther how you may argue, ma, a principle's a principle.

Voice of Johnny. Is Mary goin' to stay here?

Mary. No, I'm not goin' to stay here; you can't expect me to be always at your beck an' call, can you?

Voice of Johnny. I won't stop here be meself!

Mrs Boyle. Amn't I nicely handicapped with the whole o' yous! I don't know what any o' yous ud do without your ma. (*To* JOHNNY.) Your father'll be here in a minute, an' if you want anythin', he'll get it for you.

Johnny. I hate assin' him for anythin'. . . . He hates to be assed to stir. . . . Is the light lightin' before the picture o' the Virgin?

Mrs Boyle. Yis, yis! The wan inside to St Anthony isn't enough, but he must have another wan to the Virgin here!

JERRY DEVINE *enters hastily. He is about twenty-five, well set, active and earnest. He is a type, becoming very common now in the Labour Movement, of a mind knowing enough to make the mass of his associates, who know less, a power, and too little to broaden that power for the benefit of all.* MARY *seizes her jumper and runs hastily into room left.*

Jerry (*breathless*). Where's the Captain, Mrs Boyle, where's the Captain?

Mrs Boyle. You may well ass a body that: he's wherever Joxer Daly is—dhrinkin' in some snug* or another.

Jerry. Father Farrell is just afther stoppin' to tell me to run up an' get him to go to the new job that's goin' on in Rathmines; his cousin is foreman o' the job, an' Father Farrell was speakin' to him about poor Johnny an' his father bein' idle so long, an' the foreman told Father Farrell to send the Captain up an' he'd give him a start— I wondher where I'd find him?

Mrs Boyle. You'll find he's ayther in Ryan's or Foley's.

Jerry. I'll run round to Ryan's—I know it's a great house o' Joxer's.

[*He rushes out.*

Mrs Boyle (*piteously*). There now, he'll miss that job, or I know for what! If he gets win' o' the word, he'll not come back till evenin', so that it'll be too late. There'll never be any good got out o' him so long as he goes with that shouldher-shruggin' Joxer. I killin' meself workin', an' he sthruttin' about from mornin' till night like a paycock!

The steps of two persons are heard coming up a flight of stairs. They are the footsteps of CAPTAIN BOYLE *and* JOXER. CAPTAIN BOYLE *is singing in a deep, sonorous, self-honouring voice.*

The Captain. Sweet Spirit, hear me prayer! Hear . . . oh . . . hear . . . me prayer . . . hear, oh, hear . . . Oh, he . . . ar . . . oh, he . . . ar . . . me . . . pray . . . er!

Joxer (*outside*). Ah, that's a darlin' song, a daaarlin' song!

Mrs Boyle (*viciously*). Sweet spirit hear his prayer! Ah, then, I'll take me solemn affeydavey,* it's not for a job he's prayin'!

She sits down on the bed so that the cretonne hangings hide her from the view of those entering.

THE CAPTAIN *comes slowly in. He is a man of about sixty; stout, grey-haired and stocky. His neck is short, and his head looks like a stone ball that one sometimes sees on top of a gate-post. His cheeks, reddish-purple, are puffed out, as if he were always repressing an almost irrepressible ejaculation. On his upper lip is a crisp, tightly cropped moustache; he carries himself with the upper part of his body slightly thrown back, and his stomach slightly thrust forward. His walk is a slow, consequential strut. His clothes are dingy, and he wears a faded seaman's cap with a glazed peak.*

Boyle (*to* JOXER, *who is still outside*). Come on, come on in, Joxer; she's gone out long ago, man. If there's nothing else to be got, we'll furrage out a cup o' tay, anyway. It's the only bit I get in comfort when she's away. 'Tisn't Juno should be her pet name at all, but Deirdre of the Sorras,* for she's always grousin'.

JOXER *steps cautiously into the room. He may be younger than* THE CAPTAIN *but he looks a lot older. His face is like a bundle of crinkled paper; his eyes have a cunning twinkle; he is spare and loosely built; he has a habit of constantly shrugging his shoulders with a peculiar twitching movement, meant to be ingratiating. His face is invariably ornamented with a grin.*

Joxer. It's a terrible thing to be tied to a woman that's always grousin'. I don't know how you stick it—it ud put years on me. It's a good job she has to be so ofen away, for (*with a shrug*) when the cat's away, the mice can play!

Boyle (*with a commanding and complacent gesture*). Pull over to the fire, Joxer, an' we'll have a cup o' tay in a minute.

Joxer. Ah, a cup o' tay's a darlin' thing, a daaarlin' thing—the cup that cheers but doesn't . . .

JOXER's *rhapsody is cut short by the sight of* JUNO *coming forward and confronting the two cronies. Both are stupefied.*

Mrs Boyle (with sweet irony—poking the fire, and turning her head to glare at JOXER). Pull over to the fire, Joxer Daly, an' we'll have a cup o' tay in a minute! Are you sure, now, you wouldn't like an egg?

Joxer. I can't stop, Mrs Boyle; I'm in a desperate hurry, a desperate hurry.

Mrs Boyle. Pull over to the fire, Joxer Daly; people is always far more comfortabler here than they are in their own place.

JOXER *makes hastily for the door.* BOYLE *stirs to follow him; thinks of something to relieve the situation—stops, and says suddenly*

Joxer!

Joxer (at door ready to bolt). Yis?

Boyle. You know the foreman o' that job that's goin' on down in Killesther, don't you, Joxer?

Joxer (puzzled). Foreman—Killesther?

Boyle (with a meaning look). He's a butty o' yours, isn't he?

Joxer (the truth dawning on him). The foreman at Killesther—oh yis, yis. He's an oul' butty o' mine—oh, he's a darlin' man, a daarlin' man.

Boyle. Oh, then, it's a sure thing. It's a pity we didn't go down at breakfast first thing this mornin'—we might ha' been working now; but you didn't know it then.

Joxer (with a shrug). It's betther late than never.

Boyle. It's nearly time we got a start, anyhow; I'm fed up knockin' round, doin' nothin'. He promised you—gave you the straight tip?

Joxer. Yis. 'Come down on the blow o' dinner,' says he, 'an' I'll start you, an' any friend you like to brin' with you.' Ah, says I, you're a darlin' man, a daaarlin' man.

Boyle. Well, it couldn't come at a betther time—we're a long time waitin' for it.

Joxer. Indeed we were; but it's a long lane that has no turnin'.

Boyle. The blow up for dinner is at one—wait till I see what time it 'tis.

He goes over to the mantelpiece, and gingerly lifts the clock.

Mrs Boyle. Min' now, how you go on fiddlin' with that clock—you know the least little thing sets it asthray.

Boyle. The job couldn't come at a betther time; I'm feelin' in great fettle, Joxer. I'd hardly believe I ever had a pain in me legs, an' last week I was nearly crippled with them.

Joxer. That's betther an' betther; ah, God never shut wan door but he opened another!

Boyle. It's only eleven o'clock; we've lashins o' time. I'll slip on me oul' moleskins afther breakfast, an' we can saunther down at our ayse. (*Putting his hand on the shovel.*) I think, Joxer, we'd betther bring our shovels?

Joxer. Yis, Captain, yis; it's betther to go fully prepared an' ready for all eventualities. You bring your long-tailed shovel, an' I'll bring me navvy. We mighten' want them, an', then agen, we might: for want of a nail the shoe was lost, for want of a shoe the horse was lost, an' for want of a horse the man was lost—aw, that's a darlin' proverb, a daarlin' . . .

As JOXER *is finishing his sentence,* MRS BOYLE *approaches the door and* JOXER *retreats hurriedly. She shuts the door with a bang.*

Boyle (*suggestively*). We won't be long pullin' ourselves together agen when I'm working for a few weeks.

MRS BOYLE *takes no notice.*

Boyle. The foreman on the job is an oul butty o' Joxer's; I have an idea that I know him meself. (*Silence*) . . . There's a button off the back o' me moleskin trousers. . . . If you leave out a needle an' thread I'll sew it on meself . . . Thanks be to God, the pains in me legs is gone, anyhow!

Mrs Boyle (*with a burst*). Look here, Mr Jacky Boyle, them yarns won't go down with Juno. I know you an' Joxer Daly of an oul' date, an', if you think you're able to come it over me with them fairy tales, you're in the wrong shop.

Boyle (*coughing subduedly to relieve the tenseness of the situation*). U-u-u-ugh!

Mrs Boyle. Butty o' Joxer's! Oh, you'll do a lot o' good as long as you continue to be a butty o' Joxer's!

Boyle. U-u-u-ugh!

Mrs Boyle. Shovel! Ah, then, me boyo, you'd do far more work with a knife an' fork than ever you'll do with a shovel! If there was e'er a genuine job goin' you'd be dh'other way about—not able to lift your arms with the pains in your legs! Your poor wife slavin' to keep the bit in your mouth, an' you gallivantin' about all the day like a paycock!

Boyle. It ud be betther for a man to be dead, betther for a man to be dead.

Mrs Boyle (*ignoring the interruption*). Everybody callin' you 'Captain', an' you only wanst on the wather, in an oul' collier from here to Liverpool, when anybody, to listen or look at you, ud take you for a second Christo For Columbus!

Boyle. Are you never goin' to give us a rest?

Mrs Boyle. Oh, you're never tired o' lookin' for a rest.

Boyle. D'ye want to dhrive me out o' the house?

Mrs Boyle. It ud be easier to dhrive you out o' the house than to dhrive you into a job. Here, sit down an' take your breakfast—it may be the last you'll get, for I don't know where the next is goin' to come from.

Boyle. If I get this job we'll be all right.

Mrs Boyle. Did ye see Jerry Devine?

Boyle (*testily*). No, I didn't see him.

Mrs Boyle. No, but you seen Joxer. Well, he was here lookin' for you.

Boyle. Well, let him look!

Mrs Boyle. Oh, indeed, he may well look, for it ud be hard for him to see you, an' you stuck in Ryan's snug.

Boyle. I wasn't in Ryan's snug—I don't go into Ryan's.

Mrs Boyle. Oh, is there a mad dog there? Well, if you weren't in Ryan's you were in Foley's.

Boyle. I'm telling you for the last three weeks I haven't tasted a dhrop of intoxicatin' liquor. I wasn't in ayther wan snug or dh'other—I could swear that on a prayer-book—I'm as innocent as the child unborn!

Mrs Boyle. Well, if you'd been in for your breakfast you'd ha' seen him.

Boyle (*suspiciously*). What does he want me for?

Mrs Boyle. He'll be back any minute an' then you'll soon know.

Boyle. I'll dhrop out an' see if I can meet him.

Mrs Boyle. You'll sit down an' take your breakfast, an' let me go to me work, for I'm an hour late already waitin' for you.

Boyle. You needn't ha' waited, for I'll take no breakfast—I've a little spirit left in me still!

Mrs Boyle. Are you goin' to have your breakfast—yes or no?

Boyle (*too proud to yield*). I'll have no breakfast—yous can keep your breakfast. (*Plaintively*) I'll knock out a bit somewhere, never fear.

Mrs Boyle. Nobody's goin' to coax you—don't think that.

She vigorously replaces the pan and the sausages in the press.

Boyle. I've a little spirit left in me still.

JERRY DEVINE *enters hastily.*

Jerry. Oh, here you are at last! I've been searchin' for you everywhere. The foreman in Foley's told me you hadn't left the snug with Joxer ten minutes before I went in.

Mrs Boyle. An' he swearin' on the holy prayer-book that he wasn't in no snug!

Boyle (*to* JERRY). What business is it o' yours whether I was in a snug or no? What do you want to be gallopin' about afther me for? Is a man not to be allowed to leave his house for a minute without havin' a pack o' spies, pimps an' informers cantherin' at his heels?

Jerry. Oh, you're takin' a wrong view of it, Mr Boyle; I simply was anxious to do you a good turn. I have a message for you from Father Farrell: he says that if you go to the job that's on in Rathmines, an' ask for Foreman Mangan, you'll get a start.

Boyle. That's all right, but I don't want the motions of me body to be watched the way an asthronomer ud watch a star. If you're folleyin' Mary aself, you've no pereeogative to be folleyin' me. (*Suddenly catching his thigh.*) U-ugh, I'm afther gettin' a terrible twinge in me right leg!

Mrs Boyle. Oh, it won't be very long now till it travels into your left wan. It's miraculous that whenever he scents a job in front of him, his legs begin to fail him! Then, me bucko, if you lose this chance, you may go an' furrage for yourself!

Jerry. This job'll last for some time too, Captain, an' as soon as the foundations are in, it'll be cushy enough.

Boyle. Won't it be a climbin' job? How d'ye expect me to be able to go up a ladder with these legs? An', if I get up aself, how am I goin' to get down agen?

Mrs Boyle (*viciously*). Get wan o' the labourers to carry you down in a hod! You can't climb a laddher, but you can skip like a goat into a snug!

Jerry. I wouldn't let meself be let down that easy, Mr Boyle; a little exercise, now, might do you all the good in the world.

Boyle. It's a docthor you should have been, Devine—maybe you know more about the pains in me legs than meself that has them?

Jerry (*irritated*). Oh, I know nothin' about the pains in your legs; I've brought the message that Father Farrell gave me, an' that's all I can do.

Mrs Boyle. Here, sit down an' take your breakfast, an' go an' get ready; an' don't be actin' as if you couldn't pull a wing out of a dead bee.

Boyle. I want no breakfast, I tell you; it ud choke me afther all that's been said. I've a little spirit left in me still.

Mrs Boyle. Well, let's see your spirit, then, an' go in at wanst an' put on your moleskin trousers!

Boyle (*moving towards the door on left*). It ud be betther for a man to be dead! U-ugh! There's another twinge in me other leg! Nobody but meself knows the sufferin' I'm goin' through with the pains in these legs o' mine!

He goes into the room on left as MARY *comes out with her hat in her hand.*

Mrs Boyle. I'll have to push off now, for I'm terrible late already, but I was determined to stay an' hunt that Joxer this time.

[*She goes off.*

Jerry. Are you going out, Mary?

Mary. It looks like it when I'm putting on my hat, doesn't it?

Jerry. The bitther word agen, Mary.

Mary. You won't allow me to be friendly with you; if I thry, you deliberately misundherstand it.

Jerry. I didn't always misundherstand it; you were ofen delighted to have the arms of Jerry around you.

Mary. If you go on talkin' like this, Jerry Devine, you'll make me hate you!

Jerry. Well, let it be either a weddin' or a wake! Listen, Mary, I'm standin' for the Secretaryship of our Union. There's only one opposin' me; I'm popular with all the men, an' a good speaker—all are sayin' that I'll get elected.

Mary. Well?

Jerry. The job's worth three hundred an' fifty pounds a year, Mary. You an' I could live nice an' cosily on that; it would lift you out o' this place an' . . .

Mary. I haven't time to listen to you now—I have to go.

She is going out when JERRY *bars the way*.

Jerry (*appealingly*). Mary, what's come over you with me for the last few weeks? You hardly speak to me, an' then only a word with a face o' bitherness on it. Have you forgotten, Mary, all the happy evenins that were as sweet as the scented hawthorn that sheltered the sides o' the road as we saunthered through the country?

Mary. That's all over now. When you get your new job, Jerry, you won't be long findin' a girl far betther than I am for your sweetheart.

Jerry. Never, never, Mary! No matther what happens, you'll always be the same to me.

Mary. I must be off; please let me go, Jerry.

Jerry. I'll go a bit o' the way with you.

Mary. You needn't, thanks; I want to be by meself.

Jerry (*catching her arm*). You're goin' to meet another fella; you've clicked with some one else, me lady!

Mary. That's no concern o' yours, Jerry Devine; let me go!

Jerry. I saw yous comin' out o' the Cornflower Dance Class, an' you hangin' on his arm—a thin, lanky strip of a Micky Dazzler, with a walkin'-stick an' gloves!

Voice of Johnny (*loudly*). What are you doin' there—pullin' about everything!

Voice of Boyle (*loudly and viciously*). I'm puttin' on me moleskin trousers!

Mary. You're hurtin' me arm! Let me go, or I'll scream, an' then you'll have the oul' fella out on top of us!

Jerry. Don't be so hard on a fella, Mary, don't be so hard.

Boyle (*appearing at the door*). What's the meanin' of all this hillabaloo?

Mary. Let me go, let me go!

Boyle. D'ye hear me—what's all this hillabaloo about?

Jerry (*plaintively*). Will you not give us one kind word, one kind word, Mary?

Boyle. D'ye hear me talkin' to yous? What's all this hillabaloo for?

Jerry. Let me kiss your hand, your little, tiny, white hand!

Boyle. Your little, tiny, white hand—are you takin' leave o' your senses, man?

[MARY *breaks away and rushes out.*

Boyle. This is nice goins on in front of her father!

Jerry. Ah, dhry up, for God's sake!

[*He follows* MARY.

Boyle. Chiselurs* don't care a damn now about their parents, they're bringin' their fathers' grey hairs down with sorra to the grave, an' laughin' at it, laughin' at it. Ah, I suppose it's just the same everywhere—the whole worl's in a state o' chassis!* (*He sits by the fire.*) Breakfast! Well, they can keep their breakfast for me. Not if they went down on their bended knees would I take it—I'll show them I've a little spirit left in me still! (*He goes over to the press, takes out a plate and looks at it.*) Sassige! Well, let her keep her sassige. (*He returns to the fire, takes up the teapot and gives it a gentle shake.*) The tea's wet right enough.

A pause; he rises, goes to the press, takes out the sausage, puts it on the pan, and puts both on the fire. He attends the sausage with a fork.

Boyle (*singing*):

When the robins nest agen,
And the flowers are in bloom,
When the Springtime's sunny smile seems to banish all sorrow an'
    gloom;
Then me bonny blue-ey'd lad, if me heart be true till then—
He's promised he'll come back to me,
When the robins nest agen!

He lifts his head at the high note, and then drops his eyes to the pan.

Boyle (*singing*):

When the . . .

Steps are heard approaching; he whips the pan off the fire and puts it under the bed, then sits down at the fire. The door opens and a bearded man looking in says:

You don't happen to want a sewin' machine?

Boyle (*furiously*). No, I don't want e'er a sewin' machine!

He returns the pan to the fire, and commences to sing again.

Boyle (*singing*):

When the robins nest agen,
And the flowers they are in bloom,
He's . . .

A thundering knock is heard at the street door.

Boyle. There's a terrible tatheraraa—that's a stranger—that's nobody belongin' to the house.

Another loud knock.

Joxer (*sticking his head in at the door*). Did ye hear them tatherarahs?

Boyle. Well, Joxer, I'm not deaf.

Johnny (*appearing in his shirt and trousers at the door on left; his face is anxious and his voice is tremulous*). Who's that at the door; who's that at the door? Who gave that knock—d'ye yous hear me—are yous deaf or dhrunk or what?

Boyle (*to* JOHNNY). How the hell do I know who 'tis? Joxer, stick your head out o' the window an' see.

Joxer. An' mebbe get a bullet in the kisser? Ah, none o' them thricks for Joxer! It's betther to be a coward than a corpse!

Boyle (*looking cautiously out of the window*). It's a fella in a thrench coat.

Johnny. Holy Mary, Mother o' God, I . . .

Boyle. He's goin' away—he must ha' got tired knockin'.

[JOHNNY *returns to the room on left.*

Boyle. Sit down an' have a cup o' tay, Joxer.

Joxer. I'm afraid the missus ud pop in on us agen before we'd know where we are. Somethins tellin' me to go at wanst.

Boyle. Don't be superstitious, man; we're Dublin men, an' not boyos that's only afther comin' up from the bog o' Allen*—though if she did come in, right enough, we'd be caught like rats in a thrap.

Joxer. An' you know the sort she is—she wouldn't listen to reason—an' wanse bitten twice shy.

Boyle (*going over to the window at back*). If the worst came to the worst, you could dart out here, Joxer; it's only a dhrop of a few feet to the roof of the return room,* an' the first minute she goes into dh'other room, I'll give you the bend, an' you can slip in an' away.

Joxer (*yielding to the temptation*). Ah, I won't stop very long any-how. (*Picking up a book from the table.*) Who's is the buk?

Boyle. Aw, one o' Mary's; she's always readin' lately—nothin' but thrash, too. There's one I was lookin' at dh' other day: three stories, The Doll's House, Ghosts, an' The Wild Duck*—buks only fit for chiselurs!

Joxer. Didja ever rade *Elizabeth, or Th' Exile o' Sibayria* . . . ah, it's a darlin' story, a daarlin' story!

Boyle. You eat your sassige, an' never min' *Th' Exile o' Sibayria.*

Both sit down; BOYLE *fills out tea, pours gravy on* JOXER's *plate, and keeps the sausage for himself.*

Joxer. What are you wearin' your moleskin trousers for?

Boyle. I have to go to a job, Joxer. Just afther you'd gone, Devine kem runnin' in to tell us that Father Farrell said if I went down to the job that's goin' on in Rathmines I'd get a start.

Joxer. Be the holy, that's good news!

Boyle. How is it good news? I wondher if you were in my condition, would you call it good news?

Joxer. I thought . . .

Boyle. You thought! You think too sudden sometimes, Joxer. D'ye know, I'm hardly able to crawl with the pains in me legs!

Joxer. Yis, yis; I forgot the pains in your legs. I know you can do nothin' while they're at you.

Boyle. You forgot; I don't think any of yous realize the state I'm in with the pains in me legs. What ud happen if I had to carry a bag o' cement?

Joxer. Ah, any man havin' the like of them pains id be down an' out, down an' out.

Boyle. I wouldn't mind if he had said it to meself; but, no, oh no, he rushes in an' shouts it out in front o' Juno, an' you know what Juno is, Joxer. We all know Devine knows a little more than the rest of us, but he doesn't act as if he did; he's a good boy, sober, able to talk an' all that, but still . . .

Joxer. Oh ay; able to argufy, but still . . .

Boyle. If he's runnin' afther Mary, aself, he's not goin' to be runnin' afther me. Captain Boyle's able to take care of himself. Afther all, I'm not gettin' brought up on Virol.* I never heard him usin' a curse; I don't believe he was ever dhrunk in his life—sure he's not like a Christian at all!

Joxer. You're afther takin' the word out o' me mouth—afther all, a Christian's natural, but he's unnatural.

Boyle. His oul' fella was just the same—a Wicklow man.

Joxer. A Wicklow man! That explains the whole thing. I've met many a Wicklow man in me time, but I never met wan that was any good.

Boyle. 'Father Farrell,' says he, 'sent me down to tell you.' Father Farrell! . . . D'ye know, Joxer, I never like to be beholden to any o' the clergy.

Joxer. It's dangerous, right enough.

Boyle. If they do anything for you, they'd want you to be livin' in the Chapel. . . . I'm goin' to tell you somethin', Joxer, that I wouldn't tell to anybody else—the clergy always had too much power over the people in this unfortunate country.

Joxer. You could sing that if you had an air to it!

Boyle (*becoming enthusiastic*). Didn't they prevent the people in ''47' from seizin' the corn, an' they starvin'; didn't they down Parnell; didn't they say that hell wasn't hot enough nor eternity long enough to punish the Fenians?* We don't forget, we don't forget them things, Joxer. If they've taken everything else from us, Joxer, they've left us our memory.

Joxer (*emotionally*). For mem'ry's the only friend that grief can call its own, that grief . . . can . . . call . . . its own!

Boyle. Father Farrell's beginnin' to take a great intherest in Captain Boyle; because of what Johnny did for his country, says he to me wan day. It's a curious way to reward Johnny be makin' his poor oul' father work. But, that's what the clergy want, Joxer—work, work, work for me an' you; havin' us mulin' from mornin' till night, so that they may be in betther fettle when they come hoppin' round for their dues! Job! Well, let him give his job to wan of his hymn-singin', prayer-spoutin', craw-thumpin' Confraternity men!*

The voice of a COAL-BLOCK VENDOR *is heard chanting in the street.*

Voice of coal vendor. Blocks . . . coal-blocks! Blocks . . . coal-blocks!

Joxer. God be with the young days when you were steppin' the deck of a manly ship, with the win' blowin' a hurricane through the masts, an' the only sound you'd hear was, 'Port your helm!' an' the only answer, 'Port it is, sir!'

Boyle. Them was days, Joxer, them was days. Nothin' was too hot or too heavy for me then. Sailin' from the Gulf o' Mexico to the Antanartic Ocean. I seen things, I seen things, Joxer, that no mortal man should speak about that knows his Catechism. Ofen, an' ofen, when I was fixed to the wheel with a marlinspike, an' the wins blowin' fierce an' the waves lashin' an' lashin', till you'd think every minute was goin' to be your last, an' it blowed, an' blowed—blew is the right word, Joxer, but blowed is what the sailors use . . .

Joxer. Aw, it's a darlin' word, a daarlin' word.

Boyle. An', as it blowed an' blowed, I ofen looked up at the sky an' assed meself the question—what is the stars, what is the stars?

Voice of coal vendor. Any blocks, coal-blocks; blocks, coal-blocks!

Joxer. Ah, that's the question, that's the question—what is the stars?

Boyle. An' then, I'd have another look, an' I'd ass meself—what is the moon?

Joxer. Ah, that's the question—what is the moon, what is the moon?

EXPLANATORY NOTES

EDMUND BURKE

From *Reflections on the Revolution in France* (1790). In this celebrated passage, Burke prefaces his defence of ancient principle with an exalted tribute to Marie Antoinette. His eulogistic account of the Queen provoked his opponents, who accused him of romantic indulgence. Thomas Jefferson was among those who claimed that Burke had painted the Queen of France as an angel, while overlooking her considerable vices.

5 *Non satis est pulchra esse poemata, dulcia sunto*: it is not enough for poems to be beautiful; they must also be sweet (Horace, *Ars Poetica*, 99–100).

6 *swinish multitude*: Burke's critics seized upon this phrase and turned it to advantage. There were numerous ripostes such as Thomas Spence's *Pig's Meat, or Lessons for the Swinish Multitude* (1793–5) and J. Parkinson's *An Address to Edmund Burke from the Swinish Multitude* (1793).

7 *gentis incunabula nostrae*: the cradle of our people (Virgil, *Aeneid*, iii. 105).

From Letter to Richard Burke. On 19 Feb. 1792, Burke informed his son Richard, then in Dublin, that he was writing a long letter to him, but the letter was never finished. The letter considers the grievances of Irish Catholics and dwells on the significance of the term 'Protestant Ascendancy'.

10 *honestum nomen imponitur vitio*: an honourable name is given to a vice.

the touch of the Corporation: on 20 Jan. 1792, the Corporation of Dublin approved an address to the King, pleading for the preservation of the Protestant ascendancy in Ireland.

the Speaker of the House of Commons: John Foster (1740–1828).

the Lord Mayor of Dublin: Henry Gore Sankey (d. 1821).

11 *parce detorsum*: sparingly altered (Horace, *Ars Poetica*, 53).

THEOBALD WOLFE TONE

From *The Life of Theobald Wolfe Tone* (1826). Tone's journals were collected and edited by his son, William, and published under the above title in Washington in 1826, with later editions in Paris, Dublin, and London. The passage reprinted here was purportedly written in 1797.

13 *an eloquent publication*: Burke's *Reflections on the Revolution in France* (1790).

14 *coup de grâce*: a stroke of grace (i.e. a finishing blow to put someone out of misery).

15 *Russell*: Thomas Russell, political radical who assisted Tone and Henry Joy McCracken in establishing the Society of United Irishmen in 1791.

16 *the Volunteer Convention in 1783*: companies of volunteers, uniformed and partly armed, were established in the 1770s, initially to defend the coasts of Ireland against any invader while British regiments were engaged in America. Their presence, however, strengthened nationalist sentiment and helped to bring about legislative independence in 1782.

John Keogh: John Keogh (1740–1817), Catholic leader who was largely responsible for the Catholic Convention of 1792, leading to the Relief Act of 1793.

Henry Flood: Henry Flood (1732–91), statesman and orator. MP for Kilkenny and advocate of an independent Irish legislature. He lost his place as leader of the opposition to Henry Grattan (1746–1820).

ROBERT EMMET

'Speech from the Dock', from *Report of the Proceedings in Cases of High Treason* [by William Ridgeway, Barrister at Law] (Dublin: John Exshaw, 1803). See biographical entry for details of the circumstances relating to Emmet's arrest and trial.

DANIEL O'CONNELL

In 1843, O'Connell addressed a series of vast public meetings throughout Ireland, calling for the repeal of the Act of Union (1800) and the establishment of an Irish Parliament. One of the largest of these meetings was held at Tara, Co. Meath, the seat of the high kings of Ireland until the sixth century.

27 *a mess of pottage*: literally, stuff in a pot, but also a reference to the biblical instance of Esau selling the everlasting inheritance of heaven for a mess of pottage (Genesis 25: 29–34).

29 *my third son, the member for Kilkenny*: John O'Connell (1810–58), elected MP for Youghal, 1832, and later representing Athlone, Kilkenny, Limerick, and Clonmel.

JAMES FINTAN LALOR

From the *Irish Felon*, 24 June 1848. The newspaper was founded by John Martin (1812–75) to replace John Mitchell's *United Irishman*. Mitchell, his brother-in-law, had been transported to Van Diemen's Land and the paper had been suppressed. Lalor helped to edit the *Irish Felon* and in the first number reasserted the revolutionary spirit of Wolfe Tone and advocated immediate insurrection. His letter marks a militant break with the limited constitutional independence achieved in 1782 and proposes a more radical programme of political change than Daniel O'Connell's attempt to repeal the Act of Union. Lalor was arrested in the rising of 1848, just a month later.

35 *Arcades ambo*: balmy Arcadians (the suggestion is that the ideals of

Repeal are not in keeping with the needs of the real world; Arcadia, the legendary haunt of the Greeks, also implies rural simplicity).

36 *the constitution that Tone died to obtain*: see the extract above from the autobiography of Theobald Wolfe Tone (1763–98) and also the biographical entry on Tone at the end of this volume.

sub silentio: in silence, without remark being made.

41 *our gage of battle*: a pledge (traditionally, a glove thrown down) to signal readiness to fight.

CHARLOTTE BROOKE

This modest Preface to *Reliques of Irish Poetry* (1789) presents the book as 'a translation of ancient Irish poetry', comprising four species of composition: the Heroic Poem, the Ode, the Elegy, and the Song. An Irish typeface was designed for the printing of the originals, which appear at the end of the 1789 volume.

LE CHEVALIER DE LA TOCNAYE

From *A Frenchman's Walk Through Ireland (1796–7)* [*Promenade d'un Français dans l'Irelande*], translated by John Stevenson (Dublin: Hodges, Figgis & Co., 1914).

47 *the Four Courts of Justice*: one of Dublin's finest buildings, designed by James Gandon (1742–1823).

Themis: the name of the ancient Greek goddess of law and justice.

49 *'The Liberties'*: a district formerly outside the walls of the medieval city of Dublin, run by local courts and free of the city regulations on trade. From the eighteenth century onwards, it was a vibrant slum area, renowned for its rebelliousness.

51 *this Augean stable*: like the abominably filthy stable of Augeas, King of Elis, which Hercules cleansed by diverting the river Alpheus through it.

52 *anything green, ribbon or otherwise*: a display of Irish nationalist sentiment (the green ribbon was the emblem of the United Irishmen).

a company of Orangemen: members of the Orange Order, a Protestant Society founded in Co. Armagh in 1795, commemorating the victory of King William III, Prince of Orange, at the Battle of the Boyne in 1690.

54 *pot-de-vin*: literally, a pot of wine, but figuratively referring to additional benefits accrued from the lease of land.

JOHN GAMBLE

From *Sketches of History, Politics, and Manners, in Dublin, and the North of Ireland, in 1810*, new edn. (London: Baldwick, Cradock, and Joy, 1826).

59 *Allhallows eve*: the eve of All Hallows or All Saints, popularly known as Hallowe'en (31 Oct.). In the old Celtic calendar, the last night of October was 'old year's night', the night of all witches, but this was transformed by the Church into the Eve of All Saints.

shifts: underclothes (derived from a shift or change of clothing).

WILLIAM CARLETON

From *Traits and Stories of the Irish Peasantry. A New Edition* (Dublin: William Curry & Co., 1843–4). This was Carleton's first published work. Originally titled 'A Pilgrimage to Patrick's Purgatory' and printed in the *Christian Examiner* (1828), it appeared with its new title as an accompaniment to the novella, *Father Butler* (1829), and was then revised for *Traits and Stories of the Irish Peasantry*.

61 *Purgatory*: a place of suffering and expiation. Lough Derg is referred to as Purgatory because of the penance undertaken there by St Patrick. Carleton uses the name for both the lake and the lake isle, later known as Station Island.

Petigo: Pettigo, a village on the pilgrim route to Lough Derg in Co. Donegal.

63 *three Paters and Aves, and a Creed*: prayers of gratitude said by the Christian pilgrims arriving at Lough Derg (specifically, 'Our Father', 'Hail Mary', and 'I believe').

64 *stations*: holy places or designated sites for prayer, visited by pilgrims in fixed succession. The Stations of the Cross represent the incidents of Christ's Passion.

circumbendibus: a roundabout process or method; a twist.

65 *bannock*: a round, flat cake, usually made from barley-meal.

67 *Juggernaut*: in Hindu myth, the image of Krishna, annually dragged in procession on a mighty car, under the wheels of which his devotees would throw themselves to be crushed; figuratively speaking, the term refers to anything to which people blindly devote themselves or are ruthlessly sacrificed.

71 *his stole and box of chrism*: the priest's vestment (usually a narrow strip of silk or linen worn over the shoulders) and the consecrated oil and balm used in the administration of certain sacraments.

extreme unction: the sacrament in which those in extreme conditions (the sick and the dying) are anointed by a priest.

De profundis: a prayer based on Psalm 130, 'Out of the depths have I cried to thee, O Lord'; a cry from the depths of sorrow.

72 *malaproprian*: given to the ludicrous misuse of words.

73 *lanna*: from the Irish *leanbh* (young person; child).

a cushla: Irish term of endearment (my dear one).

73 *aroon*: another term of endearment, from the Irish *a rún* (loved one).

astore machree: yet another term of endearment, from the Irish *a stór* (treasure) and *mo chroí* (my heart).

THOMAS DAVIS

'Ballad Poetry of Ireland' first appeared in *The Nation*, 2 Aug. 1845, as a review of the book of that title edited by Charles Gavan Duffy. 'The History of Ireland' was also a book review in *The Nation*. Both essays are reprinted from *Essays Literary and Historical By Thomas Davis*, ed. D. J. O'Donoghue (Dundalk: Dundalgan Press, 1914).

the English Pale, the Ulster Settlement: from the late fifteenth century onwards, the term 'Pale' (a defended area with clearly defined boundaries) was applied to the English parts of the four counties around Dublin which were subject to direct royal government. The Ulster Settlement refers to the seizure and reallocation of land in Ulster, following the wars between Elizabeth I and the supporters of Hugh O'Neill, 1594–1603. The process of transferring land from Catholic to Protestant ownership continued throughout the seventeenth century, with a large influx of Scots settlers in the 1630s.

74 *on his march to Kinsale*: Hugh O'Neill, Earl of Tyrone (1550–1616), led his Irish soldiers to Kinsale to assist the Spanish expeditionary force that had landed there in 1601; encountering strong opposition from Lord Mountjoy and his allies, he was forced to retreat.

Strongbownian: a follower of Richard de Clare, Earl of Pembroke, known as 'Strongbow', who had landed in Ireland with Norman knights in 1170 prior to the arrival of Henry II.

Swift and Grattan: Jonathan Swift (1667–1745), Dublin-born writer, author of *Gulliver's Travels* (1726) and several essays on Irish social and political concerns; Henry Grattan (1746–1820), Dublin-born politician and architect of Irish legislative independence in 1782. Davis sees their ideas of Irish nationality as limited and offers a more comprehensive ideal of national culture.

Grattan and Curran . . . Griffin and Carleton . . . Maclise and Burton: John Philpott Curran (1750–1817), orator and MP in the Irish Parliament, and an eloquent spokesman in favour of Catholic Emancipation; Gerald Griffin (1803–40), author of *The Collegians* (1829) and other novels; William Carleton, see biographical entry in this volume; Daniel Maclise (1806–70), painter and book illustrator; Frederick William Burton (1816–1900), Dublin-based painter of miniatures and watercolour portraits, appointed Director of the National Gallery in London in 1874.

77 *the scarce lithograph of Moreau*: Caesar Moreau (1791–1861) published his valuable and scarce *Past and Present Statistical State of Ireland* in 1827, printed in a copperplate style.

MARIA EDGEWORTH

From *Castle Rackrent* (1800). The title of the novel is an acknowledgement of extortionate rents which often stretched impoverished tenants beyond their means. Thady Quirk, a steward, tells of the declining fortunes of three generations of the landowning Rackrent family. In the extract printed here (from the beginning of the novel), he recalls the dissolute behaviour of Sir Patrick Rackrent, who drinks himself to death; Sir Murtagh, an obsessive litigant; and Sir Kit, who is brought home in a wheelbarrow, fatally injured in a duel.

The notes printed at the foot of each page are the author's. Words and phrases accompanied with a superscript ^G are explained in the author's glossary at the end of the extract.

129 *Spencer*: Sir Edmund Spenser (1552–99), whose *View of the Present State of Ireland* (1596) Edgeworth proceeds to quote.

80 *Holantide*: Hallowe'en.

cousin-german: first cousin.

car: cart.

the three kingdoms itself: England, Scotland, and Ireland.

81 *He that goes to bed . . . honest fellow*: a traditional song, popular as early as the mid-seventeenth century.

83 *the Linen Board to distribute gratis*: the Linen Board was based in Dublin and encouraged the production of linen (from locally grown flax) throughout Ireland. It was only in parts of Ulster, however, that it flourished.

84 *replevying*: recovering cattle or other goods taken from him, having provided security for the case to be tried in a court of justice.

heriots: payments, often consisting of the best livestock, made to the landlord on the death of a tenant.

'learning is better than house or land': a proverb, as the novel suggests, but a possible written source is David Garrick's prologue to Oliver Goldsmith's comedy, *She Stoops to Conquer* (1733): 'When ign'rance enters, folly is at hand; | Learning is better far than house and land'.

fee-simple: feudal tenure or fief.

85 *abatements*: reductions in value.

loy: a narrow spade.

SYDNEY OWENSON (LADY MORGAN)

From *The Wild Irish Girl* (1806). The novel is set in Tireragh, Co. Sligo, where it was written. The extract reprinted here combines a vivid delight in Gothic scenery and mystery with an intense curiosity towards ancient Irish customs and manners.

95 *manes*: the shade of a departed person, seeking expiation through violent sacrifice.

carte du pays: a chart of the land.

98 *pontificals*: the appropriate vestments of a priest.

glory: a circle of light.

100 *outré*: out of the way; beyond the bounds of what is proper or usual.

Milton's ruined angel: Milton's description of Satan (of which this is a slight misquotation) appears in Book 1 of *Paradise Lost*, lines 589–91.

101 *Caiphas*: Caiaphas, the high priest who interrogates Jesus after his arrest (Matthew 26: 57).

cerulean blue: azure, the clear blue of the unclouded sky.

103 *the Eolian lyre*: the Eolian or Æolian lyre or harp (from Æolus, god of the winds) is a stringed instrument that produces musical sounds from a current of air. It was a popular symbol of inspiration for the Romantic poets.

CHARLES MATURIN

From *Melmoth the Wanderer* (1820), Maturin's celebrated Gothic novel. The extract reprinted here (chapter 1) is set in early nineteenth-century Dublin and introduces us to a student, John Melmoth, but the novel ranges far and wide as it traces the wanderings of an earlier Melmoth who, in a Faustian pact, exchanged his soul for worldly power and knowledge.

106 *Shakespeare*: the quotation is from *Henry VI*, III. iii.

107 *the mail*: the mail coach.

wig-blocks: for supporting wigs.

'shod with felt': 'To shoe a troop of horse with felt', Shakespeare, *King Lear*, IV. vi.

the ghost of Beatrice in the Monk: the Gothic novel *The Monk* (1796), which earned its author, Matthew Gregory Lewis (1775–1818), the nick-name of 'Monk' Lewis.

109 *'eyes that glow and fangs that grin'*: unidentified by Maturin's editors, though it possibly derives from the Gothic fiction of the time.

kish: a large wicker basket for carrying turf.

110 *cottar's hut*: a peasant cottage.

'as is beyond our element': Shakespeare, *The Merry Wives of Windsor*, IV. ii.

No one twined so well: Maturin is here describing various spells (practised in peasant Ireland) for discovering the identity of a future husband.

'ears polite': from Pope's *Epistle to Burlington*, ii. 149–50.

Anglicè: in standard English, as distinct from *Hibernicè* (in Hiberno-English).

111 *Lord Lyttleton*: Thomas Lyttleton (1744–79) was supposed to have foreseen his own death in a dream three days earlier.

imprimis: in the first place (used here to emphasize the fact that John has black hair: the housekeeper's expression, 'white-headed boy', is just a term of endearment).

Miss Edgeworth's Tales: Maria Edgeworth (1767–1849), whose novel *The Absentee* (1812) was part of a series of 'Tales of Fashionable Life'.

slink-veal: the flesh of a premature calf.

'suo periculo': at his own risk (Latin).

the Dean of Killala: the author's great-grandfather, Peter Maturin, was Dean of Killala, Co. Mayo, from 1724 to 1741.

112 *'veritable Amphitryon' of the feast*: Amphitryon, King of Thebes, was impersonated by Zeus; Maturin is recalling Molière's dramatization of the story: 'Le veritable Amphitryon est l'Amphitryon ou l'on dine'.

'even Sancho cherished his little carcase': from the final chapter of *Don Quixote*.

a Pythoness on her tripod: one of the Priestesses of Apollo at Delphi, who conducted her prophecies from a three-legged seat.

113 *the Irish præficæ*: Irish weepers, likened to the mourners in classical literature.

the story of Sinbad the Sailor: from *The Thousand and One Nights*.

'all was cold as any stone': Shakespeare, *Henry V*, II. iii.

114 *their name is Legion*: a reference to the New Testament story of a man possessed by many devils, hence the name Legion (Luke 9: 30).

sixes: candles bought in batches of six (presumably six to the pound).

115 *'her reading and writing came by nature'*: Shakespeare, *Much Ado About Nothing*, III. iii.

'churching of women': the thanksgiving of women after childbirth.

niggers: niggards, used to reduce the size of the grate and so cut down on fuel.

117 *THALABA*: Robert Southey, *Thalaba the Destroyer* (1801), Book II, verse 5, lines 10–11.

118 *poor Butler*: Samuel Butler (1612–80), who became destitute in later years. Maturin is quoting inaccurately from the second volume of Butler's *Genuine Remains* (1759).

facies Hippocratica: the look of the face just before death (as described by Hippocrates).

119 *the blue chamber of the dwelling*: possibly adopted from the story of Bluebeard, in which entry to a particular chamber is forbidden.

SHERIDAN LE FANU

From *The House by the Church-yard*, 3 vols. (London: Tinsley, Brothers, 1863), volume II, chapter XXXIV. The novel was first serialized in the *Dublin University Magazine*. It is narrated by Charles Cresseron and set in Chapelizod, near Dublin, in the eighteenth century. The extract in this volume follows the murder of an army doctor, Sturk, by a mysterious assailant. One of the chief suspects is Charles Nutter, whose body has reportedly been discovered by fishermen.

121 *rummer-glass*: a large drinking glass (from the Dutch *roemer*).

Ringsend: area of south-east Dublin, close to the River Liffey and Dublin Bay.

slack down the fire: dampen the flames.

122 *flags*: stone slabs or flagstones.

vapours: an exhalation rising from the ground or some damp place; mist or fog.

123 *press*: a large cupboard for holding clothes and other possessions.

EMILY LAWLESS

From *Hurrish: A Study* (1886). This first novel by Emily Lawless is set in Co. Clare during the time of the Land War waged in response to agricultural depression and exploitative landlord–tenant relations. The Land League was formed in 1879 and managed to win concessions by 1882, but there was sporadic violence along the way. The violence in this case affects Horatio (Hurrish) O'Brien, an innocent smallholder who finds himself in a tragic dispute with a resentful neighbour and distant relative. The extract is from chapter 1 of the novel.

126 *omnium gatherum*: quasi Latin for a gathering of all sorts of things.

'creepy' stool: a low stool, close to the ground.

A broad-shouldered, loose-limbed, genial-faced giant: James Joyce parodies this extravagant description of the hero in the Cyclops episode of *Ulysses*.

128 *that ill-starred apology for a rebellion*: the abortive Fenian rising of 1867.

myrmidons: unscrupulous supporters or hirelings.

pabulum: fodder.

ANTOINE RAFTERY

'I am Raftery' has been translated from the Irish ('Mise Raifteri') many times, and Raftery has become an emblematic figure of Irish poetic endeavour, not just for writers of the literary revival who were rediscovering the Gaelic culture of the west, but for later writers, like Derek Mahon, contemplating the seemingly bleak poetic prospects of the contemporary north. The version here is from Douglas Hyde's *Songs of Connacht* (1903).

CHARLOTTE BROOKE

'Elegy on the Death of Carolan', from *Reliques of Irish Poetry* (1789). See note above. Turlough Carolan (Toirdhealbhach Ó Cearbhalláin, 1670–1738), Irish harper, composer, and poet, was celebrated by his contemporaries (Oliver Goldsmith wrote a notable essay about him) and his music continues to be revered today. The poem is a translation from the Irish of M'Cabe.

THOMAS MOORE

Five of the songs are from *Irish Melodies* (1807–34). 'Oft, in the stilly night' is from *National Airs* (1818).

131 *'Oh! breathe not his name'*: the title echoes the sentiments of Robert Emmet's closing words in his famous speech from the dock at his trial for high treason in Sept. 1803 (see above). Emmet had asked for the charity of silence: 'When my country takes her place among the nations of the earth, *then, and not till then*, let my epitaph be written.'

132 *'She is far from the land'*: the 'she' of the title is Sarah Curran (1780–1808), who was secretly engaged to Robert Emmet at the time of his execution in 1803. She escaped her father's anger at discovering her attachment to Emmet by staying with friends in Cork. She later married a Captain Sturgeon in Cork in 1805. She died in England shortly after.

133 *'The harp that once through Tara's halls'*: Tara, Co. Meath, was the seat of the high kings of Ireland.

MARY TIGHE

The three poems written at Killarney in 1800 are all sonnets. 'Address to my Harp' should be compared with Charlotte Brooke's 'Elegy on the Death of Carolan' and Thomas Moore's 'The harp that once through Tara's halls', in which the harp is both a national emblem and a source of comfort. All four poems are from *Psyche, with Other Poems* (London: Longman, Hurst, Rees, Orme and Brown, 1811).

THOMAS FURLONG

'Roisin Dubh', from *Irish Minstrelsy*, ed. James Hardiman (1831), is an Irish poem which, according to Hardiman, was composed in the reign of Elizabeth I to celebrate the Irish hero, Hugh Ruadh O'Donnell of Tirconnell. A love song opens out into a political allegory of Ireland's struggle for liberty. 'Roisin Dubh' (meaning 'little black rose') has been translated many times (by Samuel Ferguson and Aubrey de Vere and James Clarence Mangan, among others).

'Eileen a Roon', from *Irish Minstrelsy*, ed. James Hardiman (1831). 'A Roon' is a term of endearment, from the Irish *a rún* (loved one).

'The Spirit of Irish Song' is thought to be the last work Furlong composed.

JAMES CLARENCE MANGAN

'To My Native Land' was published in the *Comet*, 15 July 1832. It is generally considered to be Mangan's earliest nationalist poem.

140 *The harp remaineth where it fell*: the harp, a potent image of Irish national culture, lies broken, signifying the country's defeat and ruin.

'The Woman of Three Cows' was first published in the *Irish Penny Journal*, 29 Aug. 1840. It is based on an anonymous Irish poem, probably given to Mangan in a literal translation by Eugene O'Curry.

142 *agragh*: from the Irish *a ghrá* (love, as in 'my love').

Momonia: Munster, the home of the legendary Owen More (Eoghan Mór).

brave sons of the Lord of Clare: the Lord of Clare was Domhnall Ó Briain (Daniel O'Brien), the 3rd Viscount of Clare, who provided military support for James II in 1689. His elder son, Domhnall, commanded 'Clare's dragoons', and his younger son, Cormac, commanded the infantry. Both died in exile after the Treaty of Limerick.

Movrone: from the Irish *mo Bhrón* (my sorrow).

Donnell of the Ships: Donal O'Sullivan Beare (1560–1618), Gaelic chief from West Cork, who left Ireland for Spain in 1602 after the destruction of the family stronghold, Dunboy Castle. He was later assassinated in Madrid by an Anglo-Irishman, John Bathe.

O'Ruark, Maguire, those souls of fire: Brian Óg Ó Ruairc, who offered shelter to Donal O'Sullivan Beare at Leitrim Castle, and Brian Maguidhir of Fermanagh, another supporter.

143 *the O'Carrolls*: probably the prominent O'Carroll family of Éile (Ely) in Co. Tipperary.

inagh: from the Irish *an ea* (is it?), but Mangan's own note suggests 'forsooth'.

'Lamentation of Mac Liag for Kincora' was first published in the *Irish Penny Journal*, 9 Jan. 1841. MacLiag's existence seems doubtful, but the mid-seventeenth-century Irish original on which this poem is based takes its bearings from stories of Brian Boru and his victory at Clontarf in 1014. Kincora was where Brian Boru had his palace, on the banks of the River Shannon, near Killaloe, Co. Clare.

144 *Dalcassians*: the sept or tribe of which Brian Boru was chief.

Morogh: Brian's eldest son, Murchadh, killed at Clontarf.

Donagh: Brian's surviving son and successor, Donnchadh.

Conaing: his nephew, slain at Clontarf.

Kian: the son of Maolmhuaidh, an ally at Clontarf.

Corc: a Dalcassian ancestral hero.

son of Erin the Brave: Domhnall, son of Eimhin.

great King of Onaght: Scannlán, King of the Eoghanacht sept, killed at Clontarf.

hosts of Baskinn: a tribe from south-west Clare.

Duvlann: possibly Dúnlaing, King of Life (Liffey).

Lonergan: the nephew of Brian Boru.

Prince of the Scots: Domhnall, son of Eimhin.

'Kathaleen Ny-Houlahan' was first published in the *Irish Penny Journal*, 16 Jan. 1841. Kathaleen Ny-Houlahan (or Cathleen Ní Houlihan), like Roisin Dubh, is one of the names given to Ireland personified as the poet's beloved. The earliest version is thought to be by the eighteenth-century Jacobite poet, Liam Dall Ó hIfearnáin, and appears in a 'translation' by Mangan, under the title 'Caitlin Ni Uallachain' in *Poets and Poetry of Munster: A Selection of Irish Songs* (Dublin: John O'Daly, 1849).

145 *Saxoneen*: a little Saxon.

146 *the Young Deliverer*: the Stuart Pretender.

    Let us pray to Him: in the final two stanzas, the poem draws on Christian exhortation based on Genesis and Exodus.

'Dark Rosaleen' was first published in *The Nation*, 30 May 1846. Mangan's version is probably based on Samuel Ferguson's literal translation of the original (thought to be by a Father Costello of Co. Cork). Mangan infuses the poem with the nationalist spirit of the 1840s and produces a powerful political lyric.

    And Spanish ale shall give you hope: this, like the wine from the Pope in line 5, suggests support for Ireland from sympathetic Catholic countries.

    The Erne . . . at its highest flood: the name of both the river and the lake in Co. Fermanagh.

'Black-Haired Fair Rose' is a version of 'Roisin Dubh' (see note on Thomas Furlong above). It appeared posthumously in *The Poets and Poetry of Munster* (1849).

148 *Erne*: see note on 'Dark Rosaleen'.

'The Nameless One' was published in the *Irishman*, 27 Oct. 1849, but probably composed in the autumn of 1848. The references to William Maginn (1793–1842) and Robert Burns (1759–96), both victims of alcoholism, hint at one of the sources of the poem's deep misery.

150 *eld*: old age.

151 *dreeing*: enduring.

FRANCIS SYLVESTER MAHONY

'The Bells of Shandon' was included in *The Reliques of Father Prout* (1836) in an essay titled 'The Rogueries of Thomas Moore', in which Moore is jestingly accused of borrowing heavily from sources in a variety of languages. Father Prout, the fictitious author of the book, claims that he had written 'The Bells of Shandon' while a student at the Irish College in Rome, and that Moore had plagiarized it for his 'Evening Bells: A Petersburg Air'. The eight bells are in the handsome bell-tower of St Anne's Church, just off Shandon St. in Cork.

152 *Inscrip. on an old Bell*: spurious Latin: 'I mark the Sabbath, I sob at funerals, I clang on solemn occasions.'

SAMUEL FERGUSON

'Lament for the Death of Thomas Davis', from the *Dublin University Magazine* (1847). 'Cashel of Munster', from *Lays of the Western Gael* (1865). 'The Coolun' ('Maiden of the flowing locks'), from *Lays of the Western Gael* (1865).

157 *coleen oge*: from the Irish *cailín óg* (young girl).

coleen bawn: from the Irish *cailín bán* (fair girl).

'Dear Dark Head', from *Lays of the Western Gael* (1865). The title in Irish was 'Ceann Dubh Deelish'.

THOMAS DAVIS

Both poems are reprinted from *The Poems of Thomas Davis* (Dublin: James Duffy, 1846). 'A Nation Once Again' was first published in *The Nation*. The title became an oft-quoted phrase among members of the nationalist Young Ireland movement.

'The West's Asleep' was first published in *The Nation* and then reprinted in the booklet edited by Charles Gavan Duffy, *The Spirit of the Nation*, which went through several editions. An expanded edition appeared in 1845, with musical accompaniments. 'The West's Asleep' is given the old tune, 'Brink of the White Rocks'.

160 *Coirrslabh Pass and Ard Rathain*: Coirrslabh (Coirrshliabh) Pass is in the Curlew Hills, near Boyle, Co. Roscommon. A battle between Irish and Norman forces was fought there in 1230. Ardrathan, Co. Galway, was the site of another battle in 1225.

Aughrim's slopes and Shannon's wave: the Clanricarde family fought against the English at Aughrim, Co. Galway, in 1691.

AUBREY DE VERE

'The Little Black Rose' is a version of 'Roisin Dubh' (see the note on Thomas

Furlong above). It was published in *The Sisters, Inisfail, and Other Poems* (1861).

161 *The Silk of the Kine*: the silken heifer, one of the many emblems of Ireland in early poems and songs. It continued to be used by later writers such as Thomas MacDonagh and James Joyce.

Athenry: village (now a small town) in Co. Galway.

'Florence MacCarthy's Farewell to His English Love' was first published in *Poems* (1855). A longer version appears in *The Sisters, Inisfail, and Other Poems* (1861). De Vere offers a note on the poem, explaining that Florence MacCarthy was detained in England for many years, sometimes in prison, sometimes on parole. In 1601 he was arrested, while supposedly under the Queen's protection, and imprisoned in the Tower of London. The poem is a song of exile in which the yew tree becomes a prominent symbol of a dying Ireland.

JOHN KELLS INGRAM

'The Memory of the Dead' (often referred to by its opening line, 'Who fears to speak of Ninety-eight?') was published anonymously in *The Nation* in Apr. 1843. In extolling the patriotism and heroism of the 1798 rebellion, the ballad seeks to establish continuity between the nationalist politics of the United Irishmen and the Young Ireland spirit of its own time.

WILLIAM ALLINGHAM

'The Fairies' was written in 1849 and reprinted many times, both in Allingham's volumes of poetry and in popular anthologies. It first appeared in book form in *Poems* (1850).

'The Maids of Elfin-Mere' was originally titled 'The Maidens of the Mere' and appears in Allingham's *Poems* (1850) as such. This version is taken from *Irish Songs and Poems* (1901). Mere can mean 'lake or pond', but also 'marsh or fen'.

'A Dream', from *Poems* (1850).

'The Winding Banks of Erne' is reprinted from Allingham's *Irish Songs and Poems* (1901), though earlier versions exist. In his *Fifty Modern Poems* (1865), the subtitle was 'the Emigrant's Adieu to Ballyshannon, a local ballad', and the first line began 'Adieu to Ballyshannon'. It became 'Adieu to Ballyshanny' in 1877. Allingham explains in his notes that 'The important river Erne rises in Lough Gowna, not very far from the middle of Ireland, and, after a course of some seventy miles through a chain of islanded lakes, pours its foaming waters over the Fall of Asaroe into Balyshannon Harbour on Donegal Bay.' He goes on to explain that the name of Ballyshannon is a corrupt derivation from the Irish *Bel-atha-Seanaigh* (*Bel-atha* meaning 'mouth of the ford') and *Seanaigh* possibly suggesting old (*sean*), but more likely someone's name. He claims that Ballyshanny (not Ballyshannon) is the correct vernacular.

169 *'shanachus'*: old lore. Allingham glosses this as 'old stories, histories, genealogies', but the more usual spelling would be seanchas.

rath: an earth enclosure, usually providing a fortification on a hillside.

Laurence Bloomfield in Ireland (subtitled 'A Modern Poem') is a verse novel in twelve chapters. The extract here is from chapter VII. Laurence Bloomfield is an idealistic landlord, 'Irish born and English bred', who returns to his estate at Lisnamoy during a time of agrarian conflict. He intervenes in a dispute involving a young tenant farmer, Neil Doran, who joins the outlawed secret society of Ribbonmen, and the local landlords led by their agent, Pigot. The poem is a meditation on the land question and a plea for liberal landlordism.

POPULAR SONGS AND BALLADS

The six ballads included here were inspired by the French invasion of 1796 and the rebellion of 1798. All of them have been set to music and are still frequently sung and recorded.

'Boulavogue' appeared in the *Irish Weekly Independent*, 18 June 1898 (the centenary year of the rebellion), under the title 'Father Murphy of the County Wexford'. Father John Murphy (about whom other ballads were written) was the parish priest of Kilcormack near Boulavogue in Co. Wexford. He led his parishioners in successful campaigns against the British militia in May 1798 and was eventually killed in battle by the British yeomanry. The author of the ballad was P. J. McCall (1861–1919), a founder member (with W. B. Yeats) of the Irish National Literary Society, but his ballad has now thoroughly entered the public domain. There have been many recordings of 'Boulavogue' by the Dubliners and other musicians.

173 *Hessian*: a name given to a German mercenary in the British army (from Hesse, a grand duchy of Germany).

'The Shan Van Vocht' belongs to the late 1790s, though the first printed version was in *The Nation*, 29 Oct. 1842. The Shan Van Vocht (Sean Bhean Bhoct) is the Poor Old Woman who heralds revolutionary change in Irish writing and song.

174 *the Orange*: the Orange Order, a Protestant organization, was founded in 1795 in commemoration of the victory of King William III, Prince of Orange, at the Battle of the Boyne, 1690.

Currach of Kildare: the Curragh, a plain of over 5,000 acres in Co. Kildare. A massacre of captive rebels took place here during the 1798 rebellion.

Lord Edward: Lord Edward Fitzgerald (1763–98), a leading member of the United Irishmen involved in preparations for the French invasion. He died of wounds received while resisting arrest. See W. B. Yeats's poem, 'September 1913'.

'The Wearin' o' the Green' also belongs to the late 1790s and appeared in several versions in the nineteenth century. The version printed here is shorter and more colloquial than the song that appears in Dion Boucicault's play, *Arrah-na-Pogue* (1864). Green was the colour of national pride and revolutionary aspiration, and was frequently invoked in songs of the time, such as 'The Green Cockade'. In *A Book of Ireland* (1959), Frank O'Connor refers to 'The Wearin' o' the Green' as 'the Irish Marseillaise'.

176 *Napper Tandy*: James Napper Tandy (1740–1803). In 1791 he assisted Wolfe Tone in founding the Society of United Irishmen. For much of the 1790s he was in flight from the authorities, fleeing to America in 1793, visiting Paris to gain support from the French, and trying to avoid execution. He died in Bordeaux.

caubeen: from the Irish *cáibín* (a hat).

'The Croppy Boy' has its origins in the 1798 rebellion in Wexford. The term 'croppy' refers to the rebels who cropped their hair in the French revolutionary style. There are numerous versions of the song.

'The Rising of the Moon' was written by John Keegan Casey (1846–70) shortly before its publication in *A Wreath of Shamrocks: Ballads, Songs and Legends* (1866). It had a massive circulation in broadsheet form. Casey was arrested for his Fenian activities in 1867 and imprisoned in Mountjoy Jail. An estimated 50,000 people followed his funeral. The version printed here differs slightly from the song Casey includes in his 1866 book. 'The Rising of the Moon' acquired even greater popularity after Lady Gregory used it in her play of that title in 1907.

177 *ma bouchal*: term of endearment, from the Irish *mo bhuachaill* (my boy).

'Granuaile' recounts the heroic adventures of Grace O'Malley (Gráinne Mhaol), thought to have lived as a pirate between 1530 and 1600. At her meeting with Queen Elizabeth I in London, she is said to have claimed royal prerogatives as Queen of Ireland. Legends of Granuaile were revived in the 1790s, along with those of the Shan Van Vocht, in the context of revolutionary political ambitions. The ballad singer who sings 'The Rising of the Moon' in Lady Gregory's play also sings 'Granuaile'.

179 *My royal Brian*: Brian Bóroime, better known as Brian Boru (941–1014), King of Ireland. He fought in the battle of Clontarf and was killed shortly afterwards by fleeing Vikings.

MAUD GONNE

'The Famine Queen' was first published as 'La Reine de la disette' in the Paris journal, *L'Irlande Libre*, founded by Maud Gonne in 1897 to commemorate the centenary of the 1798 rebellion. It was reprinted in the *United Irishman* on 6 Apr. 1900, but the paper was suppressed. The occasion was the visit to Ireland of Queen Victoria, then in her final years, to boost recruitment for the Boer War. See Maud Gonne MacBride, *A Servant of the Queen*, ed. A. N. Jeffares and Anna MacBride White (Gerrards Cross: Colin Smythe, 1994) and *The Gonne Yeats Letters, 1893–1938*, by the same editors (London: Hutchinson, 1992).

PATRICK PEARSE

'The Coming Revolution' was published in Nov. 1913 in the journal of the Gaelic League, *An Claidheamh* (*The Sword of Light*). It was reprinted many times after Pearse's death in 1916 and was included in *The Collected Works of Padraic H. Pearse: Political Writings and Speeches* (Dublin and London: Maunsel and Roberts Ltd., 1922). The essay marks a decisive break with the cultural ideals of the Gaelic League, in which Pearse had been active since 1896, and shows an unwavering commitment to armed insurrection.

186   *vox clamantis*: clamorous voice.

is and tá: two forms of the Gaelic verb *to be* (Pearse is talking about the rudiments of learning Irish).

Herbert Spencer: Herbert Spencer (1820–1903), founder of evolutionary philosophy and author of numerous books on sociology, ethics, education, and psychology, the most influential of which was probably *Education: Intellectual, Moral and Physical* (1861).

187   *the Gaelic League*: the Gaelic League was founded on 31 July 1893.

Liancourt: Roger du Plessis, duc de Liancourt (1598–1674).

188   *Dr Hyde*: Douglas Hyde (1860–1949). See biographical entry.

Eoin Mac Neill: Eoin MacNeill (1867–1945), a founder of the Gaelic League and first Professor of Early Irish History at University College, Dublin.

189   *Ard-Chraobh*: the governing council of the Gaelic League.

the North has 'begun': Eoin MacNeill's article 'The North Began' helped to precipitate the founding of the Irish Volunteers in the same month that Pearse's article appeared (Nov. 1913). The article was a response to the arming of loyalists in the north.

A. O. H.: Ancient Order of Hibernians, a Catholic nationalist organization.

the Transport Workers: the Irish Transport and General Workers Union (ITGWU).

JAMES CONNOLLY

'The Irish Flag' was published in the *Worker's Republic*, 8 Apr. 1916, two weeks before the Easter Rising. Connolly's passionate commitment to Irish nationalism and international socialism is encapsulated in this essay, in what has become one of his most frequently quoted statements: 'The cause of labour is the cause of Ireland, the cause of Ireland is the cause of labour. They cannot be dissevered.'

JAMES STEPHENS

From *The Insurrection in Dublin* (1916). Stephens's account of the Easter Rising is unusual because of the startling immediacy of its present-tense, first-person narrative, conveyed through the day-by-day impressions of a diary.

CONSTANCE MARKIEWICZ

'Stephen's Green', from *Cumann na mBan*, 2: 10 (1926). Constance Markiewicz describes the involvement in the Easter Rising of women members of the Irish Citizen Army and Cumann na mBan (The Irishwomen's Council), founded in Dublin in Nov. 1913 and later to become the women's division of the Irish Volunteers.

ROGER CASEMENT

For circumstances relating to his speech from the dock, see the biographical entry on Casement.

208 *the Chief Secretary*: Augustine Birrell (1850–1933).

'*grossly illegal and utterly unconstitutional*': Casement is referring to so-called 'gun running', and in particular to the landing of arms and ammunition at Larne, Co. Antrim, by the Ulster Volunteer Force in Apr. 1914. Despite the Lord Chancellor's denunciation, there was no police or military intervention.

209 *the present Attorney-General*: F. E. Smith (1872–1930), who led the prosecution against Casement.

210 *the refusal of the Army of Occupation at the Curragh to obey the orders of the Crown*: in Mar. 1914, officers at the Curragh military camp in Co. Kildare threatened resignation rather than take action against the Ulster opponents to Home Rule.

Mausers: the Mauser was a rifle named after its German inventor.

THOMAS MACDONAGH

From *Literature in Ireland: Studies Irish and Anglo-Irish* (1916), published posthumously after MacDonagh's execution by the British for his part in the Easter Rising. At the time of his death, as W. B. Yeats recalled, 'he was coming into his force; | He might have won fame in the end'. MacDonagh's extensive knowledge of poetry, especially his appreciation of the Elizabethan English lyric, informs his view of the possibilities of an Irish literature written in English. Departing from the ultra-nationalist ideal of an Irish Ireland, MacDonagh both welcomes the Gaelic Renaissance of his own time *and* asserts that Irish writers have begun to make the English language their own.

212 *Hugh O'Neill and Hugh O'Donnell*: Hugh O'Neill (1550–1616), Earl of Tyrone, and Hugh O'Donnell (1571–1602), his son-in-law.

Eoghan Ruadh O'Neill: Owen Roe O'Neill (1584–1649), a nephew of Hugh O'Neill and commander of Irish forces in the 1640s.

the Penal Laws: anti-Catholic legislation enacted from the 1690s onwards and not fully removed until Catholic Emancipation in 1829.

213 *O'Connell*: Daniel O'Connell (1775–1847). See biographical entry.

Parnell: Charles Stewart Parnell (1846–91), leader of the Irish Parliamentary Party from 1880 to 1891.

215 *Dr Sigerson*: George Sigerson (1836–1925), translator and editor of *Bards of the Gael and Gall* (1897). MacDonagh dedicated *Literature in Ireland* to Sigerson.

216 *the silk of the kine*: the silken heifer, the strong and lustrous cow of Irish mythology (see the note for Aubrey De Vere above).

John Eglinton: John Eglinton (1868–1961), from *Bards and Saints* (Dublin: Maunsel & Co., 1906), 48.

219 *Carlyle says of Imagination*: Thomas Carlyle (1795–1881) in *Sartor Resartus* (1836), book 1, chapter IX.

aisling: Irish literary genre based on a vision or dream.

dán díreach: classical syllabic verse in Irish.

JOHN O'LEARY

From *Recollections of Fenians and Fenianism* (1896). The extract here is from the opening chapter of O'Leary's memoir, in which he describes his early youth and the impact of Thomas Davis's poems and essays on his feelings about Ireland.

220 *laudator temporis acti*: one who praises the deeds of time.

221 *poems and essays of Thomas Davis*: see the writings of Davis in this volume.

T. W. Rolleston . . . Duffy: T. W. Rolleston edited *Prose Writings of Thomas Davis* in 1890 and Charles Gavan Duffy wrote *Thomas Davis: The Memoirs of an Irish Patriot* in 1892.

West-British: having British attitudes and sympathies (as if Ireland were merely a western segment of Britain).

Moore's song: 'The Song of O'Ruark, Prince of Breffni': 'On *our* side is Virtue and Erin! | On *theirs* is the Saxon and Guilt.'

the Nation: the weekly cultural and political journal founded by Thomas Davis with John Blake Dillon and Charles Gavan Duffy on 15 Oct. 1842. It promoted the nationalist ideals of the Young Ireland Movement.

222 *'fear to speak of '98'*: an allusion to the opening line of 'The Memory of the Dead' by John Kells Ingram. See note above.

Mitchel: John Mitchel (1815–75), Fenian organizer and revolutionary; editor of the *United Irishman*. His *Jail Journal* (1854) became a celebrated text of Irish nationalism.

Hugh O'Neill and Owen Roe and Sarsfield: for Hugh O'Neill and Owen Roe, see the notes above for Thomas MacDonagh. Patrick Sarsfield (1655–93) was a commander in the army of James II during the Williamite War (1689–91).

'*Memoirs of Wolfe Tone*': see extract in this volume and note above.

Madden: R. R. Madden, *The United Irishmen: Their Lives and Times*, published in 4 vols. in Dublin, 1842–6.

The Czar Nicholas: Nicholas I (1796–1855), emperor of Russia. His expansionist ambitions, opposed by Britain and France, brought on the Crimean War.

OSCAR WILDE

From *De Profundis*, a letter to Lord Alfred Douglas from Reading Prison, written in 1897 and first published in an extracted version in 1905. Wilde's letter, adopting as its title the prayer based on Psalm 130 ('Out of the depths have I cried to thee, O Lord'), is one of the great works of nineteenth-century autobiography. In a style characteristic of modern Irish literature, it sees tragedy in the raiment of comedy: 'We are the zanies of sorrow. We are clowns whose hearts are broken.'

225 *the Captain of my Soul*: 'I am the master of my fate, | I am the captain of my soul', from William Ernest Henley's poem, 'Invictus' (1875).

Wordsworth: the lines that follow are from Act 3, Scene 5 of William Wordsworth's play *The Borderers* (1796–7).

Vita Nuova: New Life, the title of a principal early work by Dante Alighieri (1265–1321).

226 *Robbie*: Robert Ross, Wilde's close friend and the editor of his *Collected Works* (1908).

228 *Verlaine*: Paul Verlaine (1844–96), French poet.

Prince Kropotkin: Prince Peter Kropotkin (1842–1921), anarchist author of *Mutual Aid* (1897).

230 *Marsyas*: in Greek mythology, a celebrated player on the pipe, who challenged Apollo to a musical contest and was flayed alive after suffering defeat. His song is the song of sorrow.

Baudelaire: Charles Baudelaire (1821–67), French poet, best known for *Les Fleurs du Mal* (1857).

Lamartine: Alphonse de Lamartine (1790–1869), French poet, best known for his *Méditations Poétiques* (1820).

Chopin's music: the music of the Polish composer Frederic Chopin (1809–49) was immensely popular among the aesthetes of Wilde's generation.

Wilde alludes to Chopin's compositions, especially the nocturnes, in his poetry, essays, and fiction.

230 *Burne-Jones's women*: Edward Burne-Jones (1833–98), Pre-Raphaelite painter, whose idealized women have a distinctive androgynous quality.

Matthew Arnold: Victorian poet and critic (1822–88). Wilde is referring to his early poem *Empedocles on Etna* (1852).

J. M. SYNGE

From *The Aran Islands* (1907). Part of this opening section was originally published as an article, 'An Impression of Aran', in the *Manchester Guardian* on 24 Jan. 1905. Part autobiography, part travel writing, the book describes Synge's growing familiarity with the life and customs of Inishmore and Inishmaan. The stories and songs he translated provided an impulse for the vigorous colloquial idiom of his plays and typified the Gaelic culture of the west of Ireland that so inspired the Literary Revival.

232 *Aranmor*: the largest of the Aran Islands, better known as Inishmore.

234 *Petrie and Sir William Wilde . . . Mr Curtin*: all of them antiquarians and collectors of folk lore. Sir George Petrie (1790–1866) established the monastic origin of the round towers of Ireland and wrote extensively on Irish architecture and music. Sir William Wilde (1815–76), the father of Oscar Wilde, wrote a number of topographical and ethnological works. Jeremiah Curtin (1838–1906) was born in Detroit to Irish parents and was the author of *Myths and Folklore of Ireland* (1890) and *Tales of the Fairies and Ghost World* (1893).

236 *beyond the bay*: this was the closing sentence of the article, 'An Impression of Aran'.

GEORGE MOORE

Hail and Farewell, Moore's memoir of literary culture in the first decade of the twentieth century, was published in three volumes: *Ave* (1911), *Salve* (1912), and *Vale* (1914). Swaying between a detached chronicle and an obsessive monologue, the book provides some brilliant cameos of personalities and events, especially those associated with the Literary Revival. The extract reprinted here is from *Ave* and recalls a meeting with W. B. Yeats and Edward Martyn, when the idea of an Irish literary theatre was in the air. It is entirely characteristic of Moore's comic perspective and his deep appreciation of the visual arts that he should recall how, in the lamplight, his visitors appeared 'as fantastic as anything ever seen in Japanese prints'.

240 *the Temple*: the Inns of Court, just off Fleet Street, London.

242 *when I cut the painter*: after training as a painter, Moore came to realize that he was better suited to being a writer, hence his wariness about wrong starts and misdirections.

the summer at Coole: Coole Park, Co. Galway, was the home of Lady Gregory, and both Yeats and Martyn were visitors there.

243 *The Heather Field*: Martyn's play was produced in 1899, one of the first plays to be associated with the Irish Literary Theatre.

The Land of Heart's Desire: Yeats's play of this name was first performed in London on 29 March 1894. It was the first of his plays to be given regular production in London.

244 *the days when I was a Frenchman*: Moore lived in Paris between 1873 and 1879, nurturing his aspirations as a painter and then as a writer.

the Book of Kells: one of the finest early medieval illuminated manuscripts, from the eighth or ninth century, possibly from a monastery in Kells, Co. Meath. It is preserved and exhibited in Trinity College, Dublin.

the Cheshire Cheese: Ye Old Cheshire Cheese (a pub at 145 Fleet St., London), well known to Samuel Johnson and a popular meeting place for the poets of the Rhymers' Club, with whom Yeats was associated in the 1890s.

the legends of the Fianna: the Fionn or Ossianic cycle of stories centred on the exploits of the mythical hero Fionn mac Cumhaill (Finn Macool), his son Oisín (Ossian), and the Fianna warriors.

245 *a work on Blake*: as well as editing a 3-vol. edition of Blake's poems with Edwin J. Ellis (1893), Yeats also wrote about this time an essay titled 'William Blake and the Imagination' (1897).

EARNÁN O'MALLEY

From *On Another Man's Wound* (1936). O'Malley commanded the Second Southern Division of the IRA in Munster during the closing months of the War of Independence (1919–21). In this episode of his memoir, from May–July 1921, he describes the execution of three British officers in Co. Tipperary.

247 *the Brigade Q.M.*: the IRA Quartermaster.

Slievenamon: (mountain of the fairy women) a conical mountain north of Clonmel and a county landmark in Tipperary.

JAMES JOYCE

'A Painful Case', from *Dubliners* (1914). The story was written in 1905 (the original title was 'A Painful Incident'), but publication was delayed because of publishers' fears over libel actions against *Dubliners*. The story effectively illustrates Joyce's repeated suggestion that Dublin is a centre of paralysis by showing us Mr James Duffy's cold and loveless treatment of the musical Mrs Sinico. It also demonstrates what Joyce in his letters described as a style of 'scrupulous meanness', being both attentive to detail and unflinching in its depiction of what might be considered low and sordid. While being strongly naturalistic in style, however, the story also contains symbolic elements. The ending of the story is puzzling. Some readers sense the presence of a Joycean 'epiphany' and argue that Mr Duffy experiences enlightenment and renewal, while others find his egotism and hypocrisy unrelieved.

252 *Duffy*: from the Irish 'dubh' (black or dark).

Chapelizod: a village about three miles west of Dublin city centre, also the setting for *The House by the Church-yard* by Sheridan Le Fanu. It is used again by Joyce in *Finnegans Wake*. The name derives from the French 'Chapel d'Iseult' and is associated with the unhappy love of Tristan and Iseult in Celtic legend.

double desk: a small desk which functions both as a storage space and as a writing surface.

Maynooth Catechism: the standard text for religious instruction in Catholic schools in Ireland, issued by the National Synod at the Royal College of St Patrick in Maynooth in 1883.

Michael Kramer: a play written by the German author Gerhart Hauptmann in 1900 and translated by Joyce in 1901. It ends with the suicide of Kramer's son, Arnold.

Bile Beans: a popular cure for bilious ailments.

253 *Rotunda*: a group of buildings on the south-east corner of Rutland Square, housing a theatre, a concert hall, and assembly rooms.

254 *Leghorn*: the English name for the Italian city of Livorno in Tuscany.

255 *Parkgate*: the main entrance to Phoenix Park in north-west Dublin.

256 *Mail*: presumably the *Dublin Evening Mail*, a Unionist daily newspaper, printed on light brown paper.

257 *Secreto*: silently or quietly.

258 *a league*: a temperance league.

259 *Herald*: presumably the *Evening Herald*, a nationalist daily newspaper.

SEÁN O'FAOLÁIN

'Lilliput', from *Midsummer Night Madness and Other Stories* (1932). In *Vive Moi! An Autobiography* (1963), O'Faoláin refers to 'Lilliput' as the 'very first story that is recognisably mine'. It was first published in the *Irish Statesman* on 6 Feb. 1926, with the title 'In Lilliput'. The story is set in O'Faoláin's birthplace, the city of Cork, at the beginning of the 1920s. During this phase of the War of Independence, curfews were in force and military patrols were on the streets. The title comes from the opening book of Jonathan Swift's *Gulliver's Travels* (1726). O'Faoláin writes in a realist mode, quite unlike Swift's satirical fantasy, but he shares Swift's acute sense of observation and unusual shifts of perspective, and he shows us a place in which people's lives appear diminished. The woman traveller, however, takes on heroic proportions: O'Faoláin presents her as a female Gulliver observed by 'a changing little crowd'.

260 *Shandon*: the handsome Tower of Shandon on St Anne's Church, Shandon Street, Cork. The peal of the eight bells of Shandon is celebrated in the poem by Francis Sylvester Mahony (Father Prout) reprinted here: ' 'Tis the bells of Shandon | That sounds so grand on | The pleasant waters of the River Lee.'

the valley of the Lee: the River Lee in Cork.

261 *jarvey-cars*: small horse-pulled traps, popular in parts of rural Ireland.

porther: porter (a dark beer also known as stout).

262 *the first Angelus*: Roman Catholic devotional prayer commemorating the Incarnation ('The Angel of the Lord said unto Mary . . .'). Traditionally, as here, it was said three times a day: morning, noon, and sunset.

263 *the Tans*: the Black-and-Tans were non-Irish members of the Royal Irish Constabulary who fought against the IRA between March 1920 and July 1921 during the War of Independence. Due to shortages, they wore mixed police and army uniforms. The name was derived from a well-known pack of hounds belonging to the Skarteen Hunt in Co. Limerick and came to be applied to any irregular forces used by the British in Ireland. They were renowned for their brutality.

265 *Mary Mac*: as well as irreverently likening the sleeping woman to Mary, the Corporal also offers a jibe in the common Celtic prefix 'Mac'.

LIAM O'FLAHERTY

'The Mountain Tavern', from *The Mountain Tavern and Other Stories* (1929). O'Flaherty's story is set during the Civil War of 1922–3. It gives a specifically political dimension to the idea of 'the dead' and to the symbolism of the snow in James Joyce's story, 'The Dead'.

Snow was falling: the snow falling silently at the opening of O'Flaherty's story recalls the snow falling faintly at the end of Joyce's story.

268 *It's gone west*: euphemism for death and destruction, especially among soldiers.

We're up the pole: in a state of desperation.

270 *Free Staters*: the army of the new Irish State, after the 1921 Treaty ending the War of Independence.

Irregulars: Republican soldiers opposed to the Treaty.

FRANK O'CONNOR

'The Majesty of the Law', from *Bones of Contention* (1936). The story was first published in the *Fortnightly Review* in Aug. 1935.

273 *brosna*: a bundle of sticks for fire-wood.

Marcus Stone print: Marcus Stone (1840–1921), Victorian painter, popular for historical genre pictures and book illustrations. He was a political radical and a friend of Charles Dickens.

274 *Begor*: (begorra) by god.

     Faix: faith.

     Wisha: Well, indeed.

275 *Dhe, whisht*: be quiet, hold your tongue.

     Ah, sha: see Wisha.

276 *Musha*: see Wisha.

278 *Erra*: (arrah) But, now, really.

279 *begod*: by god.

280 *butt*: a small cart.

SOMERVILLE AND ROSS

From *The Real Charlotte* (1894). In this, their most popular novel, Edith Somerville and Violet Martin ('Martin Ross') dramatized the uncertain fortunes of the Protestant Ascendancy in a compelling narrative of desire for land and love. The heroine of the novel plots against her young cousin, Francie Fitzpatrick, and contrives to cheat her out of her inheritance. The novel is set in the West Cork village of Lismoyle. In this extract from chapter 2, the rivalry between the two women is introduced in the context of a farcical deathbed scene involving Charlotte's elderly aunt, Mrs Mullen.

282 *Norry the Boat*: a household servant.

     the Banshee: from the Irish *bean sí* (woman of the sídh or 'host of the air'). The banshee is a mythological figure whose cry of lamentation portends a family death.

BRAM STOKER

From *Dracula* (1897). The novel opens with Jonathan Harker's record of a journey undertaken to Transylvania on behalf of his law firm to meet the mysterious Count Dracula. The passage included here has fascinated generations of readers with its suggestive eroticism, but the relationship between vampire and victim has also been read in terms of colonizer and colonized.

290 *'My tablets . . . put it down,' etc.*: a mistaken recollection of Shakespeare's lines in *Hamlet*, I. v: 'My tables—meet it is I set it down | That one may smile and smile and be a villain.'

291 *water-glasses*: glasses filled with different levels of water to produce musical notes.

JAMES JOYCE

From *Ulysses* (1922). Episode 1: Telemachus. The opening of the novel recalls the first two books of Homer's *Odyssey*, in which Odysseus' son Telemachus is urged by the goddess Athena to seek his father. The novel opens at 8 a.m. on

Thursday, 16 June 1904. The setting is the Martello tower, Sandycove (Dublin Bay), in which Stephen Dedalus, newly returned from Paris, is living with his friend Malachi ('Buck') Mulligan and an English admirer of Irish culture by the name of Haines. Stephen is a lonely son, likened to both Telemachus and Hamlet, but he is also caught in a tense political and cultural relationship with Haines (a colonial Englishman) and Mulligan (an Irish collaborator). Mulligan irreverently mocks the communion rites of the mass, the first of many parodies and inauthentic experiences in the novel. Later, the milkwoman is presented as a parodic version of the legendary Old Woman of Ireland, the Shan Van Vocht.

294 *Introibo ad altare Dei*: I will go unto the altar of God (from the opening of the Latin mass).

blood and ouns: blood and wounds: Mulligan is mocking Stephen's Catholicism, parodying the form of the mass and the priest's consecration of bread and wine as the body and blood of Christ.

Chrysostomos: 'golden-mouthed', from the Greek orator Dion Chrysostomos (*c.*50–*c.*117), a reference to Mulligan's gold fillings and also his eloquence.

Two strong shrill whistles: the mailboat is leaving Ireland.

an ancient Greek: Daedalus, the father of Icarus, who fashioned wings for himself and his son to fly.

295 *Algy*: Algernon Charles Swinburne (1837–1909), Victorian poet, whose poem 'The Triumph of Time' (1866) contains the line Mulligan quotes: 'the great sweet mother . . . the sea'.

296 *Epi oinopa ponton*: 'over the wine-dark sea' (from Homer's *Odyssey*).

Thalatta! Thalatta!: The sea! The sea!, the cry of the Ten Thousand Greek mercenary soldiers when they reach the sea in Xenophon's *Anabasis*, IV. vii. 24.

hyperborean: a term used by Friedrich Nietzsche to describe those who, like the superman (Übermensch), were 'above the crowd' (*The Will to Dominate*, 1896).

297 *Dottyville*: the lunatic asylum.

Ursula: St Ursula, renowned for her chastity.

The rage of Caliban: Oscar Wilde, in his preface to *The Picture of Dorian Gray* (1891): 'The nineteenth-century dislike of Realism is the rage of Caliban seeing his own face in the glass. The nineteenth century dislike of Romanticism is the rage of Caliban not seeing his own face in the glass.'

The cracked lookingglass of a servant: the idea of art as a cracked lookingglass occurs in Wilde's essay, 'The Decay of Lying' (1889). Stephen, who is bitterly conscious of Ireland's oppression, finds it appropriate that the looking-glass Mulligan hands him should belong to a servant.

298 *oxy chap*: Haines is from Oxford, but there are also suggestions of foolish behaviour (behaving like an ox).

298 *Hellenise it*: Matthew Arnold, in *Culture and Anarchy* (1869), identifies two prominent cultural tendencies: the Hebraic (founded on the stern recognition of law and duty) and the Hellenic (founded on the love of beauty and sensuous pleasure). Wilde was to characterize aestheticism as 'the New Hellenism'.

evening in the quadrangle: Stephen conjures up a picture of Oxford.

new paganism . . . omphalos: new paganism is another epithet for the return to Greek (Hellenic) ways. Omphalos is Greek for navel and is associated with Delphi, the centre of the earth in Ancient Greek culture.

299 *Sir Peter Teazle*: character in Richard Brinsley Sheridan's play *The School for Scandal* (1777).

some hired mute from Lalouette's: hired mourner from the Dublin undertaker of that name.

300 *Loyola*: St Ignatius Loyola (1491–1556), founder of the Society of Jesus (the Jesuit order) in 1534.

For Fergus rules the brazen cars: from the lyric 'Who Goes with Fergus', originally part of W. B. Yeats's 1892 play *The Countess Cathleen*.

Turko the terrible: a pantomime in which Edward Royce, a member of the Gaiety Theatre Company in London, took part. Joyce saw it in Dublin as a child.

301 *Liliata . . . excipiat*: Catholic prayer for the dying: 'May the lilied throng of radiant confessors encompass thee; may the choir of rejoicing angels welcome thee.'

302 *On coronation day*: 'De Golden Wedding', a song by the African-American songwriter James A. Bland (1854–1911).

Clongowes: Clongowes Wood College, the Jesuit school where Joyce was a pupil.

A server of a servant: the altar boy serving the Priest, who is servant of God, but also the Irishman serving the Englishman, who is servant of the Empire.

303 *In nominee . . . Sancti*: in the name of the father, and of the son, and of the Holy Ghost'.

the year of the big wind: a humorous dig at the folklore and occultist interests in Yeats's book, *In the Seven Woods* (1903), published by the Dun Emer Press in Dundrum in 1903, with the assistance of Elizabeth and Lily Yeats. The two sisters are likened to the witches ('the weird sisters') in Shakespeare's *Macbeth*.

304 *Mabinogion*: a group of eleven medieval Welsh tales.

Upanishads: ancient Hindu scriptures, studied by Yeats.

prepuces: foreskins.

a tilly: from the Irish *tuile* (a drop more).

Silk of the kine and poor old woman: traditional names for Ireland. For silk of the kine see notes above on Aubrey De Vere and Thomas MacDonagh.

For the poor old woman (*Sean Bhean Bhocht*) see the note for the song of that title above.

305 *cuckquean*: female cuckold.

the serpent's prey: Old Testament descriptions of woman.

306 *All I can give you I give*: this and the 'tender chant' that follows are from Swinburne's poem, 'The Oblation', from *Songs Before Sunrise* (1871).

stony: stony-broke (Mulligan, who is short of money, expects Stephen to bring some money from his teaching job).

Ireland expects . . . his duty: Mulligan mimics Lord Nelson's famous declaration at the Battle of Trafalgar (1805): 'England expects that every man this day will do his duty.'

307 *Agenbite of inwit*: remorse of conscience (Middle English).

stripped of his garments: a parody of the tenth Station of the Cross, in which Christ is stripped of his garments.

308 *Mercurial Malachi*: Stephen's view of his friend Mulligan, from a combination of the Greek and Hebrew words for 'messenger'.

Latin quarter hat: a reference to Stephen's visit to the Latin Quarter in Paris.

when the French were on the sea: an allusion to the Irish ballad, 'The Shan Van Vocht', recalling the support given to the United Irish movement by the French in the 1790s. William Pitt the Younger (1759–1806) was Prime Minister when the Martello towers were built in the early 1800s as fortifications against the French during the Napoleonic Wars.

Thomas Aquinas: St Thomas Aquinas (1225–74), Dominican theologian and scholastic philosopher, whose *Summa Theologiae* (1266–73) includes the famous 'five ways' or proofs of the existence of God.

309 *Japhet in search of a father*: the title of a novel (published in 1836) by Captain Frederick Marryat.

That beetles o'er his base into the sea: from *Hamlet*, I. iv. 71.

The seas' ruler: England (or Britannia), represented here by Haines.

310 *Goodbye, now, goodbye*: based on verses written by Oliver St John Gogarty.

a green stone: an emblem of Ireland, but the stone is held in a silver case by the Englishman Haines, suggesting colonial possession.

311 *et unam sanctam catholicam et apostolicam ecclesiam*: and in one holy, catholic and apostolic church (from the Nicene Creed).

pope Marcellus: a mass was written for Pope Marcellus II (1501–55) by Palestrina.

the vigilant angel: the Archangel Michael (depicted here as the guardian of the Catholic Church against Protestant heresy in the sixteenth century).

311 *Photius*: patriarch of Constantinople (*c.*815–97), whose appointment in 857 went against the wishes of Pope Nicholas I and resulted in the schism between the Eastern Orthodox and Roman Catholic Churches.

Arius: heretic (*c.*256–336), who refused to conform with established belief regarding the Father and the Son.

Valentine: Egyptian Gnostic who challenged established belief on Christ's humanity and suffering.

Sabellius: heretic who questioned orthodox beliefs regarding the Trinity.

313 *Uebermensch*: superman (German), as used by Friedrich Nietzsche in *Thus Spake Zarathustra* (1883).

lendeth to the Lord: parody of the biblical proverb: 'He that hath pity upon the poor lendeth unto the Lord!'

Horn of a bull, hoof of a horse, smile of a Saxon: three things the Irish should be wary of.

ELIZABETH BOWEN

From *The Last September* (1929). In one of the classic 'Big House' novels recounting the fortunes of the embattled Anglo-Irish ascendancy, Elizabeth Bowen sets a young woman's sexual awakening against the traumatic politics of the War of Independence (1919–21). The setting of the novel is Danielstown, the home of the Naylor family in Co. Tipperary. In this extract (from chapter 4), Lois Farquhar, the lonely niece of Sir Richard and Lady Naylor, tries to make sense of her own hyphenated Anglo-Irish identity.

314 *Mrs Montmorency*: Hugo and Francie Montmorency are cousins of the Naylors, visiting Danielstown. Hugo had been in love with Lois's mother.

317 *Madder*: a local river.

320 *'Has he come for the guns?'*: the suspicion is that the IRA has hidden weapons in the woods.

'by so great a cloud of witnesses': St Paul's Epistle to the Hebrews 12: 1.

SAMUEL BECKETT

From *Murphy* (1938). The two passages (from chapter 1 and chapter 4) are set in London and Dublin. The novel engages with the philosophical dilemmas that were to become a hallmark of Beckett's later work (Murphy seeks release from the Cartesian mind–body distinction), but it also has a distinctively Irish, post-Literary Revival dimension. The episode in the Dublin General Post Office, in which Wylie dashes his head against the buttocks of Cuchulain, is an irreverent response to what Beckett called the 'Cuchulainoid clichés' of the Revival. James Joyce saw the novel as neatly complementing Flann O'Brien's novel *At Swim-Two-Birds*, published the following year, and referred to Beckett and O'Brien as *Jean-qui-pleure* and *Jean-qui-rit*.

The sun shone ... on the nothing new: 'there is nothing new under the sun' (Ecclesiastes).

321 *the poor old sun in the Virgin*: the sun enters the constellation Virgo at the end of August.

Neary: thought to be based on the Trinity College philosopher, H. S. Macran, who liked to drink in Neary's pub in Dublin.

the Nerbudda: a river in India.

322 *Apmonia*: a joke word, coined from the Greek for 'harmony', as employed by Pythagoras.

Petrouchka: the persecuted puppet in Stravinsky's 1911 ballet of that title.

the statue of Cuchulain: the statue placed in the General Post Office to commemorate the heroism of Easter 1916, designed by Oliver Sheppard (1865–1941).

323 *Dalkey*: Dalkey village, a few miles south of Dublin.

324 *Cathleen na Hennessey*: a joke at the expense of Cathleen ni Houlihan (Hennessy is an Irish brandy).

that Red Branch bum: reference to the earlier episode involving Cuchulain, who belongs to the Ulster Red Branch cycle of tales.

FLANN O'BRIEN

From *At Swim-Two-Birds* (1939). O'Brien's scintillating modernist medley makes extensive use of parody and pastiche. Clearly influenced by Joyce and (like Beckett's *Murphy*) mildly contemptuous in its attitude to the pieties of the Literary Revival, the novel grafts layer upon layer of narrative, swerving from modern Dublin to the mythological realm of Finn MacCool and the mad King Sweeney. The passage included here is a playful and skilful adaptation of the twelfth-century Irish text, *Buile Shuibne* (translated by Seamus Heaney as *Sweeney Astray*). After being cursed by the cleric Rónán, Sweeney goes mad with the din of battle and takes to wandering through Ireland, living in naked destitution, dwelling in tree tops and celebrating his close attachment to nature. Much of the comedy in the novel is generated by its dramatic shift from one parodic mode to another, in this case from the medieval Irish text to the knockabout vernacular of Shanahan, Furriskey, Lamont, and the indomitable poet of the working class, Jem Casey.

AUGUSTA GREGORY

'Grief of a Girl's Heart', from the essay 'West Irish Ballads' (1901), reprinted in *Poets and Dreamers: Studies and Translations from the Irish* (1903) and also in *The Kiltartan Poetry Book: Prose Translations from the Irish* (1918). The stanzaic arrangement of the poem printed here is taken from the *Oxford Book of Irish Verse*, ed. Donagh MacDonagh and Lennox Robinson (Oxford:

Clarendon Press, 1958). The name Donal Oge is a version of the Irish *donal Óg* (Young Donal). A recital of this poem was added to the script of *The Dead* in John Huston's 1987 film of James Joyce's short story.

337 *ochone*: cry of lamentation.

   O, aya!: expression of sorrow.

OSCAR WILDE

'Requiescat' ('May She Rest') mourns the death of Wilde's sister, Isola, who died on 23 Feb. 1867, aged 9. It was probably written when Wilde was a student at Oxford in the 1870s. He may have visited Avignon on his way to Italy in 1875, though his use of the place name is no guarantee that the poem was written there. It was first published in *Poems* (1881).

'Impression du Matin' ('Impression of the Morning') was first published in *The World: A Journal for Men and Women* (2 Mar. 1881) and was included in Wilde's *Poems* (1881). As well as showing the influence of French impressionist painting on Wilde's artistic ideals, the poem also draws on the example of the American painter, James McNeill Whistler. 'Nocturne in Blue and Gold' and 'Harmony in Grey' are titles of paintings by Whistler.

'Helas!' ('Alas!') was printed as the introductory sonnet to Wilde's *Poems* (1881).

339 *stringed lute on which all winds can play*: the Æolian harp, a common image in Romantic poetry.

   virelay: an old French lyric form.

   with a little rod: the final three lines allude to an Old Testament quotation (I Samuel 14: 43): 'I did but taste a little honey with the end of the rod that was in mine hand, and, lo, I must die'.

'The Harlot's House' was first published in the *Dramatic Review* (11 Apr. 1885) and included in Wilde's *Poems* (1908).

340 *'Treues Liebes Herz'*: 'Faithful Dear Heart'.

   quadrille: a square dance (also referred to in James Joyce's story, 'The Dead').

'Sonnet. On The Sale by Auction of Keats' Love Letters' was written in 1885 and published in the *Dramatic Review* (23 Jan. 1886). It was later included in Wilde's *Poems* (1908). The sonnet was prompted by Sotheby's auction of the letters Keats had written to Fanny Brawne. Wilde attended the sale on 2 Mar. 1885.

341 *Endymion*: Wilde gives to his fellow poet the name of the mythological hero who inspired Keats's epic poem *Endymion* (1818).

'Symphony in Yellow' was first published in the *Centennial Magazine: An Australasian Monthly Illustrated* (5 Feb. 1889) and later included in Wilde's *Poems* (1908). The title recalls the musical titles of paintings by Whistler (see note on 'Impression du Matin' above).

342 *the Temple*: the Inns of Court, just off Fleet Street, London. The bridge in line 1 is presumably Blackfriars Bridge.

DOUGLAS HYDE

'My Grief on the Sea' is one of the translations from the Irish which Hyde printed with a prose commentary in his *Love Songs of Connacht* (1893).

W. B. YEATS

'The Lake Isle of Innisfree', from *The Countess Kathleen and Various Legends and Lyrics* (1892). Innisfree, from the Irish *Inis Fraoigh* (Island of Heather), is a small island on Lough Gill, Co. Sligo. The meaning of the name helps to explain the 'purple glow' in line 7 (the colour of heather reflected in the water).

'To Ireland in the Coming Times', from *The Countess Kathleen and Various Legends and Lyrics* (1892). The original title was 'Apologia addressed to Ireland in the coming days'. The version given here is that which appears in the section of poems Yeats titled *The Rose* (1893) in later editions of his work.

343 *rann*: verse or stanza.

the red-rose bordered hem: a fleeting vision of the rose of ideal beauty, here acknowledged as pre-Christian in origin.

344 *Davis, Mangan, Ferguson*: see biographical entries in this volume.

'The Song of Wandering Aengus', originally titled 'A Mad Song', from *The Wind Among the Reeds* (1899). Yeats saw Aengus as the Celtic god of youth, beauty, and poetry. In the mythological cycle of tales in medieval Irish, he falls ill after longing for a woman seen in his dreams.

345 *hazel wand*: an instrument with magical powers of divination and transformation.

'To a Shade', from *Responsibilities* (1914), written in memory of Charles Stewart Parnell (1846–91), discredited as leader of the Irish Parliamentary Party after the exposure of his affair with a married woman, Katherine O'Shea.

346 *A man*: Sir Hugh Lane (1874–1915), who offered to donate his collection of French impressionist paintings to the Dublin Municipal Gallery on condition that the Dublin Corporation would build a new gallery. His offer was rebuked.

Your enemy, an old foul mouth: probably William Martin Murphy (1844–1914), who owned two newspapers opposed to Parnell; he also objected to Hugh Lane's proposal.

the Glasnevin coverlet: Glasnevin Cemetery, Dublin, where Parnell is buried.

'September 1913', from *Responsibilities* (1914). Yeats contrasts the commercial

ethic of modern, democratic Ireland ('the greasy till') with the inspiring
heroism of an earlier generation of Irish patriots.

346 *O'Leary*: see the biographical entry on John O'Leary and the extract
     from his *Recollections of Fenians and Fenianism*.

347 *the wild geese*: Irish soldiers serving in Europe after the evacuation of
     the Irish army to France under the terms of the Treaty of Limerick,
     1691. The term was also applied to later recruits to Irish brigades in
     continental and American armies.

     Edward Fitzgerald: Lord Edward Fitzgerald (1763–98), one of the leaders
     of the 1798 rebellion, who died while resisting arrest.

     every mother's son: the modern age would fail to comprehend the passion-
     ate commitment and sacrifice of the earlier generation and attribute it to
     lovesickness.

'Easter 1916', from *Michael Robartes and the Dancer* (1921). The poem was
inspired by the execution of fifteen leaders of the Easter Rising of 24 Apr.
1916, when Irish Republican forces occupied the centre of Dublin and came
under fierce opposition from the British army (see the accounts by James
Stephens and Constance Markiewicz in this volume).

348 *That woman's days*: Constance Markiewicz (see biographical entry).

     This man ... wingèd horse: Patrick Pearse (see biographical entry). The
     wingèd horse is Pegasus (emblematic of poetic inspiration).

     This other: Thomas MacDonagh (see biographical entry).

     This other man: Major John MacBride (1865–1916), estranged husband of
     Maud Gonne.

349 *For England may keep faith*: the Home Rule Bill, granting Ireland a meas-
     ure of independence, had been passed in the British Parliament but then
     suspended for the duration of the First World War.

     Connolly: see biographical entry on James Connolly.

'The Wild Swans at Coole', from *The Wild Swans at Coole* (1919). Yeats first
visited Coole Park, Lady Gregory's home in Co. Galway, in 1897.

    'Meditations in Time of Civil War', from *The Tower* (1928). The poem was
written in 1922 during the fierce and bitter conflict between the newly formed
government of the Irish Free State and those Republicans opposed to the
partition of Ireland required by the Anglo-Irish Treaty of 1922. The poem is
in seven parts.

351 *Juno*: Queen of the Roman gods and wife of Jupiter; the peacock is sacred
     to Juno and later in the poem its cry heralds a new era.

352 *Il Penseroso's Platonist*: a reference to John Milton's poem, 'Il Penseroso'
     ('The Thinker').

     Sato's ... sword: the ceremonial Japanese sword was a gift to Yeats
     from Junzo Sato, an admirer of his poetry, whom he met when visiting
     Portland, Oregon.

354 *Primum Mobile*: First Moving: a reference to the outermost revolving sphere in medieval theories of the cosmos.

   Irregular: Anti-Treaty Republican, opposed to the new Free State government.

   Falstaffian man: like the robust, jocular character in Shakespeare's *Henry IV*.

   national uniform: soldiers of the Free State army.

355 *stare*: a starling.

356 *Jacques Molay*: Jacques de Molay (1244–1314), Grand Master of the Order of Knights Templar, burned at the stake for heresy. Yeats associates the cry for revenge with mob rule and the perpetuation of violence.

   Babylonian almanacs: books containing astrological predictions.

'The Tower', from *The Tower* (1928). The tower is Thoor Ballylee, an ancient Norman tower in Co. Galway that Yeats bought in 1917. As well as providing Yeats and his wife with a home, it also provided a wealth of symbols, being both the artist's lonely tower and a storehouse of local myths and memories. In section II of the poem, Yeats dwells on local stories of people who lived in the vicinity, including Mrs French, an eighteenth-century grandee, and Mary Hynes, a peasant girl celebrated in the poetry of Antoine Raftery.

357 *Ben Bulben's back*: Ben Bulben is a mountain in Co. Sligo, not far from where Yeats is buried.

   Choose Plato and Plotinus: turn to ancient philosophy and 'abstract things' instead of poetry.

358 *the great bog of Cloone*: in Co. Galway, near Gort.

   the man who made the song was blind: Antoine Raftery (see biographical entry).

   Helen has all living hearts betrayed: the powerful image of Helen of Troy, from Homer's epic poem *The Iliad*.

   Hanrahan: Red Hanrahan is a character who appears in stories and poems by Yeats, including 'Red Hanrahan's Song about Ireland'.

359 *the Great Memory*: the *Anima Mundi*; the collective unconscious.

360 *the people of Burke and of Grattan*: both Protestant statesmen committed to political reform in Ireland (see biographical entry for Burke and note on Grattan above, p. 476).

   fabulous horn: horn of plenty: in Greek mythology, a horn forever full of fruit, possessed by Zeus.

361 *daws*: jackdaws.

'Sailing to Byzantium', from *The Tower* (1928). The poem takes the form of an imagined journey, a spiritual quest, to the holy city of Byzantium, later Constantinople, at the time of its greatest artistic splendour (*c.* AD 560).

362 *That is no country*: Ireland (and perhaps the Celtic paradise, *Tír na nÓg*, the country of the young).

363 *the gold mosaic of a wall*: Yeats had seen the mosaic procession of martyrs
in the church of S. Apollinaire Nuova in Ravenna, which he visited in
1907, and knew of other examples of Byzantine art.

perne in a gyre: spin in the spirals of time.

set upon a golden bough: the image of a golden bird on a golden bough has
been attributed to both Hans Christian Anderson's story 'The Nightingale' and Sir Walter Scott's novel *Count Robert of Paris*.

'The Circus Animals' Desertion', from *Last Poems* (1939). Yeats considered a
number of titles for this late poem, including 'Tragic Toys', 'Despair', and
'On the lack of a theme'.

364 *Oisin . . . his fairy bride*: Yeats's poem *The Wanderings of Oisin* (1889) tells
of how Oisin was enchanted by Niamh, one of the fairy host or Sidhe,
and taken to distant realms.

'The Countess Cathleen': in Yeats's 1899 play, the Countess sells her soul to
save the people from starvation, but she is saved at the end. Maud Gonne
played Countess Cathleen in the first production.

my dear: Maud Gonne (see biographical entry).

Cuchulain fought the ungovernable sea: Cuchulain, the legendary warrior,
having unknowingly killed his own son, battles with the waves in grief
and pain.

ETHNA CARBERY

Five poems from *Four Winds of Eirinn* (1902). A later edition of the book with
a memoir by the poet's husband, Seumas MacManus, was published in 1918.
The intense patriotism of poems like 'Rody McCorley' and 'The Passing of
the Gael' is in keeping with the nationalist politics that informed her editorship of the journal *Shan Van Vocht*.

'Rody McCorley' commemorates the hanging of the young rebel, Rody
McCorley, in the 1798 rising. It has become a well-known song.

367 *the banks of Bann*: the River Bann separates Co. Antrim and Co. Derry
and flows through Toomebridge, Co. Antrim.

368 *sash of green*: the green sash was a popular declaration of nationalist
politics in the 1790s. See the popular song, 'The Wearin' o' the Green'.

'The Passing of the Gael' became a favourite recitation piece in the early years
of the twentieth century. Seán O'Casey has the hypocritical Seumas Shields
recite the line 'Kathaleen Ní Houlihan, your road's a thorny way' in his 1923
play, *The Shadow of a Gunman*.

'Beannacht Leat': the title and refrain are versions of 'Beannacht libh'
(a farewell greeting akin to 'Bless you'). See Miss Ivors's farewell in James
Joyce's story, 'The Dead'.

LIONEL JOHNSON

'By the Statue of King Charles at Charing Cross', from *Poems* (1895). The equestrian statue of Charles I (1600–49) stands on the south side of Trafalgar Square. It was designed by Hubert Sueur and cast in 1633, but disposed of as scrap metal when the Civil War broke out. After the Restoration, it was recovered and eventually erected in 1675. It looks towards Whitehall, where Charles I was executed. Like Andrew Marvell, in his 'Horatian Ode', Johnson commemorates the King's noble death, but also recruits him as an exemplar of the ideals of art and beauty upheld by many of the poets of the 1890s.

372 *Speak after sentence?*: Charles was not allowed to speak during his trial.

'Mystic and Cavalier', from *Poems* (1895). 'The Dark Angel', from *Poems* (1895).

374 *Furies*: the avenging spirits of the underworld.

375 *Apples of ashes*: temptation that proves disappointing; very likely a reference to the biblical story of the apples of Sodom that turn to ashes when picked.

   dark Paraclete: the Paraclete is the Holy Ghost; the dark Paraclete suggests Lucifer.

'Ninety-Eight', from *Ireland, and Other Poems* (1897). Although written as early as 1893, the poem was published just one year before the centenary of the 1798 rebellion by the United Irishmen. Johnson is obviously recalling the famous ballad by John Kells Ingram, 'The Memory of the Dead' (p. 162).
   'Parnell', from *Ireland, and Other Poems* (1897). First published in the journal *United Ireland*, 7 Oct. 1893, to mark the second anniversary of Parnell's death. The closing lines anticipate W. B. Yeats's 'Easter 1916': 'our part | To murmur name upon name, | As a mother names her child | When sleep at last has come'.

GEORGE RUSSELL (AE)

'Carrowmore', from *Collected Poems* (1913).

379 *colleen*: from the Irish *cailín* (girl, young woman).

EVA GORE-BOOTH

'The Little Waves of Breffny', from *The One and the Many* (1904). 'The Land to a Landlord', from *The One and the Many* (1904).

380 *merely a stranger*: 'the stranger' is often a euphemistic reference to the British or to the Anglo-Irish landowning class in Ireland. See *Cathleen ni Houlihan* (p. 426).

'Women's Rights', from *The Egyptian Pillar* (1906).

381 *Glencar* is a lake in Co. Sligo; see W. B. Yeats, 'The Stolen Child'.

JOHN MILLINGTON SYNGE

The poems included here are all from the posthumously published *Poems and Translations* (1909).

382 *Wicklow*: Synge had a deep attachment to Co. Wicklow from his childhood onwards. Some of his walks through Wicklow in later life were recorded in a collection of his travel writing titled *In Wicklow and West Kerry* (1911).

383 *peeler*: policeman.

porter: a dark beer also known as stout.

OLIVER ST JOHN GOGARTY

'To the Liffey with the Swans', from *An Offering of Swans* (1923). Both titles refer to an event that took place during the Civil War of 1922–3. Gogarty was a Senator in the Free State and a target for dissident Republicans. He was abducted in Dublin one evening, but managed to escape by diving into the River Liffey. In gratitude, he presented the river with two swans.

384 *alban*: pure white.

that doubled Bird: Zeus in the form of a swan.

Twin Sportsmen: Love and War. From the union of Leda and the swan came two pairs of children: Pollux and Clytemnestra, and Castor and Helen (of Troy).

THOMAS MACDONAGH

'John-John', from *Songs of Myself* (1910). 'Of a Poet Patriot', from *Lyrical Poems* (1913). 'The Yellow Bittern', from *Lyrical Poems* (1913). The poem is a translation of the famous Irish poem 'An Bonnán Buí', by Cathal Buí Mac Giolla Gunna (*c.*1680–1756).

387 *Constantine's halls*: Constantine the Great, Roman emperor (*c.* AD 288–337), granted Christians freedom of worship after the Edict of Milan in 313 and embarked upon an ambitious building project, constructing new halls of worship or basilicas. He later made Byzantium (Constantinople) his capital. The island in the poem is presumably somewhere in the Mediterranean.

'The Night Hunt', from *Lyrical Poems* (1913).

JOSEPH CAMPBELL

'My Lagan Love', from *Songs of Uladh* (1904). Now a well-known song, 'My Lagan Love' was heard by Campbell in Fanad, Co. Donegal, in 1903–4, accompanied by fiddle. When he first wrote it down, it had five stanzas, but the version printed here is the most popular.

389 *leanannsidhe*: from the Irish *leanann sidhe* (fairy mistress).

390 *the cricket's singing-stone*: where the cricket or grasshopper sings (presumably the stone hearth).

   spares: in renditions of the song this is usually 'stirs'.

SEUMAS O'SULLIVAN

'The Lamplighter', from *The Lamplighter and Other Poems* (1929). 'The Geese', probably written shortly before the publication of O'Sullivan's *Collected Poems* (1940), in which it appears in a section of 'later poems'.

PATRICK PEARSE

The six poems are all from *Collected Works of Padraic H. Pearse: Plays, Poems and Stories* (1917), published the year after his execution at Kilmainham Jail for his role in the Easter Rising.
   'A Rann I Made': a rann is a verse or stanza. The term is also used by W. B. Yeats in his early poem 'To Ireland in the Coming Times'.
   'I Am Ireland' is Pearse's own translation of an old Irish poem.

391 *Cuchulainn*: see the note for W. B. Yeats, 'The Circus Animals' Desertion'.

'On the Strand of Howth': Howth (from the Danish *hoved*, meaning 'head') is the northern end of Dublin Bay; it was once Dublin's main harbour. 'The Mother' was probably written in the autumn of 1915. 'Christmas 1915': these four lines are a characteristic embodiment of Pearse's religious and political fervour. 'The Wayfarer' is reputed to have been written by Pearse on the night before his execution (3 May 1916).

PADRAIC COLUM

'She Moved Through the Fair', from *Wild Earth and Other Poems* (1916). The poem has been so successfully adapted to the Irish folk repertoire that it is now regarded as a popular song and has been recorded numerous times (by Van Morrison, Sinead O'Connor, and others).

FRANCIS LEDWIDGE

'A Twilight in Middle March', from *Songs of The Fields* (1916). Composed 16 Mar. 1914.

396 *Delphi*: home of the Delphic oracle (source of wisdom and inspiration) in Greek mythology.

'June', from *Songs of the Fields* (1916). Probably composed in 1914.

> *Elmo's light*: a luminous discharge caused by electricity in the atmosphere (sometimes seen around church spires and the masts of ships).

> *like drunken Noah*: inactive and surrounded by animals.

'August', from *Songs of the Fields* (1916). Composed Aug. 1914.

'Thomas MacDonagh', from *Songs of Peace* (1917). Composed in Manchester, May 1916. See the biographical entry on Thomas MacDonagh and also the poetry and prose included in this volume. The opening line of Ledwidge's lament recalls MacDonagh's version of 'The Yellow Bittern'. This and the two poems that follow are clearly inspired by the Easter Rising of 1916.

'The Wedding Morning', from *Songs of Peace* (1917). Composed in Derry in 1916, commemorating the wedding of fellow poet Joseph Mary Plunkett and Grace Gifford in Kilmainham Jail on the eve of Plunkett's execution for his part in the Easter Rebellion.

'The Blackbirds', from *Songs of Peace* (1917). Composed in Derry in July 1916. The blackbird had been a nationalist emblem since Jacobite times. Charles Stewart Parnell was commemorated in song and verse as 'The Blackbird of Avondale'.

'The Herons', from *Songs of Peace* (1917). Composed in Derry in 1916. Ledwidge is possibly remembering Fr. Edward Smyth, one of his early supporters, who drowned in Lough Sheelin.

F. R. HIGGINS

'Father and Son' and 'To My Blackthorn Stick', from *Arable Holdings* (1923).

PATRICK KAVANAGH

All poems from *Patrick Kavanagh: Collected Poems* (London: MacGibbon and Kee, 1964). Individual dates of composition are given in the contents pages.

402 *Billy Brennan*: a likely name for a local farmer.

403 *Alexander Selkirk*: the fugitive sailor on whom Daniel Defoe based Robinson Crusoe.

JOHN HEWITT

All poems from Frank Ormsby (ed.), *Collected Poems* (1992). Individual dates of composition are given in the contents pages.

LOUIS MACNEICE

All poems from *Collected Poems 1925–1948* (1949). Individual dates of composition are given in the contents pages.

405 *basalt*: part of the geology of the north of Ireland; volcanic activity produced basalt lavas which then cooled, producing strange formations like
the Giant's Causeway.

mica: mineral deposits in granite and other rocks.

carrion water: suggesting (like 'stained water') unclean or putrid, but
water has been a source of wealth, both in the linen trade and in
shipbuilding.

banging of Orange drums: Protestant ritual commemorating the victory of
the Battle of the Boyne (1690) by King William III, Prince of Orange.

406 *the list of Christ on the cross*: the skewed alignment of the aisle is one of the
unusual features of St Nicholas's church.

the Chichesters knelt in marble: a large Elizabethan monument to the
powerful Chichester family.

407 *The troops*: a hundred men of the Yorkshire Light Infantry were deployed
in Carrickfergus at a time of increased sectarian tension accompanying
the Home Rule debate. At the outbreak of the First World War, many of
them went off to fight in France.

school in Dorset: Acreman House Preparatory School in Sherborne,
Dorset.

408 *Maud Gonne*: see biographical entry.

Casement: see biographical entry.

Orange bands: see note above.

Kathaleen ni Houlihan: see notes on James Clarence Mangan's poem of
that title above and also the play of that title by W. B. Yeats and Lady
Gregory.

409 *King William . . . To the Boyne*: King William III, Protestant victor of the
Battle of the Boyne in 1690.

Griffith, Connolly, Collins: Arthur Griffith (1871–1922), James Connolly
(1868–1916), Michael Collins (1890–1922), all prominent nationalist
leaders.

Ourselves alone: common mistranslation of *Sinn Féin* (We ourselves).

410 *Ireland, my Ireland*: an ironic echo of William Ernest Henley's patriotic
poem, 'England, My England' (1892), later retitled 'Pro Rege Nostro'
(For Our Kingdom): 'What have I done for you, | England, my
England'.

Odi atque amo: I hate and love (Catullus, *Carmina*, lxxxv).

OSCAR WILDE

From *The Importance of Being Earnest*, first performed at St James's Theatre,
London, 14 Feb. 1895, and published in 1899.

414 *The Divorce Court*: established in England in 1857.

415 *Scotland Yard*: headquarters of the London Metropolitan Police.

418 *Willis's*: popular restaurant in the 1890s, close to St James's Theatre.

419 *sent down*: asked to escort a guest to dinner.

420 *Wagnerian manner*: loud and disturbing, as some Victorians thought Wagner's operas were.

W. B. YEATS AND AUGUSTA GREGORY

Cathleen ni Houlihan was composed by Yeats and Lady Gregory between Sept. and Nov. 1901 and first produced by the Irish National Dramatic Company in Dublin on 2 Apr. 1902. Maud Gonne played the title role. Yeats explained in a letter to Lady Gregory that he had dreamed of an old woman in a long cloak: 'She was Ireland herself, that Kathleen ni Houlihan for whom so many songs have been sung and for whose sake so many have gone to their death.' The play is set in Killala, a village on the western shore of Killala Bay, Co. Mayo, at the time of the French landing in support of the 1798 rebellion. After some initial successes against British government forces, the Irish rebels and their supporters were defeated.

421 *hurling*: Gaelic sport, similar to hockey.

423 *Ballina*: town in Co. Mayo.

424 *Enniscrone*: Inishcrone, a coastal town in Co. Sligo, across the bay from Killala.

426 *Too many strangers in the house*: a covert allusion to the colonial history of Ireland and the loss of land to English and Scottish settlers.

My four beautiful green fields: the four ancient provinces of Ireland: Ulster, Munster, Leinster, and Connaught.

Kilglass: village close to Killala.

yellow-haired Donough is dead: the song is based on an Irish poem that became well known at the time of the Literary Revival. It was translated by Patrick Pearse, among others.

427 *red man of the O'Donnells ... Clontarf*: Red Hugh O'Donnell (1571–1602), Gaelic chief from Donegal, who fought the English at the Battle of Kinsale; Donal O'Sullivan Beare (1560–1618), Gaelic chief from West Cork, who left Ireland for Spain in 1602 after the destruction of the family stronghold, Dunboy Castle; Brian Boru (926–1014), high king of Ireland, who helped to defeat the Danes at the Battle of Clontarf (1014), but was killed at the end of the battle.

429 *the Poor Old Woman ... Cathleen, the daughter of Houlihan*: the legendary Sean Bhean Bhoct; see the song 'The Shan Van Vocht', in which the Poor Old Woman heralds the arrival of the French in Ireland. See also the poem 'Kathaleen Ny-Houlahan' by James Clarence Mangan.

keening: from the Irish *caoine* (funeral cry).

the white-scarfed riders: possibly priests with white stoles.

430 *the touch*: affected by a supernatural visitation; troubled mentally; as if in a trance.

AUGUSTA GREGORY

The Rising of the Moon was first performed at the Abbey Theatre in Mar. 1907. The play is set at the time of the Fenian rising of 1867 and takes its title from a popular nationalist ballad in which the rising of the moon is equated with the political rising of Fenian rebels (see song and notes above).

433 *assize time too*: periodic legal proceedings.

437 *Granuaile*: see the version of the song reprinted in this volume.

    'Shan Bhean Bhocht': see the version of the song printed in this volume.

    'Green on the Cape': one of a number of songs to do with the wearing of the nationalist colour green (see the song 'The Wearin' o' the Green' in this volume).

439 *the Rising of the Moon*: see the version of the song reprinted in this volume.

J. M. SYNGE

Riders to the Sea was written in the summer of 1902, published in 1903, and first performed in Dublin (by the Irish National Theatre Society) in Feb. 1904. It is based on Synge's experiences on Inishmaan, one of the Aran Islands (see the extract from *The Aran Islands* printed in this volume).

442 *pot-oven*: the cake is traditional Irish soda bread, baked in a clay pot on the turf (peat) fire.

443 *turf-loft*: an upper room or platform for storing turf and keeping it dry.

444 *the green head*: grassy headland overlooking the sea.

    the hooker's tacking from the east: small sailing boat running a course against the wind.

    the pig with the black feet: perhaps an omen.

445 *the jobber*: travelling salesman or tradesman.

    another cock for the kelp: kelp (seaweed) was dried in conical heaps (cocks) and used as fertilizer.

446 *destroyed*: with hunger, but the word anticipates the tragic events of the play.

447 *poteen*: illicitly distilled whiskey.

    there's a black knot on it: another omen.

448 *no one to keen him but the black hags*: keen is from the Irish *caoine* (funeral cry); the black hags are cormorants flying close to the water.

450 *Bay of Gregory of the Golden Mouth*: Gregory Sound, separating Inishmore and Inishmaan.

451 *curagh*: small traditional rowing boat.

red petticoats over their heads: the women have used their petticoats as shawls, though the colour of the garments strangely reflects the torn red sail in Maurya's speech. Synge comments on the prominence of red garments in *The Aran Islands*.

452 *Samhain*: Celtic Feast of the Dead, coinciding with All Souls' Day (1 November), when the spirits of the dead were thought to move among the living.

SEÁN O'CASEY

From Act I of *Juno and the Paycock*. Seán O'Casey's play was first produced at the Abbey Theatre in 1924. Set in a Dublin tenement during the Civil War of 1922–3, when Republican opinion split over the Anglo-Irish Treaty, the play charts the fortunes and misfortunes of the Boyle family. Juno, according to her husband, 'The Captain', takes her name from a felicitous series of events: she was born in June, they met in June, and their son Johnny was born in June. However, as with other O'Casey plays, there is a comic deflation of heroic myth: for the goddess Juno in classical mythology, the peacock was a sacred bird; for the Juno of the Dublin tenements, the only 'paycock' is her strutting, idle husband.

455 *Die-hard*: a Republican 'Irregular' opposed to the Anglo-Irish Treaty of 1921 and the creation of the Irish Free State.

457 *the Free State*: the Anglo-Irish Treaty of 1921 created an Irish Free State of twenty-six counties, leaving six northern counties loyal to the Crown and so institutionalizing the partition of the island. Continuing disagreements over the government of Ireland led to the Civil War of 1922–3.

458 *snug*: a small, comfortable side-room in a public house.

459 *affeydavey*: affidavit or sworn statement (one of numerous comic malapropisms in the play).

Deirdre of the Sorras: *Deirdre of the Sorrows* (1910) was a play by J. M. Synge, based on the tragic love story of Derdriu in the Ulster cycle of tales. There were numerous accounts of Deirdre in works by Yeats and others.

466 *Chiselurs*: children.

a state o' chassis: a state of chaos (another malapropism).

468 *the bog o' Allen*: large area of turf bog to the south-west of Ireland, associated by Boyle with rural backwardness. It is also a prominent image at the end of James Joyce's story, 'The Dead'.

return room: an outbuilding or extension to the house.

The Doll's House, Ghosts, an' The Wild Duck: all naturalist plays by Henrik Ibsen (1828–1906).

469 *Virol*: a food supplement for children.

470 *the people in ' '47' . . . the Fenians*: Boyle accuses the clergy of interfering in the struggles of the people in three historical events: the Famine of 1845–8; the Home Rule campaign led by Charles Stewart Parnell in the 1880s; the political uprisings of the Fenian rebels in the late nineteenth century.

Confraternity men: the Confraternity of the Sacred Heart (a Catholic organization).

BIOGRAPHIES

William ALLINGHAM (1824–89), poet and editor, is known mainly through a small group of poems that regularly appear in anthologies of Irish verse. These include 'The Maids of Elfin-Mere', 'The Fairies', and 'The Winding Banks of Erne'. In his own day, however, Allingham was well known to poets such as Robert Browning, Dante Gabriel Rossetti, and Alfred Tennyson, and his work inspired later Irish poets, including W. B. Yeats and John Hewitt. He was born in Ballyshannon, Co. Donegal, and his first job was in the local bank, where his father was manager. In 1846, he took a post with the national excise service and spent the next twenty-four years working as a customs officer. He first visited England in 1843 and eventually settled there in 1863. He befriended the influential poet, critic, and editor, Leigh Hunt, to whom he dedicated his first book of poems in 1850. Among his later publications were *Day and Night Songs* (1854), *Fifty Modern Poems* (1865), *Songs, Ballads and Stories* (1877), *Irish Songs and Poems* (1887), and *Flower Pieces and Other Poems* (1888). His most ambitious work was the verse novel, *Laurence Bloomfield in Ireland* (1864), in which he tried to promote reform of land ownership and tenants' rights.

Samuel BECKETT (1906–89), novelist, playwright, and poet, was born in Dublin, and educated at Portora Royal School, Enniskillen, and Trinity College, Dublin. He taught French at Campbell College, Belfast, before working as a lecteur d'anglais at the École Normale Supérieure in Paris (1928–30). While in Paris, he met James Joyce, and one of his earliest published works was 'Dante . . . Bruno. Vico . . Joyce', which he contributed to a collection of essays on *Finnegans Wake* in 1929. His early poem *Whoroscope* (1930) initiated a profound interest in Descartes and in problems of self and identity. The same year, he returned to Dublin and taught French at Trinity College, but resigned the post at the end of 1931, his mental and emotional health in a state of deterioration. Between 1932 and 1937, he moved between France, Germany, England, and Ireland. During this time he worked on his collection of Dublin short stories, *More Pricks than Kicks* (1934) and the unfinished novel, *Dream of Fair to Middling Women*, which remained unpublished until 1992. Unimpressed by post-Independence Ireland (as his 1938 novel *Murphy* suggests), Beckett eventually settled in Paris. He was living in Paris at the time of the Occupation and joined the French Resistance, but later escaped to Roussilon in south-east France, where he wrote *Watt* (not published until 1953), much of it in hiding. He received the Croix de Guerre in 1945. After the war, he chose to write in French as well as English, often producing his own translations. His major work of fiction was the trilogy consisting of *Molloy* (1955), *Malone Dies* (1958), and *The Unnamable* (1959), originally written in French between 1951 and 1953. Increasingly, Beckett was to combine a harrowing exploration of the conditions of knowledge and social being with an often caustic humour. This was also evident in the plays, especially *Waiting for Godot* (1955) and *Endgame* (1956), in which the influence of popular culture, especially the slapstick routines of the music hall and the comic pathos of Charlie Chaplin and Laurel and Hardy, is clearly evident. Beckett continued to experiment with language and dramatic form, composing radio plays like *All that Fall* (1957), television plays like *Eh Joe* (1966), and a single film, simply titled *Film* (1965). He also continued to explore the possibilities of narrative in a flourish of prose works written in the 1970s and 1980s. He was awarded the Nobel Prize in 1969.

Elizabeth BOWEN (1899–1973), novelist and short story writer, was born in Dublin into an Anglo-Irish family that had settled in Cork in the seventeenth century. Her childhood years, which are vividly recounted in her memoir, *Seven Winters* (1942), were divided between Dublin and Bowen's Court, the ancestral house in Co. Cork. At the age of 7, she moved with her family to southern England, but frequently returned to Cork, especially after inheriting Bowen's Court in 1930. Her history of the house and her family, from Cromwellian times to the early twentieth century, is recorded in *Bowen's Court* (1942). In 1923, she published her first collection of short stories, *Encounters*, and married Alan Cameron. Two further collections of stories appeared in the 1920s—*Ann Lee's* (1926) and *Joining Charles* (1929)—and others were to follow in the next two decades. Her final collection of stories, *A Day in the Dark*, was published in 1965. Her first two novels were *The Hotel* (1927) and *The Last September* (1929), the latter set in Ireland in the closing months of the War of Independence. Bowen lived in London during the Second World War, working as an air-raid warden, but she also visited Ireland on numerous occasions, reporting back to the Ministry of Information. Her anxious wartime experience is captured in the short stories of *The Demon Lover* (1945) and the novel *The Heat of the Day* (1949). Among her other novels are *The House in Paris* (1935), *The Death of the Heart* (1938), and *A World of Love* (1955).

Charlotte BROOKE (*c.*1740–93) was born in Rantavan, Co. Cavan, and brought up in Co. Kildare. She was the daughter of Henry Brooke (poet, playwright, and novelist), who educated her and encouraged her to study the Irish language. She contributed translations from the Irish to *Historical Memoirs of the Irish Bards* (1786), compiled by Joseph Cooper Walker, but she is best known for the translations which appear in her *Reliques of Irish Poetry* (1789), modelled on *Reliques of Ancient English Poetry* (1765) by Bishop Thomas Percy. In the preface to the book, she pays tribute to her father, whom she cared for until his death in 1783. She edited a selection of her father's work for publication in 1792, and also produced a moral instruction book for children, *The School for Christians* (1791).

Edmund BURKE (1729–97) was born in Dublin to a father who had abandoned his Catholicism for the Established Church, and a mother who retained her Catholic faith. He was educated at the Quaker School in Ballitore, Co. Kildare, and at Trinity College, Dublin. In 1750 he began to study law in London, but he soon developed an interest in politics and a political career.

His first book, *A Vindication of Natural Society* (1756), sought to defend the established social order and expose what he saw as fraudulent reformist policies. In 1757, the year he married Jane Nugent, he published his highly influential work on aesthetics, *A Philosophical Enquiry Into the Origin of our Ideas of the Sublime and the Beautiful*. In 1758, he began to edit the *Annual Register*, a compendium of topical political, historical, and cultural issues. After briefly serving as private secretary to Lord Rockingham, the Prime Minister, he was elected as MP for Wendover. His insights as a parliamentarian are evident in his *Thoughts on the Cause of the Present Discontents* (1770), and in numerous letters, pamphlets, and speeches. In 1774, the year he became MP for Bristol, he delivered his controversial *Speech on American Taxation*, and the following year he argued once again for cautious, sympathetic policies in his *Speech on Conciliation with America*. He took a strong interest in Indian affairs, condemning the mismanagement of the East India Company and denouncing Warren Hastings, Governor-General of Bengal, for cruel and corrupt behaviour. In the wake of political events in 1789, he began writing his celebrated defence of custom and tradition in *Reflections on the Revolution in France* (1790). Afraid that revolutionary discontent would ignite Catholic grievances in Ireland, Burke supported the efforts of the Catholic Committee in Dublin in campaigning for further social and political reform. His letters to Sir Hercules Langrishe in 1792 and 1795 reveal his acute concern over the plight of Catholics and his frustration over the failure of the Protestant ascendancy to adopt a more enlightened and responsible attitude to government. Burke continues to be widely regarded as an influential exponent of conservative political thought. His views on Ireland had considerable impact on Matthew Arnold, who edited his writings and speeches on Irish affairs (1881), and also on W. B. Yeats.

Joseph CAMPBELL (1879–1944), poet and playwright, was born in Belfast and educated at St Malachy's College. He was drawn to the Ulster Literary Theatre, for which he wrote a play, *The Little Cowherd of Slaigne* (1905). He also composed lyrics for traditional tunes collected by the composer Herbert Hughes. These were published as *Songs of Uladh* (1904), with illustrations by his brother John. One of the songs, 'My Lagan Love', was to gain immense popularity. He moved to Dublin for a brief spell, then lived in London for a number of years. Several volumes of poetry appeared in quick succession, including *The Rushlight* (1906), *The Gilly of Christ* (1907), and *The Mountainy Singer* (1908). He settled in Lackendarragh, Co. Wicklow, with his wife, Agnes Maude, in 1912. That year, he composed another play, *Judgement*, which was produced at the Abbey Theatre. An organizer for the Irish Volunteers, he acted as a rescue worker during the Easter Rising. Having opposed the Anglo-Irish Treaty, he was held captive for eighteen months during the Civil War. After the Rising, he published another volume of poetry, *Earth of Cualann* (1917), illustrated with his own line drawings. After the Civil War he emigrated to the United States and founded the School of Irish Studies in New York in 1925. He also lectured in Anglo-Irish literature at Fordham University for ten years. He returned to Ireland in 1939 and resettled in Co. Wicklow.

Austin Clarke's edition of his work, *Poems of Joseph Campbell*, was published in Dublin in 1963.

Ethna CARBERY (1866–1902) was the pen-name of poet and short story writer, Anna MacManus, née Anna Isabel Johnston, who was born in Ballymena, Co. Antrim. She was a frequent contributor to nationalist papers such as *The Nation* and *United Ireland*, and with Alice Milligan she founded the journal *Shan Van Vocht* in 1896. Her patriotic poetry, published in *The Four Winds of Eirinn* (1902), included the ballad 'Rody McCorley' and 'The Passing of the Gael' (recited by Seumas Shields in Seán O'Casey's play, *The Shadow of a Gunman*). Her fiction was collected in *The Passionate Hearts* (1903), with a preface by her husband, the Donegal short story writer and playwright, Seumas MacManus. Another collection of stories, *In the Celtic Past*, appeared the following year. A memoir by Seumas MacManus appears in the revised 1918 edition of *The Four Winds of Eirinn*.

William CARLETON (1794–1869), novelist and short story writer, was the youngest of fourteen children born to an Irish-speaking family in Prillisk, Co. Tyrone. His early upbringing provided much of the detail for his later written accounts of hedge schools, weddings, wakes, and dances. In his early twenties, he left Tyrone and sought work as a teacher in various parts of Ireland before reaching Dublin. He claims in his *Traits and Stories of the Irish Peasantry* (1830) that the experience of a pilgrimage to Lough Derg destroyed his hopes of becoming a priest, but his encounter in 1828 with the Reverend Caesar Otway, a fierce anti-Catholic proselytizer, undoubtedly contributed to his turning from Catholicism and eventual acceptance of the Church of Ireland. His earliest writings, including the serialized novella, *Father Butler*, appeared in Otway's *Christian Examiner*, and Carleton began to acquire a reputation as a satirist of Catholic ritual and superstition. His first novel, *Fardorougha the Miser*, was published serially in the *Dublin University Magazine* in 1837–8. The 1840s were prolific years, with four novels appearing in 1845: *Valentine M'Clutchy, Art Maguire, Rody the Rover*, and *Para Sastha*. Three of his best-known novels were written in the aftermath of the Famine: *The Black Prophet* (1847), *The Emigrants of Ahadarra* (1848), and *The Tithe Proctor* (1849). The later writings, including *The Squanders of Castle Squander* (1852), struggle to accommodate a tension inherent in Carleton's attitude to the rural Irish poor, who are both endearingly depicted in all their quaint eccentricity and increasingly castigated for their unenlightened ways. Carleton's popularity, however, continued to flourish. *Willy Reilly and his Dear Colleen Bawn* (1855) ran to thirty editions. His *Autobiography* was never finished, but was published as *The Life of William Carleton* (ed. D. J. O'Donoghue) in 1896.

Roger CASEMENT (1864–1916) was born in Sandycove, Co. Dublin, and educated at Ballymena Academy. In 1892 he joined the British consular service in Africa. He became known as a human rights activist after he exposed the corruption and brutality of the colonial regime in the Belgian Congo. He was later appointed as consul-general in Rio de Janeiro and investigated conditions in the Peruvian rubber plantations and elsewhere. He was knighted in

1911 for his public services and retired from the colonial services the following year. He joined the Irish Volunteers in 1913, having already shown a strong commitment to nationalist politics through his involvement with the Gaelic League in Ulster as early as 1903. At the outset of the First World War, he sought German help in winning Irish independence, and travelled to Berlin in November 1914. After the dispatch of a German ship carrying arms to support the Easter Rising was intercepted in April 1916, Casement was arrested and taken to England to stand trial. He was found guilty of high treason and sentenced to be hanged. Pleas for leniency were made by George Bernard Shaw and others, but Casement was effectively discredited by the circulation of diaries revealing his homosexual relationships. The diaries, released by the British government, were thought by many to be forgeries. Casement was hanged in Pentonville Prison, London, on 3 August 1916. His remains were returned to Ireland and re-interred in Glasnevin Cemetery after a state funeral on 1 March 1965.

Padraic COLUM (1881–1972), poet, novelist, and dramatist, was born in Longford and educated at University College, Dublin. He began to write for the theatre in 1903, when *Broken Soil* (later *The Fiddler's House*) was produced by the Irish National Theatre Society, the forerunner of the Abbey Theatre, followed by *The Land* (1905) and *Thomas Muskerry* (1910). Two of his best-known lyrics, 'She Moved Through The Fair' and 'A Cradle Song', belong to these early years. His first collection of poems, *Wild Earth*, was published in 1907, and his first novel, *Castle Conquer*, in 1923. With James Stephens and Thomas MacDonagh, he founded the *Irish Review*. In 1912 he married Mary Maguire, and in 1914 they moved to America, where they both became literature teachers at Columbia University, New York. Together, they collaborated on *Our Friend James Joyce* (1958). Colum also wrote memoirs, travel books, short fiction, including stories for children, and a late novel, *The Flying Swans* (1957). He made frequent visits to Ireland from America and was President of the United Arts Club, Dublin, for many years.

James CONNOLLY (1868–1916), founder of the Irish Labour Party, was born of Irish immigrant parents in Edinburgh. He enlisted with the British army at the age of 14, and was briefly based in Dublin. He married an Irish woman, Lillie Reynolds, in 1890. Back in Edinburgh, he became involved in socialist politics and trade union organization. He returned to Dublin in 1896 as an organizer of the Dublin Socialist Club and founded the *Workers' Republic*, the first Irish socialist newspaper. He also founded the Irish Socialist Republican Party in 1898. Between 1903 and 1910 he worked in America for Daniel DeLeon's Socialist Labour Party and the Industrial Workers of the World. On his return to Dublin in 1910, he organized the Socialist Party of Ireland, and in 1911 he was appointed as Belfast agent to the Irish Transport and General Workers' Union, later succeeding James Larkin as leader of the ITGWU. In 1913 he established the Citizen Army to protect workers' rights during the Dublin lock-out strike. In 1916 he was appointed military commander of the Republican forces in Dublin. He was in command of the

General Post Office during Easter week and was badly wounded. One of the seven signatories of the Proclamation of the Irish Republic, he was shot by firing squad in Kilmainham Jail, 12 May 1916. Connolly's writings on labour issues and international socialism have been reprinted numerous times. *Labour in Irish History* (1910) was probably his most influential work, though he also wrote poetry and a play titled *Under Which Flag?*, now lost but allegedly performed at Liberty Hall in March 1916.

Thomas DAVIS (1814–45) was born in Mallow, Co. Cork, the son of a British army surgeon. He was educated at Trinity College, Dublin, and called to the bar in 1838. His 1839 address to the Trinity College Historical Society, 'The Young Irishman of the Middle Classes', instructed young educated Protestants to help in the regeneration of Ireland and was instrumental in establishing the so-called 'Young Ireland Movement'. He joined the Repeal Association and became the leader of a younger generation of Irish patriots impatient with O'Connell's constitutional methods. With Charles Gavan Duffy and John Blake Dillon, he founded *The Nation* in 1842. His writings on Irish history and culture in *The Nation* inspired his contemporaries, while his ballads, including 'A Nation Once Again', were to influence a later generation of nationalist writers, including W. B. Yeats.

Aubrey DE VERE (1814–1902), poet, was born at Curragh Chase, Co. Limerick, the son of Sir Aubrey de Vere (1788–1846). During visits to England, he made the acquaintance of William Wordsworth, Thomas Carlyle, and Alfred Tennyson. Through John Henry Newman, he came under the influence of the Tractarian Movement in Oxford. During the Famine he assisted his elder brother, Sir Stephen de Vere, in relief activities and later wrote *English Misrule and Irish Misdeeds* (1848). In 1851 he was accepted into the Catholic Church, and much of his subsequent poetry, including *May Carols or Ancilla Domini* (1857), was devoted to the Virgin Mary and the saints. In 1856, he was invited by Newman to give a series of lectures on literature at the Catholic University in Dublin, and two of these were published in his *Essays Literary and Ethical* (1889). His best-known poetic work is *Inisfail* (1861), though he also gained recognition for *The Foray of Queen Maeve* (1882), based on the heroic legends of *Táin Bó Cualinge*.

Maria EDGEWORTH (1767–1849), novelist, was born at Black Bourton, Oxfordshire, England, but in 1782 she moved to the family estate in Ireland, Edgeworthstown, Co. Longford. She assisted her father, Richard Lovell Edgeworth, in running the property and caring for her brothers and sisters. Her first publication was *Letters to Literary Ladies* (1795), closely followed by *The Parent's Assistant* (1796), a collection of stories for children. With her father, she wrote a two-volume work titled *Practical Education* (1798). Her first novel, *Castle Rackrent* (1800), was praised by Sir Walter Scott and came to be regarded as the first regional novel in English. Her second novel, *Belinda*, was published in 1801. *Essays on Irish Bulls* (written with her father) appeared in 1802, and two further works of her own, *Popular Tales* and *The Modern Griselda*, were written over the next three years. With her father, she visited

Brussels and Paris in 1802. During her travels she refused an offer of marriage from the Swedish diplomat, Chevalier Edelcrantz, for whom she wrote *Leonora* (1806). *Tales of Fashionable Life* appeared in six volumes between 1809 and 1812, and included one of her best-known works, *The Absentee* (1812). In 1813 she visited London with her father and was warmly received by admirers of her work. *Ormond* was speedily written for her father's seventy-third birthday in 1817, but she wrote relatively little after his death that year. She edited and completed his *Memoirs* in 1820. She made further visits to London and also to Abbotsford, where Scott was her host. A late novel, *Helen*, was published in 1834. Her later years were preoccupied with the management of the Edgeworthstown estate and the relief of victims of the Famine.

Robert EMMET (1778–1803) was born at St Stephen's Green, Dublin. He was a prominent member of the Historical Society at Trinity College, and a youthful member of the United Irishmen. After the United Irishmen's rebellion of 1798, a warrant was issued for his arrest, but not enforced. In France he planned another rising with his brother, Thomas Addis Emmett, hoping for French support. After returning to Dublin, he began preparations for an armed rebellion to coincide with the expected Napoleonic invasion of England in August 1803. The explosion of an arms depot led to a premature and ineffective rising on 23 May 1803. En route to Dublin Castle, Emmet's followers murdered Lord Kilwarden, the Chief Justice, and his nephew, who were travelling in a coach. Emmet went into hiding but was arrested by Major Henry Sirr, tried for treason, and found guilty. He was hanged and beheaded outside St Catherine's Church on Thomas Street, Dublin, on 20 September 1803.

Samuel FERGUSON (1810–86) was born in Belfast and educated at Belfast Academical Institution, Lincoln's Inn, London, and Trinity College, Dublin. He was called to the bar in 1838. From an early age, he showed a strong interest in literary journalism, poetry, and translation. He became a regular contributor to *Blackwood's Magazine* and the *Dublin University Magazine*, in which he published a controversial four-part review of James Hardiman's *Irish Minstrelsy* in 1834, condemning some of the translations of early Irish poems in the volume and offering his own versions, which sought to recover some of the narrative vigour and emotional power of the originals. His later work was to have a considerable impact on the Literary Revival, especially on the early writings of W. B. Yeats. Many of his best-known versions of Irish stories and legends appeared in *Lays of the Western Gael and Other Poems* (1864). Although a liberal unionist by temperament, Ferguson was a founding member of the Protestant Repeal Association in 1848 and was friends with Thomas Davis, for whom he wrote an impassioned elegy in 1845, expressing sympathy for the ideals of the Young Ireland Movement. In 1848 he married Mary Catherine Guinness, of the well-known Dublin brewing family. He continued to combine an active career in the legal profession with an enthusiastic interest in Irish archaeology and antiquities. He became QC in 1859 and Deputy Keeper of the Public Records of Ireland in 1867. He was knighted in 1878, and in 1881 was elected president of the Royal Irish Academy.

Thomas FURLONG (1794–1827) was born to a family of tenant farmers in Scarawalsh, in the township of Ballylough, between Enniscorthy and Fens in Co. Wexford. When he was 9 years old, the family moved to Clovass and his father began to expand his business interests by providing public transport to Dublin. A trip to Dublin with his father led to Furlong being apprenticed to a Dublin grocer, for whom he later wrote an elegy, 'The Burial'. The publication of the poem brought him to the attention of the famous Jameson whiskey distilling family and he was offered patronage (probably by John Jameson). Although he wrote extensively for magazines such as the *Dublin and London Magazine* and also established and edited *The New Irish Magazine and Monthly National Advocate*, only two small volumes of his poetry appeared in his lifetime. He was himself responsible for the publication of *The Misanthrope* in London in 1819. His satirical work *The Plagues of Ireland* was published in Dublin in 1824. A strong and outspoken supporter of Catholic Emancipation, he won the trust and friendship of Daniel O'Connell. Despite the support of Thomas Moore, Lady Morgan, and others, his work did not receive a great deal of acclaim. However, he was asked by James Hardiman to versify the literal translations of Irish poems that Hardiman was preparing for his two-volume *Irish Minstrelsy* (1831), and Furlong obliged with some striking and memorable versions of poems such as 'Roisin Dubh' and 'Eileen a Roon'. The first volume of *Irish Minstrelsy* contains a memoir of Furlong, who never lived to see the work in print. In addition to the translations he worked on with Hardiman, he also worked devotedly on translating the songs of the great Irish harpist, Turlogh Carolan. His long Gothic poem *The Doom of Derenzie* was published posthumously in London in 1829, the year of Catholic Emancipation. An excellent collection of Furlong's work with valuable commentary has been produced by Sean Mythen: *Thomas Furlong: The Forgotten Wexford Poet* (Co. Wexford: Clone Publications, 1998).

John GAMBLE (1770–1831), army surgeon and author, was born in Strabane, Co. Tyrone, and educated in Edinburgh. After an eye infection ended his career in the army, he began a literary career, touring Ireland for material he might use in both fictional and non-fictional works. His political sympathies were with the Protestant radical wing of the United Irishmen. His fiction includes *Sarsfield* (1814), *Howard* (1815), *Northern Irish Tales* (1818), and *Charlton* (1827). His *Sketches of History, Politics, and Manners, in Dublin, and the North of Ireland, in 1810* was published in 1812 and appeared in a new edition in 1826. Gamble claims in his preface that 'the History of Ireland is a melancholy history' and that in his book he 'endeavours to make known a very peculiar people, and a state of society, unhappily unparalleled on the civilized earth'.

Oliver St John GOGARTY (1878–1957), surgeon and writer, was born in Dublin and studied medicine at Trinity College. As a student, he showed a great flair for poetry and went to Oxford for a term in 1904, hoping to emulate Oscar Wilde's success in winning the Newdigate Prize. He was unsuccessful in his aims, but while in Oxford met R. S. Chenevix Trench, with whom he later shared the Martello tower he had rented near Dublin.

James Joyce made up the trio of intellectuals in the tower, and Gogarty, Trench, and Joyce became the models for Mulligan, Haines, and Dedalus in *Ulysses*. Gogarty married Martha Duane in 1906 and went to Vienna the following year for postgraduate research in otolaryngology. On returning to Dublin, he established a flourishing medical practice, but also pursued his interests in a literary career. He wrote a number of plays about Dublin poverty, including *Blight: The Tragedy of Dublin* (1917), which was staged at the Abbey Theatre. A supporter of the Free State, he escaped Republican kidnappers by swimming down the River Liffey. In gratitude, he presented two swans to the river, an event recounted in his first major collection of poetry, *An Offering of Swans* (1923). W. B. Yeats was to include a generous selection of Gogarty's poems in *The Oxford Book of Modern Verse* (1936). He served as a Senator from 1922 to 1926. Gogarty greatly disliked de Valera and became increasingly disillusioned with the new Ireland of the 1930s. After losing a libel action arising from the publication of his memoir, *As I was Going Down Sackville Street* (1937), he moved to London and then to America, finally abandoning his medical work. In addition to further volumes of autobiographical writings, he wrote the novels *Going Native* (1940), *Mad Grandeur* (1941), and *Mr Petunia* (1945). His *Collected Poems* appeared in 1951.

Maud GONNE (1866–1953), revolutionary and women's rights campaigner, was born in Aldershot, the daughter of a British army officer of Irish descent. She was educated by a governess in France after her mother's early death and moved to Ireland when her father was posted to Dublin in 1882. While in the south of France, recovering from a tubercular haemorrhage, she met Lucien Millevoye, who proposed that they work together for Irish freedom and the recovery of Alsace and Lorraine from German dominion. On returning to Ireland, she led protests against evictions in Donegal and helped to secure the release of Irish political prisoners. In 1890 she returned to France and resumed her friendship with Millevoye. Their daughter, Iseult, was born in 1895, but the relationship came to an end four years later. Throughout the 1890s she travelled widely in Ireland, France, and America, addressing political meetings and raising funds for nationalist causes. She met W. B. Yeats in 1889, the beginning of a passionate and impossible devotion on the part of the poet. Yeats proposed to her for the first time in 1891 and wrote *The Countess Cathleen* for her in 1892. In 1902 she played the leading role in *Cathleen ni Houlihan*. In Paris, in 1903, she married John MacBride, the former commander of the Irish Brigade in the Boer War, and their son Seán was born the following year. The marriage was not successful; she was living in France when MacBride was executed for his part in the Easter Rising in Dublin in 1916. She rejected the Anglo-Irish Treaty in 1922, and continued to work for the Republican cause, assisting prisoners and their families. In 1938 she published a memoir of her early life, *A Servant of the Queen*.

Eva GORE-BOOTH (1870–1926), poet, and sister of Countess Markiewicz, was born at Lissadell, Co. Sligo. After moving to Manchester at the age of 22, she became active in radical politics, campaigning on behalf of feminist and socialist causes. She edited *Women's Labour News* and wrote numerous essays and pamphlets on women's parliamentary representation and right to work. Her strong interest in mysticism is evident in her early books of poetry. Her collected poems were edited with a biographical introduction by Esther Roper in 1929. She wrote five verse plays, though only one was performed in her lifetime. The letters exchanged with her sister, while Constance Markiewicz was in prison, were published in 1934 with a preface by Eamon de Valera.

Augusta (Lady) GREGORY (1852–1932), dramatist, folklorist, and translator, was born in Roxburgh, Co. Galway, and privately educated. In 1880 she married Sir William Gregory of Coole Park, a former MP and Governor of Ceylon. Her husband, who was 63 years old when they married, died in 1892. Their only child, Robert, was killed in the First World War and elegized in a number of poems by W. B. Yeats, including 'An Irish Airman Foresees His Death'. Lady Gregory first met Yeats in 1894, and from 1897 onwards the poet was a frequent visitor to Coole Park, sharing her enthusiasm for Irish literature, mythology, and folklore. In 1897 she collaborated with Yeats and Edward Martyn in founding an Irish national theatre that would eventually become the Abbey Theatre, Dublin. During the 1890s and early 1900s she was intensely active in collecting local stories and translating Gaelic poems and tales. In 1901 she edited *Literary Ideals in Ireland*, a collection of essays typifying the cultural nationalism of the Literary Revival. With Yeats, she wrote *Cathleen ni Houlihan* (first performed in 1902), and in the same year she finished her translation of tales from the Ulster cycle, published as *Cuchulain of Muirthemne*. Further collections of local folklore, poetry, and myth appeared in *Poets and Dreamers* (1903), *Gods and Fighting Men* (1904), and *A Book of Saints and Wonders* (1906). The first play to be released under her own name was *Twenty Five*, which was produced by the Irish National Theatre Society in Dublin on the same night as Yeats's play *The Hour-Glass* (14 March 1903). *Spreading the News* was staged with Yeats's *On Baile's Strand* on the opening night of the Abbey Theatre (27 December 1904). She was to become a prolific playwright and energetic organizer. Among her best-known plays are *Kincora* (1905), *The White Cockade* (1905), *The Canavans* (1906), *Dervorgilla* (1907), *The Rising of the Moon* (1907), *The Deliverer* (1911), and *Grania* (1911). Her extensive field work on Irish folklore culminated in her two-volume *Visions and Beliefs in the West of Ireland* (1920). She also recorded her views of the Abbey Theatre in *Our Irish Theatre* (1913) and the history of her family home in *Coole* (1931).

John HEWITT (1907–87) was born in Belfast and educated at the Methodist College and Queen's University. He worked at the Belfast Museum and Art Gallery throughout the 1930s and 1940s, eventually leaving for a more senior appointment as Director of the Herbert Art Gallery in Coventry, where he remained for twenty years (1952–72). He was writer in residence at Queen's from 1976 to 1979. From an early age he developed a strong interest in radical politics and religious dissent, and this was later combined with a passionate commitment to Ulster regionalism and local dialect. His early poems pay tribute to James Connolly for his unswerving dedication to both Irish nationalism and international socialism, though his later work becomes more acutely concerned with the complexities of Ulster identity. Fourteen volumes of his poetry were published over the space of forty years, ranging from *Conacre* (1943) to *Freehold* (1986). His *Collected Poems* appeared posthumously in 1992. He was also a prolific critic of literature and painting, and his *Art in Ulster 1557–1957* (1977) is an illuminating guide.

Frederick Robert HIGGINS (1896–1941) was born in Foxford, Co. Mayo, but grew up in Co. Meath. At the age of 14 he began work as a clerk in a building firm, later becoming a trade union activist. In 1915 he befriended Austin Clarke, with whom he shared an interest in Gaelic civilization as well as an enthusiasm for writing poetry. His first two books of poems, *Island Blood* (1925) and *The Dark Breed* (1927), share some of the ideals of the Literary Revival, but also show his skill in metrical innovation. His later books, *Arable Holdings* (1933) and *The Gap of Brightness* (1940), are more boldly rhetorical, perhaps influenced by the later work of W. B. Yeats. He was joint editor with Yeats of a series of broadsheets published by the Cuala Press in 1935. His one-act play *A Deuce o' Jacks* was produced by the Abbey Theatre in 1935. He became a director of the Abbey and managed the company during its 1937 American tour, later becoming its business manager.

Douglas HYDE (1860–1949), cultural historian and translator, was born in Frenchpark, Co. Roscommon, where he first heard Irish and learned to speak the language. As a student at Trinity College, Dublin, he joined the Society for the Preservation of the Irish Language and also the Young Ireland Society, where he met W. B. Yeats. He began to publish poems in Irish and also became a collector of Irish books and manuscripts. He preserved and translated poems and stories that were part of the oral tradition, and contributed three folk tales to Yeats's collection of *Fairy and Folk Tales of the Irish Peasantry* (1888). His own collection of tales in *Beside the Fire* (1890) made a great impact on Irish folklore studies and demonstrated the creative potential of Hiberno–English speech. In 1891 *The Nation* began to print his series of 'The Songs of Connacht', with commentaries and translations, an initiative that was to result in the publication of his *Love Songs of Connacht* (1893). After teaching at the University of New Brunswick, Canada, for a year, he became President of the National Literary Society, and presented his inaugural address, 'On the Necessity for De-Anglicising Ireland', on 25 November 1892. He resigned the office to become President of the Gaelic League after its foundation in July 1893. He was a pioneering scholar of Irish literature, producing *The Story of Early Gaelic Literature* (1895) and *A Literary History of Ireland* (1899), and becoming first Professor of Modern Irish at University College, Dublin, in 1905. He served as an Irish Free State Senator (1925–6), and was later appointed first President of Ireland, a position he held from 1938 to 1945.

John Kells INGRAM (1823–1907) was born at the Rectory, Temple Carne, Co. Donegal, and educated at Dr Lyons's School, Newry, and Trinity College, Dublin. He became Professor of Oratory, Professor of Greek, College Librarian, and finally Vice-Provost at TCD, before retiring in 1899. He helped to found the Dublin Statistical Society in 1847. In 1873 he founded and edited *Hermathena*, a series of occasional papers on science, philosophy and literature. His *History of Political Economy* (1888) was translated into ten languages. The authorship of his famous ballad was not formally acknowledged until the publication of his *Sonnets and Other Poems* in 1900.

Lionel JOHNSON (1867–1902), poet, was born in Broadstairs, Kent, the son of an Irish army officer. He was educated at Winchester and New College, Oxford. Along with W. B. Yeats, Ernest Dowson, and others, he joined the Rhymers' Club, which met at the Old Cheshire Cheese pub on Fleet Street, London, and acquired a reputation as one of the decadent poets of the 1890s. Yeats offers a vivid portrait of Johnson in 'The Tragic Generation' (in *Autobiographies*). In 1891 he converted to Catholicism and also developed a strong interest in Irish cultural nationalism. He visited Dublin in 1893, and the following year published two books: *Poems* and *Ireland and Other Poems*. Yeats's selection of *Twenty One Poems* by Johnson was published in 1904. Johnson's austere style was greatly admired by Ezra Pound.

James JOYCE (1882–1941) was born in Rathgar, Dublin, the eldest of ten children in a middle-class Catholic family that fell from prosperity into poverty. He was educated by the Jesuits at Clongowes Wood School and Belvedere College, and then studied languages at University College, Dublin. In his student years, he published an article on Henrik Ibsen in the *Fortnightly Review* (April 1900), which came to the attention of the Norwegian dramatist. In 1902, he went to Paris with the intention of studying medicine, but his interests became increasingly preoccupied with art and literature. His mother's fatal illness in April 1903 brought him back to Dublin. In the summer of 1904 he met Nora Barnacle, who came from Galway but was then working as a chambermaid in Dublin. He persuaded her to go abroad with him, initially to Paris for a teaching post that failed to materialize. After a few months in Pola (now in Croatia), they moved to Trieste, which was to become their home until June 1915. They had two children, a son and a daughter. Despite the struggle he faced in getting his work published, Joyce persisted with his vocation as a writer. *Chamber Music*, a collection of his poems, was published in 1907, and *Dubliners* (a collection of stories he had first tried to publish in 1905) eventually appeared in 1914. His semi-autobiographical novel, *A Portrait of the Artist as a Young Man*, was published in 1916 and *Exiles*, his only play, in 1918. In July 1915, as Italy became entangled in the First World War, Joyce and his family moved to Zurich, where they stayed until 1919, briefly returning to Trieste, then settling in Paris at Ezra Pound's advice. By 1915, Joyce was already at work on *Ulysses*, which after partial publication in the *Little Review* was suppressed. The novel was eventually published in Paris on his fortieth birthday and quickly established him as one of the most inventive European modernist authors. The same year, he began work on *Finnegans Wake*, which was to occupy him for another sixteen years. It was published in 1939. During the Second World War, the family went to live in unoccupied France, eventually returning to Zurich in December 1940. Joyce died just a few weeks later, on 13 January 1941.

Patrick KAVANAGH (1904–67) was born in the parish of Inniskeen, Co.
Monaghan. He assisted his father, the village shoemaker, and also helped to
work his father's few acres of land. He began to 'dabble in verse' at an early
age and his work came to the attention of George Russell (AE), who published
three of his poems in the *Irish Statesman* in 1929–30. His first book, *Ploughman and Other Poems*, was published in London in 1936, and was followed by
his autobiographical work, *The Green Fool*, in 1938. In 1939 Kavanagh moved
to Dublin, hoping for regular employment, but had to scrape a living as
a freelance journalist and was often penniless and in poor health. Through
his acquaintance with John Betjeman, then British press attaché in Dublin,
he manged to obtain some work with the BBC. Like his Dublin associates,
Seán O'Faoláin and Frank O'Connor, he became a fierce critic of post-
Independence Ireland. His anti-pastoral vision in *The Great Hunger* (1942)
provided a critique of the idealized rural Ireland promoted by both the Literary Revival and the Free State government of Éamon de Valera. The same
year, he produced his narrative poem, *Lough Derg*, though it was not published
until 1971. A second collection of poems, *Soul for Sale*, was published in 1947,
and an autobiographical novel, *Tarry Flynn*, appeared the following year. A
new collection of poems, *Come Dance With Kitty Stobling*, was published in
1960. Kavanagh's *Collected Poems* appeared in 1964 and his *Collected Prose* in
1967. His haunting love lyric, 'Raglan Road' (sung to the air of 'The Dawning
of the Day'), was written in 1946 and has been recorded many times. The
definitive version was made by Luke Kelly of the Dubliners.

James Fintan LALOR (1807–49) was born in Tenakill, Co. Laois, the son of
a wealthy farmer and Repeal MP. He was educated at home and at Carlow
College. He was to become one of the most vociferous and radical members of
the Young Ireland movement and a powerful advocate of land reform. In 1845
he founded the Tenant League with Michael Doheny and campaigned on
behalf of rent refusal in Co. Tipperary. He wrote a series of letters to *The
Nation*, proposing rent strikes and resistance to eviction. After the arrest of
John Mitchel, the editor of the *United Irishman*, he moved to Dublin and
helped to edit the *Irish Felon*, in which he openly called for armed insurrection
rather than gradual measures such as the repeal of the act of union. He
was arrested after the rising of July 1848. His health suffered badly during
his imprisonment and he died a month after his release. His courage and
conviction inspired a later generation of writers and thinkers, including James
Connolly and Patrick Pearse.

Emily LAWLESS (1845–1913), novelist and poet, was born at Lyons Castle,
Co. Kildare, the daughter of the 3rd Lord Cloncurry. A good part of her youth
was spent with her mother's people in Co. Galway. Her first novel, *Hurrish*
(1882), was admired by Gladstone for its analysis of the land question. Despite
her family's history of support for the United Irishmen and Catholic Emancipation, she remained a loyalist in her politics, although sympathetically
responsive to the work of the Land League at the end of the nineteenth
century. Her later novels included *Grania* (1892), and *Maelcho* (1894). She
also wrote a fictionalized diary, *With Essex in Ireland* (1890), and a book on

Maria Edgeworth (1904). A collection of poems, *With the Wild Geese*, appeared in 1902. On medical advice she moved to England in later life and died in Surrey.

Francis LEDWIDGE (1887–1917), poet, was born in Slane, Co. Meath, where he worked in mining and road-building before taking a job as a shop assistant in Dublin. From an early age he was interested in the activities of the Literary Revival and the Gaelic League. His first poems were published in the *Drogheda Independent*. In 1912 he made the acquaintance of Lord Dunsany, who arranged the publication of his first collection of poems, *Songs of the Field* (1916). He was an Irish Volunteers organizer and a supporter of Sinn Féin, but in October 1914 he joined the Royal Inniskilling Fusiliers (Dunsany's regiment), to fight 'neither for a principle nor a people nor a law, but for the fields along the Boyne, for the birds and the blue skies over them'. He served as a corporal, survived Gallipoli, and was killed by a shell at Ypres on 31 July 1917. He was deeply moved by the events of Easter 1916 and by the execution of his friend and fellow poet, Thomas MacDonagh. Some of his best-known poems, including his elegy for MacDonagh, were written in 1916 and published in *Songs of Peace* (1917). *Last Songs* appeared posthumously in 1918 and Dunsany edited the *Complete Poems* in 1919.

Joseph Sheridan LE FANU (1814–73), novelist, was born in Dublin. He studied classics at Trinity College and later trained as a barrister. His legal profession was soon overshadowed by his interests in literature and the press. He was proprietor and editor of several Dublin publications. From 1861 to 1869 he was editor of the *Dublin University Magazine*. He began to write fiction in the 1830s (his first published story was 'The Ghost and the Bone-Setter', 1838). His earliest novels included *The Cock and Anchor* (1845) and *The Fortunes of Colonel Torlogh O'Brien* (1847), but he became best known for *The House by the Church-yard* (1863) and *Uncle Silas* (1864), and also for the chilling collection of mystery stories, *In a Glass Darkly* (1872). He also wrote poems, including the popular ballad, 'Shamus O'Brien'.

Thomas MACDONAGH (1878–1916), poet, playwright and revolutionary, was born in Cloughjordan, Co. Tipperary, and educated at Rockwell College, Cashel. He contemplated taking orders, before abandoning ideas of a religious vocation in 1901. He taught in schools in Kilkenny and Fermoy until 1908, the year in which he met Patrick Pearse in Aran. He moved to Dublin to work with Pearse as 'his helper and his friend' at St Enda's School, becoming the first teacher on the staff. He studied part-time at University College, Dublin (1909–11), and wrote an MA thesis on Thomas Campion and the English lyric. He was subsequently appointed lecturer in English at UCD, and in the same year founded *The Irish Review* with Padraic Colum, James Stephens, and Mary Maguire. His essays on Irish writing were published posthumously in *Literature in Ireland* (1916). His books of poetry include *April and May and Other Verses* (1903), *Through the Ivory Gate* (1903), *The Golden Joy* (1906), and *Songs of Myself* (1910). He also wrote a number of plays, including *When the Dawn is Come* (1908), *Metempsychosis* (1912), and *Pagans* (1915). His passionate nationalist sentiments were evident at an early age. He joined the Gaelic League in 1902, but by 1909 became disillusioned with its activities and later joined the Irish Volunteers (1913), for which he was Director of Training. In 1915 he was co-opted on to the military council of the Irish Republican Brotherhood, and in April 1916 he was one of the signatories of the Proclamation of the Irish Republic. He took part in the Easter Rising in Dublin and was executed by firing squad on 3 May 1916. He was remembered by Yeats in 'Easter 1916' as one who 'might have won fame in the end, | So sensitive his nature seemed, | So daring and sweet his thought'.

Louis MACNEICE (1907–63), poet, playwright, and critic, was born in Belfast, son of a Church of Ireland clergyman who later became a bishop. His childhood was spent in Carrickfergus, which is vividly recalled in his poem of that title. He was educated at Sherbourne, Marlborough, and Oxford. He lectured in classics at Birmingham University from 1929 to 1936 and in Greek at Bedford College, University of London, from 1936 to 1940. His strong interest in the classics continued to pervade his poetry and was evident, too, in his acclaimed translation, *The Agamemnon of Aeschylus* (1936). In 1941 he joined the BBC as a feature writer and producer, a post he held for over twenty years. During the Second World War he served as a fire warden. His first volume of poems, *Blind Fireworks*, was published in 1929, while he was still a student. In the 1930s he was associated with a group of poets that included W. H. Auden, Stephen Spender, and Cecil Day-Lewis. His increasing rapprochement with the politically committed writing of the 1930s is evident in his *Poems* of 1935, in *The Earth Compels* (1938), and especially in his *Autumn Journal* of 1939, prompted by the Munich Crisis, the Spanish Civil War, and events in pre-war London. Towards the end of his career, he experienced a fresh burst of creative energy, evident in his last three volumes of poetry, *Visitations* (1957), *Solstices* (1961), and *The Burning Perch* (1963). He also wrote a number of radio plays, including *The Dark Tower* (1946), a critical study of the poetry of W. B. Yeats (1941), and an unfinished autobiography, *The Strings Are False* (published posthumously in 1965). He is buried in Carrowdore churchyard in Co. Down.

Francis Sylvester MAHONY (1804–66), the humorist and journalist known as 'Father Prout', was born in Cork and educated at Clongowes Wood College. He hoped to become a Jesuit and, after studying in Amiens, Paris, and Rome, he returned to Clongowes as a teacher. He was forced to resign after allegedly taking the boys on a late-night drinking spree. He left for Italy, entered the Irish College in Rome, and was ordained a priest in Lucca in 1832. He was assigned to a parish in Cork, where he assisted with relief work during a cholera epidemic, but he left for London in 1834 after a disagreement with his bishop. He became a contributor to *Fraser's Magazine*, adopting as his pseudonym the title of a real Father Prout who had died in Cork in 1830. His *Reliques of Father Prout*, a collection of his witty sketches, verses, and parodies, was published in 1837. He contributed verse to *Bentley's Miscellany*, founded by Charles Dickens, and in 1846 became Rome correspondent for the *Daily News*. In 1848 he settled in Paris, where he became correspondent for the

Globe (1858–66). He is buried in the vault of St Nicholas's church on Shandon St., Cork, beneath his own famous 'Bells of Shandon'.

James Clarence MANGAN (1803–49), poet and translator, was born in Dublin and showed an early flair and facility with European languages. His first job was as a copy clerk, but from the late 1820s he tried to establish himself as a writer with occasional employment in the Ordnance Survey Office (1833–9) and Trinity College library (1841–6). In the 1830s he was a frequent contributor to the *Comet* and the *Dublin Penny Journal*. A number of scholars, including John O'Donovan and Eugene O'Curry, provided him with literal translations of old Irish poems, which he would then re-work in an effort to preserve something of Gaelic antiquity. He wrote autobiographical sketches that bordered on the fantastic, and regularly contributed translations of modern German poetry to the *Dublin University Magazine* (these were reprinted in an anthology in 1845). He was fond of using pseudonyms such as 'Clarence' (adopted from Shakespeare's *Richard III*) and 'The Man in the Cloak'. In addition to reading contemporary German literature, Mangan also had a wide-ranging appreciation of French, Spanish, Persian, Hungarian, and Icelandic poetry. He contributed an inaugural poem to the first number of *The Nation* in 1842, and submitted some of his best-known work to the journal, including 'Dark Rosaleen'. A revolutionary fervour informs a good deal of the work he produced in the Famine years. His lurid autobiography first appeared in *The Irish Monthly* in 1882 and helped to promote the image of Mangan as an eccentric and dissolute genius. Weakened by malnutrition and alcohol abuse, he fell victim to the cholera epidemic of 1849. Both Yeats and Joyce were to acknowledge his vital contribution to Irish literary tradition.

Constance MARKIEWICZ, née Gore-Booth (1868–1927), was born at Buckingham Gate, London, and educated at the family estate at Lissadell, Co. Sligo. An aspiring artist, she studied painting at the Slade art school in London in 1893, and then in Paris from 1898 to 1900. In Paris she met Count Casimir Dunin-Markiewicz, a painter descended from a landed Polish family settled in Ukraine. They were married in London in September 1900 and had one child, Maeve Alys, who was born in Lissadell in November 1901. After brief spells in Paris and Ukraine, they settled in Dublin, and Constance was soon drawn to the work of the Gaelic League and the Abbey Theatre. Wishing to contribute to the nationalist cause, she joined Sinn Féin and Inghinidhe na hÉireann (Daughters of Ireland) in 1908, and in the following year she founded Fianna Éireann, a Republican youth organization. During the lock-out of Dublin workers in 1913 she ran a soup kitchen in Liberty Hall. In the 1916 Rising she served as an officer and was based at the College of Surgeons on St Stephen's Green. Although condemned to death, she had her sentence commuted to life imprisonment. She was briefly imprisoned in Aylesbury Jail, but released under the General Amnesty of June 1917. In the general election of December 1918 she was returned for St Patrick's division of Dublin, the first woman to be elected to the British Parliament, but in accordance with Sinn Féin policy she refused to take her seat. She opposed the Anglo-Irish Treaty of 1921, and continued to hold Republican views, but joined Fianna

Fáil when it was founded by de Valera in 1926. As well as being one of the prominent figures acknowledged by W. B. Yeats in 'Easter 1916', she is also the subject of two other poems: 'On a Political Prisoner' and 'In Memory of Eva Gore-Booth and Con Markiewicz'.

Charles Robert MATURIN (1780–1824), novelist and playwright, was born in Dublin of a Huguenot family, and educated at Trinity College. He was ordained in 1803 and served as an Anglican curate at Loughrea, Co. Galway. He married Henrietta Kingsbury the following year. In 1805 he became curate of St Peter's church, Aungier Street, Dublin. His first novel, *Fatal Revenge* (1807) was based on the Gothic style of Ann Radcliffe, and was reviewed by Sir Walter Scott in the *Quarterly Review*, while *The Wild Irish Boy* (1808) and *The Milesian Chief* (1812) showed the influence of Sydney Owenson (Lady Morgan). His tragic drama, *Bertram* (1816), a success on the London stage, was followed by three other less successful plays: *Manuel*, *Fredolfo*, and *Osmyn the Renegade*. He is best known for his Gothic, Faustian novel, *Melmoth the Wanderer* (1820), a work greatly admired by Baudelaire and Balzac. Oscar Wilde, a distant relation of Maturin, chose the name 'Melmoth the Wanderer' on his release from Reading Gaol.

George MOORE (1852–1933), novelist and memoirist, was born into a well-established land-owning family at Moore Hall, Ballyglass, Co. Mayo. He was educated at Oscott College, Birmingham, and originally planned to become a painter. In London and Paris, he came under the influence of French naturalism and impressionism. In the early 1870s he met a number of the French painters he most admired, including Manet, Degas, Pissarro, and Renoir. His fiction was to adopt a naturalistic style in the manner of Zola, as with *A Mummer's Wife* (1885) and the better known *Esther Waters* (1894). In 1887 he published *Parnell and his Ireland*, a series of acerbic social commentaries on contemporary Irish life. In *The Confessions of a Young Man* (1888) he struck the pose of a bohemian aesthete, recalling his days in the vicinity of Montmartre. During the late 1880s and early 1890s, he was prolific in writing critical essays on art and literature, and these were gathered in *Impressions and Opinions* (1889) and *Modern Painting* (1893). His cousin Edward Martyn introduced him to W. B. Yeats in 1897 and he was briefly involved in the plans for an Irish national theatre that would eventually become the Abbey. His dealings with W. B. Yeats, Lady Gregory, Edward Martyn, and others is memorably captured in his three-part memoir, *Hail and Farewell* (1911–14). As a short story writer, he was to make a considerable impact with *The Untilled Field* in 1903. After 1911, he was based primarily in London and concentrated on the writing of historical romances such as *The Brook Kerith* (1916) and *Heloise and Abelard* (1921).

Thomas MOORE (1779–1852), poet, was born in Dublin and educated at Samuel Whyte's academy on Grafton Street and Trinity College. In 1799 he entered the Middle Temple in London, but his love of verse and music took precedence over a career in law. In 1800 he published his *Odes of Anacreon*, a series of translations from the works of the Greek poet, and his less successful

Poetical Works of the Late Thomas Little, Esq. appeared the following year. In 1803 he was appointed registrar to the Admiralty Prize Court in Bermuda, but the seclusion of the islands was not to his liking, and he returned via the United States and Canada, gathering material for his *Odes and Epistles* (1806). The following year he prepared the first instalment of his *Irish Melodies*, with music arranged by Sir John Stevenson from popular Irish tunes. The remainder of the *Irish Melodies* appeared at irregular intervals over the next twenty-seven years and earned Moore both public esteem and considerable financial income. He was offered £3,000 by Longmans to compose an oriental romance, the result of which was *Lalla Rookh* (1817). His later publications include satirical works such as *The Fudge Family in Paris* (1818) and *The Loves of the Angels* (1823). Moore had become a friend of Lord Byron in 1811 and was entrusted with the poet's memoirs, but at the behest of Byron's widow and half-sister, the papers were burned. Moore did, however, produce the two-volume *Letters and Journals of Lord Byron, with Notices of his Life* in 1830.

Lady MORGAN, née Sydney Owenson (1776–1859), was allegedly born at sea, though she claimed Dublin as her birthplace. Her father, Robert Owenson, an Irish Catholic patriot, was an unsuccessful actor-manager, with whom she toured Ireland. Her mother, Jane Hill, was an English Protestant who died at an early age. Owenson was sent to boarding school with her younger sister, Olivia. A talented musician and singer, she wrote a series of English lyrics to accompany Irish tunes, and the resulting *Twelve Original Hibernian Melodies* (1805) anticipated the similar endeavours of Thomas Moore. Two early novels, *St Clair, or the Heiress of Desmond* (1803) and *The Novice of Dominick* (1805), met with little success. *The Wild Irish Girl* (1806) was hugely popular, however, and brought her great acclaim. The Marchioness of Abercorn invited her to become her companion, and in 1812 she married Sir Charles Morgan, the family surgeon. Despite adverse criticism, she continued to attract a wide readership for her novels, including *O'Donnel* (1814), *Florence Macarthy* (1818), and *The O'Briens and the O'Flahertys* (1827). She travelled widely, writing books on French and Italian society. She also produced an essay on absentee landlordism and a collection of autobiographical sketches. In 1837 she became the first female recipient of a literary pension from the British government. She settled in London the same year.

Flann O'BRIEN was the pseudonym of Brian Ó Nualláin (1911–66), novelist and columnist, who also wrote as Myles na gCopaleen. He was born in Strabane, Co. Tyrone, but his family moved to Dublin in 1923. He was taught by the Christian Brothers, then by the Holy Ghost fathers at Blackrock College, before attending University College, Dublin. His talent for comedy found expression in student magazines, including his own publication, *Blather*, which promoted itself as a 'publication of the Gutter'. In 1935 he joined the Civil Service, eventually becoming principal officer for town planning. His first novel, *At Swim-Two-Birds* (1939), was well received, but *The Third Policeman* failed to find a publisher in 1940 and appeared posthumously in 1967. From 1940 onwards, he contributed his humorous column, 'Cruiskeen Lawn' ('Full Jug'), to the *Irish Times*, under the name of Myles na gCopaleen. The column was written in Irish at the outset, but then adopted English and gained huge popularity for its colourful mix of fantasy and satirical invective. A satirical novel in Irish, *An Béal Bocht,* made little impact when it was published in 1941, but the English version, *The Poor Mouth,* fared better in 1964. O'Brien's plays had a disappointing reception: *Faustus Kelly* ran for only two weeks at the Abbey Theatre in 1943 and *The Insect Play* for less than a week at the Gate. After leaving the Civil Service in 1953, he made a productive new start on fiction writing, producing *The Hard Life* in 1961 and *The Dalkey Archive* in 1964. An unfinished novel, *Slattery's Sago Saga,* was included in *Stories and Plays* (1974), and selections from 'Cruiskeen Lawn' were reprinted in *The Best of Myles* (1985).

Seán O'CASEY (1880–1964), playwright, was born in Dublin of working-class Protestant parents and christened John Casey. His father's death in 1886 plunged a large family into desperate poverty. He left school at 14 and worked as a labourer until 1926. He continued to educate himself and read widely, despite an eye complaint that persisted all his life. He joined the Gaelic League and the IRB, learned Irish, and was active in James Larkin's Irish Transport and General Workers' Union, becoming secretary of its political wing, the Irish Citizen Army. He took part in the lock-out strike in 1913, but left the Citizen Army the following year when it came under the revolutionary influence of James Connolly and Patrick Pearse. Encouraged by Lady Gregory, he began to submit plays to the Abbey Theatre. His first notable success was *The Shadow of a Gunman* (1923), followed by the other plays in his Dublin Trilogy: *Juno and the Paycock* (1924) and *The Plough and the Stars* (1926). His next play, *The Silver Tassie* (1928), a more experimental work dealing with the impact of the First World War, was rejected by the Abbey, and had only a lukewarm reception when it was staged in London. Disillusioned with the ethos of post-Treaty Ireland, O'Casey eventually settled in England. In 1927 he married Eileen Carey, an actress who had started her career with the D'Oyly Carte opera company. They settled in Devon in 1940. In 1939 he published *I Knock at the Door,* the first part of a six-volume autobiography. O'Casey's socialist ideals continued to inform the plays that followed, including *The Star Turns Red* (1940), *Red Roses for Me* (1942), and *The Purple Dust* (1945), but these later plays seemed to lack the vitality and vigour of the Dublin Trilogy. Among his later experimental and allegorical plays are *Cock-a-Doodle Dandy* (1949), *The Bishop's Bonfire* (1955), and *The Drums of Father Ned* (1959). His theatrical criticism is collected in two volumes: *Feathers from the Green Crow* (1956) and *Under a Coloured Cap* (1963).

Daniel O'CONNELL (1775–1847) was born at Cahirciveen, Co. Kerry, the eldest of ten children. He was brought up by his uncle Maurice at Derrynane House and was educated in France and England, before embarking on a legal career in Dublin in 1798. He quickly established himself as a brilliant advocate and outstanding orator. He protested against the Act of Union in 1800 and became increasingly involved in the struggle for Catholic Emancipation. With the foundation of the Catholic Association in 1823, he effectively became head of a nationwide movement that achieved Emancipation in 1829. He was elected MP for County Clare in 1826, being the first Catholic to stand for Parliament since the seventeenth century. He created the first Irish parliamentary party in Westminster during the 1830s and supported a wide range of reforms, including the Reform Act of 1832. After co-operating with the Whig government in the late 1830s, he founded the Repeal Association (1840) and initiated a new campaign against the Act of Union. He was persuaded to cancel one of his 'monster' meetings at Clontarf in October 1843, under threat from the Peel government. Nevertheless, he was prosecuted and tried for seditious conspiracy in May 1844. His sentence of one year's imprisonment was quashed by the House of Lords in September that year. His career was then effectively at an end: clashes with the spirited Young Ireland movement, impatient with gradual reforms, led to a split in the Repeal Association in July 1846. Before embarking on a pilgrimage to Rome at the beginning of 1847, he appealed to the House of Commons to alleviate the sufferings of a famine-stricken Ireland. He died in Genoa before he reached his destination.

Frank O'CONNOR was the pseudonym of Michael O'Donovan (1903–66), short-story writer, novelist, and translator. O'Connor was the maiden name of his mother, Minnie, affectionately recalled in his autobiography, *An Only Child* (1961). He was born in Cork and educated at St Patrick's National School, where Daniel Corkery encouraged his literary interests. He fought in the War of Independence, and took the Republican side in the Civil War, being interned in Gormanstown in 1923. His experience of the bitter struggle for independence shaped two of his earliest works: his first collection of short stories, *Guests of the Nation* (1931) and a biography of Michael Collins, *The Big Fellow* (1937). After his release, he became a librarian, moving from Wicklow to Cork to Dublin, where he made the acquaintance of George Russell and W. B. Yeats. He wrote a novel, *The Saint and Mary Kate* (1932); a volume of translations from the Irish, *The Wild Bird's Nest* (1932); and two plays for the Abbey Theatre, *In the Train* (1937) and *Moses' Rock* (1938). He was a director of the Abbey, 1935–9. In 1936 he produced another collection of short stories, *Bones of Contention*, and a collection of poems, *Three Old Brothers*. His novel *Dutch Interior* was banned in 1941, but he persisted with short story writing, despite the constraints of censorship, and later collections included *Crab Apple Jelly* (1944), *The Common Chord* (1947), and *Traveller's Samples* (1951), the latter reprinted from the *New Yorker*. His teaching in American colleges towards the end of his career led to the publication of three books of literary criticism: *The Mirror in the Roadway*, a study of the novel (1956); *The Lonely Voice*, a study of the short story (1962); and *The Backward Look*, a study of Irish literary history (1967). With David Greene, he edited *A Golden Treasury of Irish Poetry 600–1200* (1959).

Seán O'FAOLÁIN (1900–91), short story writer, novelist, and biographer, was born in Cork (christened John Whelan) and educated at the Presentation Brothers' school and University College, Cork. In his early student days, he joined the Irish Volunteers and later fought with the Republicans in the Civil War, becoming director of propaganda. He resumed his studies after the war, and took an MA in English literature at Harvard on a Commonwealth scholarship. In Boston, in 1928, he married Eileen Gould, another Cork graduate and teacher. He was teaching at St Mary's College, Strawberry Hill, Twickenham, when his first collection of short stories, *Midsummer Night Madness*, was published in 1932. He returned to Ireland soon after and produced a series of novels, including *A Nest of Simple Folk* (1934), *Bird Alone* (1936), and *Come Back to Erin* (1940). Also in the 1930s, he began the first of several biographies, including studies of Eamon de Valera, Constance Markiewicz, and Daniel O'Connell. His second volume of stories, *A Purse of Coppers*, appeared in 1937, and he was to develop the short story form with increasing assurance in subsequent collections such as *I Remember, I Remember* (1948), *The Heat of the Sun* (1966), *The Talking Trees* (1971), and *Foreign Affairs* (1976). His *Collected Stories* appeared in three volumes (1980–2). In 1940 he founded the literary journal, *The Bell*, which encouraged the work of young writers and gave a voice to liberal, progressive opinion during a sometimes stifling era of religious and cultural traditionalism. He published two travel works, *Summer in Italy* (1949) and *South to Sicily* (1953), an autobiography, *Vive Moi* (1964), and a late novel, *And Again* (1979).

Liam O'FLAHERTY (1896–1984), novelist and short story writer, was born in Gort na gCapall on Inishmore in the Aran Islands. He was educated at Oatquarter National School, Inishmore, and at Rockwell College, Co. Tipperary, encouraged by the Holy Ghost Fathers. Abandoning his vocation in 1915, he went to fight for the Irish Guards Regiment in the First World War. He was wounded in September 1917 and discharged with shellshock. He travelled aimlessly through Canada, the United States, and Latin America, finding casual work as he went. On his return to Ireland in the immediate post-Treaty years, he joined the Communist Party and in January 1922 staged an occupation of the Rotunda Rooms for several days. His first novel, *Thy Neighbour's Wife*, was published in 1923 and was quickly followed by *The Black Soul* (1924) and *The Informer* (1925), which became a powerful film in the hands of John Ford a decade later. His later novels included *The Assassin* (1928), *The House of Gold* (1929), *The Martyr* (1935), and *Skerrett* (1932). His trilogy— *Famine* (1937), *Land* (1946), and *Insurrection* (1950)—charts the rise of nationalist politics in modern Ireland. He also wrote several volumes of autobiography, including *Two Years* (1930) and *A Tourist's Guide to Ireland* (1929), an acerbic commentary on the social and political values of the time. O'Flaherty excels in his short fiction and continues to receive acclaim for the stories in volumes such as *Spring Sowing* (1924), *The Tent* (1926), and *The Mountain Tavern and Other Stories* (1929).

John O'LEARY (1830–1907) was born in Tipperary, where he inherited a small amount of property. He was educated at Erasmus Smith School and Trinity College, Dublin. He abandoned studies in law after refusing to take an oath of allegiance to the British crown, and turned instead to medicine, attending the Queen's Colleges in Cork and Galway, but failing to qualify. In 1848 he spent several weeks in Clonmel Jail after clashes with local police. He was strongly associated with the Fenian movement, although never a sworn member. In 1863, with Charles Kickham, he founded the *Irish People*, an anti-clerical nationalist newspaper, for which he was imprisoned and later exiled. On his return to Dublin in 1885, he promoted Irish culture and nationalist ideals, giving lectures and publishing his *Recollections of Fenians and Fenianism* (1896). He helped to establish the Irish National Literary Society in 1892, and the following year formed the Celtic Literary Society, a forerunner of Sinn Féin, with William Rooney, Arthur Griffith, and others. Yeats mourned the loss of all he stood for in his elegy, 'September 1913': 'Romantic Ireland's dead and gone, | It's with O'Leary in the grave'.

Earnán O'MALLEY (1898–1957) was born in Castlebar, Co. Mayo, and raised in Dublin. He was a medical student at Trinity College in 1916 and fought in the Easter Rising. He served with the IRA during the War of Independence, being highly valued for his skills in intelligence. He was arrested in December 1920 and interrogated in Dublin Castle. After his escape in February 1921, he took over the command of the newly formed Second Southern Division of the IRA in Munster. He opposed the Treaty in 1922 and took part in fierce fighting around the Four Courts in Dublin during the Civil War. During his arrest at a 'safe house' in Dublin he received multiple bullet wounds, but nevertheless took part in a Republican hunger strike during his imprisonment in Kilmainham Jail. While in prison he was elected to Dáil Éireann, but after his release he left Ireland for nearly ten years. He travelled in the United States, where he married Helen Hooker Roelofs. He later wrote articles and features for Irish and foreign journals and for broadcast on Radio Éireann and the BBC. His memoir, *On Another Man's Wound* (1936), is one of the most candid and powerful accounts of Ireland's struggle for political freedom. A sequel, *The Singing Flame*, was published posthumously in 1978. O'Malley's journalistic writings are collected in *Raids and Rallies* (1982) and his Civil War letters have been edited by Richard English and Cormac O'Malley (1991).

Seumas O'SULLIVAN was the pseudonym of the poet James Sullivan Starkey (1879–1958). He was born in Dublin and educated mainly at home. He was a pupil at Wesley College for two years and also attended the Catholic University Medical School before becoming an apprentice in his father's pharmacy. He took a strong interest in the activities of the Literary Revival, playing the Blind Man in W. B. Yeats's play, *On Baile's Strand*, on the opening night of the Abbey Theatre, 27 December 1904. The following year he published a volume of poems, *The Twilight People*, followed by *Verses Sacred and Profane* (1908), *The Earth Lover* (1909), *Requiem and Other Poems* (1917), *Personal Talk* (1936), and *Collected Poems* (1940). He was a supporter of Sinn Féin and a friend of Arthur Griffith, Oliver St John Gogarty, and James Joyce. He founded the *Dublin Magazine* (1923–58), one of the important channels of creative expression and cultural debate in the early Free State years. In 1926 he married the Dublin painter Estella Francis Solomons. His prose works include *Essays and Recollections* (1944) and *The Rose and the Bottle* (1946).

Patrick PEARSE (1879–1916) was born in Dublin at 27 Great Brunswick Street (now Pearse Street), the son of an English stonemason father and an

Irish mother. He was educated at the Christian Brothers' school in Westland Row and at the Royal University, Dublin. While at school and university, he developed a deep interest in the Irish language. He joined the Gaelic League in 1896, becoming editor of its journal, *An Claidheamh Soluis*, in 1903. His abiding belief was that educational reform was the necessary accompaniment to political self-determination. He founded St Enda's School in 1908, with the purpose of offering a progressive bilingual education, informed by a desire for 'freedom and inspiration'. In 1910 the school moved from the Dublin suburbs of Rathmines to The Hermitage, Rathfarnham. In 1913 Pearse helped to found the Irish Volunteers and was recruited into the Irish Republican Brotherhood. In 1916 he was appointed commandant-general of the Republican forces and president of the Provisional Government. The Easter Rising commenced with Pearse's reading of the Proclamation of the Irish Republic outside the General Post Office in Dublin on 24 April 1916. Five days later he agreed to an unconditional surrender. Following a court-martial, he was executed by a firing squad in Kilmainham Jail on 3 May 1916. His brother was also executed. His writings included a good number of educational and political essays, some of which were collected in *From a Hermitage* (1915). Numerous political pamphlets appeared in 1916. His play *The Singer* (1915) embodies his belief in the redemption of the nation through blood sacrifice. He wrote poems in English and Irish, and published two collections of short stories in Irish. His *Collected Works* appeared in five volumes in 1917.

Antoine RAFTERY (1779–1835) was born at Killedan, Co. Mayo, the son of a weaver from Co. Sligo. He was blinded by smallpox in childhood and he became a travelling musician and poet, spending most of his life in the Gort-Loughrea area of Co. Galway. His poems and songs are topical, dealing with such events as Daniel O'Connell's victory in the Clare election of 1828. 'Eanach Dhúin' commemorates a boating accident on Lough Corrib in September 1828. His love songs for Máire ní Eidhin (Mary Hynes) were popular many years after, as W. B. Yeats and Lady Gregory discovered when gathering stories in Co. Galway. Raftery was celebrated by the writers associated with the Literary Revival and was recalled by Yeats in his 1926 volume, *The Tower*. Douglas Hyde translated his poems and Lady Gregory wrote a play about him (*An Pósadh*), in which Hyde played Raftery in the first performance in Galway in 1902.

George RUSSELL (AE) (1867–1935) was born in Lurgan, Co. Armagh. His family moved to Dublin and he was educated at Rathmines School. From the age of 12 he studied at the Metropolitan School of Art, where he met W. B. Yeats. After working as a clerk, he joined the Irish Agricultural Organization Society. He spent much of his time encouraging agricultural co-operation in Ireland. Writing under the anonym 'AE' (from the Greek Æon), he edited the *Irish Homestead* from 1906 to 1923 and the *Irish Statesman* from 1923 to 1930. His early literary ideals overlapped with those of the Literary Revival, and he was briefly vice-president of the Irish National Theatre Society when Yeats was president. His version of *Deirdre* (1902) was performed in Dublin with Constance Markiewicz in the title role. His first book of poems was

Homeward: Songs by the Way (1894), and this was followed by *The Earth Breath and Other Poems* (1897) and *The Divine Vision and Other Poems* (1904). Two editions of his *Collected Poems* appeared in 1913 and 1926, and new books were to appear in the 1930s, including *Enchantment and Other Poems* (1930) and *The House of the Titans and Other Poems* (1934). He was deeply interested in mysticism and joined the Theosophical Society in 1886. In 1898 he founded the Hermetic Society, dedicated to pursuing the work of Madame Blavatsky and in 1918 he published *The Candle of Vision*, a collection of short essays describing his mystical experiences. In 1932 he went to live in England, settling in London and then in Bournemouth.

SOMERVILLE AND ROSS was the joint pseudonym of cousins Edith Somerville (1858–1949) and Violet Martin (1862–1915). They met for the first time at Castletownshend in 1886, and their first joint novel was *An Irish Cousin* (1889). They were to find their distinctive subject-matter in the decline of the Anglo-Irish landed gentry. By the time Violet Martin died in 1915, they had also written *Naboth's Vineyard* (1891), *The Real Charlotte* (1894), *The Silver Fox* (1898), and *Dan Russel the Fox* (1911). In 1899 they achieved widespread recognition through their stories in *Some Experiences of an Irish R.M.* (Resident Magistrate) and in two later volumes, *Further Experiences of an Irish R.M.* (1908) and *In Mr Knox's Country* (1915). They travelled together in Ireland and abroad, in Wales, France, and Denmark, recording their experiences in travel books such as *Through Connemara in a Governess Cart* (1892), *In the Vine Country* (1893), and *Beggars on Horseback* (1895). Edith Somerville continued to write and publish as Somerville and Ross and gave her account of the literary partnership in *Irish Writing* (1946). *Irish Memories* appeared in 1917, followed by other books of reminiscence, and a further five novels were published between 1919 and 1938, including *The Big House at Inver* (1925).

James STEPHENS (1880–1950) was born in Dublin. His father died and when his mother remarried he was sent to an orphanage. He ran away and eventually found work as a solicitor's clerk. In 1907 he began contributing poems, stories, and essays to Arthur Griffith's newspaper, *Sinn Féin*, and in the same year he befriended George Russell, who introduced him to W. B. Yeats and Lady Gregory. His first volume of poems was *Insurrections* (1909) and his first novel was *The Charwoman's Daughter* (1912). His next book, *The Crock of Gold* (1912), established him as a highly original and distinctive writer of fiction, by turns philosophical and fantastic. Another collection of poems, *The Hill of Vision*, also appeared in 1912, and a collection of short stories, *Here Are Ladies*, was published the following year. He went to Paris in 1912 and returned to Dublin in 1915, taking the post of registrar at the National Gallery. His experiences of the Easter Rising in 1916 are vividly recorded in *The Insurrection in Dublin*. A new collection of poems, *Green Branches*, also appeared in 1916, and a volume of poems based on Irish originals, *Reincarnations*, was published in 1918. He married Cynthia Kavanagh in 1919. In 1925 he settled in London and over the next ten years he gave lecture tours in the United States. Between 1937 and 1950 he gave numerous talks for the BBC. Three further collections of poetry appeared in the 1930s—*Theme and*

Variations (1930), *Strict Joy* (1931), and *Kings and the Moon* (1938)—and an autobiography was commissioned, though only part of it was written (it was published as 'A Rhineroceros, Some Ladies and a Horse' in 1946).

Bram [Abraham] STOKER (1847–1912) was born in Dublin and educated at Trinity College. Like his father, he became a civil servant, and his first book was *Duties of the Clerks of Petty Sessions in Ireland* (1878). As drama critic for the *Dublin Evening Mail*, he befriended the celebrated actor Henry Irving. After his marriage to Florence Balcombe, he moved to London and acted as Irving's manager. His *Personal Reminiscences of Henry Irving* appeared in 1906, a year after Irving's death. He published a collection of short stories, *Under the Sunset*, in 1882, and a novel, *The Snake's Pass*, set in Co. Mayo, in 1891. The success of *Dracula* in 1897 prompted a steady outpouring of romantic and occultist novels, including *Miss Betty* (1898), *The Mystery of the Sea* (1902), and *The Jewel of Seven Stars* (1903). His last novel was *The Lair of the White Worm* (1911).

John Millington SYNGE (1871–1909) was born into an ecclesiastical family (descendants of Bishop Edward Synge) at Newtown Little, Rathfarnham, Co. Dublin. His father died when he was only a year old, and he was greatly influenced by his fervently evangelical mother. His interest in natural history and his reading of Darwin came into sharp conflict with his mother's religious teachings. His nationalist ideals were in some ways a substitute religion: he later claimed that he gave up the kingdom of God for the kingdom of Ireland. He took a pass degree at Trinity College, but learned Irish as a student in the School of Divinity. He also studied piano, flute, and violin at the Royal Irish Academy of Music, and travelled to Germany in 1893, hoping to train as a professional musician. In 1895, however, he settled in Paris, attending lectures at the Sorbonne and deepening his knowledge of Celtic civilization. In May 1898 he visited both Inishmore and Inishmaan. He spent the next four summers (1899–1902) in the Aran Islands, gathering material that would eventually appear in *The Aran Islands* (1907). His other travel writings, written mainly for the *Manchester Guardian*, were illustrated by Jack B. Yeats, and collected as *In Wicklow and West Kerry* (1911). His growing interest in the possibilities of Hiberno–English speech as a language for modern drama, combined with stories he had heard on his travels, led to the production of two plays for the newly founded Irish National Theatre: *In the Shadow of the Glen* (1903) and *Riders to the Sea* (1904). When the Abbey Theatre opened at the end of 1904, Synge became literary adviser and later co-director with Yeats and Lady Gregory. *The Well of the Saints* (1905) was one of the first plays to be produced at the Abbey, and *The Playboy of the Western World* (1907) provoked a riot. Two of Synge's plays were not produced in his lifetime: *The Tinker's Wedding* (1909) because of its alleged anti-clericalism, and *Deirdre of the Sorrows* (1910), which was never finished. Synge's poetry was published in *Poems and Translations* (1911).

Mary TIGHE (1772–1810) was born in Dublin, the daughter of Reverend William Blachford, who died in her infancy, and Theodosia Blachford, who brought her up in the Methodist faith and provided her early education. Her mother founded the Dublin House of Refuge for Unprotected Female Servants. In 1793 she married her cousin, Henry Tighe, and moved to London. She wrote poetry in her childhood, and probably composed her Spenserian allegory, *Psyche, or the Legend of Love*, in 1795. The poem was published privately in 1805, and then commercially. A popular third edition appeared posthumously with other poems in 1811. Her sensuous imagery was sometimes compared with that of John Keats, and like Keats she suffered from consumption. Her journal entries for 1787–1802 reveal that she also suffered from acute depression and occasional suicidal tendencies. She spent her later years in Rosanna, Co. Wicklow.

Le Chevalier de la TOCNAYE (*c.*1767–?), Jacques Louis de Bougrenet, was a French royalist and military officer from an aristocratic family in Brittany. Having fled the French Revolution, he arrived in London on 29 December 1792, not knowing English. After travelling through various parts of England and Scotland, he wrote an account of his journey titled *Promenade dans la Grande Bretagne*, which was published in Edinburgh in 1797. He visited Ireland in 1796–7 and toured the country mainly on foot, seeing both city conditions (including Dublin, Cork, and Belfast) and rural environs. His *Promenade d'un Français dans l'Irlande* was published in Dublin in 1797 and reveals its author's fears of revolutionary tendencies in Ireland prior to the 1798 rebellion. John Stevenson's translation, *A Frenchman's Walk through Ireland (1796–7)*, was published in Dublin in 1914.

Theobald Wolfe TONE (1763–98) was born into a Church of Ireland family in Dublin and educated at Trinity College. He was called to the bar in 1789 and briefly practised law, but he discovered a more pressing vocation in the radical politics of the time. His *Review of the Conduct of the Administration* (1790) was followed by his *Argument on Behalf of the Catholics of Ireland* (1791), which led to his involvement as a paid agent with the Catholic Committee, pressing for political rights among Irish Catholics. Influenced by French revolutionary theory, he helped to found a Dublin branch of the Society of United Irishmen and argued for a non-sectarian Republic that would break the connection with England and 'substitute the common name of Irishman in the place of the denominations of Protestant, Catholic and Dissenter'. After his complicity in a planned French invasion of Ireland was discovered in 1795, he left for America, but received encouragement from the French minister in Philadelphia. He travelled to Paris in 1796 and assisted General Hoche in the organization of two expeditions to Ireland, neither of which was successful. The third attempt in September 1797 ended in defeat by the English navy in Lough Swilly. Tone was court-martialled in Dublin, convicted of treason, and sentenced to hang. After his request for execution by firing squad was refused, he took his own life by cutting his throat.

Oscar WILDE (1854–1900) was born in Dublin, the second son of Sir William Wilde, a renowned surgeon and antiquary, and Jane Francesca Agnes Elgee, otherwise known as the Irish nationalist poet 'Speranza'. He was educated at Portora Royal School, Enniskillen, and Trinity College, Dublin. He then studied at Magdalen College, Oxford, where he came under the influence of Walter Pater and established himself as the leading proponent of the Aesthetic Movement. In 1878 he won the coveted Newdigate Prize for his poem 'Ravenna'. His first book, simply titled *Poems*, was published in 1881. The following year he was invited to the United States and Canada, a visit timed to coincide with a tour of the Gilbert and Sullivan opera *Patience* (satirizing the Aesthetic Movement), and lectured throughout North America on the decorative arts and other topics. He married Constance Lloyd in 1884, and their two sons, Cyril and Vyvyan, were born in 1885 and 1886. Wilde made a controversial impact as a critic, with essays like 'The Decay of Lying', 'The Critic as Artist', and 'The Soul of Man Under Socialism' appearing in leading journals in the later 1880s and early 1890s. His novel *The Picture of Dorian Gray* was equally controversial when it appeared in 1891. His skills as a storyteller were evident in collections of tales such as *Lord Arthur Savile's Crime and Other Stories* (1891) and *A House of Pomegranates* (1892). Wilde's artistic reputation, however, rests heavily on his work as a dramatist, especially on the sparkling social comedies which appeared in quick succession in the closing decade of the nineteenth century: *Lady Windermere's Fan* (1892), *A Woman of No Importance* (1893), *An Ideal Husband* (1895), and *The Importance of Being Earnest* (1895). His erotic play *Salome* was refused a licence by the Lord Chamberlain in 1892, being published in French and only later in English. By this time, he had met Lord Alfred Douglas, a much younger man and an aspiring poet, who became his lover. In 1895, following an unsuccessful libel action against the Marquess of Queensbury (the father of Lord Alfred Douglas), he was sentenced to two years' imprisonment with hard labour on charges of gross indecency. The great comedian was to turn to the tragic mode in two of his most memorable and moving works, *The Ballad of Reading Gaol* (1898) and *De Profundis* (written in 1897, but published posthumously in 1905). After his release from prison in 1897, Wilde left England and travelled through France and Italy, homeless and bankrupt. He died in the Hotel d'Alsace in Paris, and is buried in Père Lachaise cemetery beneath an imposing sphinx monument by Jacob Epstein.

William Butler YEATS (1865–1939) was born at Sandymount Avenue, Dublin, the eldest child of John Butler Yeats and Susan Pollexfen. Much of his early life, until his middle teens, was spent in London, with return trips to Ireland, mainly to visit his mother's family in Co. Sligo. From 1881 to 1887, he lived in Dublin, enrolling as a student at the Metropolitan School of Art in Dublin, developing his interests in poetry, and exploring the attractions of mysticism and the occult. He helped to found the Dublin Hermetic Society in 1885 and joined the Hermetic Order of the Golden Dawn in 1890. From 1887 onwards, he worked in both London and Dublin, energetically committing himself to the ideal of a distinctive Irish literary movement. His meeting with the Fenian John O'Leary in 1885 was instrumental in turning his attention to an existing Irish tradition of poetry, songs, and stories, and in giving a strongly nationalist dimension to his early work. His involvement in nationalist politics was intensified through his meeting in 1889 with the revolutionary Maud Gonne, to whom he unsuccessfully proposed on numerous occasions throughout his life. In the same year he published *The Wanderings of Oisin and Other Poems*. Yeats saw theatre as having a powerful role to play in the emergence of a unified culture, and with Lady Gregory, Edward Martyn, and George Moore he founded the Irish National Dramatic Society out of which the Abbey Theatre was born. Maud Gonne was to play the title role in one of his earliest plays, *The Countess Cathleen*, in 1899, though the play had already been published with a selection of poems (*The Countess Kathleen and Various Legends and Lyrics*) in 1892. His influential collection of Irish folklore, *The Celtic Twilight*, was published in 1893. His later books of poems included *The Wind Among the Reeds* (1899), *Responsibilities* (1914), and *The Wild Swans at Coole* (1919). After the execution of Maud Gonne's husband, John MacBride, following the Easter Rising of 1916, Yeats once more proposed to Maud Gonne and also to her daughter Iseult, but was refused by both. In 1917 he married George Hyde-Lees, and two children (Anne and Michael) were born in 1919 and 1921. Also in 1917 he purchased the Norman tower in Ballylee, Co. Galway, which was to become their home during the difficult years of the War of Independence and the Civil War, and which provided the inspiration for some of his major poems in *The Tower* (1928) and *The Winding Stair and Other Poems* (1933). After the establishment of the Irish Free State in 1922, he became a Senator. He won the Nobel Prize for literature in 1923. Yeats remained intensely active in his later years, editing *The Oxford Book of Modern Verse* in 1936, publishing *New Poems* in 1938, and preparing his play *Purgatory* for its production at the Abbey Theatre, also in 1938. He died at Roquebrune, France, and in September 1948 was reburied in accordance with his own wishes in Drumcliff Churchyard, Co. Sligo.

PUBLISHER'S ACKNOWLEDGEMENTS

The editor and publisher gratefully acknowledge permission to reprint the following copyright material:

Samuel Beckett: extracts from *Murphy* (Routledge, 1938), copyright © 1938 by Samuel Beckett, reprinted by permission of Calder Publications Ltd. and Grove/Atlantic, Inc.

Elizabeth Bowen: extract from *The Last September* (Constable, 1929), copyright © Elizabeth Bowen 1929, reprinted by permission of Curtis Brown Group Ltd., London, on behalf of the Estate of Elizabeth Bowen.

Joseph Campbell: 'My Lagan Love' from *Songs of Uladh* (Maunsel, 1904), reprinted by permission of Simon Campbell.

Padraic Colum: 'She Moved Through the Fair' from *Wild Earth and Other Poems* (Maunsel & Co., 1916), reprinted by permission of Máire Colum O'Sullivan.

Oliver St John Gogarty: 'To the Liffey with the Swans' from *Wild Apples* (The Cuala Press, 1928), reprinted by permission of Colin Smythe Ltd. on behalf of Veronica Jane O'Mara.

Maud Gonne: 'The Famine Queen' ('La Reine de la disette') as published in *United Irishman*, 7 April 1900, first published in French in *L'Irlande Libre*, *numéro exceptionnel* (Paris, 1 April 1900), reprinted by permission of Anna McBride White.

John Hewitt: 'To a Modern Irish Poet', 'Easter Tuesday', and 'Mourne Mountains' from *The Collected Poems of John Hewitt*, edited by Frank Ormsby (Blackstaff Press, 1991), reprinted by permission of the publisher.

F. R. Higgins: 'Father and Son' and 'To My Blackthorn Stick' from *Arable Holdings: Poems* (Cuala Press, 1933); copyright holder not traced.

Douglas Hyde: 'My Grief on the Sea' from *Love Songs of Connaught* (Gill, 1893), reprinted by permission of Douglas Sealy.

James Joyce: Episode 1 from *Ulysses* and 'A Painful Case' from *Dubliners*, copyright © the Estate of James Joyce, reprinted by permission of the Estate.

Patrick Kavanagh: 'To A Blackbird', 'Inniskeen Road: July Evening', and 'Shancoduff from *Collected Poems* (McGibbon and Kee, 1964), reprinted by permission of the Trustees of the Estate of the late Katherine B. Kavanagh, through the Jonathan Williams Literary Agency.

Louis MacNeice: 'Belfast', 'Snow', 'Carrickfergus', and '*Autumn Journal* XVI' from *Collected Poems* (Faber & Faber, 1949), reprinted by permission of David Higham Associates Ltd.

George Moore: extract from *Hail and Farewell* (Wm. Heinemann, 1911–14), reprinted by permission of Colin Smythe Ltd. on behalf of the literary heirs of Charles Douglas Medley.

Flann O'Brien: extract from *At Swim-Two-Birds* (Longmans & Co., 1939), copyright © The Estate of the late Brian O'Nolan, reprinted by permission of A. M. Heath & Company Ltd., on behalf of the Estate.

Seán O'Casey: extract from *Juno and the Paycock* (1924) in *Two Plays by Sean O'Casey* (Macmillan, 1927), reprinted by permission of Macnaughton Lord 2000 Ltd., representatives of the Estate of Seán O'Casey.

Frank O'Connor: 'The Majesty of the Law' from *Bones of Contention and Other Stories* (Macmillan, 1936), copyright © Frank O'Connor 1936, reprinted by permission of PFD on behalf of the author.

Seán O'Faoláin: 'Lilliput' from *Midsummer Night Madness and Other Stories* (Jonathan Cape, 1932), copyright © Seán O'Faoláin 1932, reprinted by permission of Rogers, Coleridge & White Ltd., 20 Powis Mews, London WII IJN.

Liam O'Flaherty: 'The Mountain Tavern' from *The Mountain Tavern and Other Stories* (Jonathan Cape, 1929), copyright © Liam O'Flaherty 1929, reprinted by permission of PFD on behalf of the author.

Earnán O'Malley: extract from *On Another Man's Wound* (London and Dublin, 1936, Anvil Books, 1979), reprinted by permission of Anvil Books Ltd.

Seumas O'Sullivan: 'The Lamplighter' and 'The Geese' from *Seumas O'Sullivan: Collected Poems* (The Orwell Press, 1940), reprinted by permission of Frances Sommerville.

George Russell (AE): 'Carrowmore' from *Collected Poems* (Macmillan, 1913), reprinted by permission of Colin Smythe Ltd. on behalf of Estate of Diarmuid Russell.

Somerville and Ross: extract from *The Real Charlotte* (Ward & Downey, 1894), copyright © Somerville & Ross 1894, reprinted by permission of Curtis Brown Group Ltd., London, on behalf of the Estate of Somerville & Ross.

James Stephens: extract from *The Insurrection in Dublin* (Maunsel & Co., 1916), reprinted by permission of the Society of Authors as the Literary Representative of the Estate of James Stephens.

W. B. Yeats: 'The Lake Isle of Innisfree', 'To Ireland in the Coming Times', 'The Song of Wandering Aengus', 'September 1913', 'To a Shade', 'The Wild Swans at Coole', 'Easter 1916', copyright © 1924 by the Macmillan Company; copyright © renewed 1952 by Bertha Georgie Yeats; 'Sailing to Byzantium', 'The Tower', 'Meditations in Time of Civil War', copyright © 1928 by the Macmillan Company, copyright © renewed 1956 by Georgie Yeats; 'The Circus Animals' Desertion', copyright © 1940 by Georgie Yeats, copyright © renewed 1968 by Bertha Georgie Yeats, Michael Butler Yeats, and Anne Yeats; all poems reprinted from *The Collected Works of W. B. Yeats*, volume 1: *The Poems*, revised, edited by Richard J. Finneran (Scribner, 1997) by permission of Scribner, an imprint of Simon & Schuster Adult Publishing Group, and from *W. B. Yeats* edited by Edward

Larrissy (OUP, 1997), by permission of A. P. Watt Ltd. on behalf of Michael B. Yeats.

W. B. Yeats and Augusta Gregory: *Cathleen ni Houlihan*, reprinted by permission of A. P. Watt Ltd. on behalf of Michael B. Yeats.

INDEX OF NAMES

Page numbers of works by Irish writers included in the anthology are given in bold.

The Oxford World's Classics Website

www.worldsclassics.co.uk

- Browse the full range of Oxford World's Classics online

- Sign up for our monthly e-alert to receive information on new titles

- Read extracts from the Introductions

- Listen to our editors and translators talk about the world's greatest literature with our Oxford World's Classics audio guides

- Join the conversation, follow us on Twitter at OWC_Oxford

- Teachers and lecturers can order inspection copies quickly and simply via our website

www.worldsclassics.co.uk

American Literature

British and Irish Literature

Children's Literature

Classics and Ancient Literature

Colonial Literature

Eastern Literature

European Literature

Gothic Literature

History

Medieval Literature

Oxford English Drama

Poetry

Philosophy

Politics

Religion

The Oxford Shakespeare

A complete list of Oxford World's Classics, including Authors in Context, Oxford English Drama, and the Oxford Shakespeare, is available in the UK from the Marketing Services Department, Oxford University Press, Great Clarendon Street, Oxford OX2 6DP, or visit the website at www.oup.com/uk/worldsclassics.

In the USA, visit www.oup.com/us/owc for a complete title list.

Oxford World's Classics are available from all good bookshops. In case of difficulty, customers in the UK should contact Oxford University Press Bookshop, 116 High Street, Oxford OX1 4BR.

JANE AUSTEN	Emma
	Mansfield Park
	Persuasion
	Pride and Prejudice
	Sense and Sensibility
MRS BEETON	Book of Household Management
LADY ELIZABETH BRADDON	Lady Audley's Secret
ANNE BRONTË	The Tenant of Wildfell Hall
CHARLOTTE BRONTË	Jane Eyre
	Shirley
	Villette
EMILY BRONTË	Wuthering Heights
SAMUEL TAYLOR COLERIDGE	The Major Works
WILKIE COLLINS	The Moonstone
	No Name
	The Woman in White
CHARLES DARWIN	The Origin of Species
CHARLES DICKENS	The Adventures of Oliver Twist
	Bleak House
	David Copperfield
	Great Expectations
	Nicholas Nickleby
	The Old Curiosity Shop
	Our Mutual Friend
	The Pickwick Papers
	A Tale of Two Cities
GEORGE DU MAURIER	Trilby
MARIA EDGEWORTH	Castle Rackrent

TROLLOPE IN OXFORD WORLD'S CLASSICS

ANTHONY TROLLOPE

An Autobiography
The American Senator
Barchester Towers
Can You Forgive Her?
The Claverings
Cousin Henry
Doctor Thorne
The Duke's Children
The Eustace Diamonds
Framley Parsonage
He Knew He Was Right
Lady Anna
The Last Chronicle of Barset
Orley Farm
Phineas Finn
Phineas Redux
The Prime Minister
Rachel Ray
The Small House at Allington
The Warden
The Way We Live Now